HTML

CSS/JavaScript/DHTML

HTML/CSS/DH

HTML/CSS/DHTML

Steve Callihan

EMCParadigm

Senior Editor	Christine Hurney
Editorial Assistant	Susan Capecchi
Production Team	Jim Patterson, Desiree Faulkner
Copy Editor	Julie McNamee
Cover and Text Designer	Jennifer Wreisner
Desktop Production	Desktop Solutions
Indexer	Larry Harrison

Publishing Management Team

George Provol, Publisher; Janice Johnson, Director of Product Development; Tony Galvin, Acquisitions Editor; Lori Landwer, Marketing Manager; Shelley Clubb, Electronic Design and Production Manager

Acknowledgements

The author and publisher wish to thank the following reviewers for their technical and academic assistance in testing exercises and assessing instruction:

- Velda James, Citrus College, Glendora, CA
- Jon Storslee, Ph.D., Paradise Valley Community College, Phoenix, AZ

Library of Congress Cataloging-in-Publication Data

Callihan, Steven E.
    HTML: CSS, JavaScript, and DHTML / by Steve Callihan.
        p. cm.
    Includes index.
    ISBN 0-7638-1653-1
    1. HTML (Document markup language) 2. Cascading style sheets. 3. JavaScript (Computer program language) 4. DHTML (Document markup language) I. Title.

  QA76.76.H94 C34 2004
  005.7'2--dc21

                                       2002033883

Text ISBN: 0-7638-1653-1
Product Number: 01581

Care has been taken to verify the accuracy of information presented in this book. However, the author, editor, and publisher cannot accept responsibility for Web, e-mail, newsgroup, or chat room subject matter or content, or for consequences from application of the information in this book, and make no warranty, expressed or implied, with respect to its content.

Trademarks: Some of the product names and company names included in this book have been used for identification purposes only and may be trademarks or registered trademarks of their respective manufacturers and sellers. The author, editor, and publisher disclaim any affiliation, association, or connection with, or sponsorship or endorsement by, such owners.

© 2004 by Paradigm Publishing Inc.
    Published by **EMC**Paradigm
    875 Montreal Way
    St. Paul, MN 55102

    (800) 535-6865
    E-mail: educate@emcp.com
    Web site: www.emcp.com

Printed in the United States of America.
10 9 8 7 6 5 4 3 2 1

Contents

Chapter 5

Working with Tables 171

Chapter 6

Working with Multi-Page Web Sites 221

Chapter 7

Working with Forms 267

Team Project

HTML Essentials 303

PART TWO: DESIGNING FOR THE WEB 309

Chapter 8

Designing with Style Sheets 311

Chapter 9

Designing with Graphics 345

Chapter 10

Adding Bells and Whistles 381

Team Project
Designing for the Web 415

PART THREE: WEB DESIGN TECHNOLOGIES 419

Chapter 11
Working with JavaScript 421

Chapter 12

Working with Dynamic HTML   457

Chapter 13

Working with XHTML and XML   497

Team Project
Web Design Technologies   523

Appendix A
HTML Quick Reference   A-1

Appendix B
Special Characters Chart   A-28

Appendix C
Web-Safe Colors Chart   A-37

Appendix D
CSS Quick Reference   A-39

Appendix E
Miscellaneous Technologies and Features   A-57

Index   I-1

Preface

In a short period of time, the Web has become a ubiquitous presence in the lives of many people, be they workers, students, business people, or even children. Today, many rely on the Web for research, communication, and entertainment.

HTML IS FOR EVERYONE

From the beginning, the Web was conceived as a two-way medium. Anyone who surfs the Web can also create and publish documents that others can surf. These Web sites are created using HTML, or *Hypertext Markup Language*. Many think HTML must be overly technical or too difficult for the average person to learn and master. From the beginning, however, HTML was conceived as a tool that anyone could use without a great deal of previous technical experience or know-how.

Graduated Learning Process

The chapters in this book break down the material covered and skills taught into logically consistent steps that move from basic to intermediate and then to advanced topics. In each chapter, the student develops new skills, which can then be applied to addressing more challenging examples in the next chapter, and so forth, with each chapter representing a higher step upon which the student can stand toward mastery of the subject.

Chapter work might take one to two class periods to complete, with review exercises, quizzes, online research, and independent projects requiring additional time. Examples, exercises, and projects can be done in class, in a computer lab, or at home. Students can break off at any time, save their work, and then later pick up where they left off, in the same or another place.

Special Features

This book is designed to make learning Web development with HTML both easy and productive by including these special features:

- **Downloadable Example Files.** These files are used to complete each chapter's examples and exercises and can be easily downloaded by the instructor or by students from this book's Internet Resource Center (IRC) at www.emcp.com/. Additional student resources and instructional support are also available at this book's IRC.

- **Differentiation of Action from Content.** This book makes it easy for students to differentiate between material included for understanding and material that should be acted upon. The in-context code examples enable the student to see and complete the tasks quickly and easily.
- **Notes, Tips, and Margin Hints.** These features highlight additional information the student might find useful or helpful in comprehending information or completing examples.
- **Trouble Spots.** Trouble Spots highlight points at which problems might occur and provide relevant advice and solutions.
- **Real-World Case Examples and Scenarios.** Examples and scenarios are used in each chapter to demonstrate topics, features, and methods.
- **Online Research and Extended Learning.** These opportunities are frequently referenced at relevant points within each chapter; margin icons call out the location of Web addresses within the text that can be accessed to find out more about different topics or subjects.
- **Chapter Summaries.** This feature summarizes the topics that should be comprehended and the skills that should be gained in each chapter.
- **Code Reviews.** This section reviews all elements, attributes, or other codes introduced in a chapter.
- **Online Quizzes.** These quizzes are available online at this book's IRC to check comprehension and retention of key topics and information. Students receive immediate feedback, highlighting areas in which further study or review might be helpful.
- **Review Exercises.** These exercises can be done by students who finish the chapter work early. Review exercises also can be completed during lab time or at home.
- **Projects.** Projects present real-world Web publishing projects that students can independently undertake or the instructor can assign to provide additional opportunities for, and practical experience in, applying the skills and knowledge gained in each chapter.
- **Team Projects.** These projects are included at the end of each Part to provide students with the opportunity to work together in teams to plan, produce, and publish real-world Web publishing projects.

WHAT THIS BOOK COVERS

This book is organized into three parts, covering the basic, intermediate, and more advanced aspects of HTML-based Web development:

- The Introduction includes background information and perspectives on the Internet, the Web, and HTML.
- Part One, *HTML Essentials*, covers all the key aspects of HTML, including using common elements such as paragraphs, headings, and lists; inserting inline highlighting and special characters; creating hypertext links; inserting and working with inline images; working with colors and backgrounds; working with tables; creating multi-page Web sites; and creating user-input forms.

- Part Two, *Designing for the Web*, covers additional aspects and features of HTML and Web design, including creating Web page designs and layouts using Cascading Style Sheets (CSS); working with image maps, image slicers, and tables to create graphical front-ends and wraparound graphical interfaces; and designing sticky Web sites that retain visitors, motivate return visits, and leverage visitor traffic.
- Part Three, *Web Design Technologies*, covers key technologies that are used in conjunction with HTML, including JavaScript, dynamic HTML, XHTML, and XML.
- The Appendixes contain additional reference information, including an HTML quick reference, a special characters chart, a Web-safe colors chart, a CSS quick reference, and a compendium of miscellaneous additional Web design technologies and features that can be implemented by Web designers, including Server-Side Includes (SSI), password protection, cookies, online databases, Web programming, secure forms and servers, and wireless Web protocols.

Standards-Based Instruction

All instruction in this book is based on the official specifications and standards for HTML, XHTML, Cascading Style Sheets (CSS), JavaScript, the Document Object Model (DOM), and other covered technologies as established by the World Wide Web Consortium and other responsible standards-setting organizations. Non-standard or proprietary methods and techniques are presented in this book only when there is no corresponding standards-based method or technique to achieve an important or necessary result. Any non-standard or proprietary methods and techniques covered in this book are clearly identified as such.

It is important that students learn not merely what happens to work at the moment in current Web browsers, but what will continue to work in future Web browsers as well. There is no guarantee that non-standard methods and techniques will continue to be supported in the future.

Software Requirements

Although most of the figures in this book use screen captures taken on a Windows system, the execution of the examples, projects, and other assignments does not require system-specific software or facilities. The example files used in this book are available for download in Windows, Macintosh, or UNIX/Linux format from this book's Internet Resource Center at www.emcp.com/.

The only software required to complete this book's examples, assignments, and projects is a simple text editor and a relatively current graphical Web browser:
- **A text editor.** You do not need anything fancy to create HTML files, which are just straight text files. Most operating systems include text editors you can use, such as Windows Notepad or SimpleText on the Macintosh. More full-featured text editors can be downloaded and installed from the Web.
- **A graphical Web browser.** To preview and debug all the examples, assignments, and projects, you need a relatively current HTML 4-compatible graphical browser installed on your system. The examples have been tested in Microsoft Internet

Explorer 6 for Windows, Microsoft Internet Explorer 5 for the Macintosh, Netscape 6, Opera 6, and Mozilla 1. Earlier versions of these browsers can be used, but they might not be able to preview all the examples.

- **A connection to the Internet.** You can create Web pages without being connected to the Web, but if you want to download additional software tools or Web art images, or want to publish projects you create on the Web, you will need an Internet connection. An Internet Resource Center (IRC) has also been created for this book that provides downloadable example files and many additional resources that complement and extend the material in the book.

No other software tools are required to create and preview this book's examples and assignments. Students, however, may choose to use optional software tools for creating individual and team projects, such as image editors, GIF animators, image map editors, image splicers, Java animation programs, and so on. Students also will need to use an FTP program if they want to publish Web pages or projects they create on the Web. Additional software tools that students can choose to employ will be discussed in more depth in the relevant chapters.

ABOUT THE AUTHOR

Steve Callihan has authored several books on Web design, HTML, Web animation, and Cascading Style Sheets; published articles on Web publishing in major computer magazines; and worked extensively as both a technical writer and desktop publisher, designing and producing hardware and software user documentation. He has more than 15 years experience as a team member, team leader, department supervisor, and independent contractor, working in a wide variety of computer document processing and production capacities.

Introduction

Before you start working with HTML, you should understand what HTML is and where it came from. HTML is a key aspect of the World Wide Web, which is an evolution of the Internet.

WHAT IS THE INTERNET?

How the Internet came to be is an interesting story. The Internet actually is rooted in the Cold War, in that the initial impetus to establish the network that was to eventually become the Internet was motivated by a desire to establish a communication system that could survive an atomic attack.

Following the launch of the Sputnik satellite by the Soviet Union in 1957, the U.S. Defense Department established the Advanced Research Projects Agency (ARPA) to develop the first U.S. satellite, which was launched 18 months later. Later, ARPA undertook a new challenge, establishing a communication system to command and control the U.S.'s ICBM missile system and strategic bomber fleet. In 1963, the Rand Corporation was asked by ARPA to conceptualize the design principles behind such a system, a primary requirement being the ability to survive and remain functioning after a nuclear attack.

The ARPAnet

The Rand Corporation responded that the system would need to have "no central authority" and would need to be designed from the beginning to "operate while in tatters." These two characteristics define the essence of what later was to become first the ARPAnet and then later the Internet: a communication system, or network, that has no central authority (that could be knocked out in nuclear strike) and operates in a condition of assumed unreliability (cities destroyed by nuclear blasts, telephone lines down). The irony, of course, is that what was to eventually become the anarchic Internet we know today, which even nation states are unable to control, had its roots in a severe case of Cold War paranoia.

The ARPAnet was commissioned by the Department of Defense in 1969, initially linking research centers at four universities involved in defense research (UCLA, Stanford, University of California at Santa Barbara, and the University of Utah). Within the next two years, the ARPAnet grew to 15 nodes (including MIT, Harvard, NASA/Ames, and others). By 1973, the ARPAnet had expanded to England and Norway.

A number of key technologies that are associated with the Internet were also developed in the early days of the ARPAnet. Telnet was introduced in 1972, standardizing the capability to dial in and log on to a computer on the network. FTP (File Transfer Protocol) was introduced in 1973, standardizing how files were transferred between computers on the network. The first network-wide e-mail system was established in 1977. Newsgroups (USENET) were introduced in 1979.

A Network of Networks

The problem initially faced by the founders of the Internet was that many different network topologies were in use. What would work to communicate with one network might not work with another network. The system needed a shared set of *protocols*, or agreed upon rules, by which these different networks could all communicate which each other.

It doesn't matter what kind of system or device is connected to the Internet—it only matters that systems or devices connected to the Internet speak the same language when sending and receiving data over the Internet. That language, in the form of a set of common protocols, is TCP/IP (Transmission Control Protocol/Internet Protocol), which was introduced in 1982. Thus was born a "network of networks," or an *Internet*.

TCP/IP

In 1982, the ARPAnet adopted *TCP/IP* (Transmission Control Protocol/Internet Protocol) as the standard set of rules for sending and receiving data across the network. Today, TCP/IP remains the key suite of protocols that enables the exchange of data over the Internet. TCP/IP actually comprises two different protocols:

- **TCP (Transmission Control Protocol).** Breaks the message down into smaller packets, which makes the transmission of larger files or messages across the network more efficient. Each packet is individually labeled, identifying its origin, destination, and position within the file. When the packets arrive at their destination, TCP checks the packets for errors, verifies that all the packets that belong to the file have arrived, and then reassembles them in the proper order to reconstitute the full file. If errors are found or a packet fails to arrive, a request is sent to the sender to resend the file.

- **IP (Internet Protocol).** At each node along the way, a *router* reads a packet's address and then, if the current node is not its destination, forwards it on toward its destination.

Any system, whether a network gateway, a mainframe computer, a Web server delivering content over the Web, or your own personal computer you use to dial in and connect to the Internet, uses TCP/IP to connect to and share information over the Internet (see Figure I.1).

FIGURE I.1 • *The Internet uses a common language (TCP/IP) that connects systems and devices to share (send and receive) data between them.*

TCP has been compared with packing up the contents of your house and moving it across the country. The movers come in and pack everything up into boxes (or "packets"), which are then shipped across country. When they finally arrive at their destination, simply checking the shipment's manifest shows whether all the packets have arrived, or whether any have been lost along the way. The movers then unpack the packets, which then become the contents and furniture of your new house. This way of transferring data over a network is also called *packet switching*. For an illustration of how this works, see Figure I.2.

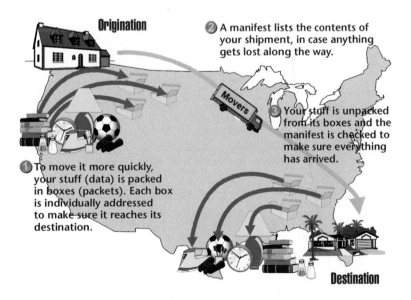

FIGURE I.2 • *Breaking data into smaller packets can speed its transmission to its destination.*

IP has been compared with sending a letter across the country. You place the letter in an envelope and as long as the address on the envelope is correct, barring mishaps, the letter should eventually be delivered safely to its address. A mail sorter doesn't have to know anything about the contents of the letter; a mere look at the zip code for the letter is sufficient to send the letter off in the right direction.

Over the Internet, the packets that compose a message might take different routes to get to the same destination. In other words, based upon changing traffic conditions, one packet might go from New York to Seattle by first going via St. Louis, San Francisco, and Portland, before finally arriving, safe and sound, in Seattle. Another packet, on the other hand, due to sudden congestion on the route to St. Louis, might go from New York to Seattle by following an entirely different route, traveling via Chicago, St. Paul, Missoula, and Spokane, before arriving in Seattle (see Figure I.3). On the Internet, if any packets that are part of a message fail to arrive (are lost along the way), the receiver of the message simply requests that the sender resend the message. After all the packets have arrived, they are reassembled into the full message, which is then read or executed.

The advantage of packet switching is that it makes it easier for multiple message streams to share the same network space. If only whole files, for instance, could be sent over the Internet, one large file could block other smaller files from getting through. Breaking messages and files—transmissions—into smaller packets is more efficient and much less prone to bottlenecks.

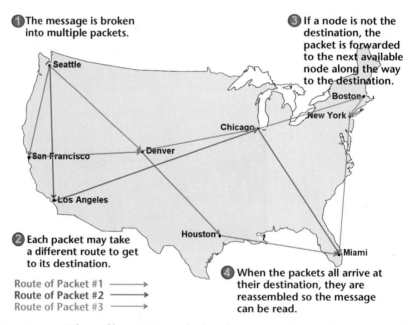

FIGURE I.3 • *When a file or message is broken down into packets, each packet can take a different route to get to its destination.*

NOTE

For TCP/IP, TCP (Transmission Control Protocol) defines the "packet," and IP (Internet Protocol) does the "switching" that routes the packets to their destination. You can think of TCP as boxcars in a train and IP as a train switch that moves the train from one track to another, except that in the case of TCP/IP, the individual boxcars could be switched onto different tracks.

One of the main points to remember about TCP/IP is that the essence of what makes up the Internet is not the wire, or the means of transmission, but the protocols that determine how information is sent, forwarded, and received over the wire. The Internet, in other words, is not the wires and connections (the hardware) that makes up the physical network, but rather the intelligence (or software) that directs and orders the traffic, or transmission stream, over the Internet. That directing and ordering intelligence is TCP/IP.

Thus, many and varied systems can be connected to the Internet. The only thing that matters is that they all use the same set of protocols—TCP/IP—to communicate with each other. When you dial in and connect to the Internet, you are connected to the Internet in exactly the same fashion as a whole network of computers might be connected at your local university, through TCP/IP.

The standardization upon TCP/IP as the common means for exchanging information across the network allowed the ARPAnet to grow and expand to eventually become the Internet we know today. In 1986, the National Science Foundation (NSF) formed the NSFNet, which initially linked five supercomputing centers to form the first high-speed backbone, running at what was then a blazing speed of 56 KBps. Unlike the ARPAnet, which linked together academic centers that were involved in defense research, the NSFNet opened up the network to the rest of the academic community, allowing anyone connected through a university to exchange information and ideas with anyone else who was also connected. Soon afterwards, the speed of the NSFNet backbone increased to 1.544 Mbps (called a "T1" connection). In 1990, the ARPAnet ended and was absorbed into the NSFNet. In the same year, the first commercial provider of dial-up access to the Internet, the World (world.std.com), came online, with many other ISPs (Internet Service Providers) coming along shortly after. The NSFNet finally became the full Internet, to which anyone could connect, that we know today.

In 1991, a new organization, the Internet Society, was founded in response to the growing internationalization of the Internet and the need to consolidate responsibility for establishing Internet infrastructure standards.

NOTE

Look at the Internet Society's site at **www.isoc.org/** for additional resources and information about the history and development of the Internet—just click on the Internet History link in the site's menu bar.

The Client-Server Model

TCP/IP enables the exchange of information and data over the Internet, but it does not, by itself, enable the distribution of services or the sharing of resources. Over a network, whether your local-area network (or LAN) or the Internet, this is done by means of a process by which computers make and respond to requests over the Internet, a process that is often referred to as the *client-server model*. A *client* is a computer that requests a service from another computer (a server). A *server* is a computer that responds to requests for services from another computer (a client).

A computer can be both a client and a server. A server is simply a computer operating on the Internet running software that enables it to function as a server. Besides Web servers, for instance, Gopher, FTP, e-mail, news, and other servers also function on the Internet. The same computer might function as a Web, FTP, and e-mail server, simply by running software that enables these functions. A server also can request a service from another server, in which case it is functioning as a client.

Most personal computers connected to the Internet are not running as servers, but only as clients—such computers are normally connected at a transmission speed of 56 KB or slower, which is just too slow to successfully function as a server, unless they are connected through DSL, ISDN, or some other form of broadband connection. Also, when you dial up to connect your computer to the Internet, most ISPs (Internet Service Providers) randomly assign an available *IP address*. An IP address is a series of numbers that uniquely identifies any computer (server or client) that is connected to the Internet. To be continually available as a server on the Internet, a computer needs to have the same permanent IP address during all the time it is connected to the Internet, and not a different IP address each time it is connected. You can think of an IP address as a street address: if you were to continually change your street address, nobody would be able to find you. They would be showing up looking for you where you were last, but not where you are.

You can think of the client-server model functioning much like a pizza delivery service. You, the client, feeling the irresistible urge for a three-cheese pizza with mushrooms and anchovies, call up the pizza delivery service, the server, and make your request: a 16-inch pizza with three cheeses (mozzarella, parmesan, and romano), mushrooms, and anchovies. As part of your request, you also tell the pizza order person what your address is, so the pizza delivery person can deliver it to your front door. The person taking your order confirms that they can supply the request. After the pizza is cooked according to your specification, it is loaded into a truck and rushed to your door, so you can eat it while it is still hot and steaming. Transactions occurring over the Internet happen in much the same manner, with a client requesting a service from a server, and then the server delivering the requested service to the client (see Figure I.4).

A client is simply software running on a computer. You should already be familiar with one client: your Web browser. Another term for a Web browser is a *user agent* (which might also encompass non-visual browsing agents as well, for instance). Web browsers aren't the only kind of clients that operate across the Internet. Other clients

FIGURE I.4 • *The client-server model is similar to a pizza delivery system, in which a customer places an order for a pizza, specifying size and toppings, to be delivered to her door.*

include Gopher, WAIS, Archie, and FTP clients, for instance. In each case, these all work relatively the same: a Gopher client makes a request of a Gopher server or an FTP client makes a request of an FTP server, which then responds by delivering the service that is being requested by the client. A Web browser, on the other hand, can function as several different clients in one—functioning as a Gopher, FTP, or WAIS client, for instance. All it needs to know is the IP address on the Internet of the particular server to which it wants to make a request.

As you learn more about using HTML and other related technologies to create your own Web pages or sites, you also will find out about server-side and client-side applications and processes. A *server-side* application is a program or script that is run on a server, whereas a *client-side* application is downloaded to and executed by a client. An example of a server-side application is a script on a server that processes responses from online forms included in Web pages, directing those responses to an e-mail address, a folder location, or a database, for instance. A Web page is the most obvious example of a client-side application, in that the codes included within a Web page are first downloaded to a Web browser, to be executed, or parsed. JavaScript scripts and Cascading Style Sheets (CSS) are also first downloaded to a browser before they are executed.

WHAT IS THE WORLD WIDE WEB?

If the Internet is said to have begun with the formation of the ARPAnet around 1970, then it predates the *World Wide Web* ("the Web") by over 20 years. If the start of the Internet is dated, however, from the formation of the NSFNet, which came about in 1986, then it predates the World Wide Web by a mere 4 or 5 years. In fact, without the formation of the NSFNet, such a development as the Web could not have come about in the first place. NSFNet opened up the Internet to allow the participation of anyone connected through participating universities and research centers, which allowed the Web—the brainchild of an academic and scientist who was also connected to the Internet—to come to fruition.

The Inventor of the Web: Tim Berners-Lee

In 1989, a British scientist working at CERN (*Conseil European pour la Recherche Nucleaire* or European Organization for Nuclear Research) in Bern, Switzerland, made a radical proposal to facilitate the sharing and exchange of information and ideas between academics across the Internet. That scientist was Tim Berners-Lee and his radical proposal was for something he called "the World Wide Web." In his original proposal for the World Wide Web, Berners-Lee described it as "a wide area hypermedia information retrieval initiative aiming to give universal access to a large universe of documents." More recently, he provided an updated description and definition for the Web: "the universal space of all network-accessible information." He also has used the term "universal space" in online presentations to describe the nature and character of the Web. A close variant of this that Berners-Lee has published on the Web replaces "the universal space" with a somewhat less redundant phrase, "the universe."

NOTE You can find CERN's home page at **www.cern.ch/**. To learn about CERN's role in the invention and early evolution of the Web, click the "general public" link, the Highlights link, and the World Wide Web link.

The Universal Medium

Another way of looking at the Web is as a universal medium. The Web, in other words, encompasses all media—print, radio, television, and so on—within a single universal medium. This is actually already implicit in the term "hypermedia" that Berners-Lee used in his initial description of the Web (hypertext and hypermedia are discussed in a later section, "The History of Hypertext").

The original focus of the Web was on the sharing and exchanging of textual information. Web documents are referred to as "pages" for that reason. The term *Web page*, however, is a bit of a misnomer, in that a document on the Web can be of virtually any length. It would be more accurate to refer to a Web document as a *Web scroll*, but somehow that just does not have the right ring.

The Original Purpose of the Web

As it was originally conceived, the Web was designed to facilitate the exchange of ideas and the sharing of information between individuals or groups, with little distinction between those who create and those who consume what was being exchanged and shared. From the beginning, it was intended that the Web would be a medium (or "information retrieval initiative") that would allow anyone to communicate with anyone. The initial participants on the Web were mostly academics and scientists, only because the Internet at the time of the introduction of the Web was still largely an academic affair. The first ISP, the World (world.std.com), made access to the Internet available outside of connected universities and other research facilities 1990, a year after the Berners-Lee's initial proposal for the formation of the Web. From the beginning, however, Berners-Lee's vision for the Web was one in which no group, community, or individuals held privileges over any other, with all having equal rights to not only consume, but also to originate and create, the content that composes the Web.

Thus, although the Web has evolved into much more than its initial vision, becoming both an entertainment medium and a platform for the distribution of commercial applications, programs, and services, the original vision of the Web as a "universal space" within which everyone could, and should, be able to communicate and interact with everyone else, remains at the heart of what the Web is and will continue to be.

In other words, on the Web, large-scale economic or political concerns, such as General Motors, Universal Studios, or the federal government, for instance, really have no greater privilege to conceptualize, produce, and distribute (or share) information, ideas, or even software products, across the Web than the plain ordinary individual. On the Web, all addresses are coequal; in other words, Joseph Schmoe's Web address of www.joseph-schmoe.com/, to cite an entirely fictional example, is just as easily reachable as Yahoo!'s Web address of www.yahoo.com/. Joe, of course, being just an ordinary guy, does not have the advertising budget of a Yahoo!, nor would the traffic limitations of his Web hosting account stand up to even a small fraction of the traffic Yahoo!

attracts, but anyone knowing his address should be able to reach his site just as quickly and easily as they can reach Yahoo! From that perspective, Yahoo!'s multi-billion dollar presence and Joseph Schmoe's presence on the Web (very much a shoestring affair) are equal. The same holds for a grandmother in Ireland, a schoolboy in France, or even a homeless person in Seattle—anyone with access to the Internet and the Web can be a creator and producer, not just a consumer, of content on the Web.

The World Wide Web Consortium

Although the World Wide Web was born at CERN in Switzerland, the fostering of a worldwide communication network was neither CERN's primary mission nor its mandate. In 1994, under the auspices of INRIA (the National Institute for Research in Computer Science and Controls, located in France), the World Wide Web Consortium (W3C) was formed in collaboration with the Laboratory of Computer Science at MIT (Massachusetts Institute of Technology) in the United States, where Berners-Lee took up a research position.

NOTE

You can find the W3C's home page at **www.w3.org**/ (see Figure I.5). To find out about the W3C's work on the different HTML standards, just click the HTML link in the left sidebar.

FIGURE I.5 • *The World Wide Web Consortium is in charge of establishing consensus on Web standards, including HTML.*

The W3C's stated mission is "to lead the Web to its fullest potential." The W3C is responsible for fostering and developing the specifications, guidelines, protocols, software, and tools that provide the standard foundation upon which the Web can stand and grow. Without the W3C, we might otherwise have ended up with a bevy of less-than-worldwide "webs," each based on separate proprietary protocols and accessed through different interfaces. As a standards-setting organization, the W3C is responsible for creating consensus among the various member organizations and vendors in the

W3C, forging a path forward that all agree they can follow. The W3C, in other words, is not a governing organization charged with enforcing dictates from some kind of elite council of technological elders, but rather simply establishes the forums and working groups within which organizations and vendors with a stake in the future development of the Web can come together and work out common agreements and commitments. The W3C is a bottom-up, "grass roots" organization that is run by and functions on the basis of consensus among its members, in other words, and not a top-down organization charged with enforcing rules and regulations. In fact, the W3C does not even refer to its specifications as "standards," but merely as "recommendations."

Basic Web Protocols

As is the case with the Internet, the Web is really nothing more than a set of agreed upon protocols and specifications. The essential protocols and specifications that comprise the Web are:

- **HTTP (HyperText Transfer Protocol).** This protocol formalizes the interchange (requests and responses) that occurs between Web-based clients (Web browsers, for instance) and Web-based servers (Web servers). All Web addresses, for instance, begin with "http://".

NOTE

In this book, the "http://" is omitted from Web addresses referenced in order to lessen the chance that a Web address will take up more than the available space on a line. All current browsers allow you to omit "http://" when typing a Web address in their Address or Location bars. Non-HTTP URLs (such as FTP or Gopher URLs, for instance) still need to be typed in full.

- **HTML (Hypertext Markup Language).** This specification establishes the common language that allows for the universal exchange of information over the Web. HTML defines elements and attributes that facilitate the presentation of structured information and data. User agents (Web browsers, for instance) then interpret the HTML coding within the document to determine how it should be presented.
- **URL (Uniform Resource Locator).** For resources to be accessible over the Web, there must be a means by which they can be located. That means is provided by a URL, which defines the "Web address" of any resource on the Web. A URL specifies how a resource is to be accessed (the protocol), where the resource is located (the host server), and what the resource is (its path and name).
- **CGI (Common Gateway Interface).** This specification provides a common means by which Web server software running HTTP can interface with the host computer on which it is running. CGI allows server-side programs and scripts to be executed across the network. An example of this might be a CGI script written in Perl (a programming language common to UNIX servers) that processes requests sent from HTML forms embedded in Web documents.

An HTTP request, for instance, might use the following commands to ask a server to
- **GET** a particular document or file, providing the name and location of the file on that server.
- **SEARCH** for keywords within a particular document or subset of documents.
- Request only return documents created **SINCE** or **BEFORE** a particular date and/or time.
- Return a document's **HEAD** (header information), which allows Web browsers, or other client software, to compare the creation date of a cached copy of a document (residing on the browser's local machine) against the non-cached remote copy of the document (residing on the server). That way, if the remote copy has not been updated since the local copy was cached, the browser can just open and display the local copy, rather than having to download the entire remote copy.
- Identify the **USER**, the user's **HOST**, and the client software that is making the request so that requests can be logged and tracked.

After receiving a request, an HTTP server informs the client of the *status* of the requested resource or service. A server can signal back to a client the status of requests for resources or services in a variety of ways. For instance, a Web server might
- Respond that the request is a success (the document is present and available for delivery).
- Forward the client to a new address, if the resource has been moved.
- Inform the client that the document cannot be found (does not refer to a valid document path and name on the server).
- Inform the client that access to the document is not authorized, forwarding the client to a form for inputting a user name and password, for instance, or simply telling the client that access has been refused.
- Inform the client that the resource is not available due to a server error.
- Inform the client that the resource is temporarily unavailable and that the client might check back later.
- Tell the client that a keyword search of documents came up with no results.
- Tell the client the format on the server to which the requested document corresponds.

After the server signals back to the client, the client can then request that the server deliver the resource if it is available. The client also can go to a forwarded address and start the whole transaction over again, or simply relay the information to the user that the resource is not available for one reason or another and wait for the user to provide a different address to go to. The client also can decide to display a locally cached copy of the resource, if it is available.

HTTP is just one of several protocols used to exchange documents and information over the Internet. Other protocols that share the Internet with HTTP include FTP, Gopher, Archie, Telnet, and WAIS. All of these other protocols require server software that can respond to requests and deliver the requested resource, as well as client software that can communicate and interact with the specific server software.

NOTE

For links to resources on the Web that discuss the history of the Internet and the Web, see this Introduction's section on the IRC for this book at **www.emcp.com/**.

WHAT IS HTML?

The acronym HTML stands for Hypertext Markup Language. HTML was a key part of the original proposal for the Web. Without HTML, the Web would be much different than it is now. HTML was originally conceived as a subset of SGML (Standard Generalized Markup Language). SGML is the standard markup language used to prepare computer-generated documents for publishing on a printing press. HTML has a similar function, except it is used to prepare computer-generated documents for publishing on the Web.

HTML Documents Are ASCII Files

HTML documents are straight ASCII text documents. ASCII (American Standard Code for Information Interchange) defines a standard set of characters and control codes that are automatically recognized by almost all computer systems. The only exceptions are IBM's mainframe computer systems that use EBCDIC (Extended Binary Coded Decimal Information Code), a standard that predated ASCII. Because the standard ASCII codes are represented by 7-bit binary numbers (0000000 to 1111111), there are 128 standard ASCII codes. These include the alphabetic characters (a to z and A to Z), numbers (0 to 9), punctuation (period, comma, colon, semicolon, and so on), the space character, and various other commonly used characters (@, #, $, and so on). Also included are a number of control characters that command actions (tab, carriage return, line feed, backspace, delete, and so on).

NOTE

ASCII is also referred to as US-ASCII because it includes the "$" symbol for U.S. currency. It doesn't include any of the accented characters used by many European languages. Many international variants of ASCII have been developed; in UK-ASCII (BS 4730), for instance, the number symbol (#) is replaced by the British pound symbol (£).

ASCII text files can be read and written by simple text editors, such as Notepad on the Windows platform, SimpleText on the Macintosh platform, and vi (pronounced "vee eye") on the UNIX (or Linux) platform.

You do not need to know the ASCII codes, however, to create HTML files. In Chapter 1, *Creating a Basic Web Page*, you use a simple text editor to create an HTML file. A text editor has one purpose, to read and write ASCII text files. An ASCII text file is also sometimes referred to as a "plain" text file because it does not include any additional formatting codes (such as for bold, italics, indents, and so on) that a word processor might include in a word processing document. Text editors are also commonly used to read and write program code, which also does not require any formatting or extra characters.

HTML Is Not a Proprietary Format

HTML is not a proprietary document format, such as is the case with documents created by word processing programs, for instance. When you create a document in a word processing program, such as Microsoft Word or Corel WordPerfect, you can include all sorts of additional formatting and other characteristics that are invisibly coded beneath the surface. You might decide to bold a phrase, set a heading in a different font face or size, apply a color to a paragraph, set margins, create footnotes, add page numbers, and so on. You are limited only by the capabilities of the program you are using.

There is a penalty, however, for being able to format word processing documents in various and fancy ways—a word processing document will be much larger than an equivalent ASCII text file containing the same textual characters. On your local computer system, the difference in file sizes between the two formats is not very important because the speed of processing files locally renders the difference in file sizes as having a negligible effect on how fast a file is displayed or updated. For that reason, you undoubtedly use a word processor to create any documents you create for local use (or for sharing across your local network or via "sneakernet").

HTML documents, however, need to be transmitted across the Internet and the Web, which means they need to be no larger than is absolutely necessary. Using only ASCII codes to compose HTML documents achieves that. The choice of using ASCII for HTML files, in other words, is an important aspect of ensuring that HTML files can easily and quickly be transmitted and exchanged over the Internet and the Web. If a proprietary format had been used for HTML instead, the Internet traffic jams would have been much worse much earlier, and special software would have been required to interpret and read HTML documents.

HTML Is a Markup Language

Many people think HTML is a programming language because it is represented by an acronym. However, HTML is actually a *markup language*. The term *markup* originates from the world of printing and publishing. A formatter or designer would actually "mark up" the copy or layout, indicating how different elements should be printed. For instance, markup might be added to indicate that a heading at the top of the document should be printed in a bold 24-point Helvetica font. Other markup on the document might indicate color, margins, indents, leading, kerning, and so on. Back before mechanical or electronic typesetters, a person would then physically set the type for the document in the specified typefaces and sizes. Later, mechanical and electronic typesetting machines were invented that automated this process. Markup in an HTML file works in a somewhat similar fashion, with a Web browser functioning as a kind of typesetter.

With HTML, you mark up your textual copy to specify the structural elements that compose your document, such as headings, paragraphs, bulleted lists, bolding, italics, superscripts, and so on. A Web browser then interprets (or "parses") your markup code to appropriately display your document according to your instructions.

A primary difference between markup for printing and for the Web is that when designing a flyer, for instance, you already know the size of the media on which the flyer will be printed, whereas a Web page may be displayed on monitors of widely different sizes, at different resolutions, and using different default font-pitches. The actual dimensions of a Web page, in other words, are unknown and variable and might even have no dimensions at all, if presented through a Braille or speech browser, for instance. Because of this, the original philosophy of HTML has been to indicate what an element is, with the identity of the element indicating its function and structural import, rather than to try to describe what an element should look like.

HTML is based on SGML (Standard Generalized Markup Language). SGML is generally used to mark up electronic documents for processing, whether for printing on a printer or for display on a computer monitor. A desktop publisher, for instance, might use SGML conventions to identify (or tag) the different elements that compose an electronic document (whether a newsletter, a brochure, a calendar, a catalog, and so on). A separate program (a desktop publishing application such as PageMaker, Quark Express, or Ventura Publisher) then applies the formatting characteristics specified for the indicated elements.

HTML shares many common characteristics and features with SGML. Both are used to specify the hierarchical structure of a document in the form of elements and their attributes. An HTML standard is defined by means of a DTD (Document Type Definition), which originates from SGML. A DTD defines the elements, attributes, and other conventions that pertain to the processing of a specific type of document—an HTML file versus some other kind of file, such as some kind of DTP (Desktop Publishing) file that is intended for printing on a printing press, for instance. HTML is much simpler than SGML, however because it is intended for a specific purpose (specifying the structure of electronic documents for presentation over the Web), while SGML is intended to take into account any and all purposes that an electronic document might be used for.

Two other markup languages are also in use: XHTML (Extensible HyperText Markup Language) and XML (Extensible Markup Language). XHTML is a version of HTML that has been brought into conformance with XML. XML is intended to facilitate the presentation of structured data (database records, spreadsheets, catalogs, address books, financial transactions, bibliographies, or any data that can be given a structure). XML also makes possible the formulation of more specific markup languages, or modules, to be used for presenting documents and data over the Web—XHTML is, in fact, an XML module. Any individual or organization can formulate an XML-based markup language simply by publishing its DTD on the Web, as long as it is otherwise in conformance with XML. Other XML-based markup languages that have been or are being developed include MathML (Mathematical Markup Language), SMIL (Synchronized Multimedia Integration Language), RDF (Resource Description Framework), SVG (Scalable Vector Graphics), and XForms (Next-Generation Web Forms).

HTML Is a Client-Side Application

In its original conception at least, HTML markup was not intended to specify individual formatting characteristics. Rather, it was intended to specify only the structural aspects of a document, leaving the question of how the different elements in the document should be displayed entirely up to the Web browser (or other user agent used to interpret the HTML code). Thus, the idea was to specify only that an element was a level-one heading, for instance—a browser might then decide to display the heading in whatever typeface and font size it determined to be appropriate. As a result, the same HTML document might look different in different browsers because the browsers were free to determine on their own how different elements should be displayed.

Doing it this way enables HTML files to remain relatively small because information does not need to be included in the file to specify how a level-one heading is to be formatted. Rather, an element is simply marked up as being a level-one heading and the browser determines on its own how to display it.

This means that decisions about how a document is to be displayed do not have to be made until the document has been downloaded to the client (the Web browser). In other words, the load of determining formatting characteristics is assigned to the client (the local Web browser), while the server (the Web server) is only responsible for conveying the structural components of the documents to the client. This is referred to as a *client-side* application or process, in that instructions are downloaded and delivered to a client (your local Web browser, for instance) before they are executed. With a *server-side* application or process, on the other hand, a script or program located on the server might be executed (via CGI), with the results then downloaded and delivered to the client.

WHAT IS HYPERTEXT?

Besides being a markup language, HTML is a language that facilitates the dynamic and nonlinear interlinking of documents by means of *hypertext*. The prefix, *hyper-*, is from the Greek and is generally translated as meaning "over" or "above." *Hyper*text, thus, indicates an additional set of nonlinear and nonsequential relations or linkages that can be defined within and between textual documents, over and above the normal flow that a straight linear or sequential reading of a document's text would encompass. This is actually not an entirely new or radical idea. Regular books, for instance, include something similar to hypertext links—they are called cross-references, footnotes, and endnotes. With a book's cross-reference, however, you have to thumb through to the page that is being referenced to find the object of the cross-reference. With a footnote, you might have to put on your hat, coat, and shoes, head on down to the library, search through the catalog or shelves to retrieve the actual book, and then turn to the chapter and page being referenced.

With a hypertext link, however, you can immediately jump to the object of the link. That object might be another HTML document, a map or chart, a figure illustration, a section in another document, and so on. The object can be in the same file, in the same folder, in the same Web site, on the same server, or located anywhere else in the Web or on the Internet. A hypertext link, for instance, can jump to a location two-thirds down from the top of another HTML file that is located halfway around the World. Besides HTML files and locations within HTML files, other objects also can be linked, including images, audio files, animations, videos, and more. In fact, anything that has an address on the Internet can be linked to, including many Internet services that predate the Web but still continue to exist on the Internet along with the Web, including Gopher files, FTP directories, WAIS files, Archie databases, Veronica searches, and so on.

In July 1945, Vannevar Bush, who had been the head of the Office of Scientific Research and Development during World War II, wrote an article, "As We May Think," that was published in *Atlantic Monthly*. In the article, he made the earliest proposal for what might be interpreted as a hypertext system. He proposed a system called a *memex*, which he described as working along similar lines to the human brain, being characterized by the association of an "intricate web of trails."

NOTE

You can read Vannevar Bush's article, "As We May Think," online at the *Atlantic Monthly* site (**www.theatlantic.com/unbound/flashbks/computer/bushf.htm**).

Twenty years later, in 1965, Ted Nelson, a graduate student at Harvard, inspired by reading Vannevar Bush's article, coined the term *hypertext* and worked out the basic characteristics of what a hypertext system might be. Nelson described hypertext as being "nonsequential writing" in *Literary Machines*, a book that he self-published in 1974. He worked for many years on elaborating a full-fledged hypertext system that he called Zanadu, but which was never completed. Nelson also coined the term *hypermedia* to describe the nonsequential linking of different media, as well as another wonderfully apt term, the *docuverse*, which encompasses the universe of hypertext-linked documents.

Prior to the invention of the Web, a number of hypertext systems were implemented. The earliest was Xerox's NoteCards system created in 1985. The Owl Guide hypertext system was released in 1986, and Apple released the HyperCard system, created by Bill Atkinson, in 1987. Asymmetrix Toolbox, a clone of the HyperCard system, was later developed for Windows.

In 1989, Berners-Lee was directly influenced by Nelson's ideas when he formulated his concepts for the creation and formation of what soon became the World Wide Web. It is no accident that the term *hypermedia* is prominently featured in Berners-Lee's initial description of the Web as a "wide-area hypermedia information retrieval initiative." Nelson's term, *docuverse*, is also a very close analog for Berners-Lee's description of the Web as "the universal space of all network-accessible information." Figure I.6 provides a graphic illustration of how hypertext and hypermedia interact within the universal space, or docuverse, that they inscribe.

FIGURE I.6 • *A hypertext link can jump to another document, a subsection within a document, a hypermedia object (image, audio, video, animation, and so on), or any other object or resource that has an address on the Internet.*

NOTE For links to resources on the Web that discuss the history of hypertext, see this Introduction's section at the IRC for this book at **www.emcp.com/**.

HOW DID HTML EVOLVE?

Although Berners-Lee defined the original principles and specifications for HTML, HTML has undergone change. Many other individuals, organizations, companies, and factors have had a hand in determining what HTML was eventually to become.

The Original Version of HTML

HTML has evolved over time. Berners-Lee introduced the original version of HTML in 1989 along with the proposal for the formation of the World Wide Web. The original version of HTML provided for the following features:

- A document title.
- Heading elements used to structure an HTML document hierarchically.
- Standalone paragraph elements, but used as separators, not as containers, as in later versions of HTML. (There was no provision for adding line breaks, however.)
- Hypertext anchors (the A element) for creating hypertext links to documents or locations within documents.
- Bulleted and glossary lists, but not numbered lists.
- Non-keyboard character entities (such as for the copyright and registered symbols).
- An address block designator (the ADDRESS element).

NOTE To find out more about the original version of HTML at the W3C site at **www.w3.org/History/19921103-hypertext/hypertext/WWW/MarkUp/MarkUp.html**. Reading the earlier versions of HTML can be a great way to find out more about why HTML is what it is and how it has evolved and changed in response to the evolution and growth of the Internet and the Web.

HTML 2.0

The original version of HTML, although functional, was simple and missing many of the key features taken for granted by today's Web authors. A number of proposals were made for extending the original version of HTML, which as a group were generally referred to as "HTML+," but which were never formalized into a final recommendation (or standard).

The first official new version of HTML, following the original version, was HTML 2.0, which was formalized as an official recommendation in 1995. HTML 2.0 added the following features:

- HTML, HEAD, and BODY elements, to provide a more explicit structure to an HTML document (specifying separate "header" and "body" sections within an HTML document).

- The paragraph element goes from being a standalone "separator" to being a container element, but with an implied ending.
- Display of inline images.
- Bold, italic, and monospace highlighting.
- Horizontal rules and line breaks.
- Numbered lists.
- Various other elements still in common use in HTML, including block quotes, preformatted text, metadata, HTML comment codes, and input forms.

NOTE To find out more about HTML 2.0, you can read its specification at the W3C site at **www.w3.org/MarkUp/html-spec/**.

Vendor Extensions to HTML

Early on, browser vendors began adding their own extensions to HTML in response to the clear desire of authors and surfers for more richly formatted documents. For instance, the capability to display inline images in an HTML document was originally an extension to HTML created by the makers of the first widely distributed graphical Web browser, Mosaic. Many of these extensions to HTML are commonly referred to as "Netscape extensions" because the makers of the Netscape Navigator browser, the first widely distributed commercial Web browser, introduced them. Some of these extensions allowed authors of HTML documents to specify changes in font colors and sizes, as well as background colors and images, for instance. Later, Microsoft, when its Internet Explorer browser began to overtake the Netscape browser in popularity, introduced some of its own extensions to HTML, which are commonly referred to as "Microsoft extensions." Examples of Microsoft extensions include changing the typeface being used to display an element (using the FONT element's FACE attribute) and creating text that scrolls horizontally across the screen (the MARQUEE element).

Many of the extensions originally introduced as extensions to HTML have since been incorporated into the official specifications (or "standards") for HTML. Some extensions to HTML, however, remain as unofficial and proprietary extensions of HTML. For instance, a Netscape extension, the ability to specify blinking text, has not been incorporated into standard HTML. Microsoft's MARQUEE element has also never been incorporated into standard HTML.

HTML 3.2

After failing to come to consensus on a more comprehensive reformulation of HTML (the proposed HTML 3.0 specification), the W3C ended up approving a somewhat less ambitious proposal in January of 1997, which it termed HTML 3.2. This new HTML standard brought into the fold a number of extensions to HTML that had been introduced by Netscape, as well as several features that had originally been proposed as part of HTML 3.0:

- Variable font sizes and colors, text and link colors, and background colors and images
- Flowing text around images and image borders

- Tables for displaying data in rows and columns
- Horizontal alignment of document divisions (new), headings, paragraphs, and rules
- Superscripts and subscripts, strikethrough, and underlining
- Client-side image maps
- Scripts and styles (the latter, however, not implemented until HTML 4.0)

NOTE To find out more about HTML 3.2, you can read its specification at the W3C site at **www.w3.org/TR/REC-html32**.

HTML 4

Less than a year later, in December of 1997, the W3C recommended a new specification, HTML 4.0. HTML 4.0 included the following new features:
- Frames and inline frames
- Fully implemented style sheets
- Font typeface changes
- New form and table elements
- New text highlighting elements, including insertions and deletions, quotations, abbreviations, acronyms, and text spans
- Java applets and multimedia objects (not just inline images, but other hypermedia objects such as videos, animations, audio consoles, and so on)
- Triggering of scripts in response to mouse and user actions

The W3C has since come out with an HTML 4.01 recommendation. The HTML 4.01 recommendation is largely a fine-tuning of the HTML 4.0 specification. The W3C has announced that HTML 4.01 is the final version of HTML—there should be no new HTML elements or attributes added in the future. HTML 4.01 will remain a recommended specification, but future development will be focused in other related technologies (style sheets, scripting technologies, the document object model, as well as XHTML and XML). This is actually a good thing because it provides stability to what has been a tumultuous evolution—the HTML 4.01 you learn today should still be fully usable and an approved specification 5, 10, or even 20 years from now. Unlike many other technologies, you do not have to worry that what you learn today will become almost completely obsolete in the next 5 to 10 years.

NOTE To find out more about HTML 4.01, you can read its specification at the W3C site at **www.w3.org/TR/html4/**. For links to resources on the Web that discuss the history of HTML, see this Introduction's section at the IRC for this book at **www.emcp.com/**.

XML AND XHTML

The W3C recommended the XML 1.0 specification in February of 1998 and the XHTML 1.0 specification in January of 2000. The W3C describes XML as "a universal format for structured documents and data on the Web." Unlike HTML, XML does not possess a specific set of named elements and attributes, but allows authors to freely invent the elements and attributes that describe the structure of a document or data set. Elements and attributes can be created to take advantage of specific applications, or applications can be created to take advantage of specific element and attribute sets. XML, by itself, provides no formatting or display characteristics, but relies on style sheets to determine the presentation or appearance of an XML document.

XHTML, on the other hand, is an attempt to reformulate HTML as a conforming XML application. An XHTML document, however, is much closer to an HTML document in structure and function than it is to an XML document. XHTML adopts certain syntactical rules from XML, which account for most of the differences between HTML 4 and XHTML, but lacks the freedom to liberally create new elements and attributes that is present in XML. Like HTML 4, XHTML possesses a specific set of elements and attributes that possess specific meanings and functions: a <p> start tag signals the beginning of a paragraph element in both XHTML and HTML, but in XML might signal the beginning of a process, priority, practice, or just about anything that an author might determine the letter "p" to mean.

XHTML 1 possesses the ability to be further extended and modularized in ways not provided for in HTML 4. The main body of XHTML, apart from the differences in its syntactical rules and its ability to be further extended and modularized in the future, is simply HTML 4, so you need not worry that learning HTML 4 first will be a waste of time. In fact, having a good grasp of HTML 4 is essential if you later decide to also learn XHTML.

XHTML is just one of a family of new XML-based applications. Other XML-based applications include MathML (Mathematical Markup Language), SMIL (Synchronized Multimedia Integration Language), and RDF (Resource Description Framework). Additionally, XML is at the heart of a new W3C initiative called the Semantic Web, which proposes the creation of a layer of semantic relations on the Web, so that Web-based objects can be identified, not just by name and object type, but by meaning as well. A semantic meaning of "game" could be attached to a certain type of object (a game application), while a meaning of "tutorial" could be attached to another type of object (an educational application), and so on, which could help facilitate finding and identifying relevant data in what is otherwise threatening to become a haystack composed entirely of needles.

NOTE

Tim Berners-Lee, along with co-authors James Hendler and Ora Lassila, originally proposed the idea for the Semantic Web in an article published in the May 2001 issue of *Scientific American*. If you would like to read the article, it is available online at **www.sciam.com/issue.cfm?issueDate=May-01**. To find out about the current work being done to develop the Semantic Web, see the W3C's page on the Semantic Web at **www.w3.org/2001/sw/**.

THE IMPORTANCE OF WEB STANDARDS

Even though the W3C does not term its recommended specifications as being standards, the intent is clearly to arrive at a degree of agreement and consensus that can result in the establishment of a standard. For instance, browser vendors are members of the W3C and vote, along with other members, on whether proposed specifications should be formally recommended by the W3C. While the W3C has no power to force anyone to follow a recommendation, those who are expected to follow the recommendation, such as browser vendors, for instance, have been directly involved in formulating the recommendation and voted for its approval. The likelihood of their implementing the recommendation is therefore considerably enhanced. Only a broad-based implementation of a recommendation will cause it to become a "standard."

This brings up an important consideration for anyone who wants to produce HTML documents for wide distribution over the Web. Only by sticking to the agreed upon recommendations for HTML (the HTML "standards") can you be relatively assured that your documents will be reliably displayed not only in all current Web browsers, but in future Web browsers as well. Browser vendors are committed to supporting standard features in future browsers, but can drop non-standard ("proprietary") features at their whim. Netscape, for instance, supported a proprietary feature, the LAYER element, in its Navigator 4.x browsers, but has dropped support for it in its Netscape 6.x browsers. Netscape, however, is not at similar liberty to drop support for features that have been included in the recommended HTML specifications. By sticking to using only standard elements and attributes in your HTML documents, you help to ensure that your documents will remain *forward-compatible* with future browsers and user agents.

Does that mean you should never use non-standard (or proprietary) HTML codes? Not really. Sometimes, the only way to do a particular thing is by means of non-standard HTML codes. For instance, when creating a framed Web site, you cannot create absolutely "seamless" frames (with no visual indication of the separation between frames) using standard HTML that will work in all browsers. Thus, to have that effect, you must use non-standard HTML codes. All the same, you need to be aware that a cross-browser trick that works today may no longer work when a new generation of browsers arrives on the scene. This is a trade-off you may have to live with, however, if it is important to take advantage of a non-standard method to achieve a particular result.

If you are creating HTML documents for distribution over an intranet that is limited to users of your local network who all use the same browser, there should be no immediate harm in using proprietary extensions provided by that browser. When creating HTML documents for distribution across the Web, however, you should try to stick as much as possible to using standard HTML codes, except where there is absolutely no alternative other than to use a non-standard code.

In providing HTML instruction, this book stresses the importance of using standard HTML codes to create HTML documents. Only a few instances exist in which the added facility provided by a non-standard code might justify its use. Even so, you should carefully consider the possible impacts whenever you use a non-standard code. In the rare instances they are presented, this book clearly identifies any non-standard codes that are included in its examples, so you can decide for yourself whether you want to use them or not.

This book teaches the latest HTML standard, HTML 4.01. The W3C has stabilized the current element and attribute set that composes HTML 4.01, so what you learn this year will not be outmoded next year, as has frequently happened in the past. HTML 4.01 is also almost entirely incorporated into XHTML, forming an HTML core component that should remain largely unchanged as new extensions and modules are added to XHTML in the future.

NOTE For links to resources on the Web that discuss the importance of Web standards, see this Introduction's section at the IRC for this book at **www.emcp.com/**.

RELATED WEB TECHNOLOGIES

Additional client-side and server-side technologies have been developed over the years that are used as adjuncts to HTML. These include Cascading Style Sheets (CSS), JavaScript and other scripting languages (such as VBScript, for instance), the Document Object Model (DOM), the Java programming language, Server-Side Includes (SSI), Active Server Pages (ASP), Structured Query Language (SQL), Cold Fusion, PHP (PHP: Hypertext Preprocessor), Macromedia Flash, Wireless Application Protocol (WAP), Virtual Reality Modeling Language (VRML), Microsoft.NET, and more.

NOTE For links to resources on the Web describing many of the Web technologies that are used in conjunction with HTML, see this Introduction's section at the IRC for this book at **www.emcp.com/**.

WEB-BASED LEARNING ACTIVITIES

In this book's text, Find It icons in the margin highlight the Web addresses of additional resources you might find helpful or informative. To further extend your learning using the Web, you can

- Go back and visit any of the Web addresses highlighted in this Introduction that you have not yet visited. Look for additional resources and information that add to your understanding and knowledge of the Internet, the Web, and HTML. When you find a relevant page or site with information or resources you might want to access later, add it to your Favorites (in Internet Explorer) or your Bookmarks (in Netscape or Mozilla).
- Visit this book's Internet Resource Center at **www.emcp.com** to find additional Web addresses of resources that you can investigate and explore.
- Do further research a specific topic discussed in this Introduction. For instance, do further research on the Web on packet-switching networks, what they are, how they work, and so on. Compile your research into a report that can be shared with your fellow students. You can also team up with other students to create a class presentation on particular topic. Look for other topics mentioned in this introduction that you could further research and report upon.

PART ONE

HTML Essentials

HTML/CSS/DHTML

1

Creating a Basic Web Page

PERFORMANCE OBJECTIVES

After finishing this chapter, you should understand the basics involved in creating a typical Web page, including how to:
- Use your text editor and a graphical Web browser to create and preview your HTML files.
- Create your page's top-level elements.
- Use heading and paragraph elements to structure and create the base content for your page.
- Create hypertext links, lists, and link lists.
- Align elements horizontally on the page.
- Insert inline images in your page.
- Create an address block for your page.

Learning how to use HTML to create a Web page is similar to learning how to ride a bicycle. No amount of theorizing or reading about it is going to teach you how to ride, in other words. You just have to get on and ride, although some training wheels, and someone to grab the handlebars if you start to teeter after the training wheels come off, can definitely be helpful.

   In this chapter, you learn how to use this book's example files, review basic HTML pointers, and create a basic Web page. You will not be doing anything particularly fancy, but you will use everything you learn in this chapter in virtually every Web page you create in the future.

USING THE EXAMPLE FILES

In this book's chapters, you use the author-prepared example files to complete the included tutorials and exercises. Your instructor might provide these to you or ask you to download them from the Web.

Downloading the Example Files

If your instructor provided the example files to you in a network folder, on a CD-R disc, or on floppy disks, skip to the next section. If your instructor wants you to download the example files, go to this book's Internet Resource Center (IRC) at the EMCParadigm

Web site at **www.emcp.com/**, click on College Division, and then click on the Internet Resource Centers link in the sidebar.

The example files are available for download in Windows, Macintosh, and Linux/UNIX formats, all as ZIP-formatted files. If you do not have software capable of expanding ZIP files installed on your computer, the following programs for Windows, the Macintosh, and Linux can be downloaded from the Web:

- WinZip at **www.winzip.com/** (shareware/Windows)
- Stuffit Expander at **www.stuffit.com/expander/** (freeware/Macintosh, Linux, and Windows)

For additional links to file-compression utilities you can download and use, visit this book's IRC at **www.emcp.com/** or the Tucows site at **www.tucows.com/**.

See this book's IRC for more pointers and tips on how to download the example files. Ask your instructor for additional help if you still have trouble successfully downloading and expanding them.

NOTE — Although the example files for this book are available in Windows, Macintosh, and Linux/UNIX formats, this book only includes procedure steps, notes, tips, and cautions for using Windows or the Macintosh, which are more likely to be used in a classroom or computer lab.

Creating a Working Folder or a Working Disk

You can use a working folder on your computer or your network or you can use a working disk to work with this book's examples.

CREATING A WORKING FOLDER The easiest way to work with the examples is to create a working folder on the computer you are using or in your network folder. Your instructor will let you know whether you should use a working folder to do the examples and exercises.

If your instructor has provided the example files to you in a network folder or on a CD-R disk, or if you have downloaded and expanded the example files, you will find all of the example files available in an **HTML_Examples** folder. To create your working folder, you just need to copy the HTML_Examples folder and rename it as **My_HTML_Examples**:

- If using your network folder, copy the HTML_Examples folder to your network folder and rename it as your working folder.
- If using Windows, copy the HTML_Examples folder to the **My_Documents** folder and rename it as your working folder.
- If using a Macintosh, copy the HTML_Examples folder to your **Desktop** and rename it as your working folder.
- If using a Linux or other UNIX-based operating system, copy the HTML_Examples folder to your root folder or to any other folder where you are storing your data files and rename it as your working folder.

The My HTML Examples folder name for your working folder is just a suggestion. You can use any name you want for your working folder (**Gillian's_HTML_Examples**, for instance). In this book, this folder is referred to as "your working folder."

In your working folder, you will now find separate folders (**chap01**, **chap02**, and so on) that contain the example files for each chapter. When working on a chapter's examples and exercises, you need to save the files you create in that chapter's folder within your working folder.

If your instructor has provided the example files to you on floppy disks, you need to create and name your own working folder, and then copy the individual chapter files from the floppy disks into your working folder.

CREATING A WORKING DISK Your instructor might want you to create and work on a working disk. To create a working disk, you should have two formatted 3.5-inch floppy disks. From the example files provided by your instructor or that you have downloaded from this book's IRC, copy the example folder for the chapter you are working on. For this chapter, for instance, copy the **chap01** folder. Save any files you create while doing this chapter's examples or exercises in that folder. For each following chapter, copy its example folder to your working disk and save your work for that chapter in that folder. When you fill up your working disk, just copy the most recent chapter folder you are working in to a new working disk.

At the end of each work session, you should copy your working disk onto a second floppy disk. If your working disk becomes damaged or lost, you will have a backup.

If you need more help in using the example files, ask your instructor for assistance. You also can find additional help and instructions at the IRC at the EMCParadigm Web site.

When working with the example files and saving files you create, you might need to perform basic operations, such as copying, moving, renaming, deleting, or opening folders or files. You should already be familiar with these kinds of basic operations. If you are confused about how to complete a particular folder or file operation on the system you are using, ask your instructor for assistance.

UNDERSTANDING THE BASICS

Before you actually start creating an HTML file, it might be helpful to review some basic pointers about how an HTML file is organized and composed.

Tags, Elements, and Attributes

The *element* is the basic building block of an HTML document. Anything included within an HTML document is either an element or is contained within an element.

HTML uses codes called *tags* to delimit elements within an HTML document. For any element, a range of *attributes* can be set to further qualify the presentation or function of an element, some of which are required, while others are optional.

In HTML, you can set two different element types: a *container element* and an *empty element*.

CONTAINER ELEMENTS A container element brackets text (or other elements) between two tags, a *start tag* and an *end tag*, with the end tag distinguished from the start tag by a leading forward slash, like this:

```
<tagname>element content</tagname>
```

NOTE
In this book, HTML code or other code that you need to key is printed in a magenta color. Code printed in a black color is presented for example purposes or for context and need not be keyed. You will be prompted later in this chapter when you need to run your text editor and start keying in any HTML codes.

For instance, the following is an example of setting a level-one heading element (a container element) using start and end tags:

```
<h1>This Is a Level-One Heading</h1>
```

In this case, the start of the container is *tagged* with a **<h1>** start tag, while its end is tagged with a **</h1>** end tag. Both start and end tags are enclosed inside of left and right angle-brackets (< and >), while in the end tag, the element name is preceded by a forward slash (/).

HTML elements are often loosely referred to as tags. It is important to stress, however, that an HTML element comprises both the tags that are used to mark the start and end of the element *and* anything that is enclosed within those two tags (see Figure 1.1).

FIGURE 1.1 • *An HTML element is not only the tags (codes) used to delimit it, but everything in between as well.*

EMPTY ELEMENTS An empty element uses a single tag, without an end tag, and does not contain text or other elements. An empty element is also called a *standalone element*, because it stands on its own and does not bracket anything.

In the following example, the HR (Horizontal Rule) element, which is an empty element, indicates where a browser should draw a horizontal rule across the page:

```
<h1>This Is a Level-One Heading</h1>
<hr>
```

HTML does not have many empty elements; most HTML elements are container elements. Besides the HR element, some other empty elements that are frequently used include the IMG (Image) and BR (Line Break) elements.

You will also run into some instances where a container element will look like an empty element, with just a start tag, but no end tag. Rather, the element actually has an implied end tag, where the end of the element is implied by the start of a following element. (You will be alerted to this when such an element is first utilized in the examples.)

BLOCK AND INLINE ELEMENTS An HTML element that is contained in the body of an HTML document (in the BODY element) also can function as a *block element* or an *inline element*. Block elements are presented as separate blocks, starting on a new line with vertical spacing inserted above and below the element. Inline elements are presented "in a line" in the position where they are inserted, without starting a new line (and without any additional vertical spacing inserted above or below the element).

Nesting and Overlapping

Because an HTML document is organized in a hierarchical fashion, elements must always either bracket or be nested inside of other elements. You should never overlap elements in an HTML document. For instance, the following two examples apply both italics and bolding to text within an HTML document:

```
<b><i>bolded and italicized</i></b>
<i><b>italicized and bolded</b></i>
```

Both of these are correct—all that matters is that one be nested inside the other.

On the other hand, here is an example of how you should not do it:

```
<b><i>bolded and italicized</b></i>
```

In this case, the B (Bold) element overlaps the I (Italic) element, which might confuse a browser about what should be nested inside of what.

Attributes and Attribute Values

In HTML elements, attributes can be used to further specify the presentation or function of an element. An attribute has two parts, the name of the attribute and its value, which are included in an HTML element in the following manner:

```
attribute="value"
```

The following example shows a series of attributes being applied to the IMG (Image) element:

```
<img src="myimage.jpg" height="200" width="150">
```

In HTML, you are free not to quote an attribute value as long as it contains only letters (a–z and A–Z), digits (0–9), hyphens, periods, underscores, and colons. The W3C recommends, however, that all attribute values be quoted.

Case-Insensitivity

In HTML, both element and attribute names are case-insensitive. Both of the following lines of code are perfectly valid, for instance:

```
<img src="myimage.jpg" height="200" width="150">
<IMG SRC="myimage.jpg" HEIGHT="200" WIDTH="150">
```

In this book, element and attribute names included in code examples are all presented in lowercase. Part of the reason for this is that XHTML, unlike HTML, is case-sensitive—XHTML requires that all element and attribute names be lowercased. Following the same rule in your HTML documents will make your task much easier if you ever decide you need to convert any of them to XHTML.

CASE EXAMPLE: CREATING A PERSONAL WEB PAGE

To gain experience creating a basic Web page, you will create one of the most common pages found on the Web: a *personal Web page*. A personal Web page might include information about a person's life, family, and other interests, for instance. It might provide further details about a person's educational, professional, or career background and involvements. It might also focus on particular interests or hobbies that the person creating the page might have. In other words, a personal page can include just about anything under the sun that is related to the person creating the page.

Johnny Watson is a college student who wants to create his own personal Web page. He does not yet know a lot about HTML, so he wants to keep things simple. He has two primary interests—sports and gardening—that he wants to feature in his page, although he wants to include other information, too. Soon to be graduating, he wants to include links to his biography and his resume. He also wants to share links to his favorite sports and gardening Web sites, and to Web pages created by his friends.

RUNNING YOUR TEXT EDITOR

You will be using a text editor to create, edit, and save your HTML documents. If using Windows, you can use Notepad. If using the Macintosh, you can use SimpleText.

Windows. In Windows 95, 98, and higher, to run Notepad, click the Start button and select Programs, Accessories, and Notepad. In Windows XP without the Classic Desktop theme selected, you need to select All Programs before you select the Programs option.

For a shortcut for running Notepad, click the Start button, select Run, key **notepad**, and press Enter.

TROUBLE *spot*

Word Wrap is turned off by default in Windows Notepad. That is fine for writing program code, but when creating and editing HTML documents, you want Word Wrap turned on. To turn Word Wrap on in Notepad in all versions of Windows except Windows XP, select Edit and Word Wrap; in Windows XP, select Format and Word Wrap. When Word Wrap is on, a checkmark is displayed next to the Word Wrap option.

If you are using Windows 95, you will need to turn Word Wrap on each time you run Notepad. If you are using Windows 98 or any other later version of Windows, Word Wrap in Notepad remains turned on until you turn it off.

Macintosh. To run SimpleText for OS 8 and higher, double-click on the Macintosh HD icon, the Applications folder, and the SimpleText program icon. (Mac OS X users can find SimpleText in their folder of OS 9 applications.) If you cannot find the SimpleText program in the Applications folder, use the Finder to search for its location. (Select File, Find, and then search for **simpletext**.)

Users of earlier versions of the Macintosh OS (OS 7 or earlier) can use the TeachText text editor to edit and save HTML files.

Users of Macintosh OS X can also use TextEdit, which is included in the Applications folder, to edit and save HTML files. Note, however, that TextEdit defaults to saving files in RTF (Rich Text Format), so you need to first select Format, then Make Plain Text, when creating and saving an HTML file. To turn on word wrap, select Format, then Wrap to Page.

Other Platforms. If you are using a platform other than Windows or Macintosh, you should still be able to do the examples, exercises, and assignments included in this book. See your system documentation or help system to find out how to run any text editor that is included with your system's software. You also can download text editors for many platforms, including Linux, OS/2, BeOS, and QNX, from Tucows at **www.tucows.com/**.

STARTING YOUR PAGE

For this example, you will be creating an HTML file from scratch. You do not need to open an example file to get started. Just key the indicated example codes directly into your text editor's window. Any text that you need to key is displayed within a code example in a magenta font.

Let any long lines wrap—you do not need to insert a hard return at the end of every line in the example codes. Additional leading is inserted between code blocks to indicate where you need to insert a hard return.

Starting with the Top-Level Elements

The HTML, HEAD, and BODY elements specify the top-level hierarchy of a Web page. The HTML element identifies that the document is an HTML document, while the HEAD and BODY elements are nested inside the HTML element.

Key the following codes into your text editor's window to create the top-level elements for your page:

```
<html>
<head>
</head>
<body>
</body>
</html>
```

In the HEAD element you will be including elements that define characteristics of the document, such as a title, a style sheet, meta data elements that describe the document, and so on.

In the BODY element you will be including elements that will be displayed in a browser, such as headings, paragraphs, lists, and so on. Because you have not yet included anything in the BODY element, opening your document in a browser at this point would just display a blank browser window. I will prompt you later when you should run your browser to check out the visual results of your work.

The specifications for HTML make including the start and end tags for the HTML, HEAD, and BODY elements optional. If you leave out the tags for these elements, the elements will still be there; they are implied, rather than absent. The original version of HTML (from 1992) did not even include HTML, HEAD, or BODY elements. When first learning HTML, it is a good idea to include these elements to help clarify how an HTML document is structured and organized.

Creating a Title for Your Page

The TITLE element is a required element that is nested inside the HEAD element. Every HTML document should have a TITLE element (even if you choose to omit the optional start and end tags for the HEAD element).

Add the following TITLE element to your HTML document:

```
<html>
<head>
<title>Johnny Watson's Home Page</title>
</head>
<body>
</body>
</html>
```

The content of the TITLE element is generally displayed in a browser's title bar. Including additional text in your title that summarizes the content of your page may improve the chances of your page being displayed, or cause it to be displayed earlier, in a search engine's list of search results. There is effectively no limit on the amount of text you can include in your title, but search engines vary on how much of an extended title content they will display or index. The Google search engine (**www.google.com/**), for instance, only displays up to 60 characters in a page's title.

Add additional text to your title that more specifically indicates the actual content of your page to make your title more informative and more likely to be found in a search engine's list of search responses. Because Johnny Watson's two favorite interests are sports and gardening, add additional text to the title to indicate that:

```
<html>
<head>
<title>Johnny Watson's Home Page: Sports and Gardening</title>
</head>
<body>
</body>
</html>
```

A number of other elements can be included in the HEAD element. These include the META, BASE, LINK, STYLE, SCRIPT, OBJECT, and ISINDEX elements. Because you are creating a basic Web page in this chapter, these other elements are not discussed at this point. You will learn about using the META element in Chapter 2, *Working with Online Documents*. For more information on the other HEAD elements, see Appendix A, *HTML Quick Reference*.

Saving a Starting Template

All HTML files start out the same. You can save your HTML file now as a template, so you can use it later to create additional HTML files without having to retype the same starting HTML elements every time.

Earlier in this chapter, you were prompted to create a working folder or disk to hold the HTML files you will be creating in this book. If you have not done that yet, return to "Using the Example Files" earlier in this chapter and follow the instructions that are given there.

Windows. Save your HTML document as a starting template, so you can reuse it later:

1. In Notepad, select File and Save. The My Documents folder should be displayed in the Save As dialog box.
2. If using a working folder (located in your My Documents folder), just double-click the folder to open it. If using a working disk, click on the Save in box and click the drive where your working disk is located. (If your working folder is located in your network folder, use the Save in box to navigate to the folder and open it.)
3. Click on the Save as type box and select All Files (*.*).
4. In the File name box, key a name for your starting template. For instance, you might key **start.html** as the file name. Click the Save button (or press the Enter key) to save your starting template.
5. Resave your HTML document under another name, so you will not overwrite your starting template. Select File and Save As, open your working folder or working disk, and then open the chap01 folder. Key **watson.html** as the file name (see Figure 1.2) and click Save.

FIGURE 1.2 • *The HTML document, watson.html, is to be saved in the chap01 folder.*

TROUBLE spot

Windows. If you have display of known file extensions turned off and save an HTML file with Text Documents selected in the Save as type box, Windows tacks a hidden ".txt" file extension to the end of your file name. Thus, watson.html, for instance, would actually be saved as watson.html.txt. When you go to open this file, you will just see the "watson.html" part of the file name, since the .txt file extension is hidden. The file icon, however, will indicate it is a text file, rather than an HTML file. Internet Explorer will display this file as an HTML file, but all other browsers will treat it as a straight text file, displaying the raw HTML codes instead.

To avoid this problem and make working with files much easier in Windows, you should turn on the display of file extensions. On the Web, files are identified by their file extensions, so it is important that they be visible to you. To turn on display of file extensions, double-click My Computer on your Desktop, select View and Folder Options (or Tools and Folder Options in Windows XP), click the View tab, and uncheck the Hide file extensions for known file types (or similar) check box.

Turning on the display of file extension also can help reduce your vulnerability to e-mail viruses. Many e-mail viruses use a visible and a hidden file extension to fool you into thinking that a file is a type of file that is safe to open.

Macintosh. Save your HTML document as a starting template, so you can reuse it later:

1. In SimpleText, select File and Save. The contents of your Desktop should be displayed in the dialog box.
2. If using a working folder (located on your Desktop), just double-click it to open it. If using a working disk, insert the disk into your floppy disk drive (it should

automatically be opened in the Save dialog box). (If your working folder is located in your network folder, you can use the Network Browser, located on the Apple menu, to open any shared network drives.)

3. In the Save this document as box, key a name for your starting template. For instance, you might key **start.html** as the file name. Press Return (or the Enter key) or click the Save button to save your starting template.

4. Resave your HTML document under another name, so you will not overwrite your starting template. Select File and Save As, open your working folder or working disk, and then open the chap01 folder. Key **watson.html** as the file name and click the Save button.

When saving an HTML file, do *not* include any spaces in the file name. Although this is allowed in both Windows and the Macintosh, it is not allowed on a UNIX server (and most Web servers run UNIX). More recent UNIX Web servers will substitute the space character's escape code (**%20**) for spaces in folder and file names, but any link to the file would also have to reduplicate the escape character in place of the space, or the link will not work. Other UNIX Web servers will simply generate a "file not found" or other error when encountering spaces in folder or file names. Substitute underscores (_) for spaces, if necessary.

Also, always add the file extension **.html** (or **.htm**) to any HTML file that you save (even if working on the Mac, which does not use file extensions to identify the file type). Internet Explorer will display an HTML file without the file extension as an HTML file, but other browsers will treat it as a straight text file and simply display the raw HTML codes.

ADDING A LEVEL-ONE HEADING

HTML includes six heading-level elements (H1, H2, H3, and so on) that can be used to create headings. Generally, only one H1 heading is included, at the top of the BODY element, functioning as a heading, or title, for the whole document. The other heading elements are then used to indicate sections and subsections within a document.

Unlike the content of the TITLE element, which is only displayed on a browser's title bar, the content of the H1 element is displayed within the browser window and serves as the displayable title for the document.

Edit the H1 element as shown here to include keywords in the level-one heading:

```
<html>
<head>
<title>Johnny Watson's Home Page: Sports and Gardening</title>
</head>
<body>
<h1>Sports, Gardening, and Other Interests</h1>
</body>
</html>
```

PREVIEWING YOUR WORK

To preview your work while creating the document examples that are presented in each chapter, you need to have your HTML document open in both your text editor and your browser. You should frequently switch between your text editor and your browser, saving your work in your text editor and then refreshing the display of your document in your browser.

Previewing Your HTML Document in Your Browser

Now that you have added something to your HTML document that will be displayed within a browser's window, you should preview your results in your browser.

Save your document and then open it in your browser, so you can see your results for yourself:

1. Resave **watson.html**. In Windows Notepad or SimpleText on the Macintosh, select File and Save to resave your document. In SimpleText, you also can press Command+S to resave your document.

Although you can press Ctrl+S to resave a document in most Windows applications, that will not work in Windows Notepad. In Windows Notepad, you need to select File, then Save to resave your document.

2. Run your browser. You do not need to connect to the Internet to preview a local file, so if you are prompted to connect or if your dialer starts to dial up your connection, just click the Cancel button. Depending upon which browser you are using, your browser might generate an error message, saying it is unable to open its default start page; just click OK.

3. Open **watson.html** in your browser. The steps for doing this can vary between browsers, and even between different versions of the same browser.

   In Internet Explorer 6 for Windows, for instance, select File, Open, and click the Browse button; in Netscape 6 for Windows, select File, Open Page, and click the Choose File button; in Internet Explorer 5 and Netscape 6 for the Macintosh, select File and Open File.

4. Next, open your working folder or working disk, open the folder for the chapter (chap01) you are working in, and then open **watson.html**. Figure 1.3 shows watson.html opened in a Web browser.

Title element

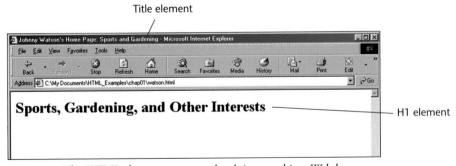

H1 element

FIGURE 1.3 • *The HTML document, watson.html, is opened in a Web browser.*

Alternatively, you can open a local HTML file in your browser by dragging it from its folder and dropping it in your browser's window. You will need to arrange your HTML file's open folder and your browser's window so you can drag your file from one and drop it in to the other. Whether this is easier than just using the File menu, however, is debatable.

As you add more example code to your HTML document, do not just rely on the figures to show you what your results should look like. Instead, use the figures as prompts to save your HTML document in your text editor and switch over to your browser. Just click the Refresh (or Reload) button in your browser to refresh the display of your page.

Hopping between Your Text Editor and Your Browser

Both Windows and the Macintosh support similar shortcut key combinations that you can use to quickly hop back and forth between your text editor and your browser.

Practice hopping back and forth between your text editor and your browser:

Windows. Hold down the Alt key and tap the Tab key to cycle through the icons for any open applications. Release the Alt key when the icon for the application you want to hop to is highlighted to bring its window to the foreground. You also can just press Alt+Tab once to jump to the previously opened application window.

Macintosh. Hold down the Command key and tap the Tab key to cycle through any open application windows. Release the Command key when the application window you want to hop to is displayed.

Stopping and Restarting Your Work

Depending on your learning style and computer experience, the amount of time required to complete this chapter's examples and exercises varies. It is not how fast you learn HTML that matters, but how well you learn it, so do not feel that you have to rush to complete a chapter within any specific time frame. You can stop at any point within a chapter, save your work, and then pick up where you left off at another time or location.

Follow these steps to resume work on a chapter's examples and exercises at home or in a computer lab, for instance:

1. In your text editor, save your HTML file in the chapter folder in which you are working.
2. Copy the chapter folder you are working in (the chap01 folder for Chapter 1) to a formatted 3.5-inch floppy disk.
3. Take the floppy disk to any other location where you want to resume working on a chapter's examples or exercises. In the new location, just run your text editor, select File, then Open, and reopen the HTML file you are working on.

Windows. When opening a file in Notepad, the Open dialog box defaults to displaying only text files (with a .txt extension). To see HTML files (with a .html extension), you need to first select All Files (*.*) in the Files of type box.

WRITING AN INTRODUCTORY PARAGRAPH

The P (Paragraph) element is used to tag regular text paragraphs in an HTML document. An HTML document should contain no untagged text.

Using an introductory paragraph in an HTML document allows you to include additional keywords that search engines and Web directories can index, improving the chances of visitors finding your page.

Add the following introductory paragraph to your HTML document (see Figure 1.4):

```
<body>
<h1>Sports, Gardening, and Other Interests</h1>
<p>Welcome to my home page! My name is Johnny Watson and I'm a
big nut about two things: sports and gardening! You may think
that is an odd combination, but they really have more things in
common than you might suppose. First they are both largely
outside activities: I enjoy participating in, rather than just
watching, sports, for one thing. When the weather is bad, there
can be an indoor component to both activities. I enjoy following
some of my favorite teams on TV, while watering my indoor
plants at the same time!</p>
</body>
</html>
```

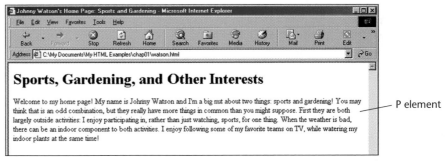

FIGURE 1.4 • *An introductory paragraph can both describe your page and include keywords that search engines and Web directories can use to index your page.*

NOTE

Beginning HTML authors often think they can just insert multiple empty P elements to add vertical spacing within a Web page. That will not work. Browsers completely ignore multiple empty P elements in an HTML document. In Chapter 2, you will learn how to use the PRE element, which is the only element in which nested spaces, tabs, and returns are displayed and can be used to insert vertical spacing within an HTML document (by nesting two or more returns).

SPACING, TABS, AND RETURNS

Web browsers ignore any spacing, tabs, and hard returns you insert into an HTML document. You can use these to make your document's raw codes easier to read and interpret visually.

Insert hard returns where ¶ characters are shown and insert spaces where · characters are shown:

```
<html>
<head>
¶
···<title>Johnny Watson's Home Page: Sports and Gardening</title>
¶
```

```
</head>
<body>
¶
···<h1>Sports, Gardening, and Other Interests</h1>
¶
···<p>Welcome to my home page! My name is Johnny Watson and I'm
a big nut about two things: sports and gardening! You may think
that is an odd combination, but they really have more things in
common than you might suppose. First they are both largely
outside activities: I enjoy participating in, rather than just
watching, sports, for one thing. When the weather is bad, there
can be an indoor component to both activities. I enjoy following
some of my favorite teams on TV, while watering my indoor plants
at the same time!</p>
¶
</body>
</html>
```

You also can use tabs, instead of three spaces, to indent the first line of nested elements within your text editor.

To test this yourself, save your HTML file in your text editor (select File, Save), switch over to your Web browser, and refresh the display of your page by clicking the Refresh (or Reload) button. You should not see any change in your page, which should still look like Figure 1.4. That is because spaces, tabs, and hard returns, while visible in your text editor, should have no effect when displayed in a Web browser.

INSERTING COMMENTS

You can annotate your HTML document by inserting comments, which can be helpful if you or someone else has to revise your document at a later date, for instance. Later you might not remember why you did something a certain way, but a comment can remind you.

In HTML, bracket anything you want to include as a comment within `<!--` and `-->` codes. Any text or codes included within these two codes can be read within your text editor, but will not be displayed in a browser.

Test using HTML comments in your document:

1. Add the following HTML comments to your document:

```
<body>
<!--Top-level heading for document-->
   <h1>Sports, Gardening, and Other Interests</h1>
<!--Introductory paragraph-->
   <p>Welcome to my home page! My name is Johnny Watson and I'm
a big nut about two things: sports and gardening! You may think
that is an odd combination, but they really have more things in
common than you might suppose. First they are both largely
outside activities: I enjoy participating in, rather than just
watching, sports, for one thing. When the weather is bad, there
can be an indoor component to both activities. I enjoy following
some of my favorite teams on TV, while watering my indoor
plants at the same time!</p>
```

2. Select File, then Save to save your document, switch over to your Web browser, and refresh the display of your page by clicking the Refresh (or Reload) button.

After refreshing the display of your page, you should not see any change in your page, which should still look like Figure 1.4, since HTML comment codes and any text or other elements contained within them, although visible in your text editor, have no effect when displayed in a Web browser.

Although you can nest both text and HTML elements inside HTML comment codes, you cannot nest an HTML comment inside another HTML comment.

You also should make sure that any HTML comment codes you add to your document are properly nested and not overlapping any elements. When commenting out an element's start tag, make sure that its corresponding end tag, if it has one, is also commented out.

CREATING A HYPERTEXT LINK

In HTML, the A (Anchor) element is used to add hypertext links to Web pages. Hypertext links can be added anywhere you can add text within an HTML document.

Johnny Watson wants to link the word "sports" in the first sentence of his introductory paragraph to his favorite sports-related Web site.

Add the following codes to link the word "sports" to ESPN.com:

```
Welcome to my home page! My name is Johnny Watson and I'm a big
nut about two things: <a href="http://www.espn.com/">sports</a>
and gardening!
```

Johnny Watson also wants to link the word "gardening" in his introductory paragraph's first sentence to his favorite gardening site.

To get some practice creating a hypertext link on your own, follow the previous example of linking the word "sports" to the ESPN Web site, but this time link the word "gardening" in the same sentence to the BBC's Lifestyle/Gardening site, using **http://www.bbc.co.uk/gardening/** as the value of the HREF attribute.

You should have now inserted two inline hypertext links, linking the words "sports" and "gardening" to actual sites that exist on the Web (see Figure 1.5).

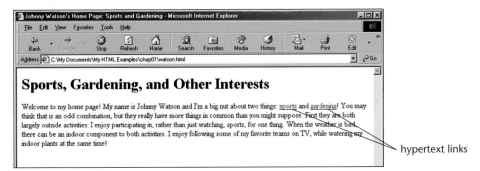

FIGURE 1.5 • *Any word or phrase within an HTML document can be turned into a hypertext link.*

If you are connected to the Internet, you can test any links you create on your local machine, without having to publish your page to the Web.

Test the "sports" and "gardening" links you just created:

1. If not already connected, run your dialer and connect to the Internet.
2. Save your document in your text editor, switch to your browser, and refresh the display of your page.
3. Click the "sports" and "gardening" links to test them. Your browser should jump to the ESPN site and the BBC gardening site, respectively. Click your browser's Back button to return to your example page.

A common error when creating hypertext links is to leave off the second quotation mark that encloses the A element's HREF value. This omission causes most browsers to simply ignore anything that follows because it is considered to still be part of the HREF value, until a following A element start tag is encountered. This can result in a single word, a whole paragraph, or even the rest of a page not being displayed. Figure 1.6 shows what this looks like in a browser.

missing link

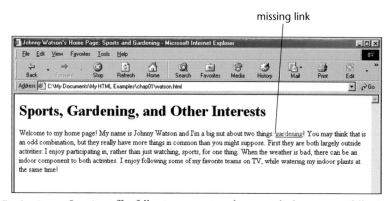

FIGURE 1.6 • *Leaving off a following quote in a hypertext link can cause following text to disappear.*

Other common errors when creating hypertext links include leaving off the closing > character of the A element's start tag and leaving out the / character in the A element's end tag. Browsers may react to either of these errors by considering all following text to be part of the same hypertext link (and underlining it), until another A element is encountered.

These link examples illustrate that you can turn any word (or phrase) within an HTML document into a hypertext link. Additionally, if Johnny Watson also had created a biography page for himself, he could have linked his name to that page.

The A element must include either an HREF (Hypertext Reference) attribute or a NAME attribute. To create a hypertext link, you use the HREF attribute. The NAME attribute is used for targeting a location within an HTML document that can be jumped to via a hypertext link—you will learn about doing that in Chapter 2.

The HREF attribute references the Web address, or *URL (Uniform Resource Locator)*, of an object or resource on the Web. For an explanation of the different components that make up a URL, see the "What Is a URL?" sidebar later in this chapter.

In this chapter's code examples, two types of URLs are used: *absolute URLs* that point to locations on the Web and file names. When you use just a file name to link to a file, you are telling a browser that the linked file is located in the same folder as the linking file. A URL that only references a file name is actually a form of a *relative URL*. A relative URL states the position of the linked object *relative to* the location of the linking file (with just a file name, for instance, indicating that both the linked and the linking files are located in the same folder). You also can use relative URLs to link to files located in other folders within your own site. For a full explanation of how to use relative URLs in your Web pages, see the "Using Relative URLs" sidebar in Chapter 6, *Creating Multi-Page Web Sites.*

Links are generally displayed in a browser as blue underlined type (as shown previously in Figure 1.6), while links to sites you have already visited are generally colored purple.

For a graphical illustration of the different parts that compose a hypertext link, see Figure 1.7.

FIGURE 1.7 • *A hypertext link is composed of several parts.*

ADDING A NEW SECTION

As was stressed earlier, an HTML document is structured hierarchically. Heading-level elements are generally used to indicate the hierarchical structure of a document, with an H1 element marking the document heading, H2 elements marking major section headings, and H3 elements marking subsection headings within major sections. If an additional heading level is required, an H4 element can mark subsection headings within other subsections. Six heading-level elements are available, from the largest (H1) to the smallest (H6). Of these, only the four largest are normally used because the two smallest (H5 and H6) are displayed in font sizes that are smaller than the default paragraph text font.

To see this for yourself, look at the HTML document included with this chapter's example files, which shows all six heading-level elements in relation to the default paragraph text. Just open **headings.html** in your browser from the chap01 folder (see Figure 1.8).

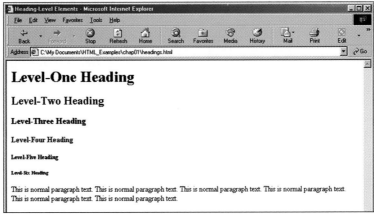

FIGURE 1.8 • *Six different heading-level elements are available, but only four are as large as or larger than normal paragraph text.*

Johnny Watson wants to add a list of links to his page linking to both local Web pages, such as his biography and resume, and to other Web pages that are located at other sites on the Web. He also wants to include his link list inside its own section, with an H2 element heading the section and a following text paragraph introducing the list of links.

What Is a URL?

The Web forms a space (a "universal space," as Tim Berners-Lee puts it) through which users ("surfers") can navigate to find information, objects, or other resources. To locate something, however, that something must have a discreet and unique location and identity. On the Web, a *Uniform Resource Locator* (URL) identifies the location and identity of any object. An object's URL is also commonly referred to as a *Web address*. A URL can be divided into the following functional parts:

- **Scheme.** A URL's scheme identifies the service (and protocol) being requested. For a URL linking to an object located on a Web server, `http:` specifies that HyperText Transfer Protocol (HTTP) be used to transfer the requested object. Any other valid URL scheme can be used (`ftp:`, `gopher:`, `telnet:`, and so on). A double forward-slash (//) following the scheme indicates it is a hierarchically structured service (organized in folders and subfolders). For instance, Web servers and FTP servers organize the documents and objects they contain in folders (and subfolders) and thus require the double forward-slash following their URL's scheme: `http://www.yahoo.com/` or `ftp://ftp.netscape.com/`, for instance. On the other hand, USENET news servers and e-mail addresses are not hierarchically organized and thus should not have the double-slash following the scheme (`news:comp.infosystems.www.authoring.html` or `mailto:peterpiper@picklepicker.com`, for instance).

- **Host (IP Number or Alias/Domain Name).** Every device connected to the Internet has an IP (Internet Protocol) number that uniquely identifies it (221.196.64.21, for instance). In place of an IP number, the combination of an *alias* and a *domain name* also can be used, which is how most people connect to servers on the Web. An alias is a prefix to a domain name that stands for (is an alias for) a resource located within that domain. It precedes, rather than follows, the domain name because it is not a hierarchically located object under that domain, but rather is an alias for such an object. The most commonly

---

  Add a level-two heading and a following paragraph element (remove the horizontal spacing and the HTML comments that you inserted previously; see Figure 1.9):

```
<p>Welcome to my home page! My name is Johnny Watson and I'm a big
nut about two things: <a href="http://www.espn.com/">sports</a>
and <a href="http://www.bbc.co.uk/gardening/">gardening</a>! You
may think that is an odd combination, but they really have more
things in common than you might suppose. First they are both
largely outside activities: I enjoy participating in, rather than
just watching, sports, for one thing. When the weather is bad,
there can be an indoor component to both activities. I enjoy
following some of my favorite teams on TV, while watering my
indoor plants at the same time!</p>
<h2>Biography, Interests, and Friends</h2>
<p>In the following list, I've included links to biographical
and career info, resources focused on topics that I'm especially
interested in, and pages that have been created by friends of
mine:</p>
```

used URL alias on the Web is www (as in `http://www.altavista.com/`). Not all Web addresses use a www alias. For instance, `http://maps.yahoo.com/`, uses an alias, maps, to point to the location of the Yahoo! Maps home page within the yahoo.com domain. A domain name, such as yahoo.com, on the other hand, is a unique name that identifies a resource on the Internet and the Web.

- **Port Number (Optional).** A port number is included in a URL only if a server is using a port number other than the default: `http://www.somehost.org:81/`, for instance. The default port number for a Web server is 80, whereas the default port number for an FTP server is 21; generally, you should only have to include a port number in your own URLs if your hosting server requires it (a rarity).

- **Resource Path.** If the linked object is not located in the host's root folder, the resource path specifies the folder path to the object's location. For instance, `http://www.somehost.org/users/jwatson/` specifies that the URL's object is located in the **jwatson** folder, which is located in the **users** folder, which is itself located in the root folder of www.somehost.org.

- **Object.** The object of a URL is the actual file that is being linked to. For instance, `http://www.somehost.org/users/jwatson/watson.html` specifies that the object of the URL is a file named watson.html. Note, however, that a Web server administrator can specify a default file name, usually index.html, which is implied if an object file name is not included in a URL. This file is often called an *index page*. Thus, `http://www.somehost.org/users/jwatson/` and `http://www.somehost.org/users/jwatson/index.html` may represent the same URL. Other default file names also can be used (index.htm, default.html, welcome.html, or main.html, for instance), but index.html is by far the most commonly used.

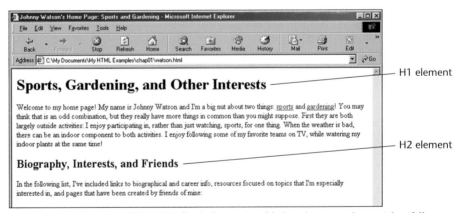

FIGURE 1.9 • *An H2 (Level-Two Heading) element is added to the page, along with a following text paragraph.*

Creating a Bulleted List

You can add two basic kinds of lists to an HTML document: *bulleted lists* and *numbered lists*. A bulleted list is also called an *unordered list* and is created using the UL (Unordered List) element; a numbered list is also called an *ordered list* and is created using the OL (Ordered List) element. In this section, you will add a bulleted list to your HTML document.

To create a bulleted list, you use two HTML elements: a UL element brackets the list as a whole, indicating that it is a bulleted (or unordered) list, while LI (List Item) elements indicate the individual items that are included in the list.

Use the UL and LI elements to create a bulleted list, following the introductory paragraph you added previously (see Figure 1.10):

```
<h2>Biography, Interests, and Friends</h2>
<p>In the following list, I've included links to biographical
and career info, resources focused on topics that I'm especially
interested in, and pages that have been created by friends of
mine:</p>
<ul>
<li>My biography
<li>My resume
<li>Get the latest sports scores
<li>Get indoor gardening tips and advice
<li>My friend Joe's site
<li>My friend Jane's site
</ul>
```

Biography, Interests, and Friends

In the following list, I've included links to biographical and career info, resources focused on topics that I'm especially interested in, and pages that have been created by friends of mine:

unordered list ———
- My biography
- My resume
- Get the latest sports scores
- Get indoor gardening tips and advice
- My friend Joe's site
- My friend Jane's site

FIGURE 1.10 • *A series of bulleted list items are added to the page.*

That is all you have to do to create a bulleted (or unordered) list. Lists are simple to create and add to your Web pages, so do not hesitate to use them.

Notice that the LI element, used to create a list item, has no end tag. The LI element is not an empty element, but its end tag is implied, either by the start of a following LI element or by the end of the list.

TROUBLE *spot*

Including the P element end tag (**</p>**) is also optional in all versions of HTML. In many instances, however, this omission can cause problems or produce differing results in different browsers—for that reason, you should always add the end tag at the end of your paragraph elements.

Creating a Link List

After you have created a bulleted list, you only need to add the links to create a link list (or list of hypertext links).

Create a link list and test it in your browser:

1. Create a link list by nesting the list item text within hypertext links (see Figure 1.11):

```
<ul>
<li><a href="mybio.html">My biography</a>
<li><a href="myresume.html">My resume</a>
<li><a href="http://www.usatoday.com/sports/scores.htm">Get the
latest sports scores</a>
```

```
<li><a href="http://www.about-house-plants.com/">Get indoor
gardening tips and advice</a>
<li><a href="http://www.blank.com/jshmoe/">My friend Joe's site</a>
<li><a href="http://www.wherever.com/jdoe/homepage.html">My friend
Jane's site</a>
</ul>
```

link list ———

Biography, Interests, and Friends

In the following list, I've included links to biographical and career info, resources focused on topics that I'm especially interested in, and pages that have been created by friends of mine:

- My biography
- My resume
- Get the latest sports scores
- Get indoor gardening tips and advice
- My friend Joe's site
- My friend Jane's site

FIGURE 1.11 • *A link list is just a list with links.*

2. Save your file, switch over to your browser, and refresh the display of your page.
3. Test the biography and resume links. Dummy example pages are included with the example files that should display in your browser when you click on the links. Click the Back button to return to your example page.
4. The next two links are to actual sites on the Web; test them if you are connected. The last two links, however, to Joe's and Jane's sites, are fictional links that should not connect to anything—test either one to find out what happens when the object of a link does not exist.

In Windows and on the Macintosh, file and folder names are case-insensitive. However, on a UNIX computer, file and folder names are case-sensitive. For example, on a UNIX computer the file names MyPage.html and mypage.html actually represent two different file names.

This UNIX naming convention matters because most Internet Web servers are UNIX servers. If you find that links that worked on your local Windows or Macintosh machine suddenly stop working after you transfer your Web page files to a Web server, the problem might be due to the case-sensitivity of file and folder names on a UNIX server. To avoid the problem, make sure that file and folder names included in your URLs match the actual file and folder names *exactly*.

The same holds true for absolute URLs that link to sites located on the Web. Although domain names are case-insensitive, any folder or file names may be case-sensitive—so whenever you include an absolute URL in your page, make sure that you include it exactly as it is given (including any uppercase characters).

Linking Etiquette

At one time it was considered proper *netiquette* to request permission before linking to someone else's page. That was because unwanted traffic could easily push a page or site beyond its traffic allowance, when such allowances were much smaller than they are now. If running a major site, you should still request permission to link to a smaller site for that very reason. In general, especially when linking to a site's front page, you should not feel constrained to ask permission to link. These days most people want all the links they can get. However, if someone requests that you not link to their page, especially if it is a personal or family page, it is only good manners to comply.

Even linking to a page within someone else's site should not be a problem, as long as you properly identify both the site and page you are linking to. It is the responsibility of the Web author to code a site's pages so that the home or front page can easily be reached from any page within the site. The basic nature of hypertext and the Web, as enunciated in the visions of Ted Nelson and Tim Berners-Lee, is that any page can be linked to from any other page. Without links, there would be no Web, after all. Links are what make the Web valuable.

If using frames, however, you should not link to another's page so that it is displayed within a frame within your site without first getting permission. Always include `target="_blank"` or `target="_top"` in your link's A element when linking within a framed page to an external site or page, so the page will be displayed outside of your frame. You will learn about using frames in Chapter 6.

On the other hand, some authors design pages to be displayed only within a frame in their own site. If at all possible, you should try to link to the page containing the frame, rather than simply the page within the frame. Where this is not possible, you might include a link to the site's front page, along with a link to their framed page.

It is, however, unethical to link to someone else's images or other media files without permission, whether using the A, IMG, EMBED, or OBJECT elements, because doing so can significantly increase someone else's traffic, which they have to pay for. Such linking on the Web is usually considered to be a form of theft (stealing someone else's bandwidth). Instead, you should always link to the site or page where the image or other media file is located, rather than directly to the file. If the image or media file is the only content of a page, you should link to a page that links to that page, has content that identifies the site, and provides a link to its front page.

Gathering URLs

If you later want to create your own list of hypertext links, you will need to gather the URLs and other link information you want to use. You can gather URLs for use in your Web pages in several ways:

- **While Surfing.** Open the page you want to create a link to in your browser, click and drag to highlight the contents of the Address (or Location) box, and press Ctrl+C (Windows) or Command+C (Macintosh). Press Ctrl+V (Windows) or Command+V (Macintosh) to paste the URL into your text editor. Copy and paste the level-one heading content to use it as your link text.
- **Copying a Link.** Just right-click on the link (on the Macintosh, hold down the Ctrl key and click) and select to copy the link. The actual menu option varies from browser to browser: Copy Shortcut, Copy Target, Copy Link Address, Copy Link Location, and so on.
- **From Internet Explorer Favorites.** Open your Favorites in the Explorer bar (select View, Explorer Bar, and Favorites). Locate a favorite you want to use, right-click on it (on the Mac, hold down the Ctrl key and click), and select Properties. Copy the contents of the URL box and paste it into your text editor. For the link text, you can type in the name of the Favorite (or any other text you want to use).
- **From Netscape or Mozilla Bookmarks.** In Netscape 6, select Bookmarks and Manage Bookmarks. Find the Web page you want to link to, right-click on it (on the Macintosh, hold down the Ctrl key and click), and select Properties. Copy the contents of the Location box and paste it into your text editor; copy the contents of the Name box and paste it to use it as the link text.

HORIZONTALLY ALIGNING HEADINGS, PARAGRAPHS, AND DIVISIONS

So far, all of the elements you have added to your example page are left-aligned (horizontally aligned with the left margin). That is because left-alignment is the default horizontal alignment for block elements, except for the CENTER element.

Using the ALIGN Attribute

You can use the ALIGN attribute to center, right-align, left-align, or justify text contained in a number of block elements, including heading level and paragraph elements. You only need to explicitly set left-alignment for a block element if a different horizontal alignment has been set for it, by being nested inside of a CENTER element, or inside of a center- or right-aligned DIV element, for instance.

Right-align the level-one heading, justify the text paragraphs, and center the level-two heading (see Figure 1.12):

```
<h1 align="right">Sports, Gardening, and Other Interests</h1>
<p align="justify">Welcome to my home page! My name is Johnny
Watson and I'm a big nut about two things: <a
href="http://www.espn.com/">sports</a> and <a
href="http://www.bbc.co.uk/gardening/">gardening</a>! You may
think that is an odd combination, but they really have more
things in common than you might suppose. First they are both
largely outside activities: I enjoy participating in, rather than
just watching, sports, for one thing. When the weather is bad,
there can be an indoor component to both activities. I enjoy
following some of my favorite teams on TV, while watering my
indoor plants at the same time!</p>
<h2 align="center">Biography, Interests, and Friends</h2>
<p align="justify">In the following list, I've included links to
biographical and career info, resources focused on topics that
I'm especially interested in, and pages that have been created
by friends of mine:</p>
```

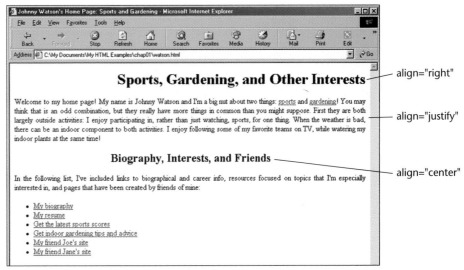

FIGURE 1.12 • *The H1 element is right-aligned, the H2 element is centered, and the P elements are justified.*

Using the DIV Element

You cannot use the ALIGN attribute to horizontally align the UL (or OL) element. You can, however, horizontally align a list by nesting it inside a centered or right-aligned DIV (Division) element. The DIV element is used to delineate a division within a document. Any element that can be nested in the BODY element can also be nested in a DIV element.

Center the link list by nesting it inside a center-aligned division (see Figure 1.13):

```
<div align="center">
<ul>
<li><a href="mybio.html">My biography</a>
<li><a href="myresume.html">My resume</a>
<li><a href="http://www.usatoday.com/sports/scores.htm">Get the
latest sports scores</a>
<li><a href="http://www.about-house-plants.com/">Get indoor
gardening tips and advice</a>
<li><a href="http://www.blank.com/jshmoe/">My friend Joe's
site</a>
<li><a href="http://www.wherever.com/jdoe/homepage.html">My
friend Jane's site</a>
</ul>
</div>
```

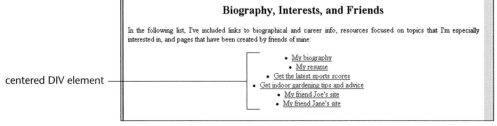

centered DIV element

FIGURE 1.13 • *The bulleted list is nested inside a centered DIV element.*

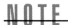

By itself, a DIV element has no formatting. Using HTML alone, you can only change the horizontal alignment of text or other elements nested in a DIV element. To apply additional formatting directly to a DIV element, you need to use styles. You will learn about using styles in Chapter 3, *Working with Fonts, Colors, and Backgrounds.*

INSERTING AN INLINE IMAGE

The IMG (Image) element is used to insert an *inline image* in an HTML document. The IMG element is an inline element and not a block element. When you insert an inline image, it is displayed in the position—in the middle of a line of text, for instance—where it is inserted. The IMG element is also an empty (or standalone) element.

An example *banner image*, banner.gif, is included with the example files for this chapter. A banner image is an image that is displayed along the top of a Web page and thus is normally wider than it is high. A logo image is similar to a banner image and is also displayed at the top of a Web page, but is usually of relatively equal height and width.

NOTE Image formats other than GIF (Compuserve Graphics Interchange Format) can be used to insert inline images, including JPEG (Joint Photographic Experts Group) and PNG (Portable Network Graphics) graphic formats. GIF, JPEG, and PNG images are compressed; non-compressed image formats, such as TIF or BMP, should not be inserted as inline images. Differences between image formats and how to decide which image format is best to use in a given situation are discussed in Chapter 4, *Working with Images and Other Media*.

action

Remove the H1 element's right-alignment and then use the IMG element to insert a banner image as an inline image at the top of the page (see Figure 1.14):

```
<p><img src="banner.gif"></p>
<h1 align="right">Sports, Gardening, and Other Interests</h1>
```

IMG element —

FIGURE 1.14 • *A banner image can add visual appeal to a Web page.*

In the IMG element, the SRC (Source) attribute specifies the URL of the image file that is to be inserted into the HTML document. This attribute works just like the HREF attribute in the A element. To specify an image file that is located in the same folder as the HTML file in which it is to be inserted, you just need to specify the image's file name.

Notice in the code example that the IMG element is nested inside a P element. That is because the IMG element is an inline element and should not be nested directly inside the BODY element. An inline element should always be nested inside a block element.

 Alternatively, you can nest the banner image at the start of the level-one heading, with a line break providing vertical separation between the image and the following heading text:

```
<h1><img src="banner.gif"><br>Sports, Gardening, and Other
Interests</h1>
```

Nesting in this way adds less vertical spacing between the inline image and the following heading text than nesting the inline image in a separate P element. Use of the BR (Break) element to add a line break is discussed later in this chapter, in the "Creating an Address Block" section.

Horizontally Aligning an Inline Image

Because the IMG element is an inline element, you cannot directly align it horizontally relative to the page. Instead, you must nest it inside a block element that is horizontally aligned.

Center the inline image by nesting it inside the centered paragraph element (see Figure 1.15):

```
<p align="center"><img src="banner.gif"></p>
<h1 align="center">Sports, Gardening, and Other Interests</h1>
```

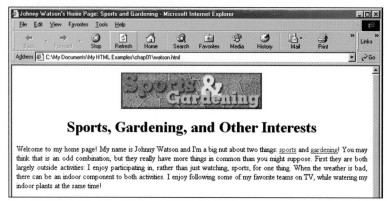

FIGURE 1.15 • *Nesting it in a centered paragraph centers the inline image.*

Using the CENTER Element

Alternatively, you also can use the CENTER element to center nested text or other elements. In HTML 4, the CENTER element is considered a shortcut for a center-aligned DIV element. Current browsers should treat **`<center>element content</center>`** as equivalent to **`<div align="center">element content</div>`**.

Remove the **`align="center"`** attribute from both the P element and the following H1 element, and then nest both elements within a CENTER element:

```
<center>
<p align="center"><img src="banner.gif"></p>
<h1 align="center">Sports, Gardening, and Other Interests</h1>
</center>
```

When you view this in your browser, the result should be identical to using the ALIGN attribute to center the P and H1 elements (refer to Figure 1.15). Because the CENTER element was originally a Netscape extension, it has been around longer than the DIV element, which was introduced with HTML 3.2. Thus, older browsers that are not HTML 3.2-compliant might support the CENTER element, but not the DIV element. For that reason, you might want to use the CENTER element, rather than a DIV element, when you want to center nested text or other elements.

Including Alternative Text

Not everyone uses a graphical Web browser to access Web pages. Some surfers still use text browsers, such as Lynx, which cannot display images. Individuals with visual impairments may use a Braille browser or a speech browser to access Web pages. Inclusion of alternative text for images is required for Web pages created for government organizations and agencies, which must comply with the Americans with Disabilities Act (ADA). Schools, libraries, businesses, or other entities that accommodate the public may have their own policies that mandate the inclusion of alternative text in Web pages, as well as other requirements, to ensure accessibility.

If you only include an SRC attribute in an IMG element, users of text-only or non-visual browsers may have a hard time identifying what the import of your image is or even that it is an image. Other surfers might be accessing your page through a Web-enabled cell-phone display, for instance, that shows only the text in your page, but not the images. Figure 1.16 shows watson.html as it is displayed in Lynx, a text-only browser.

To make it easier for anyone using these alternative means to access a Web page, you should include an ALT (Alternative Text) attribute in your IMG elements to further identify your image.

without ALT attribute

FIGURE 1.16 • *When viewing a Web page in Lynx, a text-only browser, a user might have difficulty identifying that an image is an image or what its function or content is.*

Use the ALT attribute to add alternative text to the IMG element's start tag, indicating the function and content of the image:

```
<center>
<p><img src="banner.gif" alt="Banner Image: Sports &
Gardening"></p>
<h1>Sports, Gardening, and Other Interests</h1>
</center>
```

As shown in Figure 1.17, the inline image is now more helpfully identified in Lynx.

with ALT attribute

FIGURE 1.17 • *Alternative text helps users of text-only or non-visual browsers to identify the function and content of images used in your Web pages.*

NOTE

You can download versions of Lynx for Windows, UNIX, and Macintosh at **lynx.browser.org**/. To open a local HTML file in Lynx, just press the G key to select G(o); type a standard URL for a local file, replacing any spaces in folder names with the **%20** escape sequence; and press the Enter key. The following is an example of a standard local URL:

```
file:///C:/My%20Documents/My%20HTML%20Docs/mypage.html
```

Some people also surf the Web with the display of graphics turned off in their browsers because they can find and access information on the Web faster by just downloading text and not the accompanying images. If you do not include alternative text in your images, these surfers will be presented with an image icon, but with no information to help them interpret the function or content of your image.

NOTE

For additional information and resources on Web design accessibility issues, see the Blindness Resource Center's "Access to the Internet and Web" site at **www.nyise.org/access.htm**. Accessibility is an important issue in Web design, so look for additional comments, notes, and tips in the remainder of this book that highlight measures you can take to make your own Web designs accessible to everyone.

Specifying an Image's Height and Width

Whenever you include an inline image in your page, you should specify its dimensions. That way, browsers can allocate display space for your image before it has been completely downloaded, which can allow the remainder of the page to be displayed quicker. The HEIGHT and WIDTH attributes are used in the IMG element to set the dimensions, in pixels, of an inline image.

Add HEIGHT and WIDTH attributes to the IMG element that specify the actual dimensions of the image:

```
<p><img src="banner.gif" alt="Banner Image: Sports & Gardening"
height="75" width="300"></p>
```

In most cases, you should not use the HEIGHT and WIDTH attributes to change the dimensions of an inline image, but should use these attributes to specify the actual dimensions of the image. Instead of resizing an image in the browser, you should open it in your image editor and resize it there. Reducing the size of an image in a browser is a waste of bandwidth because the full-size image still must be downloaded over the Internet. Increasing the size of an image in a browser might magnify any image flaws or deficiencies.

CREATING AN ADDRESS BLOCK

In HTML, the ADDRESS element is used to create an *address block* within your page. The address block should identify the author or owner of a page and provide a means for visitors to provide feedback. Most often, the address block is inserted at the bottom of the page.

Use the ADDRESS element to add an address block to the example document that contains the author's name and e-mail address:

```
<address>
Johnny Watson<br>
E-mail: jwatson@whatnot.com
</address>
</body>
</html>
```

Spam is unsolicited and unwanted e-mail messages. Spammers use spiders (or robots) to crawl the Web looking for e-mail addresses listed in Web pages. Including your e-mail address in your Web page might expose you to more spam than you are already receiving.

One option is to sign up for a free *Web-mail* (Web-based e-mail) address and include it in your Web pages to provide visitors a way to contact you or give you feedback. A Web-mail account is accessed through a Web site's address using your browser, rather than through a mail server using a mail program (such as Outlook Express, for instance) that you may have installed on your computer. If your Web-mail address starts to get spammed too much, just dump it and sign up for another Web mail address and use it instead, editing your pages to include the new address. Most Web-mail accounts limit the amount of space available to store messages (anywhere from 1Mb - 4Mb), so you should delete messages after you have read them, or move them to your own hard drive. You can then only let close friends and relatives know your permanent e-mail address, which should help limit the amount of spam sent to that address.

For a comprehensive listing of free Web-mail providers, just go to Yahoo! and do a search on **free e-mail**.

Most browsers display text nested in an ADDRESS block in an italic font. Nothing in the HTML specifications, however, dictates that text in an ADDRESS element should be italicized. Some earlier browsers do not italicize address block text and nothing compels future browsers to do so, either.

Nest the text in the address block inside an I (Italic) element to insure that every browser italicizes it:

```
<address><i>
Johnny Watson<br>
E-mail: jwatson@whatnot.com
</i></address>
```

Inserting a Line Break

You might notice in the previous example that a BR (Break) element is used. This element, as its name implies, is used to insert a line break. The BR element is an empty element that is useful for causing a break in a line when you do not want additional vertical spacing added, like the spacing that is automatically added between paragraph elements. It also can be used to demarcate the ends of lines in the stanzas of a poem, for instance.

Although current browsers generally support it, using multiple BR elements to create vertical blank space within an HTML document generally should be avoided. The HTML 4 specifications do not specify at all how multiple BR elements should be treated in browsers. Earlier HTML specifications stated that multiple BR elements should be collapsed to a single BR element and that may be how they are treated in some browsers. To add vertical blank space within an HTML document, you should use either the PRE (Preformatted) element or styles. You will learn about using the PRE element in Chapter 2 and about styles in Chapter 3.

Adding a Horizontal Rule

To help demarcate your address block from the remainder of your document's body, you can use the HR (Horizontal Rule) element as a separator. The HR element is an empty element that draws a horizontal line between the margins of the page.

Insert an HR element to separate the address block from the rest of the page (see Figure 1.18):

```
<hr>
<address><i>
Johnny Watson<br>
```

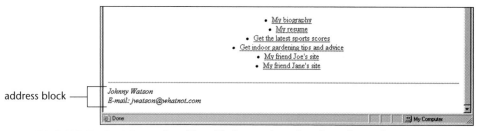

address block ———

FIGURE 1.18 • *An address block is used to identify, and provide a means to contact, the author or owner of a Web page.*

Linking to Your E-Mail Address

You can use a special form of URL to link to your e-mail address. This type of URL is commonly referred to as a *mailto address*. A link to a mailto address is created the same way you create a link to a regular Web address, except that mailto: is used as the URL scheme, instead of http:// and an e-mail address is used instead of a domain name address.

Add the following codes to turn Johnny Watson's e-mail address into a mailto link (see Figure 1.19):

```
Johnny Watson<br>
E-mail: <a
href="mailto:jwatson@whatnot.com">jwatson@whatnot.com</a>
```

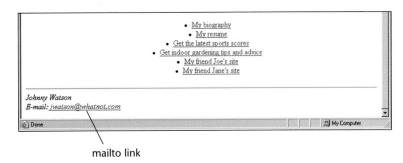

mailto link

FIGURE 1.19 • *You can use a mailto address to link to your e-mail address.*

A mailto link provides a convenient and easy way for visitors to your page to give you feedback by sending you an e-mail message. Not everyone can use a mailto link, however. Users of the Netscape and Mozilla browsers can, as long as they have installed the e-mail programs that come with those browsers and configured them to send mail. Users of Internet Explorer 5 or 6, however, need to install Outlook Express and configure it to send mail and then configure Internet Explorer to use that e-mail program as its default e-mail program (select Tools, Internet Options, click the Programs tab, and select Outlook Express as the e-mail client), before they can use a mailto link.

Because not everyone can use a mailto link, it is important to always include your e-mail address *both* as the mailto URL and as the link text, for instance:

```
<a href="mailto:your@address.com">your@address.com</a>
```

That way, if someone cannot use your mailto link, they can still click and drag to copy your e-mail address and then paste it into their e-mail program's mail composition window.

Horizontally Aligning Your Address Block

The content of the ADDRESS element is left-aligned by default. However, as is the case with the UL element, the ALIGN attribute cannot be used to horizontally align the content of the ADDRESS element. To horizontally align the content of your ADDRESS element, you need to nest it inside a CENTER element or a horizontally aligned DIV element.

Center the content of the ADDRESS element by nesting it in a CENTER element (see Figure 1.20):

```
<hr>
<center>
<address><i>
Johnny Watson<br>
E-mail: <a
href="mailto:jwatson@whatnot.com">jwatson@whatnot.com</a>
</i></address>
</center>
```

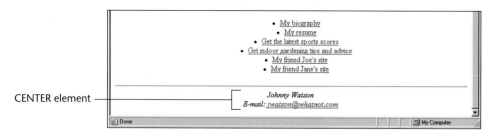

CENTER element

FIGURE 1.20 • *For a different look, you can center your address block.*

Including Other Items in the Address Block

You can include other things in your address block. If you are representing a business, you could include your toll-free number, fax number, and so on. You can include a link to your home page, for instance—this can be a good thing to do, even if the current page is your home page, because it lets others know that it is your home page. Some authors like to include the date when the page was created or last updated, as well.

Another option is simply to include a link in your address block to a contact page. This can be helpful if you have multiple e-mail contacts, phone numbers, and so on, especially if you need to update them frequently. If you use a link to a contact page, you will only need to update that page if you need to make a change, rather than updating your address block on every page.

CHAPTER SUMMARY

In this chapter, you set up your working folder or working disk, learned how to use the example files, reviewed basic HTML pointers, and created a basic Web page. You should now be familiar with many of the most commonly used HTML elements, including the top-level elements of an HTML document and the elements used to create headings, paragraphs, unordered (bulleted) lists, hypertext anchors, inline images, horizontal rules, line breaks, and address elements.

Code Review

HTML element	Contains all other elements within an HTML document.
HEAD element	Contains any elements used to provide "header information" about a document that is not displayed in a browser window.
BODY element	Contains any elements that compose the "body" of an HTML document and that are directly displayed within a browser window.
TITLE element	A required element within the HEAD element that specifies the title of the document. The title is not displayed within a browser window, but is displayed on a browser's title bar.
H1 element	A level-one heading (or displayable title) that is displayed in a browser's window.
H2 element	A level-two heading that marks the beginning of a major section within an HTML document. The H3 and H4 elements can be used to mark further subsection levels.
P element	Contains paragraph text that is included in an HTML file. There should be no untagged text within an HTML document.
HTML comments	Anything nested between <!-- and --> is not displayed in a browser.
A element	When used in conjunction with the HREF attribute, specifies that included text or elements operate as a hypertext anchor (or link).
HREF attribute	Within an A element, specifies the URL of a linked object.
UL element	A bulleted list (or unordered list).
LI element	List items that are included within a list.
ALIGN attribute	Used in the H1, H2, P, DIV, and ADDRESS elements, among others, to horizontally align their content on the page.
DIV element	Defines a document division, which can contain any other "body" elements.
CENTER element	A shortcut for `<div align="center">`*division content* `</div>` centers nested inline content.
IMG element	An inline image in an HTML document.
SRC attribute	Specifies the URL of an image to be displayed.
ALT attribute	Provides alternative text that can be displayed in place of an image.
HEIGHT attribute	Specifies the actual vertical dimension of an image in pixels.
WIDTH attribute	Specifies the actual horizontal dimension of an image in pixels.

ADDRESS element	Specifies an address block within an HTML document, in which the author or owner is identified and a means for feedback is provided.
HR element	Creates a horizontal rule that can be used as a separator in an HTML document.
BR element	Inserts a line break inside another element.

ONLINE QUIZ

Go to this text's IRC at **www.emcp.com/** and take the online self-check quiz for this chapter.

REVIEW EXERCISES

This section provides hands-on practice exercises to reinforce your understanding of the information and material included within this chapter. Save **watson.html** under another file name (**watson_practice.html**, for instance) and then use the new document to practice using the elements, attributes, and other features that were covered in this chapter:

1. Combine H2 or H3 elements with paragraph elements to add additional sections or subsections to your HTML document. Type dummy text for the paragraphs, if you wish—the main thing is to experiment with how heading and paragraph elements work, without worrying about the actual content.

2. Practice using the HTML comment codes (<!-- and -->). Do not worry at this point whether the comments you add help to annotate your code or not—the idea is to just get practice inserting comments, so feel free to use dummy text to create the comments.

3. Experiment using the ALIGN attribute to center, right-align, or justify headings, paragraphs, and divisions (DIV elements). Experiment using the CENTER element to center nested text and elements.

4. Practice creating additional in-context hypertext links. Look for additional words or phrases that can be turned into hypertext links. For instance, turn the word "weather" into a link to the Weather Channel (**www.weather.com/**). Look for or add other words or phrases that you can turn into in-context hypertext links to related sites you have discovered on the Web.

5. In the link list, add additional link items that link to sites on the Web. For instance, do research on the Web to find the URLs for any of the following: a major newspaper (Washington Post, Los Angeles Times, Chicago Tribune, and so on), a TV or cable news outlet (ABC News, PBS News, BBC News, and so on), a friend's Web site, or any other links you want to try creating.

WEB-BASED LEARNING ACTIVITIES

In this book's text, Find It icons inserted in the margin highlight the Web addresses of additional resources you might find helpful or informative. To further extend your learning using the Web, you can:

- Go back and visit any of the Web addresses highlighted in this chapter that you have not yet visited. Look for additional resources and information that add to your understanding and knowledge of the material covered in this chapter. When you find a relevant page or site with information or resources you might want to access later, add it to your Favorites (in Internet Explorer) or your Bookmarks (in Netscape or Mozilla).

- Visit this book's Internet Resource Center at **www.emcp.com/** to find additional Web addresses of resources related to the material covered in this chapter that you can further investigate and explore.

- Further research a specific topic introduced in this chapter. For instance, do further research on different text editors that are available for your platform (Windows, Macintosh, or UNIX). Create a catalog or database of the different features offered by different text editors (search and replace, spell checker, macros, and so on). Note whether the program is free to use or requires a registration fee for continued use (some programs are free for educational use). Download some text editors and write a report or review that can be shared with your fellow students. Individually, or teamed up with other students, provide an onscreen demonstration of how some different text editors work.

- It was stressed in this chapter that you should not use copyrighted images in your Web pages. You will find links to additional resources on this issue at this book's IRC. Use those resources, or other resources you can discover through Yahoo!, Google, or Altavista, to further research the issue of the use of copyrighted material (or images) on the Web. Discover at least three sources of public domain images that you are free to use. Write a report on this issue that can be shared with your fellow students.

PROJECTS

These projects can be done either in class, in a computer lab, or at home. Use the skills learned in this chapter to create any of the following projects.

Project 1. Create your own personal Web page.

Plan, write, and create your own personal Web page:

1. Plan and write the content of your personal page, including content to be used for a title, level-one heading, and introductory paragraph.

2. Gather any URLs, site names, or titles, and accompanying descriptive text you want to use in creating hypertext links, to be used either in-context or in a link list. Remember that any word or phrase in an HTML document can be a link, so look for opportunities to create interesting links to other sites or resources on the Web.

3. At the bottom of your text document, type the text you want to use as your address block. At minimum, type your name and an e-mail address. *Note: See the caution earlier, however, about the danger of exposing your e-mail address to spammers.* Use a dummy e-mail address here, if you like, or you can sign up for a free Web mail address that you can use.

4. Optionally, gather any JPEG or GIF images you want to include as inline images. Scan a snapshot of yourself, for instance, in the image-editing software that came with your scanner, and resize the image (keep it under 500 pixels wide, and 250 pixels wide is not too small for a personal snapshot). (You do not need to include any images, and you also do not need to include more than one, so you should not go overboard adding images at this stage.)

5. Tag your file with HTML tags to define the HTML elements of your page. Create your top-level elements (HTML, HEAD, TITLE, and BODY). Tag the level-one heading and any paragraphs. Tag any sublevel headings, bulleted lists, hypertext links, and your address block (inserting line breaks where needed). Insert any GIF or JPEG image you want to include as an inline image (adding HEIGHT and WIDTH attributes and alternative text).

Project 2. Create a topical Web page.

Plan, write, and create a basic Web page based on a topic you are interested in or know something about. Follow the directions given previously for creating a personal Web page, but substitute text and links (and any images you want to use) focused on the topic you want to present (instead of on yourself).

Project 3. Create a Web page for a club or organization.

Do you belong to or participate in a club or organization that does not yet have its own Web page? Create a Web page that includes a description of the club or organization, a list of its activities, and an e-mail link that visitors can use to find out about joining or contributing. Include a link list to other related clubs, organizations, and sites.

CHAPTER

2

Working with Online Documents

PERFORMANCE OBJECTIVES

In this chapter, you will learn to add features and execute formatting tasks that are common to a broad selection of online documents, including how to:
- Add a DocType declaration to identify the HTML version and compatibility level of your document.
- Use the META element to add a document description, a list of keywords, and other meta data.
- Add emphasis, such as bolding, italics, and underlining to text.
- Format quotations, citations, and definitions.
- Create superscripted footnote and endnote links.
- Insert copyright, register, and trademark symbols.
- Create a document menu (table of contents).
- Use monospaced highlighting.
- Work with numerical lists.
- Use preformatted text.

In Chapter 1, *Creating a Basic Web Page*, you learned how to create a simple personal Web page. In this chapter, you will learn more about how you can use HTML to format online documents, including creating an online academic paper, a frequently asked questions (FAQ) page, and online technical documentation.

USING THE EXAMPLE FILES

If you have created a working folder for storing files you create, you will find the example files for this chapter located in the **chap02** folder within your working folder. You should save any HTML files you create in this chapter in that folder.

If you have created a working disk, you should copy the chap02 folder to your working disk from the HTML_Examples folder that you or your instructor downloaded from this book's Internet Resource Center, or from a CD-R disc or floppy disk provided by your instructor. You should be able to include your work from both Chapter 1 and Chapter 2 on the same working disk. Ask your instructor for assistance if you do not know where you can find the HTML_Examples folder or how to copy the chap02 folder. You should save any HTML file you create in this chapter in the chap02 folder that you have copied to your working disk.

CASE EXAMPLE: FORMATTING AN ONLINE ACADEMIC PAPER

Increasingly, both students and teachers are choosing to publish academic papers and essays online, rather than just in paper form. Publishing a paper online can be a great way to get feedback and to stimulate discussion on a topic or position. In this exercise, you will add formatting to an example academic paper that is included with this book's example files.

Crystal Porter is a junior in college majoring in sociology. She is writing a paper titled "Commerce and Civilization" for her "Origins of Civilization" class. In this paper, she is arguing for commerce as a root cause, rather than simply a consequence, of the transition from simpler and more primitive "folk societies" to more complex urbanized civilizations.

Crystal wants to format her online document so that it looks and works like a regular academic paper that she would print out on a printer. However, she also wants to take advantage of some of the additional facilities afforded by HTML, such as using hypertext links to connect footnote numbers with their respective footnote text.

Although still in draft form and incomplete, she wants to put the paper online to start getting feedback from her professor and fellow students while she is still writing the paper.

Opening an HTML File in Your Text Editor

In this case example, you will be working with an example file, acad_paper_ex.html, which has been created for you. If using a working folder, you will find this file in the chap02 folder located inside your working folder. If you are using a working disk and have not already copied the chap02 folder (from the example disk or folder provided by your instructor) to your working disk, you need to do that to start working with the case example.

Open **acad_paper_ex.html** in your text editor:
1. Run your text editor (Notepad or SimpleText, for instance).
2. Select File, Open, and then open your working folder (My HTML Examples, or whatever you named it).

If you created your working folder in My Documents (Windows) or on your Desktop (Macintosh), you should just have to double-click on your working folder to open it.

If you created your working folder in your network folder, you need to navigate to and open that folder in your text editor's Open dialog box. In Windows, for instance, click on the Look in box to go to and open your network folder, and then open your working folder.

If you are using a working disk, you need to navigate to and open your floppy disk drive where your working disk is inserted. In Windows, for instance, click on the Look in box to go to and open your floppy disk drive.

3. If you are using Windows, click on the Files of type box and select All Files (*.*); otherwise, you will not be able to see files with other than a .txt extension.
4. With your working folder open, double-click the **chap02** folder to open it, and then double-click **acad_paper_ex.html**.

Saving and Previewing Your HTML File

To avoid overwriting the example file, you can resave it under another name. That way, you can use it as a reference point, or backtrack to the beginning and start over fresh, if you need to.

1. Select File, Save As, and resave the example file as **acad_paper.html** in the chap02 folder in your working folder or working disk.
2. Run your browser (or switch over to it if it is already open) and open **acad_paper.html** from the chap02 folder in your working folder or disk. (If you are unclear about how to open a local HTML file in your browser, see "Previewing Your HTML Document in Your Browser" in Chapter 1.)

When working through this chapter's examples, be sure to frequently save your HTML file, switch over to your browser, refresh the display of your Web page, and then test and debug the example code you have created. Use the screen captures in this chapter's figures as prompts to switch over to your browser to check out the results of your work for yourself, rather than simply depending upon the figures to show you how your code should look.

DECLARING THE DOCUMENT TYPE

According to the HTML 4.01 specification, a valid HTML document should declare the version of HTML that is used in the document. This is done by inserting a special code, a *Document Type Declaration* (or *DocType declaration*), at the top of the document, above the HTML element. The DocType declaration specifies the HTML version used in a document and the level of conformance being enforced.

Understanding Conformance Levels

The W3C has defined three different conformance levels for HTML 4 and XHTML 1:
- **Strict.** Disallows any deprecated or frameset elements or attributes and is intended for use with browsers that fully implement the HTML 4.01 standard.

- **Transitional (or "loose").** Allows deprecated elements or attributes and is intended for use in pages that use elements and attributes that have been deprecated in HTML 4.01.
- **Frameset.** Allows both deprecated and frameset elements or attributes and is intended for use in pages that use the FRAMESET element, the FRAME element, and other related elements or attributes to create framed Web sites.

Deprecation means that you are either discouraged from using an element or attribute, which has been superceded by newer elements or attributes, for instance, or encouraged to use an alternative. For instance, several elements and attributes have been deprecated in HTML 4 and XHTML 1 in favor of using Cascading Style Sheets (CSS) to achieve similar or superior results. Deprecated elements and attributes are perfectly legal in HTML 4 and XHTML 1 and you are free to use them. You will learn more about deprecated elements and attributes, and about using styles to achieve similar or superior results in Chapter 3, *Working with Fonts, Colors, and Backgrounds*.

Frameset element refers to the FRAMESET, FRAME, and NOFRAMES elements that are used to create a framed Web page. A page containing frameset elements is often referred to as a *frameset page*. You will learn more about using frames in Chapter 6, *Working with Multi-Page Web Sites*.

Following are three examples of DocType declarations that can be included in an HTML document to specify conformance to the strict, transitional, or frameset definitions for HTML 4.01:

```
<!DOCTYPE HTML PUBLIC "-//W3C//DTD HTML 4.01//EN"
 "http://www.w3.org/TR/html4/strict.dtd">

<!DOCTYPE HTML PUBLIC "-//W3C//DTD HTML 4.01 Transitional//EN"
 "http://www.w3.org/TR/html4/loose.dtd">

<!DOCTYPE HTML PUBLIC "-//W3C//DTD HTML 4.01 Frameset//EN"
 "http://www.w3.org/TR/html4/frameset.dtd">
```

Unless you are creating a frameset page, you should stick to declaring your Web pages as conforming to the transitional definition for HTML 4.01. You should only declare it as conforming to the strict definition for HTML 4.01 if it contains no deprecated or frameset elements or attributes.

Generally, a browser will not care if you slip up on this, but if you try to validate your page using the W3C's *HTML Validator*, you will likely get an error if you have declared your document to be in conformance with the transitional definition for HTML 4.01 and a TARGET attribute is included in it. You will learn more about validating your Web pages in Chapter 6.

Understanding DocType Switching

The newest browsers, such as Internet Explorer 6 and Netscape 6, however, use the DocType declaration to do *DocType switching*. Based on the DocType declaration included in your document, a newer browser can run in either of two modes: *standards mode* or *quirks mode*. In standards mode, current HTML standards are strictly adhered to, even if that will cause problems when displaying a page that was coded to take advantage of the non-standard quirks of an earlier browser version. In quirks mode, earlier non-standard quirks are reduplicated, even if that will cause problems when displaying a page that was coded to be standards-compliant.

If you use any of the previously listed DocType declarations in your document, browsers that do DocType switching should switch to using standards mode. If you omit a DocType declaration, such browsers will default to using quirks mode. DocType declarations other than those previously listed might also trigger quirks mode. When you are just using straight HTML, whether a browser is running in standards or quirks mode should not make much, if any, difference. It can make a difference, however, if you are using styles, scripts, or dynamic HTML features in your document. For links to additional resources on the Web that discuss DocType declarations and DocType switching, see this book's IRC at **www.emcp.com/**.

Adding a DocType Declaration

The DocType declaration is inserted at the top of an HTML document, above the HTML element.

Insert a DocType declaration declaring that your HTML document is compatible with the transitional definition for HTML 4.01:

```
<!DOCTYPE HTML PUBLIC "-//W3C//DTD HTML 4.01 Transitional//EN"
 "http://www.w3.org/TR/html4/loose.dtd">
<html>
<head>
```

USING META ELEMENTS

The META (Meta Data) element is an empty element that allows authors to include *meta data* in their HTML documents. Meta data is information that is about, or describes, a document, rather than content that is displayed in a document. META elements are inserted in a document's HEAD element.

Specifying the Document's Character Set

As the Web becomes more and more of a global phenomenon, pages are being published in many languages, many of which do not use the Latin-based alphabet used by Western European languages (such as Chinese and Japanese, for instance). Because of this, the specific character set being used in a document is a much more important issue than it once was (when virtually all Web pages were published in English). If you try to display a page originating from China or Japan and square blank boxes appear where text characters would normally be, the character set being assumed by your browser (most likely ISO 8859-1) does not match the character set being used by the page you are trying to access.

Also, you are required to specify your document's character set when validating an HTML document using the W3C's HTML Validator. The W3C recommends that Web authors specifically declare their document's character set.

You declare your document's character set by inserting it as meta data in your document's HEAD element. This should be inserted ahead of any other element within the HEAD element.

Insert the following META element at the start of your document's HEAD element to declare that your document is using the ISO 8859-1 character set (used by most Western European languages, including English):

```
<head>
<meta http-equiv="Content-Type" content="text/html; charset=ISO-
8859-1">
<title>Commerce and Civilization by Crystal Porter</title>
```

The various ins and outs of using different character sets can get complex. See Appendix B, *Special Characters Chart*, for all of the displayable characters included in the ISO 8859-1 character set, as well as a discussion of using other character sets or Unicode characters in your HTML documents. For links to resources on the Web that discuss using the ISO 8859-1 and other character sets, see this book's IRC at **www.emcp.com/**.

Including a Description and Keyword List

Probably the two most common uses of the META element are to include a description of your page and a list of keywords that are related to the content of your page. Many search engines use these META elements when listing or indexing your site. These kinds of META elements are included in an HTML document using the following general format:

```
<meta name="meta data name" content="meta data content">
```

Add a META element below your document's TITLE element that provides a description of the document's content:

```
<title>Commerce and Civilization by Crystal Porter</title>
<meta name="description" content="Discussion of the impact of
commerce on the development of civilization, contrasting folk
and urban societies, and debating the role of trade and commerce
in the transition between the two.">
</head>
```

Search engines and Web directories that support the use of META elements might display your META element description, instead of the initial text of your document, in a list of search responses. This can be useful, for instance, if the initial text of your document does not provide a good description or is short on information about your document. A good META element description makes it more likely that someone interested in a document such as yours will actually click on its link in a search engine list, rather than pass on to the next link.

Add a META element below the one you just added that provides a list of keywords a search engine might use in indexing your document:

```
<title>Commerce and Civilization by Crystal Porter</title>
<meta name="description" content="Discussion of the impact of
commerce on the development of civilization, contrasting folk and
urban societies, and debating the role of trade and commerce in
the transition between the two.">
<meta name="keywords" content="civilization, society, societies,
culture, higher societies, folk society, folk societies,
sociology, primitive, tribal, urban, egypt, sumeria, trade,
commerce, import, export, market, generalist, specialist">
</head>
```

Search engines and directories that support use of the META element can use your keyword list to help index your document. This can increase the likelihood that someone doing a search on any of the keywords you have listed will be able to find your document. For links to resources on the Web that further discuss these and other uses of the META element, see this book's IRC at **www.emcp.com/**.

ADDING INLINE HIGHLIGHTING

Bold and italic often are used to add highlighting and emphasis to text within a document. HTML includes a number of inline elements that can be used to add bolding or italics to an HTML document.

Using the I and B Elements

The I (Italic) and B (Bold) elements are used to add italic or bold highlighting to enclosed text. They are sometimes referred to as *literal* elements because they literally specify a display characteristic, italics or bolding.

Use the I and B elements to apply italics and bolding to the example text:
1. Use the I element to italicize the included text (see Figure 2.1):

```
<p>Civilizations have often been referred to as <i>advanced
societies</i>, in contrast to less developed societies.
```

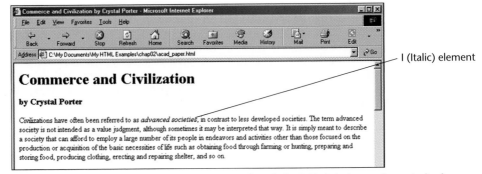

FIGURE 2.1 • *A Web browser displays text tagged with the I (Italic) element in an italic font.*

2. Use the B element to create bolded lead-in headings for the first two items in the bulleted list (see Figure 2.2):

```
<ul>
<li><b>Geographical expansion.</b> A civilization occupies a
relatively wide expanse of territory.
<li><b>Population growth and concentration.</b> A civilization
requires sufficient population and sufficient population density
to be able to employ large numbers of individuals in activities
with no direct economic return. These individuals include those
involved in government, ceremonial activities, art, philosophy,
and scientific inquiry.
```

B (Bold) element ——

FIGURE 2.2 • *A Web browser displays text tagged with the B (Bold) element in a bold font.*

Using the EM and the STRONG Elements

The EM (Emphasis) and STRONG (Strong Emphasis) elements are used to emphasize or strongly emphasize enclosed text. They are inline elements and are sometimes referred to as *logical* elements because they specify a logical display characteristic, emphasis or strong emphasis, rather than a literal one (italics or bolding). In a graphical Web browser, an EM element is displayed in an italic font, while a STRONG element is displayed in a bold font.

It is customary in publications to use italics to emphasize book, journal, or magazine titles, rather than set them in quotes. In HTML, you can use either the I or the EM element to italicize (or emphasize) these kinds of text strings.

Use the EM and STRONG elements to add emphasis and strong emphasis to the example document:

1. Use the EM element to emphasize the journal and book titles included in the following example (see Figure 2.3):

```
<h2>Distinguishing Between Folk and Urban Societies</h2>
<p>In an article published in the <em>American Journal of
Sociology</em>, Robert Redfield described the more primitive and
pre-urbanized state of society as forming "folk societies."(1)
John A. Wilson, in <em>The Culture of Ancient Egypt</em>,
summarizes Redfield's conclusions in the following manner:</p>
```

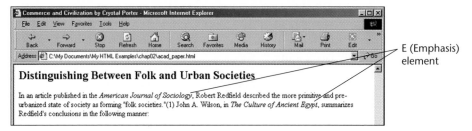

E (Emphasis) element

FIGURE 2.3 • *A Web browser displays text tagged with the EM element in an italic font.*

2. Use the STRONG element to add stronger emphasis. Scroll down to the bottom part of the document and insert the following codes where indicated to strongly emphasize the included text (see Figure 2.4):

```
<hr>
<p><strong>Notes</strong></p>
<p>
1. Robert Redfield, "The Folk Society," American Journal of
Sociology, LII (1947), pp. 293-308.<br>
```

STRONG (Strong Emphasis) element

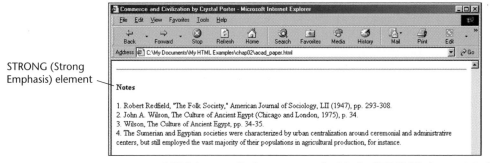

FIGURE 2.4 • *A Web browser displays text tagged with the STRONG element in a bold font.*

Whether you use logical or literal highlighting elements to apply italics to your Web pages is up to you; all graphical browsers, at least, treat the I and EM elements and the B and STRONG elements as interchangeable. The I and B elements are more economical and easier to type. The logical character of the EM and STRONG elements, however, still holds when the presentation media is not a visual media. In a speech browser, for instance, emphasized text might be preceded and followed by a pause and expressed through a somewhat louder voice, while strongly emphasized text might be expressed through both a louder and deeper voice.

Creating Bold Italic Highlighting

You can create text that is both italicized and bolded by nesting an I and a B element. It does not matter which is nested inside of which; just do not overlap them. You can also nest an EM and a STRONG element to get the same bold italic text. You can even nest an I and a STRONG element, or an EM and a B element, to get bold italic text.

Nest the STRONG element you defined in the last code example inside of an EM element (see Figure 2.5):

```
<p><em><strong>Notes</strong></em></p>
<p>
1. Robert Redfield, "The Folk Society," American Journal of
Sociology, LII (1947), pp. 293-308.<br>
```

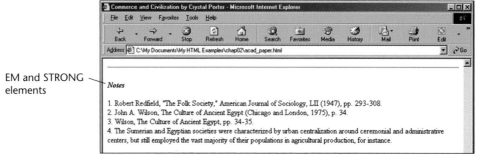

EM and STRONG elements

FIGURE 2.5 • *A Web browser displays text tagged with both the EM and STRONG elements in a bold italic font.*

Using Underlining

The U (Underline) element is an HTML 4 element that can be used to apply underlining to text in an HTML document.

Use the U element to underline the same text you previously tagged with the STRONG and EM elements (see Figure 2.6):

```
<hr>
<p><em><strong><u>Notes</u></strong></em></p>
```

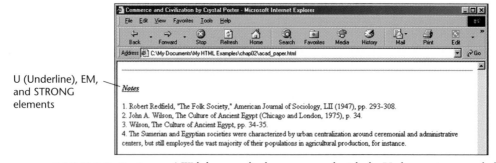

U (Underline), EM, and STRONG elements

FIGURE 2.6 • *A Web browser displays text tagged with the U element in an underlined font.*

The U element was not included in versions of HTML prior to HTML 4, so some earlier browsers do not support it. Some Web authors also avoid using the U element because underlined text is too easily confused with a hypertext link, which also is usually displayed in an underlined font. Underlining in a computer document is also somewhat of an anachronism, dating back to when early computer displays and printers lacked the capability to produce an italic font. Underlining was also commonly used in typewritten documents to indicate emphasis when using a typewriter lacking an italic font. Because modern displays and printers have no problem producing italics, there is little reason to use underlined text in a Web page. The U element is also deprecated in HTML 4.01, in favor of using styles or the DEL (Delete) element to produce an underlined font.

So far you have only marked up some of the instances in the example file where the I (Italics), B (Bold), EM (Emphasis), STRONG (Strong Emphasis), and U (Underline) elements could be used to further mark up the document for display on the Web. To gain more practice, look for other places in the document where you can use these elements. For instance:

- The I element was used to italicize a phrase that benefited from being so high-lighted in the text. Look for other instances within the document's text paragraphs where you might use the I element.
- The B element was used to bold the lead-in phrases of the first two bulleted list items. Use the B element to bold the remaining lead-in phrases in the bulleted list.
- The EM element was used to emphasize (and thus italicize) the titles of a journal and a book. Look for other journal or book titles in the footnote items at the bottom of the document and use the EM element to emphasize those titles as well.

WORKING WITH QUOTATIONS

Crystal's paper includes two extended quotations. For print publications, the general rule is that any quote that is four lines or longer should be formatted as a block quote (as a separate text block indented from the margins). In HTML, the BLOCKQUOTE element is used to tag a block of text as a block quote.

Nest the indicated paragraph inside of a BLOCKQUOTE element to format it as a block quote and delete the quotation marks, since block quotes do not need to be quoted (see Figure 2.7):

```
<h2>Distinguishing Between Folk and Urban Societies</h2>
<p>In an article published in the <em>American Journal of
Sociology</em>, Robert Redfield described the more primitive and
pre-urbanized state of society as forming "folk societies."(1)
John A. Wilson, in <em>The Culture of Ancient Egypt</em>,
summarizes Redfield's conclusions in the following manner:</p>

<blockquote><p>"This ideal folk society is homogenous, small,
and has a strong sense of community. It is nonliterate, and its
economy is one of self-sufficiency rather than of buying and
selling. In general, the ties of family provide the community.
The society is deeply rooted in religious belief and custom, and
relations are personal, so that the secular and impersonal have
not yet come into being. The behavior of such a society is
strongly traditional, so that there is no encouragement to
speculation or to experimentation, since sanctified tradition
has provided all the answers. Such a folk society could exist
as a pure culture only if the conditions of its maintenance and
security from disturbance were assured."(2)</p></blockquote>
```

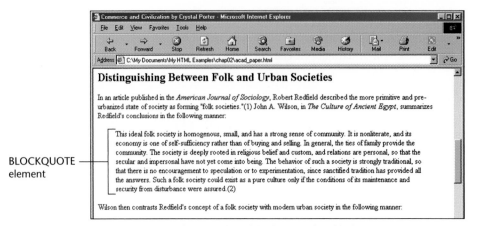

BLOCKQUOTE element

FIGURE 2.7 • *Extended quotes should be formatted as block quotes.*

Nesting Paragraphs in Block Quotes

In the example, you nested a P element, rather than raw text, within a BLOCKQUOTE element. This is not required by the transitional and frameset versions of HTML 4.01 or XHTML 1.0, which allow both block and inline elements to be nested directly inside of a BLOCKQUOTE element. The strict versions of HTML 4.01 and XHTML 1.0, however, only allow block elements to be nested directly inside of a BLOCKQUOTE element.

Nesting P elements (or other block elements) instead of raw text inside of a BLOCK-QUOTE element is a good idea, nonetheless. Nesting P elements, for one thing, lets you include more than one paragraph of text in a block quote. An additional consideration comes into play when using styles, in which case a P element and raw text nested inside of a BLOCKQUOTE element might differ in their display characteristics if the styles for the P and BLOCKQUOTE elements are not identically defined.

Nesting Other Block Elements in Block Quotes

Besides paragraph elements, you can nest any other block element inside of a BLOCK-QUOTE element that can be nested inside of the BODY element. Some Web authors take advantage of this capability to indent a whole page by nesting all of the other BODY elements within a BLOCKQUOTE element. Although using the BLOCKQUOTE element in this manner—purely as a formatting device—is legal in all versions of HTML, you might decide against it for a couple of good reasons.

The first reason is that using the BLOCKQUOTE element purely as a formatting device violates the meaning and purpose of the BLOCKQUOTE element, which is to present a block of quoted text—users of non-visual user agents, such as a Braille browser or speech browser, for instance, might be confused by BLOCKQUOTES that are used for purposes other than quoting blocks of text. The second reason is that the level of support for Cascading Style Sheets in current browsers provides a much better means for effecting margin changes for elements in HTML documents.

Just a little further down in the document, another paragraph is enclosed within quotation marks. Delete the quotation marks and then use the BLOCKQUOTE element to turn that paragraph into a block quote also.

MARKING REVISIONS

HTML includes a number of elements that can be used to mark up insertions or deletions within an HTML document.

Using the DEL and INS Elements

The DEL (Delete) and INS (Insert) elements let you mark deletions and insertions within an HTML document. Browsers that support these inline elements display deletions as strikethrough text and insertions as underlined text.

Cynthia wants to display deletions and insertions as she revises her online paper.

Use the INS and DEL elements to mark insertions and deletions in the following example text (see Figure 2.8):

```
<p><ins>As described</ins><del>Admittedly</del>, these
characteristics of folk societies and urban societies
<ins>place</ins><del>situate</del> them as extremes at either
end of a<ins>n overall</ins> continuum<ins> that is defined by
society in all of its forms</ins>. However, in reality,
societies tend to contain characteristics of both of these
societ<ins>al</ins><del>y</del> types. For example, most
societies have both generalists and specialists, but in a
community considered to be a folk society, generalists
predominate. In a community considered to be an urban society,
specialists predominate at least in rank, if not necessarily
always in numbers.(4)</p>

<h2>Commerce as a <ins>Cause of</ins><del>Means Toward</del>
Urbanization</h2>
```

INS (Insert) element

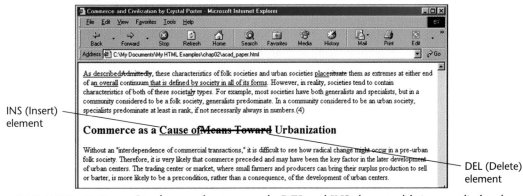

DEL (Delete) element

F I G U R E   2 . 8 • *In a browser that supports the DEL and INS elements, deletions are displayed as strikethrough text, while insertions are displayed as underlined text.*

One of the main drawbacks of using the DEL and INS elements is lack of support in earlier browsers. As with the Q element, these elements do not degrade gracefully in non-supporting browsers, with both deletions and insertions indistinguishably displayed as normal text in those browsers. In Chapter 3, you will learn some methods you can use to redirect or alert visitors using browsers that do not comply with the latest HTML standards.

Cascading Style Sheets provide a rather neat trick that can be done with deleted text. Setting a style property of **display: none** for the DEL element causes nested text not to be displayed in browsers that support this. For instance, the following style might be defined in the document's HEAD element:

```
<title>Commerce and Civilization by Crystal Porter</title>
<style type="text/css">
del { display: none }
</style>
</head>
```

The result of this in a supporting browser is that the deleted text is not displayed, while the inserted text is still displayed as underlined (see Figure 2.9).

INS element only

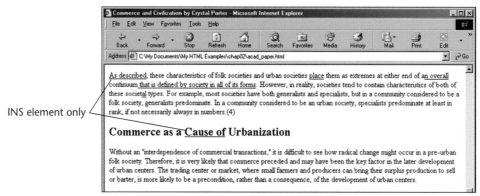

FIGURE 2.9 • *When the display of deletions (DEL elements) is turned off using CSS, a supporting browser displays only the insertions (INS elements).*

Striking Out Text

HTML provides two additional inline elements that can create strikeout text: the STRIKE and S elements. The STRIKE element had a long history as a Netscape extension before it was included in HTML 3.2. The S element was proposed for the failed HTML 3.0 proposal, but was not included in standard HTML until HTML 4.0, primarily because it is more concise than the STRIKE element. Both of these elements are deprecated in HTML 4.01, in favor of using the DEL element or styles to achieve similar or better results.

All the same, of all the elements that are displayed as strikeout text, the STRIKE element is still the most universally supported, particularly by older browsers. So, if you just want to display strikeout text, using the STRIKE element is a better choice than using the S element.

CREATING FOOTNOTES AND ENDNOTES

Footnotes or endnotes are often needed in academic papers. In this section, you learn how to incorporate both footnotes and endnotes in an online document, including how to superscript note numbers and create hypertext footnote and endnote links.

Superscripting Note Numbers

Note numbers are superscripted in documents. In HTML, the SUP (Superscript) element is used to superscript text. Example note numbers are already included in the example document.

action

Find the first note number and use the SUP element to superscript it, as shown here (see Figure 2.10):

```
<h2>Distinguishing Between Folk and Urban Societies</h2>
<p>In an article published in the <em>American Journal of
Sociology</em>, Robert Redfield described the more primitive and
pre-urbanized state of society as forming "folk
societies."<sup>(1)</sup> John A. Wilson, in <em>The Culture of
Ancient Egypt</em>, summarizes Redfield's conclusions in the
following manner:</p>
```

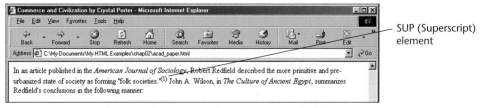

SUP (Superscript) element

FIGURE 2.10 • *The SUP element is used to superscript included text.*

Notice in the example that the superscripted note number is enclosed within parentheses. The primary reason for doing this is to avoid *ungraceful degradation* in non-supporting browsers or in browsers, such as text browsers, that cannot display superscripted text. In those browsers, an unsuperscripted note number would be displayed immediately following the preceding text, displaying **text1**, instead of **text[1]**, for instance.

NOTE

An element or attribute is not determined to ungracefully degrade merely because it produces an unexpected or unpleasant visual effect in a browser. The effect is only deemed ungraceful degradation if it also makes accessing or understanding the content of the element or document more difficult or impossible.

practice

Three additional footnote numbers (within parentheses) are included in the example document. Find each additional footnote number and use the SUP element to superscript the number and the surrounding parentheses.

tip

Although not included in the current example, just as you can use the SUP element to superscript nested text, you also can use the SUB (Subscript) element to subscript nested text. For instance, to format the chemical formula of water you might do this:

```
H<sub>(2)</sub>0
```

This should then display in a browser as **H$_{(2)}$0**, for instance.

Creating Hypertext Footnote Links

Besides simply formatting superscripted note numbers, you can turn them into hypertext links that will jump from the note number to a footnote located at the bottom of the page.

When creating a hypertext link that jumps to a location within a document, you need to create two separate anchor elements (A elements): a destination anchor that marks the location in the document that you want to jump to and a linking anchor (or jump link) that links to the destination anchor.

CREATING A DESTINATION ANCHOR A destination anchor marks a location within a document to which a hypertext link can jump. A destination anchor is created using the A element, but with a NAME attribute, instead of an HREF element. A destination anchor is also sometimes referred to as a named anchor, for that reason. A destination anchor is created in the following general format:

```
<a name="anchorname"></a>
```

Each destination anchor you create within your document must have a unique name. If you create two destination anchors that have the same name, a browser will not be able to decide which one it should jump to and, therefore, will not jump anywhere.

You can find several example footnotes at the bottom of the example document.

Add a destination anchor to mark the location of the first footnote:

```
<hr>
<p><em><strong><u>Notes</u></strong></em></p>
<p>
<a name="note1"></a>1. Robert Redfield, "The Folk Society,"
<em>American Journal of Sociology</em>, LII (1947), pp. 293-
308.<br>
```

Notice that the destination anchor you inserted is not bracketing anything. That is fine because this element is not tagging any text for presentation; it is merely marking a location.

CREATING A FOOTNOTE LINK Now that you have created a destination anchor, you can create a hypertext link that will jump to the location you have marked. A jump link that jumps to another location in a document is created in the following general format:

```
<a href="#anchorname">link text</a>
```

The # character and the following *anchorname* string together also are referred to as a *fragment identifier*. The *anchorname* specifies the name of the destination anchor to which the link will jump.

Create a jump link that jumps from a note number in the text to a footnote at the bottom of the document:

1. Return to the first note number that you previously superscripted and apply the following codes to turn it into a jump link (see Figure 2.11):

```
<h2>Distinguishing Between Folk and Urban Societies</h2>
<p>In an article published in the <em>American Journal of
Sociology</em>, Robert Redfield described the more primitive and
pre-urbanized state of society as forming "folk
societies."<sup><a href="#note1">(1)</a></sup> John A. Wilson,
in <em>The Culture of Ancient Egypt</em>, summarizes Redfield's
conclusions in the following manner:</p>
```

jump link

FIGURE 2.11 • *The superscripted note number has been turned into a jump link that, when clicked on, will jump to the specified destination anchor.*

2. Save your document, switch over to your browser, refresh the display of your page, and then click on the **(1)** note link. Your browser should jump to the first footnote at the bottom of the page (see Figure 2.12).

destination anchor

FIGURE 2.12 • *A note at the bottom of a page can be linked with its corresponding note number in the body of the document.*

At the bottom of the BODY element, a PRE (Preformatted Text) element has been inserted that contains 30 hard returns. The reason for doing this is to add vertical spacing at the bottom of the document, so that when a hypertext footnote link jumps to one of the footnotes at the bottom of the page, the footnote will be displayed at the top of the browser window, rather than partway down in the window. The PRE element can be used for this because it is the only element that does not ignore nested hard returns. Alternatively, a style could be used to add additional margin space at the bottom of the page.

CREATING A RETURN LINK Visitors can just click the browser's Back button to return to the location they were at before clicking a hypertext link. It is not a bad idea, however, to provide a more explicit means by which visitors can return to their previous position within the document. You can do this by creating another link that jumps the other way, from the end of a footnote back up to its corresponding note number in the document's text.

An anchor element can include both an HREF and a NAME attribute, so you do not have to create a separate destination anchor next to the jump link you created previously. By including both HREF and NAME attributes in an A element's start tag, you can create an anchor element that can serve as both a jump link and as a destination anchor.

Create a hypertext link that jumps back up from the footnote to its corresponding note number in the text:

1. Edit the hypertext note link you previously created, giving it a unique name using the NAME attribute:

```
<p>In an article published in the <em>American Journal of
Sociology</em>, Robert Redfield described the more primitive and
pre-urbanized state of society as forming "folk
societies."<sup><a href="#note1" name="return1">(1)</a></sup>
John A. Wilson, in <em>The Culture of Ancient Egypt</em>,
summarizes Redfield's conclusions in the following manner:</p>
```

2. Scroll back down to the list of footnotes at the bottom of the document body. At the end of the first footnote, create a jump link that will jump back to the note number link that you just named (see Figure 2.13):

```
<p><em><strong><u>Notes</u></strong></em></p>
<p>
<a name="note1"></a>1. Robert Redfield, "The Folk Society,"
<em>American Journal of Sociology</em>, LII (1947), pp. 293-308.
<a href="#return1">[Return]</a><br>
```

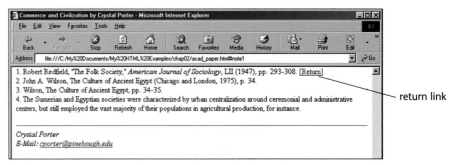

right: return link

FIGURE 2.13 • *Including a return link following a footnote provides visitors with an explicit means to return to their previous location in the document.*

3. Save your file, switch over to your browser, refresh the display of your page, and click on the **[Return]** link at the end of the first footnote. Your browser should jump back to the first note number (see Figure 2.14).

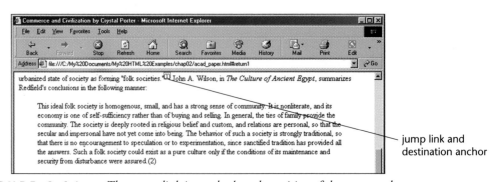

right: jump link and destination anchor

FIGURE 2.14 • *The return link jumps back to the position of the note number.*

The easiest way to keep jump links and destination anchors straight in your mind is to remember these simple differences between the two:

• A jump link always includes an HREF attribute with a fragment identifier (beginning with a # character) that identifies the name of the destination anchor it jumps to (for example: `href="#anchorname"`).

- A destination anchor (or named anchor) includes a NAME attribute (*not* beginning with a # character) that identifies (or names) it, so it can be targeted by a jump link (for example: `name="anchorname"`).

Fragment identifiers and anchor names are case-sensitive. Whatever you specify as the name of a destination anchor must be duplicated exactly, including any uppercase characters, in the fragment identifier used to jump to it. In other words, if you specify `name="note1"` as the name of a destination anchor, then `href="#note1"` must be used in the corresponding jump link, and not `href="#Note1"` or `href="#NOTE1"`.

practice

So far, you have created one hypertext note link (a jump link) that jumps from the first note number in the document to the first footnote listed at the bottom of the page (marked by a destination anchor). Using that experience as a guide, do the same for the three remaining note numbers and footnotes:

1. Create the destination anchors that mark the location of the remaining three footnotes at the foot of the page. Using the A element's NAME attribute, give each one a unique name (**note2**, **note3**, and **note4**).
2. Find each of the remaining note numbers in the document (they are the same note numbers, surrounded by parentheses, that you superscripted earlier). Turn each note number (and surrounding parentheses) into a jump link by nesting it inside of an A element with an HREF attribute targeting the name of the destination anchor you want it to jump to (**#note2**, **#note3**, and **#note4**).
3. In your browser, test each of the links you have created.

You also previously created a return link at the end of the first footnote that jumps back up to the corresponding note number in the document's text. Using that experience as a guide, create return links at the end of the other three footnotes:

1. Find the three remaining note numbers. In the jump links you created for them, use the NAME attribute to give each one a unique name (**return2**, **return3**, and **return4**). These anchor elements now serve as both jump links and destination anchors.
2. Use the A element's HREF attribute to create return links at the end of the remaining footnotes that jump back up to the corresponding note numbers. For the HREF attribute value, use fragment identifiers that target the names of the destination anchors you want to return to (**#return2**, **#return3**, and **#return4**).
3. In your browser, test each of the return links you have created.

CREATING A FOOTNOTE SEPARATOR LINE In the example text, an HR (Horizontal Rule) element is inserted above the footnotes to create a separator line between them and the rest of the document's text. An HR element, however, draws a line all the way across the page, while in printed documents with footnotes, a footnote separator line is usually drawn only part of the way across the page. By using the HR element's WIDTH, SIZE, ALIGN, and NOSHADE attributes, you can alter the dimensions, position, and appearance of a horizontal rule.

Create a footnote separator line:

1. Reduce the width of the horizontal rule to 150 pixels and set left-alignment, as shown in the following example code (see Figure 2.15):

```
<hr width="150" align="left">
<p><em><strong><u>Notes</u></strong></em></p>
<p>
<a name="note1"></a>1. Robert Redfield, "The Folk Society,"
<em>American Journal of Sociology</em>, LII (1947), pp. 293-308.
<a href="#return1">[Return]</a><br>
```

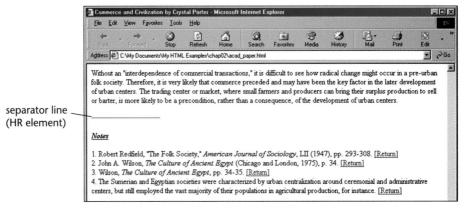

separator line (HR element)

FIGURE 2.15 • *The horizontal rule is set to 150 pixels wide and left-aligned.*

NOTE

You also can set the width of a horizontal rule using a percentage value. For instance, **width="25%"** would set the width of the horizontal rule to 25 percent of the width of the browser window.

To right-align the horizontal rule, insert **align="right"**. Horizontal rules are center-aligned by default.

2. To create a thinner footnote separator, set the size of the rule to 1 pixel and turn off 3-D shading (see Figure 2.16):

```
<hr width="150" align="left" size="1" noshade>
<p><em><strong><u>Notes</u></strong></em></p>
<p>
<a name="note1"></a>1. Robert Redfield, "The Folk Society,"
<em>American Journal of Sociology</em>, LII (1947), pp. 293-308.
<a href="#return1">[Return]</a><br>
```

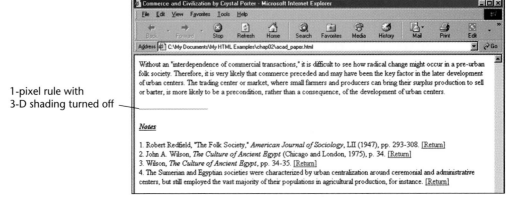

1-pixel rule with 3-D shading turned off

FIGURE 2.16 • *The size (height) of the horizontal rule is set to 1 pixel and 3-D shading is turned off.*

The NOSHADE attribute can be confusing. You might assume, for instance, that it is used to fill the horizontal rule with a shade. In fact, it is just the opposite. With the NOSHADE attribute present, some browsers fill the interior of the rule with a gray tone, whereas others fill it with black. When NOSHADE is absent, browsers fill the interior of the rule with white, while adding a variable amount of "shading" to the sides of the rule to provide relief against the page's background.

To test this, increase the size of a horizontal rule (size="6" and then view it in your browser with the NOSHADE attribute both present and absent.

All of these attributes are deprecated in HTML 4.01 in favor of using styles to achieve similar or better results. Standalone attributes are also illegal in XHTML. If used in an XHTML document, you would need to insert **noshade="noshade"** instead of just **noshade.**

If you want to reduce the amount of vertical spacing following a horizontal rule, you can nest the HR element within a following block element. This trick works in all major browsers. You can try it out for yourself if you wish.

Insert a P start tag in front of the HR element and delete the following P start tag (see Figure 2.17):

```
<p><hr width="150" align="left" size="1" noshade>
<p><em><strong><u>Notes</u></strong></em></p>
```

vertical spacing
reduced by nesting
HR element inside
of P element

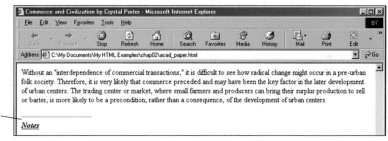

FIGURE 2.17 • *A quirk supported by most browsers reduces the vertical spacing following a horizontal rule when it is nested inside of a following block element.*

You should be aware that this is not standard HTML, in that an HR element is a block element and thus should not be nested inside of a P element. According to the standard, an HR element should terminate a preceding P element, with an implied end tag assumed for the P element, which would also then leave the following text ("Note") as untagged raw text (with an end tag, but no start tag). That the implied termination of the P element would also render it as an empty P element (which browsers should entirely ignore), only adds to the soup of non-standard features included in this trick. This trick is also not very friendly to text browsers or non-visual browsers, which might not know what to make of a horizontal rule nested inside of a P element.

Your document will also, of course, not be a valid HTML 4.01 document if you use this trick and will generate an error if you try to validate it using the W3C's HTML Validator. The only way to achieve this effect using valid HTML 4.01 code is to use a style. Styles (in the form of Cascading Style Sheets, or CSS) are used to specify formatting (or "styling") for HTML elements. Styles can be included in documents using style sheets (using the STYLE element) or they can be inserted inline within document elements (using the STYLE attribute).

Use an inline style in the following paragraph to reduce the element's top margin space (see Figure 2.18):

```
<p><hr width="150" align="left" size="1" noshade>
<p style="margin-top: -0.25em">
<em><strong><u>Notes</u></strong></em></p>
```

vertical spacing
reduced by an inline
style in P element

FIGURE 2.18 • *You can use a style to decrease the amount of vertical spacing following the HR element.*

This has the effect of eliminating any top margin set by the P element, while reducing the bottom margin set by the HR element by a quarter of an em (or one quarter of the current line height). It is not important that you understand styles in any depth at this point (nor what an em is, for that matter). It is important to understand, however, that when creating HTML documents, there are often ways to achieve effects that are supported by browsers but which are not part of the HTML standard (HTML 4.01). Often, the only way to achieve these effects in a standard fashion is by using styles. The use of styles will be discussed in more depth in Chapter 3 where the use of styles to specify font sizes, colors, and faces will be introduced.

Creating Endnote Links

In a published article or book, the only difference between footnotes and endnotes is that footnotes are listed at the bottom of a page and endnotes are listed at the end of an article or chapter (or possibly at the end of a book). A Web page, of course, is a single page of indeterminate length, so the foot and the end of the document are really the same. When working in HTML, endnotes are generally grouped in a separate document, whereas footnotes are displayed at the foot of the current document.

You might want to consider using endnotes, rather than footnotes, if you have many notes in your document or they include an extensive amount of text. If you only have a handful of relatively brief notes, then you might want to consider using footnotes.

You link to an endnote in the same way that you link to any location in another document. You create such a link in the following fashion:

```
<a href="url#anchorname">link text</a>
```

In the example, *url* stands for the object file that is targeted by the link, which can be just a file name (if the name of the file you are linking to is located in the same folder), an absolute Web address (`http://www.yourhost.com/yourfolder/yourpage.html`), or a relative Web address that points to a file located in your own site (`yoursubfolder/yourpage.html`). See "Using Relative URLs" in Chapter 6 for guidance on using relative URLs.

When working with Web pages, endnotes are generally grouped in their own separate document. You might want to do this, for instance, if you have a lot of notes that need to be listed, and for the sake of brevity or design, you do not want to display them at the foot of your page. You might also want to group notes from a collection of documents (or chapters) in a single file, which can then be referenced from those documents (these notes would function like endnotes at the end of a book, for instance).

This example uses an endnotes_ex.html example file that is included with the other example files for this chapter (in the chap02 folder). In creating the following example, you will be instructed to open endnotes_ex.html in your text editor and resave it as endnotes.html in the chap02 folder in your working folder or disk.

Edit the jump links for the note numbers so they also point to the name of the file containing the endnotes (endnotes.html):

1. Locate the first note number link and, in the HREF element, insert the name of the file that will contain the endnotes (endnotes.html) in front of the fragment identifier (#note1):

```
<h2>Distinguishing Between Folk and Urban Societies</h2>
<p>In an article published in the <em>American Journal of Sociology
</em>, Robert Redfield described the more primitive and pre-
urbanized state of society as forming "folk societies."<sup><a
href="endnotes.html#note1" name="return1">(1)</a></sup> John A.
Wilson, in <em>The Culture of Ancient Egypt</em>, summarizes
Redfield's conclusions in the following manner:</p>
```

2. Do the same with the three other note number links you have created, so they each also point to endnotes.html. Resave your file.
3. Run a second copy of your text editor and open **endnotes_ex.html** from the chap02 folder in your working folder. (If using a text editor that lets you open multiple windows, just open endnotes_ex.html in a separate window.)
4. Resave **endnotes_ex.html** in the chap02 folder as **endnotes.html**, so you will not overwrite the original example file.

In viewing the example file in your text editor, you will notice that the endnotes in endnotes.html are identical to the footnotes in your other document, including the destination anchors and return links you added to your footnotes. This demonstrates that you can link to a location within any document anywhere, even halfway around the world, as long as a destination anchor marks it.

5. Edit the return links, so they target your academic paper's file name (if you resaved your document under a different file name, substitute that file name in the following code). Resave your file.

```
<p>
<a name="note1"></a>1. Robert Redfield, "The Folk Society,"
American Journal of Sociology, LII (1947), pp. 293-308. <a
href="acad_paper.html#return1">[Return]</a><br>
<a name="note2"></a>2. John A. Wilson, The Culture of Ancient
Egypt (Chicago and London, 1975), p. 34. <a
href="acad_paper.html#return2">[Return]</a><br>
<a name="note3"></a>3. Wilson, The Culture of Ancient Egypt, pp.
34-35. <a href="acad_paper.html#return3">[Return]</a><br>
```

```
<a name="note4"></a>4. The Sumerian and Egyptian societies were
characterized by urban centralization around ceremonial and
administrative centers, but still employed the vast majority of
their populations in agricultural production, for instance. <a
href="acad_paper.html#return4">[Return]</a>
</p>
```

6. Switch to your browser and refresh the display of your page (it should still be displaying your academic paper). Find the first note number link and click on it. Your browser should open endnotes.html and jump down to the position of the first endnote (see Figure 2.19).

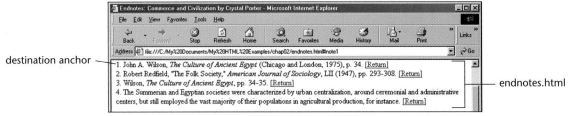

destination anchor

endnotes.html

FIGURE 2.19 • *Note links can be created that jump to a list of endnotes grouped in a separate file.*

7. Click the **[Return]** link at the end of the first endnote. Your browser should reopen your academic paper's file and return to the note number link that you just jumped from. You also can click the Back button to do the same thing.

8. Test the remaining note number links. They should each jump to endnotes.html, displaying the corresponding endnote at the top of the browser window.

NOTE

The endnotes.html example file also includes a PRE element containing multiple hard returns at the bottom of the page to help ensure that the endnotes are displayed at the top of the browser window when they are jumped to. The actual number of returns needed to cause this can vary depending upon the length of the page and the width and height of the browser's viewport.

INSERTING A COPYRIGHT SYMBOL

If you publish original material on the Web, you might want others to understand that your material is copyrighted and not part of the public domain. Including a copyright notice will not necessarily stop someone else from copying and reusing your material, but it will at least put them on notice that it is illegal for them to do so.

The copyright symbol is not included on your keyboard, so you have to use a special means to insert it into your page. To insert a non-keyboard character (sometimes called a "special character") in your document, you use an *entity code*, in the form of either a *numerical entity code* or a *named entity code*.

A numerical entity code identifies a character by its numerical position in the ISO 8859-1 character set and is inserted in this general format:

```
&#entitynumber;
```

The HTML specifications list many entity names that can be used to reference many special characters. A name entity code is inserted in this general format:

```
&entityname;
```

For instance, the copyright symbol's numerical entity code is **©**, whereas its named entity code is **©**.

action

Use the named entity code for the copyright symbol to add a copyright notice at the bottom of your example document (see Figure 2.20):

```
<hr>
<address>
Crystal Porter<br>
E-Mail: <a
href="mailto:cporter@pinebough.edu">cporter@pinebough.edu</a><br>
</address>
<p>&copy; Copyright 2003 by Crystal Porter. All rights
reserved.</p>
```

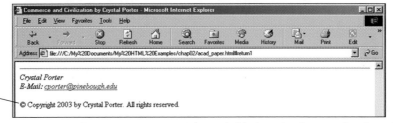

copyright symbol
(©)

FIGURE 2.20 • *You can insert a copyright symbol by inserting its named entity code.*

You also can use the copyright symbol's numerical entity code to insert it into your document. Just replace **©** with **©**.

Although many named entity codes are allowed by the HTML specifications, some earlier browsers, such as versions of Netscape Navigator prior to Version 4.75, might not recognize many of them. This is a case of ungraceful degradation because the raw code is displayed instead of the character in a non-supporting browser, as shown in Figure 2.21.

trademark
named entity
code (raw code)

FIGURE 2.21 • *If a browser does not recognize a named entity code, it displays the raw code.*

In Figure 2.21, the raw code of the named entity code of the trademark symbol is shown, as displayed in Netscape Navigator 4.75. Later in this chapter, including a trademark symbol is covered in the "Inserting the Registered and Trademark Symbols" section.

Because named entity codes do not degrade gracefully in non-supporting browsers, you should only use named entity codes to insert the characters shown in Table 2.1, and use numerical entity codes to insert all other characters.

TABLE 2.1 • *Named Entity Codes Supported by Versions of Netscape Earlier than 4.75*

Description	Named Entity Code	Character/Symbol
Copyright	&copy;	©
Registered	&reg;	®
Left Angle	&lt;	<
Right Angle	&gt;	>
Ampersand	&amp;	&
Double-quote	&quot;	"
Most accented characters	À, Õ, and ä for instance	À, Ô, and ä, for instance

You do not generally have to substitute entity codes for left angle, right angle, ampersand, or double-quote characters, except where they are part of an HTML code that you want to display "as is" in a Web page. For instance, to display `<img src="myimage.jpg">` as it appears, rather than as it is parsed by a browser, you would include the following in an HTML document:

```
&lt;img src=&quot;myimage.jpg&quot;&gt;
```

Even among the accented characters, a number of these characters cannot be displayed on a Macintosh even when using a numerical entity code, because they are not included in the Macintosh's native character set. For full details on which accented characters have this problem, see Appendix B.

Do not use keyboard shortcuts, or Window's Character Map or the Macintosh's Key Caps, to insert non-keyboard characters into an HTML document. Different systems might have different characters included at different locations in their native character sets, meaning that what displays as one character on one system might be displayed as an entirely different character on another system. Always use HTML entity codes to insert non-keyboard characters into HTML documents. See Appendix B for a listing of non-keyboard characters that can be included in an HTML document and their respective entity codes.

CASE EXAMPLE: CREATING A FREQUENTLY ASKED QUESTIONS PAGE

A frequently asked questions (or FAQ) page is one of the most common types of pages that can be found on the Web. On the Web, you can find FAQ pages on just about every topic or subject. Most FAQ pages are organized as a series of questions and answers, with a menu at the top of the page to make it easier to find the answer to a particular question.

Eddie Lopez is a support technician at CD Bunson Burners, Inc., which manufactures multi-drive CD-R recording systems. He has been given the task of creating a frequently asked questions (FAQ) page that compiles answers to questions that are frequently asked by customers. While compiling the questions and answers, Eddie noticed that a menu system at the top of the page would make it easier for users to find the particular question for which they are seeking an answer.

This example uses the cdr-faq_ex.html example file that is included with the other example files for this chapter (in the chap02 folder).

To start using the example file for this case example:
1. Open **cdr-faq_ex.html** in your text editor from the chap02 folder within your working folder or disk.
2. Resave your document as **cdr-faq.html** in the chap02 folder.
3. Open **cdr-faq.html** in your browser from the chap02 folder.

If you need more help opening and resaving an HTML file in your text editor, see "Opening an HTML File in Your Text Editor" earlier in this chapter. If you need more help opening an HTML file in your Web browser, see "Saving and Previewing Your HTML File" earlier in this chapter.

Many of the HTML codes have already been added to this example document. You will be adding codes to the example document to help demonstrate a variety of different features, including creating a document menu (or table of contents), making text bigger or smaller, creating multi-level numbered lists, inserting registered and trademark symbols, and using monospaced text to format input, output, and program code.

CREATING A DOCUMENT MENU

A document menu presents a list of links at the top of a document that jump to corresponding section headings within a longer, multi-part document. A document menu is also called a table of contents.

HTML actually provides three different elements—the UL, MENU, and DIR elements—that can be used to create a bulleted menu. Browsers have always displayed lists created using the MENU and DIR elements exactly the same as lists created using the UL element. As a result, the W3C has deprecated both the MENU and DIR elements and now strongly recommends that Web authors use the UL element instead.

Creating the Menu Links

A bulleted list is already included at the top of the example document. You just have to add the links to turn it into a menu. The menu links you will be creating work the same as the note links you created in the previous case example, except that they link to document sections, instead of to footnotes at the bottom of the page.

Add the following codes to turn the text in the list items into hypertext links (or jump links) that will jump to locations in your document (see Figure 2.22):

```
<h3>CD Bunson Burners, Inc.</h3>
<h1>CD-R Frequently Asked Questions</h1>

<ul>
<li><a href="#quest1">What is CD-R?</a>
<li><a href="#quest2">What is the difference between CD-R and
CD-ROM?</a>
```

```
<li><a href="#quest3">How long is a CD-R disc?</a>
<li><a href="#quest4">How do I back up an audio CD?</a>
<li><a href="#quest5">Can I batch process recording jobs?</a>
</ul>
```

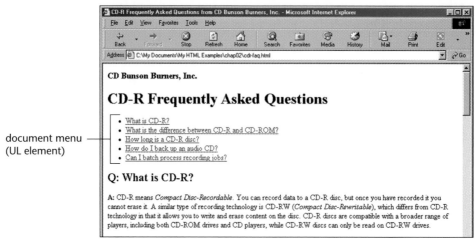

FIGURE 2.22 • *A document menu makes it easier to access the different parts of a longer document.*

Inserting the Destination Anchors

Before your menu links will work, destination anchors need to be inserted to mark the locations to which the menu links are going to jump.

The questions in the document are formatted as level-two headings (H2 elements). For the menu links to be able to jump to them, they need to be marked with named destination anchors.

Insert the destination anchor that marks the first question and answer section and then test the link that jumps to it to make sure it works:

1. Scroll down to the first H2 element and insert a destination anchor that will be jumped to from the first menu link:

```
<h2><a name="quest1"></a>Q: What is CD-R?</h2>
<p><b>A:</b> CD-R means <i>Compact Disc-Recordable</i>. You can
record data to a CD-R disc, but once you have recorded it you
cannot erase it.
```

2. Save your file in your text editor, switch over to your browser, and refresh the display of your page. Click on the first menu link to test it. Your browser should jump down to the position of the destination anchor you inserted, displaying the first question and answer at the top of the browser window (see Figure 2.23).

FIGURE 2.23 • *After the menu link is clicked on, a browser jumps to the location of the corresponding named destination anchor.*

3. Create the other destination anchors. Using the first destination anchor you created as a guide, insert destination anchors that mark the locations of the other question and answer sections. Name these destination anchors so they match the anchor names that are used in the menu links (**quest2**, **quest3**, **quest4**, and **quest5**).

4. Save your file, switch over to your browser and refresh your page, and then test the other links in your menu. For instance, click on the third menu link ("How long is a CD-R disc?"); your browser should jump down to the third question and answer section (see Figure 2.24).

destination anchor →

FIGURE 2.24 • *After the third menu link is clicked, the browser jumps to the third question and answer section.*

Creating Return Links

Whenever you create a menu that jumps to different sections within an HTML document, you should also add links at the end of each section that will return a visitor to the menu. These links are similar to the return links you added at the end of the footnotes in the previous case example, except they all return to the same destination anchor.

Add a destination anchor at the top of the document menu and then create the return links that jump back up to it:

1. Add a destination anchor at the top of your menu that your return links can jump back to:

```
<ul><a name="menu"></a>
<li><a href="#quest1">What is CD-R?</a>
<li><a href="#quest2">What is the difference between CD-R and
CD-ROM?</a>
```

2. Create the return link following the first question and answer section (see Figure 2.25):

```
<h2><a name="quest1"></a>Q: What is CD-R?</h2>
<p><b>A:</b> CD-R means <i>Compact Disc-Recordable</i>. You can
record data to a CD-R disc, but once you have recorded it you
cannot erase it. A similar type of recording technology is CD-RW
(<i>Compact Disc-Rewritable</i>), which differs from CD-R
technology in that it allows you to write and erase content on
the disc. CD-R discs are compatible with a broader range of
players, including both CD-ROM drives and CD players, while CD-
RW discs can only be read on CD-RW drives.</p>
<p>Return to the <a href="#menu">Menu</a>.</p>
```

FIGURE 2.25 • *Return links can be added that jump back to a document menu.*

3. Copy the return link you just created and paste it in following the other question and answer sections to create the other return links. All of your return links are identical because they all jump back to the same destination anchor.

4. Test your return links in your browser. Figure 2.26 shows a browser window after a return link has jumped back to the document menu.

FIGURE 2.26 • *After a return link is clicked on, a visitor is returned to the top of the document menu.*

MAKING BIGGER AND SMALLER TEXT

The BIG and SMALL elements are used to increase or decrease the size of nested text. You can also increase and decrease the size of text using the FONT element. You should be aware, however, that while the FONT element is deprecated in HTML 4.01, the BIG and SMALL elements are not. Use of the FONT element to control font sizes and the issue of deprecation are covered in more detail in Chapter 3.

Making Text Bigger

In the example file, increasing the size of the "Q:" and "A:" text strings that precede each question and answer can help the reader identify them.

Use the BIG element to increase the size of the "Q:" and "A:" text strings for the first question and answer (see Figure 2.27):

```
<h2><a name="quest1"></a><big>Q:</big> What is CD-R?</h2>
<p><b><big>A:</big></b> CD-R means <i>Compact Disc-
Recordable</i>.
```

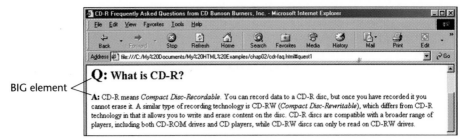

BIG element

FIGURE 2.27 • *The BIG element increases the size of nested text.*

You also can nest multiple BIG elements to further increase the size of nested text.

action

Nest the "A:" text string within another BIG element to further increase its size (see Figure 2.28):

```
<h2><a name="quest1"></a><big>Q:</big> What is CD-R?</h2>
<p><b><big><big>A:</big></big></b> CD-R means <i>Compact Disc-
Recordable</i>.
```

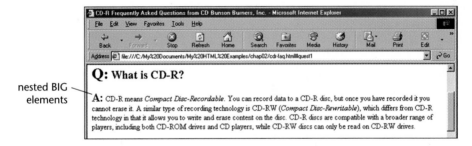

nested BIG elements

FIGURE 2.28 • *Two BIG elements increase the size of nested text even more.*

You can nest up to four BIG elements to increase the text size (more than four nested BIG elements will not further increase the text size). That is because HTML only provides for seven font sizes, only four of which are larger than the default paragraph font size. Text in heading-level elements can be increased even fewer times—the size of text can be increased once in an H1 element, twice in an H2 element, three times in an H3 element, and so on. You will learn more about setting font sizes in Chapter 3.

practice

Use the BIG element to increase the "Q:" and "A:" text strings for the other four question and answer sections. Be sure you nest the two BIG elements used to increase the size of the "A:" text strings inside of the B element's start and end tags, rather than overlap them.

Making Text Smaller

In some situations, you might want to make text smaller. For example, you might not want certain text to be as noticeable as the other text on your page, while still being legible.

Use the SMALL element to decrease the size of the copyright statement at the bottom of the page (see Figure 2.29):

```
<p><small>&copy; Copyright 2003 by CD Bunson Burners, Inc. All
rights reserved.</small></p>
</body>
```

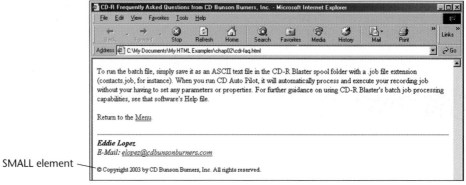

SMALL element

FIGURE 2.29 • *The SMALL element decreases the size of nested text.*

Generally, it is not a good idea to nest SMALL elements to decrease the size of text even further, because doing so might render the nested text unreadable on some systems.

USING NUMBERED LISTS

The FAQ includes one answer that provides instructional steps formatted as numbered lists. Technical documents often include numbered instructional steps. In HTML, the OL (Ordered List) element is used to create a numbered list.

In the example document, one question and answer section contains instructions formatted as separate paragraphs instead of numbered steps. The paragraphs are marked by single **<p>** start tags, without corresponding end tags, which is legal in HTML, since including end tags for paragraph elements, although generally advisable, is not required. You will be deleting the **<p>** start tags anyway, so leaving off the end tags just means you do not have to delete them as well. You create a numbered list in exactly the same way you created a bulleted list in the previous chapter, except you use an OL element, rather than a UL element.

Delete the **<p>** start tags and use the OL and LI elements to create a numbered list (see Figure 2.30):

```
<h3>Create an Image File:</h3>
<ol>
<li><p>Click the Start button and select Programs, Adaptec Easy
CD Creator 4, and Create CD.
<li><p>Click the Audio CD button.
<li><p>Insert the audio CD you want to copy in your CD-ROM or
CD-R drive. Click on the first track to highlight it. Hold down
the Shift key and click on the last track to highlight all of
the tracks. Click the Add button on the Toolbar.
<li><p>Select File, then Create CD Image. Change to the folder
where you save your image files (or you can create a folder for
this) and then save your image file, ending the file name with
a .cif file extension. For instance, type myimage.cif as the
name of your image file.
```

```
<li><p>The message "CD created successfully" will be displayed
when the image file has been successfully created. Click the OK
button.
</ol>
```

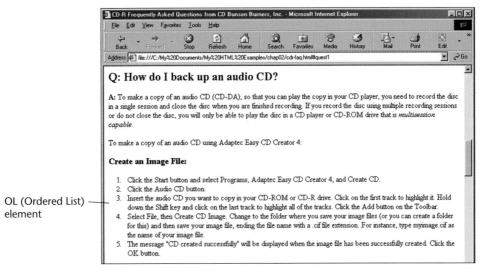

OL (Ordered List) element

FIGURE 2.30 • *The OL element is used in combination with the LI element to format a numbered list.*

The next two H3 elements ("Select Recording Options" and "Select Advanced Options") are also followed by paragraphs that can be turned into numbered lists. To gain more practice creating numbered lists, use the OL and LI elements to turn paragraphs following those headings into numbered list items as well.

Creating Multi-Level Numbered Lists

If you nest bulleted lists inside each other, a browser automatically changes the bullet type for each nested list level. Nesting numbered lists inside each other does not work in the same way; each nested list level still has the same number type (Arabic numerals).

The TYPE attribute is used in the UL or OL elements to change the bullet or number type, respectively. The OL element's TYPE attribute takes the following values: **I** (uppercase Roman), **i** (lowercase Roman), **A** (uppercase alphabetic), **a** (lowercase alphabetic), and **1** (Arabic numerals).

Change the H3 elements into list items in an ordered list and then set an uppercase alphabetic number type for the list:

1. Nest all of the H3 elements (and following numbered steps) inside an OL element, and then change the H3 elements into LI elements:

```
<ol>
<li><h3>Create an Image File:</h3>
<ol>
<li>Click on the Start button and select Programs, Adaptec Easy
CD Creator 4, and Create CD.

[...]
```

```
<li><h3>Select Recording Options:</h3>
<ol>
<li>Insert a blank (unrecorded) CD-R disc in your CD-R drive.

[...]

<li><h3>Select Advanced Options:</h3>
<ol>
<li>If the Advanced options are not displayed, click the
Advanced button.

[...]

<li>The message "CD created successfully" will be displayed when
the image file has been successfully recorded to the CD-R disc.
Click the OK button.
</ol>
</ol>
```

2. Use the TYPE attribute in the OL element to specify that it should be numbered using uppercase alphabetic characters (see Figure 2.31):

```
<ol type="A">
<li>Create an Image File:
<ol>
<li>Click on the Start button and select Programs, Adaptec Easy
CD Creator 4, and Create CD.
```

FIGURE 2.31 • *You can nest numbered lists inside each other that use different numbering schemes.*

Adding Vertical Spacing between List Items

By default, browsers do not add extra vertical spacing above or below list items (in the OL or UL elements). When creating instructional steps, however, it is nice to include a little more air in the list. One way to do that is to insert two BR (Line Break) elements at the end of the list items.

Add two BR elements at the end of all the LI elements in your nested OL elements:

1. Insert two BR elements at the end of the following LI elements (at the end of the first list item in the top-level list and the first nested list, respectively):

```
<ol type="A">
<li>Create an Image File:<br><br>
<ol>
<li>Click on the Start button and select Programs, Adaptec Easy
CD Creator 4, and Create CD.<br><br>
```

2. Insert double BR elements at the end of all the other LI elements in the numbered lists (see Figure 2.32).

FIGURE 2.32 • *Double BR elements can add vertical spacing in a list.*

This works because browsers have traditionally added vertical space when more than one BR element is combined. Earlier HTML standards seemed to imply that multiple BR elements should be collapsed to a single BR element, but the browser vendors ignored that injunction. The current specifications for HTML and XHTML do not define any specific behavior for multiple BR elements, so you cannot rely on this working in all browsers. Inserting multiple BR elements, however, also cannot be considered to be non-standard, at least according to the latest HTML specifications, as long as they are nested inside of a block element. If some browser does not support inserting multiple BR elements, little harm is done, however, because less space between list items just means they will be more closely spaced in those browsers.

There are only two other alternatives for adding vertical spacing between list items: inserting a PRE element containing one or more hard returns between the list items (hard returns are preserved when nested in a PRE element) and using a style to set a top margin for the list items.

INSERTING THE REGISTERED AND TRADEMARK SYMBOLS

Earlier, in the academic paper example, you learned how to insert the entity code for the copyright symbol. The named entity code for the registered symbol was also mentioned, although no example was given. Another common symbol that you may want to include in an HTML document is the trademark symbol.

The named entity code for the registered symbol (**®**) is supported by both current and earlier browsers. The named entity code for the trademark symbol (**™**), however, while supported in current browsers, is not supported in Netscape Navigator prior to version 4.75 and should be avoided.

Complicating matters somewhat, in the ISO 8859-1 character set, the trademark symbol is listed outside of the range of displayable characters, among the "unused characters," which means that it is not a legal character that should be included in an HTML document, even when inserted using its numerical entity code (**™**). In practice, however, the trademark symbol's numerical entity code works in Windows, Macintosh, and UNIX browsers, but since it is not a legal character, there is no guarantee that it will display on every possible system.

The only standard way to insert a trademark symbol that should display in most current browsers is to insert it as a Unicode character (**™**). As its name implies, Unicode is a universal character set that aims ultimately to include all characters that are used in every language. As it stands, Unicode includes many thousands more characters than the ISO 8859-1 character set.

Eddie Lopez's boss told him to insert trademark or registered symbols wherever required.

Insert the registered and trademark symbols as shown in the following example (see Figure 2.33):

```
<h2><a name="quest4"><big>Q:</big> How do I back up an audio
CD?</h2>
<p><b><big><big>A:</big></big></b> To make a copy of an audio CD
(CD-DA), so that you can play the copy in your CD player, you
need to record the disc in a single session and close the disc
when you are finished recording. If you record the disc using
multiple recording sessions or do not close the disc, you will
only be able to play the disc in a CD player or CD-ROM drive
that is <i>multisession capable</i>.</p>
<p>To make a copy of an audio CD using Adaptec&reg; Easy CD
Creator&#8482; 4:</p>
```

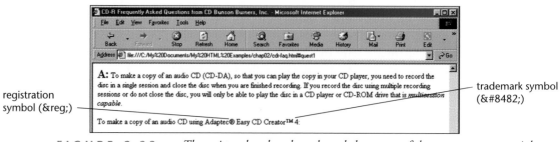

FIGURE 2.33 • *The registered and trademark symbols are two of the more common special characters that can be displayed on a Web page.*

The main problem with using the Unicode trademark symbol, however, is that it does not display in all browsers. It displays in the Netscape Navigator 4 browsers for Windows and the Macintosh, which is a big plus, but it does not display in the same browser versions for the X-Windows platform (UNIX).

If it is important to include a trademark symbol that can be displayed by all browsers (your lawyers, for instance, might insist that it be used wherever required within any corporate documents), even in non-graphical browsers, you do have an alternative. You can include a trademark symbol in a Web page by parenthesizing and superscripting the "tm" letter pair: `<sup>(tm)</sup>`. This is the same, somewhat ungraceful workaround that you used before to get around the problem of superscripted note numbers in browsers that do not support superscripting.

For more information about the ISO 8859-1 and Unicode character sets, see Appendix B.

USING MONOSPACED TEXT

HTML provides a number of elements that cause text to be displayed in a *monospaced* font. In a monospaced font, also called a *fixed-pitch* font, all characters, including letters, numbers, punctuation marks, and even spaces, are the same width, taking up exactly the same amount of horizontal space. When monospaced text is displayed in a Web page, most computer systems default to a Courier font (Courier New on a Windows system or Courier on a Macintosh system). By contrast, text in other non-monospaced elements is displayed in a *proportional* font, such as Times New Roman or Times Roman, for instance, in which each character may have a different (or "proportional") width.

Monospaced text is most common in technical documents, where it is generally used to represent different kinds of computer-generated text and to distinguish it from other surrounding text that is purely informational (rather than representational).

In HTML, the TT (Teletype) element is a generic element for producing monospaced text. The name of the element comes from a device, the *teletype*, which was used for both input and output on mainframes and minicomputers before the introduction of computer monitors using cathode ray tubes. The teletype was both a typewriter and a printer, which is why the TT element is a generic monospaced element that can be used to highlight both input and output text. Timothy Berners-Lee, and many others who helped pioneer the formation of the Web, worked with teletypes both as computer science students and later on the job, which is undoubtedly how the teletype element got its name in the first place. Bill Gates and Paul Allen, the founders of Microsoft, first learned how to program on a teletype at Lakeside Prep School in Seattle. (To read more about Bill Gates' early computer learning experiences, see "William H. Gates III: Before Microsoft" by John Mirick at **ei.cs.vt.edu/~history/Gates.Mirick.html**.) Perhaps to accommodate younger users who have never heard of nor seen a teletype, the TT element is sometimes referred to as the "typewriter text" element.

HTML provides other elements that are intended for marking up more specific types of monospaced text. These include the KBD (Keyboard), CODE (Program Code), and SAMP (Sample Code) elements. Many Web authors just stick to using the TT element for producing monospaced text, since none of these other elements display any differently than a TT element. A non-visual browser, such as a speech browser, might distinguish between a TT and a KBD element, with the KBD element indicating that nested text is input text (rather than output text). A style sheet can also be used to specify additional unique formatting to distinguish these elements, causing a KBD element to be displayed in both a monospaced and a bold font, for instance. You also can nest a B element inside a KBD element to achieve the same effect (although you also could nest the B element inside a TT element, for that matter, to indicate input text).

Use the TT element to highlight screen labels (options, buttons, and so on), the KBD element in combination with the B element to highlight keyboard input, and the SAMP element to highlight computer output (and replace the quotation marks), as shown here (see Figure 2.34):

```
<li>Select <tt>File</tt>, then <tt>Create CD Image</tt>. Change
to the folder where you save your image files (or you can
create a folder for this) and then save your image file, ending
the file name with a .cif file extension. For instance, type
<kbd><b>myimage.cif</b></kbd>, as the name of your image
file.<br><br>
<li>The message <samp>CD created successfully</samp> will be
displayed when the image file has been successfully created.
Click the <tt>OK</tt> button.<br><br>
```

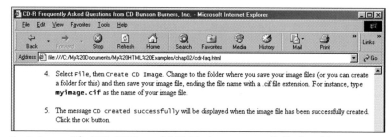

FIGURE 2.34 • *The TT, KBD, and SAMP elements are all displayed in a monospaced font.*

You also might want to display strings or blocks of computer code as monospaced text. The CODE element is an inline element, the purpose of which is to display strings of computer code. By inserting BR elements at the end of lines, the CODE element also can be used to display short blocks of computer code.

Format the example document's listing of a computer batch file in a monospaced font using the CODE element (the BR elements have already been inserted for you), as shown here (see Figure 2.35):

```
<p><code>[CD-R Blaster Job]<br>
Job Name = Contact Database<br>
Image File = F:\contacts.cif<br>
Label File = F:\Label templates\contacts.lbl<br>
Merge File = F:\contacts.mrg<br>
Type = Disk-At-Once<br>
Session = Single<br>
Disk = Close<br>
Number of Discs = 20<br>
Verify Type = None<br>
CRC32 = FFFFFFFF<br>
Serialize = No<br>
Serial Number Field = 1<br>
Serial Number Start = 123<br>
Serial Number Step = 1</code></p>
```

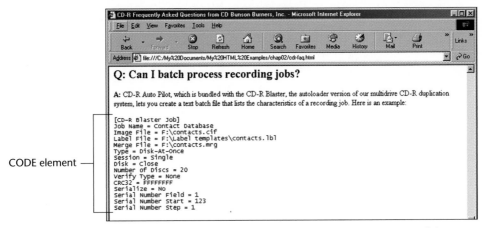

FIGURE 2.35 • *The CODE element is also displayed in a monospaced font.*

For formatting longer blocks of programming code, however, you might want to use the PRE (Preformatted Text) element, which also preserves any hard returns, spaces, or tabs that have been used to visually organize the code. The PRE element can be used to format any text that you want to display "as is" (that is, as "preformatted").

Nest the code text inside a PRE element and space out the text following the "=" character to form a second column:

1. Nest the code text inside a PRE element and delete the tags for the P, BR, and CODE elements:

```
<pre>
<p><code>[CD-R Blaster Job]<br>
Job Name = Contact Database<br>
Image File = F:\contacts.cif<br>
Label File = F:\Label templates\contacts.lbl<br>
Merge File = F:\contacts.mrg<br>
Type = Disk-At-Once<br>
Session = Single<br>
Disk = Close<br>
Number of Discs = 20<br>
Verify Type = None<br>
CRC32 = FFFFFFFF<br>
Serialize = No<br>
Serial Number Field = 1<br>
Serial Number Start = 123<br>
Serial Number Step = 1</code></p>
</pre>
```

2. To complete the next step, the text used to display the code text inside the PRE element must be displayed in your text editor using a monospaced font. If using SimpleText on the Macintosh, click and drag to highlight the code text, and then select Font and Courier New (or Courier). (If using Notepad, your text is displayed in a monospaced font by default.)

3. Insert spaces (shown by dot characters) following the "=" characters so that a second, left-aligned column is formed (see Figure 2.36):

```
<pre>
[CD-R Blaster Job]
Job Name = ·············Contact Database
Image File = ···········F:\contacts.cif
Label File = ···········F:\Label templates\contacts.lbl
Merge File = ···········F:\contacts.mrg
Type = ···············Disk-At-Once
Session = ·············Single
Disk = ················Close
Number of Discs = ·······20
Verify Type = ···········None
CRC32 = ················FFFFFFFF
Serialize = ·············No
Serial Number Field = ···1
Serial Number Start = ···123
Serial Number Step = ····1
</pre>
```

space characters

PRE (Preformatted) element

FIGURE 2.36 • *The PRE element displays a block of text in a monospaced font, while preserving any included spaces, tabs, or hard returns.*

CHAPTER SUMMARY

You should now be familiar with many of the HTML features and elements that are commonly used in creating and formatting online documents, including adding DocType declarations, META elements, inline highlighting (italics, bolding, underlining, monospacing, and so on), commonly used special characters (copyright, registered, and trademark), superscripted notes, hypertext note links, big and small text, and document menus.

Code Review

DocType declaration	Specifies the version of HTML (or XHTML) that the document is compatible with.
META element	Standalone element that is used to include meta data in an HTML document's HEAD element.
I and B elements	Literal inline elements for displaying italics and bolding.
EM and STRONG elements	Logical inline elements for adding emphasis (normally displayed as italics and bolding).
U element	Inline element that applies underlining to a text string (deprecated).
BLOCKQUOTE element	Specifies that a text block is to be formatted as a block quote, indented in from the margins.
DEL element	Specifies that nested text is a deletion.
INS element	Specifies that nested text is an insertion.
STRIKE element	Specifies strikeout text (deprecated).
S element	A more concise, but less universally supported element that specifies strikeout text (also deprecated).
SUP element	Inline element that superscripts a nested character or characters.
SUB element	Inline element that subscripts a nested character or characters.
NAME attribute	Used in the A (Anchor) element to create a destination anchor that can be jumped to from a hypertext link (or jump link).
WIDTH attribute	Used in the HR (Horizontal Rule) element to set the width of the rule (either in pixels or as a percentage).
ALIGN attribute	Used in the HR element to left-align or right-align a rule when the width of the rule is less than the width of the page (center alignment is the default).
SIZE attribute	Used in the HR element to specify the height of a horizontal rule in pixels.
© and ®	Named entity codes for the copyright and registered symbols.
&#8482;	Unicode numerical entity code for the trademark symbol.
BIG and SMALL elements	Increases and decreases the size of a text string.
OL element	Creates an ordered list (or numbered list).

TYPE attribute	Used with the OL or UL elements to change the number or bullet type that is displayed for the list.
TT element	The Teletype element, a generic element that can be used wherever a monospaced text string is desired.
KBD element	The Keyboard element, which can be used to indicate keyboard input (normally displayed in a monospaced font).
SAMP element	The Sample element, which can be used to indicate sample text or output (normally displayed in a mono-spaced font).
CODE element	Can be used to indicate program or script code (normally displayed in a monospaced font).
PRE element	The Preformatted Text element used to display a text block with all spaces, tabs, and hard returns displayed rather than ignored (normally displayed in a mono-spaced font).

ONLINE QUIZ

Go to this text's IRC at **www.emcp.com/** and take the online self-check quiz for this chapter.

REVIEW EXERCISES

This section provides some hands-on practice exercises to reinforce the information and material included within this and the previous chapter.

Save **acad_paper.html** and **cdr-faq.html** under new file names (**paper_practice.html** or **faq_practice.html**, for instance) and then use the new documents to practice using the elements, attributes, and other features that were covered in this chapter.

1. In either document (or both), delete the META element description and keyword list in the HEAD element and create a new description and keyword list based on the actual topic and content of the document. Do not use the description and keyword list provided in the chapter, but write your own from scratch.
2. Look for additional instances in both case example documents where you can apply any of the inline highlighting elements (I, B, EM, STRONG, U, and TT).
3. Find a poem that you like and format it using the BLOCKQUOTE element. Do not worry about context or realism; this is merely to get some practice formatting poetry as a block quote. Write an introductory paragraph that cites the poem and its author and then insert the poem as a block quote. For a single-stanza poem, nest the entire poem within a paragraph element; for a multi-stanza poem, nest the stanzas inside paragraph elements. Insert line breaks at the end of the individual verse lines.
4. In the academic paper document, add a fifth note number (following the other four note numbers). Do not worry about it being related to the text where you insert it; this is just for practice. Superscript the note number. Create a mock fifth footnote at the bottom of the page (following the other footnotes). Finally, turn the super-scripted note number into a hypertext link (a jump link) that jumps to a destination anchor that marks the location of the corresponding footnote. Create a return link that jumps back from the end of the footnote to the corresponding note number in the document text.

5. In the CD-R FAQ document, create a mock question and answer section. Do not worry about it relating to CD-R; any question and answer will do. Format it exactly like the other question and answer sections. Finally, add a new option to the document menu (using the question as the link text) that jumps to your new question and answer section. Add a return link below the question and answer section that jumps back up to the document menu.

6. In the CD-R FAQ document, add a mock nested number list following any of the answer sections. Do not worry about the content; use dummy text if you wish. Just make sure that you create a numbered list that has at least three levels of nested lists (including a list nested in a list that is nested in a list, in other words). Use the OL element's TYPE attribute to assign a different number-type (or letter-type) to each level of nested list. Use any of these values: **I** (uppercase Roman), **i** (lowercase Roman), **A** (uppercase alphabetic), **a** (lowercase alphabetic), **1** (Arabic numerals).

7. Experiment further with using the BIG and SMALL elements. Do not worry about context or content. The point is to see what the BIG and SMALL element will do when applied in different circumstances. Try nesting up to four BIG elements to get even bigger text. Try nesting multiple instances of SMALL elements, just to see in your browser why you should not nest SMALL elements.

8. In either document, experiment with using the HR element's WIDTH, SIZE, ALIGN, and NOSHADE attributes. Try different combinations and then check them out in your browser.

9. In the CD-R FAQ document, experiment further with inserting non-keyboard characters. Look for any additional instances in the document where you think a copyright, registered, or trademark symbol might be appropriate, or write additional example text of your own. Use named entity codes referenced in the chapter to insert the copyright and registered symbols. Use the Unicode numerical entity code referenced in the chapter to insert the trademark symbol. Alternatively, insert a trademark symbol that can be viewed in all browsers, by using the somewhat inelegant solution mentioned in the chapter to insert a trademark symbol by superscripting a parenthesized "tm" text string.

10. In either document, experiment with creating a nested bulleted list. Using dummy text, if you wish, create a nested bulleted list with at least three nested levels. A browser automatically displays different bullet characters for different nested bullet list levels, in this sequence, corresponding to the TYPE attributes that assign bullet-types: disc, circle, and square. Using these TYPE attribute values, assign bullet types to each nested bullet level that are different than the default sequence.

WEB-BASED LEARNING ACTIVITIES

In this book's text, Find It icons inserted in the margin highlight the Web addresses of additional resources you might find helpful or informative. To further extend your learning using the Web, you can:

- Go back and visit any of the Web addresses highlighted in this chapter that you have not yet visited. Look for additional resources and information that add to your understanding and knowledge of the material covered in this chapter. When you find a relevant page or site with information or resources you may want to access later, add it to your Favorites (in Internet Explorer) or your Bookmarks (in Netscape or Mozilla).

- Visit this book's Internet Resource Center at **www.emcp.com/** to find additional Web addresses of resources related to the material covered in this chapter that you can further investigate and explore.
- Further research a specific topic introduced in this chapter. For instance, do research on using DocType declarations or META elements within Web pages. Compile your research into a report that can be shared with your fellow students. You also can team up with other students to create a class presentation on a particular topic.

PROJECTS

These projects can be done in class, in a computer lab, or at home. Use the skills you have developed in this and the previous chapter to create any of the following projects.

Project 1. Format a paper or essay you have authored as an online document.

Take the lessons learned in this chapter and apply them to formatting a paper or essay that you have written so it can be displayed as an online document. Some guidelines for completing this assignment follow:

1. In your word processor, save your paper or essay under another name as a text file in this chapter's folder (chap02). For instance, you might save it as mypaper.html. (*Note: Do not save your paper or essay as an HTML file in your word processor—that is likely to generate a bunch of unnecessary and redundant HTML codes, sometimes referred to as spaghetti code.*)

2. Using the example online paper you created in this chapter, in your text editor, tag the text file you saved with the appropriate HTML elements, including the top-level HTML elements, a title element, heading elements, paragraph elements, bulleted or numbered list elements, block quote elements, and so on. No untagged text should be nested directly inside your BODY element. Optionally, also add a DocType declaration and META elements specifying your document's character set, a description of your page, and a list of keywords.

3. Scan your document's text for any special characters or symbols that have been carried over from your word processing document. Replace them with appropriate entity codes (see Appendix B) or type a substitute (replacing an *e* character with a grave accent, for instance, with a simple *e* character).

4. Look for instances in your original word processing document where you included italicized, bolded, or underlined text. Tag the same text in your text file using the I and B elements (or the EM and STRONG elements). Decide whether you want to carry over any underlined text—a better solution may be to simply format underlined text as italicized text.

5. Look for instances where you have included footnotes in your document. Use the SUP element to superscript footnote numbers and create hypertext links that jump to any footnotes listed at the bottom of your page.

6. Use the ADDRESS element to create an address block at the bottom of your page's BODY element. At minimum, type your name and an e-mail address. Sign up for a free Web-mail address that you can use here, if you do not want to expose your regular e-mail address to spammers.

Project 2. Create a Frequently Asked Questions page.

Using the FAQ page you worked with in this chapter as an example, create an FAQ page on a topic or subject about which you have some expertise. Create a list of questions and then write answers to them. Create a menu at the top of the page (listing only the questions) that uses hypertext links to jump to the corresponding question and answer sections. Insert loop-back links following each question and answer section that loop back to the menu. Add an address block to the bottom of your page.

Project 3. Write instruction steps for a computer or application procedure you are familiar with.

Create a Web page that features instruction steps that will give you an opportunity to use the TT, KBD, SAMP, CODE, and PRE elements in appropriate circumstances, as well as the I and B (or EM and STRONG) elements.

Project 4. Create a poetry page.

If you write poetry, create a Web page to show off your poems. Insert the poems inside block quote elements to indent them from the margin. Nest stanzas inside paragraph elements and insert BR elements to break the verse lines. Use any other elements or attributes you have learned to use.

CHAPTER

3

Working with Fonts, Colors, and Backgrounds

PERFORMANCE OBJECTIVES

In this chapter, you learn how to change the appearance of your Web page by using different fonts, colors, and backgrounds, including how to:

- Change the size and face of fonts for elements and text.
- Change the color of fonts, text, and links.
- Use background colors and images in Web pages.
- Set element backgrounds using styles.

In the first two chapters, you learned how to use basic and common features of HTML to create typical Web pages. In this chapter, you will learn how to change the appearance of your Web pages by changing font sizes and faces, applying color changes to fonts and links, and using background colors and images.

USING THE EXAMPLE FILES

If you have created a working folder for storing files you create, you will find the example files for this chapter located in the **chap03** folder within your working folder. You should save any HTML files you create in this chapter in that folder.

If you have created a working disk, you should copy the chap03 folder to your working disk from the **HTML_Examples** folder that you or your instructor downloaded from this book's Internet Resource Center (IRC), or from a CD-R disc or floppy disk provided by your instructor. If the working disc you used in previous chapters is getting full, create a new one. Ask your instructor for assistance if you do not know the location of the HTML_Examples folder or how to copy the chap03 folder. You should save any HTML file you create in this chapter in the chap03 folder that you have copied to your working disk.

CASE EXAMPLE: UPDATING THE APPEARANCE OF A PERSONAL WEB PAGE

In this example, you revise the personal Web page you created in Chapter 1, *Creating a Basic Web Page*, by using fonts, colors, and backgrounds to make it more attractive and visually appealing.

Johnny Watson made some changes to his personal Web page, adding a DocType statement, a META element declaring the character set his page uses, and two other META elements that provide a description and keyword list that search engines and directories can use to index or list his page. He also made a few other minor changes to the text in his page, but not to the HTML codes. His friends like the content and links he included in his page, but have commented that it might look better if he varied the size and face of his fonts and incorporated colors and backgrounds into his page's design. When Johnny Watson first created his personal Web page, he was still learning HTML and had not learned yet how to make font or color changes. He has since learned more about using these features and wants to apply them to update the appearance of his personal Web page.

To get started working with this example:
1. Run your text editor and open **watson2_ex.html** from the chap03 folder in your working folder or working disk.
2. Save watson2_ex.html as **watson2.html** in the chap03 folder.
3. Run your browser and open **watson2.html** from the chap03 folder.

If you need more guidance on opening and saving an HTML file in your text editor and opening and previewing it in your Web browser, see "Opening an HTML File in Your Text Editor" and "Saving and Previewing Your HTML File" in Chapter 2, *Working with Online Documents*.

CHANGING FONT SIZES

In HTML, the FONT element can be used to change the appearance of nested text, including the size, color, and face of the font in which text is displayed. In this section, you will focus on the first of these features, changing the size of the font used to display nested text. In the FONT element, the SIZE attribute is used to change the size of nested text.

Using Absolute Font Sizes

The FONT element's SIZE attribute enables you to specify seven different absolute font sizes, by using an integer value from 1 to 7. An absolute font size will not change, even if the default base font size is changed. For instance, the following sets an absolute font size of 5 for the nested text:

```
<font size="5">nested text</font>
```

Figure 3.1 shows the seven font sizes in relation to the default sizes of a level-one heading and paragraph text.

FIGURE 3.1 • *Seven absolute font sizes can be set in HTML.*

NOTE

The HTML file shown in Figure 3.1 is available with the example files for this chapter. To look for yourself, open **fontsizes.html** in your browser from the chap03 folder. After viewing it, click the Back button to return to watson2.html in your browser.

As shown in Figure 3.1, two of the font sizes (sizes 1 and 2) are smaller than the default size of paragraph text, one (size 3) is the same size, and four (sizes 4 through 7) are larger.

Johnny Watson discovered that by using the FONT element he can set a font size that is one size larger than the default font size of a level-one heading. He decided to take advantage of this to increase the size of the initial letters in each word of his level-one heading.

Use the FONT element's SIZE attribute to increase the initial letters in the level-one heading to size 7 (see Figure 3.2):

```
<h1><font size="7">S</font>ports, <font size="7">G</font>ardening,
and <font size="7">O</font>ther <font size="7">I</font>nterests</h1>
```

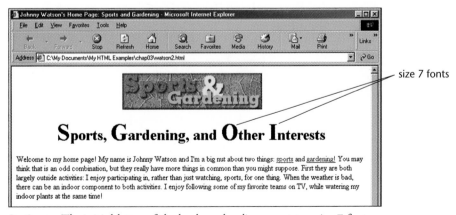

FIGURE 3.2 • *The initial letters of the level-one heading are set to a size 7 font.*

Johnny liked the result of increasing the size of the initial letters in his level-one heading so much, he decided to do the same with his level-two heading.

 Use the FONT element's SIZE attribute to increase the initial letters in the level-two heading to size 6 (see Figure 3.3):

```
<h2 align="center"><font size="6">B</font>iography, <font
size="6">I</font>nterests, and <font
size="6">F</font>riends</h2>
```

size 6 fonts

FIGURE 3.3 • *The initial letters of the level-two heading are set to a size 6 font.*

Using Relative Font Sizes

Alternatively, you can set font sizes relative to the default base font size. Relative font sizes are adjusted, up or down, if the default base font size is increased or decreased. A relative font size is indicated by a "+" or "-" character in front of the SIZE attribute integer value. For instance, the following increases the font size of text one size above the base font size:

```
<font size="+1">nested text</font>
```

Johnny wants to increase the font size of the two in-context hypertext links that are in his introductory paragraph. He has decided to try using relative font size changes to do this.

 Set relative font sizes that will increase the size of text nested inside of the two hypertext links in the introductory paragraph (see Figure 3.4):

```
<p>Welcome to my home page! My name is Johnny Watson and I'm a
big nut about two things: <a href="http://www.espn.com/"><font
size="+1">sports</font></a> and <a
href="http://www.bbc.co.uk/gardening/"><font
size="+1">gardening!</font></a>
```

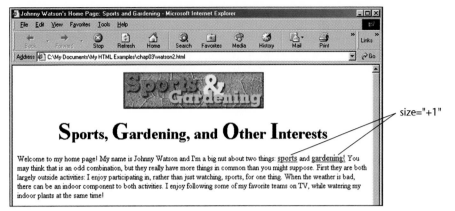

FIGURE 3.4 • *A relative font size increases the size of text relative to the default base font size.*

In the previous chapter, you used the BIG and SMALL elements to increase and decrease the size of nested text. At first glance, a BIG element and a FONT element with a `size="+1"` attribute seem to do the same thing, but that is not true.

A BIG element increases the font size of nested text relative to the font size of the current element. A FONT element with a `size="+1"` attribute increases the size of nested text one size relative to the base font size.

action

Add the following text and codes to the example page (temporarily) to see this for yourself (see Figure 3.5):

```
<h1><font size="7">S</font>ports, <font
size="7">G</font>ardening, and <font size="7">O</font>ther <font
size="7">I</font>nterests</h1>
<h2>by <big>Johnny</big> <font size="+1">Watson</font></h2>
</center>
```

When you are finished viewing the example in your browser, delete the text and codes you just added.

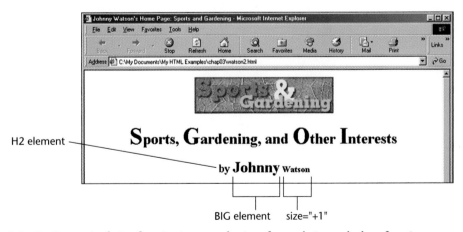

FIGURE 3.5 • *A relative font size increases the size of text relative to the base font size.*

As the callout for Figure 3.5 indicates, a BIG element changes the size of nested text relative to the font size of the element in which it is nested (the H2 element, in this case). A relative font size, on the other hand, changes the size of nested text relative to the size of the base font (the default size of the P or LI elements, for instance).

Changing the Base Font Size

The BASEFONT element is an empty element that changes the base font size for any following text. Among current major browsers, only Internet Explorer and Netscape support the BASEFONT element. The Mozilla and Opera browsers completely ignore it.

Test what changing the base font size looks like in your browser (if using Internet Explorer or Netscape):

1. Use the BASEFONT element to increase the size of the base font one size (see Figure 3.6):

```
<body>
<basefont size="4">
```

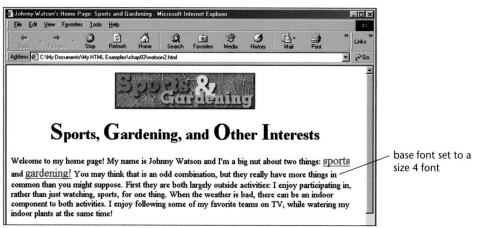

base font set to a size 4 font

FIGURE 3.6 • *The BASEFONT element is used to change the base font size in browsers that support it.*

2. After viewing the effect of the BASEFONT element on your page in your browser, delete the BASEFONT element you just set.

Later in this chapter, in "Controlling Fonts, Colors, and Backgrounds Using Styles," you will learn how to use styles to change the font size of paragraph and other body text elements.

CHANGING THE FONT FACE

The FONT element's FACE attribute lets you specify a font face (or typeface) or a comma-delimited list of font faces to be used in displaying nested text.

Understanding Font Realities

You might see some neat font on the Web and think you would like to use that font in your Web page. You download and install it, reference it in your Web page, and it works! You publish your page to the Web and then ask all your friends to check out your page, adding as your final words, "Be sure to check out the snazzy font I'm using!" One by one, however, your friends report that all they can see is the same font that is displayed on almost every Web page (Times New Roman or Times).

The problem is that your friends, unlike yourself, have not downloaded and installed the font you are using, and thus do not have it available on their systems. For a font to be displayed in a Web page using the FONT element's FACE attribute, it must be available on a user's system. Just because a particular font is available on your system does not mean that others will have the same font available on their systems, and no one font is guaranteed to be available on all systems. When specifying fonts for display in your Web page, you need to stick with specifying the most commonly available fonts, avoiding less commonly available fonts you may have installed on your system or can download from the Web. See "Specifying a Font List" a little later in this chapter for a rundown on some of the more commonly available fonts.

Specifying a Single Font Face

To specify that a particular font face, if available, should be used to display an element, you specify the name of the font as the value for the FACE attribute.

To add some visual variety to his page, Johnny Watson wants to change the look of his heading-level elements by displaying them using a sans serif font. He has decided to use the Arial font because it is one of the more common sans serif fonts. He understands that the Arial font may not be available on every system, but is willing to have a serif font displayed instead on systems that do not have the Arial font because that does not cause any accessibility problems.

He has also removed the font size changes he added earlier to his level-one and level-two headings to get a cleaner, less busy look.

Use the FONT element to specify that the level-one and level-two heading elements should be displayed in an Arial font, if available:

1. Delete the font size changes that you added earlier and set a single FONT element that sets an Arial font for the H1 element.

```
<h1><font face="Arial">Sports, Gardening, and Other
Interests</font></h1>
```

2. Do the same for the H2 element (see Figure 3.7):

```
<h2 align="center"><font face="Arial">Biography, Interests, and
Friends</font></h2>
```

Arial (sans serif) font

FIGURE 3.7 • *Using a sans serif font for headings can add visual variety to a page.*

The FONT element is an inline element and thus should always be nested inside of a block element and should not have block elements nested inside of it. For instance, you should *not* apply a font face change to the H2 element like this:

```
<font face="Arial"><h2>Biography, Interests, and
Friends</h2></font>
```

Specifying a Font List

The problem with only specifying a single font face is that there are many systems that may not have that font installed. The Arial font is a TrueType font that should be present on every Windows system, but many Macintosh and UNIX users might not have that font. To get around that problem, HTML enables you to specify a comma-delimited list of fonts. The second listed font can be displayed if the first font is not available, the third listed font if the second font is not available, and so on.

Johnny Watson wants to specify a list of fonts, rather than just a single font, to increase the chances that one of the listed fonts will be available on a user's system.

Specify a list of fonts to be used to display the level-one and level-two headings:

1. Specify a list of fonts for the H1 element:

```
<h1><font face="Arial, Geneva, Helvetica">Sports, Gardening, and
Other Interests</font></h1>
```

2. Make the same change for the H2 element.

Because some Macintosh and UNIX systems only have PostScript fonts available, it is a good idea to include a PostScript font in a font list.

The Geneva font is a sans serif TrueType font often available on Macintosh systems, whereas the Helvetica font is an Adobe PostScript font that should be available on most Macintosh and UNIX systems.

TROUBLE *spot*

Some browsers treat font-face names as case-sensitive. When specifying font-face names, you should type them using any initial uppercase characters that are included in the font-face name. For instance, you should type **Arial** and not **arial** as the FACE attribute value.

Current Windows browsers ignore most PostScript fonts in a font list. Internet Explorer 6 and the Opera browser display Courier, a PostScript font, but completely ignore Helvetica, as well as any other PostScript fonts, displaying the default text font (usually a serif font) instead. Netscape 4 and 6, as well as the Mozilla browser, substitute Arial for Helvetica and Courier New for Courier, but ignore any other PostScript fonts.

NOTE

Microsoft provides a selection of Web core fonts that Windows, Macintosh, and UNIX/Linux users can download and install if they are not already available on their systems. You can download any these fonts from **www.microsoft.com/typography/fontpack/default.htm**. Fonts included are Andale Mono, Arial, Arial Black, Comic Sans MS, Courier New, Georgia, Impact, Times New Roman, TrebuchetMS, Verdana, and Webdings (Windows only). UNIX/Linux users can download the Windows versions of these fonts (which are available as self-extracting archives). For additional links to font resources on the Web, see this chapter's section at this book's IRC at **www.emcp.com/**.

Table 3.1 shows the names of some of the most commonly available fonts for Windows, the Macintosh, or UNIX/Linux systems.

TABLE 3.1 • *Fonts Commonly Available on Different Systems*

System	Should Be Available	May Be Available
Windows	Arial, Courier New, and Times New Roman	Andale Mono, Arial Black, Century Gothic, Comic Sans MS, Georgia, Impact, Marlett, Monotype.com, Tahoma, Trebuchet MS, and Verdana
Macintosh	Times, Helvetica, Courier, and Palatino (PostScript fonts)	Arial, Arial Black, Charcoal, Chicago, Comic Sans MS, Courier New, Espy Sans, Gadget, Geneva, Georgia, Impact, Minion Web, Monaco, New York, Sand, Techno, Textile, Times New Roman, Trebuchet MS, and Verdana (TrueType fonts)
UNIX/Linux	Times, Helvetica, Courier, and Palatino (PostScript fonts)	Charter, Charter BT, Lucida, LucidaTypewriter, New Century Schoolbook, and Utopia (UNIX/Linux user can also download and install Microsoft's Web core fonts)

You cannot rely on any one font being available on all systems. Any font face you specify using the FONT element's FACE attribute is a suggestion only that may or may not be displayed on someone else's system. To maximize the chance that a particular font will be available on a user's system, you should stick to specifying Arial and Helvetica sans serif fonts, Times New Roman and Times serif fonts, and Courier New and Courier monospaced fonts.

You should also realize when using uncommon fonts that different fonts can have the same name. Thus, the Carumba font installed on your system might be an entirely different font than the Carumba font installed on someone else's system. This is another good reason to stick to using only commonly available fonts in your Web pages.

Different fonts of the same size can have different *x-heights*. The x-height is the height of the lowercase letters in a font (the height of the lowercase "x"). A font with a larger x-height will take up more horizontal space on a line than another font of the same size, but with a smaller x-height. Figure 3.8 shows a series of different fonts specified for the H2 element. (To check this out for yourself, open **fontfaces.html** in your browser from the chap03 folder.) Notice that the amount of horizontal space occupied by these fonts varies, even though they are the same size and contain the same text. When specifying a list of fonts, be aware that, while your preferred font (Arial, for instance) may not cause an H1 heading to wrap, another font in your font list with a larger x-height (Verdana, for instance) may cause the heading to wrap to a second line.

FIGURE 3.8 • *Fonts of the same size can have different x-heights, which can affect the amount of horizontal space the fonts take up.*

Specifying a Generic Font-Family Name

The Cascading Style Sheets specification includes a list of generic font-family names that can be used to refer to generic classes of fonts. These font-family names are serif, sans-serif, monospace, cursive, and fantasy. Current browsers also support these generic font-family names when using the FONT element's FACE attribute, although earlier browsers generally do not support them. Because generic font-family names used with the FACE attribute might not be supported by earlier browsers and are not part of the HTML 4.01 specification, you should include a generic font-family name only at the end of a font list as a stop-gap in case none of your listed fonts are available on a user's system.

Johnny Watson discovered that most current browsers also support using a generic font-family name in a list of font names for the FACE attribute. He has decided to include the sans-serif generic font-family name in his font list to increase the chances that a browser will display a sans serif, rather than a serif font.

Include a generic font-family name at the end of the document's font lists to increase the chances of a sans serif font being displayed on a user's system:

1. Add a generic font-family name, sans-serif, to the end of the font list for the H1 element:

```
<h1><font face="Arial, Geneva, Helvetica, sans-serif">Sports,
Gardening, and Other Interests</font></h1>
```

2. Make the same change for the H2 element.

Of the generic font-family names, only the serif, sans-serif, and monospace names are consistently supported by browsers. Browsers that support using these names generally display a Times New Roman or Times font when a serif generic font-family name is specified, Arial or Helvetica when a sans-serif generic font-family name is specified, and Courier New or Courier when a monospace generic font-family name is specified. The other generic font-family names are inconsistently supported by browsers and should be avoided.

Using Sans Serif and Serif Fonts

Most browsers use a serif font for displaying text, generally some variant of Times or Times New Roman. The Times font is so named because it was first used to print columnar text in the London Times newspaper. A serif font, such as is used in this book's paragraph text, has strokes (serifs) that accentuate the ends of the letterforms, whereas a sans serif font, such as is used in this book's headings, lacks any accentuating strokes. Serifs make larger amounts of text displayed in a smaller-sized font, such as paragraph text, for instance, easier to read and scan because the serifs guide your eyes along as you read. For that reason, books and newspapers generally use a serif font for body text that needs to be read for content, and a sans serif font only in headings and display type.

Designers, on the other hand, often use sans serif fonts in advertising copy, especially where the text also serves as a design element, but also to create a contrast with serif fonts used in a magazine's text columns. Some magazines have gone to printing body text in a sans serif font, to give their pages a look they consider more modern and stylish; when that is done, however, the space between the text lines, called the leading, is usually also increased to help make the sans serif body text easier to read.

Web page designers also sometimes opt for using sans serif fonts for body text (paragraph text), for much the same reasons print designers do, because it gives their pages more of a "designed" (and less "bookish") look. This is fine in a shorter page, such as Johnny Watson's personal page, which contains less than two screens worth of text, but if you are presenting larger amounts of text that need to be read for comprehension, a serif font is probably the better choice. Crystal Porter, for instance, would not want to present her online academic paper in a sans serif font, not simply because that is what is expected, but also because it would make her text more difficult to read and comprehend.

Compare reading the text of the *Declaration of Independence* in a serif and a sans serif font:

1. Open **textcompare.html** in your browser from the chap03 folder (see Figure 3.9).

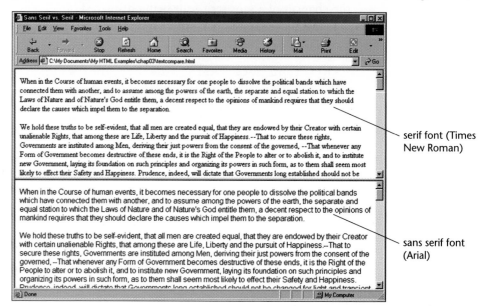

FIGURE 3.9 • *According to one school of thought, text displayed in a serif font is easier to read and comprehend than text displayed in a sans serif font.*

2. The two versions are displayed in separate frames. Read the text in each frame. You can grab the divider line between the two frames with the mouse pointer and pull it up or down to display more text in either frame.

3. Understanding that you are making an entirely subjective and unscientific judgment, make a note in your book next to Figure 3.9 indicating which of the two fonts you feel is the most readable.

NOTE

To find out more about readability and comprehension issues related to using serif and sans serif fonts, you can read Wendy Priestly's article, "Instructional typographies using desktop publishing techniques to produce effective learning and training materials," available online at **cleo.murdoch.edu.au/gen/aset/ajet/ajet7/su91p153.html**. See the section for this chapter at this book's IRC at **www.emcp.com/** for additional links to resources on typography and the Web.

WORKING WITH COLORS

The FONT element's COLOR attribute is used to specify a foreground color to be displayed for nested text. Font colors can be assigned by using either color names or hexadecimal color codes.

Using Color Names

These are the 16 standard color names that can be used as values for the FONT element's COLOR attribute: white, black, gray, silver, white, maroon, red, fuchsia, green, lime, olive, yellow, navy, blue, teal, and aqua. These color names are derived from the 16 colors available on a 16-color VGA display.

Johnny Watson's friends told him that, other than his banner graphic, his page is a drab affair that could stand to be touched up with a little color. Johnny learned that he can use the FONT element's COLOR attribute to specify any of 16 standard color names.

Use the FONT element's COLOR attribute to assign foreground colors to the text nested inside the H1 and H2 elements:

1. Specify that text nested inside the H1 element should be displayed in a blue color:

```
<h1><font color="blue" face="Arial, Geneva, Helvetica, sans-serif">Sports, Gardening, and Other Interests</font></h1>
```

2. Specify that text nested inside the H2 element should be displayed in a red color:

```
<h2 align="center"><font color="red" face="Arial, Geneva, Helvetica, sans-serif">Biography, Interests, and Friends</font></h2>
```

As shown in Figure 3.10, the text nested inside the H1 element is now displayed in a blue color and the text nested inside the H2 element is now displayed in a red color.

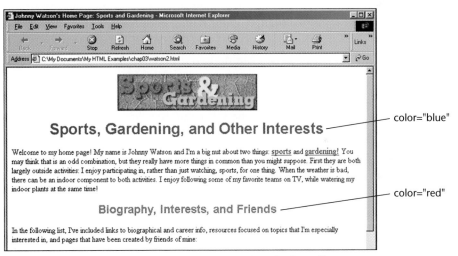

FIGURE 3.10 • *A Web page need not be a purely black-and-white affair.*

An example file, colornames.html, is included in the chap02 folder with the other example files for this chapter. You can open and view **colornames.html** in your browser, as shown in Figure 3.11.

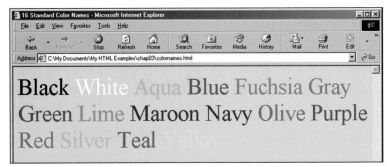

FIGURE 3.11 • *There are 16 standard color names that can be used to specify colors in Web pages.*

Most current browsers actually support many more than the standard 16 color names specified in the HTML 4 specifications. There are 140 color names that date back to the beginnings of the Web—they were part of the X-Windows system under UNIX. Many current browsers still recognize these same color names. The main problem with using these color names, however, is that the same color name may correspond to different colors on different systems. You will also likely get an error message if you try to validate your page's HTML if it contains any of these non-standard color names. Also, not all current browsers support all of these color names, which means that you could end up displaying a foreground color that is supported against a background color that is not supported, for instance.

You do not need to use non-standard color names, however, to make use of a much wider selection of colors in your Web pages. Any of the non-standard color names can also be specified using a hexadecimal RGB code, which all browsers that recognize colors support.

Using Hexadecimal RGB Codes

The 16 color names are admittedly somewhat limiting. You might have noticed that there is no "orange" color name, even though there are "green" and "purple" color names. That is because the original 16-color VGA display did not include an orange color, but derived it from combining two different colors (red and yellow). To display a different color than those specified by the standard 16 color names, you can use a *hexadecimal RGB code*. A hexadecimal RGB code states the RGB (red-green-blue) values for a color in hexadecimal numbers, in the following format:

```
color="#rrggbb"
```

The hash character (#) indicates that the following six characters correspond to three hexadecimal color values (*rr*, *gg*, and *bb*) that together represent a specific RGB color value.

 The U.K. keyboard for the Macintosh does not have the "#" (hash) character at the Shift+3 position, but has the "£" (British pound) symbol instead. To insert the "#" character using a U.K. keyboard, just press Option+3 (or Alt+3).

The hexadecimal numbering system uses a 16-number base (0, 1, 2, 3, 4, 5, 6, 7, 8, 9, A, B, C, D, E, and F), as opposed to the 10-number base that forms the decimal numbering system. Programmers tend to prefer using hexadecimal numbers because up to 256 numerical values can be stated using only 2 characters, while using a decimal numbering system 3 digits are required. Table 3.2 shows the 16 hexadecimal numbers and their decimal equivalents.

TABLE 3.2 • *The 16 Hexadecimal Base Numbers and Their Decimal Equivalents*

Hex = Dec	Hex = Dec	Hex = Dec	Hex = Dec
0 = 0	4 = 4	8 = 8	C = 12
1 = 1	5 = 5	9 = 9	D = 13
2 = 2	6 = 6	A = 10	E = 14
3 = 3	7 = 7	B = 11	F = 15

To derive the decimal value of a hexadecimal number, just apply the following formula:

$$(h^1 \times 16) + h^2 = d$$

The variable h^1 corresponds to the decimal value of the first hexadecimal digit, h^2 corresponds to the decimal value of the second hexadecimal digit (as shown previously in Table 3.2), and d equals the number's decimal value. In other words, the decimal value of AD (where the hexadecimal numbers A and D are equal to decimal values of 10 and 13, respectively) can be calculated in this fashion:

$$(10 \times 16) + 13 = 173$$

By using hexadecimal RGB codes, you can set 256 different values for each RGB color component, meaning that a total of 16,777,216 (16.7 million) separate colors (256 × 256 × 256) can be set using hexadecimal RGB codes.

A number of sites on the Web list the hexadecimal codes for the non-standard color names supported by most current browsers. Although you should not use the color names, you can use them to identify a particular color that you like, and then use its listed hexadecimal code to apply it to your Web page. Thus, instead of using the non-standard DarkGoldenRod color name to specify a gold-like color, just use its hexadecimal equivalent (#b8860b). There are many sites on the Web that provide color charts that show the non-standard color names along with their corresponding hexadecimal RGB codes. See this chapter's section at this book's IRC at **www.emcp.com/** for a selection of links to where you can find color charts, color pickers, and other color resources.

Use hexadecimal RGB codes to change the colors of the level-one and level-two heading elements:

1. Use the hexadecimal RGB code, **#b8860b**, to change the color of the level-one heading to a color corresponding to the non-standard "DarkGoldenRod" color:

```
<h1><font color="#b8860b" face="Arial, Geneva, Helvetica, sans-serif">Sports, Gardening, and Other Interests</font></h1>
```

2. Use the hexadecimal RGB code, **#2e8b57**, to change the color of the level-two heading to a color corresponding to the non-standard "SeaGreen" color (see Figure 3.12):

```
<h2 align="center"><font color="#2e8b57" face="Arial, Geneva, Helvetica, sans-serif">Biography, Interests, and Friends</font></h2>
```

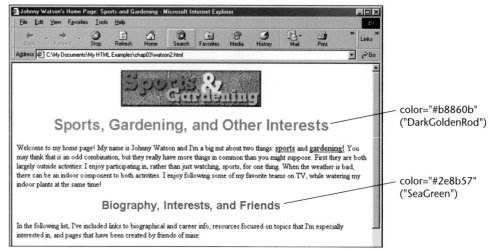

color="#b8860b"
("DarkGoldenRod")

color="#2e8b57"
("SeaGreen")

FIGURE 3.12 • *Use hexadecimal color codes to set colors other than those specified by the 16 standard color names.*

A common mistake when setting colors using hexadecimal RGB codes is to omit the # character at the start of the code. Internet Explorer actually lets you get away with doing this, but most other browsers will not display your color if the # character is missing.

Using Web-Safe Colors

Not everyone is surfing the Web on a system that can display colors from a palette of 16.7 million colors (also known as a True Color palette). Some users are still using graphic cards or monitors that limit them to 256 or fewer colors. For these users, if a specified color is not available on their system, their system uses *dithering* to approximate the color. Dithering is the adjustment of the colors in adjacent pixels so that they appear to the eye to be a single color. When successful, dithering realistically reproduces a color that is not otherwise available; when unsuccessful, it produces a noticeably splotchy or speckled color that may only remotely resemble the desired color.

An option for dealing with such users is to use only colors from *the Web-safe palette*. The Web-safe palette is also sometimes called the Netscape palette, because Netscape originally introduced it. The Web-safe palette has 216 colors that are guaranteed to be displayable on virtually all computer systems without having to be dithered. The Web-safe palette is composed entirely of colors with hexadecimal RGB codes that include only these hexadecimal numbers: 00, 33, 66, 99, CC, and FF. For instance, the hexadecimal RGB code of #996600 produces a color that is somewhat darker than the "DarkGoldenRod" color used previously, but which still produces a recognizably "gold" color.

Use the #996600 hexadecimal code to apply a Web-safe "gold" color to the H1 element (see Figure 3.13):

```
<h1><font color="#996600" face="Arial, Geneva, Helvetica, sans-
serif">Sports, Gardening, and Other Interests</font></h1>
```

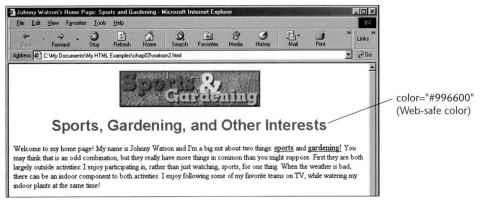

color="#996600"
(Web-safe color)

FIGURE 3.13 • *A Web-safe RGB color, including only the 00, 33, 66, 99, CC, or FF hexadecimal numerical values, will not be dithered on a 256-color system.*

Appendix C, *Web-Safe Colors Chart*, shows all the Web-safe colors along with the hexadecimal RGB codes you need to use to apply them to your Web pages. Using the chart, choose a Web-safe color and apply it to your document's H2 element. Be sure to check out the result in your browser. If you do not like how your first choice looks, try another one. Experiment with setting different Web-safe colors for your H1 element as well. Repeat until you are satisfied with your choices of Web-safe colors for the H2 and H1 elements.

You can also find an HTML file, **colorchart.html**, included with the example files for this chapter in the chap03 folder that you can open in your browser. It shows all of the Web-safe colors along with their corresponding hexadecimal RGB codes.

Setting Text, Link, and Background Colors

The BODY element's TEXT, LINK, VLINK, ALINK, and BGCOLOR attributes enable you to set colors for your page's text, unvisited links, visited links, activated links, and the background. Unvisited and visited links connect to sites you have not visited and sites you have already visited. An activated link's color is displayed when the mouse is held down on a link.

Use a combination of color names and hexadecimal RGB codes to set colors for text, links, and the page background (see Figure 3.14):

```
<body text="navy" link="#ff6600" vlink="#996699" alink="blue"
bgcolor="#ffffcc">
```

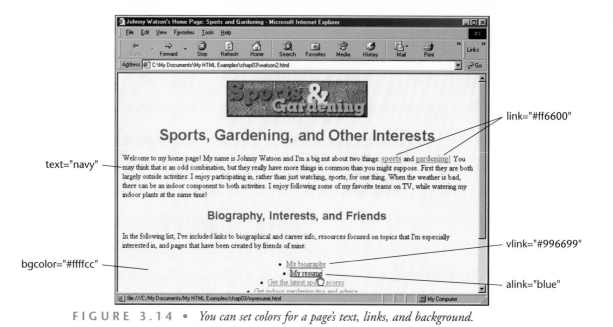

link="#ff6600"

text="navy"

vlink="#996699"

bgcolor="#ffffcc"

alink="blue"

FIGURE 3.14 • *You can set colors for a page's text, links, and background.*

Although most browsers default to a white background color when they are installed, that is not universally the case. The Mosaic browser, for instance, defaults to a gray background color, as does Netscape Navigator 4 for the Macintosh. If you want to insure that your page's background is displayed as white, you should insert a **bgcolor="white"** attribute in the BODY element.

You also should be mindful when setting foreground and background colors that some people have color-vision deficiencies that make it difficult to distinguish between certain color combinations. About ten percent of males have some form of color-vision deficiency. Some people see red text as yellow text, for instance, while others may have trouble distinguishing between red and green. Others may see blue text as yellow text.

NOTE

Make sure that you have sufficient tonal contrast between foreground and background colors in your pages in order to assist people with color-vision deficiencies. Do not rely simply on a color contrast, especially between red and green, to distinguish foreground and background colors. Visit this chapter's section at this book's IRC at **www.emcp.com/** for links to resources where you can learn more about color blindness and other accessibility issues related to the use of color in Web sites.

USING A BACKGROUND IMAGE

The BODY element's BACKGROUND attribute lets you assign a background image to your page. Using a background image can add to the visual appeal of your page; however, it also can make your page more difficult to access and read, if the image is busy or high contrast, or if its colors clash or do not provide sufficient contrast with your page's foreground and link colors. An example background image, **back_light.jpg**, is included with this chapter's example files.

Displaying a Background Image

The BODY element's BACKGROUND attribute is used to display a background image in a Web page. Its value is a URL or file name of an image, which can be any of the same kinds of image formats that are normally used for displaying inline images, including JPEG (.jpg), GIF (.gif), and PNG (.png) images. A background image is normally a smaller image, often less than 100 pixels wide or high, which is then tiled to fill a browser's background.

Use the BODY element's BACKGROUND attribute to assign a background image to your page (see Figure 3.15):

```
<body text="navy" link="#ff6600" vlink="#996699" alink="blue"
bgcolor="#ffffcc" background="back_light.jpg">
```

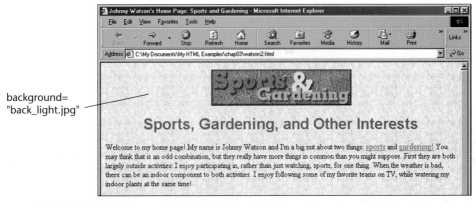

FIGURE 3.15 • *A carefully chosen background image can further enhance the appearance of a Web page.*

Notice that both a background color and a background image are specified for the BODY element. That is because some users surf the Web with the display of graphics turned off to speed up access to Web pages over a slow connection. By specifying a background color that is close in color to your background image, you can insure that such users will still see your intended foreground-background color combination. This is especially important when displaying light text against a dark background image, which could end up displaying light text against a white background if the background image is not displayed.

Creating Your Own Background Images

Some image editors, such as Jasc Software's Paint Shop Pro and Ulead PhotoImpact, include features that allow you to create your own seamless background images. In Paint Shop Pro, for instance, select the area you want to convert to a seamless pattern, select Selections, and then select Convert to Seamless Pattern.

Even if your image editor does not support creating background images, you can still create your own seamless background image from scratch, if you like. Select or crop an image that you want to use. For instance, you might want to select and crop a section of cloudy sky from a photograph of a sunset. To turn the cropped image into a seamless background:

1. Select or create an image (Image A) that you want to use and size it to 50 × 50 pixels. Open a second image (Image B) that is sized at 100 × 100 pixels. Copy and paste Image A into the upper-left corner of Image B.

2. Flip Image A horizontally, so that what was on the left is now on the right, and vice versa. Copy and paste this image into the upper-right corner of Image B.

3. Using the mirrored image you created in step 2, flip Image A vertically, so that what was the top is now the bottom, and vice versa. Copy and paste this image into the lower-right corner of Image B.

4. Using the mirrored image you created in step 3, flip Image A horizontally, so that what was on the left is now on the right, and vice versa. Copy and paste this image into the lower-left corner of Image B (see Figure 3.16.)

5. Optionally, resize Image B to a smaller size (75 × 75 pixels, for instance) and then save it as a JPEG image (as myback.jpg, for instance).

The result is that myback.jpg matches up on all four sides, creating a seamless background tile (see Figure 3.17.)

FIGURE 3.16 • *A seamless background image can be created by mirroring an image horizontally and vertically.*

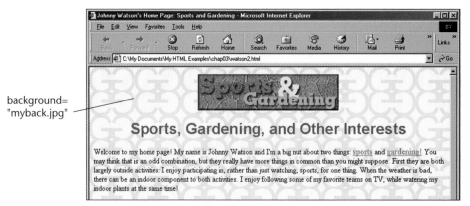

background= "myback.jpg"

FIGURE 3.17 • *The seamless background image shown in Figure 3.16 is shown here displayed in a Web page.*

CONTROLLING FONTS, COLORS, AND BACKGROUNDS USING STYLES

The FONT and BASEFONT elements, as well as the BODY element's TEXT, LINK, VLINK, ALINK, BGCOLOR, and BACKGROUND attributes, have been depreciated in HTML 4.01 and XHTML 1.0 in favor of using Cascading Style Sheets (CSS) to achieve similar or better results. The primary reason for this is to provide for improved accessibility by separating appearance and presentation from structure and content. Deprecated elements and attributes are entirely legal, as long as you declare your document to conform to the transitional or frameset definitions of HTML 4.01 or XHTML 1.0.

The W3C, however, in the HTML 4 and 4.01 specification, advises the following: "In general, authors should use style sheets to achieve stylistic and formatting effects rather than HTML presentational attributes." All current browsers provide sufficient support for CSS to enable the design of colorful and attractive Web pages without the use of deprecated elements and attributes.

Government agencies, educational institutions, non-profit organizations, or larger companies may also decide on their own to require the use of styles in place of deprecated elements and attributes, in order to help ensure that documents they publish on the Web are accessible to all and compliant, not only with the letter, but also with the spirit of the Americans with Disabilities Act (ADA). Many of these agencies, organizations, and companies have subscribed to the W3C's Web Accessibility Initiative (WAI), which mandates the use of styles in place of deprecated elements and attributes in Web pages. Screen readers, for instance, used by individuals with visual impairments, can easily ignore any CSS styling added to a page while conveying the page's structure and content as indicated by its HTML coding. Separating appearance from content is a much more difficult task, however, if HTML elements and attributes are also being used to determine a page's visual presentation and appearance.

The main difficulty in implementing CSS in Web pages is not with early browsers that do not support CSS (such as Internet Explorer 2 or Netscape 3), in that they completely ignore any CSS styles included in a page, but with more recent browsers that support CSS, but do it badly (such as Internet Explorer 3 or Netscape 4). Many Web designers choose to continue to use deprecated elements and attributes, rather than implement styles, because of the backward-compatibility issues that the use of styles pose.

For these reasons, anyone contemplating a career in Web design should be proficient in the use of both deprecated elements and attributes (for creating documents that maximize backward-compatibility) and in the use of CSS styles (for creating documents that maximize accessibility).

The purpose of this section is not to teach you everything you need to know about using styles, but to provide you with examples of and some hands-on experience with using styles in place of deprecated elements and attributes to control fonts, colors, and backgrounds. It also directs you to some solutions for dealing with earlier browsers with poor support for CSS.

Save your current file so you can reference it later and then resave it under another file name for doing this section's examples:

1. In your text editor, first save **watson2.html** (File, Save) to keep any changes you have made to that file.
2. Resave watson2.html as **watson3.html** in the chap03 folder.
3. Open **watson3.html** in your browser from the chap03 folder.

Later, you can refer to your finished version of watson2.html to refresh your understanding of using the FONT element to set font changes and your finished version of watson3.html to refresh your understanding of using styles to set font changes.

Understanding Why the FONT and BASEFONT Elements Are Deprecated

The FONT and BASEFONT elements, along with the BODY element's TEXT, LINK, VLINK, ALINK, BGCOLOR, and BACKGROUND attributes, were originally introduced as unofficial extensions to HTML by Netscape, later adopted by other browsers, and finally officially included in HTML 3.2. These elements were introduced in response to a demand for HTML features that provided Web designers with more control over the visual appearance of Web pages than was possible in HTML 2, the standard version of HTML at the time. Little thought was taken at the time, however, over how these and other presentational HTML elements might impact the accessibility of HTML documents for individuals with visual disabilities. For instance, size and color changes made using the FONT and BASEFONT elements can prevent users with visual disabilities from setting their own font size and color preferences, making pages less accessible, or even inaccessible, to such users. A user with visual acuity problems, for instance, might need to set white as the text color and black as the background color in order to gain sufficient contrast to read the text, but be foreclosed from doing so because a Web author has chosen instead to specify font colors for text and other elements using the FONT element or BODY element attributes that control the color of text, links, and the page background. Another user with poor eyesight might need to increase the size of the default font size in order to read a page's text, but be foreclosed from doing so by a Web designer using the FONT and BASEFONT elements to dictate at which size text and other elements in a page must be displayed. The result is that the Web author might be pleased with the visual appearance of the page, but at the cost of denying individuals with visual impairments the ability to access the page's content.

NOTE This section provides a brief explanation of using styles to set font characteristics within an HTML document, but does not provide any extended discussion of the syntax and rules that govern the use of CSS. To learn more about the use of CSS in broader and different contexts than are presented in this section, see the W3C's CSS site at **www.w3.org/Style/CSS/**. Also, see this book's IRC at **www.emcp.com/** for additional resources on using styles in your HTML documents.

Changing Font Sizes Using Styles

You can use a style to change the size of the font used to display any element. This can be done using either an inline style or a style sheet. Font sizes set using styles are generally set using pixels or ems.

SETTING FONT SIZES USING PIXELS The term *pixel* is short for *picture element*. A computer's graphical display is composed entirely of pixels, with the total number of pixels determined by the resolution of the display. Common screen resolutions include 640 × 480 pixels, 800 × 600 pixels, 1024 × 768 pixels, 1152 × 864 pixels, and 1280 × 1024 pixels. Generally, the larger the monitor, the higher the screen resolution it will support. The screen grabs for most of the figures in this book were captured at a screen resolution of 800 × 600 pixels. Instead of using the BASEFONT element (which is not supported by all current browsers) to set the base font size, you can use an inline style set in the BODY element to set its font size to 18 pixels.

Set the font size of the BODY element to 18 pixels:

1. Delete the BODY element attributes you set earlier:

```
<body text="navy" link="#ff6600" vlink="#996699" alink="blue"
bgcolor="#ffffcc" background="back_light.jpg">
```

2. Set an inline style, using the STYLE attribute, in the BODY element that sets its font size to 18 pixels (see Figure 3.18):

```
<body style="font-size: 18px">
```

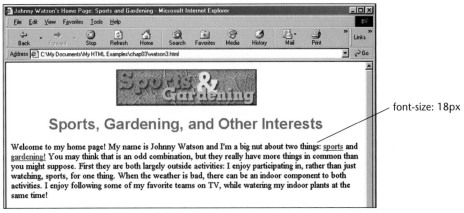

font-size: 18px

FIGURE 3.18 • *The size of body text is set to 18 pixels.*

Alternatively, you can also use a style sheet to set style properties for the BODY or other elements:

```
<style type="text/css">
body { font-size: 18px; }
</style>
</head>
```

In most browsers, the result of using a style to set the font size of the BODY element to 18 pixels should look the same as setting a size 4 font using the BASEFONT element because a size 4 font usually has a size of 18 pixels (although nothing in the HTML specifications dictates that a size 4 font must have a size of 18 pixels). This assumes, however, that a user has not increased the size of the browser's text font to make it more visible, which also would increase the size of a size 4 font.

A major problem with using pixel measurements to set font sizes for the BODY element or other body text elements (P, LI, BLOCKQUOTE, ADDRESS, and so on) is that users are no longer able to adjust their own default font size in their browser preferences or user style sheets. A person with a visual handicap might increase the default font size of text to 32 pixels, for instance, to make it more readable. For such a user, a font size of 18 pixels would actually reduce, rather than increase, the size of their text font, rendering it less readable or even possibly unreadable. Setting font sizes using the FONT or BASEFONT elements causes the same problem because it locks in a specific font size in pixels.

A better solution that insures that your Web pages are accessible to everyone is to use em measurements to set font sizes for the body text elements (but not for the BODY element). Em measurements scale relative to any font size preferences a user might set. Using em measurements is covered in the next section, "Setting Font Sizes Using Ems."

The best solution of all, however, might be to simply leave the font size of the BODY element and other body text elements (P, BLOCKQUOTE, LI, and so on) unchanged, allowing users to determine the right font size they need to be using.

SETTING FONT SIZES USING EMS Setting font sizes using ems allows your font sizes to scale relative to user preferences. In CSS, nested elements are related to each other as a parent to a child. A *parent element* is an element that brackets another element, whereas a *child element* is an element that is nested inside another element. A child element can inherit style properties that are set for its parent element.

A font size of one em for an element is one times the size of (or the same size as) that element's parent element. For instance, if a font size of 1.1 ems is set for the P element, that is 1.1 times the size of the BODY element's font size (where the BODY element is the parent of the P element).

Setting a font size for the BODY element using a style is generally frowned upon because users in some browsers, such as Internet Explorer 6 for Windows, can set their own font size for the BODY element using a user-defined style sheet. If an author also sets the font size of the BODY element, that can conflict with the user's preferred body text size. If you want to increase the size of body text elements (P, BLOCKQUOTE, LI, ADDRESS, and so on), you should set sizes for those elements, rather than for the BODY element.

Delete the inline style you set in the BODY element and add a style sheet that sets the font size of the P, LI, and ADDRESS elements to 1.1 ems (see Figure 3.19):

```
<style type="text/css">
p, li, address { font-size: 1.1em; }
</style>
</head>
<body style="font-size: 18px">
```

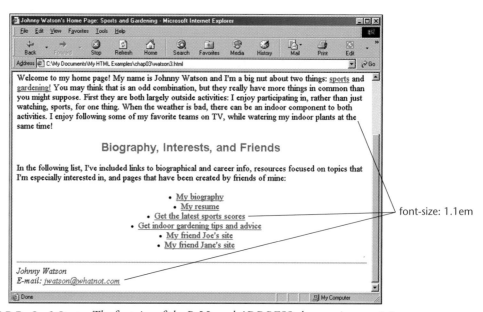

font-size: 1.1em

FIGURE 3.19 • *The font size of the P, LI, and ADDRESS elements is set to 1.1 ems.*

A common error when typing styles within a style sheet is to type regular parentheses, "(" and ")", rather than squiggly brackets, "{" and "}".

An example style sheet file, **bigfont.css**, is included with this chapter's example files. If you are using Internet Explorer 6 for Windows, you can specify it as a user-defined style sheet to see what happens when a user employs a user-defined style sheet to increase their browser's default font size.

action

Internet Explorer 6 for Windows Only. Specify a user-defined style sheet that increases the browser's base font size to 32 pixels:

1. Select Tools, Internet Options, and click the Accessibility button (in the lower-right corner of the dialog box).
2. Check the Format documents using my style sheet check box, and then click the Browse button.
3. Open your working folder or working disk, and then open this chapter's folder (**chap03**). Double-click **bigfont.css** to open it.
4. Click OK twice to return to the document window. As shown in Figure 3.20, notice that the page's BODY text is now 1.1 times the size of the user-defined font size of 32 pixels, or 35 pixels. Also notice that the two links ("sports" and "gardening"), which have relative font sizes set using the FONT element's SIZE attribute, have not scaled in relation to the user-defined font size preference.

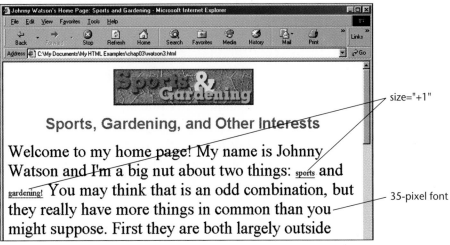

FIGURE 3.20 • *The BODY text is set to a size of 1.1 times a 32-pixel base font size set in a user-defined style sheet.*

5. For the time being, leave bigfont.css selected as a user-defined style sheet in Internet Explorer 6 (you will turn it off in the next section).

SETTING FONT SIZES USING THE SPAN ELEMENT Previously, in Chapter 1, you set relative font sizes for the "sport" and "gardening" in-context links. As shown in Figure 3.20, when a user increases his preferred font size, the relative font sizes do not scale relative to the user's preferred font size. To have the size of those links also scale relative to a user's preferred font size, you need to use styles to set a font size with an em measurement.

The SPAN element is a generic inline element that, by itself, has no display characteristics. By combining it with the CLASS attribute, which allows you to apply styles to a separate class of elements, you can create as many custom inline elements as you want.

Replace the FONT elements that are nested inside the "sports" and "gardening" anchor elements with SPAN elements that set the font size to 1.1 ems:

1. Delete the FONT elements that were set previously and add SPAN elements with **class="link"** attributes:

```
<p>Welcome to my home page! My name is Johnny Watson and I'm a
big nut about two things: <a href="http://www.espn.com/"><span
class="link">sports</span></a> and <a
href="http://www.bbc.co.uk/gardening/"><span
class="link">gardening!</span></a>
```

2. Add a style to the style sheet that applies a font size of 1.1 ems to SPAN elements belonging to the "link" class (see Figure 3.21):

```
<style type="text/css">
p, li, address { font-size: 1.1em; }
span.link { font-size: 1.1em; }
</style>
</head>
```

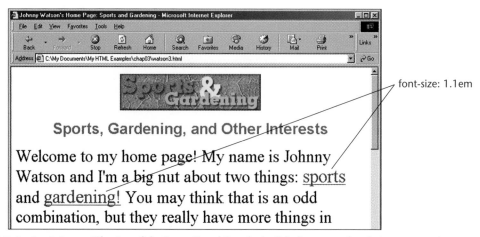

FIGURE 3.21 • *The size of the "sports" and "gardening" links now scale relative to a user's preferences.*

In a style rule, the "." character indicates that the following text references the name of an element class. The ".link" text in the style specifies that the style is to be applied only to SPAN elements with a **class="link"** attribute. The ".link" text also can be listed by itself, without the preceding "span" element reference, in which case the style can be applied to any element, and not just the SPAN element, that has a **class="link"** attribute.

As shown previously in Figure 3.21, the "sports" and "gardening" link sizes are now scaled relative to the font size of the SPAN elements' parent element (the P element). Each link is now 1.1 times the size of the P element's text, which in turn is 1.1 times the size of the BODY element's font size. If you previously set a user-defined style sheet in Internet Explorer 6 for Windows, you should now turn it off.

Internet Explorer 6 for Windows. Turn off the user-defined style sheet you set previously:

1. Select Tools, Internet Options, and click the Accessibility button.
2. Uncheck the Format documents using my style sheet check box. Click OK twice to return to the document window.

UNDERSTANDING COMPATIBILITY ISSUES WITH FONT SIZES USING EMS

All current browsers handle setting font sizes using ems just fine. Browsers that do not support styles, or that have styles turned off, completely ignore the font size changes. Earlier browsers that only partially support CSS might have problems with em measurements that can impact the readability of your page, however. Internet Explorer 3.x, for instance, treats one em as equal to one pixel, meaning that a font size measurement of 1.1 ems would cause paragraph text in that browser to be displayed in a 1.1-pixel font, rendering the text completely illegible.

NOTE The Web Standards Project's Browser Upgrade Campaign at **www.webstandards.org/upgrade/** provides a number of ways to deal with older browsers with poor support for current Web standards. Just click on the "Developer Tips" link to find out about easy-to-implement methods for alerting users of older browsers that they need to upgrade their browsers.

Web Standard's DOM Sniff Method, for instance, uses a simple JavaScript script that automatically redirects users of Internet Explorer 3.x, Netscape Navigator 4.x, and other less than standards-compliant browsers to the Web address shown in the previous paragraph. You also can use it to direct users to a browser-upgrade page that you have created as part of your own site.

For a somewhat less radical solution (which does not risk losing visitors), the site also provides an Invisible Object Method. This method displays an alert at the top of the page to users of browsers that are less than standards-compliant. Such users are alerted that the page they are viewing would look much better in a standards-compliant browser, while providing a link they can use to find out how to upgrade their browser.

Use the Web Standards Project's Invisible Object Method to alert users of less than standards-compliant browsers that they need to upgrade their browsers:

1. Create a style that turns off the display of elements belonging to the "oops" class and add an IFRAME element to the top of the BODY element belonging to that class:

```
<style type="text/css">
p, li, address { font-size: 1.1em; }
span.link { font-size: 1.1em; }
.oops { display: none; }
</style>
</head>
<body>
<iframe class="oops">
<center><font size="5" color="maroon">This site will look much
better in a browser that supports <a
href="http://www.webstandards.org/upgrade/"
title="Download a browser that complies with Web standards.">
Web standards</a>,<br>but it is accessible to any browser
or Internet device.</font>
```

```
</center>
<hr>
</iframe>
```

2. Save your document. If you have a version of Netscape 4 installed on your computer, open **watson3.html** in that browser. You will see the content of the IFRAME element you added in step 1 displayed at the top of the page (see Figure 3.22). If you refresh the display of the page in a browser that supports the display property, the IFRAME element will be invisible.

IFRAME element (invisible to standards-compliant browsers)

FIGURE 3.22 • *By using the Web Standards Project's Invisible Object Method, you can alert users of less than standards-compliant browsers, such as Netscape Navigator 4, as shown here, that they need to upgrade their browsers.*

3. If viewing the page in Netscape 4, click on the "Web standards" link. (If using a browser that supports the display property, use the Address or Location box to go to www.webstandards.org/upgrade/.) If connected to the Internet, you will be taken to the Web Standard Project's Browser Upgrade Campaign page (see Figure 3.23).

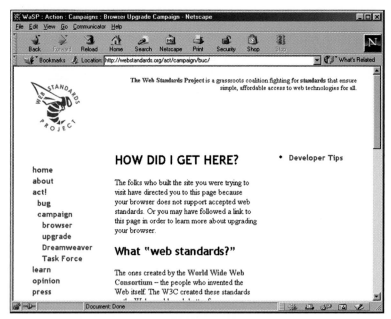

FIGURE 3.23 • *After clicking on the "Web standards" link in a browser that displays the IFRAME "oops" alert, a user is taken to the Web Standards Project's Browser Upgrade Campaign page.*

To find out more about using the DOM Sniff and Invisible Object methods, click on the Developer Tips link in the Browser Upgrade Campaign page. To find links to where users can upgrade their browsers, on the same page, scroll down to the "What can I do?" section.

The Invisible Object method works in two ways. First, any browser that does not recognize the **display: none** style property displays the alert message; in browsers that do recognize it, the message is invisible. Netscape 4, however, which has poor support for CSS, does recognize the **display: none** style property, but does not recognize the IFRAME (Inline Frame) element; because Netscape 4 does not recognize the IFRAME element, it also ignores the **display: none** style property that is assigned to it.

To cause this alert to display in Internet Explorer 3, but not in Netscape Navigator 4, just apply the **class="oops"** attribute to any standard element other than the IFRAME element that contains the alert text. If you do, however, be sure to test your page out in Netscape Navigator 4 to make sure that it displays your page in an acceptable manner.

Reducing the font size of body text elements (P, LI, BLOCKQUOTE, ADDRESS, and so on) can affect the legibility of body text for some users, depending on their system or browser font settings. If you must decrease the font size for body text in a page you are creating, reduce it only slightly using an em measurement and not a pixel measurement, in conjunction with one of the Browser Upgrade Initiative's methods for dealing with earlier browsers that have trouble with em measurements. Here is an example of reducing the size of body text elements:

```
p, li, blockquote, address { font-size: .9em; }
</style>
```

As mentioned previously, you should not set this directly for the BODY element, since that is more likely to conflict with a user's own font-size setting in a user-defined style sheet. By setting it in the body text elements, the font-size will scale relative to a user's font-size set for the BODY element.

When setting CSS font sizes for documents to be displayed on the Web, you should use either pixels or ems. Other measuring units, such as inches (in), centimeters (cm), millimeters (mm), points (pt), or picas (pc), should never be used when setting font sizes for display on the Web. That is because they are absolute measurements that have no meaning relative to a Web page, the size and dimensions of which are always indeterminate.

Use of points (pt) is to be avoided especially when specifying measurements in CSS. That is because, while points and pixels are equivalent by default on a Macintosh system, they are not equivalent on a Windows system, because of the different default dot pitches at which fonts are displayed on those systems (72 dpi on the Macintosh and 96 dpi in Windows). The result is that text set in an 8-point font, for instance, which is legible on a Windows browser, will be illegible on a Macintosh browser that does not readjust font sizes to match the Windows display.

Specifying Font Families Using Styles

Authors must be careful when setting font sizes using styles because of the poor support for font measurements using ems in early CSS-supporting browsers, and accessibility issues involved in specifying font measurements in pixels. The only real problem with specifying font families using styles, however, is non-support in earlier browsers that do not support the use of styles (but might support the use of the FONT element's FACE attribute).

When specifying font families using styles, you use the same font names you used when specifying font-face names using the FONT element's FACE attribute.

Set a style that specifies a list of font families to be used in displaying the H1 and H2 elements:

1. Delete the FONT element that was previously nested in the H1 element:

```
<h1><del>font color="#996600" face="Arial, Geneva, Helvetica, sans-serif"</del>Sports, Gardening, and Other Interests<del></font></del></h1>
```

2. Make the same deletion in your document's H2 element.
3. Add the following style to your page's style sheet (see Figure 3.24):

```
<style type="text/css">
p, blockquote, li, address { font-size: 1.1em; }
span.link { font-size: 1.1em; }
.oops { display: none; }
h1, h2 { font-family: Arial, Geneva, Helvetica, sans-serif; }
</style>
</head>
```

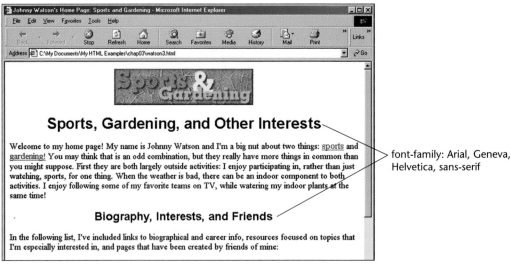

FIGURE 3.24 • *A single style causes the H1 and H2 elements to be displayed in an Arial font on systems that have that font available.*

Notice in the previous example that the H1 and H2 elements are both included in the same style. By using a comma-delimited list of element names, you can group elements to which you want to apply the same style.

USING STYLES AND THE FONT ELEMENT TOGETHER   To catch both browsers that support styles and browsers that only support the FONT element's FACE attribute, you can combine using inline styles and the FONT element. You cannot do that by applying a style to an element while nesting a FONT element within that element, however, because the formatting of the nested element (the FONT element) takes precedence. Nothing in the HTML or CSS specifications, however, forbids using a style within the FONT element (as long as you are declaring your document to be in conformance with the transitional version of HTML 4.01). For instance, in the following code example, browsers that support styles will ignore the FACE attribute, while browsers that support the FACE attribute, but not styles, will ignore the STYLE attribute:

```
<h1><font style="font-family: Arial, Geneva, Helvetica, sans-
serif" face="Arial, Geneva, Helvetica, sans-serif">Sports,
Gardening, and Other Interests</font></h1>
```

In CSS, font-family names are officially case-insensitive. However, because some computer systems might separately dictate case-sensitive font names, font-family names used in styles should be treated as though they were case-sensitive, with all uppercase and lowercase letters typed in exactly as shown.

QUOTING FONT-FAMILY NAMES THAT INCLUDE SPACES   When specifying font-family names using styles, any font names with spaces in them must be quoted. For instance, in the following example, the font-family name of Comic Sans MS needs to be quoted because there are spaces in the font-family name:

```
<h1 style="font-family: 'Comic Sans MS', Arial, Geneva,
Helvetica, sans-serif">Sports, Gardening, and Other
Interests</font></h1>
```

Single quotes are used because double quotes are already being used around the STYLE attribute. When specifying a font-family name with spaces in it in a style sheet, double quotes can be used:

```
<style type="text/css">
h1 { font-family: "Comic Sans MS", Arial, Geneva, Helvetica,
sans-serif; }
</style>
```

Setting Colors Using Styles

You also can set the foreground color of elements using styles. You use the same 16 standard color names or hexadecimal RGB codes that you used previously to specify colors using the FONT element's COLOR attribute.

Use styles to specify different colors for the H1 and H2 elements (see Figure 3.25):

```
h1, h2 { font-family: Arial, Geneva, Helvetica, sans-serif; }
h1 { color: #996600; background: transparent; }
h2 { color: #2e8b57; background: transparent; }
</style>
```

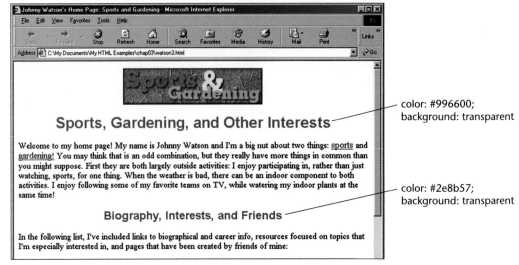

color: #996600;
background: transparent

color: #2e8b57;
background: transparent

F I G U R E   3 . 2 5   •   *Different colors are set for the H1 and H2 elements using styles.*

As shown in the previous example, you can specify a series of style properties that can be applied to a specific style element. A style element and the properties that are assigned to it are referred to as a *style rule*. Semicolons are used to separate style properties within a style rule.

A common error when typing styles is to type a colon where a semicolon is called for, or vice versa. Another common error is to type a regular opening or closing parenthesis, rather than an opening or closing squiggly bracket ("{" or "}"), before or after a style rule's properties. Also, if your style is not nested inside of a properly formed STYLE element (starting with `<style type="text/css">` and ending with `</style>`), it might not be displayed. If you find that a style is not working, check to make sure you have not made any of these errors.

Notice that a transparent background is also specified for the H1 and H2 style rules. Whenever you specify a foreground color using styles, you usually should also specify a background color, if only as transparent. The reason for this is that a user might be using a user-defined style sheet that assigns foreground and background colors to the H1 and H2 elements—if you only set a foreground color, it could end up being displayed against a user's background color. You could end up with yellow text against a yellow background, for instance, or red text against a green background that someone who has red-green color-blindness might have difficulty reading.

Setting Text, Link, and Background Colors Using Styles

The BODY element's TEXT, LINK, VLINK, ALINK, and BGCOLOR attributes also are deprecated in HTML 4.01 in favor of using styles to achieve similar or better results. Alternatively, you can control the display characteristics of your page's text, link, and background colors using only styles.

Use styles to control text, link, and background colors:

1. Delete the SPAN elements you earlier nested inside the "sports" and "gardening" links:

```
<p>Welcome to my home page! My name is Johnny Watson and I'm a
big nut about two things: <a href="http://www.espn.com/"><span
class="link">sports</span></a> and <a
href="http://www.bbc.co.uk/gardening/"><span
class="link">gardening!</span></a>
```

2. Set styles that specify foreground and background colors for text and links (see Figure 3.26):

```
<style type="text/css">
body { color: navy; background: #ffffcc; }
p, blockquote, li, address { font-size: 1.1em; }
span.link { font-size: 1.1em; }
.oops { display: none; }
h1, h2 { font-family: Arial, Geneva, Helvetica, sans-serif; }
h1 { color: #996600; background: transparent; }
h2 { color: #2e8b57; background: transparent; }
a:link { color: #ff6600; background: transparent; }
a:visited { color: #996699; background: transparent; }
a:hover { color: green; background: transparent; }
a:active { color: blue; background: transparent; }
</style>
</head>
```

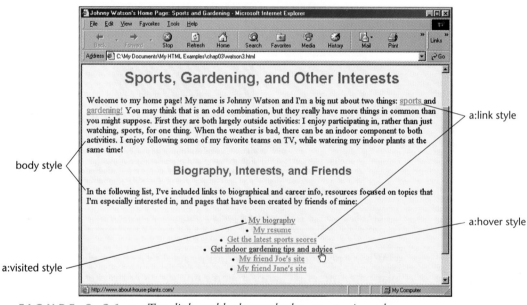

FIGURE 3.26 • *Text, link, and background colors are set using styles.*

This example reproduces the color scheme you set previously using the FONT element and the BODY element attributes, with the exception of the "hover" link style that controls the color of a link when the mouse pointer hovers over it. The "hover" link style can be set only using styles. The "active" link style is not shown in the figure since "hover" and "active" cannot be displayed at the same time. The a:link, a:visited, a:hover, and a:active style elements are a special class of style elements referred to as *anchor pseudo-classes* in CSS.

When using the anchor pseudo-classes to set link properties, you should always list the a:hover and a:active pseudo-classes after the a:link and a:visited pseudo-classes. If you do not, the hover and activated link states will not be displayed. You can list the a:hover and a:active pseudo-classes in whichever order you like; if you list a:hover after a:active, for instance, the activated state will not be visible when the mouse pointer is held down on the link.

In Internet Explorer, however, the activated state still will be visible after the user clicks the Back button to return to the page. To stop the activated state from being visibly displayed at all, just insert a:active before a:hover in the style sheet and set it to the same color as a:visited. Another option is to set a:link, a:visited, and a:active to the same color, while setting a:hover to a different color.

Setting a Background Image Using a Style

The final touch you need to add now is a background image.

Add a background image to your style sheet that will display behind the BODY element (see Figure 3.27):

```
<style type="text/css">
body { color: navy; background: #ffffcc; url(back_light.jpg); }
```

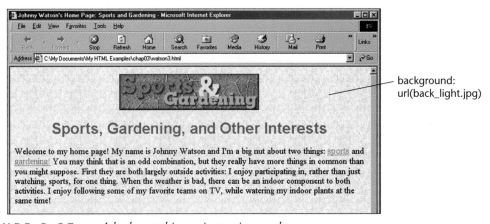

background:
url(back_light.jpg)

FIGURE 3.27 • *A background image is set using a style.*

When specifying a background image URL in a style, be sure to surround it with regular parentheses ("(" and ")") and not squiggly brackets ("{" and "}"). As with setting a background image using a BODY element attribute, when setting a background image using a style, you should always specify a background color that is similar to your background image's coloration because some users surf the Web with the display of graphics turned off.

SPECIFYING A BACKGROUND IMAGE To make a more dramatic statement, you can use a dark background image. To do this, you must adjust your page's foreground colors so they provide proper contrast, as well as the background color you have specified. A dark background image, back_dark.jpg, is included with the other example files in the chap03 folder.

Set a dark background image and reset your page's foreground and background colors to match (see Figure 3.28):

```
<style type="text/css">
body { color: #ffffcc; background: navy url(back_dark.jpg); }
p, li, address { font-size: 1.1em; }
span.link { font-size: 1.1em; }
.oops { display: none; }
h1, h2 { font-family: Arial, Geneva, Helvetica, sans-serif; }
h1 { color: #ffcc33; background: transparent; }
h2 { color: #99ccff; background: transparent; }
a:link { color: #33ffcc; background: transparent; }
a:visited { color: #00cccc; background: transparent; }
a:hover { color: yellow; background: transparent; }
a:active { color: aqua; background: transparent; }
</style>
```

FIGURE 3.28 • *A dark background image with light foreground colors can give a page a more dramatic look.*

When printing a Web page, most browsers do not print background colors or images, which can result in light-colored text being printed against a white background. If displaying white text against a dark background, the result can be white text against a white background (or no visible text, in other words). One way to deal with this problem is to create and link to a "printer-ready" version of your page that substitutes dark text against a white background.

Computer systems often do not come with good software utilities for viewing graphic files. When choosing a background image to use in a Web page, it helps to easily view, and possibly open and edit, any background images that you have available. For links to some freeware and shareware image viewers you can download, see this chapter's section at this book's IRC at **www.emcp.com**/. For additional links to freeware and shareware image viewers that you can download and use with Windows, the Macintosh, and other platforms, go to Tucows at **www.tucows.com**/.

USING OTHER BACKGROUND PROPERTIES There are a number of other background properties you can set using styles. The background-attachment, background-repeat, and background-position properties can be used to vary how a background image displays in a browser.

The background-attachment property specifies whether the background image is fixed relative to the browser window or scrolls along with the page. The default value is **scroll**, which causes the background to scroll along with the page. A **fixed** value, on the other hand, causes the background image to remained fixed relative to the browser window (so the document text scrolls within the browser window, but the background image remains fixed).

The background-repeat property specifies whether the background image is to be repeated (or tiled) and whether it should be repeated vertically or horizontally. The default value is **repeat**, which caused a background image to be tiled both vertically and horizontally within the browser background. The **repeat-y** value causes the background image to be repeated vertically only, while a **repeat-x** value causes it to be repeated horizontally only. The **no-repeat** value causes the background image to be displayed only once (not tiled). The no-repeat value is usually used in conjunction with the background-position property (otherwise the background image is displayed, untiled, in the upper left corner of the page).

The background-position property specifies the position of a non-tiled background image. Percentage or length (pixels or ems) can be used to space the background image in from the top left corner of a page or element's padding area. If only one value is given, it is assumed that only the horizontal position of the background image is being set. If two values are given, the first is used to set the horizontal position and the second to set the vertical position. The keywords of **left**, **center**, and **right** can also be used to set the horizontal position of the background image, while the keywords of **top**, **middle**, and **bottom** can be used to set the background image's vertical position. The keyword values cannot be combined with the percentage or length values. Here are some possible styles that could be set using these properties:

```
body {
background-image: url("backimg.jpg");
background-attach: fixed;
background-repeat: no-repeat;
background-position: 50% 50%;
}
```

or

```
body {
background-image: url("backimg.jpg");
background-repeat: repeat-y;
background-position: center;
}
```

or

```
body {
background-image: url("backimg.jpg");
background-repeat: no-repeat;
background-position: 50% 100px;
}
```

You can also use the background property to set all background properties at once. For instance:

```
body { color: #ffffcc; background: navy url("watermark.gif") no-repeat fixed 50% 50%; }
```

When vertically positioning a non-tiled background image, using a percentage value or a keyword value (middle or bottom), some browsers position the background image relative to the browser window, while others position it relative to the length of the document. To insure that your watermark background image will always be displayed the same distance from the top of the page in all browsers that support this feature, set a specific length amount from the top of the page.

Creating Rollover Links

Using CSS, you also can set a background color or background image for specific elements. By using this capability with the a:hover pseudo-class, you can create a "rollover" effect that is displayed when the mouse pointer is passed over a link. A rollover effect generally refers to a dramatic change, often a flipping of color values, for an object or element that results in response to a user interaction. Using rollover links is one way to increase the interactivity of your page.

Create a rollover link:

1. Set contrasting foreground and background colors for the a:hover pseudo-class, to create a rollover effect for your page's links:

```
a:hover { color: red; background: yellow; }
a:active { color: aqua; background: transparent; }
```

2. In your browser, pass the mouse pointer over a link to activate the rollover effect (see Figure 3.29).

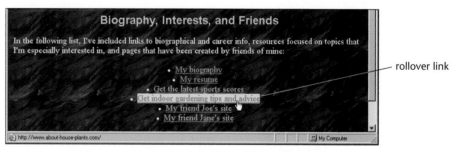

rollover link

FIGURE 3.29 • *Rollover links can increase the interactivity of your page.*

Turning Link Underlining Off

Using styles, you also can turn off the underline that is displayed under a hypertext link. Be careful when doing this, however, because it can cause some surfers not to recognize that a link is a link. In some circumstances turning off this feature can be useful and effective. Using rollover links is one of those circumstances because the user will already have recognized that the link is a link before passing the mouse over it.

Turn the underlining off for the a:hover pseudo-class (see Figure 3.30):

```
a:hover { color: red; background: yellow; text-decoration: none; }
```

underlining turned off
(text-decoration: none)

FIGURE 3.30 • *A rollover link is one circumstance in which turning off the underlining of a link is appropriate.*

Using Downloadable Fonts

The CSS2 specification includes a feature called the @font-face rule, which can be used to specify the name of a font to be downloaded from the Web. When this feature is used, a browser is supposed to look first to determine whether the specified font or a close match is available on a user's computer; if the font or a close match is not available, the browser can download the font from a URL specified by the author.

Of current browsers, only Internet Explorer (Version 4 and above) supports displaying downloadable fonts. Netscape Navigator 4 earlier supported a different format for downloadable fonts, but Netscape 6 (up to Version 6.22) does not include support for downloadable fonts.

To make a downloadable font available to users of Internet Explorer 4 and above, you need to convert a TrueType font into an Embedded Open Type (EOT) font. A free tool, Microsoft WEFT (Web Embedding Fonts Tool), is available from Microsoft—you can find out more about WEFT at **www.microsoft.com/typography/web/embedding/weft2/**.

The following is a simple example of an @font-face rule that can be included in a style sheet to specify an EOT font as available for download:

```
@font-face {
    font-family: Christmas;
    font-style: normal;
    font-weight: bold;
    src: url("http://www.someserver.com/somefonts/Christmas.eot");
    }
h1 { font-family: Christmas.eot; }
```

Although you can provide most TrueType fonts for download with a Web page using WEFT and EOT font files, the TrueType font format allows embedding permissions to be set to no embedding. The WEFT utility reports the permissions for any local TrueType fonts installed on a Windows system.

Be aware, however, that using embedded fonts in a Web page can significantly increase the amount of time required for that page to display. Before opting to use a downloadable font, consider whether achieving a specific look for some users (of Internet Explorer 4 and above) is worth the additional time required to download and display the page.

NOTE — In this chapter, you have just barely scratched the surface of using styles within Web pages. Following are some online resources that provide more information about using styles in Web pages:

- The W3C's CSS site: **www.w3.org/Style/CSS/**
- The Web Design Group's Guide to CSS: **www.htmlhelp.com/reference/css/**
- The HTML Writers Guild CSS FAQ: **www.hwg.org/resources/faqs/cssFAQ.html**
- Web Review.com's Style Sheet Reference Guide: **www.webreview.com/style/**
- The CSS Pointers Group: **www.css.nu/**
- Visit the newsgroup: **comp.infosystems.www.authoring.stylesheets**

CHAPTER SUMMARY

You should now be familiar with using both HTML and CSS to control fonts, colors, and backgrounds in Web pages you create. You should know how to set absolute and relative font sizes, specify font-face names and font lists, apply colors using the 16 standard color names and hexadecimal RGB codes, use Web-safe colors in your pages, set foreground and background colors, use background images, set CSS font sizes using pixels and ems, use the SPAN element to create your own custom inline elements, and create interactive rollover links. You also should be aware of accessibility concerns that can arise when setting fonts, colors, and backgrounds in Web pages.

Code Review

FONT element	Specifies the font size, color, or face for an element. Deprecated in HTML 4.
SIZE attribute	In the FONT element, specifies the font size for an element. You can set seven absolute font sizes (1 to 7), or relative font sizes (+1 or -1, for instance).
FACE attribute	In the FONT element, specifies the font face of an element, in the form of a font-face name or font list.
COLOR attribute	In the FONT element, specifies the foreground color of nested text. Colors can be specified using any of the 16 standard color names or hexadecimal RGB codes.
BASEFONT element	An empty element that specifies font characteristics for the base font, with changes taking effect at the position where the element is inserted. Earlier browsers recognize only the SIZE attribute. The Opera and Mozilla browsers ignore it. Deprecated in HTML 4.
TEXT attribute	In the BODY element, sets the color of body text.
LINK attribute	In the BODY element, sets the color of unvisited links.
VLINK attribute	In the BODY element, sets the color of visited links.
ALINK attribute	In the BODY element, sets the color of activated links.
BGCOLOR attribute	In the BODY element, sets a background color for a page.
BACKGROUND attribute	In the BODY element, sets a background image for a page.
STYLE element	Element in the document head that specifies nested text in a style sheet.
STYLE attribute	Used to insert an inline style within an element's start tag.
font-size property	In CSS, sets the font size of an element.
SPAN element	A generic inline element that has no formatting characteristics of its own, but which can be used to create custom inline elements by using styles.
CLASS attribute	Assigns an element to a class. Any styles assigned to the class are then applied to the element.
display property	Style property that can be used to turn the display of an element off and on in supporting browsers.
IFRAME element	Specifies that nested text is to be formatted as an inline frame.
font-family property	In CSS, specifies a specific or generic font-family name or a font-family list.

color property	In CSS, specifies the foreground color of an element, using a color name or hexadecimal RGB code.
background property	In CSS, specifies a background color or background image for an element.
a:link	In CSS, an anchor pseudo-class that specifies the properties of an unvisited link.
a:visited	In CSS, an anchor pseudo-class that specifies the properties of a visited link.
a:hover	In CSS, an anchor pseudo-class that specifies the properties of a link when the mouse pointer is hovering over it.
a:active	In CSS, an anchor pseudo-class that specifies the properties of an activated link.
@font-face rule	In CSS, can specify a downloadable font.

ONLINE QUIZ

Go to this text's IRC at **www.emcp.com/** and take the online self-check quiz for this chapter.

REVIEW EXERCISES

This section provides some hands-on practice exercises to reinforce the information and material included within this and previous chapters.

Save **watson2.html** and **watson3.html** under new file names (**watson2_practice.html** and **watson3_practice.html**, for instance) and then use the new documents to practice using the elements, attributes, styles, and other features that were covered in this chapter.

1. In the first practice document (watson2_practice.html, or whatever file name you gave it), further experiment with using the FONT element's SIZE attribute to set font sizes. Practice setting both absolute and relative font sizes.

2. In the first practice document, further experiment with using the FONT element's FACE attribute to set font faces. Try specifying some of the other fonts that are available on your own system, just to see what they look like. If you are not sure which fonts are available on your system, you should be able to find a list of available fonts in your word processing program. Realize, however, that if users do not have the font you specify available on their systems, they will not be able to see the font you specify. For that reason, you should provide alternative fonts in your list of fonts that are more likely to be available on another's system.

3. In the first practice document, experiment with just specifying a sans-serif generic font-family name as the value of the FONT element's FACE attribute. See whether you can identify which specific font your browser defaults to when displaying a sans serif font. (Hint: Compare it with a list of fonts displayed in your word processor or other software that shows you what the fonts on your system look like.)

4. In the first practice document, experiment further with using the 16 standard color names to set font colors. Experiment with using all the standard color names except for black and white in setting colors for the H1 and H2 elements, as well as for the two in-context links included in the introductory paragraph. Make a note of which of the 16 standard colors you do and do not like and why.

5. In the first practice document, experiment further with using hexadecimal RGB codes to set colors. Use one of the links provided in the chapter to find a resource listing the hexadecimal RGB codes for the 140 or so non-standard color names. Use those codes to set colors using the FONT element's COLOR attribute and the BODY element's TEXT, LINK, VLINK, ALINK, and BGCOLOR attributes. Try to find at least three different color schemes that you think are both attractive and readable, with at least one of the three featuring light text displayed against a dark background color. Save each scheme as a separate file (**watson2_color1.html**, **watson2_color2.html**, **watson2_color3.html**). Ask at least two of your classmates to judge which one of the three schemes they like the best and which one they like the least. Try to find out what they like or do not like about the color schemes you have created.

6. Do the same as in exercise 5, but add using background images into the mix. You can find additional background images that you can use in the **art** folder included with this book's example files. See also this book's IRC at **www.emcp.com/** for links to resources where you can find and download background images on the Web.

7. In the second practice document (watson3_practice.html, or whatever file name you gave it), further experiment with using styles to set font sizes, using both pixels and ems.

8. In the second practice document, further experiment with using styles to specify font-family names to be used to display different elements.

9. In the second practice document, experiment further with using the 16 standard color names and hexadecimal RGB codes with styles to set colors. Create at least three color schemes for your page, using only styles to control foreground colors and background colors, with at least one of the three featuring light text displayed against a dark background color. Ask at least two of your classmates to judge which one of the three schemes they like the best and which one they like the least. Try to find out what they like or do not like about the color schemes you have created.

10. Do the same as in exercise 9, but add using background images into the mix. You can find additional background images that you can use in the **art** folder included with this book's example files. See also this book's IRC at **www.emcp.com/** for links to resources where you can find and download background images on the Web.

WEB-BASED LEARNING ACTIVITIES

In this book's text, Find It icons inserted in the margin highlight the Web addresses of additional resources you might find helpful or informative. To extend your learning using the Web, you can:

- Go back and visit any of the Web addresses highlighted in this chapter that you have not yet visited. Look for additional resources and information that add to your understanding and knowledge of the material covered in this chapter. When you find a relevant page or site with information or resources you might want to access later, add it to your Favorites (in Internet Explorer) or your Bookmarks (in Netscape or Mozilla).

- Visit this book's IRC at **www.emcp.com/** to find additional Web addresses of resources related to the material covered in this chapter that you can further investigate and explore.

- Further research a specific topic introduced in this chapter. For instance, do further research on the readability of serif versus sans serif fonts or the problems those with different forms of color-blindness can have viewing different color combinations on the Web.
- A good image viewer can make working with background images and other clip art much easier. Visit this chapter's section at this book's IRC at **www.emcp.com/** to see a listing of image viewers you can download. See Tucows at **www.tucows.com/** for additional freeware and shareware image-viewing utilities that are available for your platform. Download several and test them. Ask your instructor if you can give a demonstration to your fellow classmates of the best image-viewing software you have discovered.

PROJECTS

These projects can be done either in class, in a computer lab, or at home. Use the skills you have developed in this and the previous chapters to create any of the following projects.

Project 1. Update the appearance of a personal Web page using fonts, colors, and backgrounds.

If you created your own personal Web page as a project at the end of Chapter 1, apply the lessons learned in this chapter to update the appearance of your personal page, using the FONT element's SIZE, FACE, and COLOR attributes and the BODY element's TEXT, LINK, VLINK, ALINK, BGCOLOR, and BACKGROUND attributes. Experiment with using different color schemes and background images, until you find the combination you like best. You can find additional background images you can use in the **art** folder included with this book's example files. Also, see this book's IRC for links to where you can find additional background images on the Web that you can download and use in your Web pages.

Project 2. Update the appearance of a personal Web page using styles.

If you created your own personal Web page as a project at the end of Chapter 1, apply the lessons learned in this chapter to update the appearance of your personal page, using only styles (without using the FONT element's SIZE, FACE, and COLOR attributes or the BODY element's TEXT, LINK, VLINK, ALINK, BGCOLOR, and BACKGROUND attributes). Experiment with using different color schemes and background images, until you find the combination you like best. Pay special attention to making your page accessible to visitors with visual handicaps, by using em measurements for font sizes and avoiding color combinations that can cause difficulties for users with different forms of color-blindness, for instance. If using em measurements, be sure to also use one of the methods provided by the Web Standards Project to redirect or alert users of earlier, less than CSS-compliant Web browsers.

Project 3. Update the appearance of a topical Web page using fonts, colors, and backgrounds.

If you created a topical page as a project at the end of Chapter 1, apply the lessons learned in this chapter to update the appearance of your personal page, using the FONT element's

SIZE, FACE, and COLOR attributes and the BODY element's TEXT, LINK, VLINK, ALINK, BGCOLOR, and BACKGROUND attributes. See the guidelines for Project 1 for more details.

Project 4. Update the appearance of a topical Web page using styles.

If you created a topical page as a project at the end of Chapter 1, apply the lessons learned in this chapter to update the appearance of your topical page, using only styles. See the guidelines for Project 2 for more details.

Project 5. Update the appearance of a page you created for a club or organization.

If you created a page for a club or organization at the end of Chapter 1, apply the lessons learned in this chapter to update the appearance of that page, using either HTML elements and attributes or styles to control fonts, colors, and backgrounds. See the guidelines for Projects 1 and 2 for more details.

Project 6. Create a new Web page from scratch that uses fonts, colors, and backgrounds.

Create any kind of new page from scratch: a personal page, a topical page, a page for a club or organization, or a page created for any other purpose. If you are not sure what kind of page you want to create, look on the Web for examples that you can try to emulate. Apply the lessons learned in this chapter or previous chapters to create an effective and visually attractive page featuring font size, face, and color changes, combined with a background color or background image. Try to combine features learned in this chapter with features learned in earlier chapters. For instance, you might combine a document menu that jumps to subsections within a document, as was demonstrated in Chapter 2, with rollover links, as was demonstrated in this chapter.

4

Working with Images and Other Media

PERFORMANCE OBJECTIVES

In this chapter, you will learn to use inline images and other media to enhance the presentation and functionality of your Web pages, including how to:
- Flow text and other elements around a floating image.
- Create a thumbnail image gallery.
- Use graphic rules, banners, and buttons.
- Create GIF and JPEG Web graphics.
- Work with Web-safe and optimized color palettes.
- Create interlaced and transparent GIF images.
- Use and create GIF animations.
- Embed sound and video.

In Chapter 1, *Creating a Basic Web Page*, you learned how to include an inline image in an HTML document using the IMG element. In this chapter, you will learn much more about working with and using images and other media in HTML documents.

The original version of HTML had no means for including images. As has often happened in HTML, the market perceived a deficit, and supplied it. The IMG element was actually the first unofficial extension to HTML, supported by the first widely available graphical browser, the Mosaic browser.

The old adage that a picture is worth a thousand words is proven true by how the deft usage of carefully chosen images augments and supplements the textual content of a page. In fact, an image or a group of images can even stand by itself as the main content of a page.

USING THE EXAMPLE FILES

If you created a working folder for storing files you create, you will find the example files for this chapter located in the **chap04** folder within your working folder. Save any HTML files you create in this chapter in that folder.

If you created a working disk, you should copy the chap04 folder to your working disk from the **HTML_Examples** folder that you or your instructor downloaded from this book's Internet Resource Center (IRC). Ask your instructor for assistance if you need help copying the chap04 folder. Save any HTML files you create in this chapter in the chap04 folder on your working disk.

CASE EXAMPLE: CREATING A REPORT WITH FLOATING IMAGES

In this example, you will create a report on the history of NASA's Project Mercury space program to place a manned space vehicle into orbit around the earth. To supplement the textual content of the report, you will include actual NASA photographs at key points, which are included with the example files for this chapter.

Shirley Johnson is a science major who is particularly interested in astronomy and space exploration. For a class, she is writing a report on the history of the Project Mercury space program, which placed the first American, John Glenn, into orbit around the earth.

Shirley has already done quite a bit of work developing her page. She has written the report text, set up a document menu that jumps to sections within the report, created note links that jump to footnotes at the bottom of the page, and set up the colors, fonts, and backgrounds she wants to use. For the background, she created her own seamless background image, taken from one of NASA's photographs of a star cluster in outer space.

To get started working with this example:

1. Run your text editor and open **mercury_ex.html** from the chap04 folder in your working folder or working disk.
2. Save mercury_ex.html as **mercury.html** in the chap04 folder.
3. Run your browser and open **mercury.html** from the chap04 folder (see Figure 4.1).

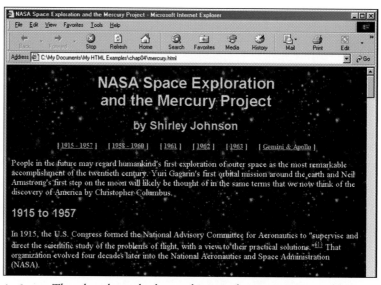

FIGURE 4.1 • *The color scheme, background image, document menu, and hypertext note links have already been created for mercury.html.*

This chapter uses a number of image files that are included with this chapter's example files in the chap04 folder. Any HTML files you create in this chapter must be saved in the same folder in which the example graphic files for this chapter are located; otherwise, the example graphics will not display when you preview the HTML files in your browser.

FLOATING IMAGES

You added an inline image to an HTML document in Chapter 1, but nested it by itself inside an otherwise empty P element, which added vertical spacing above and below the image, separating it from other elements. You had to do that because an IMG element is an inline element that is displayed in a line at the point at which it is inserted and, as such, does not insert line breaks or vertical spacing above or below an image.

Shirley decided to illustrate her report by using actual NASA photographs that are available online. She researched NASA's copyright and reproduction guidelines and discovered that most of NASA's photographs are not copyrighted, so she is free to use them for non-commercial or educational purposes.

action

Insert an inline image at the start of a paragraph containing text (see Figure 4.2):

```
<h2><a name="sect1"></a>1915 to 1957</h2>
<p>In 1915, the U.S. Congress formed the National Advisory
Committee for Aeronautics to "supervise and direct the
scientific study of the problems of flight, with a view to
their practical solutions."<sup><a href="#note1"
name="return1">(1)</a></sup> That organization evolved four
decades later into the National Aeronautics and Space
Administration (NASA).</p>
<p><img src="atlas_mercury.jpg" alt="Atlas rocket with Mercury
spacecraft" width="175" height="238">The Atlas rocket launch
vehicle, which lifted John Glenn into orbit, began being used
following World War II. Its initial test occurred in
1948.<sup><a href="#note2" name="return2">(2)</a></sup> The
first launch was not attempted until June 11, 1957, however,
just four months prior to the launching of the Sputnik I.
Unfortunately, the first Atlas launch ended with the missile
exploding at 10,000 feet. A second Atlas test launch also ended
in failure on September 25, 1957. It was not until January 10,
1958, that the Atlas rocket was successfully launched.</p>
```

HINT

Setting WIDTH and HEIGHT attributes for inline images can speed up display of the rest of the page, since the browser can allocate space for images before they have finished downloading.

inline image (non-floating)

FIGURE 4.2 • *An inline image is displayed at the position where it is inserted within a line.*

Flowing Text around a Left-Aligned Image

The IMG element's ALIGN attribute has two different functions. It can be used to vertically align an image relative to the line of text it is inserted on (you will learn how to do that later in this chapter). ALIGN also can be used to float an image to the left or right margin and cause following text or elements to flow around the image.

Set the inline image you just added so that it floats to the left margin, with following text and elements flowing around the right side of the image (see Figure 4.3):

```
<p><img src="atlas_mercury.jpg" align="left" alt="Atlas rocket
with Mercury spacecraft" width="175" height="238">The Atlas
rocket launch vehicle, which lifted John Glenn into orbit, began
being used following World War II.
```

left floating image
(align="left")

FIGURE 4.3 • *A left-aligned image floats to the left margin, with following text and elements flowing around the right side of the image.*

Setting Horizontal Spacing

The only problem with the floating image is that no horizontal spacing separates it from the flowing text. The IMG element's HSPACE attribute lets you set horizontal spacing that will be added on each side of the image.

Add 10 pixels of horizontal spacing to the inline image (see Figure 4.4):

```
<p><img src="atlas_mercury.jpg" align="left" hspace="10"
alt="Atlas rocket with Mercury spacecraft" width="175"
height="238">The Atlas rocket launch vehicle, which lifted John
Glenn into orbit, began being used following World War II.
```

horizontal spacing
(hspace="10")

FIGURE 4.4 • *Ten pixels of horizontal spacing are added to both sides of the image.*

Use the VSPACE attribute,
which works the same
as the HSPACE attribute,
to add vertical spacing
above and below an
inline image.

As shown in Figure 4.4, any horizontal spacing you add to the image is added to both sides of the image.

Flowing Text around a Right-Aligned Image

You also can float an image to the right margin, with following text and elements flowing around the left side of the image.

action

Insert a right-aligned inline image with 10 pixels of horizontal spacing set (see Figure 4.5):

```
<h2><a name="sect2"></a>1958 to 1960</h2>
<p>In June, 1958, the initial specifications were established for
what was to become the Project Mercury manned spacecraft. On
November 5, the Space Task Group was formed to implement a manned
satellite program; on November 26, the manned satellite program
was officially designated as Project Mercury.</p>
<p><img src="astronauts.jpg" align="right" hspace="10" alt="The
seven original Mercury astronauts" width="200"
height="197">Project Mercury was approved on October 7, 1958,
which led to the first orbital flight by an American astronaut,
John Glenn, in the "Friendship 7" spacecraft, about three years
and four months later, on February 20, 1962.</p>
```

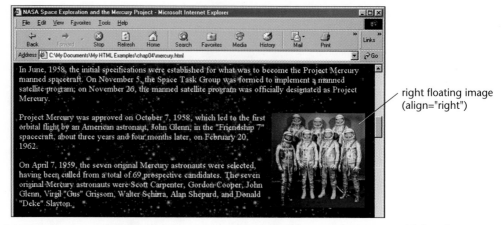

FIGURE 4.5 • *A right-aligned image with 10 pixels of horizontal spacing is added to the page.*

right floating image
(align="right")

Notice that an ALT attribute is included in both IMG elements you have added so far. Adding an ALT element to any inline image you include in a Web page informs someone using a non-visual browser, such as a Braille or speech browser, of the content or purpose of the image. In some, although not all, browsers, the content of the ALT attribute is displayed when the mouse is passed over the image (see Figure 4.6).

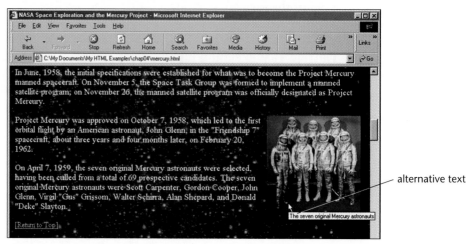

alternative text

FIGURE 4.6 • *Some browsers display the content of the ALT attribute when the mouse pointer is passed over an image.*

Flowing Text between Two Images

You also can flow text between a left-aligned and a right-aligned image.

Add both a left-aligned and a right-aligned image at the same location within the page (see Figure 4.7):

```
<h2><a name="sect3"></a>1961</h2>
<p><img src="chimp_ham.jpg" align="left" hspace="10" alt="Ham, the
first chimpanzee to go into outer space" width="175"
height="211"><img src="glenn_grissom_shepard.jpg" align="right"
hspace="10" alt="John Glenn, Virgil Grissom, and Alan Shepard in
front of the Redstone rocket" width="191" height="211">On January
31, 1961, a Redstone rocket launched a Mercury space vehicle from
Cape Canaveral with Ham, a 37-pound chimpanzee, as its passenger
```

in a suborbital flight. Ham survived the flight in good shape, but when he was shown the space vehicle again later, made clear he wanted no part of it. On February 1, John Glenn, Virgil Grissom, and Alan Shepard were selected to train for the first manned space flight.</p>

left floating image (align="left")

right floating image (align="right")

F I G U R E   4 . 7 • *Text flows between a left-aligned and a right-aligned image.*

Overlapping Floating Images

You also can overlap floating images, so that text first flows just around the right side of the first image, then between both images, and finally just around the left side of the second image.

Move the second image down, so the two floating images overlap (see Figure 4.8):

```
<h2><a name="sect3"></a>1961</h2>
<p><img src="chimp_ham.jpg" align="left" hspace="10" alt="Ham, the
first chimpanzee to go into outer space" width="175"
height="211"><img src="glenn_grissom_shepard.jpg" align="right"
hspace="10" alt="John Glenn, Virgil Grissom, and Alan Shepard in
front of the Redstone rocket" width="191" height="211">On January
31, 1961, a Redstone rocket launched a Mercury space vehicle from
Cape Canaveral with Ham, a 37-pound chimpanzee, as its passenger
in a suborbital flight. Ham survived the flight in good shape,
but when he was shown the space vehicle again later, made clear
he wanted no part of it. <img src="glenn_grissom_shepard.jpg"
align="right" hspace="10" alt="John Glenn, Virgil Grissom, and
Alan Shepard in front of the Redstone rocket" width="191"
height="211">On February 1, John Glenn, Virgil Grissom, and Alan
Shepard were selected to train for the first manned space
flight.</p>
```

overlapping floating images

FIGURE 4.8 • *You can overlap a left-aligned and a right-aligned image.*

Practicing Using Floating Images

You should now have a good understanding of left-aligning and right-aligning inline images, as well as of flowing text between floating images and overlapping left-aligned and right-aligned images. A number of additional example graphics are included with this chapter's example files that you can use to get more practice using floating images.

Using the previous examples of inserting left-aligned and right-aligned images as a guide, insert additional floating images at appropriate points within the document. Be sure to specify the actual height and width of the images, add horizontal spacing, and include alternative text that describes the image. The following are some images included with the example images for this chapter that you can use:

- **alan_shepard.jpg** Close-up view of Astronaut Alan Shepard in his pressure suit for the first manned Mercury suborbital flight (MR-3). Width: 175; height: 201.
- **mercurylaunch.jpg** Launch of the Mercury-Atlas 6 mission that put John Glenn into orbit around the earth. Width: 200; height: 214.
- **glenn_orbit.jpg** View of earth taken by Astronaut John Glenn during his space flight. Width: 200; height: 153.
- **john_glenn.jpg** Astronaut John Glenn poses in Mercury Space Suit. Width: 175; height: 199.
- **schirra_splash_down.jpg** Navy frogman secures tow line to Sigma 7 flotation collar. Width: 200; height: 184.
- **white_eva.jpg** Astronaut Edward White during first EVA performed during Gemini 4 space flight. Width: 200; height: 171.
- **flagonmoon.jpg** Astronaut Edwin Aldrin poses for photograph beside deployed U.S. flag (Apollo 11 landing on moon). Width: 200; height: 171.
- **earth_apollo17.jpg** View of the Earth seen by the Apollo 17 crew traveling toward the moon. Width: 200; height: 192.

VIEWING IMAGES

When you are choosing an image to use, it helps to view it first. Windows users can use My Computer to view images. Just double-click the My Computer icon on your desktop and then locate and double-click on any image file. If the image format is recognized by Windows, the image is displayed in the left side panel (see Figure 4.9).

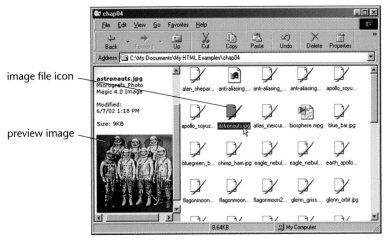

FIGURE 4.9 • *Windows users can use My Computer to see what an image looks like.*

You also can open an image in a Web browser, if it is a GIF, JPEG, or PNG image. Just open it as you would open a local HTML file (select All Files to see non-HTML files). Many image editors, such as Jasc Paint Shop Pro or Ulead PhotoImpact, also allow you to view a thumbnail gallery of all the images in a particular folder. Many image-viewing utilities are also available on the Web that let you view thumbnail galleries (see Figure 4.10). Following are some image viewers that you can download from the Web:

- CoffeeCup Free Viewer Plus at **www.coffeecup.com/viewer/** (freeware/Windows)
- XnView at **www.xnview.com/** (freeware/Windows, Macintosh, and Linux)
- ACDSee Classic at **www.acdsystems.com/English/Products/Other/ACDSeeClassic/** (Windows)
- Quick and Dirty Image Viewer at **www.epicware.com/** (freeware/Mac OS X)

For additional links to image viewers you can download and use, see this chapter's section at the IRC for this book at **www.emcp.com/** or visit the Tucows site at **www.tucows.com/**.

FIGURE 4.10 • *A thumbnail image viewer can make working with multiple images much easier.*

CASE EXAMPLE: CREATING AN ONLINE PICTURE GALLERY

A common way to present images on the Web is in an online picture gallery. Web authors might choose to display many different kinds of images in an online picture gallery, including personal snapshots, vacation photos, photographic artworks, paintings, drawings, sculptures, and so on.

Images can be presented as a gallery in many ways as well. One common way is to use left-aligned and right-aligned images in conjunction with caption text that describes the images. Additionally, online picture galleries usually use thumbnail images that link to fuller-sized images that can be viewed in a separate window. This method maximizes the number of images that can be shown on a gallery page, while keeping the size of the page as small as possible.

In addition to creating her online report on the Mercury spaceflight program, Shirley Johnson decided to create an online picture gallery of NASA space exploration images. Shirley already has a good start on her online gallery. She created her color scheme, set a background image, inserted images she wants to use, and wrote headings and captions for the gallery images.

To get started working with this example, from the chap04 folder, open **spacegallery_ex.html** in your text editor and resave it as **spacegallery.html** in the same folder. Open **spacegallery.html** in your browser (see Figure 4.11).

FIGURE 4.11 • *The color scheme, background image, images, headings, and captions are already set.*

CREATING A FLOWING LEFT-RIGHT GALLERY LAYOUT

To create this example you alternate left-aligned and right-aligned floating images, with headings and captions flowing around the images. You also set up the floating images to function as hypertext links to larger-sized versions of the images.

Floating the Gallery Images

Starting out, the gallery images are just inserted as regular inline images. You can float an image to either the left or right margin, but you need to be careful that following floating images do not also flow around the image. The BR (Break) element's CLEAR attribute lets you stop following text or elements from flowing around a floating image.

Float the first image and use the BR element's CLEAR attribute to stop following elements from flowing around the image (see Figure 4.12):

```
<hr>
<h2><img align="left" hspace="10" src="spacecapsules_th.jpg"
width="200" height="166" alt="Mercury, Gemini, and Apollo
spacecraft."> Mercury, Gemini, and Apollo Spacecraft</h2>
<p>The Mercury spacecraft carried one pilot, the Gemini
spacecraft carried two crew members, and the Apollo spacecraft
carried three crew members.<br clear="all"></p>

<hr>
<h2><img align="right" hspace="10" src="flagonmoon2_th.jpg"
width="200" height="169" alt="Astronaut Edwin Aldrin posing next
to U.S. flag on the moon.">U.S. Flag and Edwin "Buzz" Aldrin on
the Moon</h2>
<p>The Lunar Module "Eagle" is on the left. You can see the
footprints of the astronauts on the surface of the moon. The
picture was taken by Neil Armstrong on July 20, 1969.<br
clear="all"></p>
```

FIGURE 4.12 • *The gallery images are floating at the left and right margins.*

The CLEAR attribute value of **all** in the BR element causes following text or elements to clear any floating image. You also can set a CLEAR attribute value of **left** or **right**, which causes following text or elements to clear a left-aligned or right-aligned floating image, respectively.

practice

Four more images are included in the online gallery. Using the first two images that have already been set up as floating images, do the same with the remaining images in the gallery. Alternate the image float from the left to the right and use BR elements with a `clear="all"` attribute at the end of the caption text to stop following text or elements from also flowing around the images.

Creating Image Links

An *image link* is an image that also functions as a hypertext link. To create an image link, you nest an inline image inside a hypertext link. An image link need not link to another image. It can link to any object that has an address on the Web.

A smaller-sized image that links to a larger-sized image is sometimes called a *thumbnail* image. For that reason, in the example file, the smaller-sized images have a "_th" at the end of their file names, while the larger-sized images do not have "_th" at the end of their file names.

action

Set up the first two floating images as image links:

1. Bracket the first two floating images with hypertext links that link to the corresponding fuller-sized images (see Figure 4.13):

```
<hr>
<h2><a href="spacecapsules.jpg"><img align="left" hspace="10"
src="spacecapsules_th.jpg" width="200" height="166"
alt="Mercury, Gemini, and Apollo spacecraft."></a>Mercury,
Gemini, and Apollo Spacecraft</h2>
<p>The Mercury spacecraft carried one pilot, the Gemini
spacecraft carried two crew members, and the Apollo spacecraft
carried three crew members.<br clear="all"></p>


<hr>
<h2><a href="flagonmoon2.jpg"><img align="right" hspace="10"
src="flagonmoon2_th.jpg" width="200" height="169" alt="Astronaut
Edwin Aldrin posing next to U.S. flag on the moon."></a>U.S.
Flag and Edwin "Buzz" Aldrin on the Moon</h2>
```

FIGURE 4.13 • *The first two floating images are set as image links.*

2. In your browser, click on the first image link to test it. The full-sized image should be displayed in the browser window (see Figure 4.14). Click your browser's Back button to return to the gallery page.

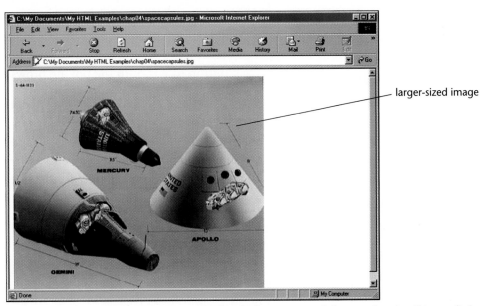

larger-sized image

FIGURE 4.14 • *A full-sized image is displayed when a visitor clicks on a thumbnail image link.*

When an image is set as an image link, a border is displayed around it. This border appears in whatever color is being displayed for unvisited and visited links, respectively, and serves the same function as the underline under a hypertext link.

practice

HINT

Copy the first A element start tag, paste it in before the remaining floating images, and then edit the copies so they target the correct full-size images. Copy the A element end tag and paste it in following the remaining floating images.

Using the first two image links you created as a guide, also set the four remaining images as image links. Remember that the smaller-sized images have "_th" at the end of their file names, while the larger-sized images do not. After creating the image links, test each one in your browser.

CONTROLLING LINK TARGETS In the example, when you click on one of the image links, the object of the link is displayed in a browser window that replaces the current browser window. Some Web authors like to cause linked pages that are external to their own site to display in a second browser window, while the first browser window remains open in the background. They do this in order to keep visitors from simply taking an exit and never coming back. That way, when a visitor closes the second browser window, the first browser window should return to the foreground. The A element's TARGET attribute can be used to cause the object of a link to be displayed in a new browser window that does not replace the current browser window.

action

Cause the gallery's linked images to be displayed in a new browser window, rather than replacing the current browser window:

1. Insert a **target="_blank"** attribute in the first gallery image's link:

```
<h2><a href="spacecapsules.jpg" target="_blank"><img align="left"
hspace="10" src="spacecapsules_th.jpg" width="200" height="166"
alt="Mercury, Gemini, and Apollo spacecraft."></a>Mercury, Gemini,
and Apollo Spacecraft</h2>
```

2. Do the same for the other gallery images' links.
3. Test any of the image links. To return to the gallery page, close the new window that has been opened (click on the Close button in the upper-right corner).

To have the linked image display in the same browser window, rather than open a new browser window, substitute `target="_top"` for `target="_blank"`. A visitor then only has to click the Back button to return to the linking browser window.

TURNING OFF AN IMAGE LINK'S BORDER The introductory paragraph tells the visitor that the thumbnail images can be clicked on to view the full-size images. In this case, you can thus safely turn off the display of the image link border. You need to be careful, however, turning off image link borders, because visitors to your page might not be able to tell that an image link is a link if there is no border displayed around the image.

Turn off the image link borders:

1. Turn off the first image link border:

```
<h2><a href="spacecapsules.jpg" target="_blank"><img border="0"
align="left" hspace="10" src="spacecapsules_th.jpg" width="200"
height="166" alt="Mercury, Gemini, and Apollo
spacecraft."></a>Mercury, Gemini, and Apollo Spacecraft</h2>
```

2. Do the same for the other image links (see Figure 4.15).

FIGURE 4.15 • *The image link borders are turned off.*

Although the image link borders are turned off, when a visitor passes the mouse pointer over one of the image links, as shown in Figure 4.15, the image still behaves as a link, with a "hand" cursor displayed over the image and the link URL displayed on the browser's status bar.

USING RULES, BANNERS, AND BUTTONS

Using graphic rules and banners can add visual appeal to your page, as well as give it more of a 3-D look.

Using Graphic Rules

A *graphic rule* is an image of variable width (usually 400 to 500 pixels in width), but which usually does not have a height of more than 5 to 10 pixels. Graphic rules are generally used as decorative separators and can be used in place of horizontal rules, giving your page a more colorful and 3-D look. An example graphic rule, **bluegreen_bar.jpg**, is included with this chapter's example files.

Replace the HR element with a graphic rule:

1. Replace the first HR element with the example graphic rule:

```
<hr>
<p align="center"><img src="bluegreen_bar.jpg" height="8"
width="100%" alt="Horizontal separator"></p>
<h2><a href="spacecapsules.jpg" target="_blank"><img border="0"
align="left" hspace="10" src="spacecapsules_th.jpg" width="200"
height="166" alt="Mercury, Gemini, and Apollo
spacecraft."></a>Mercury, Gemini, and Apollo Spacecraft</h2>
```

2. Replace the remaining HR elements with the same example graphic rule (see Figure 4.16).

FIGURE 4.16 • *Graphic rules can add visual impact to a page.*

Notice that a percentage value (`width="100%"`) is used to set the width of the graphic rule. This is an exception to the general rule that you should specify the actual dimensions of an image and not a different size at which you want it to display. Varying the width of a graphic rule relative to the width of the browser window allows it to reduplicate the function of a horizontal rule (the width of which is also dynamically resized relative to the width of the browser window). This method also does not generally cause problems with image quality because a graphic rule's height is small (usually less than 10 pixels), so that increasing only its width is unlikely to magnify flaws within the image.

You can easily create your own graphic rules in your image editor. Most image editors allow you to add various effects to a graphic rule. The example graphic rule, for instance, was created in Paint Shop Pro, using its buttonize effect. A good width for a graphical rule is 450 pixels, which is short enough that it should not have its width reduced and is long enough that it should not undergo much distortion when being stretched to fill 100 percent of a browser's window.

Using a Transparent Banner Image

When displaying a background image, a banner image with one of its colors set to be transparent can make an effective visual impact. An example banner image with a transparent background color is included with this chapter's example files.

Add a banner image and turn off the display of the H1 element:

1. Add a style to the CENTER element that reduces the bottom margin of that element and then insert a banner image above the H1 element:

```
<center style="margin-bottom: -1em">
<p><img src="spacegallery.gif" width="450" height="75"
alt="Space Gallery Banner Image"></p>
<h1>Space Exploration Gallery</h1>
</center>
```

2. Edit the style sheet in the HEAD element to turn off display of the H1 element (see Figure 4.17):

```
h1 { color: aqua; background: transparent; display: none; }
```

transparent banner image

FIGURE 4.17 • *A transparent banner image can help give a page more of a 3-D look.*

Notice in the example that the H1 element is left in the page, but with its display turned off (by the **display: none** style property), instead of simply being replaced by the banner image. The reason for this is that some search engines place special weight on the content of your H1 element when indexing your page, so it pays to leave it in, even though turning off its display.

Using Navigation Icons and Button Links

A *navigation icon* is an image that portrays an action a visitor can take by clicking on the image. For instance, a graphic of a house functioning as an image link conveys the idea that it is a link to the home page of the site or author. A left-pointing arrow conveys the idea that the link goes to the previous page, while a right-pointing arrow conveys that the link goes to the next page in a series of pages.

A button link is similar to a navigational icon because its design (with 3-D borders) conveys its function (that it can be clicked on), while its label conveys the action or result that will occur when a visitor clicks on the button.

Because they graphically indicate their function and purpose, it is customary to turn off the border of navigation icons and button links. An example button image, gobutton.gif, with the word "Go" as its label, is included with the other example files for this chapter.

Add an image link to the bottom of the page, below the address block, that uses a button link to link to Shirley Johnson's home page (see Figure 4.18):

```
</address>
<p align="center"><a href="home.html" style="text-decoration:
none"><img src="gobutton.gif" width="100" height="50" alt="Go
button" border="0" hspace="8" align="middle">to my Home
Page</a></p>
```

button link

FIGURE 4 . 1 8 • *A button image link graphically conveys that it can be clicked to go to an object or resource.*

Notice that the ALIGN attribute is used here to vertically align the image relative to the text line on which it is inserted—in this case, the middle of the image is aligned with the image's text line. You also can specify `align="top"` to align the top of the image relative to its text line. Bottom-alignment is the default. If you set top-, middle-, or bottom-alignment, you cannot also set left- or right-alignment. A style is also used to turn off underlining of the link to the right of the button.

The inline style in the A element, `text-decoration: none`, turns off the underline for the text following the button, which still functions as part of the link.

Finding Images on the Web

Many repositories of images are available on the Web. Always carefully read any terms of use that are posted relative to images you find on the Web (if you do not see a terms of use page, look for an FAQ page). Some images are true public domain images that you are free to use in any manner that you choose, either due to the lapsing of their copyright or a creator releasing them into the public domain. Many other images, however, are free to use only if you can satisfy the terms of use. Some images, for instance, are free for personal, non-commercial, or educational purposes, but not for commercial or for-profit purposes. Some providers also require a credit and a link back to their site if you use their images on your site.

A number of sites specifically provide clip art images that can be freely used by instructors and students in an educational environment. Many other Web art repositories allow free use of their art images for non-commercial or educational purposes. Following are some of these sources of clip art on the Web:

- Classroom Clipart at **www.classroomclipart.com/**
- Discovery School's Clip Art Gallery at **school.discovery.com/clipart/**
- Art Images for College Teaching (AICT) at **www.mcad.edu/AICT/**
- The Clip Art Connection at **www.clipartconnection.com/**
- GifArt.com at **www.gifart.com/**

For additional clip art resources, visit this book's IRC at **www.emcp.com/**.

CREATING YOUR OWN WEB IMAGES

You can create your own Web art images to give your page or site a unique or personalized appearance. To create your own Web art images, you need an image editor that can create and save GIF and JPEG images. A wide array of image editors can be used to create Web art images. If you do not already have an image editor you can use, here are some you can try out:

- **Adobe Photoshop (www.adobe.com/products/photoshop/).** The tool of choice preferred by many professional graphic designers (Windows and Macintosh).
- **Paint Shop Pro by Jasc Software (www.jasc.com/products/psp/).** A full-feature image editor that is both powerful and easy to use (Windows).
- **WebPainter by Totally Hip Software (www.totallyhip.com/).** A full-feature, but inexpensive, image editor (Windows and Macintosh).
- **Corel Draw Graphics Suite (www.corel.com/** for Windows and Macintosh; **www.linux.corel.com/** for Linux). Includes both Corel Draw and Corel PhotoPaint, either can be used to create Web graphics (Windows, Macintosh, and Linux).

For links to additional image editors and graphic utilities, see this chapter's section at the IRC for this book at **www.emcp.com/** or visit the Tucows site at **www.tucows.com/**.

Determining which Format: GIF or JPEG?

Beginning Web authors are often perplexed by which image format—GIF or JPEG—to use for displaying images on the Web. The GIF and JPEG image formats are different, so their relative strengths and weaknesses should determine which one you use to save a particular image.

The GIF image format works best for images that include line art, flat colors, and fewer than 256 colors. When such an image is saved as a GIF, it produces a smaller image, measured in bytes, than if the image is saved as a JPEG.

Photographs or other images with continuous tones or blends and with more than 256 colors should be saved as JPEG images. The exception to this rule is an image containing text. Buttons and banners with text as a prominent or primary feature, for instance, even if they contain color gradients and blends, should be saved as a GIF image because the JPEG image format, due to the kind of compression it applies, tends to blur sharp edges (such as the edges of letterforms) within an image.

For an image with a transparent background, you need to create a GIF image; JPEG images do not support transparency.

For images that contain both text and gradient blends, saving them as straight GIF images will likely produce undesirable dithering or banding effects within the image. *Dithering* is done by positioning pixels of different colors next to each other in order to simulate to the eye that a single color is present, which can result in a color with a speckled or mottled appearance that barely resembles the desired color. Without dithering, areas that use blends, gradients, or continuous tones might be displayed as a sequence of distinct color bands because only colors that are actually included in the palette can be displayed. Dithering is sometimes also referred to as *error diffusion*.

The answer to these problems is to save your GIF image using an optimized color palette, which contains only colors that are included within your image, rather than the standard GIF palette, which might contain many colors not included in your image.

Example graphics are included with this chapter's example files that show the same image saved as a JPEG image (with a 40-percent compression), an optimized GIF image, a non-optimized GIF image (with dithering), and a non-optimized GIF image (without dithering). To view these images in your browser, just open **image_compare.html** from the chap04 folder (see Figure 4.19).

FIGURE 4.19 • *An image containing text usually looks best when saved as an optimized GIF image.*

The next section, "Creating GIF Images," provides more detailed directions on how to create optimized GIF images.

Creating GIF Images

The GIF image format was originally created by the CompuServe online service, to provide a means to exchange images over its network. GIF images use a form of compression and thus have smaller sizes in bytes than the same images saved in a non-compressed image format. Although GIF images were not originally designed for display on the Web, a number of basic methods and techniques have been created by Web authors that make using GIF images over the Web effective.

USING THE WEB-SAFE COLOR PALETTE In Chapter 3, *Working with Fonts, Colors, and Backgrounds*, you learned about using the *Web-safe color palette* to set HTML colors in Web pages. GIF images saved using the Web-safe color palette include only 216 colors that are included in all system palettes, which ensures that colors in the image will not be dithered on a system that is only able to display 256 colors. To ensure that everyone, regardless of the capabilities of their graphics card, sees the same image, you can save your image using the Web-safe (or browser-safe) color palette, rather than your system's default color palette. The system palettes for Windows and Macintosh are similar, but each contain colors not present in the other. Most full-feature image editors either default to saving GIF images using a Web-safe color palette, or allow you to select it as an option.

The problem with using the Web-safe palette, however, is that it only works well for images with relatively few colors or color gradations. Images that contain many colors that are not included in the Web-safe palette are likely to suffer considerably when saved using that palette. In other words, if you are concerned that some viewers of your image will see a lot of dithered colors, making sure that everyone sees a lot of dithered colors is hardly an optimum solution.

CREATING AN OPTIMIZED COLOR PALETTE Fewer and fewer users are accessing the Web using systems only capable of displaying 256 colors. As a Web author, you need to decide whether to design your site to make sure that a small minority of viewers have an optimal viewing experience, while limiting the visual appeal of your images to the vast majority of viewers. Increasingly, Web authors are choosing to focus their design efforts on the majority of viewers who are using true-color graphics cards (capable of displaying colors selected from a palette of 16.7 million colors).

GIF images, however, can only display up to 256 colors. When you save an image that has many more than 256 colors as a GIF image using the Web-safe palette, the image quality can suffer tremendously. Such images should be saved with an *optimized palette* (also called an *adaptive palette* in Photoshop). For instance, in Paint Shop Pro 7 for Windows, you create an optimized palette for an image like this:

1. Select Colors, Decrease Color Depth, and X Colors (4/8 bit).
2. For the Number of colors, select 216. Select the Optimized Median Cut radio button and the Reduce color bleeding check box. If you are not including a transparent color, select the Error diffusion radio button (otherwise, select the Nearest color radio button) (see Figure 4.20). Click OK.
3. Save your image as a CompuServe Graphics Interchange (*.gif) file.

Optimized color palette option

Web-safe color palette option

Error diffusion (dithering)

• *In Paint Shop Pro 7 for Windows, you can create an image with an optimized color palette that contains only colors included within the image.*

As shown in Figure 4.20, when creating an optimized color palette, you can choose 256 or fewer as the number of colors. The fewer colors you can select and still retain acceptable image quality, the fewer bytes the resulting image will consume.

If you are creating a GIF image with a transparent background color, choosing the Error diffusion radio button can result in the color of your background being diffused into more than one color. Because only one color can be defined as transparent, this can interfere with setting the background of your image as entirely transparent. If you want to set a transparent background, your choices are to either turn off error diffusion or refill your image's background later with a solid color.

Many image editors also include wizards that help automate the creation of optimized GIF images. These editors often let you see the results of different settings as you are using them.

USING TRANSPARENT GIF IMAGES An additional problem can occur when creating transparent GIF images that will be displayed against a non-white background in a Web page. If you include a text object that uses anti-aliasing, the edges of the curves and diagonals are blended with the image's background to give them a smoother appearance. If your image's background is white, the anti-aliasing blends to white; the problem occurs if you set the white background color of your image as transparent and then try to display it against a non-white background set in a Web page. Especially against a darker background color or image, the result will be a noticeable white "halo" around your text's letterforms, as shown in Figure 4.21. To see this for yourself, just open **anti-aliasing.html** in your browser from the chap04 folder. This also can be a problem with any other effect that blends a color into your image's background, such as a drop shadow effect, for instance.

FIGURE 4.21 • *Anti-aliasing can cause text in a transparent GIF image to display a white halo effect if created against a white background but displayed against a dark background.*

A workaround exists that allows you to use anti-aliasing in a transparent GIF image that you want to display against a Web page's non-white background. All you have to do is set the background color you want to be transparent within your image so that it closely matches the color of your Web page's background. You can do this by trying to match the color you want to use in your image editor with the background color displayed in your Web page, or you can make an exact match.

Paint Shop Pro 7 for Windows, in fact, lets you specify a color's hexadecimal RGB code (see Figure 4.22) when selecting a color, so all you have know is the corresponding hexadecimal RGB code for the background color that is used in your Web page to set an exactly matching color in your image. Just fill the background of your image with the selected color that you want to be transparent and then create your text object using anti-aliasing or a drop shadow effect on top of that color. The anti-aliasing or drop shadow effect will now blend to the new color, rather than to white.

FIGURE 4.22 • *In Paint Shop Pro 7 for Windows, you can select a color based on its hexadecimal RGB code.*

A background image, however, can contain a number of colors. Most full-feature image editors contain an eye-dropper tool that lets you pick up a color from an image and set it as the color of your foreground or background swatch. Just open the background image in your image editor that you are using in your Web page, and then use its eye-dropper tool to assign a color included in the background image to the foreground color swatch. Figure 4.23 shows a color being picked up out of a background image using Paint Shop Pro 7's Dropper tool; with the mouse cursor hovering over the desired color, right-clicking assigns it to the foreground color swatch. The Flood Fill tool can then be used to fill an image's background with the selected color.

FIGURE 4.23 • *Paint Shop Pro 7's Dropper tool can pick up a color from a background image and assign it to the foreground color swatch.*

Picking the right color out of a background image to be used as a transparent background color in your image can take a little trial and error. Try to pick a color that is either the most prominent or one of the more common colors in the image.

USING INTERLACED GIF IMAGES *Interlacing* refers to displaying an image or display in more than one pass, with only some of the lines in the image or display appearing in any one pass. Earlier computer displays often used interlacing to display higher resolutions than they would otherwise be able to present, by displaying the odd lines in the display first, and then displaying the even lines. Interlacing in GIF images works in a somewhat similar fashion, except that four passes are used to display an interlaced GIF image, with the last two passes filling in progressively more lines than the first two passes. The result is that a viewer can start seeing what a downloaded interlaced GIF image will look like much sooner than with a non-interlaced GIF image.

Many visitors just click the Back button if they think a site's images are taking too long to display. By saving your GIF images as interlaced, you can give visitors to your site a much earlier indication of what the images will look like. When you save a GIF image, most image editors let you choose an option to save your image as interlaced.

Using JPEG Images

A photographic image or an image with a lot of colors or blends is best saved as a JPEG image. The exception to this rule is an image that includes text, which is best saved as an optimized GIF image because a JPEG image's compression method tends to blur and fuzz the edges of letterforms.

When you save a JPEG image, most image editors let you set a compression level for the image. The higher the compression level, the smaller the resulting file size will be. The smaller the file size, the quicker the image will download and display. Finding the right compression level for a JPEG image is a matter of finding the right balance between preserving image quality and saving bytes. Here is one way you can try to find the optimum compression level for an image:

1. Save your image as a JPEG with the lowest level of compression set, as **testimage1.jpg**, for instance. In most image editors, you can usually set the compression level for a JPEG image through an option in the Save dialog box. Figure 4.24 shows the compression level for a JPEG image being set in Paint Shop Pro for Windows.

FIGURE 4.24 • *When saving a JPEG image, the higher the compression level, the lower the image quality.*

2. Resave your image as a JPEG image at a compression level of 25 percent, as **testimage2.jpg**, for instance.

3. Repeat resaving your image, but at progressively higher compression levels, at 30 percent, 40 percent, 50 percent, and 60 percent, for instance. Save your images as **testimage3.jpg**, **testimage4.jpg**, and so on.

4. Close the original image and then open all the saved test images in your image editor. Position them side-by-side and compare the results. Use your image editor's zoom tool to get a closer look.

5. Compare the file sizes of the images. In Windows, for instance, in any Save or Open dialog box or in Windows Explorer, you can click the Details icon to display file details, including file sizes in kilobytes. In the Finder on the Macintosh, you can select View and choose to view the contents of a folder as a list, which displays the file size of each file (although you might need to scroll over to see it).

6. Identify which of the images provides you with the best balance of preserved image quality and savings in file size. That file represents the optimal compression settings for that particular image.

Realize, however, that some images can take much higher levels of compression than other images. The optimal level of compression can be different for each JPEG image you want to create. In general, however, you can usually compress JPEG images up to 20 to 30 percent without appreciable loss of image quality. Some images can take as much as a 50 percent compression, while others can take as high as 60 percent.

JPEG images use a *lossy* compression scheme. A lossy compression scheme results in bits in the image being thrown away, which means that a JPEG image cannot be uncompressed after it has been compressed. A *lossless* compression scheme, on the other hand, does not throw away bytes, which means that an image saved using such a scheme can later be uncompressed, with no bytes being lost. You should not store original images you create as JPEG images, but should save them in your image editor's proprietary format (PSD for Photoshop or PSP for Paint Shop Pro, for instance) or in an image format that uses a lossless compression scheme, such as PNG or TIFF.

Most image editors let you save a JPEG image as either a *standard* or a *progressive* JPEG image. A progressive JPEG image displays in a similar fashion to an interlaced GIF image, except that progressively higher resolutions of the image are displayed, starting with a low-resolution image. As with interlaced GIFs, viewers are able to see what the downloaded JPEG image will look like before it has completely downloaded. Earlier Web browsers, however, can have problems displaying progressive JPEG images. For that reason, many Web authors stick to just using standard JPEG images in their Web pages.

NOTE

Using the FONT element or styles, you are limited to displaying fonts that are available on a viewer's local computer. When creating your own Web images, however, you can use any font you have installed on your system, since you will be using them in a graphic instead of displaying them as part of your page's text. You can use a Dracula font, for instance, to create a banner graphic for your page if you have that font installed on your computer. For links to places on the Web where you can find and download fonts, see this chapter's section at the IRC for this book at **www.emcp.com/**. Before using a font, however, read the terms of use for copyright information and restrictions on use.

Using Other Image Formats

The PNG (Portable Network Graphics) image format has features in common with both GIF and JPEG images. Like GIF images, PNG images support transparency and interlacing. Although GIF images support only a single transparent color, PNG images can specify multiple transparent colors. Like JPEG images, PNG images support true-color images (up to a 48-bit palette as compared to up to a 24-bit palette for JPEGS). PNG images use a lossless compression scheme, rather than a lossy compression scheme, as is the case with JPEG images. Thus, although a PNG image can be uncompressed whereas a JPEG image cannot be uncompressed, the additional overhead required to encode every byte within the image means that the same image saved as a PNG image will likely be larger in bytes than if it were saved as a JPEG image.

Because earlier browsers and even some more recent browsers might not display PNG images, most Web authors still stick to using GIF and JPEG images. Eventually, PNG images are expected to replace GIF images on the Web, but not JPEG images. To find out more about the PNG image format, see the Portable Network Graphics site at **www.libpng.org/pub/png/**.

Another image format that shows a lot of promise is the SVG (Scalable Vector Graphics) format. Using SVG graphics, Web authors can create vector graphics and animations that will scale relative to a system's display. GIF and JPEG images are saved at fixed pixel dimensions, which do not scale relative to a system's display. To view SVG graphics, you can install the free Adobe SVG Viewer (for Windows or the Macintosh) at **www.adobe.com/svg/**.

Many other image formats are available, including BMP, WMF, TIFF, PCX, PICT, and more. Although these image formats are fine for using in a desktop publishing program where you only need to display them on your local computer and print them on your printer, they should not be used for display in a Web page.

Because Internet Explorer displays BMP images, many beginning Web authors mistakenly think that it is okay to use BMP images in Web pages. Many other browsers, such as Netscape Navigator, for instance, do not display BMP images. The BMP image format also does not use any compression, so images saved in that format can be many times larger than the same image saved as a GIF, JPEG, or PNG image. An image that has a size in the tens of kilobytes when saved as a JPEG image, for instance, can have a size of hundreds of kilobytes when saved as a BMP image. In other words, do not use BMP or WMF images in Web pages, even if you know everybody accessing your page will be using Internet Explorer.

USING ANIMATIONS

You can include media other than still graphics in a Web page. By adding animations to your pages, you can make them more dynamic and eye-catching than pages that include only still images (or no images at all).

Using GIF Animations

The GIF image format allows for the inclusion of multiple image frames within a single image. When displayed in a Web browser, the image frames within the image are displayed at a frame rate that can be set when the image is created. An example GIF animation, go_anim.gif, is included with this chapter's example files.

Replace the previous navigation icon at the bottom of the page with a GIF animation, go_anim.gif, set the image's vertical spacing to 5 pixels, and insert a BR element to move the following text below the image (see Figure 4.25):

```
</address>
<p align="center"><a href="home.html" style="text-decoration:
none"><img src="go_anim.gif" vspace="5" width="100" height="50"
alt="Go button" border="0" hspace="8" align="middle"><br>to my
Home Page</a></p>
```

GIF animation

FIGURE 4.25 • *A GIF animation also can function as an image link and a navigation icon.*

Notice that a BR element is added that moves the following text below the GIF animation, and 5 pixels of vertical spacing is added to provide extra spacing between the animation and the following text. The `align="middle"` attribute is deleted because it has no effect with the following text moved below the image.

To create your own GIF animations, you need a GIF animation editor. Here are some GIF animation editors you can download and try:

HINT

For links to additional GIF animation editors, visit this chapter's section at the IRC for this book at **www.emcp.com/** or the Tucows site at **www.tucows.com/**.

- **Animation Shop (www.jasc.com/).** An excellent GIF animation editor included with Paint Shop Pro for Windows.
- **GIF Construction Set Professional (www.mindworkshop.com/alchemy/ gifcon.html).** A shareware GIF animation editor for Windows.
- **GIFfun (www.stone.com/GIFfun/).** A freeware GIF animation editor for the Macintosh.
- **Gifsicle (www.lcdf.org/~eddietwo/gifsicle/).** A freeware GIF animation utility for Linux.

Many GIF animation editors include animation wizards that make creating GIF animations as simple as selecting the images you want to use, the order in which you want them to appear, and the frame rate at which you want your animation to display. After you have created an animation, you can change the settings for individual frames, create transitions between frames, add and delete frames, preview the animation, and so on. Figure 4.26 shows go_anim.gif open in Animation Shop for Windows.

FIGURE 4.26 • *Using a GIF animation editor, you can create, edit, and preview your own GIF animations.*

GIF animations, although they can include multiple image frames, are still GIF images. The color palette used to display all the frames within a GIF animation is still limited to no more than 256 colors. The result is that some GIF images included in a GIF animation can suffer visually, due to additional dithering, for instance. Some GIF animators also let you import JPEG, PNG, or other true-color images that can suffer considerably from dithering when converted to GIF format within a GIF animation.

One way to try to fix this problem is to edit the individual images in your image editor and create optimized color palettes for each one that include only the minimal number of colors required to produce acceptable image quality. For instance, if you can reduce the total number of colors used by each image to 128 or 64 colors, you will reduce or eliminate the dithering that can result when the images are combined within a GIF animation.

File size is another issue to consider with GIF animations. For instance, a 4-frame GIF animation created in Animation Shop with the highest image quality settings produces an 8-KB (kilobyte) file, an 8-frame animation produces a 14-KB file, and a 16-frame animation produces a 27-KB file. If you add any transition effects between frames, that can add many additional frames to your animation, depending on the effect being used. Also, the more image frames you include in your animation, the more likely that individual images in your animation will be dithered. For these reasons, it is usually best to limit the number of frames included in a GIF animation; you would not want to include a 200-KB GIF animation in a Web page, for instance (a more reasonable size would be 30-KB to 50-KB, or less).

Using Other Animations

GIF animations are not the only kinds of animations that can be included in a Web page. Flash or Java animations can include many more effects than GIF animations. These types of animations can also do much more than just provide dynamic movement; they can create multimedia effects (animation, video, and audio effects) that interact with user actions or respond to events. Here are some software tools that can be used to create interactive Flash or Java animations for the Web:

- **Macromedia Flash for Windows or the Macintosh (www.macromedia.com/).** The program that introduced the Flash animation format.
- **Adobe LiveMotion (www.adobe.com/products/livemotion/).** Another full-feature Flash animation editor for Windows and the Macintosh.
- **CoffeeCup Firestarter (www.coffeecup.com/firestarter/).** A Flash animation editor for Windows that is much less expensive to purchase than Flash or LiveMotion.

For links to additional animation programs, see this chapter's section at the IRC for this book at **www.emcp.com/** or visit the Tucows site at **www.tucows.com/**.

- **AnFX (www.stepaheadsoftware.com/anfx.htm).** An inexpensive Java animation editor for Windows that lets you create interactive Java animations that conform to Sun's Java standard.

ADDING SOUND

You can add background sound that plays automatically when a Web page displays. An example WAV-format audio file, kennedy.wav is included with this chapter's example files.

Embedding Audio Files

The EMBED element is not actually a standard HTML element, but is an unofficial extension to HTML that was introduced by Netscape and is supported by most browsers.

PLAYING AN AUDIO FILE AUTOMATICALLY IN THE BACKGROUND You can embed an audio file that will play automatically in the background when the page is opened in a browser.

Add and test a WAV file that plays automatically in the background when the page is opened:

1. At the bottom of the page, use the EMBED element to insert an audio file that plays automatically in the background:

```
<p><embed src="kennedy.wav" autostart="true" loop="false"
width="2" height="2"></p>
</body>
```

2. Save your HTML file, switch to your browser, and click the Refresh (or Reload) button.

If your computer has a sound card and is otherwise configured to play WAV audio files, an audio file of President John F. Kennedy announcing the program to land a man on the moon will start playing in the background.

If the WAV file does not play in your browser, you may need to download and install a player or plug-in that will play WAV files. See this chapter's section at the IRC for this book at **www.emcp.com/** for a selection of audio/video players.

In the example, the `width="2"` and `height="2"` attribute values have the effect of hiding the WAV player console from view. These settings are necessary for the background sound to play in some versions of the QuickTime player, which will not play the audio file if the width and height are set to **0**. Because the 2-pixel × 2-pixel dimensions that are set might impact the formatting of the page if the EMBED element is inserted at the top of the page, it is inserted at the bottom of the page where it will have no impact on the page's formatting.

The **autostart="true"** attribute causes the audio file to start playing automatically as soon as it is finished downloading. The **loop="false"** attribute causes the audio file to only play once, rather than being looped indefinitely. Especially when hiding the player console, indefinitely looping an audio file that plays automatically in the background is strongly discouraged because users have no way of turning it off, except by accessing their system's audio volume controls. Because some visitors find audio annoying, you could also set **autostart="false"**, especially if the embedded audio is on your front page.

A common error is to specify a numerical value for the EMBED element's LOOP attribute, to specify a set number of loops, such as **loop="2"**, for instance. This causes varying results in different players, with some defaulting to looping the media file only once, while others loop it indefinitely. Always set either **true** or **false** as the LOOP attribute's value.

PLAYING AN AUDIO FILE AUTOMATICALLY IN THE FOREGROUND If you want to automatically play an indefinitely looping audio file, you should set the dimensions of the player console to make it is visible in the browser window, so users can turn off the audio if they wish.

Move the EMBED element from the bottom to the top of the page and edit it to cause the player console to be visible:

1. First, place HTML comment codes around the EMBED element that is already in the document (that way, you can go back to using it later, just by removing the comment codes):

```
<!--
<p><embed src="kennedy.wav" autostart="true" loop="false"
width="2" height="2"></p>
-->
</body>
```

2. Highlight and copy the EMBED element (but not the P element start and end tags).
3. Paste the EMBED element above the banner image's IMG element, as shown here:

```
<center style="margin-bottom: -1em">
<embed src="kennedy.wav" autostart="true" loop="false" width="2"
height="2">
<img src="spacegallery.gif" class="banner" width="450"
height="75" alt="Space Gallery Banner Image">
```

4. Edit the EMBED element to set an indefinite loop, specify width and height dimensions for the player console, and add a BR element:

```
<embed src="kennedy.wav" autostart="true" loop="true"
width="145" height="45"><br>
```

5. Save the document, switch over to your browser, and click the Refresh (or Reload) button (see Figure 4.27).

Stop button

player console
(EMBED element)

FIGURE 4.27 • *Displaying the player console on the page lets a user turn off the playing of a looping or long audio file.*

The width and height dimensions (145 and 45 pixels) are the minimum required to display the slider bar showing the progress of the playing of the audio file in the Windows Media player console. The player console displayed, however, depends upon which audio player is associated with WAV files. If that is the QuickTime player, for instance, then the QuickTime player console is displayed instead.

Even if you are not looping your audio file, you might want to display the player console, rather than hide it, if your audio file is longer than 10 to 15 seconds. That way, those who might be irritated by a background audio file playing can easily turn it off. Others might click the Back button as soon as they hear a background audio playing, especially if they are working in an office environment; if the player console is clearly visible and available, they can just as easily click the player console's Stop button.

USING THE NOEMBED ELEMENT The NOEMBED element provides content that is displayed for visitors using browsers that do not support the EMBED element. The content of the NOEMBED element is generally a link that a visitor can click to play the media file.

Add a NOEMBED element that provides a link to the audio file if a visitor's browser doesn't support the EMBED element:

```
<embed src="kennedy.wav" autostart="true" loop="true" width="145"
height="45">
<noembed>Listen to <a
href="kennedy.wav">kennedy.wav.</a></noembed>
<br>
```

SPECIFYING A PLUG-IN PAGE One problem with including audio in Web pages is that a user needs to have an appropriate player or plug-in to play the audio. The EMBED element's PLUGINSPLAYER attribute can be used to specify a URL for downloading an appropriate plug-in player for the audio format being played.

Use the PLUGINSPAGE attribute to specify the URL where the QuickTime player can be downloaded:

```
<embed src="kennedy.wav" autostart="true" loop="true"
width="145" height="45"
pluginspage="http://www.apple.com/quicktime/download/">
<noembed>Listen to <a
href="kennedy.wav">kennedy.wav.</a></noembed>
<br>
```

If a browser does not have the appropriate plug-in player to play a particular media file, it will present the URL provided by the PLUGINSPAGE attribute, so that the user can download a plug-in player capable of playing the media file.

Using the OBJECT Element to Insert Audio Files

The OBJECT element is a standard element included in HTML 4 that is intended as a generic means to insert objects into Web pages. An object might be an image, a sound file, a video, a Java applet, and so on. You can even embed an HTML file inside another HTML file as an object. The PARAM (Parameter) element can be nested inside the OBJECT element to set display, behavior, and other parameters.

PLAYING AN AUDIO FILE AUTOMATICALLY IN THE FOREGROUND Previously, you used the EMBED element to insert a WAV audio file that plays automatically when the page is opened. The same thing can be accomplished using the OBJECT element.

Comment out the EMBED element you added previously and then use the OBJECT element to automatically play and loop a WAV audio file with the player console displayed (see Figure 4.28):

```
<center style="margin-bottom: -1em">
<!--<embed src="kennedy.wav" autostart="true" loop="true"
width="145" height="45"
pluginspage="http://www.apple.com/quicktime/download/">
<noembed>Listen to <a
href="kennedy.wav">kennedy.wav.</a></noembed>
<br>
-->
<img src="spacegallery4.gif" class="banner" width"450" height="75"
alt="Space Gallery Banner Image"><br>
<object data="kennedy.wav" type="audio/wav" width="145"
height="45" vspace="5">
<param name="src" value="kennedy.wav">
<param name="autostart" value="true">
<param name="controller" value="true">
<param name="loop" value="true">
President Kennedy calling for landing a man on the moon.
</object>
<h1>Space Exploration Gallery</h1>
</center>
```

player console
(OBJECT element)

FIGURE 4.28 • *The OBJECT element, a standard HTML 4 element, is used to embed an audio file in a Web page.*

To not automatically play the audio file in the foreground, set a value of **false** for the **autostart** parameter. To listen to the audio file, the user must click the player console's Play button.

The OBJECT element's TYPE attribute specifies the MIME type (or content type) of an object file. MIME stands for *Multipurpose Internet Mail Extensions* and was originally devised to identify different e-mail attachments, but is now used more generally to identify files on the Internet. For instance, **audio/wav**, **image/gif**, and **text/css** are all MIME types for files that can be downloaded over the Web. MIME types have two parts, a type and a subtype, with **audio** specifying the type and **wav** specifying the subtype, for instance. Including the TYPE attribute in the OBJECT element is optional, but recommended; if a browser does not recognize the MIME type, it can simply not download the object.

Various additional attributes can be used with the OBJECT element. For a listing, see Appendix A, *HTML Quick Reference*. For further explanation of how to use the OBJECT element, see the W3C's HTML 4.01 specification at **www.w3.org/TR/html401/**.

PLAYING AN AUDIO FILE AUTOMATICALLY IN THE BACKGROUND You also can use the OBJECT element to automatically play an audio file in the background when a Web page is opened.

Use the OBJECT and PARAM elements to automatically play, but not loop, a WAV audio file with the player console hidden:

```
<object data="kennedy.wav" type="audio/wav" width="0" height="0"
vspace="5">
<param name="src" value="kennedy.wav">
<param name="autostart" value="true">
<param name="controller" value="true">
<param name="loop" value="true">
President Kennedy calling for landing a man on the moon.
</object>
```

Setting the width and height of the OBJECT element to **0** hides it from view. The **controller** parameter is deleted because it is not needed to display the player console. The **loop** parameter is also deleted to not loop the audio file (**value="false"** is the default value).

HANDLING EARLIER BROWSERS The main problem with using the OBJECT element is that earlier browsers might not support it. Netscape Navigator 4, for instance, does not support the OBJECT element. The EMBED element, although not a standard

HTML element, is more widely supported by earlier browsers that are not HTML 4-compliant.

When using the OBJECT element, you might want to use a method or technique for shielding or redirecting users of earlier browsers, such as those provided by the Web Standards Project's Browser Upgrade Initiative that was described in Chapter 3. You could also use a browser-sniffer JavaScript script to detect earlier browsers and redirect them to a different page.

Choosing Audio Formats

Many different audio formats can be used to play audio in a Web page. Some of the most commonly used audio formats are WAV, AIFF, MIDI, MP3, AU, and RealAudio. Table 4.1 shows many of the audio formats, along with their MIME types, that can be used in Web pages.

TABLE 4.1 • *Common Audio MIME Types*

Media Object	Extensions	MIME Types
AU (Sun/Next Audio format)	AU, SND	audio/basic
AIFF (Audio Interchange File Format)	AIF, AIFF, AIFC	audio/x-aiff
MIDI (Musical Instrument Digital Interface)	MID, MIDI, RMI	audio/mid
MPEG (Moving Picture Experts Group)	MPG, MPEG, MP2, MPE	audio/mpeg
MP3 audio	MP3	audio/mpeg3
RealAudio	RA	audio/x-realaudio
Windows (WAV) audio	WAV	audio/wav
Windows Media Audio file	WMA	audio/x-ms-wma

The WAV audio format is native to the Windows system, the AIFF format originated from the Macintosh, and the AU format originated from the Sun and Next computer platforms. The MIDI and MP3 formats are popular for playing music files.

ADDING VIDEO

You are not limited to including only still images or GIF animations in Web pages. Many video formats also can be inserted into a Web page using the EMBED or OBJECT elements. An example video file, biosphere.avi, is included with this chapter's example files.

Using the EMBED Element to Insert a Video

You can use the EMBED element to insert a video file in a Web page.

Embed a video file at the bottom of the page:

1. Copy and paste the graphical rule at the bottom of your page, as shown here:

```
<p align="center"><img src="bluegreen_bar.jpg" height="8"
width="100%" alt="Horizontal separator"></p>
```

```
<p align="center"><img src="bluegreen_bar.jpg" height="8"
width="100%" alt="Horizontal separator"></p>
<address>
```

2. Use the EMBED element to insert a video file:

```
<p align="center"><img src="bluegreen_bar.jpg" height="8"
width="100%" alt="Horizontal separator"></p>
<center>
<h2>Earth Biosphere Animation from NASA</h2>
<p><embed src="biosphere.mpg" autostart="false" loop="true"
width="320" height="255"></p>
</center>
<p align="center"><img src="bluegreen_bar.jpg" height="8"
width="100%" alt="Horizontal separator"></p>
<address>
```

3. Save your file, switch over to your browser, and click the Refresh (or Reload) button.
4. If the video and player console are displayed, click the Play button to start the video (see Figure 4.29).

FIGURE 4.29 • *The embedded MPEG video file, biosphere.mpg, starts to play when the Play button is clicked.*

Depending on the browser you are using, how it is configured, and which players or plug-ins are installed, what you see on your system might differ from what is shown in Figure 4.29. If you have trouble playing video files in your browser, download and install the latest video players from Apple (**www.apple.com/quicktime/**), Real Networks (**www.real.com/realone/**), and Microsoft (**www.microsoft.com/windows/windowsmedia/**).

If after installing the QuickTime player, you are unable to view a video format in Internet Explorer, just reinstall all components of the Windows Media Player.

A visitor's browser, player, or plug-in settings also can affect the ability to view video files inserted in Web pages.

Using the OBJECT Element to Insert a Video

You also can use the OBJECT element to insert a video in a Web page.

Comment out the EMBED element and use the OBJECT element to insert an AVI video:

```
<!--
<p><embed src="biosphere.avi" autostart="false" loop="true"
width="320" height="255"></p>
-->
<p align="center"><object data="biosphere.avi" type="video/avi"
width="320" height="255" vspace="5">
<param name="src" value="biosphere.avi">
<param name="autoplay" value="false">
<param name="controller" value="true">
<param name="loop" value="false">
</object></p>
</center>
```

If your browser supports the OBJECT element, the result you see in your browser should look the same as when using the EMBED element (refer to Figure 4.29) to embed the video file in your Web page. Table 4.2 shows some of the more common video formats, along with their MIME types, that are used on the Web.

TABLE 4.2 • *Common Video MIME Types*

Media Object	Extensions	MIME Types
ASF (Advanced Streaming Format)	ASF	video/x-ms-asf
MPEG video	MPEG, MPG, MPE	video/mpeg
MPEG-2 video	MPV2, MP2V	video/mpeg2
QuickTime video	MOV, QT	video/quicktime
RealMedia meta file	RM, RAM	application/vnd.rn-realmedia
RealVideo	RV	video/vnd.rn-realvideo
Video for Windows (Audio/Video Interleave)	AVI	video/avi
Windows Media Video file	WMV	video/x-ms-wmv
VDOLive streaming video	VDO	video/vdo
Vivo streaming video	VIV	video/vnd.vivo

UNDERSTANDING COPYRIGHT ISSUES

A lot of images, audio clips, and video files can be downloaded easily from the Web, but that does not mean you are free to use them. Always make sure you have the right to use an image or other media file before you use it.

When using images or other media files from online sources, be sure to save any pages or documents that provide permission for usage or guidelines for fair or allowed usage of images or other media files. Also, the use of an image of a recognizable living person

For links to additional resources on copyright issues as they apply to the Web, see this chapter's section at the IRC for this book at **www.emcp.com/**.

might require separate permission from that person. In its guidelines, for instance, NASA advises that images of such persons in its collection can be used without permission if for communicative purposes, rather than for commercial exploitation.

Additional considerations apply to musical copyrights, because a particular musical work's score (sheet music), arrangement, performance, recording, and sequencing might all be separately copyrighted. Both performance and distribution fees can be deemed due when offering copyrighted audio recordings for download over the Web.

If you are creating a commercial Web site, many sites on the Web offer access to images, music, and video for a membership or subscription fee. These media files are usually referred to as royalty-free, to distinguish them from public domain media files. To locate vendors of royalty-free images, music, or video files, search at AltaVista (**www.altavista.com/**) or Yahoo! (**www.yahoo.com/**) on the words "royalty free."

CHAPTER SUMMARY

You should now be familiar with using images and other media files in Web pages. When working with images, you should understand how to use floating images, image links, graphic rules, transparent banner images, navigation icons, button links, and GIF animations. You also should understand the differences between the GIF and JPEG image formats, including which format to use to save which kinds of images, how to optimize your GIF and JPEG images, and what transparent and interlaced GIFs are used for. You also should have experience using audio and video files in a Web page, including using both the EMBED element and the OBJECT element to play an audio file in the background, playing an audio file with the player console displayed at the top of the page, and inserting and playing a video in a Web page.

Code Review

ALIGN attribute	In the IMG element, floats an image to the left or right margin or vertically aligns it relative to a line of text.
CLEAR attribute	In the BR element, stops following text or elements from wrapping around a floating image.
HSPACE and VSPACE attributes	In the IMG or OBJECT element, these attributes add horizontal space on the left and right sides of an image or vertical space above or below an image.
BORDER attribute	In the IMG or OBJECT element, draws a border around the element; border="0" turns off the border displayed around an image link.
GIF image	CompuServe Graphics Interchange Format, an image format, which supports a color palette of up to 256 colors, transparency, and multiple frames (animation).
JPEG image	Joint Professional Experts Group image format, which supports a color palette of up to 16.3 million colors, but does not support transparency or animation.
PNG image	Portable Network Graphics image format, which supports 48-bit True Color (compared with 24-bit True Color for JPEG images). PNG images also support transparency and are slated eventually to replace GIF images on the Web. PNG images do not support animation.
EMBED element	A non-standard element introduced by Netscape, but supported by current browsers, that allows audio and video to be embedded into a Web page.
AUTOSTART attribute	In the EMBED element, causes an audio or video file to start playing automatically after the page where it is embedded is opened in a browser.
LOOP attribute	In the EMBED element, causes an audio and video file to loop indefinitely, rather than only play once.

PLUGINSPAGE attribute	In the EMBED element, indicates the URL where an appropriate plug-in player for a media file can be downloaded, which a browser can convey to a user if no plug-in player for the media file is installed.
HEIGHT and WIDTH attributes	In the EMBED or OBJECT element, these attributes specify the dimensions of the player console, but also can be used to hide the console.
OBJECT element	An element introduced in HTML 4 that is used to include objects in HTML documents, including images, audio, video, Java animations, and more.
PARAM element	In conjunction with the OBJECT element, specifies display or behavior parameters for an object.

ONLINE QUIZ

Go to this text's IRC at **www.emcp.com/** and take the online self-check quiz for this chapter.

REVIEW EXERCISES

This section provides some hands-on practice exercises to reinforce the information and material included within this and previous chapters.

Save **mercury.html** and **spacegallery.html** under new files names (**mercury_practice.html** and **spacegallery_practice.html**, for instance) and then use the new documents to practice using the elements, attributes, styles, and other features that were covered in this chapter.

1. In the first or second practice document (mercury_practice.html or spacegallery_practice.html), use any of the example images included with this chapter's example files to experiment further with floating images using the IMG element's ALIGN attribute and the BR element's CLEAR attribute.

2. Experiment with finding and downloading images from the Web. Go to NASA's Photo Gallery at **www.nasa.gov/gallery/photo/** and download several images you want to experiment with. To save an image, just right-click on it and then select to save the picture or image to your hard drive.

3. If you do not have an image viewer, use one of the links provided earlier in this chapter or in this chapter's section at the IRC for this book at **www.emcp.com/** to download an image viewer you can experiment with. Practice viewing images that are located on your computer. Practice viewing thumbnail galleries of images, if your image viewer has that capability. Practice using your image viewer to open, copy, and rename images on your computer.

4. If you do not have an image editor, use one of the links provided earlier in this chapter or in this chapter's section at the IRC for this book at **www.emcp.com/** to download an image editor you can experiment with. Practice opening, cropping, and resizing the images you downloaded from the NASA site in Exercise 2. Practice

saving the images as optimized JPEG images, by trying to choose a compression level that sets the file size as small as possible, while still preserving acceptable image quality. Experiment with adding text to photographic images and then save them as optimized GIF images.

5. Use your image editor to save smaller-sized thumbnail images of the images you have downloaded from the Web. Use the second practice document (spacegallery_practice.html) to experiment further with using thumbnail images to link with larger-sized images.

6. Use your image editor to experiment with creating your own banner images. Experiment with using different fonts, color combinations, and special effects. Experiment with saving your banner as a transparent GIF. If you created your own personal page at the end of Chapters 1 and 3, create a personalized banner image to use on your personal page. If you created a page for a club or organization, create a banner image for that page.

7. Experiment further with using different graphic rules in the second practice document. You can find additional graphic rules with this chapter's example files and in the art folder that accompanies this book's example files. The file names of graphic rules all end with "_bar." You also can search for graphic rules on the Web that you can download and use. If you have an image editor, experiment with creating your own graphic rules.

8. If you have a GIF animation editor, use it to experiment with creating GIF animations. The four button images (go1.gif, go2.gif, go3.gif, and go4.gif) that were used to create the go_anim.gif GIF animation are included with this chapter's example files and can be used to create your own GIF animation. If you have an image editor, you also can create your own images to use in a GIF animation.

9. Use any of the links provided earlier in this chapter or at this book's IRC at **www.emcp.com/** to download additional WAV, MIDI, or other audio files and practice using the EMBED and OBJECT elements to include them in Web pages. Experiment with playing audio files automatically in the background or with the player console displayed. Experiment with turning looping on or off.

10. Go to NASA's Video Gallery at **www.nasa.gov/gallery/video/** and download one or more additional videos you can use to experiment further with including videos in your Web pages.

WEB-BASED LEARNING ACTIVITIES

In this book's text, Find It icons inserted in the margin highlight the Web addresses of additional resources you might find helpful or informative. To further extend your learning using the Web, you can:

- Go back and visit any of the Web addresses highlighted in this chapter that you have not yet visited. Look for additional resources and information that add to your understanding and knowledge of the material covered in this chapter. When you find a relevant page or site with information or resources you might want to access later, add it to your Favorites (in Internet Explorer) or your Bookmarks (in Netscape or Mozilla).

- Visit this book's Internet Resource Center at **www.emcp.com/** to find additional Web addresses of resources related to the material covered in this chapter and that you can further investigate and explore.

- Further research a specific topic introduced in this chapter. For instance, do further research on using copyrighted, restricted license, and public domain image, audio, and video files in Web pages. Create a report on the topic you have chosen or team up with classmates to create a presentation.

PROJECTS

These projects can be done either in class, in a computer lab, or at home. Use the skills you have developed in this and the previous chapters to create any of the following projects.

Project 1. Add images to a page you have already created.

Add floating images, graphical rules, a banner graphic, and a navigation icon to a page you have already created, such as a personal page, a page for a club or organization, a topical page, or any other page. Incorporate lessons you learned in previous chapters, including using a document menu, return links, and colors and backgrounds, for instance. Use images downloaded from the Web or create your own images in an image editor. Optionally, incorporate audio or inline video.

If downloading images, use any of the links provided previously in the "Finding Images on the Web" section or at this book's IRC at **www.emcp.com/** to find links you can use in your page, or use Google (**www.google.com/**), AltaVista (**www.altavista.com**), or Yahoo! (**www.yahoo.com/**) to find additional sources for images you can download and use. Use an image editor to resize, crop, and optimize the images.

If creating your own images, you can create your images from scratch in an image editor or use images that you have scanned in using a scanner or imported from a digital camera. Here are some additional resources on using images from a scanner or a digital camera:
- A Few Scanning Tips by Wayne Fulton (**www.scantips.com/**)
- Scanning Tips (**www.graffiti.org/faq/scan.html**)
- A Short Course in Using Your Digital Camera (**www.shortcourses.com/using/**)
- Use Digital Camera Support to Import Photos (**www.jasc.com/tutorials/revised/pspdcs.asp**)

Visit this chapter's section at the IRC for this book at **www.emcp.com/** to find additional links to scanning and digital imaging resources on the Web.

Project 2. Create your own online gallery.

Using this chapter's online gallery example as a guide, create your own online gallery from scratch. For instance, create a gallery of vacation photos, or a gallery of other personal snapshots. If you are an artist, create a gallery of photos of your paintings, illustrations, drawings, or other artwork. If you are a photographer, create a gallery to display some of your photographic works. Use a scanner or digital camera to create the raw images you will use or create your own images in an image editor. Crop, resize, sharpen, and apply other corrections or effects to prepare your images to be displayed on the Web. Save your images as either optimized JPEGs or optimized GIFs. Save smaller-sized thumbnail versions and larger-sized versions of each image.

Project 3. Create a Web page using images.

Create any other kind of Web page from scratch that makes use of images (any kind of page you can imagine or conceive). Use images downloaded from the Web or images that you have scanned or imported from a digital camera. Optionally, incorporate audio and inline video. Apply skills learned in this chapter and any previous chapters.

5

Working with Tables

PERFORMANCE OBJECTIVES

In this chapter, you learn to use HTML tables for a variety of purposes, including how to:

- Use the PRE element to format tabular data.
- Use the TABLE element to format tabular data in rows and columns.
- Span columns and rows within tables.
- Control the width and appearance of table columns.
- Control the appearance of row groups.
- Control the appearance of tables using styles.
- Add captions to floating figures using tables.
- Create indented icon bullet lists.
- Design a two-column layout using tables.
- Format an online resume using a table.

Tables are one of the most commonly used features of HTML. They are used in Web pages for two different purposes, one being the purpose for which they were designed, to format tabular data, and the other being to create multicolumn layouts that cannot be created using other HTML elements.

USING THE EXAMPLE FILES

If you have created a working folder for storing files you create, you will find the example files for this chapter located in the **chap05** folder within your working folder. You should save any HTML files you create in this chapter in that folder.

If you have created a working disk, you should copy the chap05 folder to your working disk from the **HTML_Examples** folder that you or your instructor downloaded from this book's Internet Resource Center (IRC), or from a CD-R disc or floppy disk provided by your instructor. You should save any HTML file you create in this chapter in the chap05 folder that you have copied to your working disk.

CASE EXAMPLE: FORMATTING A WORKSHEET

When creating published reports, it is common to include worksheet tables from spreadsheet programs. You also might want to include such data in tabular format within an HTML document.

Chandra Nichols is an assistant to the president of the Parker-Ruff Corporation, a major firm with more than $80 million in quarterly sales. She is producing the company's quarterly sales report, which provides the sales results for all the company's sales representatives. Besides creating a printed sales report in Quark Express, her boss also wants her to produce a version of the sales report for posting on the Web.

action

To get started working with this example:

1. In your text editor, open **salesreport_ex.html** from the chap05 folder in your working folder or working disk.
2. Save salesreport_ex.html as **salesreport.html** in the chap05 folder.
3. In your browser, open **salesreport.html** from the chap05 folder.

FORMATTING TABULAR DATA AS PREFORMATTED TEXT

The easiest way to include tabular data in a Web page is as preformatted text. In HTML, the PRE element is used to insert preformatted text into a Web page. Before the introduction of the TABLE element, the PRE element was the only way to include tabular data in a Web page.

Chandra has created the quarterly sales report as a worksheet in Microsoft Excel (see Figure 5.1). She needs to export the worksheet data from Excel so that it can be formatted and displayed using HTML. She has opened Microsoft Excel and saved her worksheet file as a space-delimited PRN (.prn) file, which preserves all the spaces within the worksheet.

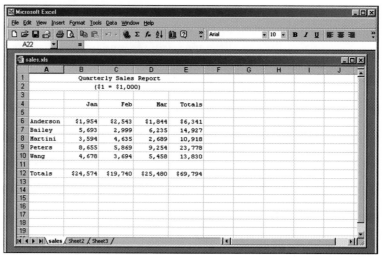

FIGURE 5.1 • *The sales report worksheet is created in Microsoft Excel.*

The PRN text file format is actually a "print" format file. It originated from Lotus 1-2-3, which provided a feature called "printing to a file." This allowed a user to save a copy of a worksheet (or range within a worksheet) as a text file with all relative spacing, as it appears in the worksheet, preserved. Then the feature was primarily used to print a worksheet on a printer connected to another computer via "sneaker net." This transportability now works just as well to import worksheet data into a Web page. In Microsoft Excel, to save your worksheet as a PRN file, select File, Save As, and then Formatted Text (Space delimited)

(*.prn) as the file type. There is nothing official or standard about the PRN file format—this is just the file extension that Lotus 1-2-3 and Excel have used when saving this type of file. Other spreadsheet programs might use different file extensions for this type of file. (For example, the Macintosh does not generally use file extensions.) An example PRN file, sales.prn, is included with the example files in the chap05 folder. This is just a regular text file that you can open directly in your text editor. To see files with file extensions other than .txt in Windows Notepad's Open dialog box, select All Files as the file type. In Excel 2000 for Windows, you cannot save a PRN file with a .txt extension—Excel will save the file as sales.txt.prn, for instance.

tip For a quick and dirty way to transfer worksheet data to your text editor, in your spreadsheet program, click and drag to highlight the data cells you want to transfer, copy the highlighted data, and then paste it into your text editor. All the spacing will not be preserved, so you will have to insert or delete spaces to line up the columns.

action Open **sales.prn** in your text editor and then paste it into salesreport.html as preformatted text:

1. Run a second copy of your text editor and open **sales.prn** from the chap05 folder in your working folder. (If you are using a text editor that lets you open multiple file windows, just open **sales.prn** in a separate window.)

2. If the data columns are out of alignment, it is because a proportional font is being used to display text in your text editor. To specify that a monospaced font is to be used to display text in Notepad for Windows, click and drag to highlight the contents of the file, and then select Edit, Set Font, and choose Fixedsys as the font. In SimpleText on the Macintosh, highlight the contents of the file, select Font, and choose Courier or Courier New as the font.

3. Insert five spaces at the start of each line to indent the text lines from the left margin. Add an additional space following each item in the month columns in each row, to further space them out horizontally.

4. Insert three additional spaces at the start of the first two lines (by keying or pasting them) to re-position them horizontally relative to the following data rows.

5. In the first data row ("Anderson…"), delete a space in front of each $ sign and then insert a space following each $ sign. The result should appear similar to the following:

```
                    Quarterly Sales Report
                        ($1 = $1,000)


                    Jan        Feb        Mar       Totals

        Anderson  $ 1,954   $ 2,543   $ 1,844   $ 6,341
        Bailey      5,693     2,999     6,235    14,927
        Martini     3,594     4,635     2,689    10,918
        Peters      8,655     5,869     9,254    23,778
        Wang        4,678     3,694     5,458    13,830

        Totals    $24,574   $19,740   $25,480   $69,794
```

6. Click and drag with the mouse cursor to highlight the contents of sales.prn, and then copy it (Ctrl+C in Windows or Command+C on the Macintosh).

7. Switch to the text editor window that contains salesreport.html. Scroll down to and highlight [**Insert worksheet file here.**], and then paste in the text that you copied in the previous step (Ctrl+V in Windows or Command+V on the Macintosh), as shown in the following example:

```
<p>At Parker-Ruff, we have one of the top firms in our field in
the country and this sales report only reinforces that. We rank
in the top tier of firms in our field, with gross annual sales
of over $250 million. We trail only three other firms, all of
which have much larger sales forces and have been competing in
the field for longer periods of time. In the all-important
category of earnings as a percentage of gross sales, we are
actually the leader, which shows that we both try harder and
can do more with less. With current sales growth at over 20
percent per quarter, we project that Parker-Ruff will be the
leader in gross sales inside of two years. The following table
shows sales figures for the quarter, broken down by individual
sales representatives and monthly sales figures:</p>
```

```
                       Quarterly Sales Report
                          ($1 = $1,000)


                      Jan        Feb        Mar       Totals

         Anderson   $ 1,954    $ 2,543    $ 1,844    $ 6,341
         Bailey       5,693      2,999      6,235     14,927
         Martini      3,594      4,635      2,689     10,918
         Peters       8,655      5,869      9,254     23,778
         Wang         4,678      3,694      5,458     13,830


         Totals     $24,574    $19,740    $25,480    $69,794
```

```
<p>We are proud of what we have accomplished. We have a
superior product line, a top-notch sales program, and a great
crew of sales representatives. Congratulations on another
outstanding quarter! We look forward to seeing even higher
results in the remaining quarters!</p>
```

8. Nest the sales report data inside a PRE element, as shown in the following (see Figure 5.2):

```
<pre>
                       Quarterly Sales Report
                          ($1 = $1,000)


                      Jan        Feb        Mar       Totals

         Anderson   $ 1,954    $ 2,543    $ 1,844    $ 6,341
         Bailey       5,693      2,999      6,235     14,927
         Martini      3,594      4,635      2,689     10,918
         Peters       8,655      5,869      9,254     23,778
         Wang         4,678      3,694      5,458     13,830


         Totals     $24,574    $19,740    $25,480    $69,794
</pre>
```

PRE element

FIGURE 5.2 • *For text nested inside a PRE element, hard returns and multiple spaces are shown, rather than ignored.*

Only inline elements can be nested inside the PRE element, such as the I, B, EM, STRONG, and FONT elements. You can even insert a hypertext link using the A element inside the PRE element. You cannot, however, insert IMG, OBJECT, BIG, SMALL, SUB, or SUP elements inside the PRE element. For instance, you could use the B element to bold the top two lines in the worksheet and the FONT element to make the Totals row red.

Use inline elements to vary the display of the data worksheet:

1. Use the B element to bold the first two lines:

```
<b>Quarterly Sales Report</b>
    <b>($1 = $1,000)</b>
```

2. Use the FONT element to apply a red color to the bottom line (see Figure 5.3):

```
    Wang          4,678     3,694     5,458     13,830
<font color="red">
    Totals      $24,574   $19,740   $25,480   $69,794
</font>
</pre>
```

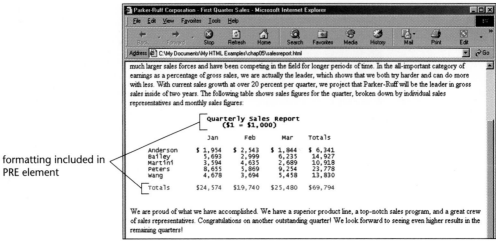

formatting included in PRE element

FIGURE 5.3 • *The B and FONT elements are used to apply bolding and a red color to the preformatted text.*

You cannot apply the B element to text included in the data columns because that alters the character width of the text. For instance, if you applied bolding to the bottom row, as well as a red color, the monthly totals would no longer line up with the text columns.

FORMATTING TABULAR DATA USING AN HTML TABLE

Another way to include tabular data in a Web page is to use the TABLE element. The TABLE element lets you format tabular data in cells that are arranged in rows and columns. The TABLE element gives you much more control over the appearance of tabular data than the PRE element.

NOTE
You also can save an Excel worksheet as an HTML file. Excel tries to duplicate the appearance and layout of your worksheet, including fonts, column widths, and so on. In doing so, however, Excel produces a large amount of both XML and HTML code, often referred to as "spaghetti code." It also includes some doubtful coding, such as setting font sizes and column widths in points, which should never be used in Web pages. By exporting your worksheet as a PRN file, you not only create a file that is many times smaller than an Excel-generated HTML file, you also maintain control over the final appearance of your worksheet because you will be doing all the formatting.

Creating the Basic Table

The TABLE element is used in conjunction with the CAPTION, TR (Table Row), TH (Table Heading), and TD (Table Data) elements. The TABLE element brackets everything that is contained within the table, the CAPTION element brackets the table caption, and the TR element brackets each table row. The TH element defines table cells that function as column and row headings, whereas the TD element defines table cells that contain data.

Use the TABLE element to format the quarterly sales report:

1. Delete the PRE, B, and FONT elements you added in the previous example, and then nest the table text inside a TABLE element (just leave any blank lines as they are, since they are only displayed when nested in a PRE element):

```
<table>
<pre>

                      <b>Quarterly Sales Report</b>
                          <b>($1 = $1,000)</b>

                    Jan        Feb        Mar      Totals

        Anderson    $ 1,954    $ 2,543    $ 1,844    $ 6,341
        Bailey        5,693      2,999      6,235     14,927
        Martini       3,594      4,635      2,689     10,918
        Peters        8,655      5,869      9,254     23,778
        Wang          4,678      3,694      5,458     13,830
<font color="red">
        Totals      $24,574    $19,740    $25,480    $69,794
</font>
</pre>
</table>
```

2. Delete the spaces at the start of the first two lines, nest the first two lines inside a CAPTION element, and insert a BR element at the end of the first line:

```
<table>
<caption>Quarterly Sales Report<br>
($1 = $1,000)</caption>
```

3. Delete the five spaces at the start of each line and nest the lines inside of TR elements to define them as table rows:

```
<tr>                Jan        Feb        Mar      Totals</tr>

<tr>Anderson    $ 1,954    $ 2,543    $ 1,844    $ 6,341</tr>
<tr>Bailey        5,693      2,999      6,235     14,927</tr>
<tr>Martini       3,594      4,635      2,689     10,918</tr>
<tr>Peters        8,655      5,869      9,254     23,778</tr>
<tr>Wang          4,678      3,694      5,458     13,830</tr>

<tr>Totals      $24,574    $19,740    $25,480    $69,794</tr>
</table>
```

4. Use TH and TD elements to tag the remaining table items, defining them as either table heading cells or table data cells (delete any more than one space between the elements; see Figure 5.4):

```
<tr><th></th> <th>Jan</th> <th>Feb</th> <th>Mar</th>
<th>Totals</th></tr>

<tr><th>Anderson</th> <td>$ 1,954</td> <td>$ 2,543</td> <td>$
1,844</td> <td>$ 6,341</td></tr>
<tr><th>Bailey</th> <td>5,693</td> <td>2,999</td> <td>6,235</td>
<td>14,927</td></tr>
```

```
<tr><th>Martini</th> <td>3,594</td> <td>4,635</td>
<td>2,689</td> <td>10,918</td></tr>
<tr><th>Peters</th> <td>8,655</td> <td>5,869</td> <td>9,254</td>
<td>23,778</td></tr>
<tr><th>Wang</th> <td>4,678</td> <td>3,694</td> <td>5,458</td>
<td>13,830</td></tr>

<tr><th>Totals</th> <td>$24,574</td> <td>$19,740</td>
<td>$25,480</td> <td>$69,794</td></tr>
</table>
```

TABLE element

FIGURE 5.4 • *The tabular data is formatted in rows and columns.*

Although the table is not very impressive at this point, you will make it look more presentable in the following sections.

Although you should first learn how to build tables from scratch, a number of utilities are available for Windows and the Macintosh that automate the creation of tables and convert comma-delimited files (which most spreadsheet and database programs should be able to save) into HTML tables. A filter is also available from Microsoft that removes Office-specific markup from documents saved in HTML format in Microsoft Excel 2000 and Word 2000. For links to these resources, see the section for this chapter at this book's IRC at **www.emcp.com/**.

Controlling the Table Border

The TABLE element's BORDER attribute draws a border around the table and its cells. Adding a border can help delineate the different parts of the table and make it easier for you to see them.

Add a one-pixel border around the table and its cells (see Figure 5.5):

```
<table border="1">
```

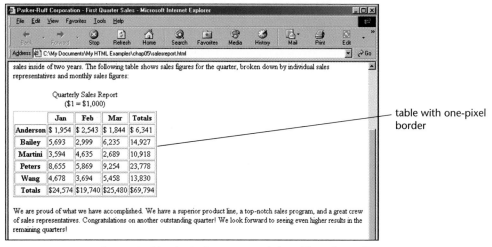

FIGURE 5.5 • *A one-pixel border is drawn around the table and its cells.*

Increasing the border size only increases the size of the border around the table, giving it a 3-D look, but the borders around the table cells remain unchanged.

Increase the size of the border to six pixels (see Figure 5.6):

```
<table border="6">
```

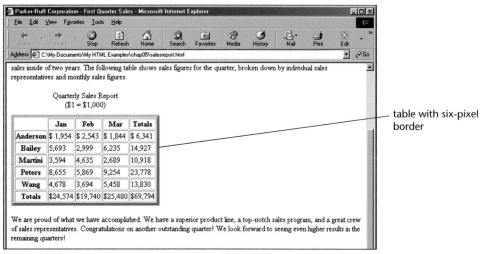

FIGURE 5.6 • *Increasing the border value only changes the style and increases the size of the outside border; the inner borders remain unchanged.*

Controlling Spacing and Padding

The TABLE element's CELLPADDING and CELLSPACING attributes let you control the amount of padding displayed inside the cells and the amount of space displayed between the cells.

Add five pixels of padding and spacing to the table (see Figure 5.7):

```
<table border="6" cellpadding="5" cellspacing="5">
```

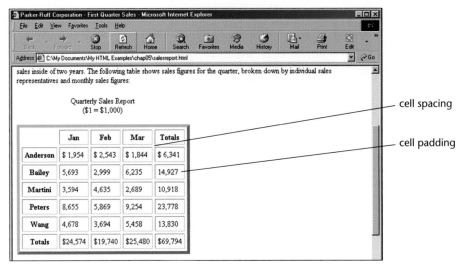

FIGURE 5.7 • *Padding and spacing are added to the table's cells.*

Some browsers, such as Internet Explorer 6 for Windows, for example, apply padding and spacing to both the table caption and the body of the table. Other browsers, including Internet Explorer 5 for the Macintosh and the Mozilla browser, however, apply padding and spacing only to the body of the table, not to the table caption. The only workaround for this is to use a style to set bottom-padding and bottom-margin values for the CAPTION element.

Use an inline style to set a bottom-padding value and a bottom-margin value for the CAPTION element, which will cause all browsers that recognize styles to add vertical spacing beneath the CAPTION element:

```
<caption style="margin-bottom: 10px; padding-bottom:
10px">Quarterly Sales Report<br>
($1 = $1,000)</caption>
```

This does not produce absolutely uniform results, but at least ensures that browsers display vertical separation between the caption and the table body. The Mozilla browser applies both the bottom-margin and bottom-padding values, inserting 20 pixels of vertical spacing between the caption and the table body. Internet Explorer 6 for Windows applies only the bottom-padding value, ignoring the bottom-margin value, while Internet Explorer 5 for the Macintosh applies only the bottom-margin value, ignoring the bottom-padding value.

According to the HTML 4 specifications, you also can use the ALIGN attribute to align a table caption above and below a table, as well as on the left and right sides of a table. Current browsers should all support using **align="bottom"** to align a table caption beneath a table, but no browsers support aligning a caption along the left or right sides of a table. Instead, **align="left"** or **align="right"** causes nested text to be left-aligned or right-aligned within the caption box. Because the ALIGN attribute for the CAPTION element is also deprecated, you should not expect the recommended usage to be implemented in future browsers.

You might notice that the empty TH cell in the first table row does not have a border drawn around it. In this case, that is the desired result, but in other situations, you might want an empty table cell to have a border. The solution is to insert an invisible non-breaking space character, ` `, in the table cell, which causes a border to be drawn around the otherwise empty cell.

Setting Table Width and Alignment

The TABLE element's WIDTH and ALIGN attributes let you control the table's width and horizontal alignment.

Set the table to a width of 85 percent and center it (see Figure 5.8):

```
<table border="6" cellpadding="5" cellspacing="5" width="85%"
align="center">
```

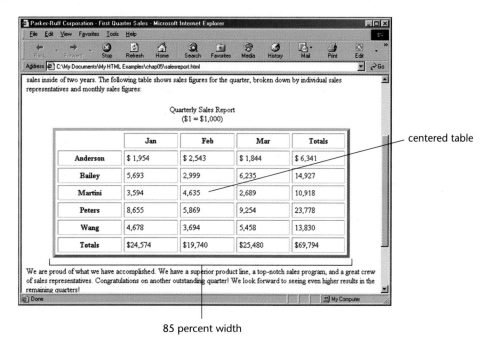

FIGURE 5.8 • *The table is centered and set to an 85 percent width.*

The WIDTH attribute can be set using a percentage or a numerical value. A percentage value sets the width of the table to a percentage of the browser window. For instance, if you set the browser width to 100 percent, the table will always be as wide as the browser window.

The ALIGN attribute sets the horizontal alignment of the table and can take a value of **center**, **left**, or **right**. Center-alignment works the same way as in the heading-level and paragraph elements. Left-alignment and right-alignment, on the other hand, work similarly to the IMG element, with the table floating to the left or right margin and following text or elements flowing around the table. As with the IMG element, the BR element's CLEAR attribute can be used to stop following text or elements from flowing around a table.

Center-aligning the table, however, causes the caption to be displayed off-center in Netscape 6. The only workaround for this problem is to use styles to center the caption. Alternatively, you can just leave the caption displaying off-center in Netscape, since it is only that one browser that does this.

Insert the following style properties to cause Netscape 6 to center the caption:

```
<caption style="margin-bottom: 10px; padding-bottom: 10px;
margin-left: auto; margin-right: auto">Quarterly Sales
Report<br>
($1 = $1,000)</caption>
```

Horizontally Aligning Cell Contents

The ALIGN attribute can be used in the TR, TH, and TD elements to horizontally align cell contents. By default, the content of TH elements is center-aligned and the content of TD elements is left-aligned, although either can inherit a horizontal-alignment setting from the TR element.

Use the ALIGN attribute to right-align the table's data rows (see Figure 5.9):

```
<tr align="right"><th>Anderson</th> <td>$ 1,954</td> <td>$
2,543</td> <td>$ 1,844</td> <td>$ 6,341</td></tr>
<tr align="right"><th>Bailey</th> <td>5,693</td> <td>2,999</td>
<td>6,235</td> <td>14,927</td></tr>
<tr align="right"><th>Martini</th> <td>3,594</td> <td>4,635</td>
<td>2,689</td> <td>10,918</td></tr>
<tr align="right"><th>Peters</th> <td>8,655</td> <td>5,869</td>
<td>9,254</td> <td>23,778</td></tr>
<tr align="right"><th>Wang</th> <td>4,678</td> <td>3,694</td>
<td>5,458</td> <td>13,830</td></tr>

<tr align="right"><th>Totals</th> <td>$24,574</td>
<td>$19,740</td> <td>$25,480</td> <td>$69,794</td></tr>
```

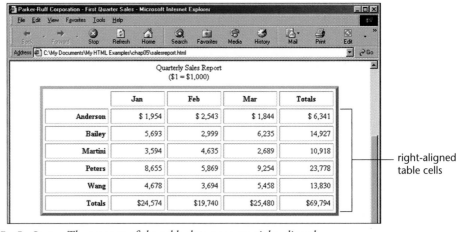

FIGURE 5.9 • *The contents of the table data rows are right-aligned.*

Setting Column Widths

The WIDTH attribute can be used in the TH or TD elements to set the width of a column. The attribute only needs to be inserted in one cell in a column to set the width of all cells within that column.

Set the width of the first cell in the second row to a width equal to 18 percent of the table width (see Figure 5.10):

```
<tr align="right"><th width="18%">Anderson</th> <td>$ 1,954</td>
<td>$ 2,543</td> <td>$ 1,844</td> <td>$ 6,341</td></tr>
```

18 percent
column width

FIGURE 5.10 • *The first column is set to a width that is 18 percent of the table width.*

You also could use the WIDTH attribute in the first cell in the first row to set the column width. It was set in the first cell in the second row, however, because you will be deleting the first cell in the first row in the next section, "Spanning Columns and Rows."

In a table without any WIDTH attributes set in the TABLE, TH, or TD elements, column widths are determined by the width of the column content. If a WIDTH attribute is only set in the TABLE element, most browsers apportion column widths equally so their sum is equal to the table width.

Because there are five columns, without any width settings, each column is equal to 20 percent of the table width. For current browsers, with a percentage width set for the table as a whole, reducing the width of one column (to 18 percent, in this case) causes the widths of the remaining columns to be increased by an equal amount necessary to keep the total width of the table at 85 percent (of the browser's viewport).

For some earlier browsers, such as Netscape Navigator 4, setting a width for only a single column causes the remaining columns to be displayed with unequal widths. To fix that, you need to set the same width value for each of the remaining columns.

Set a percentage width for each of the remaining columns to make sure that the other columns display at equal widths in Netscape Navigator 4:

```
<tr align="right"><th width="18%">Anderson</th> <td
width="20%">$ 1,954</td> <td width="20%">$ 2,543</td> <td
width="20%">$ 1,844</td> <td width="20%">$ 6,341</td></tr>
```

You might notice that percentage widths of the columns do not add up to 100 percent. That is because Netscape Navigator 4 does not include the spacing between cells when computing column width, although Internet Explorer does. The main consideration is that the sum of the percentage amounts do not exceed 100 percent.

Although not included in this example, you also can use the HEIGHT attribute to set the height of cells within a row. For instance, to increase the first row to a height of 65 pixels, you just need to insert `height="65"` in any TH (or TD) element within that row.

Spanning Columns and Rows

The COLSPAN and ROWSPAN attributes can be used in TH and TD elements to create table cells that span multiple columns or rows.

Add a row to the example table that includes a cell that spans three columns (see Figure 5.11):

```
<tr><th></th> <th colspan="3">Monthly Sales
Figures</th><th></th></tr>
<tr><th></th> <th>Jan</th> <th>Feb</th> <th>Mar</th>
<th>Totals</th></tr>
```

FIGURE 5.11 • *The "Monthly Sales Figures" cell spans three columns.*

Because the remainder of the table has five columns (five TD elements in each row), the COLSPAN value should not exceed the number of available columns. In the previous example row, two regular TH elements, each representing one column, and one spanned TH element that spans three columns, add up to five columns.

Use the ROWSPAN element to create table cells in the upper-left and upper-right corners of that table that span two rows:

1. Because they are going to be spanned, delete the first and last TH elements in the second row:

```
<tr><th></th> <th colspan="3">Monthly Sales
Figures</th><th></th></tr>
<tr><th></th> <th>Jan</th> <th>Feb</th> <th>Mar</th>
<th>Totals</th></tr>
```

2. Key **Sales Reps** as the content of the first cell and **Totals** as the content of the last cell in the first row. Use the ROWSPAN attribute in the first and last cells of that row to cause those cells to span two rows (see Figure 5.12):

```
<tr><th rowspan="2">Sales Reps</th> <th colspan="3">Monthly
Sales Figures</th><th rowspan="2">Totals</th></tr>
<tr><th>Jan</th> <th>Feb</th> <th>Mar</th></tr>
```

cells spanning two rows

FIGURE 5.12 • *The "Sales Reps" and "Totals" cells are spanning two rows.*

Vertically Aligning Cell Contents

By default, the contents of table cells are vertically aligned with the middle of the cell. The VALIGN attribute lets you vertically align the contents of table cells with the top, middle, or bottom of a cell, or along a common baseline.

Use the VALIGN attribute to vertically align the contents of the "Sales Reps" and "Totals" cells with the bottom of the cells (see Figure 5.13):

```
<tr><th rowspan="2" valign="bottom">Sales Reps</th> <th
colspan="3">Monthly Sales Figures</th><th rowspan="2"
valign="bottom">Totals</th></tr>
```

bottom-aligned cell contents

FIGURE 5.13 • *The contents of the "Sales Reps" and "Totals" cells are bottom-aligned.*

In addition to the **top**, **middle**, and **bottom** values, the VALIGN attribute also can take a **baseline** value, which causes text strings in different cells in a row to be aligned along their baselines.

USING HTML TO CONTROL TABLE APPEARANCE

There are a number of ways to control the appearance of tables by using HTML alone. For instance, you can use the FONT element to set font characteristics (sizes, colors, and faces) inside table cells and use the BGCOLOR and BACKGROUND attributes in various elements to control background colors and background images within tables.

Save the current file twice, so you can use it to experiment with setting table display characteristics using HTML attributes, and then to do the same thing using styles:

1. In your text editor, save any changes you have made to **salesreport.html** (File, Save).
2. Resave salesreport.html as **salesreport2.html** in the chap05 folder. (Later, you will return to salesreport.html and use it to experiment with using styles with tables.)
3. Open **salesreport2.html** in your browser.

Controlling Font Characteristics

You cannot bracket a table with a FONT element to change the font or color of text included in a table cell. A FONT element must be inserted inside each cell in which a change in font or color is desired.

Use the FONT and B element to change the appearance of text within the table:

1. Change the appearance of the caption and text in the first table row by using the FONT element:

```
<caption style="margin-bottom: 10px; padding-bottom: 10px;
margin-left: auto; margin-right: auto"><font size="4">Quarterly
Sales Report</font><br>
($1 = $1,000)</caption>

<tr><th rowspan="2" valign="bottom">Sales Reps</th> <th
colspan="3"><font color="blue" face="Arial, Helvetica">Monthly Sales
Figures</font></th><th rowspan="2" valign="bottom">Totals</th></tr>
<tr><th>Jan</th> <th>Feb</th> <th>Mar</th></tr>
```

2. Change the appearance of the bottom row of totals by using the FONT and B elements (see Figure 5.14):

```
<tr align="right"><th>Totals</th> <td><font color="red"
face="Arial, Helvetica"><b>$24,574</b></font></td> <td><font
color="red" face="Arial, Helvetica"><b>$19,740</b></font></td>
<td><font color="red" face="Arial,
Helvetica"><b>$25,480</b></font></td> <td><font color="red"
face="Arial, Helvetica"><b>$69,794</b></font></td></tr>
```

FONT elements

FIGURE 5.14 • *The font characteristics of the caption, top row, and bottom row are changed.*

Displaying a Background Color behind the Table

The BGCOLOR attribute lets you control the background color of the table, rows, or cells. It works exactly the same way as in the BODY element. You insert the BGCOLOR attribute in the TABLE element to display a background color behind the whole table.

Use the BGCOLOR attribute to assign a light blue color (one of the Web-safe colors) to the table background (see Figure 5.15):

```
<table border="6" cellpadding="5" cellspacing="5" width="85%"
align="center" bgcolor="#ccffff">
```

FIGURE 5.15 • *The table background is now light blue.*

Although current browsers all handle this as shown in Figure 5.15, earlier browsers vary in how they display a background color set for the whole table. Internet Explorer 4, for instance, displays the background color behind the caption, as well. Netscape Navigator 4 displays the background color only behind the table cells, but not behind the spacing between the cells (see Figure 5.16).

FIGURE 5.16 • *Netscape Navigator 4 displays a background color set for the whole table only behind the table cells, but not behind the spacing between the cells.*

The only workaround for this is to turn off the spacing between the cells, while increasing the padding to maintain the same table dimensions.

Eliminate the spacing between the table's cells and increase the padding within the table's cells to eight pixels (see Figure 5.17):

```
<table border="6" cellpadding="8" cellspacing="0" width="85%"
align="center" bgcolor="#ccffff">
```

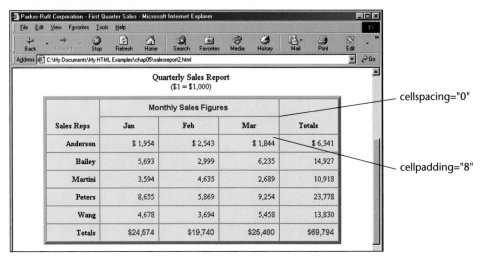

FIGURE 5.17 • *The spacing between cells is eliminated and the padding within the cells in increased to eight pixels.*

The eight-pixel padding amount roughly equals the previous padding and spacing amount, in that the spacing between cells was shared.

The table now displays the same in Netscape Navigator 4 as it does in current browsers. To cater to an older browser that is only being used by a small percentage of users, another alternative is to use the Web Standard Project's Invisible Object Method, which was demonstrated in Chapter 3, *Working with Fonts, Colors, and Backgrounds* (in the "Compatibility Issues with Font Sizes Using Ems" section). This method alerts users of Netscape Navigator 4 that they can access your page using that browser, but that your page will look better if viewed using a browser that supports current Web standards.

Displaying Background Colors behind Rows and Cells

You insert the BGCOLOR attribute in the TR, TH, or TD elements to display background colors behind table rows or table cells.

Use different background colors to highlight the different parts of the table:
1. Copy and then paste a second copy of the table below the current table. In the following steps, you will be working in the second table (the one you pasted in).
2. Set a light green background color behind the first two rows:

```
<tr bgcolor="#ccffcc"><th rowspan="2" valign="bottom">Sales
Reps</th> <th colspan="3"><font color="blue" face="Arial,
Helvetica">Monthly Sales Figures</font></th><th rowspan="2"
valign="bottom">Totals</th></tr>
<tr bgcolor="#ccffcc"><th>Jan</th> <th>Feb</th> <th>Mar</th></tr>
```

3. Set a light yellow color behind the row heading cells that contain the last names of the sales reps:

```
<tr align="right"><th bgcolor="#ffffcc" width="18%">Anderson</th>
<td width="20%">$ 1,954</td> <td width="20%">$ 2,543</td> <td
width="20%">$ 1,844</td> <td width="20%">$ 6,341</td></tr>
<tr align="right"><th bgcolor="#ffffcc">Bailey</th> <td>5,693</td>
<td>2,999</td> <td>6,235</td> <td>14,927</td></tr>
<tr align="right"><th bgcolor="#ffffcc">Martini</th>
<td>3,594</td> <td>4,635</td> <td>2,689</td> <td>10,918</td></tr>
<tr align="right"><th bgcolor="#ffffcc">Peters</th> <td>8,655</td>
<td>5,869</td> <td>9,254</td> <td>23,778</td></tr>
<tr align="right"><th bgcolor="#ffffcc">Wang</th> <td>4,678</td>
<td>3,694</td> <td>5,458</td> <td>13,830</td></tr>
```

4. Set a light pink background color behind the bottom row in the table (see Figure 5.18):

```
<tr bgcolor="#ffcccc" align="right"><th>Totals</th> <td><font
color="red" face="Arial, Helvetica"><b>$24,574</b></font></td>
<td><font color="red" face="Arial,
Helvetica"><b>$19,740</b></font></td> <td><font color="red"
face="Arial, Helvetica"><b>$25,480</b></font></td> <td><font
color="red" face="Arial,
Helvetica"><b>$69,794</b></font></td></tr>
</table>
```

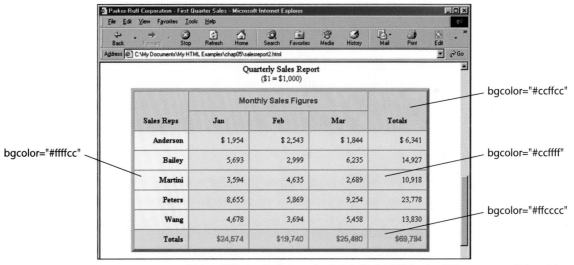

FIGURE 5.18 • *Using different background colors helps highlight the different parts of the table.*

Displaying Background Images in Tables

The BACKGROUND attribute can be used to display background images in tables. You should be aware, however, that the BACKGROUND attribute is not part of the HTML 4 standard, although all current browsers and many earlier browsers support it. An example background image, back_clouds.jpg, is included with this chapter's example files in the chap05 folder.

With current browsers, any background colors set in the TR, TH, or TD elements take precedence over a background image set in the TABLE element. Therefore, if you want to display a background image behind the whole table, you need to delete any background colors (other than transparent) that are set in the TR, TH, or TD elements.

Go back to the first table (the one without the BGCOLOR attributes in the rows and cells) and set a background image for the table (see Figure 5.19):

```
<table border="6" cellpadding="8" cellspacing="0" width="85%"
align="center" bgcolor="#ccffff" background="back_clouds.jpg">
```

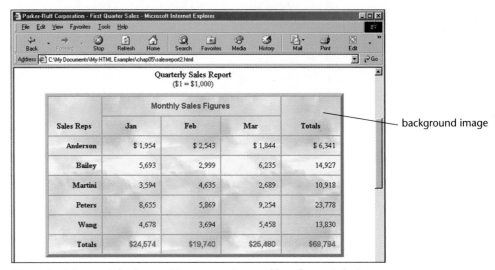

FIGURE 5.19 • *A background image can give a table a dramatic look.*

Because the BACKGROUND attribute is not a standard attribute for the TABLE element, you should expect some variability in how it displays in browsers. Current browsers all display it the same, as shown in Figure 5.19, but one earlier browser, Netscape Navigator 4, displays the background image individually behind each table cell, rather than tiling it behind the whole table. As with a background color, a background image in Netscape 4 is only displayed behind the table cells, but not behind the spacing between the cells.

Whenever displaying a background image in a table, you also should specify a background color that resembles the color of your background image. That way, if users are surfing with the display of images turned off, they will still see your background color. This is especially important when displaying light text against a dark background image because with the display of images turned off, a visitor could end up seeing (or not seeing) white text against a white background, for instance.

USING STYLES TO CONTROL TABLE APPEARANCE

The use of styles provides much more control over the appearance of tables than can be achieved through HTML alone. Styles are also much more efficient than using the FONT element to control table appearance. You have to insert the FONT element inside of each and every table cell where you want it to have effect, but a single entry in a style sheet can change the formatting of every table cell.

The use of styles to format tables also provides for better accessibility, in that they separate the presentation of the table from its content and organization. A nonvisual browser, for instance, can easily ignore any presentation features defined by styles to concentrate on conveying the table's content and organization.

A number of table elements were introduced as part of HTML 4, which require the use of styles to provide visual formatting. By themselves, the TBODY, THEAD, TFOOT, COL, and COLGROUP elements have no visual formatting, but can be used in conjunction with styles to format row groups and column groups in tables.

The disadvantage of using styles to format tables is that many earlier browsers either do not understand styles or poorly implement them. Even among current browsers, the style features supported and how some style features are implemented varies.

NOTE

The purpose of this section is to demonstrate how certain HTML 4 features and elements, in conjunction with styles, can be used to provide more control over the appearance of tables. This section is not intended to provide an in-depth understanding of the use of styles in general. For links to resources that cover the use of styles in more depth, see Chapter 3's section at the IRC for this book at **www.emcp.com/**.

NOTE

Because of variability in how different browsers implement the use of styles to control the display of tables, you should use Internet Explorer 5.5 or 6 for Windows, Internet Explorer 5 for the Macintosh, Mozilla 1.0, or any higher version of these browsers, to do the following example. You can use Netscape 6 and Opera 6 browsers to do the example, but the result you see in your browser might not exactly match what is shown in the figures.

action

Return to the copy of your example file that you saved earlier to do the following style examples:

1. Reopen **salesreport.html** in your text editor from the chap05 folder.
2. Save salesreport.html as **salesreport3.html** in the chap05 folder and open it in your browser.

Alerting Netscape 4 Users

Netscape Navigator 4 has poor support for styles. When using styles to control the appearance of tables, you need to be aware that the results might not look perfect in Netscape 4. One option to deal with users of Netscape 4 is to use the Web Standards Project's Invisible Object Method, which was covered in Chapter 3, *Working with Fonts, Colors, and Backgrounds.*

action

Set up the page to display an object that will be hidden from users of current browsers, but will alert users of Netscape 4 and other earlier browsers that they need to upgrade their browsers:

```
<style type="text/css">
.oops { display: none; }
</style>
</head>
<body>
<iframe class="oops">
<center><font size="5" color="red">This site will look much
better in a browser that supports
```

```
<a href="http://www.webstandards.org/upgrade/" title="Download a
browser that complies with Web standards."> Web
standards</a>,<br>but it is accessible to any browser or Internet
device.</font>
</center>
<hr>
</iframe>

<h1 align="center">Parker-Ruff Corporation Quarterly Sales</h1>
<h2 align="center">First Quarter Sales</h2>
```

Changing Fonts and Colors

You can use styles to easily change fonts, colors, and backgrounds used in a table.

Create a style sheet to transform the appearance of the table:

1. Create a style sheet that assigns fonts and colors to the table's contents (see Figure 5.20):

```
<title>Parker-Ruff Corporation - First Quarter Sales</title>
<style type="text/css">
.oops { display: none; }
table { color: #330000; background: #ffffcc; }
caption { color: black; background: transparent; }
th { font-family: Arial, Helvetica, sans-serif; }
</style>
</head>
```

background and foreground colors set by styles

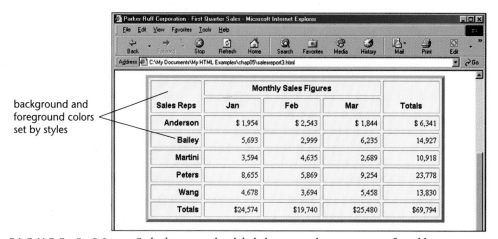

FIGURE 5.20 • *Styles let you make global changes to the appearance of a table.*

2. Use a style to add a background image to the table (see Figure 5.21):

```
<style type="text/css">
table { color: #330000; background: #ffffcc
url("back_marblebeige.jpg"); }
```

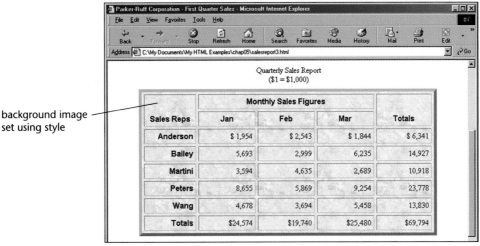

background image set using style

FIGURE 5.21 • *A background image gives a table a whole new look.*

Controlling the Appearance of Row Groups

The TBODY, THEAD, and TFOOT elements are HTML 4 elements that let you set different display characteristics for groups of rows within a table. By themselves, these elements have no visual formatting; you must use these elements in conjunction with styles to produce any visual result.

Use the TBODY, THEAD, and TFOOT elements to create separate display characteristics for the body, head, and foot of the table:

1. Add THEAD, TBODY, and TFOOT elements to the table to define table head, body, and foot groups of rows:

```
<table border="6" cellpadding="5" cellspacing="5" width="85%"
align="center">
<caption style="margin-bottom: 10px; padding-bottom: 10px; margin-
left: auto; margin-right: auto">Quarterly Sales Report<br>
($1 = $1,000)</caption>
<thead>
<tr><th rowspan="2" valign="bottom">Sales Reps</th> <th
colspan="3">Monthly Sales Figures</th><th rowspan="2"
valign="bottom">Totals</th></tr>
<tr><th>Jan</th> <th>Feb</th> <th>Mar</th></tr>
</thead>
<tbody>
<tr align="right"><th width="18%">Anderson</th> <td width="20%">$
1,954</td> <td width="20%">$ 2,543</td> <td width="20%">$
1,844</td> <td width="20%">$ 6,341</td></tr>
<tr align="right"><th>Bailey</th> <td>5,693</td> <td>2,999</td>
<td>6,235</td> <td>14,927</td></tr>
<tr align="right"><th>Martini</th> <td>3,594</td> <td>4,635</td>
<td>2,689</td> <td>10,918</td></tr>
<tr align="right"><th>Peters</th> <td>8,655</td> <td>5,869</td>
<td>9,254</td> <td>23,778</td></tr>
<tr align="right"><th>Wang</th> <td>4,678</td> <td>3,694</td>
<td>5,458</td> <td>13,830</td></tr>
<tr align="right"><th>Totals</th> <td>$24,574</b></td>
<td>$19,740</b></td> <td>$25,480</b></td>
<td>$69,794</b></td></tr>
</tbody>
```

```
<tfoot>
<tr><td colspan="5">All sales amounts are stated at $1 per
$1,000.</td></tr>
</tfoot>
</table>
```

2. Create styles to control the display of the table's head, body, and foot sections (see Figure 5.22):

```
th { font-family: Arial, Helvetica, sans-serif; }
thead { color: #330000; background: #ffff99
url("back_sandstone.jpg"); }
tbody { color: #990000; background: transparent; }
tfoot { color: #330000; background: #ffff99
url("back_goldrock.jpg"); font-weight: bold; text-align: center; }
</style>
```

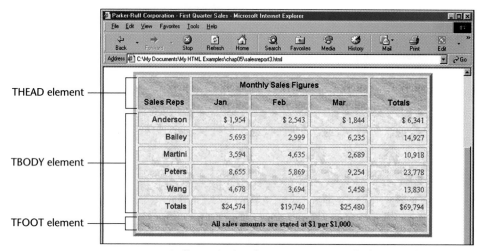

FIGURE 5.22 • *Different display characteristics are applied to the table's head, body, and foot.*

The TBODY element can be optionally left out. Any table cells not included in a THEAD or TFOOT element will be formatted using style properties assigned to the TBODY element in the style sheet.

You should be aware, however, that current browsers vary in how they display background properties set for these row group elements. Both Internet Explorer 6 for Windows and Mozilla 1 display background properties only behind the table cells in a row group, whereas Internet Explorer 5 for the Macintosh and Netscape 6 display background properties behind both the table cells and the spacing between table cells within a row group. The only way to get all these browsers to display a relatively similar result when applying background properties to row groups is to turn off the spacing between the table's cells as shown in the following section.

Turning Off Spacing between Cells

Earlier, in the salesreport2.html example, you eliminated the spacing between table cells by setting a **cellspacing="0"** attribute in the TABLE element, while increasing the padding amount within the cells by setting a **cellpadding="8"** attribute. The same result can be achieved using styles and without using the CELLSPACING or CELL-PADDING attributes.

Use styles to eliminate the spacing between the table cells and set a black one-pixel border between the cells:

1. Remove the cell padding and cell spacing currently set in the TABLE element:

```
<table border="6" cellpadding="5" cellspacing="5" width="85%"
align="center">
```

2. Collapse the spacing between the table cells:

```
table { border-collapse: collapse; border-spacing: 0; color:
#330000; background: #ffffcc url("back_marblebeige.jpg"); }
caption { color: black; background: transparent; }
```

3. For the TH and TD elements, set eight pixels of padding and set a one-pixel black border to be drawn around the table cells (see Figure 5.23):

```
th { font-family: Arial, Helvetica, sans-serif; }
th, td { padding: 8px; border: 1px solid black; }
```

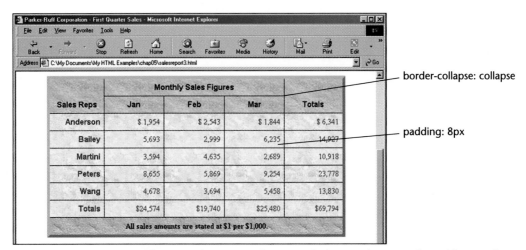

FIGURE 5.23 • *Styles are used to remove the spacing between and increase the padding inside the table cells.*

Netscape 6 does not recognize the **border-collapse: collapse** property (which is a CSS2 property), but does collapse the borders if a **border-spacing: 0** property is included.

The default setting for tables is **border-collapse: separate**. As long as that setting is active, each cell has its own separate border. To set a specific amount of spacing around the border of a cell, set the border-spacing property to the amount of spacing you want between cell borders (**border-spacing: 6px**, for instance).

Internet Explorer 5 for the Macintosh does not recognize the border-spacing property. To make sure that spacing set between cell borders is also displayed in that browser, include a corresponding CELLSPACING attribute in the TABLE element.

Controlling the Appearance of Columns

You also can control the appearance of columns using styles. You can do this by assigning table cells to a class, to which style properties can be applied, or by setting a contextual style (applying style properties to elements only within certain contexts, such as to TH elements located inside a TBODY element).

Assign separate display characteristics to the "Sales Reps" column and the "Totals" column:

1. Assign the "Totals" column to a class, so a style can be applied to it:

```
<tr align="right"><th width="18%">Anderson</th> <td
width="20%">$ 1,954</td> <td width="20%">$ 2,543</td> <td
width="20%">$ 1,844</td> <td class="totalcol" width="20%">$
6,341</td></tr>
<tr align="right"><th>Bailey</th> <td>5,693</td> <td>2,999</td>
<td>6,235</td> <td class="totalcol">14,927</td></tr>
<tr align="right"><th>Martini</th> <td>3,594</td> <td>4,635</td>
<td>2,689</td> <td class="totalcol">10,918</td></tr>
<tr align="right"><th>Peters</th> <td>8,655</td> <td>5,869</td>
<td>9,254</td> <td class="totalcol">23,778</td></tr>
<tr align="right"><th>Wang</th> <td>4,678</td> <td>3,694</td>
<td>5,458</td> <td class="totalcol">13,830</td></tr>

<tr align="right"><th>Totals</th> <td>$24,574</td>
<td>$19,740</td> <td>$25,480</td> <td
class="totalcol">$69,794</td></tr>
```

2. Define styles that apply formatting to the "Sales Reps" and "Totals" columns (see Figure 5.24):

```
tbody th { color: #ffffcc; background: #330066
url("back_blueslate.jpg"); }
tbody td.totalcol { font-weight: bold; color: navy; background:
#990000 url("back_paper.jpg"); }
</style>
```

column formatted using contextual style: tbody th...

column formatted using class selector: class="totalcol"

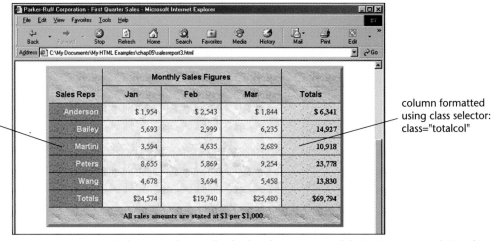

FIGURE 5.24 • *Styles are used to set the display characteristics of the "Sales Reps" and "Totals" columns.*

Two additional HTML elements, the COLGROUP and COL elements, can be used in conjunction with styles to control the appearance of column groups and individual columns. However, because support for these elements among current browsers is either inconsistent or nonexistent, you should stick to specifying column formatting using the methods shown in the previous example.

An example file, salesreport_colgroups.html, that demonstrates using the COLGROUP and COL elements is included with the other example files for this chapter. To see how these elements are used in an HTML file, open the example file in your text editor. If you are using Internet Explorer 6 for Windows or Netscape 6, or higher versions of these browsers, you can open and view the example file in your browser, although the results will vary depending on the browser you use. Neither Mozilla 1 nor Opera 6 support these elements, however.

SETTING DISPLAY CHARACTERISTICS OF SPECIFIC ROWS AND CELLS You also can apply display characteristics to specific rows and cells within the table.

Include specific cells or rows within classes and then create styles that apply display characteristics to those classes:

1. If **salesreport3.html** is not currently open in your text editor and browser, reopen it.
2. Assign classes to the first row's second TH element, to the second row's TR element, and to the next to last row's TR element:

```
<thead>
<tr class="toprow"><th rowspan="2" valign="bottom">Sales Reps</th>
<th colspan="3">Monthly Sales Figures</th><th rowspan="2"
valign="bottom">Totals</th></tr>
<tr class="months"><th>Jan</th> <th>Feb</th> <th>Mar</th></tr>
</thead>

[...]

<tr class="totalrow" align="right"><th>Totals</th>
<td>$24,574</b></td> <td>$19,740</b></td> <td>$25,480</b></td> <td
class="totalcol">$69,794</b></td></tr>
</tbody>
```

3. Create three styles that set display characteristics for the three classes:

```
.toprow { color: #003399; background: transparent
url("back_marblegreen.jpg"); }
.months th { font-weight: bold; color: #003300; background:
#336600 url("back_lightbrown.jpg"); }
.totalrow td { font-weight: bold; color: #ffcc33; background:
#990000 url("back_redstone.jpg"); }
</style>
```

4. Create an additional style that sets a separate format for the grand total cell (see Figure 5.25):

```
tr.totalrow td.totalcol { font-family: Arial, Geneva, Helvetica,
sans-serif; font-size: 1.1em; font-weight: bold; color: #ccff99;
background: #990000 url("back_bluestone2.jpg"); }
</style>
```

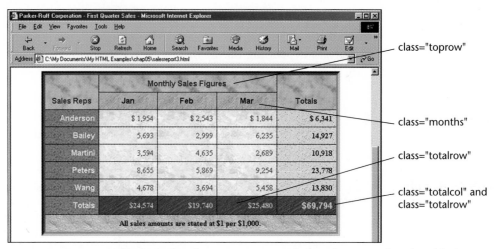

class="toprow"

class="months"

class="totalrow"

class="totalcol" and
class="totalrow"

FIGURE 5.25 • *Different display characteristics are applied to elements within the table that are assigned to specific classes.*

ADDING BORDERS TO THE TABLE Using styles, you can add a variety of different styles of borders to HTML elements.

Add borders above the first row in the table body, above the "Totals" row, and around the table:

1. Assign a class to the first row in the table body section:

```
<tbody>
<tr class="firstrow" align="right"><th width="18%">Anderson</th>
<td width="20%">$ 1,954</td> <td width="20%">$ 2,543</td> <td
width="20%">$ 1,844</td> <td class="totalcol" width="20%">$
6,341</td></tr>
```

2. Create the styles that draw the borders (see Figure 5.26):

```
.firstrow th, .firstrow td { border-top: #33ccff 6px ridge; }
.totalrow th, .totalrow td { border-top: #33cc99 6px ridge; }
</style>
```

3. Set a style to draw a border around the table (see Figure 5.26):

```
table { border: 8px #ffcc00 inset; border-collapse: collapse;
border-spacing: 0; color: #330000; background: #ffffcc
url("back_marblebeige.jpg"); }
```

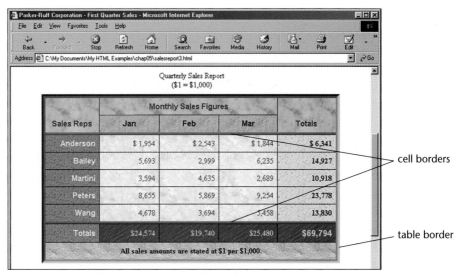

cell borders

table border

FIGURE 5.26 • *Borders are drawn above the "Anderson" and "Totals" rows in the table, and around the table as a whole.*

You can apply a variety of border styles to a table (or any other block element). The borderstyles.html example file is included with this chapter's example files, which you can open in your browser (see Figure 5.27).

FIGURE 5.27 • *A variety of border types can be applied to tables and other block elements.*

Be aware, however, that Figure 5.27 shows the interpretation of one browser (Internet Explorer 6 for Windows) of how the different border styles should be displayed. Other browsers might display many of these border styles differently, as they are free to do, because the W3C only specifies the names for these border styles, but not how they should be displayed.

CASE EXAMPLE: CREATING FLOATING FIGURE CAPTIONS

In the previous chapter, you created a report on the history of the Mercury space program that used floating images to illustrate the narrative. By using tables, you also can include figure captions with the images.

Shirley Johnson has decided that creating figure captions for the images in her report on the Mercury space program will make them more informative.

Prepare to get started with this example by following these steps:

1. In your text editor, open **mercuryfigs_ex.html** from the chap05 folder in your working folder or working disk.
2. Save mercuryfigs_ex.html as **mercuryfigs.html** in the chap05 folder.
3. Run your browser and open **mercuryfigs.html** from the chap05 folder.

With a non-floating image, you just have to insert a BR element immediately following the IMG element to display following text as a caption beneath the image. That will not work, however, if the image is floating on the left or right margin because text following a BR element would still flow around, rather than being displayed below, the image.

To display a text caption below a floating image, you need to unfloat the image and then insert it inside a floating table. In the floating table, the image is displayed in the top row, while the caption is displayed in the bottom row.

Add a caption to the first floating image:

1. Delete the ALIGN and HSPACE attributes from the IMG element and nest the image inside of a left-aligned (or floating) table:

```
<p><table align="left"><tr><td>
<img src="atlas_mercury.jpg" align="left" hspace="10" alt="Atlas
rocket with Mercury spacecraft" width="200" height="272">
</td></tr>
</table>
The Atlas rocket launch vehicle, which lifted John Glenn into
orbit, began being used following World War II.
```

2. Set the width of the table to 215 pixels, add a second row to the table that contains a caption for the figure, and add a figure reference to the page's text (see Figure 5.28):

```
<p><table align="left" width="215"><tr><td>
<img src="atlas_mercury.jpg" alt="Atlas rocket with Mercury
spacecraft" width="200" height="272">
</td></tr>
<tr><td><font color="aqua"><small>Figure 1. <i>Atlas rocket with
Mercury spacecraft<i></small></font></td></tr>
</table>
The Atlas rocket launch vehicle (see Figure 1), which lifted
John Glenn into orbit, began being used following World War II.
```

horizontal spacing

floating image

flowing text

figure caption

FIGURE 5.28 • *Adding captions to floating images can make them more informative.*

The addition of the `width="215"` attribute to the TABLE element is important. If not included, the width of the caption text determines the width of the table, which could exceed the width of the image. The value of **215** is derived from the width of the image (200 pixels) and the desired amount of horizontal spacing (15 pixels) that separates the table's content from the text flowing around its right side.

Setting the table's width to be greater than the width of its content only works for adding horizontal spacing to the right of a left-aligned table, since it relies on the default left-alignment of the table's content. To add horizontal spacing only to the left side of a right-aligned table, one option is to insert a new table column (`<td rowspan="2" width="15">`, for instance) to the left of the current table column:

```
<p><table align="right" width="215"><tr><td rowspan="2"
width="15"></td><td>
```

Another option is to use a style to set a left or right margin for the table. For instance, the following sets a 5-pixel right margin for a left-aligned table:

```
<p>table align="left" width="200" style="margin-right:
5px"><tr><td>
```

practice Using the figure caption you just created for Figure 1 as a guide, create figure captions (Figure 2, Figure 3, and so on) for the remaining images in the report. Use the content of the ALT attribute as the caption text (or write your own caption). For left-aligned images, add horizontal spacing to the right side of the table by setting the width of the table to be greater than the width of the image it contains. For right-aligned images, add horizontal spacing to the left side of the table by inserting an additional column (in the form of a row-spanned cell) at the start (left side) of the table. In either case, set the table width to be equal to the width of the image, plus the width of any horizontal spacing you want to add to the right or left side of the table. Insert figure references that point to the figures at appropriate places within the text.

CASE EXAMPLE: CREATING INDENTED ICON LINK LISTS

In previous chapters, you created bulleted link lists simply by using the UL and LI elements. You will notice on the Web, however, many instances in which bulleted lists are created using graphical bullet icons.

While surfing the Web, Johnny Watson has noticed that many sites make use of colorful graphical bullet icons when presenting lists. He decided that he wants to do the same in his personal page to add more color and visual appeal. Johnny removed the DIV, UL, and LI elements he used previously, nested his list of link items in a P element, added descriptions to the link list items in his page, and added BR elements where he wants line breaks.

Creating an Icon Link List Using a Table

A better, although somewhat more complicated, way to create an indented icon link list is to use a table.

Prepare to work with this example by following these steps:
1. Open **watson4_ex.html** in your text editor.
2. Save watson4_ex.html as **watson4.html** in the chap05 folder.
3. Open **watson4.html** in your browser from the chap05 folder.

You create an indented icon link list using a table by creating a two-column table, with the bullet icon inserted in the cells of the first column and the link text and descriptions inserted in the second column. An example icon bullet image, goldball.gif, is included with this chapter's example files.

Use a table to create an indented icon line list:
1. Create a two-column table, with the bullet icons nested in the first column and the links and link descriptions nested in the second column:

```
<table>
<tr valign="top"><td width="30">
<img src="goldball.gif" height="15" vspace="3" width="15" alt="*">
</td><td>
<a href="mybio.html">My biography</a> - Read about where I'm
from, my family history, my interests and involvements, the
accomplishments I'm most proud of, and my future plans.
</td></tr>
<tr valign="top"><td>
<p><img src="goldball.gif" height="15" vspace="3" width="15"
alt="*">
</td><td>
<a href="myresume.html">My resume</a> - Look here for details
about my studies, work experience, community involvements, and
awards and honors.
</td></tr>
<tr valign="top"><td>
<img src="goldball.gif" height="15" vspace="3" width="15" alt="*">
</td><td>
```

```
<a href="http://www.usatoday.com/sports/scores.htm">Get the latest
sports scores</a> - Learn how your favorite local sports team did
the night before and read other sports stories from around the
nation.
</td></tr>
<tr valign="top"><td>
<img src="goldball.gif" height="15" vspace="3" width="15" alt="*">
</td><td>
<a href="http://www.about-house-plants.com/">Get indoor gardening
tips and advice</a> - Learn how to deal with pests and other
problems that plague your indoor plants.
</td></tr>
<tr valign="top"><td>
<img src="goldball.gif" height="15" vspace="3" width="15" alt="*">
</td><td>
<a href="http://www.blank.com/jshmoe/">My friend Joe's site</a> -
Joe is into trading baseball and football cards. He's got a great
collection. Check it out!
</td></tr>
<tr valign="top"><td>
<img src="goldball.gif" height="15" vspace="3" width="15" alt="*">
</td><td>
<a href="http://www.wherever.com/jdoe/homepage.html">My friend
Jane's site</a> - Jane is a very talented photographer. She's put
up a gallery of photos from her recent trip to Olympic National
Park in Washington state. Don't miss it!<br><br>
</td></tr>
</table>
```

2. Reduce the width of the table and center it on the page:

```
<table width="85%" align="center">
```

3. Edit the style sheet so that text in the TD element will display at the same size as the paragraph text (see Figure 5.29):

```
p, td, blockquote, li, address { font-size: 1.1em; }
```

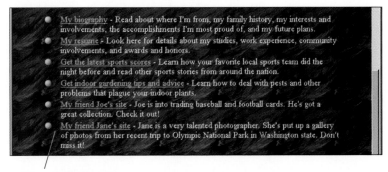

indent created using
table columns

FIGURE 5.29 • *It is easy to indent and center an icon link list created using a two-column table.*

The primary disadvantage of using tables to create indented icon link lists is that they tend to be somewhat labor-intensive to create and maintain, especially if you have a lot of list items. They also are less efficient and consume more bytes than the other methods for creating an indented icon link list.

Creating an Icon Link List Using Styles

You also can create indented icon link lists using styles.

Prepare to work with this example by following these steps:
1. Re-open **watson4_ex.html** in your text editor.
2. Save watson4_ex.html as **watson5.html** in the chap05 folder.
3. Open **watson5.html** in your browser from the chap05 folder.

You use the `list-style-image` style property to specify a bullet image to be displayed in an unordered list. This example uses another icon bullet image, blueball.gif, which is included with this chapter's example files.

Create an indented icon link list using a style:
1. Use the UL and LI elements to set up the list of links and descriptions as an unordered list:

```
<ul>
<li><a href="mybio.html">My biography</a> - Read about where I'm
from, my family history, my interests and involvements, the
accomplishments I'm most proud of, and my future plans.
<li><a href="myresume.html">My resume</a> - Look here for
details about my studies, work experience, community
involvements, and awards and honors.
<li><a href="http://www.usatoday.com/sports/scores.htm">Get the
latest sports scores</a> - Learn how your favorite local sports
team did the night before and read other sports stories from
around the nation.
<li><a href="http://www.about-house-plants.com/">Get indoor
gardening tips and advice</a> - Learn how to deal with pests
and other problems that plague your indoor plants.
<li><a href="http://www.blank.com/jshmoe/">My friend Joe's
site</a> - Joe is into trading baseball and football cards. He's
got a great collection. Check it out!
<li><a href="http://www.wherever.com/jdoe/homepage.html">My
friend Jane's site</a> - Jane is a very talented photographer.
She's put up a gallery of photos from her recent trip to
Olympic National Park in Washington state. Don't miss it!
</ul>
```

2. Edit the style sheet to assign a bullet icon image to be displayed in the list and add additional formatting (see Figure 5.30):

```
ul { list-style-image: url(blueball.gif); }
ul li { padding-left: 15px; margin-left: 15px; margin-right:
15px; padding-right: 15px; }
</style>
```

bullet icon created using a style

FIGURE 5.30 • *You also can create an indented icon link list using styles.*

The primary disadvantage of using styles to create indented icon link lists is that many earlier browsers either do not support styles or do not support the **list-style-image** style property. Such browsers, however, will simply display the list as a regular unordered list, so using this feature does degrade gracefully in earlier browsers. There is also no immediate way to adjust the vertical positioning of the bullet icon; to adjust the bullet icon down a couple of pixels, you need to add a couple of pixels at the top of the image in your image editor. An advantage of using styles to create indented icon link lists is they are much easier to create and maintain and are much more efficient than using either left-aligned bullet icons or a table.

Creating an Icon Link List Using Floating Bullet Icons

A third way to create an indented icon link list is to use floating bullet icons.

Prepare to work with this example by following these steps:
1. Open **watson4_ex.html** in your text editor.
2. Save watson4_ex.html as **watson6.html** in the chap05 folder.
3. Open **watson6.html** in your browser from the chap05 folder.

This method uses the IMG element's ALIGN attribute in conjunction with the HSPACE and VSPACE attributes to create an indented icon link list. An example icon bullet image, redball.gif, is included with this chapter's example files.

Create an indented icon link list using the IMG element's ALIGN attribute (see Figure 5.31):

```
<p><img src="redball.gif" align="left" vspace="4" hspace="15"
height="15" width="15" alt="*"><a href="mybio.html">My
biography</a> - Read about where I'm from, my family history, my
interests and involvements, the accomplishments I'm most proud
of, and my future plans.<br clear="left">
<img src="redball.gif" align="left" vspace="4" hspace="15"
height="15" width="15" alt="*"><a href="myresume.html">My
resume</a> - Look here for details about my studies, work
experience, community involvements, and awards and honors.<br
clear="left">
<img src="redball.gif" align="left" vspace="4" hspace="15"
height="15" width="15" alt="*"><a
href="http://www.usatoday.com/sports/scores.htm">Get the latest
sports scores</a> - Learn how your favorite local sports team did
the night before and read other sports stories from around the
nation.<br clear="left">
<img src="redball.gif" align="left" vspace="4" hspace="15"
height="15" width="15" alt="*"><a href="http://www.about-house-
plants.com/">Get indoor gardening tips and advice</a> - Learn how
to deal with pests and other problems that plague your indoor
plants.<br clear="left">
<img src="redball.gif" align="left" vspace="4" hspace="15"
height="15" width="15" alt="*"><a
href="http://www.blank.com/jshmoe/">My friend Joe's site</a> - Joe
is into trading baseball and football cards. He's got a great
collection. Check it out!<br clear="left">
```

```
<img src="redball.gif" align="left" vspace="4" hspace="15"
height="15" width="15" alt="*"><a
href="http://www.wherever.com/jdoe/homepage.html">My friend Jane's
site</a> - Jane is a very talented photographer. She's put up a
gallery of photos from her recent trip to Olympic National Park
in Washington state. Don't miss it!<br clear="left"></p>
```

indent created using
floating bullet icons

> Get indoor gardening tips and advice - Learn how to deal with pests and other problems that
> plague your indoor plants.
> My friend Joe's site - Joe is into trading baseball and football cards. He's got a great collection.
> Check it out!
> My friend Jane's site - Jane is a very talented photographer. She's put up a gallery of photos from
> her recent trip to Olympic National Park in Washington state. Don't miss it!

FIGURE 5.31 • *An indented icon link list can be created using floating bullet icons.*

In this example, the ALIGN attribute floats the bullet icon to the left margin, the
HSPACE attribute sets horizontal spacing on both sides of the bullet icon, and the
VSPACE attribute sets vertical spacing above and below the bullet icon. The VSPACE
attribute causes the indent by extending the height of the bullet icon beyond the height
of the text line, which causes the second text line to be indented, rather than wrap to
the left margin.

The primary advantage of using this method is that it is simpler to implement than using
a table. There are some disadvantages to creating an icon bullet list using this method,
however. You are limited to only two indented lines of text; a third line of text wraps to the
left margin. Remember that a two-line description in a maximized browser window running
at 800 × 600-pixel resolution might be a three-line description in a browser running at
640 × 600-pixel resolution. The other disadvantage is that browsers vary somewhat in
how they align the bullet icon with the following text line.

CASE EXAMPLE: FORMATTING AN ONLINE RESUME

A common type of HTML document that many people want to create is an online
resume. Having an attractive resume online can be a real asset in landing that dream job.

> *Kristine Kochanski has been the controller of a medium-sized corporation for more
> than five years. She believes she is ready to step into a management position and has
> launched a job search because the opportunities for further advancement at her cur-
> rent firm are limited.*
>
> *Kristine has decided that creating an online resume will help in her job search.
> She has already written her resume and done the initial HTML formatting. She has
> been studying using HTML tables, however, and has decided to use them to finalize
> the formatting of her resume. For instance, one of the changes she wants to implement
> is to use tables to format the dates and following paragraphs as hanging paragraphs.*

Prepare to work with this example by following these steps:
1. Open **resume_ex.html** in your text editor.
2. Save resume_ex.html as **resume.html** in the chap05 folder.
3. Open **resume.html** in your browser from the chap05 folder (see Figure 5.32).

FIGURE 5.32 • *The resume has been written and partially formatted using HTML, but is far from optimal in its appearance.*

Initially, the layout is not very efficient and it does not look much like a resume. An HTML table can be used to create a more efficient layout that also looks much more like a resume.

Create an online resume using a table:

1. Use a two-column HTML table and COLSPAN attributes to create the resume layout:

```
<table width="97%" cellpadding="3" cellspacing="3">
<tr><td colspan="2" height="15"></td></tr>
<tr valign="baseline"><th width="112" align="right">
<p><font size="5">Objective:</font></th>
<td><font size="4">Challenging and technologically innovative
financial management position</font></p>
</td></tr>
<tr><th colspan="2"><h2><h3>Experience</h3></h2>
<hr></th></tr>
<tr valign="top">
<p><th width="115" align="right">1/97 to Now </th>
<p><td><i>Controller</i>, Huffman and Company, Los Angeles,
California. Streamlined the accounting system and instituted an
automated time and billing system. Played a leadership role in
deploying financial systems and strategies to reduce operating
and interest expenses, while increasing revenues.</td>
</tr>
<tr valign="top">
<p><th align="right">6/92 to 12/96 </th>
<p><td><i>Senior Financial Analyst</i>, Management Analytics,
Inc., San Francisco, California. Prepared planning, budgetary,
operational, capital expenditure, and other analyses and reports
for management and the board of directors. Provided consulting
expertise for clients, in the area of annual planning, business
valuation, and earnings projections.</td>
</tr>
<tr valign="top">
<p><th align="right">2/86 to 5/92 </th>
```

```
<p><td><i>Financial Analyst</i>, D. Lister and Associates, Portland,
Oregon. Applied statistical methodologies in performing financial
business analyses. Constructed business simulations and models to
help anticipate business trends, clarify relations with strategic
partners, and highlight potential threats from competitors.</td>
</tr>
<tr><th colspan="2"><h2><h3>Education and Training</h3></h2>
<hr></th></tr>
<tr valign="top">
<p><th align="right">9/84 to 6/86 </th>
<p><td><i>Master of Business Administration</i>, with
concentrations in Technology/Innovation Management and Finance,
University of Colorado at Boulder.</td>
</tr>
<tr valign="top">
<p><th align="right">9/80 to 6/84 </th>
<p><td><i>Bachelor of Arts</i>, Business Administration,
University of Colorado at Boulder.</td>
</tr>
<tr><th colspan="2"><h2><h3>Certifications and
Memberships</h3></h2>
<hr></th></tr>
<tr valign="top">
<p><td colspan="2" align="center"><i>Certified Public Accountant
(CPA)</i>, San Francisco, California.<br>
<i>Personal Financial Planning (PFP)</i>, Portland, Oregon.<br>
<i>American Association of Financial Planners, senior member</i>,
Portland, Oregon.</td>
</tr>
</table>
<p align="center">References available upon request.</p>
```

2. Create a style sheet to control the spacing of the H2 and H5 elements and set a different font for the H2, H5, and TH elements (see Figure 5.33):

```
<style type="text/css">
h2, h5 { margin-top: 10px; margin-bottom: 0; padding: 0; }
h2, h5, th { font-family: Arial, Geneva, Helvetica, sans-serif; }
</style>
</head>
```

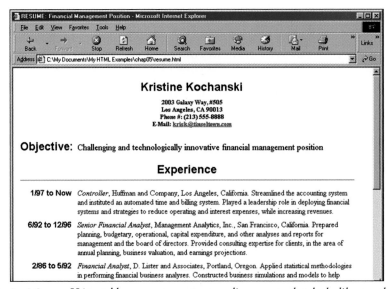

FIGURE 5.33 • *Using tables, you can create an online resume that looks like a real resume.*

Most of the techniques applied in creating the online resume layout have been used in previous examples in this chapter. One feature that is new in this example is the use of the **valign="baseline"** attribute in the "Objective" table row. Because the text strings in the two table cells in the row are differently sized (in Size 5 and Size 4 font sizes), this attribute causes the text strings to be vertically aligned along their baselines.

A nonbreaking space character (** **) is inserted following the dates to create more separation between the two table columns without having to globally increase the padding or spacing in the table.

Browsers are inconsistent in how they display block elements nested inside table cells. When a block element is nested inside a table cell, Internet Explorer does not display the vertical spacing that is normally added above a block element, but the Mozilla and Netscape browsers do. The result can be very different vertical spacing within the page if block elements are nested inside table cells, depending upon which browser is used to view the page. The solution to this problem in the example is to create a style sheet to specify the margin and padding space to be added in above block elements that are nested inside table cells, which will cause Internet Explorer, Mozilla, and Netscape 6 to add the same amount of vertical spacing above the nested block elements.

CASE EXAMPLE: CREATING A TWO-COLUMN LAYOUT

A common use for tables is to create a two-column Web page, with a menu or table of contents in a sidebar column and the main content of the page in the other column.

Shirley Johnson has decided that she wants to format her report on the Mercury space program in two columns, with a table of contents in a sidebar column.

Prepare to work with this example by following these steps:

1. Save (File, Save) any changes to **mercuryfigs.html**. If you have closed your text editor, reopen **mercuryfigs.html**. (If you have not yet created mercuryfigs.html, go back to "Case Example: Creating Floating Figure Captions" and do that case example first.)
2. Save mercuryfigs.html as **mercurycols.html** in the chap05 folder.
3. Open **mercurycols.html** in your browser from the chap05 folder.

The most basic layout you can do with tables is to create a two-column layout, with a sidebar column on the left side and a main content column on the right side. The method for doing this involves setting a width of 100 percent for the whole table, while setting the sidebar column within the table to a fixed pixel width. That way, the table as a whole can expand or contract along with the browser window, while the sidebar column remains the same width.

Create a two-column table with the content of the page in the second column (see Figure 5.34):

```
<body text="white" link="#99ff99" vlink="#99ff99" alink="yellow"
bgcolor="black" background="starcluster.jpg">

<table width="100%" border="1" cellpadding="5" cellspacing="0">
```

```
<tr><td width="150" valign="top" class="side">

</td>
<td class="main">

<a name="top"></a>
<h1 align="center">NASA Space Exploration<br>and the Mercury
Project</h1>

[...]

</td></tr>
</table>
</body>
```

left column   right column

FIGURE 5.34 • *A basic two-column layout is created, with the main content of the page in the right column.*

Using a Spacer Image

Some earlier browsers, such as Netscape 4, do not recognize using the WIDTH attribute to set the width of a column if the width of the content is less than that specified by the WIDTH attribute. A solution to this is to use a "spacer" image, which is a totally transparent single-pixel GIF image that can be resized to force the desired column width. An example image, spacer.gif, is included with this chapter's example files.

Use a spacer image to force the first column to be 150 pixels wide in all browsers:

```
<tr><td width="150" valign="top" class="side">
<p><img src="spacer.gif" height="1" width="140"></p>
```

The width of the spacer image is set to 140 pixels because the 5 pixels of cell padding is set on both the left and right sides of the cell. Thus, the image's width of 140 pixels and the 10 pixels of cell padding equal 150 pixels.

Creating a Sidebar Menu

To create a sidebar menu, you just need to create a link list in the left column that jumps to the section headings in the right column.

Add a sidebar menu to the left column:

1. Click and drag to highlight the menu in the second column and then cut it (Ctrl+X in Windows or Command+X on the Macintosh):

```
<a name="top"></a>
<h1 align="center">NASA Space Exploration<br>and the Mercury
Project</h1>
<h2 align="center">by Shirley Johnson</h2>

<p align="center" class="menu"><b>
[ <a href="#sect1">1915 - 1957</a>
]     
[ <a href="#sect2">1958 - 1960</a>
]     
[ <a href="#sect3">1961</a> ]     
[ <a href="#sect4">1962</a> ]     
[ <a href="#sect5">1963</a> ]     
[ <a href="#sect3">Gemini & Apollo</a> ]</b></p>
```

2. In the first column, paste in the menu codes and text (Ctrl+V in Windows or Command+V on the Macintosh), and then delete everything except the P element and the hypertext links, so the result looks like this:

```
<table width="100%" border="1" cellpadding="5" cellspacing="0">
<tr><td width="150" valign="top" class="side">
<p align="center" class="menu"><b>
<a href="#sect1">1915 - 1957</a>
<a href="#sect2">1958 - 1960</a>
<a href="#sect3">1961</a>
<a href="#sect4">1962</a>
<a href="#sect5">1963</a>
<a href="#sect3">Gemini & Apollo</a></b></p>
<p><img src="spacer.gif" height="1" width="140"></p>
</td>
```

3. Add a heading, remove the center-alignment from the P element that you pasted in, and then set the links up so they are all in their own paragraphs (see Figure 5.35):

```
<table width="100%" border="1" cellpadding="5" cellspacing="0">
<tr><td width="150" valign="top" class="side">
<h4>Menu:</h4>
<p align="center" class="menu"><b>
<a href="#sect1">1915 - 1957</a></b></p>
<p class="menu"><b>
```

```
<a href="#sect2">1958 - 1960</a></b></p>
<p class="menu"><b>
<a href="#sect3">1961</a></b></p>
<p class="menu"><b>
<a href="#sect4">1962</a></b></p>
<p class="menu"><b>
<a href="#sect5">1963</a></b></p>
<p class="menu"><b>
<a href="#sect3">Gemini & Apollo</a></b></p>
<p class="menu"><img src="spacer.gif" height="1"
width="140"></p>
</td>
```

sidebar menu

FIGURE 5.35 • *A sidebar menu is inserted in the left column.*

Varying the Padding Amounts

When creating a two-column layout, sometimes the amount of padding set in the TABLE element can be too much for the sidebar column, but too little for the main body column.

One way to vary padding amounts is to nest a second table inside the main body column and use its TABLE element to set increased padding for the main body column, while decreasing the padding for the sidebar column.

Turn off the padding in the table and then nest another table inside of its main body column:

1. Turn off padding in the table:

```
<table width="100%" border="1" cellpadding="0" cellspacing="0">
```

2. Nest another table inside the first table's main body column, with 10 pixels of padding set:

```
<td class="main">
<table width="100%" border="0" cellpadding="10">
<tr><td>
<a name="top"></a>
<h1 align="center">NASA Space Exploration<br>and the Mercury
Project</h1>
```

```
<h2 align="center">by Shirley Johnson</h2>

[...]

</td></tr>
</table>
</td></tr>
</table>
</body>
```

3. Set display characteristics for the H4 heading and increase the size of the sidebar menu's font (see Figure 5.36):

```
h1, h2, h3, h4 { font-family: Arial, Geneva, Helvetica, sans-
serif; }
h1 { color: #99ffff; background: transparent; }
h2 { color: #ffcc00; background: transparent; }
h3 { color: #ccccff; background: transparent; }
h4 { font-size: 1.25em; margin-top: 15px; color: #ffcc00;
background: transparent; }
.menu { color: yellow; background: transparent; font-size: 1.1em; }
```

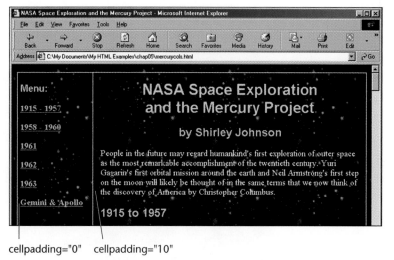

cellpadding="0" cellpadding="10"

FIGURE 5.36 • *Nesting one table within another table is one way to vary the amount of padding.*

Web pages commonly feature designs involving several levels of nested tables. Web publishing programs often create these types of designs. Although nothing in the HTML specifications forbids creating Web pages with several levels of nested tables, such pages are often difficult to edit and maintain, and can waste bandwidth. They also make it more difficult for someone using a nonvisual browser to access a page because multiple levels of nested tables make understanding the structure and order of precedence of information within a document much more difficult, if not impossible.

Therefore, although you should not necessarily avoid using nested HTML tables, since there is really no good alternative to them if you want to achieve certain design results, you should try to limit the number of nested tables you use in a page.

On the other hand, some Web designers believe that HTML tables should not be used at all for creating layouts because that violates the intended purpose of tables, which is to format tabular data, and can make it more difficult for nonvisual browsers to access and present the information in a Web page. Currently, however, if you want to create multicolumn page layouts that can be reliably viewed with the vast majority of graphical browsers in use, the only way is to use tables. Eventually, page layout will likely be done much more frequently using Cascading Style Sheets (CSS), after browsers become entirely compliant with the second level of CSS (CSS2) and older browsers are gradually phased out of use.

Creating a Seamless Table Layout

In the current layout, the table is separated by margin space between it and the edge of the browser window. That space is actually the default page margin that the browser inserts.

REMOVING THE PAGE MARGINS No standard set of attributes can be used to remove the page margin set by a browser. To achieve this result, you need to use an assortment of nonstandard attributes.

Use a mixture of nonstandard HTML attributes to turn off the page border (see Figure 5.37):

```
<body text="white" link="#99ff99" vlink="#99ff99" alink="yellow"
bgcolor="black" background="starcluster.jpg" marginheight="0"
marginwidth="0" topmargin="0" leftmargin="0">
```

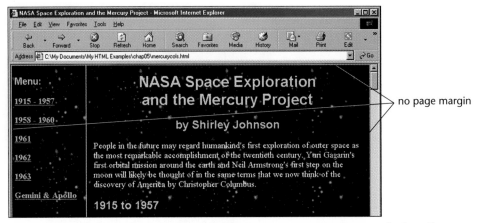

FIGURE 5.37 • *The page margin is turned off using an assortment of nonstandard attributes.*

ADDING A SEAMLESS BACKGROUND If you include a background color in the sidebar column, you no longer need the table border to show the separation between the columns.

Turn off the table borders and set a background color in the sidebar column (see Figure 5.38):

```
<table width="100%" border="0" cellpadding="5" cellspacing="0">
<tr><td width="150" valign="top" class="side" bgcolor="#660000">
```

FIGURE 5.38 • *The table borders are turned off and a background color is displayed behind the sidebar column.*

You also can add a background image to the sidebar column. A special background image, back_nebula.jpg, is included with the example files. This background image was created from a NASA photograph of the star nebula and is sized so that it will only tile vertically, but not horizontally, within the sidebar column.

action

Add a background image, **back_nebula.jpg**, to the sidebar column that is sized to tile only vertically (see Figure 5.39):

```
<tr><td width="150" valign="top" class="side" bgcolor="#660000"
background="back_nebula.jpg">
```

FIGURE 5.39 • *A background image, sized to tile only vertically, is displayed behind the sidebar column.*

GETTING THE ROLLOVER LINKS TO WORK The only problem now is that the rollover links do not work because they are nested inside a table, instead of within the page body. To fix the problem, you need to edit the rollover styles to target the links' positions within a table cell.

Edit the rollover link styles to target their locations inside a table cell (see Figure 5.40):

```
td a.return { color: #ffcc00; background: transparent; font-size:
0.9em; }
td a:link { color: #99ff99; background: transparent; }
td a:visited { color: #99ff99; background: transparent; }
td a:hover { color: maroon; background: #ffcc00; text-decoration:
none; }
td a:active { color: #99ff99; background: transparent; }
```

FIGURE 5.40 • *Rollover links are set up in the sidebar column.*

CHAPTER SUMMARY

You should now be familiar with creating tables in HTML documents, including using the PRE element and the TABLE element to format tabular data, creating floating figures with captions, formatting indented icon link lists, creating an online resume with hanging paragraphs, and designing a two-column Web page layout. You should be familiar with adding captions to tables, defining table heading and table data cells, controlling table borders, setting padding within and spacing outside of cells, setting the table width and horizontal alignment, horizontally and vertically aligning cell contents, setting column widths, spanning columns and rows, and controlling font characteristics and backgrounds in tables. You should also be familiar with formatting row groups in tables using HTML 4's TBODY, THEAD, and TFOOT elements in conjunction with CSS styles, as well as with formatting column groups using styles.

Code Review

TABLE element	Defines a table (data arranged in rows and columns) in HTML.
CAPTION element	Specifies a caption that can be displayed above or below a table.
TR element	Defines a row of cells in a table.
TH element	Defines a table heading cell, which can function as either a column heading or a row heading.
TD element	Defines a table data cell.
BORDER attribute	In the TABLE element, draws a border around the table and between the table cells.
CELLPADDING attribute	Specifies the amount of padding that is displayed inside a table's cells.
CELLSPACING attribute	Specifies the amount of spacing that is displayed between a table's cells.
WIDTH attribute	In the TABLE element, specifies the width of the table, either in pixels or as a percentage of the width of the browser window. In a TH or TD element, specifies the width of a column, either in pixels or as a percentage of the width of the table.
ALIGN attribute	In the TABLE element, either centers or floats the table to the left or right margin (with following text or other elements flowing around the table). In the TR, TH, or TD elements, it horizontally aligns nested text or other elements.
COLSPAN element	Causes a table cell (TH or TD element) to span more than one column.
ROWSPAN element	Causes a table cell (TH or TD element) to span more than one table row.
VALIGN attribute	In the TR, TH, and TD elements, vertically aligns nested text or elements with the top, middle, or bottom of a table cell.
TBODY, THEAD, and TFOOT elements	Allow the application of style properties to row groups within a table.
list-style-image property	A style property that specifies an image to be displayed as an icon bullet in an unordered list.

ONLINE QUIZ

Go to this text's IRC at **www.emcp.com/** and take the online self-check quiz for this chapter.

REVIEW EXERCISES

This section provides some hands-on practice exercises to reinforce the information and material included within this and previous chapters.

You can use any of the example files that you created in this chapter to further practice features or methods covered in this chapter. To practice with an example file, save it under a new name (as **salesreport_practice.html**, for instance), so you will not overwrite your original example file.

1. If you have access to Microsoft Excel or another spreadsheet program that can save a space-delimited text file (PRN file), practice saving a PRN file, opening it in your text editor, copying it, and then pasting it into an HTML file. You can create your own worksheet file to practice with, or you can use a worksheet file you have already created. Your spreadsheet program might also have sample worksheet files you can practice with.

2. Practice using the TABLE, CAPTION, TR, TH, and TD elements to format table data, using many of the features covered in this chapter. Focus on the features that control the structural formatting of a table, rather than its appearance, including setting a border, controlling spacing and padding, setting column widths, spanning columns and rows, vertically and horizontally aligning cell contents, and so on. Use **worksheet_ex.html** to get started, saving it under a new name, or you can create your own HTML file from scratch.

3. Practice using HTML attributes to control the appearance of HTML tables, including specifying font sizes, colors, and faces, and setting background colors and background images.

4. Practice using style properties to control the appearance of HTML tables, including controlling padding, spacing, and borders, assigning display characteristics to rows and columns, setting background colors and background images, and setting borders both within and around the table.

5. Experiment further with creating floating figure captions. For instance, instead of using a two-row table, experiment nesting the figure caption in a CAPTION element displayed underneath the table. Use **mercuryfigs_ex.html** to get started, saving it under a new name, or you can create your own HTML file from scratch. Look for images to experiment with in the chap05 folder, or you can copy additional images from the chap04 folder.

6. Experiment further with creating indented icon link lists, using each of the three methods covered in the chapter. Use **watson4_ex.html** to get started, saving it under a new name, or you can create an HTML file from scratch. Look for additional bullet icon images with this chapter's example files that you can practice with.

7. Experiment further with creating a two-column layout. For instance, instead of creating a layout with a sidebar menu on the left, create a layout with a sidebar menu on the right of the page. Use the **mercuryfigs.html** example file you created in this chapter, saving it under a different name, or any other HTML file you have created.

WEB-BASED LEARNING ACTIVITIES

In this book's text, Find It icons inserted in the margin highlight the Web addresses of additional resources you might find helpful or informative. To further extend your learning using the Web, you can:

- Go back and visit any of the Web addresses highlighted in this chapter that you have not yet visited. Look for additional resources and information that add to your understanding and knowledge of the material covered in this chapter. When you find a relevant page or site with information or resources you might want to access later, add it to your Favorites (in Internet Explorer) or your Bookmarks (in Netscape or Mozilla).
- Visit this book's IRC at **www.emcp.com/** to find additional Web addresses of resources related to the material covered in this chapter that you can further investigate and explore.
- Research a specific topic introduced in this chapter. For instance, you can research table utilities for converting and generating tables, or research different ways in which tables can be used in Web pages. Compile your research into a report that can be shared with your fellow students. You also can team up with other students to create a class presentation on a particular topic.

PROJECTS

These projects can be done in class, in a computer lab, or at home. Use the skills you have developed in this and the previous chapters to create any of the following projects.

Project 1. Incorporate tabular data into a Web page.

Take the lessons learned in this chapter and apply them in incorporating an HTML table or tables for formatting tabular data into a Web page you have already created or that you create from scratch. This can be a personal page, a topical page, an online paper, or any other page you have created or can create that can profit from the inclusion of tabular data. Focus more on the organized and structured presentation of data than on the esthetic appearance of the tables.

Project 2. Coordinate the design of a table or tables with the overall design of a Web page using HTML attributes.

Take the lessons learned in this chapter and apply them to incorporating the design of an HTML table with the overall design of a Web page, using HTML attributes. Use a Web page you have already created or that you create from scratch. In this project, focus on using HTML attributes to create a consistent overall look for the page by making use of fonts, colors, and backgrounds.

Project 3. Coordinate the design of a table or tables with the overall design of a Web page using styles.

Take the lessons learned in this chapter and apply them to incorporating the design of an HTML table with the overall design of a Web page, using CSS styles. Use a Web page you have already created or that you create from scratch. In this project, focus on using styles to create a consistent overall look for the page by making use of fonts, colors, and backgrounds. Use the Invisible Object Method to warn Netscape 4 users that they need to upgrade their browsers or the DOM Sniff method to redirect Netscape users to a browser upgrade page (see Chapter 3 for instructions). While creating your design, be sure to test your page in more than one browser (in Mozilla and Opera, for instance, in addition to Internet Explorer).

Project 4. Incorporate floating figures with captions into an online paper.

Take the lessons learned in this chapter and apply them in incorporating floating figures with captions into an online paper you have already created or that you create from scratch. Be sure to include HEIGHT, WIDTH, and ALT attributes in the IMG elements. Use either a two-row table or a one-row table with a bottom-aligned CAPTION element to create the figure captions.

Project 5. Incorporate an icon link list into a Web page.

Take the lessons learned in this chapter and apply them in incorporating an icon link list into a Web page that you have already created or that you create from scratch. Use any of the three methods for creating indented icon link lists covered in this chapter. Select the bullet icon so that it is coordinated with the overall look and color scheme of your page. Use any of the bullet icons included with this chapter's example files or look in the Art folder that accompanies this book's example files for additional bullet icons you can use. You also can look online for sources of bullet icons that you can download and use.

Project 6. Create a Web page that uses a two-column layout.

Take the lessons learned in this chapter and apply them in formatting a Web page that uses a two-column layout. Use a Web page you have already created or that you create from scratch. Create a sidebar menu that uses rollover links. Include return links that jump back to the top of the page at the end of sections in the page. Use any of the techniques covered in this chapter, such as eliminating page margins and creating a seamless table layout. If using background images, use any of the background images included in this chapter, or copy background images included in other chapter folders or in the Art folder that accompanies this book's example files. You also can look online for additional sources of background images. If you have access to Paint Shop Pro, you can experiment with creating your own seamless background patterns (select an area within any image and then choose Selections, and Convert to Seamless Pattern).

Project 7. Format an online resume using a table.

Take the lessons learned in this chapter and apply them in formatting an online resume for yourself or a friend that uses a table to create a side-by-side format (with dates in one column and following text in a second column). Use the text for a resume you have already created or that you create from scratch. Experiment with more than one way of organizing and laying out a resume, discovering solutions and methods using tables, HTML attributes, and/or styles to achieve a desired layout or organization. If using styles, be sure to also use the DOM Sniff or Invisible Object Method for shielding or warning users of earlier browsers with poor support for CSS.

CHAPTER

6

Working with Multi-Page Web Sites

PERFORMANCE OBJECTIVES

In this chapter, you will learn to perform various tasks involved in creating and publishing multi-page Web sites, including how to:
- Use frames to create a multi-windowed Web site.
- Create two-row, two-column, and combination row-column framed Web sites.
- Control the appearance of a framed site using an external style sheet.
- Use relative URLs to link to files in multiple folders.
- Validate your page's HTML and CSS.
- Publish your Web page files using FTP.

Until now in this book, you mostly have been working with single HTML documents. Web design involves more than just creating single Web pages. A Web site can be composed of many documents and files organized into separate folders. Creating, publishing, and maintaining more complex Web sites presents a unique set of opportunities and challenges.

USING THE EXAMPLE FILES

If you have created a working folder for storing files you create, you will find the example files for this chapter located in the **chap06** folder within your working folder. Save any HTML files you create in this chapter in that folder.

If you have created a working disk, copy the chap06 folder to your working disk from the **HTML_Examples** folder that you or your instructor downloaded from this book's Internet Resource Center (IRC) or from a CD-R disc or floppy disk provided by your instructor. Save any HTML file you create in this chapter in the chap06 folder that you have copied to your working disk.

CASE EXAMPLE: CREATING A FRAMED WEB SITE

A popular way to present a multi-page Web site is to use frames. HTML frames allow you to create a multi-windowed page, with individual pages displayed in the window frames.

Arturo Rodriguez is a graphic designer and printer working for a full-service printing firm, A-Plus Printers. Because Arturo is in charge of designing Web sites for customers, his boss has given him the task of creating a new Web site for the company that can effectively market its services and serve its customers online over the Web.

Arturo has decided to redesign the A-Plus Printers site to take advantage of a two-column layout using frames.

CREATING FRAME PAGE LAYOUTS

Frames were originally introduced by Netscape and have been included since HTML 4. All current graphical browsers support using frames. By using frames, you can create a wide variety of different multi-column, multi-row, and combination column-and-row layouts. Unlike tables, frame layouts can include separate windows (or *frames*) within which scrollable content can be displayed.

Creating a Two-Column Frame Page

You can arrange frames in columns or rows. In this case, you create a basic frames layout that uses two columns, with a sidebar menu in one column and the main content of the page in the other column.

CREATING THE FRAMESET PAGE A frameset page is a page that includes the instructions for laying out frames. The pages that are displayed in the frames are already created for you. A starter page, framestart_ex.html, has also been created that you will use to start creating the different frame page examples in this chapter.

To start working with this example:
1. Open **framestart_ex.html** in your text editor.
2. Save framestart_ex.html as **twocol_frame.html** in the chap06 folder in your working folder or disk.
3. Open **twocol_frame.html** in your Web browser.

A frameset page is created using the FRAMESET and FRAME elements. A frameset page does not contain any displayable content, but only pointers to the pages (or other files) to be displayed in the individual frames. In a frameset page, the FRAMESET element replaces the BODY element.

Create a frameset page that creates a two-column Web page, with a sidebar menu in the left column and the main content of the page in the right column:
1. Add a FRAMESET element that specifies a two-column layout, with a 150-pixel wide column on the left and a column on the right that will expand to fill the page:

```
<!DOCTYPE HTML PUBLIC "-//W3C//DTD HTML 4.01 Frameset//EN"
 "http://www.w3.org/TR/html4/frameset.dtd">
<html>
<head>
<meta http-equiv="Content-Type" content="text/html; charset=ISO-
8859-1">
```

Note that there is no BODY element. In a frameset file, the FRAMESET element replaces the BODY element.

```
<title>A-Plus Printers: Serving All Your Printing Needs Since
1975</title>
</head>
<frameset cols="150,*">
</frameset>
</html>
```

2. Use the FRAME element to define the frames that compose the columns and point to the documents to be displayed in them:

```
<frameset cols="150,*">
  <frame src="sidebar.html">
  <frame src="main.html" name="main">
</frameset>
```

3. Save **twocol_frame.html** (File, Save) and open it in your browser (see Figure 6.1).

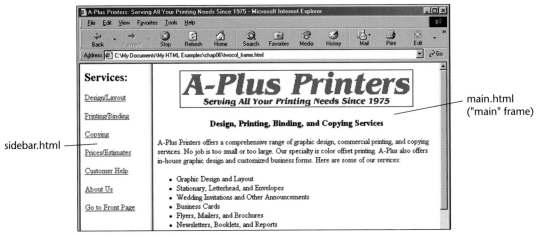

sidebar.html

main.html ("main" frame)

FIGURE 6.1 • *The A-Plus Printers page is displayed in a two-column format.*

4. Click on the Design/Layout link in the left sidebar (see Figure 6.2).

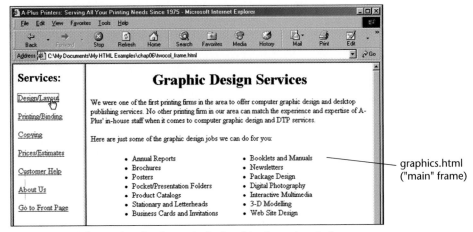

graphics.html ("main" frame)

FIGURE 6.2 • *The graphics.html page is displayed in the main window.*

5. Click on the Go to Front Page link in the left sidebar to return to the site's front page.

TROUBLE *spot*

When displaying a frameset page in a browser, only the title defined in the frameset page will be displayed in the browser's title bar. Any titles defined for pages displayed within frames will not be displayed, unless the pages are opened as standalone pages.

UNDERSTANDING THE SIDEBAR PAGE You have just activated two links whose functions are key to creating an effective navigation scheme using frames.

Open and review the sidebar page codes:

1. Open **sidebar.html** in your text editor:

```
<!DOCTYPE HTML PUBLIC "-//W3C//DTD HTML 4.01 Transitional//EN">
<html>
<head>
<meta http-equiv="Content-Type" content="text/html; charset=ISO-8859-1">
<title>A-Plus Printers</title>
</head>
<body>
<h2>Services:</h2>
<p><a href="graphics.html" target="main">Design/Layout</a></p>
<p><a href="printing.html" target="main">Printing/Binding</a></p>
<p><a href="copying.html" target="main">Copying</a></p>
<p><a href="prices.html" target="main">Prices/Estimates</a></p>
<p><a href="service.html" target="main">Customer Help</a></p>
<p><a href="about.html" target="main">About Us</a></p>
<p><a href="main.html" target="main">Go to Front Page</a>
</body>
</html>
```

2. With sidebar.html open in your text editor, use the following pointers to review the content of the page.

Notice that a foreshortened DocType declaration, **<!DOCTYPE HTML PUBLIC "-//W3C//DTD HTML 4.01 Transitional//EN">**, is inserted at the top of the sidebar.html. A foreshortened, rather than a full, DocType declaration is used to get around a bug in Internet Explorer 6 for Windows, which inserts unnecessary horizontal scroll bars in frame windows when vertical scroll bars are also displayed. This only happens, however, when Internet Explorer 6 for Windows, using DocType switching, invokes standards mode, but not when it invokes quirks mode. A foreshortened "frameset" DocType declaration (without the URL to the W3C DTD file) causes Internet Explorer 6 (and any other browser that does DocType swtiching) to revert to quirks mode (also called "bugwards compatibility mode"). In doing this, however, you need to be aware that you cannot include features in the page that will not display properly if standards mode is not invoked. Later in this chapter, in "Using Styles with Multi-Page Web Sites," you will work with an example where standards mode must be invoked for the page to display properly in Internet Explorer 6 (or later versions), even though the page is included within a frame in which scrolling is not turned off.

A couple of features of this file are key to its definition and operation:

- The **target="main"** attributes in the links target the "main" window as the location in which the objects of the links should be displayed. This corresponds to the **name="main"** that you applied to the second FRAME element in your frameset file. This combination of attributes allows you to click on a link in one frame to cause a file to be displayed in another frame. Without a TARGET attribute, the object of the link is displayed in the same frame as the linking file.

TARGET and NAME attribute values are case sensitive. If you have **target="main"** in your link, but **name="Main"** in your frameset page's FRAME element, the targeting will not work.

- The last link allows the user to redisplay the site's front page, main.html, in the main frame window.

Creating a sidebar frame on the left side of the page is only one way to lay out a framed page. You could just as easily position the sidebar frame on the right side of the page, for instance, simply by switching the positions of the FRAME elements in the frameset page.

NOTE

Only the graphics.html subpage has been fully developed for this example. Dummy files have been created for the other subpages (printing.html, copying.html, service.html, and about.html).

Creating a Two-Row Frame Page

Another common way to lay out a framed page is by using two rows, with the top row containing a menu running along the top of the page. Because the previous left-side frame was referred to as a sidebar frame, this kind of frame is called a topbar frame.

CREATING THE FRAMESET PAGE   As with creating a two-column frame page, you need to create a frameset page that specifies a two-row layout. To get started, you will be using the same starter page, framestart_ex.html, you used in creating the previous example.

To start working with this example:
1. Open **framestart_ex.html** in your text editor.
2. Save framestart_ex.html as **tworow_frame.html** in the chap06 folder in your working folder or disk.
3. Open **tworow_frame.html** in your Web browser.

You create a two-row frame page in the same way you created a two-column frame page, except you specify the layout using the ROWS attribute, rather than the COLS attribute.

Create a two-row frame layout:
1. Define a two-row frame layout containing a top row with a height of 25 pixels and a bottom row that expands to vertically fill the page. Make the first frame row link to topbar.html and the second frame row link to main.html (see Figure 6.3):

```
</head>
<frameset rows="25,*">
  <frame src="topbar.html" scrolling="no" marginheight="0">
  <frame src="main.html" name="main">
</frameset>
</html>
```

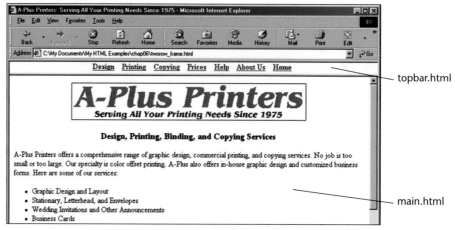

topbar.html

main.html

FIGURE 6.3 • *The A-Plus Printers page is displayed in a two-row format.*

2. Click the Design link in the topbar frame (see Figure 6.4).

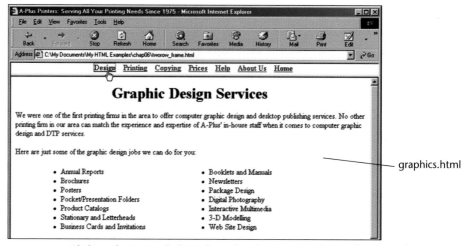

graphics.html

FIGURE 6.4 • *Clicking the Design link in the topbar frame causes the graphics.html file to be displayed in the main frame.*

This example differs from the previous example in the following ways:

- The **rows="25,*"** attribute in the FRAMESET element specifies that the following nested FRAME elements define horizontal rows, rather than vertical columns. It sets the height of the first row to 25 pixels and uses the wildcard character ("*") to set the second row to expand to fill the browser window. You also can set the height of a row using a percentage value (**rows="15%,*"**, for instance).

- The **scrolling="no"** attribute in the first FRAME element turns off any scroll bars that might be displayed in the frame window.

- The **marginheight="0"** attribute in the first FRAME element sets the top and bottom margins of the frame to 0, so that the content of the frame (topbar.html) will fit vertically within the frame. To set a positive height for the top and bottom margins in pixels, just specify an integer value.

UNDERSTANDING THE TOPBAR PAGE You have just activated two links whose functions are key to creating an effective navigation scheme using frames.

Open and review the topbar page codes:

1. Open **topbar.html** in your text editor:

```
<!DOCTYPE HTML PUBLIC "-//W3C//DTD HTML 4.01 Transitional//EN"
  "http://www.w3.org/TR/html4/loose.dtd">
<html>
<head>
<meta http-equiv="Content-Type" content="text/html; charset=ISO-
8859-1">
<title>A-Plus Printers</title>
</head>
<body>
<p align="center" style="margin-top: 0"><b>
<a href="graphics.html"
target="main">Design</a>   
<a href="printing.html"
target="main">Printing</a>   
<a href="copying.html"
target="main">Copying</a>   
<a href="prices.html" target="main">Prices</a>   
<a href="service.html" target="main">Help</a>   
<a href="about.html" target="main">About
Us</a>   
<a href="main.html" target="main">Home</a></b>
</body>
</html>
```

2. With topbar.html open in your text editor, use the following pointers to review the content of the page.

A number of features of this file are key to its definition and operation:

- The document includes a full DocType declaration, which triggers standards mode in Internet Explorer 6 (and other browsers that do DocType switching). Because the scroll bars have been turned off for the frame, you do not have to worry about Internet Explorer 6's scroll bar bug.
- The P element that contains the menu links includes a `style="margin-top: 0"` inline style to turn off the top margin that the Mozilla and Netscape 6 browsers insert when an element is the first element in a frame. (Internet Explorer does not display top margin spacing for the first element in a frame.)
- The topbar menu links are arranged horizontally in a centered paragraph, with three non-breaking space characters (`   `) separating the links.
- The `target="main"` attributes work the same way as in the sidebar file, causing the linked files to be displayed in the "main" frame.
- The last link allows the user to redisplay the site's front page, main.html, in the "main" frame.

Creating a Frame Page with Columns and Rows

For a more complex frame layout, you can create a layout that contains both columns and rows by nesting one frameset element within another.

CREATING THE FRAMESET PAGE For this example, you will start out using the two-column frame page layout you created previously. If you have not yet done that example, you should go back and do it first, before trying to do this example.

To start working with this example:
1. Reopen **twocol_frame.html** in your text editor.
2. Save twocol_frame.html as **combo_frame.html** in the chap06 folder in your working folder or disk.
3. Open **combo_frame.html** in your Web browser.

You create a combination row-column frame layout by nesting one FRAMESET element inside of another FRAMESET element, with the first defining the rows and the second defining the columns.

Create a combination frame layout that uses both rows and columns:
1. Create a frameset layout that nests one frameset element (that specifies columns) inside another frameset element (that specifies rows) (see Figure 6.5):

```
</head>
<frameset rows="85,*">
  <frame src="topbanner.html" scrolling="no" marginheight="0">
  <frameset cols="150,*">
    <frame src="sidebar2.html">
    <frame src="main2.html" name="main">
  </frameset>
</frameset>
</html>
```

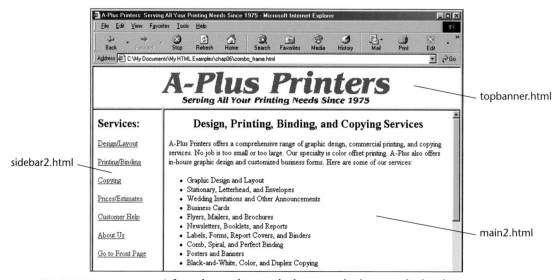

FIGURE 6.5 • *A frame layout that uses both rows and columns is displayed.*

2. Click on the Design/Layout link in the sidebar (see Figure 6.6).

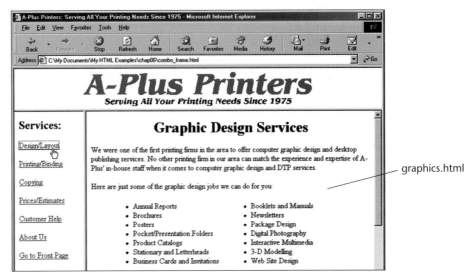

graphics.html

FIGURE 6.6 • *Clicking on the Design/Layout link causes the graphics.html file to be displayed in the "main" window.*

The following are the main features of this example:

- The outside FRAMESET element defines an initial two-row layout, with the top row set to a height of 85 pixels and the bottom row set to expand to fill the page.
- The first FRAME element defines the first row in the outside frameset. It links to a topbanner.html file that contains the A-Plus Printers' banner image. It also turns off scrolling and sets the top margin to 0, as in the previous example.
- The inside FRAMESET element forms the second row in the outside frameset. It defines a two-column layout that is nested inside of the outside frameset's bottom row.

UNDERSTANDING THE FRAMED PAGES The inside frameset links to two new files, sidebar2.html and main2.html, included with the example files. The sidebar2.html file differs from sidebar.html only in the "Go to Front Page" link, which links to main2.html, rather than main.html. The main2.html file differs from main.html only in that the banner image at the top of the page has been deleted.

The topbanner.html file is similar to the topbar.html file from the two-row frame layout example.

Open and review the content of the topbanner page:
1. Open **topbanner.html** in your text editor:

```
<!DOCTYPE HTML PUBLIC "-//W3C//DTD HTML 4.01 Transitional//EN"
 "http://www.w3.org/TR/html4/loose.dtd">
<html>
<head>
<meta http-equiv="Content-Type" content="text/html; charset=ISO-
8859-1">
<title>A-Plus Printers</title>
</head>
<body>
<p align="center" style="margin-top: 5px">
```

```
<a href="combo_frame.html" target="_top"><img src="aplusbanner.gif"
height="75" width="500" alt="A-Plus Printers banner image"
border="0"></p>
</body>
</html>
```

2. With topbanner.html open in your text editor, use the following pointers to review the content of the page.

A number of features of this file are key to its definition and operation:

- As in topbar.html, a full DocType declaration is included. Because scrolling is turned off in the frame in which this document is displayed, you do not need to worry about Internet Explorer 6 for Windows' scroll bar bug.
- The banner image is centered by nesting it in a centered paragraph. The inline style in the P element sets its top margin to five pixels. This setting also enforces the same top margin height in both Internet Explorer and the Netscape 6/Mozilla 1 browsers (otherwise, Internet Explorer 6 does not insert a top margin, but Netscape 6 and Mozilla 1 do insert a top margin for the P element).
- The banner image is set up as an image link by nesting it inside a hypertext link that causes the combo_frame.html frameset page to be displayed in the top-level browser window (by including **target="_top"** in the A element) if the image is clicked on.
- The border that was drawn around the banner image in the previous examples has been turned off (**border="0"**).

The main advantages of this layout is that the banner image remains visible in the browser window at all times, instead of scrolling off the screen if inserted at the top of page in the main frame.

NOTE You can create a "grid" layout by combining the ROWS and COLS attributes in the same FRAMESET element. For instance, to split the browser window into four equally sized frames, just create the following FRAMESET element:

```
<frameset cols="50%,50%" rows="50%,50%">
  <frame src="filename1.html" name="upperleft">
  <frame src="filename2.html" name="upperright">
  <frame src="filename3.html" name="lowerleft">
  <frame src="filename4.html" name="lowerright">
</frameset>
```

Substitute the actual file names of the pages you want to display in the grid. To increase the number of cells within the grid, just increase the number of columns and/or rows, reapportioning the percentages accordingly.

USING A NESTED FRAMESET FILE A variation on using a nested FRAMESET element is to use a nested frameset file. You do this by first creating two frameset files, with the first defining two rows, for instance, and the second defining two columns. You then link the second FRAME element in the two-row frameset to the two-column frameset. The advantage of this is that you can name the FRAME element that links to the nested frameset file, whereas you cannot name a nested FRAMESET element. You can then create a series of frameset files (containing more than one frame) that can be swapped in and out using the name of the linking FRAME element. The disadvantage of this is that you have to create and maintain at least one additional file.

Understanding Pros and Cons of Using Frames

Frames were originally introduced by Netscape and have only been a standard part of HTML since HTML 4. Both positives and negatives are involved in using frames. If you want to use frames in designing Web sites, you need to understand the possible negatives and some of the solutions that can at least partially overcome those negatives.

WHY USE FRAMES? You might choose to use frames in a Web site for a number of positive reasons:

- Multi-column and multi-row layouts can be easily created.
- The presentation of content, such as sidebar menus, masthead banners, and so on, remain fixed and visible, while other content can scroll within the page.
- If done right, frames can help create a consistent and easy-to-use navigation system because sidebar, topbar, or bottombar menus remain visible and accessible at all times.
- Creating and maintaining a more complex multi-page Web site can be more efficient and manageable because the HTML code for presenting repeating page elements, such as banners and menus, needs only to be created once and requires only a single update if a change is necessary.

WHY NOT USE FRAMES? Frames also present a number of drawbacks that you need to be aware of before deciding whether to use frames in a Web site:

- Some earlier browsers do not understand frames. Internet Explorer 2, for instance, which is the default browser for Windows NT 4, does not understand frames.
- Search engines and directories may not list a frameset page, because it does not contain any content that can be indexed.
- Search engines and directories may not list pages that are linked to in a frameset page, because most search engines' robots do not follow frame page links (set using the FRAME element's SRC attribute).
- It is difficult to bookmark a page that is linked to within a frame. For instance, if a user clicks on the Design/Layout link in the current example's sidebar menu to display graphics.html in the main window, he cannot bookmark that specific page simply by clicking on the Favorites or Bookmark button. Instead, only the initial frameset page (showing main.html) is bookmarked. To bookmark a particular page, users have to know to right-click on the page's background and select Add to Favorites (in Internet Explorer) or Bookmark This Page (in Netscape or Mozilla).
- If a Web author does not use TARGET attributes with external links (either intentionally or unintentionally), any external pages that are linked to will be displayed within a frame in the site's frameset, which also makes it impossible to bookmark the external page without right-clicking on the page's background. Most users do not know that they can open a framed page within its own window, because the procedures for doing this are not obvious—a Netscape 6 user needs to right-click on the page's background and select Open Frame in New Window, whereas an Internet Explorer 6 user needs to right-click on the page's background, select Properties, copy the page's address, and paste the address in the Address box.

NOTE There have been a number of lawsuits over Web sites deep-linking into another site's commercial content. This is generally done using frames; the other site's page is displayed in a frame within the linking site. Including another person's page or site within your own frame is generally frowned upon on the Web and might even be illegal if the content you are framing within your site is copyrighted. When linking to an external Web site from a framed page, you should *always* include a `target="_top"` or `target="_blank"` attribute in the link's A element to open the page in the top-level browser window or in a new browser window.

If you decide to link to a page that is deep within another's site, you also should include a link to the site's front page, especially if the identity of the page's parent site is neither obvious nor easy to navigate to. You should avoid linking directly to "printer-ready" pages, because doing so will likely bypass advertising that might be present on the regular version of the page.

See this chapter's section at the IRC for this book at **www.emcp.com/** for additional links to resources on the Web that discuss ethical, legal, and free speech issues involved in linking and deep-linking.

- Although content within a framed Web page—such as menus, banners, or advertising—can remain fixed and always visible, this is at the expense of the amount of space available for viewing the scrollable content of the page.
- A multi-page framed Web site can take longer to download and display than a single page because multiple pages must be downloaded.

NOTE A question that is often asked is whether an author should link to external pages (pages external to your site) from within a framed page using a `target="_top"` or a `target="_blank"` attribute. The first attribute causes the external page to be displayed in the top-level browser window, replacing the current window. The second attribute causes the external page to be displayed in a new browser window, with the current window remaining open in the background. Designers creating commercial Web sites often opt to use `target="_blank"` when linking to external pages because they are concerned that if they use `target="_top"`, a potential customer might go away and never come back. If, however, your site is informational, rather than commercial, using `target="_top"` is friendlier to visitors to your site because it does not force them to open a second browser window when they might not want to.

Using META Elements in Frame Pages

The META element allows you to provide a description and a list of keywords that search engines and directories can use in indexing and listing a framed Web site.

Use the META element to add a description and a list of keywords to the combo_frame.html frameset page:

1. If necessary, open **combo_frame.html** in your text editor and your browser.
2. In your text editor, add a description and a list of keywords:

```
<title>A-Plus Printers: Serving All Your Printing Needs Since
1975</title>
<meta name="description" content="A-Plus Printers offers a
comprehensive range of graphic design, commercial printing, and
copying services. We specialize in one-color, two-color, and
full-color offset printing, as well as embossing, binding,
laminating, and more."
```

```
<meta name="keywords" content="printer, printing, printing
services, service bureau, offset printing, 3-color, 4-color,
perfect binding, spiral binding, comb binding, linotype,
prepress, graphic design, flyers, brochures, newsletters,
booklets, banners, reports, posters, invitations"
</head>
```

When creating META element descriptions and keyword lists, you should be aware that including descriptions or keywords lists that do not correspond to the actual content of your page or site is considered spamming and may result in your page or site being penalized by receiving a lower search ranking (or no ranking).

Because the META element has been abused by Web site promoters trying to get a higher ranking in search response lists, some search engines and directories no longer use META element descriptions and keyword lists to index and list a page or site. For that reason, you should not rely upon the META element alone to provide content for a framed page. The following section details another way to include positive content within a framed page.

Using the NOFRAMES Element

The NOFRAMES element is included in HTML ostensibly to enable you to provide content to browsers that do not recognize framed pages. Perhaps even more importantly, however, you can also use the NOFRAMES element to provide content and links that search engine robots and spiders can index and follow.

CREATING A SIMPLE NOFRAMES ELEMENT The simplest way to use the NOFRAMES element is to alert users of browsers that do not support frames and provide them with an alternative means to view the content of your site. An efficient way to do this is to link to your main content page, and then link to the rest of the pages in your site through that page.

Use the NOFRAMES element to provide a means for users of browsers that do not understand frames and for search engine robots to access the content of your site:
1. If not already open, open **combo_frame.html** in your text editor.
2. Save combo_frame.html as **combo_frame2.html** in the chap06 folder.
3. Add a NOFRAMES element to the combo_frame2.html file:

```
<frameset rows="85,*">
  <frame src="topbanner.html" scrolling="no" marginheight="0">
  <frameset cols="150,*">
    <frame src="sidebar2.html">
    <frame src="main2.html" name="main">
  </frameset>
<noframes>
<h3>A frames-compatible browser is required to view this page.
Please visit the <a href="main.html">non-frames version</a> of
this site.</h3>
</noframes>
</frameset>
```

The NOFRAMES element may be nested inside the top-level FRAMESET element. A browser that recognizes frames will ignore the content of the NOFRAMES element, while a browser that does not recognize frames will ignore the FRAMESET and FRAMES elements, seeing only the NOFRAMES content (which is the only positive content in the page). This example has two primary characteristics:

- Search engines' robots can also follow the NOFRAMES link to access the rest of your site. As long as the page linked through the NOFRAMES link contains links to other pages in your site, search engine robots will also be able to find and index those other pages, as well.

- The link to the "non-frames version," in this instance actually links to the site's main page, main.html. Linking directly to your site's main content page (or front page) allows you to avoid having to create an entire separate page (or site) simply to service a rapidly diminishing body of users (users using non-frames-compatible browsers).

- You can use HTML elements within the NOFRAMES element to control how the content will be presented to users of browsers that do not recognize frames. You even can include a BODY element within the NOFRAMES element to assign a background color or background image to the NOFRAMES content.

MAKING SURE PAGES IN FRAMES CAN STAND ALONE If the page linked to through the NOFRAMES link does not link to any other pages, a search engine robot will not be able to index any more than just that one page. If you want other pages in your site to be indexed and listed, you should make sure that links also are included in the linked page that let search engine robots access the rest of your site.

A search engine robot cannot index the rest of your site if your framed pages are not linked together. Instead of simply relying on a sidebar (or topbar) menu to provide links to the other pages in your site, you should also include links in your other pages, so they can stand alone as link nodes in your site.

With all the content pages of your site linked together (with none standing apart unlinked to any other page), a search engine might index and list any page within your site. Visitors are not limited to simply visiting your site through your front door, in other words. They can "beam in" at any point within your site.

NOTE Clients sometimes instruct Web designers that they want visitors to only access their site through the front page, so they can maximize revenue from ads that are displayed there. There is, however, no way to do this other than setting up password protection and forcing visitors to log in before accessing pages within your site. Having to log in, however, will probably drive away more visitors from your site's front door, so to speak, than you will have gained from diverting them from other pages.

A much better idea is to embrace the idea that every page in your site is potentially a front page. Every content page in your site should be designed to stand on its own, as a separate and independent page. By attracting visitors to many pages within your site, you can attract more "traffic" than if you try to attract visitors only to a single page.

Add a navigation menu to the bottom of your site's content pages:

1. Open **topbar.html** in your text editor and copy everything inside the BODY element.
2. Open **main2.html** in your text editor and paste the codes and text you copied in Step 1 in the location shown here:

```
<p align="center" style="margin-top: 0"><b><a href="graphics.html"
target="main">Design</a>   
<a href="printing.html" target="main">Printing</a>   
<a href="copying.html" target="main">Copying</a>   
<a href="prices.html" target="main">Prices</a>   
<a href="service.html" target="main">Help</a>   
<a href="about.html" target="main">About Us</a>   
<a href="main.html" target="main">Home</a></b></p>
<hr>
<address>
```

3. Edit the menu you just pasted in so it references the name of your site's front page:

```
<a href="main2.html" target="main">Home</a></b></p>
```

4. Repeat Steps 2 and 3 with the graphics.html page, adding a navigation menu at the bottom of that page, as well.

Figure 6.7 shows the navigation menu displayed at the bottom of the main2.html front page.

FIGURE 6.7 • *A navigation menu at the bottom of a framed page lets it stand by itself, outside of the frameset, as a standalone Web page.*

CREATING A MORE COMPLEX NOFRAMES ELEMENT You can do more than just include a link in the NOFRAMES element to another page in your site. You can include the codes for an entire page, including a BODY element, within the NOFRAMES element. Then this embedded page also can contain links to other pages in your site.

BREAKING UP A FRAMED SITE INTO MULTIPLE FRAMESETS One way to overcome the problem of users not being able to bookmark separate pages within a framed site is to create additional frameset files for each of the major sections in your site. Then, instead of linking to the front pages for those sections, you can link to the framesets instead. For instance, the following is an example of a sidebar menu file that links to frameset files rather than to the individual section pages:

```
<h2>Services:</h2>
<p><a href="graphics_frame.html" target="_top">Design/Layout</a></p>
<p><a href="printing_frame.html"
target="_top">Printing/Binding</a></p>
<p><a href="copying_frame.html" target="_top">Copying</a></p>
<p><a href="prices_frame.html"
target="_top">Prices/Estimates</a></p>
<p><a href="service_frame.html" target="_top">Customer Help</a></p>
<p><a href="about_frame.html" target="_top">About Us</a></p>
<p><a href="combo_frame.html" target="_top">Go to Front Page</a>
```

Notice that instead of targeting the "main" frame, the links in this example use a target="_top" attribute to display the linked page in the top-level browser window.

Each of these additional frameset files is almost identical to the combo_frame.html file, for instance, except that instead of linking to the main.html in the "main" frame, they link instead to graphics.html, printing.html, copying.html, prices.html, service.html, and about.html, respectively, in their "main" frames.

The advantage of doing it this way is that a user can bookmark and return later to any of the main sections in your site. The disadvantage is that you have to create and maintain an additional file (the frameset file) for each of your site's main sections.

USING STYLES WITH MULTI-PAGE WEB SITES

By creating an external style sheet file, you can control the look and feel of an entire site from a single file. This can make changing and updating the appearance and design of a site much easier than if you are using an internal style sheet or HTML FONT elements to add colors, fonts, and backgrounds to your pages.

To get started with this example, do the following:

1. Open **combo_frame2.html** in your text editor and save it as **combo_frame4.html**.
2. In your text editor, edit **combo_frame4.html** so that it points to different files (you will be saving these files shortly):

```
<frameset rows="85,*">
  <frame src="topbanner2.html" scrolling="no" marginheight="0">
  <frameset cols="150,*">
    <frame src="sidebar3.html" marginheight="0" marginwidth="10px">
    <frame src="main3.html" name="main">
  </frameset>
<noframes>
<h3>A frames-compatible browser is required to view this page.
Please visit the <a href="main.html">non-frames version</a> of
this site.</h3>
</noframes>
</frameset>
```

Setting Up the Files to Be Styled

Before you create an external style sheet to control the appearance of your site's pages, you need to prepare the files to be displayed.

SETTING UP THE TOP BANNER FILE To set up the top banner file, you need to link the file to the external style sheet you will be creating, assign the BODY element to a class so styles can be applied to it, and repoint the top banner image link so it links to combo_frames4.html.

Set up the top banner file:
1. Open **topbanner.html** in your text editor and save it as **topbanner2.html**.
2. Edit **topbanner2.html** so it matches what is shown here:

```
<!DOCTYPE HTML PUBLIC "-//W3C//DTD HTML 4.01 Transitional//EN"
  "http://www.w3.org/TR/html4/loose.dtd">
<html>
<head>
<meta http-equiv="Content-Type" content="text/html; charset=ISO-
8859-1">
<title>A-Plus Printers</title>
<link rel="stylesheet" type="text/css" href="aplus.css">
</head>
<body class="topbanner">
<p align="center" style="margin-top: 5px">
<a href="combo_frame4.html" target="_top"><img src="aplusbanner.gif"
height="75" width="500" alt="A-Plus Printers banner image"
border="0"></p>
</body>
</html>
```

The LINK element defines the relationship, or link, between a document or other object and the current document. In this case, the relationship is of an external style sheet that is linked to the current document. The REL attribute defines the relationship (**rel="stylesheet"**) and the TYPE attribute specifies that the linked file is a CSS style sheet (the same attribute value used in the STYLE element to embed a style sheet). The HREF attribute specifies the URL of the link.

You also can include both a linked style sheet (using the LINK element) and an embedded style sheet (using the STYLE element) within the same HTML file. Styles in an embedded style sheet take precedence over the same styles included in a linked style sheet.

Another way to attach an external style sheet to an HTML file is to use CSS' @import at-rule. For instance, in browsers that support this, the following example achieves the same result as using the LINK element to link to an external style sheet:

```
<style type="text/css">
@import { url("aplus.css"); }
</style>
```

Linking to an external style sheet in this fashion also has the added side benefit of excluding Netscape Navigator 4, Internet Explorer 3, and many other early browsers with poor support for styles from accessing the style sheet. At least one early version of Netscape Navigator 4, however, crashes when it encounters an @import at-rule in a style sheet.

You also can shield Netscape Navigator 4 users accessing a style sheet by using a LINK element with a MEDIA attribute:

```
<link rel="stylesheet" media="all" type="text/css" href="aplus.css">
```

This works because Navigator 4 recognizes a LINK element containing a `media="screen"` attribute, but not if it contains any other form of the MEDIA attribute.

You can combine this method with use of the @import at-rule method to avoid the problem of early versions of Navigator 4 crashing when encountering an @import at-rule. Using a LINK element with a `media="all"` attribute to link to an external style sheet blocks all Navigator 4 users from accessing the style sheet. An @import at-rule can then be included in the external style sheet that links to a second external style sheet, thus blocking any other browsers (such as Internet Explorer 3, for instance) that do not recognize the @import at-rule from accessing that style sheet.

NOTE

The MEDIA attribute can be applied to both the LINK and STYLE elements to define styles used only for printing a document. For instance, the following LINK element links to a style sheet that will be used to specify how the Web page should be printed:

```
<link rel="stylesheet" media="print" type="text/css"
href="print.css">
```

When creating a style sheet specifically for printing a document, it is okay to use absolute measurements (points, inches, or centimeters, for instance), because the dimensions of the output media are generally known (an 8.5 × 11-inch piece of paper). You can also specify black text against a white background where light text against a dark background will cause problems when printing.

Styles can be targeted to other media types, as well. For additional information on using styles to specify a media-specific presentation, see this chapter's section at the IRC for this book at **www.emcp.com/**.

SETTING UP THE SIDEBAR FILE To set up the sidebar file to be styled, you need to add a link to the external style sheet you will be creating and assign the BODY element to a class so that styles can be applied to it.

action

Set up the sidebar file:

1. Open **sidebar3_ex.html** and save it as **sidebar3.html**.
2. Edit **sidebar3.html** so it matches what is shown here:

```
<!DOCTYPE HTML PUBLIC "-//W3C//DTD HTML 4.01 Transitional//EN"
  "http://www.w3.org/TR/html4/loose.dtd">
<html>
<head>
<meta http-equiv="Content-Type" content="text/html; charset=ISO-
8859-1">
<title>A-Plus Printers</title>
<link rel="stylesheet" type="text/css" href="aplus.css">
</head>
<body class="sidebar">
<div class="side">
<p><a href="graphics2.html" target="main">Design</a></p>
<p><a href="printing2.html" target="main">Printing</a></p>
<p><a href="copying2.html" target="main">Copying</a></p>
<p><a href="prices2.html" target="main">Prices</a></p>
<p><a href="service2.html" target="main">Help</a></p>
<p><a href="about2.html" target="main">About Us</a></p>
```

```
<p><a href="main3.html" target="main">Home</a></p>
</div>
</body>
</html>
```

Notice that a full DocType declaration is included in this version of the sidebar file, rather than the foreshortened DocType that was included previously. The foreshortened DocType declaration was used to get around the horizontal scroll bar bug in Internet Explorer 6, by triggering quirks mode in that browser. The reason you cannot do the same in this case will be explained after you have created the external style sheet file.

SETTING UP THE MAIN FRAME FILE To set up the main frame file to be styled, you need to add a link to the external style sheet you will be creating and assign the BODY element to a class so that styles can be applied to it.

Set up the main frame file:

1. Open **main2.html** in your text editor and save it as **main3.html**.
2. Edit **main3.html** so it matches what is shown here:

```
<!DOCTYPE HTML PUBLIC "-//W3C//DTD HTML 4.01 Transitional//EN">
<html>
<head>
<meta http-equiv="Content-Type" content="text/html; charset=ISO-8859-1">
<title>A-Plus Printers</title>
<link rel="stylesheet" type="text/css" href="aplus.css">
</head>
<body class="mainframe">
<h2 align="center">Design, Printing, Binding, and Copying Services</h2>

[...]

<p align="center" style="margin-top: 0"><b>
<a href="graphics2.html" target="main">Design</a>   
<a href="printing2.html"
target="main">Printing</a>   
<a href="copying2.html" target="main">Copying</a>   
<a href="prices2.html" target="main">Prices</a>   
<a href="service2.html" target="main">Help</a>   
<a href="about2.html" target="main">About Us</a>   
<a href="main3.html" target="main">Home</a></b></p>

<hr>
<address>
<b>A-Plus Printers</b><br>
Toll-Free Phone #: 1-800-000-0000<br>
E-Mail: <a href="mailto:info@aplusprint.com">info@aplusprint.com</a>
</address>
</body>
</html>
```

SETTING UP THE OTHER MAIN FRAME FILES To set up the graphics.html file to be styled, you need to add a link to the external style sheet you will be creating and assign the BODY element to a class so that styles can be applied to it.

Set up the graphics file:

1. Open **graphics.html** in your text editor and save it as **graphics2.html** in the chap06 folder.
2. Edit **graphics2.html** so it matches what is shown here:

```
<!DOCTYPE HTML PUBLIC "-//W3C//DTD HTML 4.01 Transitional//EN">
<html>
<head>
<meta http-equiv="Content-Type" content="text/html; charset=ISO-8859-1">
<title>A-Plus Printers: Graphic Design and Desktop Publishing
Services</title>
<link rel="stylesheet" type="text/css" href="aplus.css">
</head>

<body class="mainframe">
<h1 align="center">Graphic Design Services</h3>

[...]

<p align="center" style="margin-top: 0"><b>
<a href="graphics2.html" target="main">Design</a>   
<a href="printing2.html"
target="main">Printing</a>   
<a href="copying2.html" target="main">Copying</a>   
<a href="prices2.html" target="main">Prices</a>   
<a href="service2.html" target="main">Help</a>   
<a href="about2.html" target="main">About Us</a>   
<a href="main3.html" target="main">Home</a></b></p>
<hr>
<address>
<b>A-Plus Printers</b><br>
Toll-Free Phone #: 1-800-000-0000<br>
E-Mail: <a href="mailto:info@aplusprint.com">info@aplusprint.com</a>
</address>
</body>
</html>
```

The remaining files—printing2.html, copying2.html, prices2.html, service2.html, and about2.html—have not been fully developed for this example, but exist as dummy files with the other example files.

Creating the External Style Sheet

By creating a single style sheet, you can control the appearance of all the files included in the A-Plus Printers site. An external style sheet is just a regular text file with the same styles listed in it that would otherwise be listed inside the STYLE element, if the styles were embedded within an HTML file. External style sheet files should be saved with a ".css" file extension.

action

Create the external style sheet:

1. Open a blank window within your text editor.
2. Save your blank file as **aplus.css** in the chap06 folder.

STYLING THE TOP BANNER FILE You have already prepared the top banner file to be styled, so all you have to do is add the appropriate styles to the aplus.css style sheet file.

action

Edit and save the style sheet file and open the frameset file in your browser:

1. Add the following styles to the aplus.css style sheet file:

```
/* Top Banner Styles */


body.topbanner { color: navy; background: #fc9
url(back_marblegreen.jpg); }
```

2. Save the style sheet (File, Save) and then open the frameset file
   (**combo_frame4.html**) in your browser (see Figure 6.8).

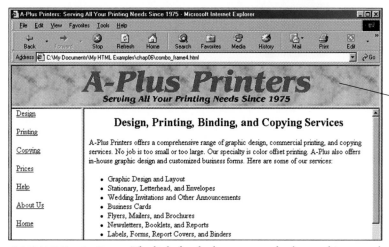

FIGURE 6.8 • *The linked style sheet causes a background image to be displayed in the page (topbanner2.html) in the top frame.*

The **body.topbanner** style applies the specified properties only to a BODY element belonging to the "topbanner" class.

STYLING THE SIDEBAR FILE You have already prepared the sidebar file to be styled, so all you have to do is add the appropriate styles to the aplus.css style sheet file.

action

Edit and resave the style sheet file and refresh the frameset file in your browser:

1. Add the following styles to the aplus.css style sheet file:

```
/* Top Banner Styles */
body.topbanner { color: navy; background: #fc9
url(back_marblegreen.jpg); }


/* Sidebar styles */
body.sidebar { color: yellow; background: teal
url(back_turquoise.jpg); }
```

```
div.side { margin-left: 10px; margin-top: 15px; }
div.side a, div.side a:link, div.side a:visited, div.side
a:active { color: #fc0; text-decoration: none; font-family:
'Comic Sans MS', Arial, Helvetica, sans-serif; font-size: 18px; }
div.side a:hover { color: yellow; text-decoration: underline; }
```

2. Save the style sheet (File, Save) and then refresh the frameset file
(**combo_frames4.html**) in your browser (see Figure 6.9).

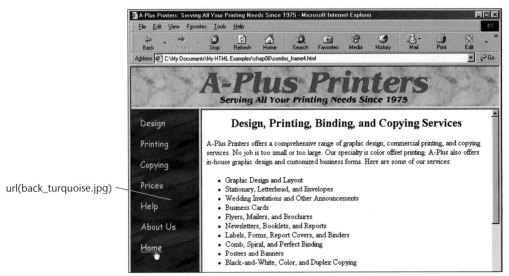

url(back_turquoise.jpg)

FIGURE 6.9 • *The linked style sheet causes a background image and rollover links to be
displayed in the page (sidebar2.html) in left sidebar frame.*

The **body.sidebar** style applies the specified properties only to a BODY element
belonging to the "sidebar" class. The **div.side** style sets the left and top margins for
nested elements. The following selector is a group of contextual selectors that assign
properties to the A element and the a:link, a:visited, and a:active pseudo-elements.
Because these are contextual selectors, the properties are assigned only to links that are
nested inside the "side" DIV element.

In this example, foreshortened color codes are used. For instance **#fc0** is the same as
#ffcc00. This only works in CSS, however, and not in HTML.

STYLING THE MAIN FRAME FILE You have already prepared the files to be styled
that will be displayed in the "main" frame.

Edit and resave the style sheet file and refresh the frameset file in your browser:

1. Add the following styles to the aplus.css style sheet file:

```
/* Top Banner Styles */
body.topbanner { color: navy; background: #fc9
url(back_marblegreen.jpg); }


/* Sidebar styles */
body.sidebar { color: yellow; background: teal
url(back_turquoise.jpg); }
div.side { margin-left: 10px; margin-top: 15px; }
div.side a, div.side a:link, div.side a:visited, div.side a:active
{ color: #fc0; text-decoration: none; font-family: 'Comic Sans
MS', Arial, Helvetica, sans-serif; font-size: 18px; }
```

```
div.side a:hover { color: yellow; text-decoration: underline; }

/* Main Frame Styles */

body.mainframe { color: #630; background: #ff9
url(back_parch.jpg); margin-top: 8px; }

h1, h2, h3 { font-family: Arial, Helvetica, sans-serif; color:
#fc0; background: #069; padding: 3px; border: 4px #f90 outset;
margin-top: 0; }
p, li, address { font-family: Arial, Helvetica, sans-serif;
font-size: 1.1em; }

li { list-style-image: url(smblueball.gif); font-size: 95%;
font-weight: bold; padding-left: -15px; margin-left: -15px;
color: #369; background: transparent; }

table { width: 100%; }
td { width: 45%; padding-left: 0; margin: 0; }
```

2. Save the style sheet (File, Save) and then refresh the frameset file
   (**combo_frames4.html**) in your browser (see Figure 6.10).

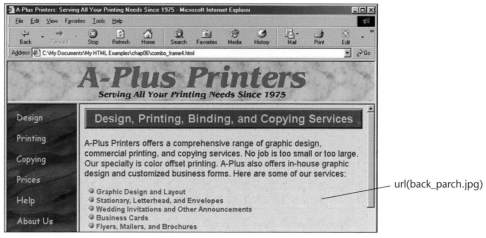

url(back_parch.jpg)

FIGURE 6.10 • *The linked style sheet determines the formatting of the page (main3.html)
displayed in the right ("main") frame.*

NOTE

In the previous code example, negative margin-left and padding-left properties are applied to the LI element. List items are indented in from the left margin by default, but some browsers, such as Internet Explorer and Opera, set this using a left margin, while others, such as Netscape and Mozilla, set this using left padding. Internet Explorer and Opera recognize the `margin-left: -15px` property, while Netscape and Mozilla ignore it. Netscape and Mozilla recognize the `padding-left: -15px` property, while Internet Explorer and Opera ignore it.

If you want to increase how far the list items are indented, you need to apply positive margin-left and padding-left property values, but to the UL (or OL) element, rather than the LI element.

Note, however, that if you validate this using the W3C CSS Validator, you will get an error report that a negative padding-left value is not allowed for the LI element. This is an example in which valid CSS coding will not work the same in all major browsers, so you have to make adjustments. To get the style sheet to validate, however, you will have to remove the negative padding-left property.

3. In your browser, click on the Design link in the sidebar to display graphics2.html in the main frame window (see Figure 6.11).

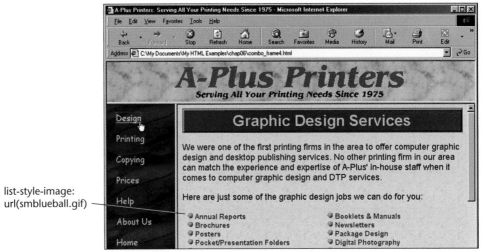

list-style-image:
url(smblueball.gif)

FIGURE 6.11 • *Clicking on the Design link in the sidebar menu causes graphics.html to be displayed in the main frame.*

In this example, a group selector assigns the same properties to the H1, H2, and H3 elements. The main3.html file contains an H2 element and the graphics2.html element contains an H1 element. The group selector sets a sans serif font (Arial or Helvetica); defines foreground and background colors; sets three pixels of padding; and specifies the color, width, and style of a border to be drawn around the element. The result is a boxed element, as shown previously in Figures 6.10, 6.11, and 6.12.

Adding Rollover Buttons

Earlier you created rollover links that change their appearance when the mouse pointer is passed over them. In the following example, you will be adding rollover buttons to the sidebar menu.

Edit the sidebar section of the style sheet as shown below, save it, and then refresh your browser's display (see Figure 6.12):

```
/* Sidebar styles */
body.sidebar { color: yellow; background: teal
url(back_turquoise.jpg); }
div.side { margin-left: 8px; margin-top: 10px; }
div.side a, div.side a:link, div.side a:visited, div.side
a:active { display: block; padding: 2px; border: 4px #f90 outset;
margin-bottom: 5px; background: #069; color: #fc0; text-
decoration: none; font-family: 'Comic Sans MS', Arial, Helvetica,
sans-serif; font-size: 18px; }

/* Start Box Model Hacks - Required for Internet Explorer 5.5 */
div.side a, div.side a:link, div.side a:visited, div.side a:active
{ width: 112px; voice-family: "\"}\""; voice-family: inherit;
width: 100px; }
```

```
html>body div.side a { width: 100px; }

div.side a:hover { color: #c00; background: #fc6; font-size:
20px; padding: 2px 4px; border: 2px #3c9 outset; width: 112px;
voice-family: "\"}\""; voice-family: inherit; width: 100px; }
html>body div.side a { width: 100px; }
/* End Box Model Hacks */

div.side p { margin: 0; padding: 0; }
```

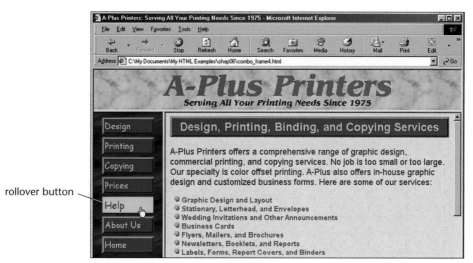

FIGURE 6.12 • *The linked style sheet causes rollover buttons to be displayed in the left sidebar frame.*

This example sets padding, border, and width values for the A element and the anchor pseudo-elements that control the appearance of unvisited, visited, active, and hover links. Internet Explorer 5 and 5.5 for Windows, however, incorrectly implement the CSS box model, by including any specified padding or border widths within the total width for the element. The correct implementation is to consider the width of an element to be independent of any padding or border widths. The result is that elements that have a specific width, set along with border, and/or padding values, will be displayed at a shorter width than in browsers that, correctly, do not calculate padding and border widths as part of the element width. When creating button links, the difference in width can be critical, in that a shorter element width in Internet Explorer 5.5 could end up not providing enough space for the button text. On the other hand, a longer element width in Netscape 6, Mozilla, and Opera, could end up exceeding the available width of the sidebar frame.

The solution to this is the *box model hack*, which was developed by Tantek Çelik, a leader of the Internet Explorer development team at Microsoft. The box model hack takes advantage of an Internet Explorer 5.5 for Windows parsing error to fool it into displaying the correct element width. In the code example, the start and end of the box model hack section are marked by CSS comments (/* and */). Here is how the box model hack works:

1. The **width: 112px;** property sets the element width for Internet Explorer 5.5 for Windows.
2. The **voice-family: "\"}\""; voice-family: inherit;** style properties cause Internet Explorer 5.5 for Windows to stop parsing the style rule (this is the parsing error).
3. The following **width: 100px;** property resets the element width to a width that is equal to the width set earlier for Internet Explorer 5.5 for Windows, but minus

the border and padding amounts (8 pixels of padding and 4 pixels of borders, or 12 pixels in total). This width is read by browsers that do not have the parsing error that Internet Explorer 5.5 for Windows has.

4. The following style rule, `html>body div.side a { width: 100px; }`, is necessary for Opera 5, which has the same parsing error as Internet Explorer 5.5 for Windows, but correctly implements the CSS box model. The style uses a CSS2 style selector, which is not recognized by Internet Explorer 5.5 for Windows, but is recognized by Opera 5, to reset the element width to 100 pixels for Opera 5.

 To see Tantek Çelik's own explanation of the box model hack, see **www.tantek.com/CSS/Examples/boxmodelhack.html**.

TROUBLE *spot*

One possible problem arises when using the box model hack in a framed page. Earlier, you were advised to use a foreshortened DocType declaration to force Internet Explorer 6 for Windows to go into quirks mode to overcome the horizontal scroll bug that is present in that browser when it is running in standards mode. Unfortunately, although running in quirks mode also causes Internet Explorer 6 for Windows to reduplicate the same incorrect implementation of the CSS box model that is present in Internet Explorer 5.5 for Windows, it does not reduplicate the parsing error that makes the box model hack possible. Therefore, to ensure that the rollover buttons are the same width in all CSS1-supporting browsers, it is necessary to include a full DocType declaration to trigger standards mode, even if that might result in unnecessary horizontal scroll bars being displayed for the frame in Internet Explorer 6 for Windows.

USING RELATIVE URLS

Until now, you have been working with examples that utilize files that are all located in the same folder. When working with a more complex Web site with many files, using a single folder can become cumbersome. To make working with a more complex Web site easier, you can organize it into separate folders. These can include separate folders for the different parts of a project, for instance. If creating an online manual or multi-part report, you could break out the different parts into separate folders. You also can create a separate images folder to store images that are reused in the different parts of your project. For instance, Arturo Rodriguez might decide to organize his A-Plus Printers project as shown in Figure 6.13.

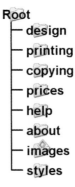

FIGURE 6.13 • *A complex Web site can be easier to work with and maintain if it is organized into multiple folders.*

You create links between two files located in different folders within your site by using a *relative URL*. A relative URL states the location of a linked object relative to the location of the linking file. You should always use relative URLs when linking between files that are internal to your own site. The same relative URL will work equally well both when creating your site on your local machine and after you have published your site to the Web. You also can easily move a site that uses relative URLs from one Web server to another, without having to fix a single internal link, but if you had used absolute URLs to link to files internal to your own site, you would need to fix every single internal link in your site.

You have actually been using relative URLs all along in this book—using only the name of file to link to it is the simplest form of a relative URL (because the linked and linking files are in the same folder, no other path information is required to create the link).

Reorganizing the A-Plus Printers Site

Before you can experiment with using relative URLs, you need to reorganize the last A-Plus Printers example you created into multiple folders.

In this section, you will be asked to create folders and then move files into those folders. The tools and steps required to perform these tasks vary according to the tool being used and the platform (Windows, Macintosh, or UNIX) that you are working on. If you need additional assistance creating folders and copying or moving files, ask your instructor for assistance.

WORKING WITH FILES AND FOLDERS IN WINDOWS Use My Computer or Windows Explorer to create new folders and copy or move files between folders.

- **Create a new folder.** In My Computer or Windows Explorer, select File, New, and Folder. In Windows Explorer, just key the folder name and press Enter. In My Computer, scroll down until you see the New Folder folder, click on the "New Folder" folder name, and then after a short delay, click on it again to highlight it (double-clicking will open the folder, which is not what you want). Then, just key the name of the folder and press the Enter key.
- **Copy or move a file.** In My Computer or Windows Explorer, right-click on the file and select Copy or Cut. Then right-click on the folder to which you want to copy or move the file, and select Paste. To copy or move multiple files between folders, first select them by clicking on them while holding down the Ctrl key, and then copy or move them the same way you do with a single file.

WORKING WITH FILES AND FOLDERS ON THE MACINTOSH Use the Finder to create new folders and copy or move files between folders.

- **Create a new folder.** Open the folder where you want to create the new folder and then select File, and New Folder. Key the name of the folder and press the Enter key.
- **Copy or move a file.** Hold down the Option key if copying the file (but not if you are moving the file), and then click and drag the file to drop it on the open folder or the icon for the folder into which you want to copy or move the file. To copy or move multiple files between folders, first select them by holding down the Shift key while clicking on the files, and then copy or move them the same way you do with a single file.

Even though both Windows and the Macintosh allow it, you should never include spaces in the names of folders or files you will be publishing to the Web, since doing so will likely result in broken links or pages not displaying. That is because UNIX does not allow spaces in the names of folders or files and most Web servers are still running UNIX.

Shortcut: Click the Start button, select Run, key **explorer**, and press Enter to run Windows Explorer.

Create a folder structure for the A-Plus Printers site and move the project's files into their appropriate folders:

1. In Windows, run Windows Explorer or open My Computer from the Desktop. On the Macintosh, if the Finder is not in the foreground, click the Applications menu in the upper-right corner and select the Finder.
2. In Windows Explorer, My Computer, or the Finder, open the chap06 folder (in your working folder or your working disk).
3. In the chap06 folder, create a new folder, keying **design** as the folder name. Do the same to create a **printing**, an **images**, and a **styles** folder.
4. Move the **graphics2.html** file into the design folder you just created. Move the **printing2.html** file into the printing folder.
5. Move the **aplus.css** style sheet file into the styles folder you just created.
6. Copy the following images into the images folder you just created: **aplusbanner.gif**, **back_marblegreen.jpg**, **back_turquoise.jpg**, **back_parch.jpg**, and **smblueball.gif**.

Creating the Relative URLs

Now that you have re-organized the A-Plus Printers site, you need to edit any of the files that need to use relative URLs to link to files in their new locations. You do not need to change the links in the frameset file, combo_frames4.html, because the files it links to are all still located in the root folder, but you do need to edit the HTML files that are linked to from the frameset file.

EDITING THE TOP BANNER FILE The top banner file, topbanner2.html, links to the style sheet file, aplus.css, and to the banner image, aplusbanner.gif, both of which have been moved to separate folders.

Open **topbanner2.html** in your text editor and edit it as follows (save the file when done):

```
<link rel="stylesheet" type="text/css" href="styles/aplus.css">
</head>
<body class="topbanner">
<p align="center" style="margin-top: 5px">
<a href="combo_frame4.html" target="_top"><img
src="images/aplusbanner.gif" height="75" width="500" alt="A-Plus
Printers banner image" border="0"></p>
```

The `images/aplusbanner.gif` relative URL creates a link from the topbanner2.html file, located in the root folder (the chap06 folder), to the aplusbanner.gif file, which is now located in the images folder that is inside the root folder.

A common error when creating relative URLs that link to files located in the child folder (or subfolder) of the linking file's folder is to insert a forward slash at the start of the URL: **/images/aplusbanner.gif**. Another common error is to use a backward slash, instead of a forward slash, in the URL: **images\aplusbanner.gif**. Earlier versions of Internet Explorer let you get away with committing both of these errors, while Internet Explorer 6 lets you get away with using backward slashes in URLs. Other browsers, however, will not complete the links if these errors are made.

EDITING THE SIDEBAR FILE   The sidebar file, sidebar3.html, links to the style sheet file, aplus.css, and to the Graphic Design page, graphics2.html, both of which have been moved to separate folders.

Open **sidebar3.html** in your text editor and edit it as follows (save the file when done):

```
<link rel="stylesheet" type="text/css" href="styles/aplus.css">
</head>
<body class="sidebar">

<div class="side">
<p><a href="design/graphics2.html" target="main">Design</a></p>
<p><a href="printing/printing2.html"
target="main">Printing</a></p>
<p><a href="copying/copying2.html" target="main">Copying</a></p>
<p><a href="prices/prices2.html" target="main">Prices</a></p>
<p><a href="help/service2.html" target="main">Help</a></p>
<p><a href="about/about2.html" target="main">About Us</a></p>
<p><a href="main3.html" target="main">Home</a></p>
</div>
```

NOTE

Other than graphics2.html and main3.html, you have not worked with the other files linked to in the sidebar file and have not created the folders that these links now point to. You will have a chance to work with these files and folders later, however, when doing the Review Exercises for this chapter. For the sake of illustrating how relative URLs work, you will just be using graphics2.html and main3.html.

EDITING THE MAIN FILE   The initial "main" frame file you have been working with, main3.html, also links to the style sheet file, as well as to the graphics and printing files that have been moved.

Open **main3.html** in your text editor and edit it as follows (save the file when done):

```
<title>A-Plus Printers</title>
<link rel="stylesheet" type="text/css" href="styles/aplus.css">
</head>

[...]

<p align="center" style="margin-top: 0"><b>
<a href="design/graphics2.html"
target="main">Design</a>   
<a href="printing/printing2.html"
```

```
target="main">Printing</a>   
<a href="copying/copying2.html"
target="main">Copying</a>   
<a href="prices/prices2.html"
target="main">Prices</a>   
<a href="help/service2.html"
target="main">Help</a>   
<a href="about/about2.html" target="main">About
Us</a>   
<a href="main3.html" target="main">Home</a></b></p>
```

EDITING THE GRAPHICS DESIGN FILE The initial graphics design file you have been working with, graphics2.html, also links to the style sheet file, as well as to the main and printing files.

Open **graphics2.html** in your text editor from the design folder (in the chap06 folder) and edit it as follows (save the file when done):

```
<title>A-Plus Printers: Graphic Design and Desktop Publishing
Services</title>
<link rel="stylesheet" type="text/css" href="../styles/aplus.css">
</head>

[...]

<p align="center" style="margin-top: 0"><b>
<a href="../design/graphics2.html"
target="main">Design</a>   
<a href="../printing/printing2.html"
target="main">Printing</a>   
<a href="../copying/copying2.html"
target="main">Copying</a>   
<a href="../prices/prices2.html"
target="main">Prices</a>   
<a href="../help/service2.html"
target="main">Help</a>   
<a href="../about/about2.html" target="main">About
Us</a>   
<a href="../main3.html" target="main">Home</a></b></p>
```

In this case, the relative URLs need to connect a linking file located in a subfolder of the chap06 folder (the design folder) with linked files that are located in other subfolders of the chap06 folder (the design and printing folders, for example). In the relative URL, **../design/graphics2.html**, the **../** part steps back one level up the folder tree (to the parent folder, which in this case is the chap06 folder), while the remainder, **design/graphics2.html**, steps one level back down the folder tree (to the design folder, which is a child folder of the chap06 folder). The design and printing folders referenced in the preceding example also can be called "sibling" folders, because they share the same parent folder (while folders sharing the same grandparent folder can be referred to as "cousins").

EDITING THE STYLE SHEET FILE The style sheet file that is linked to by all the previous files has been relocated to the styles folder. It also links to a number of background images have been relocated to the images folder.

Open **aplus.css** in your text editor from the styles folder (in the chap06 folder) and edit it as follows (save the file when done):

```
/* Top Banner Styles */

body.topbanner { color: navy; background: #fc9
url(../images/back_marblegreen.jpg); }

/* Sidebar styles */
body.sidebar { color: yellow; background: teal
url(../images/back_turquoise.jpg); }

[...]

/* Main Frame Styles */

body.mainframe { color: #630; background: #ff9
url(../images/back_parch.jpg); margin-top: 8px; }

[...]

li { list-style-image: url(../images/smblueball.gif); font-size:
95%; font-weight: bold; padding-left: -15px; margin-left: -15px;
color: #369; background: transparent; }
```

Testing the Reorganized Site

You have now created subfolders (the design, printing, images, and styles folders) within the root folder (the chap06 folder) and transferred files from the root folder to each of those subfolders. You have edited all the files included in the example (all files appending from the combo_frames4.html frameset file) to repoint the links to the new locations of the linked files using relative URLs. You can now test the reorganized site.

Test the reorganized site:

1. Open **combo_frame4.html** in your browser. All the background images that have been copied to the images folder should be displayed.
2. Click the Design button link in the sidebar menu. The graphics design file, graphics2.html, which has been moved to the design folder, should be displayed. (The background image, which has been copied to the images folder, should also be displayed.)
3. Click the Printing button link in the sidebar menu. The printing file, printing2.html, which has been moved to the printing folder, should be displayed. (*Note: this is a dummy file, which is why it is in black and white.*)
4. Click the Home button link in the sidebar menu. The main file, main3.html, should now be redisplayed in the main frame window.

TROUBLE spot If any of these links do not work correctly, double-check to make sure that you have copied or moved all the required files to the new folders you have created. Open the file in which the link is not working and double-check the URL to make sure it matches both the folder name and file name to which it is linking.

You should now have understanding and practical experience of working with at least the most commonly used forms of relative URLs. See Table 6.1 for additional examples of using relative URLs. All of the URLs shown in Table 6.1 assume a base URL of www.server.com/folder/project1/.

TABLE 6.1 • *Examples of Different Relative URLs*

Relative URLs	Absolute URL Equivalents
images/back.jpg	www.server.com/folder/project1/images/back.jpg
../project2/index.html	www.server.com/folder/project2/index.html
../../folder2/project-a/	www.server.com/folder2/project-a/
chap1/tbls/tbl1.html	www.server.com/folder/project1/chap1/tbls/tbl1.html
main.html	www.server.com/folder/pdroject1/main.html
./index2.html	www.server.com/folder/project1/index2.html
./	www.server.com/folder/project1/

Note: A double period followed by a forward slash (../) indicates the parent folder of the base folder, while a single period followed by a forward slash (./) indicates the current folder (or base folder). A double period and forward slash repeated twice (../../) indicates the grandparent folder of the current folder.

Creating Seamless Frames

A common question about creating framed Web sites is how to create seamless frames. The FRAMEBORDER attribute can be used in the FRAME element to turn the display of frame borders off and on (by specifying **0** or **1** as the value), but this attribute does not eliminate the space (or "seam") between the frames. You cannot, in fact, create seamless frames by using standard HTML. However, a collection of non-standard HTML attributes can be used that has the effect of eliminating the seams between frames in all the major browsers, at least, with some of the attributes working in some browsers, and some working in other browsers.

Apply a collection of non-standard HTML attributes to the top-level frameset element to turn off the display of the frame borders and eliminate the spaces ("seams") between the frames:

1. If it is not already open in your text editor, open **combo_frame4.html** and then resave it as **combo_frame5.html**.

2. Edit **combo_frame5.html** to create a seamless frame layout (see Figure 6.14):

```
<frameset rows="85,*" border="0" spacing="0" frameborder="0"
framespacing="0">
```

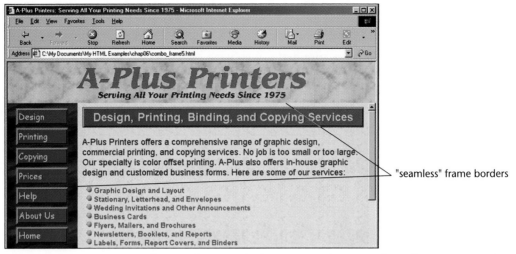

FIGURE 6.14 • *A collection of non-standard HTML attributes must be used to create a seamless frame layout.*

Controlling Frame Borders Using Styles

You also can use styles to control the display of borders in frame pages. You can do this simply by applying inline styles to the FRAMESET or FRAME elements that you want to style.

action

Use inline styles in combo_frame5.html to set a top border for the nested frameset and a left border for the main frame:

```
<frameset rows="85,*" border="0" spacing="0" frameborder="0"
framespacing="0">
  <frame src="topbanner2.html" scrolling="no" marginheight="0">
  <frameset cols="150,*" style="border-top: 5px ridge lime">
    <frame src="sidebar3.html" marginheight="0" marginwidth="10px">
    <frame src="main3.html" name="main" style="border-left: 5px
ridge lime">
  </frameset>
```

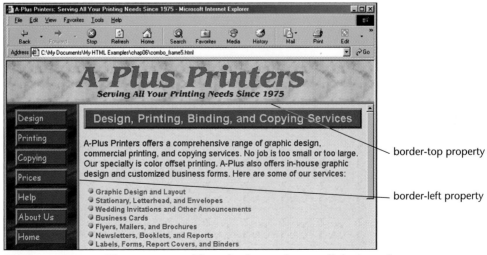

FIGURE 6.15 • *The appearance of frame borders can be controlled using styles.*

VALIDATING YOUR WEB PAGES

To make sure that a Web page includes only valid HTML codes, you can use an online HTML Validator. Validating your page is also one way to help make sure that your page will display correctly in current browsers. An HTML Validator checks your page for compatibility to the version and definition of HTML that is declared in your page's DocType declaration. If you have declared your page to be in conformance with the transitional definition of HTML 4.01, then an HTML Validator tests your page for conformance to the transitional HTML 4.01 DTD (Document Type Definition). The main online HTML Validators are discussed below.

Using the W3C HTML Validation Service

Because the W3C is in charge of defining the official recommended standard for HTML, you should start with its validation service when validating your page. The W3C HTML Validator can check the validity of both HTML and XHTML pages. You can go directly to the W3C HTML Validator at the URL given in the previous bulleted list, or you can go to the W3C home page at **www.w3.org/** and click on the HTML Validator link in the sidebar menu.

You can validate a page in two different ways. You can validate a page you have already published to the Web or you can upload a page to be validated.

UPLOADING AN HTML FILE TO BE VALIDATED To upload an HTML file to be validated, you need to specify the path on your computer on which the file you want to validate is located.

Validate the main3.html file:
1. In your browser, go to the W3C HTML Validation service at **validator.w3.org/**.
2. Scroll down on the page and click the "Upload Files" link.
3. Click the Browse button and navigate to the chap06 folder in your working folder or working disk. Double-click on main3.html (see Figure 6.16).

FIGURE 6.16 • *The file path of the HTML file to be validated is displayed in the File box.*

4. Because you have included a DocType declaration in your document, leave "(speci-fied inline)" selected in the Document type box. Leave the check boxes all unchecked.

5. Click the Validate this document button. As long as you have not introduced any errors on your own, you should see a page with the "No errors found!" message displayed (see Figure 6.17).

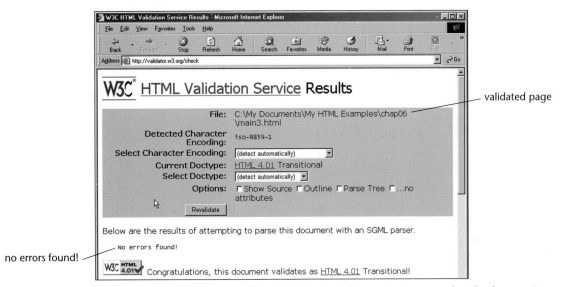

FIGURE 6.17 • *If no errors are found, the W3C validation service reports that the document's HTML is valid (for HTML 4.01 Transitional).*

If errors are found in your page, see the following section, "Correcting Errors," for pointers on interpreting error messages. The error message (or messages) should give you a good idea of what the error is. Correct your HTML code and then try to validate your page again.

6. Scroll down and click and drag to copy the HTML code you can include in your page to show that it includes only valid HTML 4.01 code.

7. Open **main3.html** in your text editor and paste in the code you just copied as shown in the following example:

```
</address>
<p>
<a href="http://validator.w3.org/check/referer"><img border="0"
src="http://www.w3.org/Icons/valid-html401" alt="Valid HTML 4.01!"
height="31" width="88"></a>
</p>
</body>
</html>
```

8. Open **combo_frame4.html** in your Web browser and scroll the page (main3.html) displayed in the main window to display the bottom of the page. If you are connected to the Internet, you will see the W3C validation icon displayed below the page's address block (see Figure 6.18).

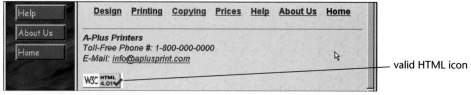

valid HTML icon

FIGURE 6.18 • *The W3C validation icon is displayed at the bottom of the main3.html page.*

CORRECTING ERRORS Of course, not every HTML file you validate is going to check out as completely valid. If any errors are reported, you need to correct the errors before you can identify your page as valid.

Add some errors to your HTML file, validate it, correct the reported errors, and then revalidate it:

1. Open **main3.html** in your text editor. Resave the file as **mainerror.html** in the chap06 folder.
2. Introduce some errors into the file and delete the HTML validation icon you added previously (resave the file when done):

```
<body class="mainframe">
<h2 align="center">Design, Printing, Binding, and Copying
Services</h3>

[...]

<address>
<b>A-Plus Printers</b><br>
Toll-Free Phone #: 1-800-000-0000<br>
E-Mail: <a href="mailto:info@aplusprint.com">info@aplusprint.com</a>
</address>
<p>
<a href="http://validator.w3.org/check/referer"><img border="0"
src="http://www.w3.org/Icons/valid-html401" alt="Valid HTML 4.01!"
height="31" width="88"></a>
</p>
</body>
```

3. In your browser, go back to the W3C HTML validation service at **validator.w3.org/**. Scroll down and click the "Upload Files" link. Click the Browse button, navigate to the chap06 folder in your working folder or working disk, and double-click on **mainerror.html**.
4. Click the Validate this document button. Instead of reporting that your document is a valid HTML 4.01 document, the W3C HTML Validator reports a series of errors (see Figure 6.19).

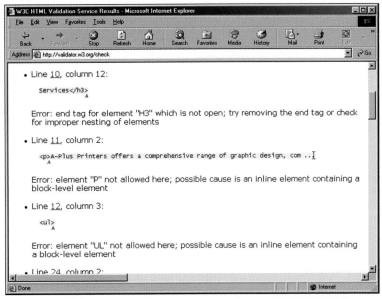

FIGURE 6.19 • *If your HTML file contains errors, the W3C HTML Validator provides a report of the errors it has found.*

The W3C error report actually includes more errors than your page actually contains because one error can trigger the reporting of additional errors. When the first error is corrected, the following errors are also corrected. For instance, the first error reported (Line 10, column 12) is for the **</h3>** end tag, which does not match the preceding **<h2>** start tag. Because of that error, the W3C HTML Validator reports errors for all the following block elements (for each instance of the following P, UL, HR, and ADDRESS elements) in the page, because it sees them as being nested inside of the H2 element (which is not allowed).

Toward the bottom of the error report, you will see the two other errors you introduced, which were the missing **</a>** and **</address>** tags, as well as the **<h2>** start tag that is missing a corresponding **</h2>** end tag:

```
Error: end tag for "A" omitted; possible causes include a missing
end tag, improper nesting of elements, or use of an element where
it is not allowed
```

and

```
Error: end tag for "ADDRESS" omitted; possible causes include a
missing end tag, improper nesting of elements, or use of an
element where it is not allowed
```

and

```
Error: end tag for "H2" omitted; possible causes include a missing
end tag, improper nesting of elements, or use of an element where
it is not allowed
```

In other words, just a few errors in an HTML file can generate the reporting of many other errors. A simple missing end tag for a block element caused all other following block elements to be reported as errors.

practice Correct the errors you added to the mainerror.html document and, following the previous examples of validating an HTML document as a guide, revalidate your document at the W3C HTML validation service.

Using Other Validators

You can use other validators to check the validity of your HTML and CSS documents. For links to HTML validators, CSS validators, and link checkers, see this chapter's section at the IRC for this book at **www.emcp.com/**.

N O T E ──── A number of other utilities are available that can be used to check HTML files, such as the Weblint utility and the CSE HTML Validator. In the strict sense, these are not actually HTML Validators (regardless of the CSE utility's name), in that they do not check the validity of your document against the official DTD for the definition and version of HTML you are using. These utilities are, more correctly, termed as style checkers—they might provide useful feedback about your HTML file, but do not actually test to determine whether your file's HTML is valid.

PUBLISHING WEB SITES

After you have planned and developed a Web page or site, you will want to publish it to the Web. The primary way of doing that is to use an FTP program to transfer your Web page files to your folder located on a Web server.

Finding a Web Host

Many options are available for finding a Web host for your Web pages:
- **Web space through your school.** Your school might provide you with free Web space on its Web server. The primary drawback of this is that you will lose the Web space when you graduate or leave.
- **Web space through your dial-up provider.** The dial-up provider you use to connect to the Internet also might provide you with free Web space. The amount of free space provided can vary, from 1 MB to 10 MB.
- **Web space through a free Web space provider.** There are also many providers of free Web space. Generally, these sorts of Web space accounts require that you display a banner or pop-up window with advertising when your Web pages are opened.
- **Web space through a for-pay Web space provider.** To gain access to more features, additional e-mail addresses, domain name registration, and higher traffic and space allotments, you can sign up for an account with a for-pay Web space provider. Costs run anywhere from $10 to $30 a month, depending on the account and its features.
- **Web space through a reseller account.** A reseller account allows you to resell Web space accounts. This can be handy, for instance, if you want to both design and manage Web sites for clients; by using a reseller account, you also can sell Web space, domain registration, and other Web services to your design clients.

For additional information on finding the right Web host for your Web pages, as well as links to resources for finding free and budget Web space providers, see this chapter's section at the IRC for this book at **www.emcp.com/**.

Understanding What You Need to Know

To transfer files from your local computer to your Web space folder on a remote Web server, you need or might need to know the following:

- **Host name (server name or Web address).** This is usually the name of the Web server on which your Web site folder is located (srv3.myhost.net, for instance). Some providers also let you use the Web address of your site, which might be different from the server name (www.myhost.net/~myfolder/, for instance).

- **Host type.** In most cases, you should not need to know this, but can specify that the host type should be automatically detected (if asked for this information). If that does not work, your Web server might require that you identify the specific host type you are trying to connect to. Your Web space provider will need to provide that information, or you can just experiment with the different available options in your FTP program until you find the right one.

- **User name.** If you are using Web space provided by your dial-up provider, this will be the same user name you use to log on the Internet. If you are using Web space provided by a separate provider, you need to use the user name assigned to you by that provider. Your user name is case-sensitive.

- **Password.** If you are using Web space provided by your dial-up provider, this will be the same password you use to log on to the Internet. If you are using Web space provided by a separate provider, you need to use the password assigned to you by that provider. Your password is case-sensitive.

- **Initial remote folder.** This is not required to connect to your Web space folder, but can specify that a particular folder, other than the root folder, be connected to. Web space folders are often organized into separate folders, one of which contains all the files and folders that are included in your Web site and into which you need to publish your Web page files. This folder can be named as **www**, **web**, or anything that your server administrator has decided to name this folder. By specifying that folder as your initial remote folder, you will go directly to it when you connect to your site.

- **Firewall settings.** If your computer is located behind a firewall, you might need to specify additional information, such as the name or IP address of your firewall and your user name and password. To set these settings, in WS_FTP, for instance, click the Connect button and then click the Firewall tab. Generally, this should not affect you in uploading files to a remote server, but might stop you from downloading files to your local computer. Check with your server administrator if you need to specify these additional settings.

NOTE

FTPplanet at **www.ftpplanet.com/** provides a number of tutorials for using WS_FTP LE for Windows to connect to your folder through various services that provide free Web space, including AOL, GeoCities, Angelfire, Tripod, Hometown, Bizland, FortuneCity, and V3space. The tutorials include what you need to specify as the host name in each case, which can easily be adapted for use with FTP programs other than WS_FTP LE. For additional FTP resources and tools, see this chapter's section at the IRC for this book at **www.ecmp.com/**.

Using an FTP Program

You can use many FTP programs to publish your Web page files to the Web. For links to where you can download FTP programs that are available for your platform, see this chapter's section at this book's IRC at **www.emcp.com/**. The following are some general tips for using an FTP program to connect to your Web space folder:

- You should uncheck any Anonymous check box or other option. An anonymous log-on is only done when a user name and password are not required.
- You usually can select to save your password, which will save you from having to retype it each time you connect. Realize, however, that your password will be saved on your local computer in an unencrypted form. If you are creating an e-commerce site or a site containing trade secrets, for instance, you would not want to save the password to access that site. If just creating a personal Web site, however, there is not much risk in saving your password.
- When transferring files, it is important to transfer them in the right format. You will need to transfer two types of files: ASCII files and binary files. ASCII files are any text files you want to transfer, including HTML (.html), CSS (.css), and JavaScript (.js) files. Binary files include any non-text files you want to transfer, including image, video, and audio files, for instance. If you transfer an ASCII text file as a binary file (or a binary file as an ASCII text file), it might not display properly.
- Although FTP programs give you the option of editing the HTML files located on your Web server, you should only make edit changes to the HTML files located on your local machine. If you directly edit the HTML files on your remote folder and your Web server crashes, you could lose all your edits. If you edit only on your local machine, after republishing your site, any changes you have made will be present on both your local machine and on your remote Web server.
- Some FTP programs include an "auto" feature that can be chosen when transferring Web page files. This is generally used when batch transferring all the contents of a folder, which can contain both ASCII and binary files. However, you might need to specify the file extensions for some ASCII text files, or they might be transferred as binary files. In WS_FTP, for instance, after connecting to your Web site, you can select Options and click the Extensions tab to specify the file extensions of ASCII text files (.htm, .html, .css, .js, .txt, and .xml).
- Some FTP programs also let you automatically convert file names to all lowercase. If you follow a policy of always naming files using all lowercase characters, this can be a handy way to insure that your link URLs and the file names they link to agree (file names on UNIX servers are case-sensitive). Windows, for instance, has a tendency to want to capitalize the first letter in file names, so selecting this option can guard against such file names sneaking through. To set this in WS_FTP, for instance, after connecting to your Web site, select Options and check the Force Lowercase Remote Names check box.

The spelling of file names referenced in links to local files within your own site should exactly match the actual file names, including all uppercase and lowercase characters. That is because file names are case-sensitive on UNIX computers and most Web servers still run some variant of UNIX. If after publishing your Web site's files to a Web server you find that links are suddenly no longer working that worked fine on your local machine, the most likely reason is that the file name referenced in the link URL does not exactly match the actual file name.

CHAPTER SUMMARY

You should now be familiar with creating multi-page Web sites using frames, understand the pros and cons of using frames, and know how to overcome some of the negatives associated with using frames. You also should understand how to create an external style sheet that can control the appearance of all the pages within a Web site, as well as how to use relative URLs to organize a multi-page Web site into multiple folders. Lastly, you should be familiar with the different Web hosting options, how to find out more about Web hosting options, and what you need to know to publish your Web pages to a Web server using an FTP program.

Code Review

FRAMESET element	Specifies a set of frames (or frameset), in columns or rows, and the files to be displayed in them.
COLS or ROWS attribute	In a FRAMESET element, specifies the number of columns or rows that are included in a frameset.
FRAME element	Defines a frame within a frameset, including specifying the file to be displayed in the frame, the name of the frame, vertical and horizontal margins, and whether borders and scrolling are turned off or on.
SCROLLING attribute	In the FRAME element, turns scrolling within the frame off (0) or on (1).
MARGINHEIGHT and MARGINWIDTH attributes	In the FRAME element, these attributes set the amount of vertical or horizontal margin spacing, in pixels, surrounding the content of a frame.
NAME attribute	Provides a name for a frame, so it can be targeted in a link.
TARGET attribute	In the A element (hypertext link), targets the name of a frame, so the link's object can be displayed in the targeted frame.
LINK element	In the HEAD element, defines the relationship of a linked file to the current document.
REL and TYPE attributes	In the LINK element, `rel="stylesheet"` declares that the link functions as a style sheet in relation to the current document and the `type="text/css"` specifies that the style sheet is a CSS style sheet.
display property	Specifies the type of element to be displayed (block, inline, list item, or none). This property can be used to specify that an inline element should be treated as a block element, so margins can be applied to it, for instance.
box model hack	A sequence of style codes that tricks Internet Explorer 5.5 for Windows to apply the correct width to a block element that also includes borders and padding.
list-style-image property	Specifies a bullet icon image to be displayed as the bullet in a bulleted list.
border property	Draws a border around an element in a variety of different styles (solid, double, dotted, dashed, groove, ridge, inset, and outset).

| padding property | Controls the amount of padding that is displayed between an element's content and its border. |
| margin property | Controls the amount of margin spacing that is displayed outside of an element's border. |

ONLINE QUIZ

Go to this text's IRC at **www.emcp.com/** and take the online self-check quiz for this chapter.

REVIEW EXERCISES

This section provides some hands-on practice exercises to reinforce the information and material included within this and previous chapters.

You can use any of the example files that you created in this chapter to further practice features or methods covered in this chapter. Because this chapter used example files that are linked together by name, to further practice with these files, make a copy of the whole chap06 folder, naming it as chap06_practice, for instance. If you are using a working disk, you can just copy the chap06 folder to another floppy disk and use that disk for further practice.

To copy the chap06 folder in Windows' My Computer or Windows Explorer, just right-click on the folder and select Copy, and then right-click in the background of your working folder or working disk and select Paste. Click on the name of the Copy of chap06 folder, click on it again, and then key **chap06_practice** as the new folder name.

On the Macintosh, in the Finder, just hold down the Option key, and click and drag the chap06 folder to create a copy. Then click on the "chap06 copy" folder name and key **chap06_practice** as the new folder name.

1. Working in the chap06_practice folder, experiment further with creating different kinds of frameset layouts. For instance, create a layout using a right sidebar frame or a bottom menu frame. Use any of the other example HTML files as the content of the frames, or create your own HTML pages to display in the frames. Experiment with using percentages to set frame widths and heights and then resize the browser window up or down to see what happens to percentage widths and heights in those situations.

2. Experiment further with creating frameset layouts that use both columns and rows. Copy and rename the **combo_frame4.html** frameset file (as **combo_frame4_2.html**, for instance). Revise the frameset layout so that the top-level FRAMESET element defines two columns, with the first column containing the sidebar menu file and the second column containing a nested FRAMESET element defining two rows. In the nested FRAMESET, set the first row as containing the top banner frame file and the second row as containing the main frame file.

3. The chapter explained how to create a grid layout by specifying both rows and columns in the same FRAMESET element. Create your own frameset from scratch to experiment with creating grid layouts. For the content of the frames, use any of the other HTML files in the folder. You also can experiment with linking to images as the content of frames within a grid layout. You can use any images you want to experiment doing this, or you can use any of the images that are included with the Chapter 4 example files (in chap04).

4. Experiment working with the aplus.css external style sheet file to specify different colors, backgrounds, or other formatting characteristics for the files linked to in by the combo_frame4.html frameset file. See Chapter 3, *Working with Fonts, Colors and Backgrounds,* to review specifying colors using hexadecimal RGB codes. For links to where you can find color charts, wheels, and pickers on the Web, see Chapter 3's section at the IRC for this book at **www.emcp.com/**.

   Experiment with assigning different background images in the aplus.css style sheet file. Coordinate the color scheme you are using with the background image, or vice versa. Use any of the other background images included with this chapter's example files. You also can find additional background images in the **art** folder that is included with this book's example files. You also can download background images from the Web or you can create your own background images. For links to image-viewing utilities that you can download and use, see Chapter 4's section at the IRC for this book at **www.emcp.com/**.

5. In the aplus.css style sheet file, experiment with creating different looks for the rollover button menu. Experiment setting different foreground and background colors, as well as different border colors, for the non-hover links (a:link, a:visited, and a:active) and the hover links (a:hover). Coordinate these colors with the color scheme for the site as a whole and with any background images you are displaying. When you have created a whole new look for the framed site that you are happy with, ask at least two other classmates for their opinions of your choices.

6. Experiment further with using inline styles to control the appearance of frame borders. Try setting different border widths, styles, and colors.

WEB-BASED LEARNING ACTIVITIES

In this book's text, Find It icons inserted in the margin highlight the Web addresses of additional resources you might find helpful or informative. To further extend your learning using the Web, you can:

- Go back and visit any of the Web addresses highlighted in this chapter that you have not yet visited. Look for additional resources and information that add to your understanding and knowledge of the material covered in this chapter. When you find a relevant page or site with information or resources you might want to access later, add it to your Favorites (in Internet Explorer) or your Bookmarks (in Netscape or Mozilla).

- Visit this book's Internet Resource Center at **www.emcp.com** to find additional Web addresses of resources related to the material covered in this chapter that you can further investigate and explore.

- Further research a specific topic introduced in this chapter. For instance, you can research issues involved with deep-linking with pages in other sites, especially when displayed within a site's own frames. Debate the pros and cons of the copyright and free speech issues that are involved with deep-linking.

   You might also further research the pros and cons of using frames in Web pages. Look for examples on the Web that show both effective and ineffective uses of frames.

   You also can research the availability of free and inexpensive Web hosting options. Find at least five sources of free Web space and five sources of inexpensive Web space ($15/month or less). Compare the features offered by each, including space and traffic allowances, e-mail addresses, domain name registration, and other services.

Sign up for a free Web space account and practice publishing a Web page to the Web space folder it provides.

You also can research available FTP programs for your platform. Download several FTP programs from the Web. If you have signed up for a couple of free Web space accounts, experiment using different FTP programs to publish a Web page to the Web. Compare the user interfaces, ease of use, and features.

Compile your research into a report that can be shared with your fellow students. You also can team up with other students to create a class presentation on a particular topic.

PROJECTS

These projects can be done in class, in a computer lab, or at home. Use the skills you have developed in this and the previous chapters to create any of the following projects.

Project 1. Create your own two-column or two-row framed Web site.

Take the lessons learned in this and previous chapters and apply them in creating your own two-column or two-row framed Web site:

- If you have already created a personal, topical, or other Web page that contains multiple sections, you can copy and save those sections as separate files and use them as the basis for creating content pages for a framed Web site. Create a sidebar or top bar menu file that accesses the content pages included in your site. Use any of the lessons you have learned in this book's chapters in creating the menu and content pages for your site.
- You can plan, write, and create a multi-page Web site using frames from scratch based on any topic of your choice. Create a sidebar or top bar menu file that accesses the content pages included in your site.

Keep it relatively simple starting out. Get a working multi-page framed Web site working first, before you spend a lot of time designing the individual pages. After you create a starter site, save a backup copy of it, and then use it as the base for experimenting with different designs and looks. With one version, for instance, create the appearance and design of the site entirely using HTML elements and attributes, without using styles. With another version, use styles to control the appearance and design of your site.

Project 2. Use an existing Web site as an example for creating a two-column or two-row framed Web site.

Look for an example of a multi-page framed Web site on the Web and use it as an example for creating your own two-column or two-row framed Web site.

For instance, to find examples of Web sites in specific categories, go to Yahoo! at **www.yahoo.com** and do a search on a keyword or key phrase of your choice. To find examples of computer consulting sites, for instance, do a search on "computer consultants." Feel free to browse any of Yahoo!'s categories to find an interesting example of the kind of Web site you would like to create.

Do not simply copy the text of the example site, but use the content of the example site as the basis for (and providing information and data for) writing your own content pages. If you have access to an image editor, create your own top banner or other graphics. If you want to publish the site on the Web (as opposed to simply creating it for practice on your own local computer), be sure to ask permission from the author or owner before using any graphics from the example Web site.

Project 3. Create a framed Web site that uses both rows and columns.

If you have done one of the first two projects, expand it to incorporate both rows and columns. Use an image editor to create your own top banner image, for instance, or you can use styles to create "styled" top banner text (using colors, borders, padding, and a background, for instance). Experiment with different layouts that combine a menu (left sidebar, right sidebar, topbar, or bottombar), a top banner frame, and a main content frame.

Project 4. Experiment with other frame schemes.

Take the lessons learned in this and previous chapters and apply them in experimenting with frame layouts (or schemes) not specifically covered in this chapter. For instance, create a layout that features the following:

- A topbar (or bottombar) menu that links to multiple frameset pages. This menu functions as a navigation bar for your whole site.
- Content pages with subsections that are marked with destination anchors (that can be jumped to using jump links).
- Sidebar menu pages for each of the content pages that use jump links (using fragment identifiers) to jump to subsections within the content pages.
- A main frameset page that links to the topbar (or bottombar) menu page, the first sidebar menu page, and the first content page. This frameset should be linked to from your topbar (or bottombar) menu through a "Home" or similar link, with a `target="_top"` attribute included in the link to cause the linked frameset file to be displayed in the top-level browser window.
- Use the first frameset page as a model for creating additional frameset pages that link to the topbar (or bottombar) menu page, as well as to each of the other sidebar menu/content page combinations you have created. These framesets should be linked to from your topbar (or bottombar) menu through the other menu link options, with `target="_top"` attributes included in the links to cause the linked frameset files to be displayed in the top-level browser window.

Project 5. Publish a Web page or site on the Web.

Using the lessons learned in this chapter, as well as any additional resources at this chapter's section in the IRC for this book at **www.emcp.com/**, validate and publish a Web page or Web site of your own creation on the Web:

- Choose any Web page or site that you have created and that you want to present to the rest of the world over the Web. If you have not yet finalized a page or site that you want to publish, do that first.
- Decide which kind of Web space account you want to use to publish your page or site. If you have Web space through your school that you want to use, but do not know how to access it, check with your system administrator, network support, or your instructor to find out what you need to do. You also can use free Web space provided by your home dial-up provider or by any other provider of free Web space. See this chapter's section at the IRC for this book at **www.emcp.com/** for links to additional resources that can help you find a provider of free Web space.

- Before publishing your site, validate your HTML files using the W3C HTML Validator. Correct any errors that are reported. When your pages are reported as valid, include valid HTML 4.01 icons at the bottom of your content pages.
- If you are using embedded style sheets or an external style sheet in your Web page or site, validate your style sheet using the W3C CSS Validator. Correct any errors that are reported. When your style sheet or sheets are reported as valid, include valid CSS icons at the bottom of your content pages.
- Publish your page or site to the Web. If you are publishing to your Web space folder on a school Web server, you might be able to simply copy and paste your Web page files into your Web space folder (ask your system administrator, network support, or your instructor for details of what you need to do). If you are publishing to Web space provided by your dial-up provider or another free provider, you might be able to use the provider's wizard or control panel to transfer your Web page files.

  You also can use an FTP program to publish your Web page files—see this chapter's section at the IRC for this book at **www.emcp.com/** for links to FTP guides and tutorials. For tutorials on how to use WS_FTP LE to connect to the many major free Web space providers (AOL, Angelfire, GeoCities, and so on), see FTPplanet at **www.ftpplanet.com/**). You also can check the support pages provided by the provider of your free Web space for details of how you need to configure your FTP software to connect to its server.
- After successfully validating and publishing a page or site to the Web, ask at least three classmates to critique your page's design, usability, and general attractiveness. Elicit other responses from friends or family members.
- Using the feedback provided by classmates, friends, and family, further refine the design and appearance of your site. Revalidate its pages and style sheets and then republish it to the Web.
- After you have created, published, and finalized your site, see this chapter's section at the IRC for additional resources on how to register your site at the major search engines and directories and how to promote your site. Be sure to include a mailto link to your e-mail address (use a free Web-mail address to protect against getting spammed), so you can receive feedback from visitors to your page or site.

Working with Forms

PERFORMANCE OBJECTIVES

In this chapter, you will learn how to create user-input forms, including how to:
- Create mailto and CGI forms.
- Create text boxes.
- Create radio buttons and check boxes.
- Create unfolding list menus.
- Create multi-line text area boxes.
- Handle form responses.
- Design form layouts.

Forms provide you with a means to gather information and data from visitors to a Web page. Forms can be as simple as a text area box that lets visitors send you a message or as complex as a survey or questionnaire that lets visitors fill out text boxes and select radio buttons, check boxes, and options from pull-down menus. You can gather information for your own use or you can format the data for presentation on the Web.

USING THE EXAMPLE FILES

If you have created a working folder for storing files you create, you will find the example files for this chapter located in the **chap07** folder within your working folder. Save any HTML files you create in this chapter in that folder.

If you have created a working disk, copy the chap07 folder to your working disk from the **HTML_Examples** folder that you or your instructor downloaded from this book's Internet Resource Center (IRC), or from a CD-R disc or floppy disk provided by your instructor. Save any HTML file you create in this chapter in the chap07 folder that you have copied to your working disk.

USING MAILTO AND CGI FORMS

You can include two basic kinds of forms in your Web pages: mailto and CGI forms. A mailto form uses a mailto URL to send form responses to your e-mail addresses. A CGI form uses a CGI script to process form responses, either saving them to a folder on your server or forwarding them to your e-mail address.

Mailto forms are easier to set up and test, but many users may not be able to use a mailto form. To use a mailto form, a user needs to be running one of the following:

- Any version of Netscape Navigator 2, 3, or 4 with Netscape's mail program (Netscape Messenger in Navigator 4) configured to send mail.
- Internet Explorer 4 with Internet Mail designated as the mail program and configured to send mail.
- Internet Explorer 5 or 5.5 with Outlook Express designated as the mail program and configured to send mail.

Many users, however, use browsers and/or mail programs that will not let them use a mailto form, including Netscape 4 users who have designated a mail program other than Messenger, Internet Explorer 4 users who have designated a mail program other than Internet Mail, and Internet Explorer 5 users who have designated a mail program other than Outlook Express. No version of the Opera browser supports sending mailto form responses. Internet Explorer 6, Netscape 6, and Mozilla 1, or later versions of those browsers, also do not support using sending mailto forms responses. In other words, users of the most current browsers will not be able to use mailto forms.

Users of mail systems that do not use SMTP (outgoing mail) servers are also not able to use a mailto form. For instance, if you are sending mail through AOL's mail system, you cannot use a mailto form. If you are using your local area network's (LAN) mail system to send mail, you also might not be able to use a mailto form.

For these reasons, if your browser/e-mail client combination allows the sending of mailto form responses, you should use a mailto form only to practice submitting and receiving form responses on your local computer. Mailto forms should not be published to the Web. Always publish forms to the Web as CGI forms. In the "Creating CGI Forms" section of this chapter, you learn how to create and use CGI forms.

Later in this chapter, you learn how to configure Internet Explorer 5 and 5.5 to send mailto forms, in case you are using either of those browsers, so you can use either of them to test sending and receiving mailto form responses, if you wish. You also learn what you need to know and do to create CGI forms and enable them in your Web pages.

CASE EXAMPLE: CREATING A SUBMISSION FORM

You can use a form to gather data from visitors to your page or site and then republish it on the Web.

Roger Yang is a computer science student who is taking a class in Web design. Through research, he found a bewildering array of Web hosting options. For a project to be completed for his class, he has decided to create a Web site that organizes different Web hosting options according to key features and characteristics. He has even registered a domain name, BestHosts.org, for his site. As part of that project, he has decided to create a user-input form that Web hosting companies can use to submit their Web hosting plans to be displayed on his site.

CREATING A FORM

In this section, you will create an HTML form containing a text area box, text boxes, radio buttons, check boxes, and pull-down lists. A starter page, hostsubmit_ex.html, also has been created for you that you will use to get started creating the example form for this chapter.

To start working with this example:
1. Open **hostsubmit_ex.html** in your text editor from the chap07 folder.
2. Save hostsubmit_ex.html as **hostsubmit.html** in the chap07 folder in your working folder or disk.
3. Open **hostsubmit.html** in your Web browser.

Starting the Form

The FORM element is used to create a user-input form in HTML. All other form elements are nested inside the FORM element.

Add a FORM element set to post the form response to a mailto e-mail address:

```
<h2 align="center">BestHosts.org</h2>
<h1 align="center">Web Hosting Plans - Submission Form</h1>
<p>To submit a hosting plan to be published on my Web Hosting
Plans page, fill out and submit the following form. This form
posts the responses to a mailto e-mail address, so not everyone
will be able to use this form. If you cannot use this form, send
the details of your hosting plan directly to <a
href="mailto:hostplans@besthosts.org">hostplans@besthosts.org</a>.
</p>

<form action="mailto:hosts@besthosts.org" method="post">
</form>
</body>
```

The ACTION attribute specifies the URL to which the form response is to be sent. This particular attribute specifies that the form data should be sent to a mailto e-mail address. A CGI form would specify the URL of a CGI script as the value of the ACTION attribute.

The METHOD attribute specifies the method to be used to transfer the form data when it is submitted. The METHOD attribute has two possible values: **post** and **get**. The post method sends the form data as an attachment to the URL (as a string of characters following a ? character in the URL); the get method sends the form response data as appended to the URL specified by the ACTION attribute. With the get method, a limit of 1,024 to 2,000 characters can be sent in a form response (the actual total number depends on the server being used). Because of the limit on the number of characters that can be sent, the get method is generally used only to send queries to and get responses from a CGI script. When submitting form data, however, you should always use the post method, not the get method.

You will notice that an introductory paragraph alerts users that they might not be able to use a mailto form and gives them an alternative means to submit their data. Because not everyone can use a mailto form, you should always provide an alternative means for submitting the form data whenever you use a mailto form.

Creating Input Controls

The INPUT element lets you specify a variety of different input controls you can add to a form, including text boxes, radio buttons, check boxes, and pull-down lists.

CREATING TEXT BOXES The INPUT element's `type="text"` attribute specifies a text box to be added to the form.

Add text boxes for specifying the provider's name, phone number, Web address, and e-mail address (see Figure 7.1):

```
<form action="mailto:hosts@besthosts.org" method="post">
<p>Provider: <input type="text" name="Provider" size="40"> Phone
#: <input type="text" name="Phone_Number" size="40"></p>
<p>Web Address: <input type="text" name="URL" size="40"> E-Mail:
<input type="text" name="EMail" size="40"></p>
<p>Plan Name: <input type="text" name="PlanName" size="30">
Setup Fee: <input type="text" name="Setup_Fee" size="15" value="$">
Monthly Fee: <input type="text" name="Monthly_Fee" size="15"
value="$"></p>
</form>
```

FIGURE 7.1 • *Four text box input controls are added to the form.*

The NAME attribute names the text field. NAME attribute values should not include spaces (use underscores instead). Each text box input control should have a unique name. When the form response data is submitted, the text keyed in the text box will be associated with the name of the text box field. If two text box input controls have the same name, the second text box's data will overwrite the first text box's data when the form is submitted.

The SIZE attribute specifies the width of the text box, according to text characters (not pixels). This attribute, however, only sets the width of the text box; it does not delimit the amount of text that can be entered in a text box. To delimit the amount of text that can be entered in a text box, use a MAXLENGTH attribute, which limits the total number of characters that can be entered in a text box to the specified value. For instance, `maxlength="40"` would limit input to a total of 40 characters. You might want to do this, for instance, if you plan on importing the form responses into a database with length limits set on specific fields.

The VALUE attribute specifies an initial value to be displayed within a text box.

CREATING RADIO BUTTONS The INPUT element's `type="radio"` attribute specifies a radio button option to be added to the form. Only one button from a group of radio buttons can be selected. The term *radio button* actually comes from car radios, which as a safety feature used push buttons for selecting radio stations. In this older radio style, pushing one button would pop up any other button that had been pushed previously.

Add a group of radio buttons that allows a user to specify the type of host plan being submitted (see Figure 7.2):

```
<p>Plan Name: <input type="text" name="PlanName" size="30">
Setup Fee: <input type="text" name="Setup_Fee" size="15"
value="$">
Monthly Fee: <input type="text" name="Monthly_Fee" size="15"
value="$"></p>

<p>Plan Type:
<input type="radio" name="PlanType" value="Non-Virtual Host"
checked>Non-Virtual Host Plan  
<input type="radio" name="PlanType" value="Basic Virtual
Host">Basic Virtual Host Plan  
<input type="radio" name="PlanType" value="Advanced Virtual
Host">Advanced Virtual Host Plan  
<input type="radio" name="PlanType" value="Reseller">Reseller
Plan  
</p>
</form>
```

FIGURE 7.2 • *A group of radio button options is added to the form.*

Notice that a CHECKED attribute is included in the first radio button INPUT element. It specifies that the radio button should initially be selected. In the absence of a CHECKED attribute, none of the radio buttons will be selected initially. The same attribute can be used with check boxes (covered in the next section) to specify that a check box should initially be checked.

Unlike with text boxes, notice that the NAME attribute in each radio button input control specifies the same name. The NAME attribute, in this case, defines a group of radio button controls.

The VALUE attribute specifies the value to be submitted with the form response data if a radio button is selected (the data value will be associated with the name of the radio button input control group).

CREATING CHECK BOXES The INPUT element's `type="checkbox"` attribute specifies a check box option to be added to the form. Unlike with radio buttons, multiple check boxes from a group of check boxes can be selected at the same time.

Add a group of check boxes to the form (see Figure 7.3):

```
<input type="radio" name="PlanType" value="Reseller">Reseller
Plan  
</p>
<p>Basic Features Included:</p>
<p><input type="checkbox" name="Basic_Features" value="stock CGI
scripts">stock CGI scripts  
<input type="checkbox" name="Basic_Features" value="FTP
upload">FTP upload  
<input type="checkbox" name="Basic_Features" value="extra e-mail
addresses">multiple e-mail addresses  
<input type="checkbox" name="Basic_Features" value="access
reports">access reports  
<input type="checkbox" name="Basic_Features" value="free domain
name registration">free domain name registration  </p>
</form>
```

Plan Type: ⦿ Non-Virtual Host Plan ○ Basic Virtual Host Plan ○ Advanced Virtual Host Plan ○ Reseller Plan ⟶ check boxes

Basic Features Included:

☐ stock CGI scripts ☐ FTP upload ☐ multiple e-mail addresses ☐ access reports ☐ free domain name registration

FIGURE 7.3 • *A group of check boxes is added to the form.*

Unlike with text boxes, notice that the NAME attribute in each check box input control specifies the same name. The NAME attribute, in this case, defines a group of check box input controls.

The VALUE attribute specifies the value to be submitted with the form response data if a check box is selected (the data value will be associated with the name of the check box input control group). If more than one check box is selected, a comma-separated list of selected values is returned.

USING OTHER INPUT CONTROLS You can use a number of additional input controls in forms, including hidden, password, file, submit, reset, image, and button input controls. Examples will be shown later in this chapter of using the hidden, submit, reset, and image input controls. The password input control works like the text input control, but displays text that is keyed as a series of asterisks. You might, for instance, use a password input control to ask for a credit card number in a secure form. The file input control allows you to create a box where the name of a file to be uploaded can be specified. The button input control allows you to create a push button that can activate a JavaScript script, for instance.

Creating List Menus

The SELECT and OPTION elements are used to include a pull-down menu in a form that lets users select from a list of options.

Add a pull-down menu to the form (see Figure 7.4):

```
<input type="radio" name="PlanType" value="Reseller">Reseller
Plan  </p>
<p>Server Type:
<select name="ServerType">
  <option selected>Unix/Linux-Based Server
  <option>Windows-Based Server
  <option>Macintosh-Based Server
  <option>Other Server</select>
</p>
<p>Basic Features Included:</p>
```

list menu —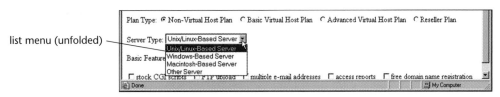

FIGURE 7.4 • *A pull-down list is displayed folded when it is included in a form.*

When you click on a pull-down list, the list options drop down (or pop-up), as shown in Figure 7.5.

list menu (unfolded) —

FIGURE 7.5 • *When a pull-down list is clicked, it unfolds to display the options.*

SETTING THE SIZE OF A LIST MENU By default, a list menu only displays one option. You can use the SELECT element's SIZE attribute to specify the number of options that will be displayed initially in a list menu. For instance, to set all four options to be displayed, set a size of 4:

```
<select name="ServerType" size="4">
```

SPECIFYING OPTION VALUES By default, the text following the selected OPTION element in a list menu is sent with the form response data. You can use the OPTION element's VALUE attribute, however, to specify alternative data values that you want to have sent. This allows you to display more descriptive text as your options, for instance, while sending more abbreviated text as data in the form response:

```
<select name="ServerType">
  <option value="unix" selected>Unix/Linux-Based Server
  <option value="win">Windows-Based Server
  <option value="mac">Macintosh-Based Server
  <option value="other">Other Server
</select>
```

ENABLING MULTIPLE SELECTIONS IN A LIST MENU Normally, a user only can select one item from a list menu. The SELECT element's MULTIPLE attribute specifies that users can select multiple options from a list menu, either by holding down the Ctrl key to select separate options or by holding down the Shift key to select a range of options.

For this to be practical, you need to preface the list menu with some kind of notice indicating that multiple options can be selected and instructing the user how to do it.

```
<p>Server Type (hold down CTRL or SHIFT to select multiple
options):
<select name="ServerType">
   <option value="unix" selected>Unix/Linux-Based Server
   <option value="win">Windows-Based Server
   <option value="mac">Macintosh-Based Server
   <option value="other">Other Server
</select>
```

Creating Text Area Boxes

The TEXTAREA element creates a multi-line text box. Text area boxes are often used to allow users to provide comments or expand on their previous selections.

Add a text area box that is 8 lines high and 75 characters wide (see Figure 7.6):

```
<input type="checkbox" name="Basic_Features" value="free domain
name registration">free domain name registration  </p>
<p>Added Comments:</p>
<p><textarea name="Comments" rows="8" cols="75"></textarea></p>
</form>
```

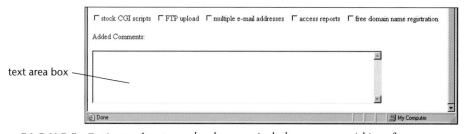

FIGURE 7.6 • *A text area box lets users include comments within a form.*

Creating Control Buttons

After you have created the elements of your form, you need to provide a means for the user to submit or reset the form.

CREATING SUBMIT AND RESET BUTTONS Two additional input controls, the Submit button and the Reset button, allow users to submit or reset the form.

Add Submit and Reset buttons to the form (see Figure 7.7):

```
<p><textarea name="Comments" rows="8" cols="75"></textarea></p>

<p><input type="submit" value="Submit"> <input type="reset"
value="Reset"></p>
</form>
```

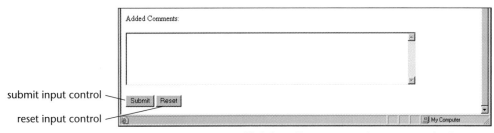

submit input control ——

reset input control ——

FIGURE 7.7 • *Buttons are added that allow users to submit or reset the form.*

The VALUE attribute specifies the label for the button. This can be whatever you want, as long as it conveys the action of the button when it is clicked. For instance, you could just as easily specify **Submit Form** and **Submit Button** as the value of these attributes. When a user clicks on the Submit button, the form is submitted to the URL specified by the FORM element's ACTION attribute.

CREATING AN IMAGE BUTTON Alternatively, you can use an image as a Submit button. An example Submit button image, submit.gif, is included with this chapter's example files. For this example, you will be including both a Submit button and a Submit image button in the same form for testing purposes; in normal practice, however, you would use one or the other, not both, in a form.

Add a Submit image button to the form (see Figure 7.8):

```
<p><input type="submit" value="Submit"> <input type="reset"
value="Reset"></p>
<p><input type="image" src="submit.gif" alt="Submit Form Button"
border="0"></p>
```

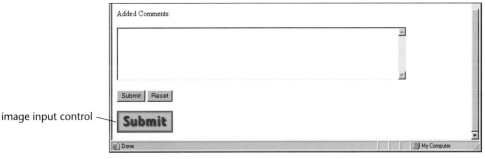

image input control ——

FIGURE 7.8 • *You also can use an image as a Submit button.*

USING THE BUTTON ELEMENT HTML 4 includes an additional element, the BUTTON element, that is supposed to work the same way as a Submit button created using the INPUT element, except with richer rendering possibilities. The main problem with using the BUTTON element is that few browsers support it and it does not degrade gracefully in browsers that do not support it, because users of such browsers are left with no way to submit the form. The BUTTON element is supported by Internet Explorer 5.5 for Windows and Internet Explorer 5 for the Macintosh, but not by the Netscape or Mozilla browsers.

Create Submit and Reset buttons using the BUTTON element (see Figure 7.9):

```
<p><input type="image" src="submit.gif" alt="Submit Form Button"
border="0"></p>
<p><button name="submit" value="submit" type="submit">
  <font size="4" color="green">Submit</font>
</button>  
<button name="reset" type="reset">
  <font size="4" color="maroon">Reset</font>
</button></p>
</form>
```

FIGURE 7.9 • *Submit and Reset buttons created with the BUTTON element are more flexible, but are supported by fewer browsers.*

You also can use a style to set the formatting of the BUTTON element, including specifying a background image for the button. An example background image, back_marblebeige2.jpg, is included with the example files for this chapter.

Create a style that defines the visual formatting of the BUTTON element (see Figure 7.10):

```
<style type="text/css">
button { font-size: 1.25em; font-weight: bold; background:
#ffffcc url(back_marblebeige2.jpg); width: 5em; }
</style>
</head>
```

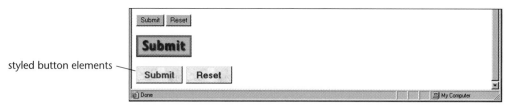

FIGURE 7.10 • *A style can be used to control the visual appearance of BUTTON elements.*

Because few browsers support the BUTTON element and it degrades ungracefully in browsers that do not support it, it is probably best to avoid using it, at least until more browsers support it. Use the INPUT element, instead, to create Submit and Reset buttons for forms.

Testing the Form

Now that you have created a form, you can test it. Depending on your browser/mail program combination and configuration, you might not be able to actually submit and retrieve a form response. You can, however, test all the elements of the form and make sure the Submit and Reset buttons are working properly.

FILLING IN THE TEXT BOXES The top of the form contains a series of text boxes. You can move from one text field to another by pressing the Tab key.

Test the form you have just created:

1. With hostsubmit.html open in your browser, key **XYZ Hosting Company** in the Provider text box.
2. Press Tab to get to the Phone # text box and key **(212) 555-8743**.
3. Press Tab to get to the Web Address text box and key **http://www.xyzhosting.com/**.
4. Press Tab to get to the E-Mail text box and key **info@xyzhosting.com**.
5. Press Tab to get to the Plan Name text box and key **ABC Host Plan**.
6. Press Tab to get to the Setup Fee text box and key **$10.00**.
7. Press Tab to get to the Monthly Fee text box (see Figure 7.11) and key **$12.95**.

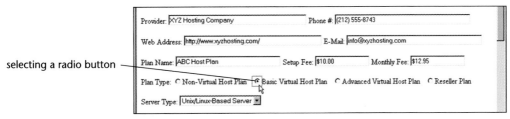

FIGURE 7.11 • *The form's text boxes are filled in.*

SELECTING A RADIO BUTTON The next section of the form contains a group of radio buttons. You can select only one radio button out of a group.

Click on the Basic Virtual Host Plan radio button to select the Plan Type (see Figure 7.12). Notice that the Non-Virtual Host Plan radio button, which was selected previously, is no longer selected.

FIGURE 7.12 • *A radio button is selected to designate the plan type.*

SELECTING A LIST MENU OPTION The next line of the form contains a list menu that lets a user specify a server type.

action

Click on the Server Type list box to unfold it and select the Windows-Based Server option (see Figure 7.13).

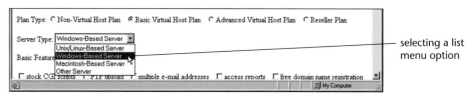

selecting a list menu option

FIGURE 7.13 • *The Windows-Based Server option is selected from the list box.*

SELECTING CHECK BOXES The next section of the form contains a series of check boxes. Unlike radio buttons, you can select multiple check boxes within a check box group.

action

In the Basic Features Included group of check boxes, click on the first, second, and fourth check boxes (stock CGI scripts, FTP upload, and access reports) to select them, while leaving the other two check boxes unchecked (see Figure 7.14).

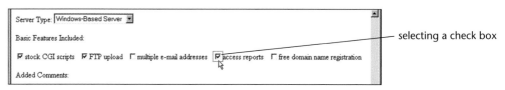

selecting a check box

FIGURE 7.14 • *You can select multiple check boxes in a group of check boxes.*

FILLING IN THE TEXT AREA BOX You cannot key more than one line of text in a text box, but you can key multiple lines of text in a text area box.

action

In the Added Comments text area box, key: **Same day e-mail support. 30-day money back guarantee. Redundant T3 connections to the Internet backbone.** (See Figure 7.15.)

text typed in a text area box

FIGURE 7.15 • *You can key a multi-line comment in a text area box.*

TESTING THE SUBMIT AND RESET BUTTONS The current form has three kinds of Submit buttons and two kinds of Reset buttons. In a normal form, you only have one set of these buttons.

action

Test the Submit and Reset buttons:

1. Click the gray Submit button. Internet Explorer 5.5 (with Outlook Express designated as the mail program) displays a pop-up box alerting you that the form is being sent via e-mail and asking you if you want to continue (see Figure 7.16). Just click Cancel at this point.

mailto pop-up window ——

submit input control ——

FIGURE 7.16 • *When submitting a mailto form, Internet Explorer alerts the user that the form is being sent by e-mail.*

2. Click the Submit image button. You should get the same pop-up box shown in Figure 7.16, if using Internet Explorer 6 (with Outlook Express). Click Cancel.
3. Click the green Submit button (the bottom Submit button). If using Internet Explorer 6 (with Outlook Express), you should see the same pop-up box as in Steps 1 and 2. Click Cancel.
4. Click the first Reset button (in the first line of buttons). You will see that the form has reverted to its original state, with none of the fields filled out.
5. Key any text in the Added Comments text area box. Click the maroon Reset button (on the bottom line of buttons). You will see that the form has reverted to its original state, with none of the fields filled out.

Setting the Tabbing Order

Users can move from one form element to the next by pressing the Tab key. Normally, the tabbing order is the same as the order in which the form elements are inserted in the document. By using the TABINDEX attribute, however, you can set a different tabbing order. The following elements accept the TABINDEX attribute: A, AREA, BUTTON, INPUT, OBJECT, SELECT, and TEXTAREA. Not all of these are form elements, but they would normally be included in the tabbing order.

The TABINDEX attribute takes a value from 0 to 32,767. The element with the lowest TABINDEX value is tabbed to first, the one with the second-lowest value is tabbed to second, and so on. The following example uses the TABINDEX value to reorder the tabbing order:

```
<p>Provider: <input type="text" name="Provider" size="40"
tabindex="1"> Phone #: <input type="text" name="Phone_Number"
size="40" tabindex="3"></p>
```

```
<p>Web Address: <input type="text" name="URL" size="40"
tabindex="2"> E-Mail: <input type="text" name="EMail" size="40"
tabindex="4"></p>
```

SENDING AND RECEIVING MAILTO FORM RESPONSES

As was stressed at the start of this chapter, many users cannot use a mailto form. For that reason, you should use a mailto form only to test sending and receiving form responses on your local computer, but not for soliciting responses from the Web. If you decide to publish a mailto form to the Web, you should always alert users that they might not be able to use the form and provide them with a link to your e-mail address, so they can submit data or provide feedback by sending you an e-mail. When including your e-mail address in the form, be sure to display your e-mail address as the link text, because some users also cannot use a mailto e-mail address (although more people can use mailto e-mail addresses than can use mailto forms) and will need to copy and paste your e-mail address into their mail programs.

Setting Up Your Browser to Send Mailto Forms

Only some browsers can send mailto form responses. The following sections provide details about using mailto forms with the Netscape, Mozilla, and Internet Explorer browsers.

USING MAILTO FORMS WITH NETSCAPE AND MOZILLA To send mailto form responses in Netscape 2, 3, or 4, you only need to have Netscape's mail client (Netscape Messenger in Netscape 4) configured to send mail. If you can send an e-mail message by clicking on a mailto link, you also should be able to send a mailto form response.

Netscape 6 (or higher) and Mozilla 1, however, do not support sending mailto form responses. Clicking on the Submit button pops up a correctly addressed blank message composition window, but without the form response data attached. If sent, the recipient would receive a blank e-mail message.

tip

One option is to download and install a copy of Netscape Communicator 4 (which includes Netscape Navigator 4 and Messenger 4) and use it to test submitting and receiving mailto form responses on your local computer. You can download and install a version of Netscape Communicator 4 for Windows, Macintosh, or UNIX at **wp.netscape.com/download/archive.html**. To get it to work, you will need to configure Netscape Messenger to send mail by specifying the outgoing (SMTP) mail server you are using.

USING MAILTO FORMS WITH INTERNET EXPLORER The most recent versions of Internet Explorer (Version 6 and higher) do not support sending mailto form responses, even if you have Outlook Express specified as your mail client and have configured it properly to send e-mail. To send mailto form responses, you must use Internet Explorer 4 (with Internet Mail installed as your mail client and configured to send mail) or Internet Explorer 5 or 5.5 (with Outlook Express installed and designated as your mail client and configured to send mail). If using Exchange or Outlook (not Express) as your mail client with Internet Explorer 5 or 5.5, you will not be able to send mailto form responses.

Internet Explorer 5 or 5.5 for Windows. If you are using Internet Explorer 5 or 5.5 for Windows as your browser, designate Outlook Express as your mail program in Internet Explorer 5 or 5.5 for Windows:

1. In Internet Explorer, select Tools and Internet Options.
2. Click the Programs tab. Make sure that Outlook Express is specified in the E-mail field (see Figure 7.17). Click OK.

Outlook Express selected as e-mail client in Internet Explorer

FIGURE 7.17 • *To use mailto links and mailto forms, you must specify Outlook Express as your mail program in Internet Explorer 6.*

If you are using Internet Explorer 5 for the Macintosh, you can specify separately the outgoing mail server (SMTP host) you are using to send mail.

Internet Explorer 5 for the Macintosh. Specify an outgoing mail server to be used when sending mailto form responses:

1. In Internet Explorer, select Edit and Preferences.
2. Scroll down to the bottom of the left panel. Expand the E-mail option, if it is not already expanded.
3. Under E-mail, click on the General option. The outgoing mail server for the e-mail account provided by your dial-up provider should be displayed in the SMTP host box. (If the SMTP host is empty or specifies an inactive mail server, you will not be able to send mailto form responses.)

It is important to stress that posting form responses to a mailto URL is not provided for in the official HTML or XHTML specifications. When using the FORM element's ACTION attribute, the HTML 4.01 specification states the following: "User agent behavior for a value other than an HTTP URI is undefined." This means that how a particular browser handles (or does not handle) posting mailto form data depends entirely upon the individual browser. The HTML 4 and XHTML 1 standards do not require that browsers support mailto forms.

Sending Mailto Form Responses

If you are using one of the browsers specified as supporting mailto forms and have properly configured it and your mail program, you should be able to send a mailto form response. If, however, your connection to the Internet does not use a standard POP3 e-mail facility (if connecting through AOL or a school LAN, for instance), you probably will not be able to send a mailto form response. If you have an alternative means to connect to the Internet (such as your home Internet account), you can try using that to test this.

If you are not using a browser that supports sending and receiving mailto forms or have difficulty configuring a browser that does, skip ahead to the next section, "Creating CGI Forms."

Set up the example form to send a mailto form response to your e-mail address and then send a form response to that address:

1. If it is not already open in your text editor, open **hostsubmit.html** in your text editor.
2. Revise the FORM element's ACTION attribute to refer to your e-mail address:

```
<form action="mailto:type your e-mail address here" method="post">
```

3. Comment out the additional Submit and Reset buttons (otherwise, the content of the BUTTON element will be sent as form data):

```
<p><input type="submit" value="Submit"> <input type="reset"
value="Reset"></p>
<!--
<p><input type="image" src="submit.gif" alt="Submit Form Button"
border="0"></p>
<p><button name="submit" value="submit" type="submit">
    <font size="4" color="green">Submit</font></button>  
<button name="reset" type="reset">
    <font size="4" color="maroon">Reset</font></button>
</p>
-->
```

4. Save the form (File, Save) and then open (or refresh) it in your browser.
5. Fill out text fields (using whatever text you like), select radio buttons, and select check boxes.
6. Click on the Submit button (the one in the first line).
7. If alerted that the form is being sent via e-mail, click OK. If further alerted that a program is trying to use Outlook Express to send an e-mail message on your behalf, just click the Send button.

Receiving Mailto Form Responses

If you have successfully sent a mailto form response to yourself, you will find a message in your e-mail account's inbox containing the form response. How this message is displayed and how the form response is accessed depends upon the browser that sent the form response and on the mail program being used to access it:

- A form response sent using Netscape 4 is displayed with a subject heading of "Form posted from Mozilla." Do not confuse this with the Mozilla browser (which cannot send mailto form responses). A form response sent using Internet Explorer 4, 5, or 5.5 is displayed with a subject heading of "Form posted from Microsoft Internet Explorer."
- To view form response data sent by Netscape 4, open the form message and then click on the Part 1 link.

- For a form response sent by Internet Explorer, click on the attachment (POST-DATA.ATT) and save it as a file (as **testresponse.txt**, for instance) to your hard drive or floppy disk. Figure 7.18 shows a fictional form response that has been saved and opened in Notepad.

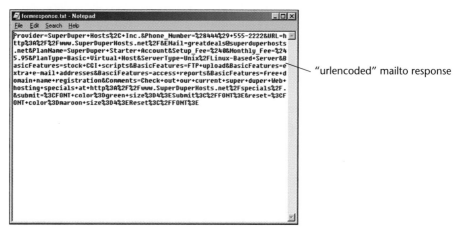

"urlencoded" mailto response

FIGURE 7.18 • *A mailto form response is opened in Windows Notepad.*

DECIPHERING MAILTO FORM RESPONSES As you will notice in Figure 7.18, mailto form data is not sent in a format that is easy for a person to read. That is because the default content type for mailto form responses (referred to as a *urlencoded* content type) substitutes control codes for any spaces, hard returns, and commas, for instance. To send mailto form responses in a format that is friendly to humans, you must change the content type for the form response.

Change the content type of the form data and then resend and receive the form data:
1. If not already open, open **hostsubmit.html** in your text editor. Edit the FORM element to change the content type, as shown here:

```
<form action="mailto:your e-mail address" method="post"
enctype="text/plain">
```

2. Save the file (File, Save) and open (or refresh) it in your browser. Fill out the form and click the Submit button to send a form response to your e-mail address.
3. In your mail program, open the form response. Now, instead of the POSTDATA.ATT attachment, you will see the form data displayed in the message body in a format that is easy for a person to read (see Figure 7.19).

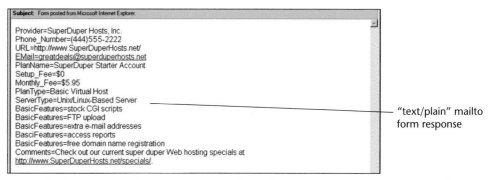

"text/plain" mailto form response

FIGURE 7.19 • *By setting the content type of a mailto form response, you get a response that is much more easily read by a human being.*

Using Mailto Form Utilities Various utilities also are available on the Web that process mailto form responses. Besides converting form responses into text format, such utilities might also translate mailto form responses into comma-delimited format so they can be easily imported into a database or spreadsheet program. For links to where you can find mailto form utilities you can download and try out, see this chapter's section at the IRC for this book at **www.emcp.com/**.

CREATING CGI FORMS

To create a form that everyone can use, you need to create a CGI form. A CGI form uses a program or script located on the Web server, generally referred to as a *CGI script*, to process and direct form responses. Many Web hosts provide a stock form-processing CGI script that you can use. If your Web host does not provide a stock form-processing CGI script and does not allow you to install your own CGI scripts, you will not be able to use a CGI form, at least not a form using a CGI script hosted by your Web host. There are, however, services that provide remotely hosted form-processing CGI scripts that you can use instead, usually in exchange for allowing them to display advertising along with the form submission confirmation.

N O T E The acronym, CGI, stands for Common Gateway Interface and refers to the standard means by which a client-side application, such as a Web browser, can communicate and interface with a server-side program or script that is located on a Web server. The term, CGI script, refers to any script or program that can be executed over the Web from a Web server.

Setting Up a CGI Form

The following includes a hypothetical example of setting up a CGI form. In real life, the ACTION attribute value will vary according to what your Web host requires, which can be different, depending upon the location and name of the script being used.

Resave your example form file (to preserve the mailto form example) and set up your form as a CGI form:

1. In your text editor, save any changes to **hostsubmit.html** (File, Save) and then resave it as **hostsubmit2.html** in the chap07 folder in your working folder or working disk.
2. Open **hostsubmit2.html** in your browser.
3. In your text editor, edit **hostsubmit2.html** so it matches what is shown here:

```
<form action="/cgi-bin/FormMail.pl" method="post"
enctype="text/plain">
<p><input type="hidden" name="recipient" value="type your email
address here"></p>
```

This is just one example of linking a form-processing CGI script. A different CGI script might be required by your Web host, so check first with your Web host to see which CGI script they provide (if they provide one). The hidden input control that follows the FORM element specifies the e-mail address to which form responses should be sent. Other form-processing CGI scripts might require a slightly different hidden input control to specify this, using a different NAME value, for instance, but they should be relatively similar to what is shown here.

CGI scripts can be written in any programming or scripting language available on the Web server. Many CGI scripts are written using Perl, which is a programming language commonly available on UNIX servers, but they also can be written using other languages, such as C or C++, Visual Basic, AppleScript, TCL, ASP, and the UNIX shell, for instance.

NOTE

Some Web authors use a CGI form instead of a mailto link to provide visitors with a means to provide feedback. This has the advantage of hiding your e-mail address from spam robots that roam the Web looking for e-mail addresses in Web pages.

Setting Up and Configuring a Form-Processing CGI Script

To use CGI scripts, your Web host must allow the use of at least stock CGI scripts that they provide for you. A Web host also might allow you to create and add your own custom CGI scripts to your site. On a Windows server or Macintosh server, you can install CGI scripts in any folder. On a UNIX server, however, most Web hosts that support the use of custom CGI scripts set up a *personal cgi-bin* folder that is part of your site's folder structure. In that folder, you can add or create CGI scripts, as well as assign permissions.

If your site is hosted on a UNIX or Linux server, before you can use a CGI script in your personal cgi-bin folder, you must set the access permissions for it. If you do not, users might not be able to access the CGI script over the Web.

Most Web servers on the Web are running under UNIX. For that reason, the following instructions are for using Telnet or FTP to set access permissions on a UNIX (or Linux) server. If your Web host's server is running under Windows or on a Macintosh, see their technical support notes for information on what you need to do to install and configure CGI scripts on those platforms.

USING TELNET TO SET PERMISSIONS FOR A CGI SCRIPT You can use a telnet program to log on to your Web hosting account, if your account allows you to do this. See this chapter's section at the IRC for this book at **www.emcp.com/** for links to telnet programs you can download and try. To use a telnet program to set permissions for a CGI script, you would do something similar to the following:

1. Run the telnet program and specify the name of the server on which your Web site folders are located (sv2.someserver.com, for instance) to connect to it.
2. After connecting to your server, you should be prompted to log in. Key your user name and press Enter, and then key your password and press Enter.
3. To see your current position, key **pwd** and press Enter. You might see something like /users/vhome/*username* (with *username* standing for your user name).
4. A personal cgi-bin folder is usually directly off the root folder. To change to your personal cgi-bin folder, key **cd cgi-bin** and press Enter.
5. To set the permissions for the CGI script, key **chmod 755 FormMail.pl** (FormMail.pl is a CGI script written in Perl; substitute a different name for the CGI script if your form-processing script is named differently), and press Enter.
6. Key **logout** and press Enter to end and close the telnet session.

USING AN FTP PROGRAM TO SET CGI SCRIPT PERMISSIONS You also might be able to use an FTP program to set CGI script permissions on a UNIX or Linux server. Using an FTP program was covered in Chapter 6, *Creating Multi-Page Web Sites*; to find freeware and shareware FTP programs you can download and use, see that chapter's section at the IRC for this book at **www.emcp.com/**.

For instance, if your site is located on a UNIX server, following are steps you can follow to use WS_FTP LE for Windows to set CGI script permissions:

1. Run WS_FTP LE and connect to your Web hosting account.
2. Change to your cgi-bin folder—if you have set up WS_FTP LE to automatically open your Web site folder, you will need to first change to the parent folder (your site's root folder) and then change to your cgi-bin folder.
3. Right-click on the CGI script (FormMail.pl, for instance), select FTP Commands, and then select SITE.

The name of the form-processing CGI script that is used on your site's server may be different from the CGI script shown in Step 3. Check your Web host's support pages for information on which CGI script is used on your server.

4. Key **chmod 755 FormMail.pl** and press Enter (substitute the actual name of the CGI script you want to set permissions for).
5. Click Close and then click Exit.

UNDERSTANDING THE CHMOD NUMBER   The CHMOD (Change Mode) command is used to set access permissions for the owner, the group, and all others. The number, 755, used to set the permissions for the FormMail.pl script is not nearly as arcane as it might appear. Rather than a three-digit number, it actually represents three separate numbers: 7, 5, and 5. The first number sets permissions for the owner, the second for the group, and the third for everyone else.

You are the owner, of course. The group is either everyone logged onto the server or a more restrictive listing of individuals who are assigned permission to access the file by the server administrator. Everyone else refers to the users on the Web who will visit your site and make use of the form. Table 7.1 shows how these access numbers are derived.

TABLE 7.1 • *How CHMOD Permission Numbers Are Derived*

Access Permission	Owner	Group	World
Read (4 = yes; 0 = no)	4	4	4
Write (2 = yes; 0 = no)	2	0	0
Execute (1 = yes; 0 = no)	1	1	1
CHMOD Number	7	5	5

Thus, as shown in Table 7.1, if you want the owner to have read, write, and execute permissions for a file, you need to assign a value of 7 (or 4 + 2 + 1) in the first number. On the other hand, if you do want group members or others to have permission to read and execute a file, but not to write to that file, you need to assign a value of 5 (4 + 0 + 1) in the second two numbers, with the full resulting CHMOD value thus being 755.

Sending and Receiving CGI Form Responses

Unlike a mailto form, you cannot test submitting CGI form responses on your local computer without accessing a Web host's server, since a CGI script needs to be located on a Web server for you to be able to access it. If you have access to a form-processing CGI script located on the Web, you can access it on your local computer by specifying an absolute URL for the script. If using a relative URL, however, you need to first publish your form to the Web before you can test it.

When you submit a mailto form, if your browser/mail program combination and configuration supports using mailto forms, a pop-up window alerts you that you are sending a form via e-mail. When you submit a CGI form, the CGI script on the server generates an HTML page that confirms that the form response has been sent. Figure 7.20 shows a form response confirmation page generated by the FormMail CGI script.

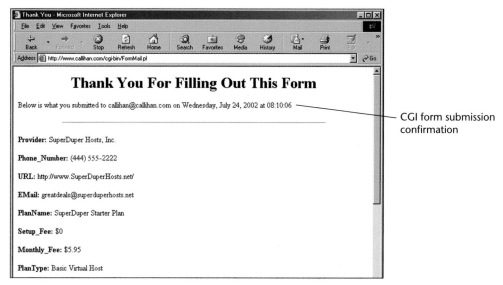

FIGURE 7.20 • *When you submit a CGI form, the form-processing CGI script generates a page confirming that the form response has been sent to the recipient's e-mail address.*

When you receive the form response in your inbox, the form response data is generally included in the body of the message. Figure 7.21 shows an example of a CGI form response.

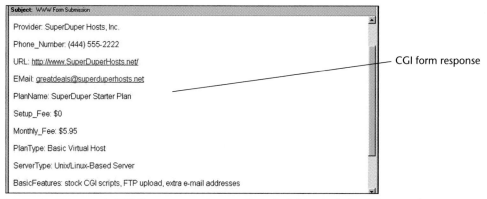

FIGURE 7.21 • *A CGI form response is generally included in the body of the e-mail message.*

DESIGNING FORMS

Until now in this chapter, you focused on using the different form elements and attributes, as well as understanding how to use, submit, and receive form responses. You also can design and format your forms further so they are more attractive and easier to read.

Using the PRE Element with Forms

You can use the PRE element to horizontally align text fields and other form elements.

Use the PRE element to horizontally align text fields and other form elements:

1. Re-open **hostsubmit.html** in your text editor and save it as **hostsubmit3.html**. Open **hostsubmit3.html** in your browser.
2. Edit **hostsubmit3.html** so it matches what is shown here (insert spaces where " · " characters are displayed).

```
<pre>Provider:·····<input type="text" name="Provider" size="40"
tabindex="1">··Phone #:··<input type="text" name="Phone_Number"
size="30">
</pre>

<pre>Web Address:···<input type="text" name="URL"
size="40">··E-Mail:····<input type="text" name="EMail" size="30">
</pre>

<pre>Plan Name:·····<input type="text" name="PlanName"
size="30">··Setup Fee:<input type="text" name="Setup_Fee"
size="10" value="$">··Monthly Fee:·<input type="text"
name="Monthly_Fee" size="10" value="$"></pre>

<pre>Plan Type:····<input type="radio" name="PlanType"
value="Non-Virtual Host" checked>Non-Virtual Host
Plan········<input type="radio" name="PlanType" value="Basic
Virtual Host">Basic Virtual Host Plan
············<input type="radio" name="PlanType" value="Advanced
Virtual Host">Advanced Virtual Host Plan··<input type="radio"
name="PlanType" value="Reseller">Reseller Plan</pre>

<pre>Server Type:···<select name="ServerType">
  <option selected>Unix/Linux-Based Server
  <option>Windows-Based Server
  <option>Macintosh-Based Server
```

```
          <option>Other Server
</select>
</pre>

<pre>Basic Features Included:

· · · · · · · · · · · · ·<input type="checkbox" name="Basic_Features"
value="stock CGI scripts">stock CGI scripts· ·<input
type="checkbox" name="Basic_Features" value="FTP upload">FTP
upload· ·<input type="checkbox" name="Basic_Features" value="extra
e-mail addresses">multiple e-mail addresses
· · · · · · · · · · · · ·<input type="checkbox" name="Basic_Features"
value="access reports">access reports· · · · ·<input type="checkbox"
name="Basic_Features" value="free domain name registration">free
domain name registration</pre>

<pre>Added Comments:

· · · · · · · · · · · · ·<textarea name="Comments" rows="8"
cols="75"></textarea></pre>

<pre>· · · · · · · · · · · · ·<input type="submit" value="Submit">· ·<input
type="reset" value="Reset"></pre>
```

Do not add additional hard returns inside of the PRE elements in the preceding example. When using the PRE element to align input controls in a form, you need to be aware that any hard returns nested inside of the PRE element will be displayed when the page is viewed in a browser.

3. Save your file (File, Save) and refresh the display of the form in your browser. Compare the horizontal spacing of your form with that shown in Figure 7.22.

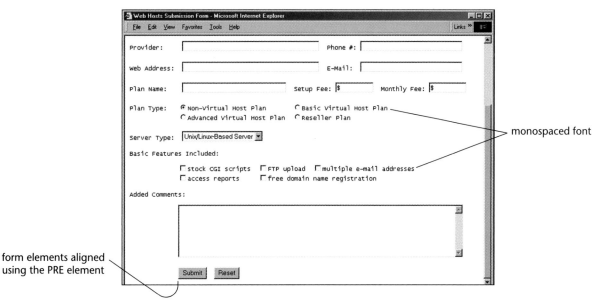

FIGURE 7.22 • *By using the PRE element, you can space out form elements to line them up vertically.*

Using Colors and Backgrounds with Forms

Using colors and backgrounds with forms can help make forms more attractive, as well as provide additional contrast between form element backgrounds (which stay white) and a background color or background image.

Specify text and background colors in the BODY element (see Figure 7.23):

```
<body bgcolor="#ccccff" text="#660000">
```

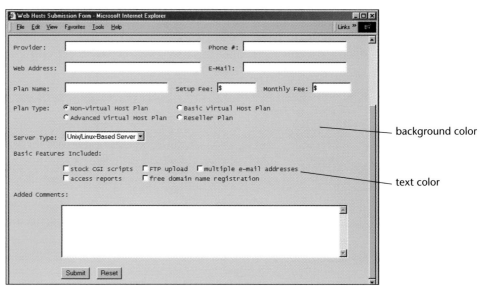

FIGURE 7.23 • *Setting text and background colors can improve the visual appeal of a form, as well as provide increased contrast between form elements and the page's background.*

Using Tables with Forms

The primary disadvantage of using the PRE element is that the form text has to be displayed in a monospaced font—otherwise, you cannot space out the input elements to line them up vertically. Alternatively, you can use a table to vertically line up elements within a form.

Format a form using tables:

1. Re-open **hostsubmit.html** in your text editor and save it as **hostsubmit4.html**. Open **hostsubmit4.html** in your browser.

2. To create visual appeal and add contrast, set background, text, and link colors:

```
<body bgcolor="navy" text="white" link="aqua" vlink="silver"
alink="blue">
```

3. Edit **hostsubmit4.html** so that it matches what is shown here (see Figure 7.24):

```
<table width="100%"><tr valign="bottom">
<td width="13%" height="20">Provider:</td> <td><input
type="text" name="Provider" size="40"></td>
<td>Phone #:</td> <td><input type="text" name="Phone_Number"
size="35"></td>
</tr><tr valign="bottom" height="35">
```

```
<td>Web Address:</td><td><input type="text" name="URL"
size="40"></td>
<td>E-Mail:</td><td><input type="text" name="EMail" size="35"></td>
</tr></table>


<table width="100%"><tr valign="bottom" height="35">
<td width="13%">Plan Name:</td> <td><input type="text"
name="PlanName" size="30">
  Setup Fee: <input type="text" name="Setup_Fee"
size="15" value="$">
  Monthly Fee: <input type="text" name="Monthly_Fee"
size="15" value="$"></td></tr></table>


<table width="100%"><tr valign="bottom" height="35">
<td width="13%">Plan Type:</td> <td><input type="radio"
name="PlanType" value="Non-Virtual Host" checked>Non-Virtual
Host Plan  <input type="radio" name="PlanType"
value="Basic Virtual Host">Basic Virtual Host Plan  
<input type="radio" name="PlanType" value="Advanced Virtual
Host">Advanced Virtual Host Plan  
<input type="radio" name="PlanType" value="Reseller">Reseller
Plan</td></tr></table>


<table width="100%"><tr valign="bottom" height="35">
<td width="13%">Server Type:</td>
<td><select name="ServerType">
  <option selected>Unix/Linux-Based Server
  <option>Windows-Based Server
  <option>Macintosh-Based Server
  <option>Other Server
</select></td></tr></table>


<table width="100%"><tr valign="bottom" height="50">
<td width="13%">Basic Features Included:</td>
<td><input type="checkbox" name="Basic_Features" value="stock
CGI scripts">stock CGI scripts  
<input type="checkbox" name="Basic_Features" value="FTP
upload">FTP upload  
<input type="checkbox" name="Basic_Features" value="extra e-mail
addresses">multiple e-mail addresses  <input
type="checkbox" name="Basic_Features" value="access
reports">access reports<br>

<input type="checkbox" name="Basic_Features" value="free domain
name registration">free domain name registration</td>
</tr></table>


<table width="100%"><tr height="10">
<td></td></tr>
<tr valign="top">
<td width="13%">Added Comments:</td>
<td><textarea name="Comments" rows="8"
cols="77"></textarea></td>
</tr></table>


<table width="100%"><tr valign="bottom" height="35">
<td width="13%"></td><td><input type="submit" value="Submit">
<input type="reset" value="Reset"></td>
</tr></table>
</form>
```

proportional font

form elements aligned
using tables

FIGURE 7.24 • *You also can use tables to vertically align table elements.*

As was previously noted, you need to be aware when displaying light text against a dark background that users can have difficulty printing such a page, which in many browsers will print as light text against a white background (or, even worse, as white text against a white background). If you believe a user might want to print a completed form, you should format it with dark text against a light or white background.

USING JAVASCRIPT WITH FORMS

Straight HTML forms do not give you much control over the data that a user enters into a form or how the form interacts with the user. JavaScript scripts enable you to include much more interactivity and intelligence in your forms. The following are some of the things that JavaScript lets you do with forms:

- Check that an input field is not blank.
- Check that an integer value (rather than an alphanumeric text string) has been keyed in a field.
- Check that an integer value between a minimum and a maximum value (between 1 and 6, for instance) has been keyed in a field.
- Check that an e-mail address has been keyed in a field requesting an e-mail address.
- Check that a valid phone number has been keyed in a field requesting a phone number.
- Check that a valid postal code has been keyed in a field requesting a ZIP or other postal code.
- Perform calculations on numerical values that have been keyed or selected in input fields. For instance, you might want to total the cost of items selected in an order form, calculate the sales tax, add shipping and handling, and then display the total amount.
- Check that text entered in a text area box does not exceed a set number of characters. Although you can use the MAXLENGTH attribute to limit the number of

characters that can be keyed in a text box, it cannot be used to do the same thing in a text area box.

- Create a button element (using an INPUT element with a **type="button"** attribute that performs an action when the button is clicked).
- Set other actions to be performed in response to user actions.
- Create drop-down menus that allow users to jump to different pages or other objects in your site.
- Redirect users to a confirmation page after submitting a mailto form (which normally provides confirmation that the form data has actually been sent).

This is just a sampling of how you can use JavaScript to add versatility and functionality to forms. For links to resources, guides, and tutorials that can help you learn more about using JavaScript in forms, see this chapter's section in the IRC for this book at **www.emcp.com/**.

CHAPTER SUMMARY

You should now be familiar with how to create all the different form elements, including text boxes, radio button groups, check box groups, pull-down list menus, multi-line text area boxes, and various kinds of Submit and Reset buttons. You gained practical experience using the PRE element and tables to create horizontally aligned form layouts, and learned how to use colors and backgrounds with forms. You should be conversant in the differences between mailto forms and CGI forms and understand the pros and cons of using one or the other. You might have gained experience sending and receiving form responses. You also should be aware of the role that JavaScript can play in validating forms and extending their functionality.

Code Review

FORM element	Defines a user-input form in an HTML file.
ACTION attribute	In the FORM element, specifies the URL to which form data is to be submitted.
METHOD attribute	In the FORM element, specifies the method of submitting the form. Possible values are **post** and **get**, with the first being the more usual method for submitting online form data.
INPUT element	Defines a range of user input controls, including text boxes, radio buttons, check boxes, and more.
type="text"	In the INPUT element, specifies that an input control is a text box.
SIZE attribute	In a text box input control, specifies the width of the text box in characters. Text entered in a text box can exceed the size of the box.
MAXLENGTH attribute	In a text box input control, specifies a maximum number of characters that can be keyed.
type="radio"	In the INPUT element, specifies that an input control is a radio button.
type="checkbox"	In the INPUT element, specifies that an input control is a check box.
type="password"	In the INPUT element, specifies that an input control allows the entry of a password. Text keyed in a password box is displayed as a series of asterisks.
SELECT and OPTION elements	The SELECT element defines a list menu (or selection list), while the OPTION element defines the individual options for the menu.
MULTIPLE attribute	In the SELECT element, specifies that multiple list options can be selected (otherwise, only one option can be selected).
TEXTAREA element	Defines a text area box, which allows users to key in multi-line comments.
ROWS and COLS attributes	In the TEXTAREA element, defines the dimensions of a text area box. The ROWS attribute value specifies the number of text lines that are included in the box and the COLS attribute specifies the width of the box in text characters (not pixels).

`type="submit"`	In the INPUT element, specifies that an input control is a Submit button.
`type="reset"`	In the INPUT element, specifies that an input control is a Reset button.
`type="image"`	In the INPUT element, specifies that an input control is an image button. Image buttons function identically to Submit buttons.
BUTTON element	An HTML 4 element that can define a Submit button or a Reset button. BUTTON element Submit and Reset buttons function identically to input control Submit and Reset buttons, except that they can be more richly rendered.
TABINDEX attribute	Resets the tabbing order for elements, including the A, AREA, BUTTON, INPUT, OBJECT, SELECT, and TEXTAREA elements.
mailto form	A form that posts form responses to a mailto e-mail address. Not supported by all browsers.
CGI form	A form that posts form responses to a CGI script on a Web server. The CGI script can either store responses in a file or database on the server or forward them to an e-mail address.
`type="hidden"`	In the INPUT element, specifies that an input control is a hidden control, which passes a value when the form is submitted, but is not displayed in the form. In CGI forms, a hidden control is often used to specify the URL of a CGI script.
chmod *755 filename*	UNIX command used to set permissions for a CGI script file, so it can be accessed over the Web.

ONLINE QUIZ

Go to this text's IRC at **www.emcp.com/** and take the online self-check quiz for this chapter.

REVIEW EXERCISES

This section provides some hands-on practice exercises to reinforce the information and material included within this and previous chapters.

You can use any of the example files that you created in this chapter to further practice features or methods covered in this chapter. To save the original versions of these files for future reference, save them under another name, such as hostsubmit_practice.html in the chap07 folder in your working folder or disk, before using them for practice.

1. Save **hostsubmit.html** under a new name (**hostsubmit_practice.html**, for instance) and practice creating additional text boxes. For instance, under the line including the Plan Name, Setup Fee, and Monthly Fee text boxes, create two more lines containing the following text boxes:

1st text box (1st line):

    lead-in text = Web Space:
    name = Space
    size = 40

2nd text box (1st line)

    lead-in text = Extra Space:
    name = Extra_Space
    size = 35

3rd text box (2nd line):

    lead-in text = Traffic:
    name = Traffic
    size = 40

4th text box (2nd line):

    lead-in text = Extra Traffic:
    name = Extra_Traffic
    size = 35

2. Still working with hostsubmit_practice.html, practice further creating a second radio button group following the Plan Type radio button group you already created:

Lead-in text = Advanced Payment Discounts?

1st radio button:

    name = Pay_Discount
    value = Y
    following text = Yes

2nd radio button:

    name = Pay_Discount
    value = N
    following text = No

3. Still working with hostsubmit_practice.html, practice further creating a second pull-down menu list on the same line following the Server Type menu list you have already created:

Lead-in text = Connection Type:

Name = ConnectType

1st list menu option:

    text = Multiple DS-3 Connections

2nd list menu option:

    text = Single DS-3 Connection

3rd list menu option:

    text = Other

4. Still working with hostsubmit_practice.html, practice further creating a second group of check boxes following the Basic Features Included check box group you have already created:

Lead-in text = Other Features Included:

1st check box:

    name = Other_Features
    value = custom CGI scripts
    following text = custom CGI scripts

2nd check box:

    name = Other_Features
    value = autoresponders
    following text = autoresponders

3rd check box:

    name = Other_Features
    value = shell account
    following text = shell account

4th check box:

    name = Other_Features
    value = access logs
    following text = access logs

5th check box:

    name = Other_Features
    value = RealMedia
    following text = RealMedia

6th check box:

    name = Other_Features
    value = FrontPage Extensions
    following text = FrontPage Extensions

7th check box:

    name = Other_Features
    value = password protected folders
    following text = password protected folders

8th check box:

    name = Other_Features
    value = database/MySQL
    following text = database/MySQL

9th check box:

    name = Other_Features
    value = Cold Fusion
    following text = Cold Fusion

10th check box:

    name = Other_Features
    value = PHP
    following text = PHP

11th check box:

    name = Other_Features
    value = ASP
    following text = ASP

12th check box:

    name = Other_Features
    value = multiple domain hosting
    following text = multiple domain hosting

13th check box:

    name = Other_Features
    value = shopping cart
    following text = shopping cart

14th check box:

    name = Other_Features
    value = 24/7 phone support
    following text = 24/7 phone support

5. If your browser supports sending mailto form responses, further test sending form responses directly to your e-mail address. Use your mail program to open and receive form responses. Experiment with sending form responses using both the "urlencoded" (the default) and "text/plain" content types.

6. If you have access to a Web space account that provides a forms-processing CGI script, check the support area to find out the URL of the forms-processing CGI script and what you need to do to call it in your form. If the CGI forms-processing script is located on a UNIX or LINUX server in a personal cgi-bin folder that has been created for you, following the instructions provided earlier in this chapter, telnet to your server, change to your personal cgi-bin folder, and then key **chmod 755** *scriptname* and press Enter to set the access permissions for your forms-processing CGI script.

7. As a continuation of the previous review exercise, after you set the access permissions for your forms-processing CGI script, do further research to see which hidden input controls you need to include in your form to instruct the forms-processing CGI script to forward form responses to your e-mail address. Open **hostsubmit2.html** and save it as **hostsubmit2_practice.html** and edit it to post form responses to the forms-processing CGI script on your server. After editing your form, publish it to your Web site folder and test submitting CGI form responses in your browser and receiving them in your e-mail program.

8. If you have a Web space account but it does not provide access to a forms-processing CGI script, see this chapter's section at the IRC for this book at **www.emcp.com/** to find services that provide remotely hosted forms-processing CGI scripts. Sign up for a service and follow its instructions to edit your form (hostsubmit2_practice.html) to use the service's forms-processing script to send form responses to your e-mail address. Publish the page with your form to your Web site and test sending and receiving form responses using the remotely hosted forms-processing CGI script.

9. Open **hostsubmit3.html** in your text editor and resave it as **hostsubmit3_practice.html**. Practice setting different text, link, and background colors in combination with your form. To refresh your memory about setting text, link, and background colors in Web pages, see Chapter 3, *Working with Fonts, Colors, and Backgrounds*. Try out several color schemes to find the color scheme you think works best with your form. When you find the color scheme you like, ask at least two classmates to critique your color choices.

10. Still working with hostsubmit3_practice.html, rearrange the organization and layout of the form, while still using the PRE element to allow the spacing and horizontal alignment of form elements. Create an entirely different layout from the current layout. Adjust text box sizes (widths) to fit your layout.

11. Reopen **hostsubmit1_practice.html** in your text editor and resave it as **hostsubmit4_practice.html**. In a separate text editor window, open **hostsubmit4.html**. Using hostsubmit4.html as a reference, use HTML tables in hostsubmit4_practice.html to create a layout design for your form. In hostsubmit4_practice.html, create a different table layout than that used in hostsubmit4.html, incorporating the new text boxes, radio buttons, list menu, and check boxes you created earlier in this section into your layout design.

WEB-BASED LEARNING ACTIVITIES

In this book's text, Find It icons inserted in the margin highlight the Web addresses of additional resources you might find helpful or informative. To further extend your learning using the Web, you can:

- Visit this book's IRC at **www.emcp.com/** to find additional Web addresses of resources related to the material covered in this chapter that you can further investigate and explore. When you find a relevant page or site with information or resources you may want to access later, add it to your Favorites (in Internet Explorer) or your Bookmarks (in Netscape or Mozilla).
- Further research a specific topic introduced in this chapter. For instance, you can further research the pros and cons of using mailto and CGI forms. You also can research services that provide remotely hosted forms-processing CGI scripts. Another topic you can research is the use of JavaScript scripts with forms.

Compile the results of your research into a report that can be shared with your fellow students. You also can team up with other students to create a class presentation or demonstration.

- Use Yahoo! at **www.yahoo.com/** to look for examples of how forms are used on the Web. Look for different form designs and different functions that forms are performing. Find at least six different form examples on the Web that you think demonstrate the effective design and use of forms. Save the examples you find as bookmarks or favorites, so you can use them as a reference later in conceptualizing and designing your own forms.

PROJECTS

These projects can be done in class, in a computer lab, or at home. Use the skills you have developed in this and the previous chapters to create any of the following projects.

Project 1. Conceptualize and design a user feedback form.

For any page that you have created for yourself or for any of the fictional case example scenarios that you have worked with so far in this book, conceptualize and design a user feedback form from scratch that allows users to fill out a form to send you feedback. For instance, create a user feedback form for the page on NASA Space Exploration that you created in Chapter 4 that asks visitors their opinions about space exploration, whether money should be spent on space exploration, whether human beings should go to Mars, and so on. Include a text area box that lets a visitor provide a longer comment.

Create a user feedback form for any other page, whether as part of a fictional case example scenario or for a personal, topical, or other page that you have created for yourself.

Project 2. Create a survey form.

Create a form that surveys visitors' opinions about a particular topic, issue, or event. This can be on any topic or subject matter, so be creative and come up with something different that you think would elicit a relatively broad response. For instance, you might create a survey asking visitors what they ate (or drank) for breakfast. You can create a survey of opinions about global warming. You can create a survey of what visitors think about recent movies, asking them to rank them on a scale from 1 to 5 in different categories, for instance. Or, you can create a survey form on any other topic or subject you can conceive.

Project 3. Create an order form.

Look on the Web for examples of order forms that allow visitors to order products or services. Save examples you find as bookmarks or favorites and use them as guides in conceptualizing and designing an order form of your own. For instance, you might create an order form that allows visitors to order a range of different size and color "widgets." You can have options for ordering 2-inch, 5-inch, and 10-inch widgets in orange, green, and purple colors.

Project 4. Create a product registration form.

When people buy a product, they are increasingly asked to register the product online. This is not just for software products, but can be for non-software products, as well.

Use Yahoo! at **www.yahoo.com/** to search for examples of product registration forms. Save good examples you find as bookmarks or favorites and then use them as guides in creating a fictional product registration form from scratch. This could be for a software product, a video camera, a car stereo, a foot massager, or just about anything. Try to make it realistic. Ask for the customer's first name, last name, title, company name, address, city, state, ZIP code, country, product name, model number, date purchased, use of the product (work, entertainment, education, or other, for instance), and any comments about the product.

Project 5. Create a dating service form.

Imagine that you are running a dating service, Lonely Hearts Unlimited. Create a form that allows people looking for dates to describe their interests, likes and dislikes, favorite things to do, favorite music, ambitions, what they are looking for in a date or partner, and so on. Make liberal use of radio buttons, check boxes, and list menus to elicit responses to an array of different kinds of questions. Have fun with it. Be creative.

Project 6. Create a form for a site of your own.

Create a form for a site that you have already created for yourself, or design a site from scratch that includes a form. This can be any kind of form you care to design (totally open-ended). Decide whether you are going to use a mailto or a CGI form. If using a CGI form, you will need access to a forms-processing CGI script on your Web host's server or from a service that provides remotely hosted forms-processing CGI scripts. When satisfied with the form, publish the form to the Web. If you do not have Web space where you can publish your site, look in Chapter 6's section at the IRC for this book for links to Web hosting resources on the Web, including information and guidance in finding a free Web space provider.

TEAM PROJECT
HTML Essentials

For this project, you will participate as a member of a team, cooperating with others in planning, preparing, creating, and publishing a multi-page Web site. Remember, it is not just the performance of the team that matters, but also your performance as a member of the team. Learning how to cooperate, communicate, and coordinate is just as important as learning how to code a page or design a graphic.

1. BRAINSTORM TOPICS, AUDIENCES, AND OBJECTIVES

With your teammates, brainstorm the kinds of topics, audiences, and objectives you might want to target. Come up with at least six topics for possible projects (with each teammate suggesting at least two topics). For each project topic, define the audience you want to address, and the goal you want to achieve by addressing that audience with the topic. Try to come to a consensus on the topic, target audience, and objective.

If you have difficulties coming up with ideas or cannot agree on a topic, audience, and objective, use Yahoo! at **www.yahoo.com/**, Google at **www.google.com/**, or any other search engine to search for sites that can suggest ideas to you.

After choosing the topic you want to cover or address through your project, further refine your understanding of your project as a team by asking and coming up with answers to the following questions:

- Why do you want to do the project? What about the project has value and significance?
- Who do you most want to do the project for? Who is the target audience of the project or what are the characteristics of the audience that will most likely be interested in the project's topic and subject matter?
- What result or results do you hope to achieve through your project? This brings together both your own impetus to do the project (why it is of value for you) and the value the project will have for your intended audience.
- How are you going to implement your project to achieve the ends you want to achieve? Think here of more specific functions and features you can implement to achieve your desired results.

2. SUBMIT YOUR PROJECT PROPOSAL FOR APPROVAL

Condense your answers to the why, who, what, and how questions into a mission statement for your project. Try to incorporate everything that is most relevant about your project in a single concise statement. Following your mission statement, include further information about your project. Include the topic of the project, the audience you will be addressing, the goals you hope to achieve, and the methods and techniques you plan to implement to achieve those goals. Keep it to less than one page, double-spaced. Be sure to share responsibility for formulating and creating this proposal.

Submit this proposal to your instructor for approval.

3. CREATE AN OUTLINE

Break down your approved project into parts. Create an outline of your site's planned content that is at least two levels deep, with the first level signifying the major branching subpages within your project's site and the second level signifying major section headings within those pages. After creating your outline, you should have a good idea of what the content of your site will be and how it will be organized.

4. ESTABLISH LAYOUT AND NAVIGATION SCHEMES

Discuss which layout and navigation schemes are appropriate and best suited for your project. Decide whether to lay out your site using regular pages, tables, or frames. Come to a team consensus on the layout scheme you want to implement. Determine the navigation scheme you will be using, whether using a link menu, a left sidebar menu, a right sidebar menu, or a topbar menu, for instance. Following are some basic types of navigation schemes:

- A link menu on a front page that jumps to subpages, with return links then jumping back to the main page's link menu.
- A navigation menu at the top and/or bottom of each page that provides access to the other main pages within the site.
- A sidebar or topbar menu using tables, which jumps to subpages that also have sidebar or topbar menus.
- A sidebar, topbar, or bottombar menu using frames, which jumps to subpages displayed within a targeted frame (the "main" frame, for instance). The menu links also can jump to additional frameset pages, so those pages can be added to a visitor's Favorites or Bookmarks.

5. CREATE A STORYBOARD

A storyboard is a kind of cartoon of your site, showing how your site's pages are ordered and related to each other. A Web site can be organized in many ways. Creating a pictorial representation of your site helps clarify the major relationships that exist between the different parts of your site. For instance, you might draw up a diagram of your site that shows it as:

- A linear series of pages, like the chapters of a book (similar to the cars of a train).
- A top-down hierarchy, in what is usually referred to as a tree structure.
- A hub and wheel, with the start or front page in the middle and the subpages arrayed around the hub like the rim of a wheel.
- A non-linear, non-hierarchical, distributed arrangement, such as a triangle, square, star, or other pattern, with three, four, five, or more co-equal entrance points. Each entrance point can highlight a significant aspect of the topic being covered or presented, without any one being foremost over the others.

Explore at least two of these options and discuss the merit of each one within your team. Then select the best model for your project.

6. DRAW A MAP

To visualize the dynamic relationships that can be achieved using hypertext links to create navigation schemes, you can draw a map of your site that shows how its pages are linked together. This is similar to creating a storyboard, except you are not outlining the order of precedence of your site's pages, but delineating the links that exist between them, outside the outward organization and structure of your site. Remember, any page can link to any other page in your site. By drawing out the links between pages, you might see ways in which pages are related to each other that you had not realized before. Look for ways to creatively cross-link your pages.

7. ESTABLISH A COLOR SCHEME

Experiment with different text, link, and background colors to establish an appropriate and effective color scheme for your project. Pay attention to legibility and accessibility when choosing color combinations. Optionally, incorporate a background image into your color scheme. Come to a team consensus on the color scheme you want to implement.

8. DEFINE RESPONSIBILITIES

Responsibilities for creating the site should be shared coequally among team members. When you start to actually create your project, however, you will need to agree on who will be responsible for which tasks. You can allocate responsibilities in a project in a couple of ways:

- Individual team members might be responsible for creating different parts of the site, but within the shared vision, layout scheme, and color scheme the team members have agreed on.
- Team members can divide up responsibilities relative to the capabilities and strengths of each member. If one team member is a visual artist, for instance, she might take a leadership role in creating and preparing graphic images that will be used in the project; if one team member is a writer, he might take a leadership role in composing and writing copy for the project.

No matter how responsibilities are assigned, it is important that each team member gain experience in all aspects of creating the project. Taking a leadership role for a particular area does not mean excluding others from participating in that area.

9. SET A TIME LINE

After agreeing on the responsibilities for the different tasks that need to be completed to finalize the project, determine the order in which those tasks need to be completed, to the best of your ability. Set a time line detailing milestones (along with their respective target dates) that everyone included within your group agrees with and that need to be achieved to complete the project. Be prepared to renegotiate these agreements, if necessary, as work on the project progresses, to take into account exigencies, problems, or changes to the project that might impact the time line. Pay close attention to those aspects of the project that must be completed first, before work on other aspects of the project can begin. In planning and executing the project, you also need to take into account any overall due date that your instructor has set for the project.

10. BUILD THE SITE

Begin building the site, considering the time line and assignment dates provided by your instructor. Some of the tasks that might need to be performed include:

- Finding or creating buttons, bars, balls, and background images to give the project a cohesive visual look.
- Creating a banner image and/or logo image for the project site.
- Writing textual copy for the site. The text that composes the content of the site is just as important as any other aspect of the site.
- Create a starter template that establishes the basic look and feel for the site's pages, which each team member can then adapt for the pages he or she is working on.
- Scan, resize, color-correct, or optimize photographic or other images you want to use in the project's site.

11. TEST AND TROUBLESHOOT

All team members should participate in testing and troubleshooting the project's site. Test the project's site in several browsers. For instance, you can test your project's site in the most recent Internet Explorer, Netscape, Mozilla, and Opera browsers. You also can test your project's site for backward compatibility in a version of Netscape Navigator 4.

When you run into problems, you might have to selectively comment out code to isolate the problem code. If you are not able to get a code to work across browsers, you should consider not using the code.

Validate your site's pages using the W3C HTML Validation Service at **validator.w3.org/**. If you are using Cascading Styles Sheets in your project, also validate your site's style sheets using the W3C CSS Validation Service at **jigsaw.w3.org/css-validator/**.

12. PUBLISH TO THE WEB

Using Web space provided by your school or by another provider of free Web space, publish your project's site so it can be viewed over the Web. Get suggestions, comments, and other feedback from fellow classmates on how you can improve your site. Make revisions to your site that incorporate positive changes suggested by your fellow classmates.

Submit your site to search engines so you can get feedback and comments from visitors to your site who are not fellow classmates.

13. CRITIQUE YOUR WORK

Write a self-critique of your participation in the team project. List some of the important lessons you learned while doing the project. Spell out where you think you performed well and where you think you performed less well, detailing some of the reasons that determined your performance. Point out areas in which you feel you need to improve and what you need to work on in order to improve.

Include a critique of your team's performance. Evaluate your team's ability to communicate, work cooperatively, complete assigned responsibilities in a timely and satisfactory manner, and any other factors you believe made either a positive or negative contribution to completing the project in a satisfactory fashion.

As part of your critique, indicate whether the site fulfilled the approved mission statement and support your evaluation with examples. Report your recommendations for improving or further enhancing the site developed by your team.

PART TWO
Designing for the Web

HTML/CSS/DHTML

CHAPTER

8

Designing with Style Sheets

PERFORMANCE OBJECTIVES

In this chapter, you will learn more about using Cascading Style Sheets (CSS) to create effective Web site designs by learning to:
- Understand the basics of CSS.
- Use single, group, class, and ID selectors.
- Flow text around floating images using CSS.
- Position images and divisions on the page.

You have already worked with Cascading Style Sheets (CSS) in Part One, *HTML Essentials*. Many of the deprecated elements and attributes in HTML 4 are deprecated in favor of using CSS to achieve similar or superior results. Thus, CSS is both an essential aspect of HTML and a means by which you can extend the capabilities of HTML in designing Web sites that are visually richer, more interactive, and more accessible.

USING THE EXAMPLE FILES

If you have created a working folder for storing files you create, you will find the example files for this chapter located in the **chap08** folder within your working folder. You should save any HTML files you create in this chapter in that folder.

If you have created a working disk, copy the chap08 folder to your working disk from the **HTML_Examples** folder that you or your instructor downloaded from this book's Internet Resource Center (IRC), or from a CD-R disc or floppy disk provided by your instructor. Save any HTML file you create in this chapter in the chap08 folder that you copied to your working disk.

UNDERSTANDING CSS

HTML began as a fairly simple set of codes (tags) designed to facilitate the sharing of text documents over the Web. In its initial conception, HTML was never intended as a design medium. Pretty soon, however, browser vendors began extending the capabilities of standard HTML, adding such things as inline images, colors and backgrounds, font size and face changes, tables, and other features that allowed Web designers to use HTML as a design medium. In doing so, however, the original ideal of universal accessibility to content that HTML promised was sacrificed in favor of the ability to create more richly designed Web sites.

CSS operates on the premise of separating presentation from content. Many of the deprecated elements and attributes in HTML 4 control how a Web page is presented, rather than designate the structural content of the page. The FONT element, perhaps the most primary of the elements that has been deprecated for these reasons, is entirely involved in determining presentation, without having any import relative to the contextual structure of a page. Some designers, however, abuse the FONT element, using it to give contextual and structural emphasis to nested text, such as substituting text enlarged with the FONT element for an H1 element. The H1 element, on the other hand, at least in its pure form, does not indicate at all how nested text should be presented, other than in a larger font to indicate a higher order of precedence. Browsers are free to determine for themselves how an H1 element should be presented. The H1 element's ALIGN attribute does control more directly the presentation of nested text, but that is also one of the attributes that has been deprecated in favor of using styles to control presentation in HTML documents.

Use of deprecated elements and attributes is entirely legal in HTML 4 and XHTML 1, as long as you do not declare your document to be in conformance with the strict definition of HTML 4 or XHTML 1. (See "Declaring the Document Type" in Chapter 1 for an explanation of DocType declarations for HTML documents. Declaring the document type for XHTML documents is covered in "Declaring the XHTML DocType" in Chapter 13.) Use of CSS is the preferred alternative, however, because it provides the ability to design Web sites that are both visually richer and more accessible. Although most people now access the Web using a select number of graphical Web browsers, increasing numbers of people are accessing the Web through alternative means, whether through TVs, cell phone displays, PDAs, or any number of other devices. People with visual impairments that make using graphical Web browsers either difficult or impossible might want to access the information and resources offered over the Web using speech, Braille, or other non-visual browsing technologies. Certainly, government agencies, educational institutions, and larger organizations and corporations will increasingly emphasize the importance of universal accessibility, so anyone who wants to work in the Web design field should be cognizant of the need to create accessible Web site designs and understand the necessary methods and approaches.

The primary obstacle to the widespread implementation of styles is not that users are still using browsers that do not support styles (such as Netscape Navigator 1.2 or Internet Explorer 2), but that some earlier browsers (such as Netscape Navigator 4 and Internet Explorer 3) have flawed implementations of CSS. Many Web designers continue to use deprecated elements and tables to achieve layout effects because they display reliably in these earlier browsers. As time goes by, however, fewer and fewer people will be using these older "legacy" browsers and the added functionality and accessibility benefits of CSS will only become more and more attractive. Those who aspire to work as Web designers and authors should know how to design using deprecated elements and tables (or frames) and design using only styles (without using any deprecated elements or tables to achieve layout effects).

NOTE

For links to resources on the Web that discuss the accessibility and other benefits of using CSS to create page layouts instead of deprecated elements/attributes and tables, see this chapter's section at the IRC for this book at **www.emcp.com/**.

Before you can effectively employ CSS to design Web pages and sites, you should understand some of the basic CSS concepts.

Understanding Style Sheets

If you have worked with word processing or desktop publishing software, you have probably already worked with style sheets to determine the visual presentation of document elements (even if you might not have known it). A *style sheet* is a list of styles that determines the appearance or display of elements to which the styles are applied. Microsoft Word, WordPerfect, Adobe PageMaker, Ventura Publisher, and Quark Express, for instance, all use style sheets that work in similar fashions to style sheets on the Web. In Microsoft Word, for instance, you might create a separate style named Body Text that you can apply to any text that forms the body of your document. You can define various properties for the Body Text style, such as the font to be used, how far the text is indented from the margins, whether the tagged paragraph is tabbed or in block format, how much vertical leading is added above or below a paragraph, the amount of line spacing to be used inside the paragraph, and so on. CSS on the Web works in a similar manner.

Understanding CSS Syntax

The basic constituent of a CSS style sheet is the *style rule*. The style rule is composed of two parts, a *selector* and a *declaration*, with the declaration set off from the selector by squiggly brackets, as shown here:

```
selector { declaration }
```

The selector portion of the rule specifies the element or elements for which the style rule is being declared, while the declaration portion specifies *properties* and their *values* that are to be applied to the selector:

```
selector { property1: value1; property2: value2; }
```

As you will notice, property names and their values are separated by colons (:), while property declarations are separated by semi-colons (;). For instance, in the following example, two properties and their values (color and background) are declared for the style rules selector (the H1 element):

```
h1 { color: blue; background: transparent; }
```

You are not limited to declaring style properties for a single element. For instance, by specifying a comma separated list of elements, you can apply style properties to a group of elements, using what is commonly referred to as a *group selector*:

```
h2, h3, h4 { color: red; background: transparent; font-style:
italic; }
```

In the previous examples, spaces are inserted following "{" and preceding "}" purely for the sake of readability. You are free to format style rules in any manner that makes it easier for you to work with them. For instance, many Web authors prefer to format their CSS style rules in the following manner:

```
h2, h3, h4 {
      color: red;
      background: transparent;
      font-style: italic;
}
```

Using group selectors allows you to create more efficient style sheets, in that you can create a single style rule to apply commonly shared properties to a group of elements. Group selectors are not the only variant of selector you can use in CSS style sheets; see "Using Style Selectors" later in this chapter for explanations of the different CSS1 and CSS2 selectors that can be used in style sheets.

Understanding How Cascading Style Sheets Differ

CSS also differ significantly from other style technologies because three separate parties determine how a Web page is styled: the author, the user, and the user agent (or browser).

The term *cascading* in Cascading Style Sheets has to do with the fact that style information for presenting a document on the Web can have multiple sources. Browsers, for instance, include their own internal style sheets that determine how specific elements will be presented. Users also can set browser preferences or even create their own user-defined style sheets to assert control over how they want documents to be displayed in their browsers. Authors need to be aware, in other words, that other players are sitting at the table when it comes to how a Web page is displayed in a browser.

Which players' preferences are displayed is largely determined by the *cascade*. In general, style properties set by the author carry heavier weight than the same style properties set by a user or a browser; style properties set by a user carry heavier weight than the same style properties set by a browser. If an author does not set a style property, however, a user or a browser is free to set it. In other words, the styling for an element first cascades to the author; then if not specified by the author, cascades to the user; and then if not specified by the user, cascades to the browser. An even further cascade is involved, in that display characteristics not determined by the browser might be set by the system preferences, such as the default dot-pitch resolution in which body text fonts are displayed.

To further complicate matters, either the author or the user can declare that their style property should have precedence by attaching an important property declaration to the property. For example:

```
p { color: navy ! important; background: white ! important; }
```

In CSS1 (Cascading Style Sheets, level 1), an author's important declaration trumps a user's important declaration. In CSS2 (Cascading Style Sheets, level 2), a user's important declaration trumps an author's important declaration.

NOTE Browsers also apply a fairly complex system of assigning weights to style declarations, depending upon origin, importance, order, and specificity. For instance, an inline style applied to a particular instance of the H3 element is more specific than a different style applied to all H3 elements. A style property set for the H1, H2, and H3 elements as a group is less specific than one set for the H1 element alone. To learn more about how the specific weight of a style declaration is calculated, see the W3C's section on Cascading Order at **www.w3.org/TR/REC-CSS1#cascading-order**.

Another important reason CSS styles differ from other style systems is *inheritance*. For many CSS style properties, child elements can inherit properties that have been set for their parent elements (or their parent elements' parents). A P element nested inside the BODY element is a child element of the BODY element and thus can directly inherit properties from its parent (the BODY element). For instance, if the BODY element's foreground color is set to be white, while its background color is set to be black, a nested P element also inherits those display characteristics, even though they have not been specifically set for the P element. On the other hand, a different P element might be nested inside a DIV element and inherit display characteristics from that element.

NOTE Styles can be included in HTML documents in three different ways: as embedded style sheets using the STYLE element, as linked (or imported) style sheets using the LINK element (or @import at-rule), and as inline styles using the STYLE attribute. All of the examples in this chapter use embedded styles. See "Using Styles with Multi-Page Web Sites" in Chapter 6, *Working with Multi-Page Web Sites*, for examples of using linked and imported style sheets. See "Using Inline Styles" later in this chapter for an example of using an inline style. For links to resources on the Web that further discuss the general capabilities and features of both CSS1 and CSS2, see this chapter's section at the IRC for this book at **www.emcp.com/**.

USING CSS SELECTORS

You can select which style properties are applied to which elements in a variety of ways. In CSS, these are called *CSS selectors*. CSS selectors fall into two categories: those defined within the CSS1 specification (*CSS1 selectors*) and those defined within the CSS2 specification (*CSS2 selectors*). When the CSS3 specification becomes final, there will be a third set of selectors (*CSS3 selectors*). CSS1 selectors form the core of the different means for selecting style properties and applying them to document elements and are supported by all CSS1-compliant browsers. CSS2 selectors provide a number of new and useful ways to select and apply style properties to elements, but are not as widely supported in browsers as CSS1 selectors.

Using CSS1 Selectors

The different kinds of selectors defined in the CSS1 specification should be supported by all CSS-supporting browsers. These include simple selectors, group selectors, contextual selectors, class selectors, and ID selectors, for instance. You already worked with some examples using all of these types of style selectors in Part One.

USING SIMPLE SELECTORS A *simple selector* applies a style property or properties to a single element. For example, this simple selector is being used in a style sheet to set display characteristics for the H1 element:

```
<style type="text/css">
h1 { font-family: Arial, Helvetica, sans-serif; }
</style>
```

USING GROUP SELECTORS A *group selector* applies style properties to a group of elements, separated by commas, as shown here:

```
h1, h2, h3 { color: red; background: yellow; }
```

USING CONTEXTUAL SELECTORS A *contextual selector* (also called a *descendant selector*) applies styles to an element relative to its context (or where it is nested). When a contextual relation is being specified, no commas are inserted between the elements. For instance, the following style specifies properties to be applied only to P elements that are nested inside a DIV element (but not to P elements that are directly nested inside the BODY element):

```
div p { margin-left: 20px; margin-right: 20px; }
```

USING CLASS SELECTORS A class selector applies properties only to elements that belong to a particular class. For instance, the following style applies the specified properties only to a SPAN element that has been assigned to the "option" class (by including a **class="option"** attribute in the SPAN element:

```
span.option { font-weight: bold; font-size: 1.1em; color: green;
background: transparent; }
```

You also can create a class selector to apply properties to any element belonging to the "option" class:

```
.option { font-weight: bold; font-size: 1.1em; color: green;
background: transparent; }
```

The second option allows you to create groups of different elements that share the same display characteristics simply by assigning them to the same class.

USING ID SELECTORS An *ID selector* allows you to assign properties to an element with a specific ID. For instance, if an H1 element is assigned to an ID of "top" (by having an **id="top"** attribute set), the following would apply style properties to that element:

```
h1#top { border-bottom: 2px black solid; }
```

or

```
#top { border-bottom: 2px black solid; }
```

The HTML 4 specification requires that each ID attribute value in a Web page should be unique, meaning you should not set the same ID for more than one instance of an element. Browsers do not seem to care whether you set the same ID attribute value in multiple elements, but doing so might cause an HTML Validator to report an error if you try to validate your page.

USING INLINE STYLES Another option for applying styles is an *inline style*. An inline style is applied directly to a specific element, using the STYLE attribute. For instance, the following is a regular style set in a style sheet:

```
h3 { font-family: "Comic Sans MS," Verdana, sans-serif; font-weight: bold; font-size: 1.5em; color: green; background: transparent; }
```

and this is the same style set in the body of the document for a particular element, using the STYLE attribute:

```
<h3 style="font-family: 'Comic Sans MS,' Verdana, sans-serif; font-weight: bold; font-size: 1.5em; color: green; background: transparent">
```

Notice that only two differences exist between the style in the style sheet and the inline style:

- The style declaration is surrounded by double-quotes.
- The font-family name—Comic Sans MS—which needs to be quoted because there are spaces in the font name, is single-quoted instead of double-quoted.

Using CSS2 Selectors

A number of additional kinds of selectors are defined in CSS2. Support for these selectors is much more sketchy among current browsers than for the CSS1 selectors. For instance, of the CSS2 selectors, Internet Explorer 6 for Windows only supports the universal selector. Only a few current browsers, such as the Mozilla 1 and Opera 6 browsers, support all of the CSS2 selectors.

USING THE UNIVERSAL SELECTOR The *universal selector*, in the form of an asterisk (*), functions as a wildcard character that matches any element. For instance, the following example uses a universal selector in combination with a contextual selector:

```
blockquote * em { color: blue; background: yellow; }
```

In this case, the blue foreground color and yellow background color are applied only to EM elements that are the grandchildren of a BLOCKQUOTE element (such as an EM element nested inside a P element nested inside a BLOCKQUOTE element). Most current browsers seem to support using the universal selector.

USING CHILD SELECTORS A *child selector* sets style properties for the child of a particular element. For instance, the following selector sets display characteristics for P elements that are the children of the BODY element:

```
body > p { color: navy; background: white; }
```

A child selector differs from a contextual selector because it sets properties only for an element's children, not its grandchildren. A contextual selector, on the other hand, sets properties for all the descendants of an element, whether they are children, grandchildren, or great grandchildren.

USING ADJACENT SIBLING SELECTORS An *adjacent sibling selector* applies style properties to two adjacent children of the same parent element. The following is an example of using an adjacent sibling selector:

```
h1 + h2 { color: red; background: transparent; }
```

In this case, the style properties are applied only to an H2 element that immediately follows an H1 element. Support for sibling adjacent selectors is the same as for child selectors, with Internet Explorer 6 for Windows, for instance, not supporting the use of adjacent sibling selectors.

NOTE An adjacent sibling selector is less specific than a simple, group, or contextual selector. If a color is set for the element by any of those selectors, it trumps any color set by an adjacent sibling selector, even if the adjacent sibling selector comes later in the style sheet.

USING ATTRIBUTE SELECTORS An *attribute selector* lets you apply style properties to an element based on the presence of an attribute or attribute value. For instance, the following example draws a solid, 3-pixel, navy border around a DIV element only if it contains a WIDTH attribute:

```
div[width] { border: 3px navy solid; }
```

You also can use an attribute value to apply property values only to an element that contains a specific attribute/value pair. For instance, the following example applies an italic font style to an OL element only if it contains a **type="A"** attribute/value pair:

```
ol[type=A] { font-style: italic; }
```

Attribute selectors can also reference multiple attributes. For instance, the following example sets a solid green 3-pixel border for the DIV element only if a navy foreground color and a yellow background color have already been set for the element:

```
div[color=navy][background=yellow] { border: 3px green solid; }
```

CSS2 also provides a number of additional ways to specify attribute matches. For instance, you would apply properties only to an element containing a font-family attribute with **Arial** as the initial value in a comma-separated list of font-family names:

```
span[font-family|=Arial] { font-size: 0.9em; }
```

On the other hand, to apply properties to an element that has an **Arial** value listed anywhere within a comma-separated list of font-family names, you could do the following:

```
span[font-family~=Arial] { font-size: 0.9em; }
```

NOTE For links to resources on the Web that discuss the use of both CSS1 and CSS2 selectors in Web page designs, see this chapter's section at the IRC for this book at **www.emcp.com/**.

CASE EXAMPLE: DESIGNING AN ONLINE GALLERY WITH STYLES

Previously, you created an online gallery that featured using the IMG element's ALIGN attribute to float images at the left and right margins. Use of the ALIGN attribute in the IMG element is deprecated in HTML 4, in favor of using styles to achieve similar or better results. Similarly, the HSPACE and VSPACE attributes, which were also used in the previous example, are also deprecated.

Shirley Johnson previously created her online gallery of images from NASA using deprecated HTML elements and attributes. She wants to learn more about using styles and has decided to design a version of her online gallery using only styles and without using any deprecated elements or attributes.

To start working with this example:

1. Run your text editor and open **spacegallery2_ex.html** from the chap08 folder in your working folder or working disk.
2. Save spacegallery2_ex.html as **spacegallery2.html** in the chap08 folder.
3. Run your browser and open **spacegallery2.html** from the chap08 folder (see Figure 8.1).

inline images

FIGURE 8.1 • *Starting out, all the images are inserted as regular inline images without any horizontal alignment or floating set.*

CENTERING AND FLOATING ELEMENTS USING STYLES

You do not need to use deprecated elements and attributes to center or float elements. Styles, at least in the current generations of browsers, can both horizontally align and float elements.

Horizontally Aligning Images and Text Using Styles

The CENTER element is deprecated, as is the ALIGN attribute, in all instances except when used in tables, in favor of using styles to achieve similar or better results. The means for setting horizontal alignment in CSS are somewhat more complex than those provided by HTML and are also affected by a major bug in Internet Explorer 5.5 for Windows.

Using only styles, center-align the page's banner image—spacegallery.gif—and the following H1 element:

1. To the P element within which the banner image is nested, assign a class, so a style can be applied to it:

```
<p class="banner"><img src="spacegallery.gif" width="450"
height="75" alt="Space Gallery Banner Image"></p>
<h1>Space Exploration Gallery</h1>
```

2. Define a class selector to the page's style sheet that centers the content of the "banner" paragraph, and set another style that centers the content of the H1 element (see Figure 8.2):

```
p.banner { text-align: center; }
h1 { text-align: center; }
</style>
```

p.banner {text-align: center;} ————

FIGURE 8.2 • *The banner image is centered using only a style.*

The **text-align: center** property center-aligns the content of the "banner" paragraph and the H1 element.

Including both a banner image and a top-level heading can be redundant, if the top-level heading closely matches the content of the banner image, but search engines place special weight upon the content of a page's H1 element when they index a page. Shirley has discovered, however, that she can use a style to turn off the display of her page's H1 element, while still leaving it in her page so search engines' robots will still index the content of her H1 heading. Browsers that do not support turning off the display of the H1 element will just display both the banner image and the H1 element.

action

Turn off the display of the H1 element (see Figure 8.3):

```
h1 { text-align: center; display: none; }
```

h1 {display: none;}

FIGURE 8.3 • *Display of the H1 element is turned off.*

When you set the display property for an element to **none**, it is treated as though it is no longer present in the page (taking up no space in the page) by browsers that support that property. The element, however, will be displayed in browsers that either do not support styles or do not support the use of the display property. Another property, the visibility property, also can be used to hide an element. When the visibility property is set to **hidden** for an element, browsers that support the property will hide the element from view. Unlike with a **display: none** property, however, a **visibility: hidden** property does not close up the space that is occupied by the element.

Floating Images Using Styles

Use of the ALIGN attribute is deprecated in HTML 4, except when used in tables, in favor of using styles to achieve similar or better results.

Float the gallery images alternately at the left and right margins:

1. Assign the first gallery image to a class (the "left" class) so style properties can be applied to it:

```
<h2><a href="spacecapsules.jpg" target="_blank"><img
src="spacecapsules_th.jpg" class="left" width="200" height="166"
alt="Mercury, Gemini, and Apollo spacecraft."></a>
Mercury, Gemini, and Apollo Spacecraft</h2>
```

2. Create styles that float the first gallery image on the left margin, turn off the image border, add right-margin spacing, and set the following HR element to clear the floating image (see Figure 8.4):

```
img.left { float: left; border-width: 0; margin-right: 12px; }
hr { clear: both; }
</style>
```

FIGURE 8.4 • *The first gallery image is floating on the left margin with the following text flowing around its right side.*

Notice that by using a style, you can add horizontal spacing on one side of the image, without having to also add it to the other side, unlike when using the deprecated HSPACE attribute, which causes any horizontal spacing to be added to both sides of the image.

3. Assign the second gallery image to a class (the "right" class) so style properties can be applied to it:

```
<h2><a href="flagonmoon2.jpg" target="_blank"><img
src="flagonmoon2_th.jpg" class="right" width="200" height="169"
alt="Astronaut Edwin Aldrin posing next to U.S. flag on the
moon."></a>U.S. Flag and Edwin "Buzz" Aldrin on the Moon</h2>
```

4. Create a style that floats the second gallery image on the right margin, turns off the image border, and adds left-margin spacing (see Figure 8.5):

```
img.left { float: left; border-width: 0; margin-right: 12px; }
img.right { float: right; border-width: 0; margin-left: 12px; }
hr { clear: both; }
</style>
```

FIGURE 8.5 • *The second gallery image is floating on the right margin with the following text flowing around its left side.*

5. Insert a **class="left"** attribute in the IMG elements for the third and fifth gallery images, to apply the style properties assigned to the img.left class selector to those images as well.
6. Insert a **class="right"** attribute in the IMG elements for the fourth and sixth gallery images to apply the style properties assigned to the img.right class selector to those images as well (see Figure 8.6).

FIGURE 8.6 • *The third and fourth gallery images are floated to the left and right margins, respectively.*

The float property causes an object (an image or any other element) to float at the left or right margin with following text and elements flowing around the object. Possible values are **left**, **right**, **both**, and **none** (the default). The clear property causes a following element to clear (stop flowing around) a floating object. A value of **left** causes the element to clear an object floating on the left margin (with the element moving down until the left margin is clear). A value of **right** causes the element to clear an object floating on the right margin (with the element moving down until the right margin is clear). A value of **both** causes the element to clear objects floating on both the left and right margins (with the element moving down until both the left and right margins are clear).

CASE EXAMPLE: CREATING AN ONLINE NEWSLETTER

A newsletter is a publication that is issued on a regular basis, such as monthly, quarterly, or semi-annually. An online newsletter functions just like a regular newsletter, except that instead of sending the newsletter out through the mail, it is issued on the Web.

Alfred Owikandi is an avid boater who has created an online newsletter on boating safety. A new issue of the newsletter is published every three months (or quarterly). Each new issue features an article on boating safety issues, authored either by Alfred or a contributor.

Alfred also has chosen to create the layout for his site by using only styles, without using any tables or deprecated elements and attributes to create layout or presentation effects.

To get started working with this example:

1. Run your text editor and open **safety_ex.html** from the chap08 folder in your working folder or working disk.
2. Save safety_ex.html as **safety.html** in the chap08 folder.
3. Run your browser and open **safety.html** from the chap08 folder (see Figure 8.7).

FIGURE 8.7 • *Starting out, safety.html includes only non-deprecated HTML, without any presentational formatting.*

SETTING COLORS AND BACKGROUNDS USING STYLES

This example uses a special background image, back_grade.jpg, which is included with the example files for this chapter. It is a two-tone background image that runs a colored vertical strip down the left side of the page, forming a gradation that blends in with the color that is displayed across the remainder of the page. This background image is very wide (1,280 pixels), to allow for the widest possible browser display, but is relatively short.

Use a style to set foreground and background colors, and specify a background image for the BODY element (see Figure 8.8):

```
<style type="text/css">
body { color: navy; background: #c0ffc0 url("back_grade.jpg"); }
</style>
</head>
```

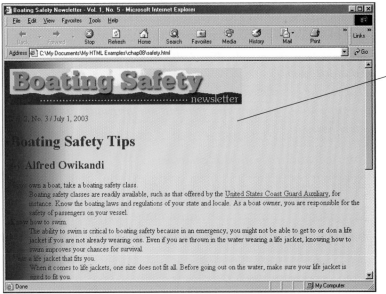

two-color background image

FIGURE 8.8 • *A style is used to set a foreground color (navy) and a background image (back_grade.jpg) for the BODY element.*

POSITIONING ELEMENTS

The position property, in conjunction with the left, right, top, and bottom properties, is used to position elements on the page. The kind of positioning that is applied depends on the value of the position property:

- **position: static** is the initial position value for all elements. Statically positioned elements are positioned relative to the normal document flow.
- **position: absolute** positions an element relative to the sides of its containing block (the block that contains it). For instance, a DIV element nested directly inside of the BODY element would be absolutely positioned relative to the sides of the page. Absolutely positioned elements are removed from the normal document flow.
- **position: relative** positions an element relative to its current (or normal) position within the document flow. For instance, a relatively positioned inline image would be positioned relative to its position within the line in which it is inserted.

- **`position: fixed`** works similarly to absolute positioning, but also positions an element in a fixed position that does not move when the page is scrolled.

All current browsers (Internet Explorer 5/5.5 for Windows, Internet Explorer 5 for the Macintosh, Netscape 6, Opera 5/6, and Mozilla 1, for instance) support absolute and relative positioning.

Not all current browsers support fixed positioning, however. Of the current browsers, Internet Explorer 5 for the Macintosh, Mozilla 1, Netscape 6.2, and Opera 5/6 support fixed positioning, but Internet Explorer 5, 5.5, or 6 for Windows does not.

At this point, the page's text is overlapping the vertical background stripe, making it partially unreadable. In this section, you will use CSS absolute positioning to first position the page's banner image and then to position the page's text within the browser window.

Positioning Images Using Styles

You can position any element on the page using absolute or relative positioning.

Alfred has decided to create his page without using any deprecated elements or attributes. Instead of using the ALIGN attribute to horizontally position the page's banner image on the page, he has decided to use CSS's position property to absolutely position the image on the page.

action

Use the position style property to position the page's banner image relative to the left and top margins of the page (see Figure 8.9):

```
body { color: navy; background: #c0ffc0 url("back_grade.jpg"); }
img.banner { position: absolute; top: 10px; left: 5px; }
```

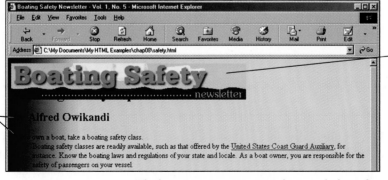

non-positioned text (overlapped by image)

absolutely positioned image

FIGURE 8.9 • *The banner image is positioned 10 pixels down from the top and 5 pixels over from the left side of the browser window.*

Notice that the image now overlaps the following text. That is because when you absolutely position an object in the browser window, it is taken out of the normal flow of text or objects within the page. Following text or elements move up on the page as though the image was no longer there.

Positioning a Runner Divider

Newsletters commonly display a runner divider that also displays the volume number, issue number, and possibly the issue date, as well.

Create a "runner" division (a DIV element assigned to a "runner" class) that runs across the browser window, below the banner image:

1. Delete the P element start and closing tags and delete the forward slash character:

~~<p>~~Vol. 2, No. 3~~/~~ July 1, 2003~~</p>~~

2. Nest the runner text inside a DIV element and two SPAN elements:

```
<div class="runner">
<span class="volno">Vol. 2, No. 3</span>
<span class="dateyear">July 1, 2003</span>
</div>
```

3. Set a style to set the display characteristics of the DIV and SPAN elements (see Figure 8.10):

```
img.banner { position: absolute; top: 10px; left: 5px; }
div.runner { position: absolute; top: 95px; left: 5px; color:
navy; background: #fcda8a; border: 1px navy solid; width: 99%;
height: 1.1em; }
span.volno { float: left; font-weight: bold; padding-left: 145px; }
span.dateyear { float: right; font-weight: bold; padding-right:
10px; }
```

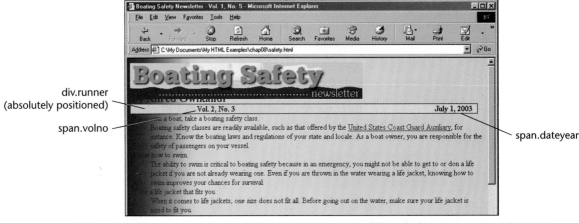

FIGURE 8.10 • *A "runner" division is set to display below the banner image, with SPAN elements floating nested text within the division.*

The "runner" division is absolutely positioned 95 pixels down from the top of the page and 5 pixels in from the left side of the page. A foreground color and background color are defined for it. Notice that the width of the division is set to 99 percent, instead of 100 percent. The reason for that is that a 100 percent width causes a horizontal scrolling bar to be displayed in the Mozilla 1 browser.

The **height: 1.1em** property is necessary for Netscape 6.2, which otherwise will collapse the borders and not display the background color behind the division.

The two SPAN class selectors, span.volno and span.dateyear, float nested text at the left side and right side of the "runner" division. The span.volno class selector also sets

145 pixels of padding on the left, spacing the "Vol. 2, No. 3" text by that amount in from the left side of the containing division element.

Positioning a Main Division

At this point, because it has yet to be positioned and is still part of the normal flow, the remaining text in the page is overlapping the darker gradation running down the left side of the page that is set by the background image.

Nest the remaining text and elements inside a "main" division. Then position that element so it is displayed below the banner image and the "runner" division, as well as in from the left so it is no longer overlapping the gradated background color on the left:

1. Nest the remaining text within the page inside of a "main" division:

```
<div class="main">
<h1>Boating Safety Tips</h1>
<h2>by Alfred Owikandi</h2>

[...]

<address align="center">
Alfred Owikandi<br>
E-mail: <a
href="mailto:alowik@safe_boating.com">alowik@safe_boating.com</a>
</address>
</div>
</body>
```

2. Create a style to absolutely position the "main" division (see Figure 8.11):

```
div.main { position: absolute; top: 125px; left: 150px; }
div.main h1 { margin-top: 0; }
</style>
```

FIGURE 8.11 • *The "main" division is absolutely positioned relative to top and left sides of the browser.*

The "main" division is positioned 125 pixels from the top of the browser window so that it is positioned under the "runner" division, and 150 pixels in from the left side of the browser window. By positioning the division in from the left side of the browser window, the text is no longer overlapping the dark background color gradation running down the left side of the window.

The top margin of the H1 element is also set to zero. This is necessary for the Opera browsers, which add top margin spacing above block elements that are positioned at the top of a division or a page, while other browsers do not.

Creating a Sidebar Menu

Now that you have positioned the "main" division in from the left side of the browser window, you can create another division to hold a sidebar menu.

Position a division that runs along the side of the page and create a sidebar menu in the division:

1. Above the "main" division, create a division holding a sidebar menu:

```
<div class="side">
<p class="toppar">Menu:</p>
<p><a href="boatarchives.html">Past Issues</a></p>
<p><a href="boatlinks.html">Boating Resources</a></p>
<p><a href="boatcheck.html">Safety Check List</a></p>
<p><a href="boatgloss.html">Boating Glossary</a></p>
<p><a href="boatcontact.html">Contact Us</a></p>
</div>
<div class="main">
```

2. Define styles to position the "side" division and control its appearance (see Figure 8.12):

```
div.main h1 { margin-top: 0 }
div.side { position: absolute; top: 125px; left: 5px; padding-top: 12px; }
div.side p { color: white; background: transparent; font-weight: bold; }
div.side a { color: yellow; background: transparent; font-weight: bold; }
p.toppar { margin-top: 0; }
```

div.side
(absolutely positioned)

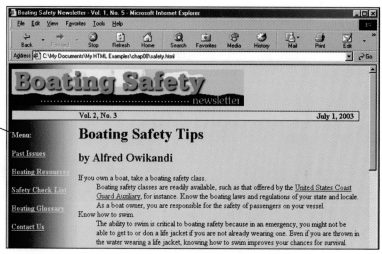

FIGURE 8.12 • *The "side" division is absolutely positioned relative to top and left sides of the browser.*

The "side" division is positioned 125 pixels down from the top of the page and 5 pixels in from the left side of the page. To move the content of the "side" division content down and position it relative to the "main" division's H1 heading, 12 pixels of padding are added at the top of the division.

Contextual selectors are also used to set the characteristics of the P and A elements inside the "side" division. The p.toppar style, which sets the top margin of the "toppar" paragraph to zero, is necessary for the Mozilla browser, which otherwise adds margin space above a block element at the top of a division or page.

Setting Height, Width, and Borders for Divisions

The "side" division does not yet have a height or width set for it. As long as it contains only short lines of text or links that do not intrude into the "main" division's space, it is not obvious that the "side" division actually extends across the page. To set a border or background for the division, or to protect text lines from intruding into the "main" division space, you need to specify a width for the "side" division. If adding a border and background, you also should set a height; otherwise, the "side" division will only extend down as far as the text or other elements that it contains.

action

Set a height and width for the "side" division and outline it with a border (see Figure 8.13):

```
div.main { position: absolute; top: 125px; left: 150px; height:
56em; }
div.main h1 { margin-top: 0; }
div.side { position: absolute; top: 125px; left: 5px; padding-top:
12px; border: 3px white ridge; width: 125px; height: 56em; }
div.side p { color: white; background: transparent; font-weight:
bold; margin-left: 3px; margin-right: 3px; }
div.side a { color: yellow; background: transparent; font-weight:
bold; }
```

border: 3px white ridge

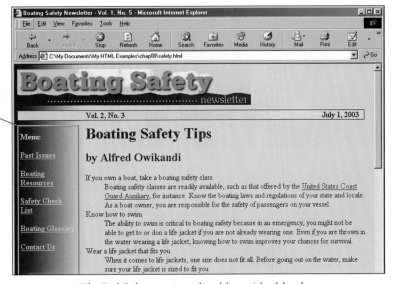

FIGURE 8.13 • *The "side" division is outlined by a ridged border.*

The height of both the "main" and "side" divisions is set to 56 ems. When ems are used to set the height or width of a block element, they are measured relative to the height of the font size that is set for (or inherited by) the element. This is different from using ems to set font sizes (using the font-size property), where the size of an em is relative to the size of the parent element's font size.

The point here is that unless you specifically set the font-size of an element in pixels (or some other non-relative measurement), you have no way of knowing for sure what the font size of an element might be. In other words, due to a visual impairment, a user might set a larger default font size in his or her browser, which might overrun a containing division for which you have set a height in pixels based on your browser's default font size.

Many browsers also support setting division heights using percentage values. A percentage height for a division or other element is set relative to the height of the browser window (or viewport) and not relative to the height of the page. Internet Explorer 6 for Windows, however, unlike earlier versions of that browser, also requires that the BODY element be set to a height of 100 percent before it will recognize percentage heights for other elements on the page.

A 3-pixel, white, ridged border is set around the "side" division, which has the effect of outlining the division while still allowing the page background to show through (because the division background is set as transparent).

A 3-pixel margin is set on the left and right of the P elements within the "side" division to create horizontal spacing separating the paragraphs from the surrounding border.

Adding the Finishing Touches

You can do more to improve the visual appearance of the newsletter and make it easier to read by setting different font characteristics for some of the elements on the page. For instance, to vary the look of the page, a sans serif font and color and weight changes can be applied to certain elements.

Add the finishing touches to the style sheet (see Figure 8.14):

```
div.main h1 { margin-top: 0; margin-bottom: 3px; }
div.main h2 { margin-top: 0; font-size: 1em; font-style: italic; }
div.main h1, div.main h2 { color: #003399; background:
transparent; font-family: Arial, Helvetica, sans-serif; }
div.side { position: absolute; top: 125px; left: 5px; padding-
top: 12px; border: 3px white ridge; width: 125px; height: 56em; }
div.side p { font-family: Arial, Helvetica, sans-serif; color:
white; background: transparent; font-weight: bold; margin-left:
3px; margin-right: 3px; }
div.side a { color: yellow; background: transparent; font-weight:
bold; font-size: .8em; text-decoration: none; }
p.toppar { margin-top: 0; }
dt { font-weight: bold; font-family: Arial, Helvetica, sans-serif;
font-variant: small-caps; color: purple; background: transparent;
margin-bottom: 3px; }
dd { font-style: italic; margin-left: 15px; margin-bottom: 3px; }
```

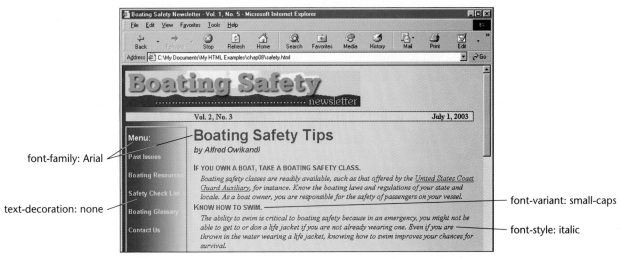

font-family: Arial

text-decoration: none

font-variant: small-caps

font-style: italic

FIGURE 8.14 • *Various finishing touches are added to the newsletter.*

A sans serif font is applied to the H1 and H2 elements in the "main" division, as well as to the P elements in the "side" division. An italic font style is applied to the H2 and DD elements. A small caps font variation is applied to the DT elements. Foreground colors are set for the H1, H2, and DT elements.

The size of the H2 element that contains the byline is reduced (to 1 em) and the margin spacing between the H1 and H2 elements is reduced to 3 pixels. The left margin of the DD element is reduced to 15 pixels. The DD element's bottom margin is set at 3 pixels to create some vertical spacing between the safety tips.

The DT (Definition Term) and DD (Definition Data) elements are used in conjunction with the DL element to define a definition list (or glossary list). The only default formatting that is applied to a definition list is that the DD element is indented under the DT element.

Lastly, the A elements in the "side" division are reduced in size (to .8 of an em), and the underlining of the links is turned off (the word "Menu:" at the head of the links clearly indicates that they are links).

Resetting the Stacking Order

Normally, objects that are positioned on the page overlap other objects in the order in which they are inserted on the page. Thus, if the "side" division were to intrude into the same space as the "runner" division, the "side" division would overlap and be displayed on top of the "runner" division, because the "runner" division was inserted later on the page. This ordering of positioned elements is called the *stacking order*. The z-index property, however, lets you reset the stacking order of positioned elements in whichever order you choose. You reset the stacking order by assigning numerical values using the z-index property for each element you want to stack. An element with a higher z-index value is stacked on top of an element with a lower z-index value.

Reposition the "side" division so it runs from near the top of the page and then set it so it is stacked beneath the banner image and the "runner" division:

1. Reposition the banner image and the "runner" division so they are both now spaced in 15 pixels from the left side of the page, and readjust the amount of left padding in the "volno" SPAN element:

```
img.banner { position: absolute; top: 15px; left: 15px; }
div.runner { position: absolute; top: 95px; left: 15px; color:
navy; background: #fcda8a; border: 1px navy solid; width: 99%;
height: 1.1em; }
span.volno { float: left; font-weight: bold; padding-left:
135px; }
```

2. Reposition the "side" division so it is 5 pixels from the top of the page and reset the top and left padding amounts (see Figure 8.15):

```
div.side { position: absolute; top: 5px; left: 5px; padding-top:
125px; padding-left: 5px; border: 3px white ridge; width: 125px;
height: 56em; }
```

"side" division repositioned at top of page

FIGURE 8.15 • *The "side" division is repositioned at 5 pixels from the top of the browser window.*

3. Set z-index values to cause the "side" division to be stacked beneath the banner image and the "runner" division (see Figure 8.16):

```
img.banner { z-index: 2; position: absolute; top: 15px; left:
15px; }
div.runner { z-index: 3; position: absolute; top: 95px; left:
15px; color: navy; background: #fcda8a; border: 1px navy solid;
width: 99%; height: 1.1em; }

[...]

div.side { z-index: 1; position: absolute; top: 5px; left: 5px;
padding-top: 125px; padding-left: 5px; border: 3px white ridge;
width: 125px; height: 56em; }
```

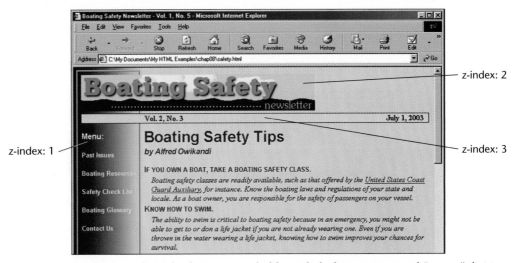

z-index: 2

z-index: 1

z-index: 3

FIGURE 8.16 • *The "side" division is stacked beneath the banner image and "runner" division.*

In the absence of a z-index value, a positioned element is assumed to have a z-index value of **0**. If two positioned elements have the save z-index value, the following element will be stacked on top of the preceding element.

TAKING CARE OF EARLIER BROWSERS

A number of features are included in this example that can cause display problems in earlier browsers, especially Netscape Navigator 4 and Internet Explorer 3.

You can use the Invisible Object Method to alert visitors that the page will look much better if they upgrade their browsers. You cannot simply place the IFRAME element containing the alert at the top of the page because the absolutely positioned elements in the page will not move down to make room for it. You can, however, place the IFRAME element at the bottom of the page and position it within an open space in the page, such as to the right of the H1 and H2 elements.

Use the Web Standards Project's Invisible Object Method to alert users of earlier browsers that they should upgrade their browsers:

1. Add the IFRAME element containing the alert at the bottom of the page:

```
<iframe class="oops">
<h3 class="alert">This site will look much better
in a browser that supports
<a href="http://www.webstandards.org/upgrade/"
title="Download a browser that complies with Web standards.">
Web standards</a>, but it is accessible to any browser
or Internet device.</h3>
</iframe>
</body>
```

2. Set the style that positions the alert in an open space in the page and draws a red border around it (see Figure 8.17):

```
.oops { display: none; }
h3.alert { position: absolute; top: 165px; left: 425px; font-
size: 16px; margin-bottom: 0; border: 1px red solid; }
</style>
```

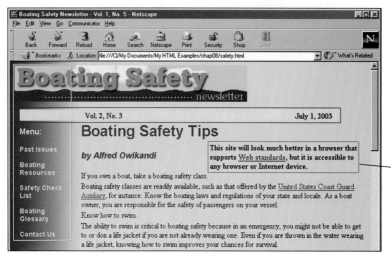

FIGURE 8.17 • *An alert is displayed for users of earlier browsers, such as Netscape Navigator 4, that might have problems displaying the page's styles.*

NOTE For links to resources on the Web that discuss creating Web page designs and layouts using CSS positioning, see this chapter's section at the IRC for this book at **www.emcp.com/**.

OVERFLOWING AND CLIPPING

The overflow property lets you determine what happens if the content of an element overflows the height or width that is set for it. The clip property lets you crop out parts of an element.

Reset the heights of the "side" and "main" divisions so they will fit inside a browser window maximized at an 800 × 600 screen resolution, and then set the overflow property to **auto** for the "main" division:

1. In your text editor, save safety.html as **safety2.html** in the chap08 folder. Open **safety2.html** in your browser.
2. Edit the style sheet in your text editor, as shown here (see Figure 8.18):

```
body { color: navy; background: #c0ffc0 url("back_grade.jpg");
height: 100%; }
[...]
div.main { position: absolute; top: 125px; left: 150px; height:
65%; width: 80%; overflow: auto; border-bottom: 1px navy solid;
padding-bottom: 5px; }
[...]
div.side { z-index: 1; position: absolute; top: 5px; left: 5px;
padding-top: 125px; padding-left: 5px; border: 3px white ridge;
width: 125px; height: 65%; }
```

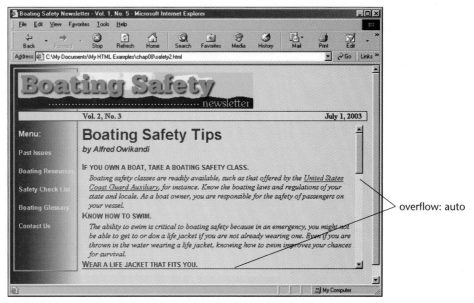

FIGURE 8.18 • *The overflow is set to auto for the "main" division.*

The 100 percent height for the BODY element (any percent value will do) is necessary for Internet Explorer 6 for Windows to recognize percentage heights set for other elements in the page. The "side" and "main" divisions are each set to a height of 65 percent. The "main" division is also set to a width of 80 percent. With the overflow property set to **auto**, this makes the content of the "main" division scrollable because it overflows the stated height of the element (see Figure 8.19).

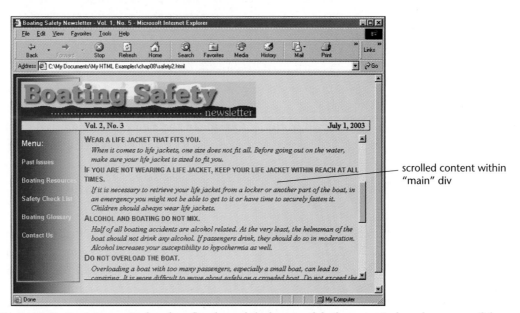

FIGURE 8.19 • *Rather than flow beyond the bottom of the browser window, the content of the "main" division scrolls within the element.*

Other values that can be set for the overflow property are: **visible**, **hidden**, and **scroll**. With a value of **visible**, the element expands to match the height or width of the element's content. With a value of **hidden**, only the content within the element borders is displayed, without scroll bars, while content extending beyond the element borders is hidden and not displayed. With a value of **scroll**, content is only displayed inside the element borders, but both vertical and horizontal scroll bars are displayed, even if the content does not extend beyond the element borders.

For the "main" division, change the overflow value from **auto** to **scroll** (see Figure 8.20):

```
div.main { position: absolute; top: 125px; left: 150px; height:
65%; width: 80%; overflow: scroll; border-bottom: 1px navy
solid; padding-bottom: 5px; }
```

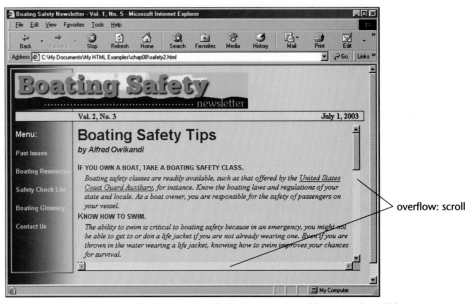

FIGURE 8.20 • *When overflow is set to scroll, both vertical and horizontal scroll bars are displayed, whether they are required or not.*

The clip property lets you clip (or crop out) part of an element. You define a clipping area within an element by specifying the offsets of its four sides from the upper-left corner of the element. For instance, the following specifies that for the clipping area, its top is 0 pixels down from the top side of the element, its right is 425 pixels over from the left side of the element, its bottom is 55 pixels down from the top of the element, and its left side is 0 pixels from the left side of the element:

```
img.banner { z-index: 2; position: absolute; top: 15px; left: 15px;
width: 500px; height: 75px; clip: rect(0px, 425px, 55px, 0px); }
```

The clip property is not widely supported. The Mozilla browser supports it, but neither Internet Explorer 6 nor Opera 6 supports it. Figure 8.21 shows the banner image in the Boating Safety newsletter page clipped as shown in the previous code example.

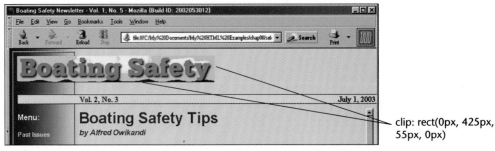

FIGURE 8.21 • *The Mozilla 1 browser supports clipping elements.*

USING PSEUDO-CLASSES AND PSEUDO-ELEMENTS

Styles are normally attached to elements according to their position in the *document tree*. Within a document, every element, with the exception of the root element, has one element that is its parent. A parent element, however, can have multiple child elements. The document tree is composed of the sum total of branchings, extending from the root element, through every parent-child branch in the document.

There are common situations, however, in which it is productive to be able to apply style properties, even though those situations are not directly attributable to the position of an element in the document tree. For instance, you might want to automatically apply style properties to the first letter or first line in an element, even though the first letter or line of an element is not itself an element within the document tree. Pseudo-elements and pseudo-classes are included in CSS to provide for exactly these sorts of situations. The *pseudo* prefix means that these selectors define selections that are similar to those made for actual elements or classes of elements that are present in the document tree, without actually referring to a real element.

Using Link and Dynamic Pseudo-Classes

The BODY element's LINK, VLINK, and ALINK attributes, which set the colors of unvisited, visited, and active links, are deprecated in HTML 4 in favor of using styles to achieve similar or better results. CSS provides a number of pseudo-classes—the :link, :visited, and :active pseudo-classes—that can be used not only to assign colors to these link states, but also to assign many other display characteristics. CSS provides two additional pseudo-classes—the :hover and :focus pseudo-classes—which, along with the :active pseudo-class, can set dynamic effects for links and for other elements as well. Of these, the :focus pseudo-class is primarily used when creating forms. In Part One, you already worked extensively using the other pseudo-classes in setting link state characteristics, both in creating rollover links and rollover buttons.

In CSS1, the :link, :visited, and :active pseudo-classes were referred to as *anchor pseudo-classes*, because they are only used to set display characteristics for various states of the A (Anchor) element—:link sets display characteristics for unvisited links, :visited for previously visited links, :active for activated links (when the mouse button is held down on a link, for instance), :hover for links over which the mouse cursor is hovering, and :focus for links that have been given focus (by being tabbed to, for instance).

In CSS2, however, the :active, :hover, and :focus pseudo-classes are no longer limited to setting the display characteristics of links, but also can dynamically control the display characteristics of other elements in response to actions or events. Thus, in CSS2, :link and :visited are referred to as *link pseudo-classes*, while :active, :hover, and :focus are referred to as *dynamic pseudo-classes*.

> *To provide some interactivity and add visual interest to his page, Alfred has decided to set up CSS rollover links in the left sidebar of his page.*

Use link and dynamic pseudo-classes to set up the sidebar links as rollover links:

1. Reopen **safety.html** in your text editor and your browser.
2. Define :link, :visited, :hover, and :active pseudo-classes for A elements that are nested inside the "side" division (see Figure 8.22):

```
div.side a { color: yellow; background: transparent; font-
weight: bold; font-size: .8em; text-decoration: none; }
div.side a:link { color: yellow; background: transparent; }
div.side a:visited { color: #ffffcc; background: transparent; }
div.side a:hover { color: navy; background: #fcda8a; }
div.side a:active { color: yellow; background: #ff0033; }
```

FIGURE 8.22 • *You can create rollover links using anchor pseudo-classes.*

The :link, :visited, and :hover pseudo-classes are shown in Figure 8.22. The :active pseudo-class is not shown. Most CSS-supporting browsers show the :active pseudo-class display characteristics when the mouse button is held down on a link. Internet Explorer 5 and 6 additionally continue to display a link in the active state after returning to a page using the Back button.

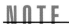

NOTE

For this example, only the Past Issues link in the sidebar menu links to an actual page. The other links are all dummy links that do not connect to actual pages. To test the visited and active link states, just click on the Past Issues link and then click the Back button to return to the current issue.

Using Other Pseudo-Classes and Pseudo-Elements

A number of additional pseudo-classes and pseudo-elements are part of CSS2.

The :first-child pseudo-class sets display characteristics for an element that is the first child of another element. For instance, the following example applies a bold font-weight only to a P element that is the first child of its parent element:

```
p:first-child { font-weight: bold }
```

The :first-line pseudo-element applies style properties only to the first line in a specified element. For instance, the following example applies a bold font-weight to the first line of any P element that is nested inside a DIV element belonging to the "main" class:

```
div.main p:first-line { font-weight: bold; }
```

The :first-letter pseudo-element applies style properties only to the first letter of a specified element. For instance, the following example formats as a drop-cap the first letter of any P element that is a descendant of a DIV element belonging to the "main" class:

```
div.main p:first-letter { font-size: 215%; font-weight: bold;
float: left; margin-bottom: 1px; }
```

The :before and :after pseudo-elements let you specify generated content to be displayed before or following an element. For instance, the following example inserts open and closed quotes before and after a SPAN element belonging to the "quote" class:

```
span.quote:before { content: open-quote; }
span.quote:after { content: close-quote; }
```

The following example inserts the text string "Note:" in front of a P element belonging to the "note" class:

```
p.note:before { content: "Note: "; color: red; }
```

The previous example inserts the generated content as inline content that is displayed on the same line as the paragraph in which it is inserted. By changing the display property value to **block**, you can cause the generated content to be displayed as a separate block:

```
p.note:before { content: "Note: "; color: red; display: block;
margin-bottom: 12px; }
```

As with the additional CSS2 selectors, not all current browsers support these CSS2 pseudo-classes and pseudo-elements. Internet Explorer 5.5 and 6 for Windows, for instance, support the :first-letter and :first-line pseudo-elements, but not the :first-child pseudo-class or the :before and :after pseudo-elements.

NOTE
For links to resources on the Web that discuss the use of both CSS1 and CSS2 pseudo-classes and pseudo-elements, see this chapter's section at the IRC for this book at **www.emcp.com**/.

CHAPTER SUMMARY

You should now have a good understanding of using styles to create Web page layouts using only styles, instead of using tables and deprecated elements and attributes to create layouts. You should know how to position elements on the page, as well as set the stacking order to determine the order in which elements overlap each other.

Code Review

single selector	Sets properties for a single element.
group selector	Sets properties for a comma-separated list of elements.
contextual selector	Sets properties for elements only within a certain context.
class selector	Sets properties for elements belonging to a certain class.
ID selector	Sets properties for an element with a specific ID.
text-align property	Horizontally aligns nested text within an element.
float property	Floats an object (image or other element) at the left or right margin, with following text and elements flowing around the floating object.
clear property	Causes an element to clear a floating object.
position property	Positions an element. Absolute positioning positions the element relative to the browser window (or viewport). Relative positioning positions an element relative to the current element position. Fixed positioning is similar to absolute positioning, except the positioned element does not scroll with the page, but remains fixed in its position.
top, right, bottom, and left properties	These properties specify the position of a positioned element. With absolute and fixed positioning, they specify the position of the element relative to the top, right, bottom, or left sides of the browser window (or viewport). With relative positioning, positive or negative values specify the position of the element from its current position, with `left: -5px`, for instance, positioning the element 5 pixels to the left of the current position.
DL element	Defines a definition list (or glossary list).
DT element	Specifies a definition term within a definition list.
DD element	Specifies definition data (or the definition of a term) in a definition list.
z-index property	Specifies the stacking order of overlapping elements. An element with a higher z-index value is stacked on top of an element with a lower z-index value.
overflow property	Determines what happens if the content of an element overflows its width and height. A value of **visible** causes the element to expand to contain the content; **hidden** hides content that overflows the element box; **scroll** causes vertical and horizontal scroll bars to be displayed, even if the content does not overflow the element box; and **auto** causes scroll bars to be displayed only if the content overflows the element box.
clip property	Lets you specify a clipping region outside of which element content is not displayed.
:first-child	A pseudo-class that applies style properties to the first child of an element.

:first-line	A pseudo-element that applies style properties to the first line in an element.
:first-letter	A pseudo-element that applies style properties to the first letter in an element.
:before	A pseudo-element that inserts generated content before the specified element.
:after	A pseudo-element that inserts generated content after the specified element.

ONLINE QUIZ

Go to this text's IRC at **www.emcp.com/** and take the online self-check quiz for this chapter.

REVIEW EXERCISES

This section provides some hands-on practice exercises to reinforce the information and material included within this and previous chapters.

You can use any of the example files that you created in this chapter to further practice features or methods covered in this chapter. To save the original versions of these files for future reference, save them under another name, such as spacegallery2_practice.html or safety_practice.html in the chap08 folder in your working folder or disk, for instance, before using them for practice.

1. Save **spacegallery2.html** under a new name (**spacegallery2_practice.html**, for instance) and practice further horizontally aligning images using styles. For instance, edit the p.banner style to right-align rather than center-align the banner image. Experiment with setting other style properties for the "banner" paragraph, such as a bottom border, a reduced bottom margin, and so on.

2. Still working with **spacegallery2_practice.html**, practice further using floating images. For instance, figure out how to switch the floating images so that the images now floating on the left margin float on the right margin and the images now floating on the right margin float on the left margin.

3. Right now, in **spacegallery2_practice.html**, the floating images are actually image links, but with their borders turned off using styles. Leaving the border-width property set to **0** for those properties, edit the img.left and img.right styles and experiment with using the border property to draw "frames" around the images. For instance, try inserting **border: 6px aqua inset** in the img.left or img.right style to see what the result will be. Experiment with different pixel-widths, colors, and border-styles (solid, double, dotted, dashed, groove, ridge, inset, or outset). Experiment with setting different padding amounts for the img.left and img.right styles. For those same styles, to add a "mat" around the images, set a background color (**background: #ffffcc**, for instance). Experiment setting different background colors to be displayed in the img.left and img.right padding areas.

4. Experiment further with setting left and right margins for the img.left and img.right styles. Try increasing or decreasing the left and right margins. Right now, only a right margin is set for the img.left style and only a left margin is set for the img.right style. Try also setting a left margin for the img.left style and a right margin for the img.right style, experimenting with different margin amounts.

5. Still working with **spacegallery2_practice.html**, experiment with any other style properties you have worked with so far in this book. Experiment with setting different colors for different elements, for instance. Try setting different fonts. Find a different background color that you like, copy it into the chap08 folder, and then use a style to display it in the page's background; adjust the page's text, links, and background colors so they complement the background image.

6. Find a graphic rule that you like, copy it into the chap08 folder. Use it, instead of the HR element, as a separator. Since the IMG element is an inline image, nest the graphic rule's IMG element in a paragraph. Assign the paragraph to a class, and then add a style to the style sheet that uses a class selector to cause the graphic rule's paragraph to clear the floating images. If you set the width of the graphical rule to less than 100% (or do not set a width), use a style to center-align the graphic rule's paragraph (see the p.banner style for an example of horizontally aligning a paragraph's content).

7. If you are using a browser that supports them, experiment with using some of the CSS2 selectors that were covered in this chapter, such as the universal, child, adjacent sibling, and attribute selectors. To experiment with all these selectors, you can use the Mozilla 1 or Opera 6 browser, for instance. Internet Explorer 5.2 for the Macintosh lacks support only for attribute selectors. Internet Explorer 6 for Windows, however, only supports using the universal selector.

8. Save **safety.html** under a new name (**safety_practice.html**) and practice further with positioning elements on the page. For instance, adjust the "top" absolute positioning that is defined for the img.banner, div.runner, and div.main styles. Adjust the "left" absolute positioning that is defined for the div.main style. Adjust the top padding amount that is set for the div.side style, to move the menu up or down in the sidebar.

9. Experiment with repositioning the banner image along its horizontal axis. For instance, in the img.banner style, replace the **left** property with the **right** property to position the banner image relative to the right side, instead of the left side, of the browser window. Try setting it using a percentage value, for instance. Experiment with different values.

10. Experiment with setting different style properties for the div.runner style. For instance, change the font family to an Arial font or another sans serif font, change the foreground and background colors, change the border characteristics, and adjust the height and the font size. Try setting an italic font (**font-style: italic**) for either of the two SPAN elements that define the content of the "runner" division. Try setting small caps font (**font-variant: small-caps**) for the other of the two SPAN elements.

11. Experiment setting a background color in the div.side style to display a color behind the sidebar. If necessary, adjust the foreground colors set for the div.side p, div.side a:link, div.side a:visited, div.side a:hover, and div.side a:active styles so they complement the background color you have set for the div.side style.

12. Experiment with moving the "side" division down and to the right on the page. Move the "runner" division to the left on the page, so that it starts to the left of the "side" division. Move the "main" division to the right, so that it is not overlapped by the "side" division.

13. Still working with **safety_practice.html**, experiment with any other style properties you have worked with so far in this book. Experiment with setting different colors for different elements, for instance. Try setting different fonts. Find a different

background color that you like, copy it into the chap08 folder, and then use a style to display it in the page's background; adjust the page's text, links, and background colors so they complement the background image.

14. If you are using a browser that supports them, experiment with using some of the CSS2 pseudo-classes and pseudo-elements that were covered in this chapter, such as using the :first-child, :first-line, :before, and :after selectors.

15. Save **safety2.html** under a new name (**safety2_practice.html**) and experiment with the overflow property. Try setting the different overflow values, **auto**, **scroll**, and **hidden** (**visible** is the default) to see the different results. If you are using the Mozilla 1 browser, or another browser that supports the clip property, experiment further with using it to "crop out" the banner image or any other element on the page.

WEB-BASED LEARNING ACTIVITIES

In this book's text, Find It icons inserted in the margin highlight the Web addresses of additional resources you might find helpful or informative. To further extend your learning using the Web, you can:

- Go back and visit any of the Web addresses highlighted in this chapter that you have not yet visited. Look for additional resources and information that add to your understanding and knowledge of the material covered in this chapter. When you find a relevant page or site with information or resources you might want to access later, add it to your Favorites (in Internet Explorer) or your Bookmarks (in Netscape or Mozilla).

- Visit this book's Internet Resource Center at **www.emcp.com/** to find additional Web addresses of resources related to the material covered in this chapter that you can further investigate and explore.

- Further research a specific topic introduced in this chapter. For instance, you can do further research on the pros and cons of using style sheets to create page layouts, instead of using tables or frames. You might also do research on the Web page accessibility issues that CSS is designed to address.

  Compile the results of your research into a report that can be shared with your fellow students. You also can team up with other students to create a class presentation or demonstration.

- Use Yahoo! at **www.yahoo.com/** to look for examples of how styles are used on the Web. Find at least six different examples on the Web that you think demonstrate the effective use of styles. Save the examples you find as bookmarks or favorites, so you can use them as a reference later in conceptualizing and designing your own Web pages using styles.

PROJECTS

These projects can be done in class, in a computer lab, or at home. Use the skills you have developed in this and the previous chapters to create any of the following projects.

Project 1. Create a Web-page design that uses floating images created using CSS.

Either using a page you have already created or starting out from scratch, create a Web-page design that uses floating images created using CSS. For instance, you can create an image gallery page of your own photographs or artwork using floating images created using CSS. You also can search for images on the Web that you can use to create a practice online gallery.

Project 2. Create a Web-page design that uses CSS positioning.

Starting out either from scratch or using a Web page you have already created, create a Web page design that does not use any deprecated elements/attributes or tables (or frames), but uses CSS positioning to create the layout design. For links to where you can find lists of all deprecated (and obsoleted) elements and attributes, see this chapter's section at the IRC for this book at **www.emcp.com/**.

The subject or topic for this project is open-ended. You can create a personal page, topical page, a page for a club or organization, or a page for a fictional commercial client. Try experimenting with different layouts than those that have been presented in this chapter.

CHAPTER

9

Designing with Graphics

PERFORMANCE OBJECTIVES

In this chapter, you will learn more about using graphics to create effective Web site designs, including how to:
- Understand graphic issues.
- Create a graphical front end using an image map.
- Split a single image into multiple images using an image slicer.
- Create a wraparound graphical interface using sliced images and a table.
- Add JavaScript rollover buttons to a page.

You have already worked with images in Part One, *HTML Essentials*, including Chapter 4, *Working with Images and Other Media*, which was specifically focused on using images with HTML. The focus of this chapter is using image maps, image slicing, and other techniques to create graphical Web designs.

USING THE EXAMPLE FILES

If you have created a working folder for storing files you create, you will find the example files for this chapter located in the **chap09** folder within your working folder. Save any HTML files you create in this chapter in that folder.

If you have created a working disk, copy the chap09 folder to your working disk from the **HTML_Examples** folder that you or your instructor downloaded from this book's Internet Resource Center (IRC), or from a CD-R disc or floppy disk provided by your instructor. Save any HTML file you create in this chapter in the chap09 folder that you have copied to your working disk.

UNDERSTANDING GRAPHIC ISSUES

When designing Web pages, many designers want to create the same kinds of designs they can create in a desktop publishing program or a graphics editor. Information presented by means of graphics, however, consumes many more bytes than the same information presented by means of straight HTML (or CSS). This does not mean that you should not create graphical Web designs, but you need to be aware that the inefficient use of graphics can slow down access to your site. Many surfers, when they encounter a page that is slow to load, automatically click the Back or Stop button.

In Chapter 4, you learned about optimizing GIF and JPEG images. If you need to review how to optimize your images, see the "Creating Your Own Web Images" section in that chapter.

Graphical front ends and interfaces also can present accessibility problems, in that someone using a text or non-visual browser will not be able to see the graphic elements of your page. In this chapter, a number of steps are discussed that you can use to help make sure your graphical Web designs are accessible.

NOTE For links to resources on the Web that discuss the use of graphics in Web design, including designing with type and bandwidth conservation, see this chapter's section at the IRC for this book at **www.emcp.com/**.

CASE EXAMPLE: CREATING A GRAPHICAL FRONT END

Using an image map to create a graphical front end is a popular way to give a site a distinctive and attractive look. An *image map* is an image in which *hotspots* have been mapped; a hotspot is an area within the image that is associated with a URL link. When visitors click on the hotspot, their browsers take them to the linked URL.

Rhonda Andrews is an amateur chef and enjoys collecting recipes from family and friends. She wants to share her collection of recipes over the Web. She has decided to create a graphical front end for her site, which will allow visitors to access different kinds of recipes by clicking on an area in the image.

To start working with this example:
1. Run your text editor and open **recipes_ex.html** from the chap09 folder in your working folder or working disk.
2. Save recipes_ex.html as **recipes.html** in the chap09 folder.
3. Run your browser and open **recipes.html** from the chap09 folder.

CREATING IMAGE MAPS

As stated previously, an image map is an image for which clickable hotspots have been mapped, and a hotspot is an area within an image that functions as a hypertext link. When a visitor clicks in a hotspot area, the browser opens the page or other object that is the target of the link.

Any image can be set up as an image map, but before you select or create an image you want to use, you should plan how you want your image map to appear and what you want it to do. It can be helpful, for instance, to first sketch out on a piece of paper the basic design you want to create.

Rhonda has sketched out the basic design for her image map. She has decided to use the different recipe categories as design elements, presenting them in 3-D relief against the image's background. To give it a distinctive look, she has used two different wood-grain textures, as well as button, cutout, and drop shadow effects.

The example image, recipes.gif, which you will be using to create an image map, is included with the example files for this chapter.

Insert recipes.gif in the example file as an inline image and center it (see Figure 9.1):

```
<body bgcolor="#003300" text="white" link="yellow"
vlink="yellow" alink="yellow">
<center>
<p><img src="recipes.gif" width="575" height="375" alt="Recipes
image map: Meats, Seafood, Pasta, Soup, Barbecue,
Salad, Bread, Dessert, and Drinks"></p>
</center>
```

FIGURE 9.1 • *The image, recipe.gif, is centered on the page and displayed against a dark green background image.*

Using Image Map Editors

Several image map editors allow you to draw hotlink areas in an image and then export the HTML codes that create the image map. Some image editors also include image mapping wizards or utilities. These all work in roughly the same way.

The following example uses Map This, a freeware image map editor for Windows, to draw image map hotspots and export them to an HTML file. If you are using Windows, you can find a link to where you can download Map This, as well as other image map editors, at this chapter's section at the IRC for this book at **www.emcp.com/**.

Following are steps for using Map This, a freeware image map editor for Windows, to draw and export image map hotspots. If you have Map This installed, an example image file, recipes.gif, is included with the example files for this chapter that you can use in experimenting with creating an image map. Other image map programs should work very similarly to how Map This works.

To create an image map using Map This, follow these steps:

1. In Map This, start a new image map (File, New) and specify the image (recipe.gif, for instance) that you want to set up as an image map.

2. Select the kind of hotspot area (rectangle, ellipse, or polygon) that you want to specify.

3. Use the mouse cursor to draw shapes around areas in the image you want to set up as hotspots (see Figure 9.2).

4. Click on the Pointer icon, click on one of the hotspot areas you defined, click on the Edit icon, and type the URL you want the hotspot to link to (see Figure 9.3). Click OK. Repeat for each hotspot you have defined.

5. Click the Save icon and save the image map codes to the HTML file (recipes.html, for instance) in which they will be used (select HTML, not NCSA or CERN as the image map type).

FIGURE 9.2 • *A hotspot area is drawn in Map This, a freeware image map editor.*

FIGURE 9.3 • *A URL (or file name) is specified for the hotspot area.*

Understanding the Image Map Codes

An image map editor inserts the image map codes into an HTML file. In most cases, you do not need to do anything additional to get your image map to work (with Map This, however, you need to edit the image's IMG element to link it to the image map codes). Because you have not actually exported the image map codes to the HTML file to see how they work, you will need to key them in.

1. In the example file, scroll to the bottom of the page (just above the **</body>** end tag) and key the image map HTML codes:

```
<map name="recipes">
<area shape="rect" coords="39,108,183,171" href="meats.html">
<area shape="rect" coords="199,107,387,175" href="seafood.html">
<area shape="rect" coords="400,106,536,177" href="pasta.html">
<area shape="rect" coords="36,189,162,251" href="soup.html">
<area shape="rect" coords="171,189,392,252" href="barbecue.html">
<area shape="rect" coords="400,188,535,252" href="salad.html">
<area shape="rect" coords="29,274,176,324" href="bread.html">
<area shape="rect" coords="191,271,371,325" href="dessert.html">
<area shape="rect" coords="381,269,544,327" href="drinks.html">
<area shape="default" href="recipes.html">
</map>
</body>
```

2. In the IMG element (for recipes.gif), turn off the display of the image's border and insert a USEMAP attribute that associates it with the MAP element's NAME attribute (this is inserted automatically by most image map editors, although not by Map This):

```
<p><img usemap="#recipes" border="0" src="recipes.gif" width="575"
height="375" alt="Recipes image map: Meats, Seafood, Pasta, Soup,
Barbecue, Salad, Bread, Dessert, and Drinks"></p>
```

3. Save **recipes.html** (File, Save) in your text editor and switch to your browser where recipes.html should be displayed. Click the Refresh or Reload button to refresh the display of the page.

4. Click on the Meats hotspot area (see Figure 9.4). The page of meat recipes, meats.html, is displayed in the browser window (see Figure 9.5).

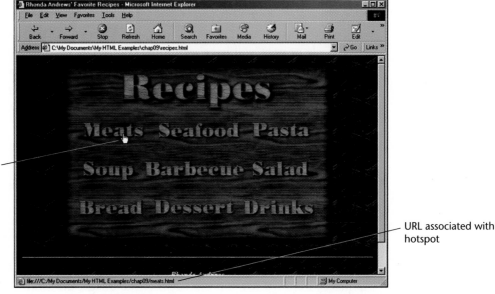

mouse cursor over hotspot

URL associated with hotspot

FIGURE 9.4 • *When the mouse passes over a hotspot, the URL link appears in the browser's status bar.*

FIGURE 9.5 • *After clicking on a hotspot, a browser displays the file specified in the hotspot's URL link.*

5. Click the Return to Front Page link to return to the front page.

Following are some pointers to help you understand the code for this example:

- The MAP element identifies that nested elements are used to define a client-side image map. (A different element, the ISMAP element, is used to specify a server-side image map.)
- The MAP element's NAME attribute names the image map, so it can be linked with the image that is being mapped.
- The nested AREA elements specify the coordinates and URL links for the hotspots.
- In the AREA element, the SHAPE attribute specifies the type of hotspot area. Possible values of the SHAPE attribute are **rect**, **circle**, **poly**, and **default**. The example uses the **rect** and **default** values, but not the **circle** or **poly** values (which define circular and polygon-shaped hotspot areas).
- In the AREA element, the COORDS attribute specifies the coordinates of the hotspot area, relative to the left and top edge of the image. For instance, in the coordinates for the Seafood hotspot area (199,107,387,175), the first two numbers specify the distance in pixels that the upper-left corner of the hotspot is spaced in from the image's left and top edges, respectively, while the second two numbers specify the same thing for the hotspot's lower-right corner. (The other shape types, circle or poly, will have additional coordinate pairs to map out their positions.)
- In the last AREA element, the `shape="default"` attribute indicates that the entire image functions as a hotspot that is linked to the specified URL; when declaring a default shape for the image as a whole, no COORDS attribute is used (because the coordinates are the same as the image).

NOTE

For links to image map editors and other graphics programs capable of creating image maps, see this chapter's section at the IRC for this book at **www.emcp.com/**.

You do not need an image map editor to create image maps. The AREA element's coordinate numbers correlate to the position of the upper-left and lower-right corners of the hotspot area. The first two coordinates specify the distance of the upper-left corner, in pixels, from the left and top edges of the image; the second two coordinates specifying the distance of the lower-right corner from the left and top edges of the image. To discover the coordinate position of any point within an image, in your image editor, just position the mouse cursor over any point in the image—the coordinate distances from the left and top edge of the image should be displayed in the image editor's status bar. For instance, the upper-left corner of the Meats hotspot area is 39 pixels in from the image's left edge and 108 pixels down from the top edge, while the lower-right corner is 183 pixels in from the left edge and 171 pixels down from the top edge.

Two kinds of image maps can be created: server-side image maps and client-side image maps. Server-side image maps are created using the ISMAP element and use scripts on a server to process link actions. The main disadvantage of server-side image maps is a noticeable delay between clicking a hotspot area and the resulting link action, due to the link request having first to be sent to and processed by a script on the server. With a server-side image map, you also cannot tell that an area in the image is a hotspot simply by passing the mouse over it, as is the case with a client-side image map, which displays the URLs of hotspot links in the browser's status bar. Server-side image maps also can present accessibility problems for visitors using a text or non-visual browsers, in that they have no way of knowing what a hotspot link is for or where it goes.

Image maps also can be defined for the OBJECT and INPUT elements, although support among browsers is not anywhere near as wide as it is for the IMG element.

Planning for Accessibility and Backward Compatibility

When using an image map in your site, be aware that some visitors will not be able to see or use your image map for the following reasons:

- Some early browsers do not support client-side image maps.
- Users of text browsers and non-visual browsers will not be able to see an image map's image. This can leave someone with a visual handicap who is using a speech or Braille browser with literally nowhere to go when they come to your page.
- A significant number of users surf the Web with the display of graphics turned off in their browsers in order to speed up access to the textual content of Web pages. These users also will not be able to see your image map's image and thus might not be able to tell the function or purpose of your hotspot links.
- Search engines might not be able to follow image map links to index the rest of your site. An image map page also might not have text content that a search engine can index.

For these reasons, it is important to provide alternative means, other than just an image map, that surfers and search engine robots can use to access the rest of your site.

INCLUDING A TEXT-BASED LINK MENU   The simplest way to do that is to include separate links below your image map that link to the main pages in your site.

Add a one-line link menu below the image map (see Figure 9.6):

```
<center>
<p><img usemap="#recipes" border="0" src="recipes.gif" width="575"
height="375" alt="Recipes image map: Meats, Seafood, Pasta, Soup,
Barbecue, Salad, Bread, Dessert, and Drinks"></p>
<p><a href="meats.html">Meats</a> - <a
href="seafood.html">Seafood</a> - <a href="pasta.html">Pasta</a> -
<a href="soup.html">Soup</a> - <a href="barbecue.html">Barbecue</a>
- <a href="salad.html">Salad</a> - <a href="bread.html">Bread</a>
- <a href="dessert.html">Dessert</a> - <a
href="drinks.html">Drinks</a></p>
</center>
```

text menu

FIGURE 9.6 • *A link menu provides an alternative means for visitors or search engine robots to access the other pages in the site.*

A neat trick that you can use here is to combine the alternative text menu with the CSS display property. By using CSS to turn off the display of the text menu, you can render it invisible to most browsers that support client-side image maps while continuing to display it for early browsers that do not support client-side image maps.

Edit the text menu's paragraph so it will be invisible in all browsers that support the display property:

```
<p style="display: none"><a href="meats.html">Meats</a> - <a
href="seafood.html">Seafood</a> - <a href="pasta.html">Pasta</a> -
<a href="soup.html">Soup</a> - <a href="barbecue.html">Barbecue</a>
- <a href="salad.html">Salad</a> - <a href="bread.html">Bread</a>
- <a href="dessert.html">Dessert</a> - <a
href="drinks.html">Drinks</a></p>
```

The result of this is that any browsers that do not support the client-side image maps will display the alternative text menu, because they also do not support the display property (or any other CSS properties, for that matter). Although some browsers that support client-side image maps do not support the display property, such as Netscape Navigator 3 or Internet Explorer 3, these browsers will display both the image map and the text menu (which is exactly what the result would be in all browsers if no display property was present). Netscape Navigator 4 supports the display property and thus will also display the image map while hiding the text menu.

You should not use this trick, however, without also including informative ALT attributes in your image map's AREA elements, as described in the next section.

USING THE ALT ATTRIBUTE IN IMAGE MAPS The ALT attribute is a required attribute for the AREA element. Many image map editors, however, do not insert ALT attributes in AREA elements when they output a MAP element's nested AREA elements. Although graphical browsers do not care whether your image map's AREA elements contain ALT attributes, you should include ALT attributes in AREA elements for a number of reasons, including

- To inform users of text-based or non-visual browsers, who are unable to see the mapped image, of the function and purpose of hotspot links.
- Pages that feature image map front ends do not have much textual content that search engine robots can index. Including ALT attributes for your image map's AREA elements can provide textual content that a search engine robot can index.

Add ALT attributes to the image map's AREA elements:

```
<map name="recipes">
<area shape="rect" coords="39,108,183,171" href="meats.html"
alt="Meat recipes: roasts, stews, beef, pork, chicken, lamb">
<area shape="rect" coords="199,107,387,175" href="seafood.html"
alt="Seafood recipes: fish, shellfish, crab, clams, oysters,
salmon, chowder">
<area shape="rect" coords="400,106,536,177" href="pasta.html"
alt="Pasta recipes: spaghetti, fettuccine, ravioli, lasagna,
pesto, macaroni">
<area shape="rect" coords="36,189,162,251" href="soup.html"
alt="Soup recipes: bisques, borsch, bouillon, broth, chowder,
cream soups, gumbo">
<area shape="rect" coords="171,189,392,252" href="barbecue.html"
alt="Barbecue recipes: ribs, pork, chicken, fajitas, marinade,
sauce">
<area shape="rect" coords="400,188,535,252" href="salad.html"
alt="Salad recipes: greens, lettuce, spinach, caesar, waldorf,
dressings">
<area shape="rect" coords="29,274,176,324" href="bread.html"
alt="Bread recipes: bread, rolls, buns, biscuits, corn bread,
pita bread, dumplings">
<area shape="rect" coords="191,271,371,325" href="dessert.html"
alt="Dessert recipes: cakes, cookies, tarts, shortcake, puddings,
doughnuts, scones, muffins">
<area shape="rect" coords="381,269,544,327" href="drinks.html"
alt="Drink recipes: coffee, espresso, tea, juices, spiced cider,
punch">
<area shape="default" href="recipes.html" alt="Favorite recipes:
meat, seafood, pasta, barbecue, bread, soup, salad, dessert,
drinks">
</map>
```

You should always include a META element description and keyword list in the HEAD element. A descriptive ALT element in the image map's IMG element can also give search engine robots something more to index. You also can include a paragraph describing your site below the ADDRESS element, but with a style property of **display: none** set. That will also provide content for search engines to index—in earlier browsers that do not support the display property, the description paragraph should not be initially visible, because it should fall below the fold (the bottom edge of the browser window).

CASE EXAMPLE: CREATING A WRAPAROUND GRAPHICAL INTERFACE

When surfing the Web, you might have noticed sites that feature a wraparound graphical interface, in which the top banner and sidebar menu areas appear as one continuous graphic that wraps around the page's text content. Although it looks like one continuous graphic, it is actually several separate graphics that are invisibly arrayed next to each other using a table. This is achieved by using an *image slicer*, which slices an image into multiple images along a grid pattern.

> *Grady Roberts is a student at Munster University and is a big fan of his school's football team, the Fighting Crawdads. He wants to create a fan page for his favorite team, featuring the current schedule and roster, articles about the team, and a discussion forum where fans can gather and discuss their favorite topic.*

Grady noticed sites on the Web that use a wraparound graphical interface and decided to create his site along the same lines.

SLICING IMAGES

Creating wraparound graphics is not the only reason to slice an image. Anytime you are using a larger image within a Web site, slicing your image into pieces can speed up the time it takes the total image to be downloaded and displayed. That is because a smaller file has a much easier time negotiating the Internet "maze," whereas a larger file is much more likely to get caught up in an Internet traffic jam. A visitor also sees your image begin to display much earlier, in that the first piece of your image is displayed as soon as it arrives. What drives visitors to click the Back button is when nothing happens when they first access your site, and not that some parts of your site might not download and be displayed immediately.

For instance, the image map example you created earlier in this chapter also can be sliced into multiple images and then pieced back together using a table. To set up the links, you either have to create an image map for each sliced section of the image or turn the relevant image slices into image links (with their borders turned off).

Grady created the graphic he wants to use in his image editor and downloaded an image slicer from the Web. He sliced his image into a 3 × 11 grid (see Figure 9.7).

FIGURE 9.7 • *You can slice an image into pieces using an image slicer, such as Shoestring's PictureDicer, as shown here.*

Example sliced images, craw001.gif, craw002.gif, craw003.gif, and so on, are included with the example files for this chapter, so you do not need to first slice the full Crawdads front end image (crawdads.gif) to create the example wraparound graphical layout. The sliced areas of the image that will be used for text display have not been included, since those (pure white) images will not be used.

Figure 9.7 shows the example graphic, crawdads.gif, being sliced in the PictureDicer image slicer, a freeware utility for Windows. In PictureDicer, to create a vertical slice, just click the mouse where you want the slice to be; to create a horizontal slice, just hold down the Shift key and then click the mouse where you want the slice to be. To delete a slice, just click on the red or blue triangle at the end of a slice line. To output the sliced images, select File, Process Image.

When slicing images for creating wraparound graphical interfaces, be mindful that the rectangles where you want to display text should not include any of the colored areas of the graphic, but should only encompass the image's white space areas. After you splice the wraparound graphic back together, you will be throwing away the pure white images and replacing them with text.

NOTE

You do not have to slice an image along the lines of only a single grid. For instance, you can first slice an image into rows, but without also slicing it into columns. You can then open a sliced row image in your image slicer and slice it vertically (into columns) at any point that you choose, while slicing the other row images vertically at other points.

PUTTING TOGETHER THE WRAPAROUND LAYOUT

After you have sliced an image into pieces, you need to stitch (or splice) it back together. You do this using a table or tables, depending on whether you have sliced your image into one or multiple grids. In this example, you will just be working with a single table to stitch the image back together again.

An example file, crawdads_ex.html, is included with the other example files for this chapter. The sliced images have already been inserted in a table for you in the example file.

To start working with this example:
1. Run your text editor and open **crawdads_ex.html** from the chap09 folder in your working folder or working disk.
2. Save crawdads_ex.html as **crawdads.html** in the chap09 folder.
3. Run your browser and open **crawdads.html** from the chap09 folder (see Figure 9.8).

table borders

FIGURE 9.8 • *The sliced images are inserted inside table cells.*

Borders are set for the example table, so you can see how the sliced images are nested inside the table cells. Unbreakable space characters ( ) have been inserted in any empty table cells, so borders will be displayed around them.

The Mozilla 1 and Netscape 6 browsers insert a margin underneath inline images nested inside table cells, which creates a space between nested images. These browsers also insert top-margin spacing above the first block element within a table cell, which can cause the content of the cell to exceed the desired height, breaking the contiguous display of the wraparound sliced images.

To solve these problems and make sure that the table and wraparound interface will be displayed in a similar fashion in all current browsers, the following styles have been included in the example file:

```
td img { display: block; margin: 0; }
td :first-child { margin-top: 0; }
```

Notice that to fix the first problem, the IMG element, which is an inline element, is redefined as a block element (vertical margins cannot be set for inline elements). To fix the second problem, the combination of a contextual selector and a :first-child pseudo-class is used to cause the top-margin to be eliminated for the first child element in any TD element. This works because Mozilla 1 and Netscape 6 both support the :first-child pseudo-class (a CSS2 feature). Whenever you are creating a wraparound graphical interface using sliced images, you should always add these styles to your page's style sheet; otherwise, your page design might not look the way you want it to look in the Mozilla 1 and Netscape 6 browsers.

Some early browsers also might not support using tables, which have only been part of the HTML standard starting with HTML 3.2. To deal with these earlier browsers that do not support tables, you could employ a browser-sniffing script that would redirect users of these browsers to an alternative page. Another option is to use the Web Standards Invisible Object Method to alert users of earlier browsers that they should consider upgrading their browsers.

Setting Up the Table

Starting out, the table is divided into a grid of cells, with quite a few empty cells (the "white" cells). Before adding text to the page, you need to turn the two columns on the right (for the bottom nine rows) into a single spanned cell.

Use the ROWSPAN and COLSPAN attributes to combine the following "white" cells into one cell (delete the table cells that are being spanned; see Figure 9.9):

```
<tr>
  <td><img src="craw006.gif" width="157" height="75" alt=""></td>
  <td colspan="2" rowspan="9"> </td>
  <td> </td>
</tr>
<tr>
  <td><img src="craw009.gif" width="157" height="75" alt=""></td>
  <td> </td>
  <td> </td>
</tr>
<tr>
  <td><img src="craw012.gif" width="157" height="75" alt=""></td>
  <td> </td>
  <td> </td>
</tr>
<tr>
  <td><img src="craw015.gif" width="157" height="75" alt=""></td>
  <td> </td>
  <td> </td>
</tr>
<tr>
  <td><img src="craw018.gif" width="157" height="75" alt=""></td>
  <td> </td>
  <td> </td>
</tr>
<tr>
  <td><img src="craw021.gif" width="157" height="75" alt=""></td>
  <td> </td>
  <td> </td>
</tr>
<tr>
  <td><img src="craw024.gif" width="157" height="75" alt=""></td>
  <td> </td>
  <td> </td>
</tr>
<tr>
  <td><img src="craw027.gif" width="157" height="100" alt=""></td>
  <td> </td>
  <td> </td>
</tr>
<tr>
  <td><img src="craw027.gif" width="157" height="100" alt=""></td>
  <td> </td>
  <td> </td>
</tr>
```

spanned table cell

FIGURE 9.9 • *The empty "white" cells are turned into a single spanned cell (spanning two columns and nine rows).*

NOTE

As shown in Figure 9.9, a horizontal scroll bar is displayed at the bottom of the Internet Explorer 6 window when displaying the example page running maximized at an 800 × 600-pixel resolution. This is caused by the table borders, which are only turned on to show how the table cells are arranged; after the table borders are turned off, the horizontal scroll bar will disappear.

The ROWSPAN and COLSPAN attributes create a table cell that spans two columns (the second and third columns) and nine rows (starting with the third row). This spanned cell will contain the main textual content of the page.

Adding the Page's Text Content

The third cell in the second table row and the spanned cell below it will contain the textual content for the page. All other cells within the table contain graphic images. An example file, crawdads.txt, is included with the example files for this chapter, which you can use to copy and paste the main content for the page (rather than having to key it all in).

action

Key a headline (and byline) for the page and then paste in the main textual content for the page:

1. Key a headline and byline for the page (see Figure 9.10):

```
<tr>
  <td><img src="craw003.gif" width="157" height="102" alt=""></td>
  <td><img src="craw004.gif" width="163" height="102" alt=""></td>
  <td valign="bottom">
  <h2 align="right">Crawdads Start New Season</h2>
  <h4 align="right">by Grady Roberts</h4>
   
  </td>
</tr>
```

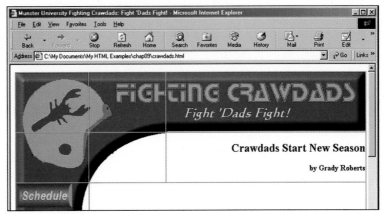

FIGURE 9.10 • *A heading and byline are added to the third cell in the second table row.*

2. An example text file that contains the main textual content for the page is included with the other example files for this chapter. Open **crawdads.txt** in your text editor, click and drag to highlight all the text in the file, and then copy it (Ctrl+C in Windows or Command+C on the Macintosh).

3. If necessary, reopen **crawdads.html** in your text editor. With that file open, first delete the non-breaking space entity code ( ) and then paste in the text you copied in Step 3 (Crtl+V in Windows or Command+V on the Macintosh), as shown here:

```
<tr>
  <td><img src="craw006.gif" width="157" height="75" alt=""></td>
  <td colspan="2" rowspan="9"> 
<table cellpadding="10" cellspacing="0"><tr><td>
<p>With only four starters not returning from a team that finished
second in the Heartland Conference last season, hopes are high for
this season. Season ticket sales are running well ahead of last
season's pace--good seats are still available, so get on down to
Snuffy Smith Field House on the Munster University campus and get
your tickets now!</p>

<h3>Offense Should Be Strong</h3>
<p>With All-Conference players returning at the quarterback, wide
receiver, and center positions, the Munster University Fighting
Crawdads should have a strong offense once again. Last season,
quarterback Jimmy Otis set a school record for pass attempts and
passing yardage, and flanker Tony Loffatt set a record for pass
receptions. Add in Anthony Rogers at the other wide receiver
position, who showed flashes of brilliance playing as a true
freshman last season, and the Crawdads should have a strong
passing attack that will threaten the record books. With a veteran
offensive line returning, led by All-Conference center Brad Bond,
Jimmy Otis should have plenty of time to find Loffatt and Rogers
downfield for pass completions.</p>
<p>The only weak point for the Crawdads offense is that All-
Conference tailback Ace Williams has graduated. Joe Jackson and
Randall Hirsch will be competing for the starting tailback spot.
Jackson, especially, showed promise during spring practice and
likely will be penciled in as the tentative starter.</p>

<h3>Key Holes to Fill on Defense</h3>
<p>Most of last season's defense is back, but with four key
starters having graduated, some key holes need to be filled. New
starters will be lining up to play at the cornerback, strong
safety, middle linebacker, and nose guard positions. All-
```

Conference cornerback Richie Toots will be missed especially. His replacement likely will be redshirt freshman Eddie Peters. The strong safety position will also be relying on redshirt freshmen to step in and perform, since no players with playing experience are back at that position.</p>

```
<hr>
<address>
Fighting Crawdads Football Fan Page<br>
E-Mail: <a
href="mailto:webmaster@fightdads.com">webmaster@fightdads.com</a><
br>
URL: <a
href="http://www.fightdads.com/">http://www.fightdads.com/</a>
</address>
</td></tr></table>
  </td>
</tr>
```

4. Vertically align the content of the spanned cell with the top of the cell (see Figure 9.11):

```
<tr>
  <td><img src="craw006.gif" width="157" height="75" alt=""></td>
  <td colspan="2" rowspan="9" valign="top">
<table cellpadding="10" cellspacing="0"><tr><td>
```

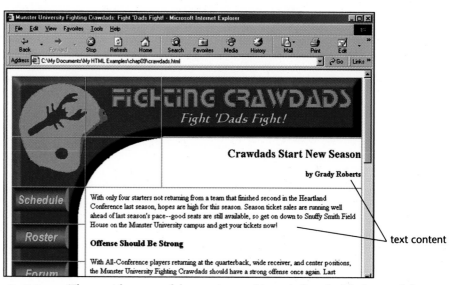

FIGURE 9.11 • *The textual content of the page is pasted in and aligned with the top of the spanned table cell.*

5. Turn off the table border (see Figure 9.12):

```
<body>
<table cellpadding="0" cellspacing="0" width="750" border="1">
```

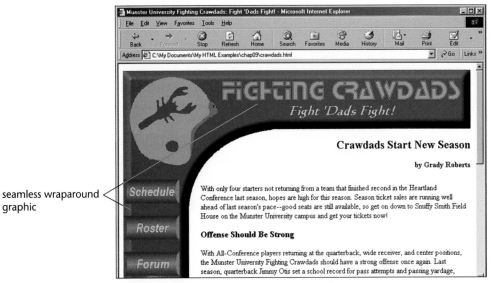

seamless wraparound graphic

FIGURE 9.12 • *With the table border turned off, the graphic seems to seamlessly wrap around the page's text.*

The content of the first text cell, which contains the article title and byline, is vertically aligned with the bottom of the cell to bring it closer to the main text content that is one row lower. The content of the spanned cell, which contains the main text content, is vertically aligned with the top of the cell. The default vertical alignment for table cells is middle-alignment, which would cause the main text content to be displayed further down the page because its height is less than the height of the cell in which it is nested.

The main text content for the page is nested inside its own table, which is then nested inside the spanned cell. This allows the setting of a different cell-padding amount than is set for the containing table.

NOTE

When nesting tables, you should always close any TR, TH, or TD cells in your tables (even though HTML 4 allows end tags for these elements to be implied), or some browsers may not display your tables properly (or at all). You should also be careful about nesting more than one table deep—that is because browsers must download everything that is in your nested tables before being able to allocate space for anything in your nested tables. Multiple nested tables can significantly increase the amount of time required to display a page.

Using a nested table here can also make your page more difficult to access for someone using a non-visual browser or a screen reader. Alternatively, you might consider dispensing with the nested table entirely and using a style instead to set a padding value for the spanned TD cell:

```
<td colspan="2" rowspan="9" valign="top" style="padding: 10px">
```

Setting Colors and Backgrounds

To further enhance your wraparound interface, you can set the colors and backgrounds for the page. An example background image, back_parch.jpg, is included with this chapter's example files.

Set colors and backgrounds for the page:

1. Set colors for the page's text, links, and background (see Figure 9.13):

```
<body text="#330000" link="red" vlink="maroon" bgcolor="#ffffcc">
```

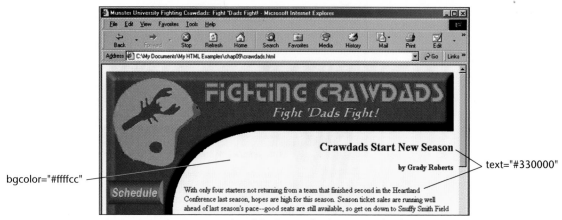

FIGURE 9.13 • *Foreground and background colors are set for the page.*

2. Set a background image to be displayed for the page (see Figure 9.14):

```
<body text="#330000" link="red" vlink="maroon" bgcolor="#ffffcc"
background="back_parch.jpg">
```

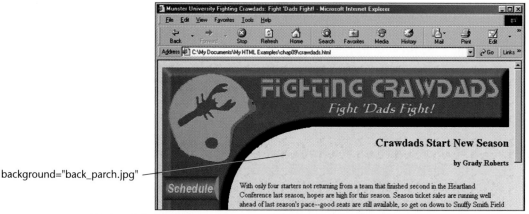

FIGURE 9.14 • *A background image is defined for the page.*

NOTE

Although not featured in this specific example, you can optionally eliminate the page margins surrounding the layout table. This was covered earlier in Chapter 5, *Working with Tables*. To do this using HTML, you need to use an assortment of non-standard HTML attributes in the BODY element:

```
<body text="#330000" link="red" vlink="maroon" bgcolor="#ffffcc"
background="back_parch.jpg" marginheight="0" marginwidth="0"
topmargin="0" leftmargin="0">
```

You also can achieve the same result using a style, by setting the margins for the BODY element to 0:

```
body { font-size: 16px; margin: 0; }
```

When designing your layout, figure into the dimensions of your wraparound graphic whether or not page margins are going to be displayed. If not, you could increase the width of your wraparound graphic by 16 pixels, without causing a horizontal scroll bar to be displayed in most browsers running maximized at 800 × 600-pixel resolution, since the default margin setting in most browsers is 8 pixels.

Creating the Menu Links

You can create hypertext links for the sidebar buttons in two different ways. The first is to use image maps to set a link just for the button area. The second is to turn the sliced image containing the button into an image link. The disadvantage of using image maps for this is that you have to create a separate image map for every button area you want to turn into a link. In the following example, you will be turning the sliced images into image links.

Set the sliced images that contain the buttons into image links:

1. Set up the link for the first button:

```
<tr>
   <td><a href="schedule.html">
   <img border="0" src="craw006.gif"
   width="157" height="75" alt="Season schedule"></a>
   </td>
```

2. Do the same with the remaining buttons:

```
<tr>
   <td><a href="roster.html">
   <img border="0" src="craw009.gif"
   width="157" height="75" alt="Team roster"></a>
   </td>
</tr>
<tr>
   <td><a href="forum.html">
   <img border="0" src="craw012.gif"
   width="157" height="75" alt="Message forum"></a>
   </td>
</tr>
<tr>
   <td><a href="news.html">
   <img border="0" src="craw015.gif"
   width="157" height="75" alt="Team news"></a>
   </td>
</tr>
<tr>
   <td><a href="articles.html">
   <img border="0" src="craw018.gif"
   width="157" height="75" alt="Featured articles"></a>
   </td>
</tr>
<tr>
   <td><a href="history.html">
   <img border="0" src="craw021.gif"
   width="157" height="75" alt="Crawdads history"></a>
   </td>
</tr>
```

```
<tr>
  <td><a href="contact.html">
  <img border="0" src="craw024.gif"
  width="157" height="75" alt="Contact us"></a>
  </td>
</tr>
```

3. Save your page in your text editor and hop over to your browser and refresh the display of your page. Click on the Schedule button. An example page, schedule.html, should be displayed in your browser (see Figure 9.15). Click the Back button to return to the front page.

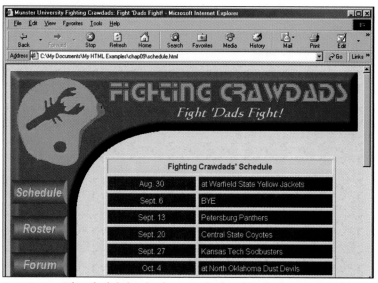

FIGURE 9.15 • *The schedule.html subpage is displayed in the browser window.*

The **border="0"** attribute in the IMG elements turns off the border that is normally displayed around an image link. The ALT attribute content identifies the purpose of the button links for visitors using text or non-visual browsers. Alternatively, in the other spliced images that are not also functioning as image links, the blank **alt=""** attribute has the contrary effect of not cluttering up a text browser with meaningless image icons, with Lynx, for instance, entirely ignoring any images with blank ALT attributes.

 When defining image maps for each sliced image that you want to function as a button link, you should also turn off the display of the image's border.

Looking at schedule.html in your browser, as shown in Figure 9.15, notice that the main text area is moved up on the page, overlapping the second and third table cells in the second table row. This is done by using relative positioning (**position: relative**), repositioning the nested table upward 60 pixels (**top: -60px**) relative to its previous position:

```
<div class="sched" style="position: relative; top: -60px">
<table align="center" cellpadding="5" cellspacing="5" width="500"
border="1">
<tr><th colspan="2">Fighting Crawdads' Schedule</th></tr>

[...]

</table>
```

```
<p class="return" align="center">Return to <a
href="crawdads.html">Front Page</a>.</p>
</div>
```

The other subpage files (roster.html, forum.html, and so on) are not included with the example files, so if you try to test those links, you will get a "page not found" error. You will have an opportunity when doing this chapter's review exercises to create one or more of these pages for yourself.

EMBELLISHING THE DESIGN

You can use either the FONT element or styles to further develop the appearance of the page. Styles let you apply characteristics globally to every instance of an element using a single style, while the FONT element must be nested inside each element where a display change is desired.

Add some formatting final touches to the page's text:

1. Format the H2 and H3 elements, setting colors, font faces, and borders (see Figure 9.16):

```
<style type="text/css">
body, td, p, address { font-size: 16px; }
td img { display: block; margin: 0; }
td :first-child { margin-top: 0; }
h2, h3, h4 { font-family: Arial, Helvetica, sans-serif; }
h3, address { border-top: 3px lime ridge; color: navy;
background: transparent; }
h2, h4 { margin-right: 10px; }
h2 { font-size: 24px; margin-bottom: 0; color: green;
background: transparent; }
h3 { font-size: 18px; }
h4 { font-size: 16px; margin-top: 6px; margin-bottom: 14px;
color: maroon; background: transparent; }
</style>
```

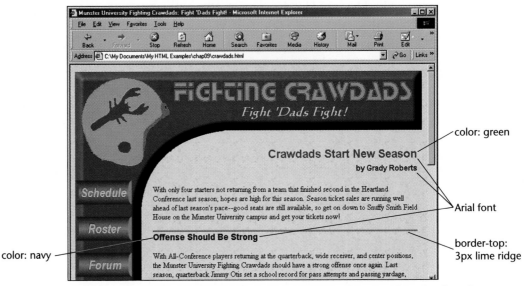

FIGURE 9.16 • *Color and font face changes are applied to the H2 and H3 heading elements and a top-border is applied to the H3 element.*

2. Delete the HR element above the ADDRESS element (since you also have set a border above the ADDRESS element; see Figure 9.17):

```
<hr>
<address>
Fighting Crawdads Football Fan Page<br>
```

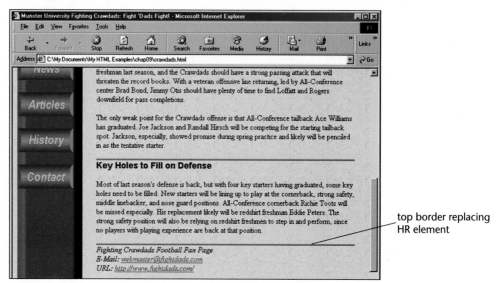

top border replacing HR element

FIGURE 9.17 • *The HR element is replaced by a top-border applied to the top of the ADDRESS element.*

An absolute font size, 16 pixels, is set for the BODY, P, TD, and ADDRESS elements. Absolute font sizes are also set for the H2, H3, and H4 heading elements. Setting absolute font sizes for these elements helps protect against the font size of these elements being increased either through browser preferences or a user-defined style sheet, which would potentially split up the seamless wraparound layout. On the other hand, this does penalize users who might need a larger font-size, although most more recent browsers allow users to easily zoom the display of text.

A sans serif font (Arial, Helvetica, or a browser's generic sans serif font) is set for the H2, H3, and H4 elements. A 10-pixel right margin is set for the H2 and H4 elements to space the article title and byline in from the right cell border. Different colors are set for the different heading elements. The bottom margin for the H2 element and the top margin for the H4 element are set to control the amount of margin spacing displayed between the article title and the byline.

To add some additional visual highlighting for the page's text content, a lime-colored, ridged border is set above the H3 and ADDRESS elements.

Adding a Drop-Cap

A drop-cap at the start of the initial paragraph can provide an additional graphical embellishment.

Add a drop-cap to the start of the initial text paragraph (see Figure 9.18):

```
<table cellpadding="10" cellspacing="0"><tr><td>
<p><span style="float: left; padding-right: 1px; font-size: 38px;
line-height: 1; font-weight: bold; color: maroon; background:
transparent">W</span>ith only four starters not returning from a
team that finished second in the Heartland Conference last season,
hopes are high for this season. Season ticket sales are running
well ahead of last season's pace--good seats are still available,
so get on down to Snuffy Smith Field House on the Munster
University campus and get your tickets now!</p>
```

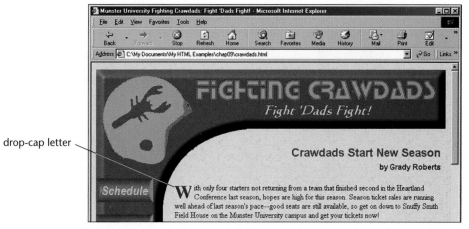

FIGURE 9.18 • *A drop-cap is added to the initial text paragraph.*

A SPAN element brackets the letter ("W", in this case) to be turned into a drop-cap. An inline style is used to create the drop-cap effect. The float property causes the SPAN element to float on the left margin, with following text flowing around the right side of the SPAN element. The font-size property set the drop-cap letter size to 38 pixels, while the line-height property sets the line height to one times the font size. Without the line-height property, additional spacing would be added above and below the spanned text, causing the "W" letter to no longer fit inside two lines of text.

Using a Gradient Element Background

Using styles, you can specify a background image that will be displayed behind an element. By using a background image that uses a vertical gradient blend between two colors, you can display a background behind an element that appears to fade into the page's background. An example gradient background image, gradient1.jpg, is included with the example files for this chapter.

Define a style that sets a gradient background image behind the H3 element (see Figure 9.19):

```
h3 { font-size: 18px; background: url("gradient1.jpg");
background-repeat: repeat-x; padding-left: 3px; padding-top: 3px;
padding-bottom: 13px; margin-bottom: -14px; }
h4 { margin-top: 6px; margin-bottom: 14px; color: maroon;
background: transparent; }
```

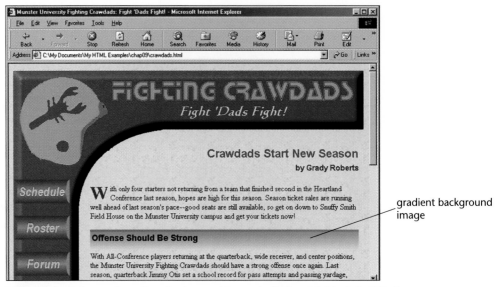

gradient background image

FIGURE 9.19 • *A gradient background image is displayed behind the H3 element.*

The gradient background image used in the current example is dimensioned at 40 × 40-pixels. Top and bottom padding values are set to expand the display space for the gradient background. The **background-repeat: repeat-x** property causes the background image to be repeated (or tiled) only along the horizontal axis (or x-axis), but not the vertical axis. Other possible values for the background-repeat property include: **repeat**, **repeat-y**, and **no-repeat**. The **repeat** value is the default and causes the background image to be repeated (or tiled) along both the x-axis and y-axis, the **repeat-y** value causes it to be repeated only along the y-axis, and the **no-repeat** value causes it to not be repeated. The **no-repeat** value, for instance, might be used in conjunction with the background-position property to display a non-repeating watermark image in a page's background.

The gradient effect in the background image was created using Paint Shop Pro's gradient fill effect. To create your own gradient backgrounds in Paint Shop Pro 7 for Windows, just do the following:

1. Select File, New, and specify a width and height for the image (40-×-40 pixels, for instance). The background should be set to white, with 72 pixels/inch set as the resolution and 16.7 million colors set as the image type. Click OK.
2. At the top of the right sidebar, click on the first color swatch and select a foreground color. Click on the second color swatch and select a background color. These two colors will be used to create the gradient fill.
3. Select the Flood Fill tool (the "paint bucket" icon). Click the triangle icon in the first Styles box in the right sidebar and select the Gradient icon.
4. Click inside the first Styles box to access the Gradient dialog box. Select the first Style and set the Angle to 180.
5. Click the Edit button and select the first gradient type (#1 Foreground-Background). You will see displayed a gradient blend of the foreground and background colors you selected in Step 2. To change the gradient balance, click and drag the diamond icon to the left or right above the gradient bar. Click OK and then click OK again.
6. Click the Flood Fill cursor inside the blank image you created in Step 1. The image background should be filled with the gradient fill (creating a vertical blend between the foreground color at the top to the background color at the bottom).

7. Save your image as a JPEG image. Set a compression level that preserves the continuous blend effect, while reducing the number of bytes consumed by the image.

NOTE — To create a gradient blend that appears to blend in with a page's background image, open the background image in your image editor and use its eye dropper tool to pick up a color from the background image and assign it as the background color. In Paint Shop Pro, just right-click the Dropper tool inside the background image to assign the color under the mouse cursor to the background color swatch. Then, select a foreground color to specify the other end of the gradient effect.

USING JAVASCRIPT ROLLOVER BUTTONS

Using JavaScript, you can create button links that *roll over*, displaying another image, when the mouse cursor hovers over the image. When the mouse cursor passes off the image, the original image is redisplayed (or alternatively, a third image could be displayed).

Grady Roberts wants to make his page more interactive and has discovered that by using JavaScript he can create rollover buttons. Grady has yet to learn much about JavaScript, but a friend of his who is much more experienced in JavaScript has created a script that Grady can easily edit to add interactive rollover buttons to his page.

Preloading the Button Images

When creating rollover buttons, you should preload the images that will be displayed by the rollover effect. Otherwise, an image to be displayed when the mouse passes over a button will not start downloading until the effect is activated, causing a noticeable delay.

Add a JavaScript to the page's HEAD element that preloads the images used in the rollover effect:

```
</style>
<script language="JavaScript" type="text/javascript">
    //Below is the code that preloads the graphics

    {
    //The first button graphics:
    var graphic1 = new Image();
    graphic1.src = "craw006.gif";
    var graphic1on = new Image();
    graphic1on.src = "craw006_rox.gif";

    //The second button graphics:
    var graphic2 = new Image();
    graphic2.src = "craw009.gif";
    var graphic2on = new Image();
    graphic2on.src = "craw009_rox.gif";

    //The third button graphics:
    var graphic3 = new Image();
    graphic3.src = "craw012.gif";
    var graphic3on = new Image();
```

```
        graphic3on.src = "craw012_rox.gif";

        //The fourth button graphics:
        var graphic4 = new Image();
        graphic4.src = "craw015.gif";
        var graphic4on = new Image();
        graphic4on.src = "craw015_rox.gif";

        //The fifth button graphics:
        var graphic5 = new Image();
        graphic5.src = "craw018.gif";
        var graphic5on = new Image();
        graphic5on.src = "craw018_rox.gif";

        //The sixth button graphics:
        var graphic6 = new Image();
        graphic6.src = "craw021.gif";
        var graphic6on = new Image();
        graphic6on.src = "craw021_rox.gif";

        //The seventh button graphics:
        var graphic7  = new Image();
        graphic7.src = "craw024.gif";
        var graphic7on = new Image();
        graphic7on.src = "craw024_rox.gif";
        }
</script>
</head>
```

The SCRIPT element identifies that text nested in the element is a client-side script.
Both the LANGUAGE and the TYPE attributes identify that the script is JavaScript.
The TYPE attribute is required. The LANGUAGE attribute is deprecated in HTML 4
in favor of using the TYPE attribute, but some earlier browsers support the LANGUAGE
attribute that do not support the TYPE attribute. Including both attributes does no harm,
however. Client-side scripting languages other than JavaScript might also be specified,
such as Microsoft's VBScript, for instance.

Although not shown in the example, an SRC attribute can be used in the SCRIPT element to link to the URL of an external script file. For instance, if the nested script text was
saved as a text file, rollover.js, in the same folder as the linking file, a **src="rollover.js"**
would link the file to the external script. This can be helpful if you want to reuse the
same script in more than one page. For instance, with the current example, instead of
including the whole rollover button script in each page (crawdads.html, schedule.html,
roster.html, and so on), you could save the script text lines as a myscript.js text file and
link to it in each page where you want to use it, like this:

```
<script src="rollover.js" language="JavaScript"
type="text/javascript">
</script>
</head>
```

The // characters at the start of a line signal that any following text on the same line
is a comment and should not be parsed by a user agent (or browser).

The images are preloaded by first declaring a variable (**var graphic7 = new Image()**) that creates a new image object. In the declaration, **var** specifies that a local variable is being declared, **graphic7** names the variable, **new** specifies that a new object is being created, and **Image()** specifies that the object to be created is an image.

In the next line, the variable name declared in the previous line is combined with the src property (**graphic7.src**) to declare the URL (or source) of the image. The image, in this case, is located in the same folder where the JavaScript that is calling it is located, so only the image's file name (**craw024.gif**) is specified as the URL.

The next two lines work the same as the previous two lines, except a variable object is created (and URL specified) for the image that will be displayed when the rollover effect is activated.

Optionally, you can omit **var** in the variable declaration, which will create a global, rather than a local, variable. A local variable is only available in the function in which it is defined, whereas a global variable is available even if no function has been defined for it.

A few rules apply when creating variable names. A variable name must begin with a letter or underscore, but not with a number. It cannot contain any spaces (use underscores instead) or punctuation (such as periods or hyphens, for instance). Variable names can only contain ASCII characters or numbers; they also must avoid duplicating any of JavaScript's reserved words, such as *class, else, for, function, goto*, and so on. For links to listings of reserved words in JavaScript, see this chapter's section at the IRC for this book at **www.emcp.com/**. You can see a table showing the ASCII text characters at **www.ascii.cl/**.

Creating the Rollover Effect

To create the rollover effect, you need to define a function that specifies the effect.

Create rollover effects for the sidebar button links:

1. Define a function that creates the rollover effect:

```
graphic7on.src = "craw024_rox.gif";
}

//The function that
//creates the rollover effect:
function imageRoll(imageID,imageName) {
{
document.images[imageID].src = eval(imageName + ".src");
}
}
</script>
```

2. For the first button image, use define event handlers that will activate the rollover effect when the mouse is passed over and off of the button image:

```
<td><a href="schedule.html"
onMouseOver="imageRoll('one','graphic1on')"
onMouseOut="imageRoll('one','graphic1')">
<img name="one" border="0" src="craw006.gif"
width="157" height="75" alt="Season schedule"></a>
</td>
```

3. Do the same for the remaining buttons:

```html
<tr>
  <td><a href="roster.html"
  onMouseOver="imageRoll('two','graphic2on')"
  onMouseOut="imageRoll('two','graphic2')">
  <img name="two" border="0" src="craw009.gif"
  width="157" height="75" alt="Team roster"></a>
  </td>
</tr>
<tr>
  <td><a href="forum.html"
  onMouseOver="imageRoll('three','graphic3on')"
  onMouseOut="imageRoll('three','graphic3')">
  <img name="three" border="0" src="craw012.gif"
  width="157" height="75" alt="Message forum"></a>
  </td>
</tr>
<tr>
  <td><a href="news.html"
  onMouseOver="imageRoll('four','graphic4on')"
  onMouseOut="imageRoll('four','graphic4')">
  <img name="four" border="0" src="craw015.gif"
  width="157" height="75" alt="Team news"></a>
  </td>
</tr>
<tr>
  <td><a href="articles.html"
  onMouseOver="imageRoll('five','graphic5on')"
  onMouseOut="imageRoll('five','graphic5')">
  <img name="five" border="0" src="craw018.gif"
  width="157" height="75" alt="Featured articles"></a>
  </td>
</tr>
<tr>
  <td><a href="history.html"
  onMouseOver="imageRoll('six','graphic6on')"
  onMouseOut="imageRoll('six','graphic6')">
  <img name="six" border="0" src="craw021.gif"
  width="157" height="75" alt="Crawdads history"></a>
  </td>
</tr>
<tr>
  <td><a href="contact.html"
  onMouseOver="imageRoll('seven','graphic7on')"
  onMouseOut="imageRoll('seven','graphic7')">
  <img name="seven" border="0" src="craw024.gif"
  width="157" height="75" alt="Contact us"></a>
  </td>
</tr>
```

4. Save your HTML file and switch to your browser. Click the Refresh (or Reload) button to refresh the display of your page.

5. Pass the mouse over any of the buttons. When the mouse passes over the button area (the sliced image), the button and its text change their texture and color (see Figure 9.20).

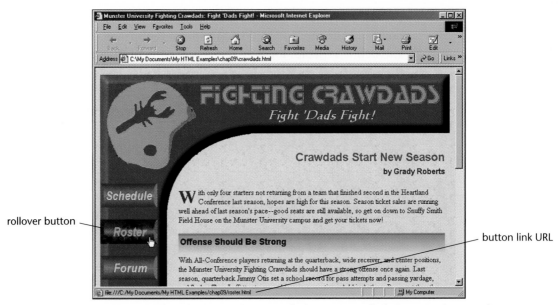

rollover button

button link URL

The remaining code in the SCRIPT element nested in the HEAD element defines the imageRoll function. A function, as its name implies, defines a function (or action) that can be executed. Generally, a function defines an action to be performed with an object. The first code line defines a function, named imageRoll, for which two parameters are defined (imageID and imageName). The next code line contains the commands to be executed by the function. In brief, when the function is called, for the specified image element (identified by the imageID parameter), the function substitutes an image URL defined by the specified variable (identified by the imageName parameter).

This will be much clearer when you look at how the function is called. For the image link A elements, onMouseOver and onMouseOut event handlers are declared. For instance,

```
<a href="contact.html"
onMouseOver="imageRoll('seven','graphic7on')"
```

specifies that when the mouse hovers over the "contact.html" link, the imageRoll function is called. The first parameter specifies that the imageRoll function is to be applied to the image element with an identify of "seven" (a **name="seven"** attribute value), while the second parameter specifies that the image URL defined by the graphic7on variable (craw024_rox.gif) is to be displayed in place of the current image (craw024.gif), creating the rollover effect.

The onMouseOver attribute is an *event handler*. Event handlers are a class of special attributes (such as onMouseOver, onMouseOut, onClick, onLoad, and so on) which can be used to trigger script actions in response to user actions or system events. In this example, passing the mouse over the link triggers the calling of a JavaScript function. For a listing of HTML 4 event handlers and the elements they can be used with, see "Generic and Other Attributes" in Appendix A, *Quick HTML Reference*. See also the "Intrinsic events" section of the W3C's HTML 4.01 specification at **www.w3.org/TR/html4/interact/scripts.html#events**.

You do not have to understand in depth how this script works to be able to use it, however. All you need to do is substitute the specific file names you want to preload and define variables for. The remaining parts of the script can be used unchanged and the event handlers also can be applied unchanged to any links from which you want to call the rollover function. The main thing to keep in mind is that in an event handler, the content of the first parameter must reference the name of the image you want to change, and the content of the second parameter must reference the name of the variable that specifies the image URL to be substituted to create the rollover effect.

NOTE

A more thorough rundown on the various characteristics and features of JavaScript, along with additional examples of JavaScript scripts, will be provided in Chapter 11, *Working with JavaScript*. If you want to learn more about using JavaScript at this time, see this chapter's section at the IRC for this book for links to basic JavaScript introductions and tutorials.

CHAPTER SUMMARY

You should now be familiar with the tools, procedures, and steps required to produce graphic Web designs using image maps and wraparound graphic interfaces. You should have an understanding of how image maps are created. You should also know how to create your own image maps from scratch, without using an image map editor, simply by plotting out the locations of hotspot areas within an image. You should be familiar with how an image slicer splits an image up into multiple sliced images, as well as understand how to seamlessly piece the sliced images back together again using a table. Finally, you should understand how to edit a JavaScript script for creating rollover buttons, so you can adapt it to other situations, even if you do not yet understand everything that is in the script.

Code Review

MAP element	Creates an image map.
NAME attribute	In the MAP element, provides a name for the image map, so it can be linked with the image map image.
AREA element	An element nested inside the MAP element, which delineates the coordinates of a hotspot area and specifies the URL that the hotspot links to.
SHAPE attribute	In the AREA element, identifies the shape of a hotspot area. Possible values are **rect**, **circle**, **poly**, and **default**.
COORDS attribute	In the AREA element, specifies the coordinates of a hotspot area.
HREF attribute	In the AREA element, specifies the URL that a hotspot area is linked to.
	Sets properties for elements only within a certain context.
	Sets properties for elements belonging to a certain class.
USEMAP attribute	In the IMG element, identifies the name of a MAP element that is to be associated with the image. The attribute value is in the form of a fragment identifier: *#mapname*.
position: relative	A style property that specifies a new position for an element relative to the element's current position.
top property	When used in conjunction with a `position: relative` property, a negative measurement (`-10px`, for instance) moves an element up relative to its current position, while a positive measurement (`10px`, for instance) moves an element down relative to is current position.
display: block	A style property that specifies that an element is to be treated as a block element, even if the element is an inline element. Other possible CSS1 values include **inline**, **list-item**, and **none**. Additional values for this property are defined in the CSS2 specification.
border-top property	Specifies the characteristics of a border (color, size, and style) to be displayed above a block element. Related properties are the border-left, border-right, border-bottom, and border properties.

background-repeat property	Specifies how or whether a background image is repeated (or tiled). Possible values include **repeat** (the default), **repeat-x**, **repeat-y**, and **no-repeat**.
SCRIPT element	Specifies that nested text is a client-side script.
LANGUAGE attribute	In the SCRIPT element, identifies the script language being used, such as JavaScript or VBScript, for instance. This attribute is deprecated in HTML 4 in favor of using the TYPE attribute.
TYPE attribute	In the SCRIPT element, this required attribute identifies the MIME-type of the scripting language being used. Possible values might include **text/javascript** or **text/vbscript**, for instance.
//	When inserted at the start of a line in a JavaScript script, specifies that following text on the line is to be treated as a comment and not parsed by the user agent.
onMouseOver attribute	An event handler that triggers a script action when the mouse cursor is passed over an element; commonly used in creating JavaScript rollover buttons, for instance.
onMouseOut attribute	An event handler that triggers a script action when the mouse cursor moves outside of an element's boundary; commonly used in creating JavaScript rollover buttons, for instance.

ONLINE QUIZ

Go to this text's IRC at **www.emcp.com/** and take the online self-check quiz for this chapter.

REVIEW EXERCISES

This section provides some hands-on practice exercises to reinforce the information and material included within this chapter.

1. If you do not already have one on your computer, download and install an image map editor or other program capable of creating image maps (see this chapter's section at the IRC for this book at **www.emcp.com/** for links to where you can find and download image map editors for your platform). If using Windows, instructions are included in this chapter for using the Map This freeware image editor.

    Open **recipes_ex.html** in your text editor and save it as **recipes_practice.html** in the chap09 folder in your working folder or disk. Open **recipes_practice.html** in your browser, as well.

    Run your image map editor and use it to draw hotspot areas for the example image, recipes.gif, and then save the image map codes to the **recipes_practice.html** file.

    In your text editor, edit **recipes_practice.html**. If not already inserted by your image map editor, insert a USEMAP attribute (usemap="#*mapname*") that links the image to the MAP element that was exported by the image map editor (Map This does not insert this for you, but Mapedit does, for instance). Also add informative ALT attributes to all the AREA elements.

Test your image map in your browser. Test it using the first hotspot area (the Meats hotspot). If it does not work, compare the codes added by your image map editor to the codes included in the example file (recipes.html) that you created earlier in this chapter. You also can check out your image map editor Help feature to look for possible reasons why your image map is not working.

2. If you do not already have one on your computer, download and install an image-slicing utility or other program capable of slicing images (see this chapter's section at the IRC for this book at **www.emcp.com/** for links to where you can find and download image-slicing utilities for your platform). There is also a link provided to an online image splicing utility that can be used on any platform. If using Windows, an example of using the PictureDicer freeware image slicer is shown earlier in this chapter.

An unsliced example file, crawdads.gif, is included with this chapter's example files in the chap09 folder. Open it in your image-slicing utility and create a slicing grid that allows you to define the sidebar buttons as image links and throw away the "white" sliced images (where you will be displaying the text content for your page). Export the sliced images—give them a root name that differs from the root name that was used to create the example sliced image that were used earlier in this chapter.

Start an HTML file from scratch, save it as **crawdads_practice.html**, and create a table that pieces the sliced images back together in a wraparound layout. Use the ROWSPAN and COLSPAN attributes to create a spanned table cell to hold the text content for the page. You can use any text that you want for the text content or you can try creating text content for one of the subpages for which example pages have not been provided. For instance, create a fictional Contacts (contact.html) page with information for how to contact the editor or other personnel of the Crawdads Football Fans Web site.

For further practice, use your sliced images to create Web pages featuring the same graphical wraparound interface for the other subpages (roster.html, forum.html, news.html, articles.html, or history.html). Create what you feel would be credible content for those pages.

3. If you have access to an image editor, use it to create images to be displayed in JavaScript rollover buttons. For instance, open the sliced image you created in Exercise 2 for the first button area (the Schedule button) and use your image editor to alter its appearance in whichever way you like. Save the file, but add "_rox" (or some other marker) to the file name. Do the same with the other sliced button images that you have created.

Using the JavaScript rollover script and event handlers that you created in the crawdads.html file in this chapter, add JavaScript rollover buttons to the crawdads_practice.html page you are creating in this exercise.

WEB-BASED LEARNING ACTIVITIES

In this book's text, Find It icons inserted in the margin highlight the Web addresses of additional resources you might find helpful or informative. To further extend your learning using the Web, you can:

- Go back and visit any of the Web addresses highlighted in this chapter that you have not yet visited. Look for additional resources and information that add to your understanding and knowledge of the material covered in this chapter. When you find a relevant page or site with information or resources you may want to access later, add it to your Favorites (in Internet Explorer) or your Bookmarks (in Netscape or Mozilla).

- Visit this book's IRC at **www.emcp.com/** to find additional Web addresses of resources related to the material covered in this chapter that you can further investigate and explore.

- Further research a specific topic introduced in this chapter. For instance, you can further research image maps or image-slicing utilities that are available via the Web. Compile the results of your research into a report that can be shared with your fellow students or team up with other students to create a class presentation or demonstration.

- Use Yahoo! at **www.yahoo.com/** to look for examples of the use of image maps, wraparound graphical interfaces, and JavaScript rollover buttons. Save the examples you find as bookmarks or favorites, so you can use them as a reference later in conceptualizing and designing your own image maps, wraparound graphical interfaces, and JavaScript rollover buttons.

PROJECTS

These projects can be done in class, in a computer lab, or at home. Use the skills you have developed in this and the previous chapters to create any of the following projects.

Project 1. Create a Web page design that uses an image map to create a graphical front end.

Conceptualize, plan, and design a graphical front end for a Web site. You can do this for a site you have already created that makes use of multiple subpages or you can design a new site from scratch. If creating a new site from scratch for the sake of this project, you can create just one of the subpages for testing purposes, or you can create all the subpages, if you like. Follow these general steps:

1. Plan out the structure and content of the site you are creating. You need to know what the topics of your main subpages are going to be before you can design the image for your image map.
2. Before actually creating the image for your image map, sketch out on paper different ideas for an image map. You can create different shaped hotspot areas, so do not feel constrained to create an image map that only uses rectangular hotspots.
3. Use an image editor to create an image to use for an image map. If your image uses text, create an optimized (or adaptive) color palette and save your image as a GIF image (saving your image as a GIF image will render sharper text than saving it as a JPEG image). For pointers on how to create an optimized (or adaptive) color palette, see Chapter 4.
4. Create an HTML file that will contain your image map codes. If you want, open **recipes_ex.html** and save it using another file name that fits your current project. Edit the TITLE element and META elements so they fit your current project. Insert the image you have created as an inline image.
5. After saving the image you want to use for your image map, run your image map editor and draw the hotspot areas, assigning URL links to them that link to the subpages for your site (these can be fictional subpages not yet created by you. At least one hotspot area, however, should link to an actual file that you have already

created or will be creating (otherwise, you will not be able to test your image map). Use your image map editor to export the image map codes to your HTML file.

6. Edit your HTML file, adding a USEMAP attribute to your image map image's IMG element and ALT attributes to the AREA elements, if your image map editor has not already done that for you.

7. Test your graphical front end in your browser. Ask at least two classmates to try out and critique your graphical front end.

Project 2. Create a Web page design that uses a graphical wraparound interface.

Conceptualize, plan, and design a Web site that uses a graphical wraparound interface. You can do this for a site you have already created that makes use of multiple subpages or you can design a new site from scratch. If creating a new site from scratch for the sake of this project, you can create just one of the subpages for testing purposes, or you can create all the subpages, if you like. Follow these general steps:

1. Plan out the structure and content of the site you are creating. You need to know the topics of your main subpages before you can design the image that will form the wraparound graphic for your site.

2. Before actually creating the image for your wraparound graphic, sketch out on paper different design ideas. Sketch out the content of the top (or masthead) and sidebar (or menu) areas of your page.

3. Use an image editor to create an image to use for a wraparound graphic. It should be no wider than 750 pixels, unless you plan to turn off the page margins, in which case you can create an image that is 766 pixels wide. That will help insure that horizontal scroll bars will not be displayed in browsers running maximized at 800 × 600-pixel resolution. Make your image 750 to 850 pixels high.

4. Use any of your image editor's features to create your image. Experiment, for instance, with different 3-D effects your image editor can create. If your image editor has a button wizard, you can use it to create buttons in the sidebar. Your buttons do not have to look anything like the buttons you created in this chapter's example. You can create round buttons, for instance, if you like. Be sure to leave sufficient "white" area in your graphic to allow for the inclusion of the text content for your site.

5. Create an optimized (or adaptive) color palette, assign the white color (where the text will be displayed) as a transparent color, and save your image as a GIF image.

6. Run your image-slicing utility and slice your image along a grid that groups the "white" parts of your image together in their own cells. Your horizontal slicing lines should equally slice the areas containing your sidebar buttons.

7. Create an HTML file that will contain your graphical wraparound interface. Construct a table to piece together your sliced images. Use the ROWSPAN and COLSPAN attributes to create a spanned table cell to hold the textual content of your page. Review the example you created earlier in this chapter for other things you need to add to your page.

8. Set up the sliced images of the button areas in your graphic as image links. At least one of these should link to an actual file that you have already created or will create (otherwise you will not be able to test your button links). Be sure to turn off the border for your button link images.

9. Test your graphical wraparound interface in your browser. Ask at least two class-mates to try out and critique your efforts.

Project 3. Create a Web page design that uses JavaScript rollover buttons.

Using a Web site you have already created or one created from scratch, create a Web site that uses JavaScript rollover buttons. Follow these general steps:

1. Conceptualize, plan, and design a Web site that uses JavaScript rollover buttons. You can do this for a site you have already created that makes use of multiple subpages or you can design a new site from scratch. If creating a new site from scratch for the sake of this project, you can create just one of the subpages for testing purposes, or you can create all the subpages. If you like, you can use the Web site you created in Project 2, adding JavaScript rollover buttons to it.

2. Use an image editor to create the rollover images. You need to create two images for each rollover button, with the first button image initially displayed on the page and the second button displayed when the mouse is passed over the button area. If using the Web site you created as Project 2, you only need to create the second button (open the sliced button image in your image editor, alter its appearance, and then save it with a different file name).

3. Using the JavaScript rollover example you created earlier in this chapter as a guide, add a JavaScript script and event handlers to your HTML file that will create a rollover effect when the mouse is passed over a button image.

4. Test your JavaScript rollover buttons in your browser. Ask at least two classmates to try out and critique your efforts.

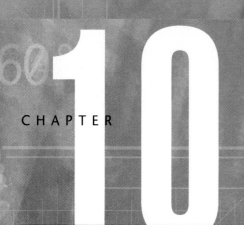

CHAPTER

10
Adding Bells and Whistles

PERFORMANCE OBJECTIVES

In this chapter, you will learn about additional features you can add to enhance the effectiveness of your Web page or site, including how to:
- Create sticky pages and get return visitors.
- Add a hit counter and track other visitor statistics.
- Add a search form that allows visitors to search the contents of a site.
- Use news and weather feeds to provide up-to-date content.
- Use guestbooks, message boards, chat rooms, instant messaging, mailing lists, and Web polls to create a Web community.
- Use link referrers, bookmark scripts, and other features to help engender the viral marketing of a site or page over the Web.

Up to this point, you have learned how to create different Web page layouts and designs, worked with using font and color changes, extended the display possibilities for your pages through the use of styles, learned how to validate your pages, made sure your pages are both backward- and forward-compatible, worked with the META element to make your pages more search-engine friendly, and used many other features that can help attract and welcome visitors to your page or site. Getting visitors to come to your site and making sure that it is easy for them to access or navigate to the key information or content you are providing is only part of the equation when it comes to creating an effective Web page or site, however. After visitors come to your site, you also want to do the following:
- Encourage visitors to stay and linger at your page or site by providing interesting and valuable content.
- Create an engaging environment so visiting your site is a fun and entertaining experience.
- Encourage visitors to interact with each other.
- Make it easy for visitors to find what they are looking for.
- Motivate a visitor to return to your site (again and again, hopefully).

USING THE EXAMPLE FILES

If you have created a working folder for storing files you create, you will find the example files for this chapter located in the **chap10** folder within your working folder. Save any HTML files you create in this chapter in that folder.

If you have created a working disk, copy the chap10 folder to your working disk from the **HTML_Examples** folder that you or your instructor downloaded from this book's Internet Resource Center (IRC), or from a CD-R disc or floppy disk provided by your instructor. Save any HTML files you create in this chapter in the chap10 folder that you have copied to your working disk.

UNDERSTANDING STICKINESS

A *sticky* Web page is able to retain visitors after they have arrived and motivates visitors to return. Stickiness might not be a big factor when designing a simple personal page, however, when creating a project designed to maximize traffic, stickiness can be a major factor in whether your page meets your performance goals and objectives. You can do a number of different things when designing a Web page to make it sticky, including the following:

- **Create effective content.** Provide interesting and valuable content for your site. None of the other methods for adding stickiness to a site will make any difference if your page or site offers little that is interesting or valuable to the visitor. Providing original material on a topic of wide interest that cannot be duplicated elsewhere is a sure way to attract and retain visitors.

- **Supply new and fresh content.** Provide new and updated content on a regular basis. For example, provide news and weather feeds, display daily or weekly announcements (or specials, if running a commercial site), and include a calendar of coming events.

- **Foster a Web community.** Create a Web community that brings visitors together via guestbooks, message boards, chat rooms, instant messaging, and mail lists.

- **Create a quick and responsive site.** Use a script on a gateway page to preload images, which will cause images on your main page to be quickly displayed when your main page is accessed. Delays caused by waiting for images to load are a major reason visitors leave Web sites.

- **Make it easy for visitors to find what they are looking for.** Become a valuable resource that helps visitors find what they are looking for by providing a site search form, a site map, or other means for easily identifying and locating key information or resources.

- **Provide feedback and create a sense of immediacy.** Create a page that provides feedback to the visitor and creates a sense of immediacy by providing a hit counter, displaying the time and date, or displaying other visitor feedback. Simply displaying the time and date can create the impression that the information on your page is current and fresh.

- **Facilitate bookmarking and link referring.** Make it easy for visitors to bookmark your page or to recommend it to others, by using bookmarking scripts and link referrers, for instance.

- **Include free products/downloads.** Offer free products or downloads on your site. For instance, you can use free services or products to create screensavers or wallpapers that visitors to your site can download and use.

- **Entertain visitors.** Provide cartoons, jokes, puzzles, contests, or games on your site to entertain your visitors.

You also can do many things to make your page or site unsticky (or slippery), including the following:

- **Fail to provide interesting and valuable content.** Fail to provide interesting, valuable, relevant, or compelling content and visitors are liable to make a quick u-turn when they arrive at your site. If your site has nothing substantive to offer, why should visitors bother to stick around?
- **Fail to refresh your site with new content.** If your site does not provide new and up-to-date content, what motivation does a visitor have to return for repeat visits?
- **Produce a poorly written or error-ridden site.** A poorly written site with frequent spelling errors, grammatical mistakes, or other errors will only discourage visitors from returning. Good writing is sticky; bad writing is not.
- **Create a sluggish site that is slow to load and full of delays.** Visitors get frustrated easily if they have to undergo long delays before a page or graphic loads and displays.
- **Create a confusing navigation scheme.** If visitors need to click through multiple links to find the information or content they are looking for, they are liable to get frustrated and leave.
- **Publish a site with broken links and images.** Create a page or site with hypertext links that do not work or images that do not display.

Nothing substitutes for real content when it comes to creating a sticky page or site. If your project offers nothing of interest or value to visitors, they are liable to take a quick look around, perhaps sample an internal link or two, but then promptly click the Back button, after which you are unlikely to ever see them again. All the bells and whistles in the world, in other words, cannot substitute for real and compelling content.

RESEARCHING REAL-WORLD EXAMPLES

When planning and creating your Web design project, you must do more than simply create a site focused on a popular topic. For a popular topic, there might already be several sites covering that topic, and it will be difficult to attract and retain an audience to a new site for that a topic.

Before starting to create your page or site, research what other sites on the same or similar topics are offering on the Web. Pay attention to the following things:

- Are there other sites already covering the same topic or doing the same thing that you want to do? What can you offer that will differentiate your site from theirs? Do not ignore your own personal experience as a key differentiating factor.
- Are there subtopics or niche areas within the topic that you are considering that are not already widely covered on the Web? There might be several sites, for instance, that cover mountain biking in your state or nationally, but few if any sites that cover that topic for your local area.
- When researching a topic for your site, pay special attention to what other sites are doing to add stickiness. Think about how you might make use of the same kinds of features in your own site. Look for features not mentioned in this chapter that help to add stickiness to a site.

Sally Rogers, a college student in Colorado, is a mountain biking enthusiast. She is considering creating a Web site about mountain biking. She is not sure what is already being covered on the Web and does not want to just duplicate someone else's efforts. She is also interested in what other mountain biking sites are doing to make their sites stickier in order to keep visitors at their site and encourage return visitors.

action

Research the topic of mountain biking and look for sticky features:

1. Run your browser, go to Yahoo! at **www.yahoo.com/**, and scroll down to see Yahoo!'s Web Site Directory.
2. Key **mountain biking** in Yahoo!'s Search (you may have to scroll up) box and click the Search button.
3. Click the Mountain Biking category match. Note how many sites are listed under the main mountain biking category, as well as how many provide general coverage of the topic and how many offer more narrowly focused coverage (see Figure 10.1).

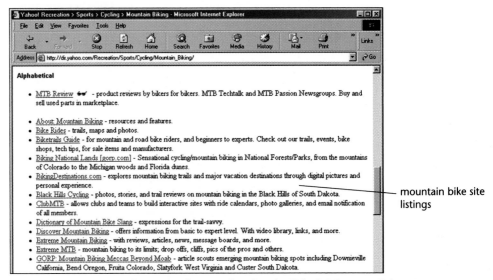

FIGURE 10.1 • *A wide variety of sites are listed under Yahoo's Mountain Biking category.*

4. Keep track of any features you believe help to create a stickier site. Visit a number of sites that are listed in the Mountain Biking category at Yahoo! and see how many different sticky features you can find. See if you can find any sticky features not already mentioned in this chapter. For instance, click on the link to the MTB Review site. Figure 10.2 shows some of the sticky features used at the MTB Review site (the current page you see on the Web will differ, of course, from the page shown in the figure).

FIGURE 10.2 • *The MTB Review site uses a variety of sticky features to help ensure that visitors will have a lot to do at the site and will want to return often.*

5. Return to the Mountain Biking category at Yahoo! and narrow the focus of your research. Because Sally Rogers is located in the state of Colorado, she would be interested in researching sites about mountain biking in her state.

6. Click on the By Region category, the U.S. States category, and then the Colorado category.

7. Investigate any sites on mountain biking listed for the state of Colorado. The first thing you should notice is that the Complete List category for the state of Colorado lists a handful of sites. Because there are so few sites, click on the Complete List link.

NOTE — Do not assume that a topic without many sites is not a worthwhile topic. It might be a topic that relatively few people have thought to cover, but for which an audience is ready and waiting, if the topic is properly presented and promoted. It might also be a topic that one or a few other sites are already doing a great job covering.

8. Check out some of the mountain biking sites listed for Colorado. For instance, click on the TrailCentral.com site, which is described as providing "Colorado mountain bike trail information, event listings, and more."

9. Note the scope and coverage that TrailCentral.com provides to mountain bike enthusiasts in the state of Colorado. For instance, TrailCentral.com is doing a great job of providing comprehensive information about mountain biking in the state of Colorado, so it probably does not make sense to create a site that would simply duplicate what they are already doing very well. A site detailing your own personal experiences and recommendations for mountain biking excursions, trails, and equipment, however, might be a valuable adjunct to the information TrailCentral.com offers.

10. Note specific things that TrailCentral.com is doing to create a stickier site. Identify at least six separate things TrailCentral.com is doing to retain visitors and motivate them to return for repeat visits.

NOTE Visit this chapter's section at the IRC for this book at **www.emcp.com/** to see a dynamic demonstration of sticky features used in the TrailCentral.com site. Click on the link and pass your mouse cursor over different areas of the site's image to see how many of the sticky features you were able to identify.

NOTE For resources on the Web that discuss methods and techniques for creating sticky sites, see this chapter's section at the IRC for this book at **www.emcp.com/**.

CASE EXAMPLE: CREATING A STICKY WEB SITE

After you have created a Web site that is targeted toward a ready audience, designed a layout and navigation scheme that makes it easy for visitors to read and peruse your site, and provided compelling content that your target audience will be interested in, the next step is to incorporate sticky features into your site that more specifically encourage visitors to spend more time at your site and come back for return visits.

Shirley Johnson is creating a Web page focused on space exploration and astronomy that she wants to serve as the front page to the other pages she has created about space and a doorway to other space resources on the Web. Because she plans to incorporate material in her site that will change on a daily basis, she wants to emphasize the immediacy of her page by displaying the current date and time.

To start working with this example:
1. Open **spacepage_ex.html** in your text editor from the chap10 folder in your working folder or disk.
2. Save spacepages_ex.html as **spacepage.html** in the chap10 folder.
3. Open **spacepage.html** in your Web browser from the chap10 folder.

PROVIDING FEEDBACK AND IMMEDIACY

Providing feedback to visitors is one way to create a sense of immediacy for your page or site. If visitors get the impression that your page is new and fresh, rather than dated and stale, they are more likely to want to return for future visits. You can provide visitor feedback in a number of ways, including adding a counter and displaying the date (and, optionally, the time as well).

NOTE A number of the examples in this chapter make use of JavaScript codes. The purpose of these examples is to demonstrate incorporating sticky features into Web pages and not to teach you everything you need to know about using JavaScript. Later in this book, in Chapter 11, *Working with JavaScript*, you will learn about using JavaScript in Web pages in more detail.

Displaying the Date and Time

You can display the date and time by using a JavaScript script. This can be either a relatively simple thing to do or, depending on how you want to format the date and time, a little more complicated. The simplest way to do this is just to create a Date object in JavaScript and then write it to your document.

Use a JavaScript script to first create a Date object, assign it to a variable, and then write it to the document (see Figure 10.3):

```
<h2><a name="sect1"></a>Read the Latest Space News<br>
<font size="3" color="#99ffff"><script language="JavaScript">
<!--
today = new Date();
document.write("for "+today);
// -->
</script>
</font>
</h2>
```

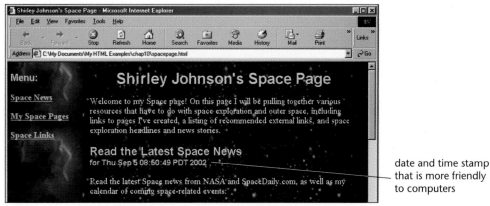

date and time stamp
that is more friendly
to computers

FIGURE 10.3 • *Using JavaScript, makes it easy to automatically generate a date and time stamp, but the format in which the date and time are displayed is friendlier to computers than it is to human beings.*

The automatically generated date and time stamp is in a format which computers can interpret easily, using abbreviations, no punctuation, and a 24-hour clock, but it is not in a format that is friendly to human beings. To display the date and time in a format that reads more like normal text is somewhat more involved than the previous example. You need to first create a script that defines the variables that will output the different parts of your formatted date, and then you need to call the variables to write out the date and time.

Create a date and time display that is friendlier to humans:
1. Delete the previous script you added.
2. In the HEAD element, add a SCRIPT element, define a variable ("thismoment") that calls JavaScript's built-in Date object, and then define a series of additional variables that call Date object methods for deriving the current minute, hour, day, month, year, and date:

```
</style>
<script language="JavaScript" type="text/JavaScript">
<!--
thismoment = new Date();
minute = thismoment.getMinutes();
hour = thismoment.getHours();
day = thismoment.getDay();
month = thismoment.getMonth();
year = thismoment.getYear();
date = thismoment.getDate();
//-->
</script>
</head>
```

3. Next, create variables that convert the date data gathered by the previously created variables into a format that is more easily read by humans:

```
date = thismoment.getDate();
var dayname = new Array ("Sunday","Monday","Tuesday","Wednesday",
"Thursday","Friday","Saturday");
var theday = dayname[day];
var monthname = new Array ("January","February","March","April",
"May","June","July","August","September","October","November",
"December");
var themonth = monthname[month];
var timeofday;
    if (hour >= 12) timeofday = "p.m.";
    else timeofday = "a.m.";
var thehour;
    if (hour > 12) thehour = hour - 12;
    else thehour = hour;
        if (hour == 0) thehour = 12
var theminute;
    if (minute < 10) theminute = '0' + minute;
    else theminute = minute;
var theyear;
    if (year >= 100 && year <= 1999) theyear = 1900 + year;
        else theyear = year;
//-->
</script>
```

4. Replace the previous date script you inserted in the document body with a JavaScript script that outputs a text string that calls the variables you defined in Step 2 (see Figure 10.4):

```
<h2><a name="sect1"></a>Read the Latest Space News<br>
<font size="3" color="#99ffff"><script language="JavaScript">
<!--
document.write ("for "+ theday +", "+ themonth +" "+ date +",
"+ theyear +" - "+ thehour +":"+ theminute +" "+ timeofday);
//-->
</script></font>
</h2>
```

date and time stamp
that is more friendly
to humans

FIGURE 10.4 • *Although a date and time format that is easier for humans to read is more difficult to generate, it provides better feedback (and is thus stickier) than simply echoing the raw computer-generated date and time.*

Adding a Counter

One of the more popular add-ons for Web pages is a counter that displays how many times the page has been accessed (or "hit"). A counter is one way you can provide feedback to visitors to your site; it also conveys to visitors the level of interest others are showing in your site. If visitors see that many others are also visiting your site, they might be more inclined to add your site to their bookmarks or favorites as a valuable and well-regarded resource.

NOTE A counter showing a low number of hits might, of course, provide a negative impression. It is a good idea when displaying a counter, to also display the date from which you are counting. That way, if you have had 100 hits to your page, but you have only been counting for a week, that will not seem like such a low number of hits.

However, the main reason Web authors like to display a counter on their page is to see how many, if any, people are visiting their site. In other words, a counter not only provides feedback to visitors to a site, but it also provides feedback to a site's creator or owner.

NOTE Some counters let you specify the number at which you want to start counting. This can be handy, for instance, if you want to switch where your site is being hosted and need to also switch the counter script you are using—that way you can start out at your new host counting at the number where you left off at your old host. Some Web authors are tempted to use this feature to artificially inflate the number of hits their site has received. If you are concerned about displaying a low hit number, a better idea is to wait until you have received a good number of visitors to your page and then start counting from a number derived from usage statistics provided by your Web host.

There are a variety of different sources and methods for adding a counter to a Web page. For instance, any of the following can be used to add a counter to a page:

- **A JavaScript script.** The advantage of using a JavaScript counter is that you can easily install it yourself because it runs as a client-side application. The disadvantage of using a JavaScript script is that a visitor needs to be using a browser with JavaScript enabled. A JavaScript counter thus cannot be relied upon to provide as accurate a count as might be provided by a CGI counter, although it can be used to show that there is significant interest in a page or site.

- **A Java counter.** A Java counter is created using a Java applet. The advantage of a Java counter is that it can be more dynamic and animated than a CGI or JavaScript counter. A Java counter has the same disadvantage as a JavaScript counter, in that it depends upon a visitor running a Java-enabled browser—in fact, even fewer visitors will be using a Java-enabled browser than will be using a JavaScript-enabled browser. Any visitors visiting your site using browsers that are not Java-enabled will not see your counter and will not be counted.

- **A CGI script provided by your Web host.** If your Web host provides a counter CGI script you can use, that is your best option. All you need to do is follow the directions provided by your Web host for inserting the counter code in your page. Not all Web hosts, especially free Web hosts, provide access to a counter script, however.

- **A CGI script you install and configure yourself.** You can find many sources on the Web where you can download counter CGI scripts you can use in your pages. To do this, however, you need to have a Web host that provides you with your own personal cgi-bin folder and allows you to install your own custom CGI scripts. You also will need to set the permissions for the script, so anybody accessing it on the Web can use it. Many free Web hosts, however, do not allow you to use custom CGI scripts.

- **A remotely hosted CGI script.** If your Web host does not provide a counter CGI script or will not let you install one, another option is to use a service that provides a remotely hosted counter script. Most remotely hosted counter scripts require that you display a logo ad for the service providing the script.

NOTE

This section and the following sections provide examples that use remotely hosted scripts and services by third-party providers, such as for adding counters, news and weather feeds, search forms, guestbooks, message boards, Web polls, and link referrers to your pages. If any of these scripts or services become unavailable, you must substitute a different script or service to recreate the example. See this chapter's section at the IRC for this book at **www.emcp.com/** for listings of alternative providers of remotely hosted scripts and services.

TROUBLE spot

It is important to understand that hits and visitors are not the same thing. A single visitor might generate several hits, for instance, generating a hit each time they return to your page during the same day. Some counters count hits, whereas others count unique visitors (ignoring multiple hits by the same visitor). Counting hits will give you a higher number, but it might also misrepresent your page's actual traffic. Counting visitors almost always is preferable to counting hits, because it provides a more accurate portrayal of your site's actual traffic.

Some counters rely on how many times the counter image is displayed to create their count. If visitors are surfing with the display of images turned off, they might not be counted. If visitors view a copy of your page stored in their cache, their visit will not be counted.

Because of variability in what is counted (hits or visitors) and how the count is done from one counter to another, you should not consider that a counter does anything more than provide a rough indication of the traffic a page or site is receiving. The main value of including a counter in your page, in other words, is to show that your page is receiving visitors with some frequency, rather than trying to show exactly how many visitors you are receiving.

NOTE

Most providers of remotely hosted scripts and services require that you give them your e-mail address, so they can send you your username and password, for instance. Although most providers will not misuse your e-mail address (selling it to e-mail marketers, or spammers, for instance), there is no guarantee that some will not. If you want to protect yourself against this, you should first sign up for a free Web mail account and then provide that e-mail address when you sign up for remotely hosted scripts and services. To find a free Web mail account you can sign up for, just go to Yahoo! at **www.yahoo.com** and do a search on "free e-mail."

If you do not want to receive additional unwanted e-mail, be sure to uncheck any check boxes asking you to opt in to receiving newsletters or other e-mailings from associated sites.

action

Add a hit counter to the bottom of the example page:

1. Visit this chapter's section at the IRC for this book at **www.emcp.com/** and go to the listing of resources.
2. Go to the "Counters and Statistics" section, where you will find a listing of free remotely hosted counters you can include in your page.
3. Visit as many of the different free counter providers as you like. When you find a style of counter that you like, sign up for the counter and then follow the provider's directions to copy and paste the counter script code into the example page.
4. For instance, to sign up for the free counter from TheCounter.com, go to **www.thecounter.com/** and scroll down to find the paragraph referring to the "The Counter.com Free Version" and click on the "Register here!" link. Read and agree to the Terms of Service, and then fill out and submit the signup form. Next, just copy the provided code and paste it into the example page at the location where you want it to be displayed.
5. Add additional formatting and text to enhance the display and meaningfulness of your counter. For instance, if you have pasted in the code for the TheCounter.com free counter, you can add the following (see Figure 10.5):

```
<address align="center">
Shirley Johnson<br>
E-mail: <a
href="mailto:sjohnson@someu.edu">sjohnson@someu.edu</a>
</address>
<center>
<p>
<!-- Start of TheCounter.com Code -->
[...]
<!-- End of TheCounter.com Code -->
<br><small>Since [key the current date here]</small></p>
</center>
```

FIGURE 10.5 • *A free counter from TheCounter.com is added to the example page.*

practice

Alternatively, if you have access to a Web hosting account that either provides a CGI counter script you can use or allows you to install your own CGI script, you can experiment with installing a CGI counter script.

If your Web host provides a CGI counter script you can use, follow its directions for inserting the code into your page to activate the counter. To actually see the counter, you will need to publish the example page to your Web site's folder on the Web.

If you have access to a Web hosting account that does not provide a counter CGI script but which allows you to install your own CGI scripts (provides you with your own personal cgi-bin folder), then you can optionally find a CGI counter script that you would like to use and install it in your personal cgi-bin folder. See this chapter's section at the IRC for this book at **www.emcp.com/** for sources of CGI scripts, including counter scripts, which you can download and install for your site. If using a UNIX server, you also will need to use telnet or FTP to set the permissions for your script using the CHMOD command (see Chapter 7, *Working with Forms*, for directions on how to set permissions for CGI scripts).

Many Web hosts also provide statistical reports that show how many visitors the pages in your site are receiving, and possibly, where those visitors are coming from as well. Some remotely hosted counters also track and report visitor statistics. Some Web hosts allow you to access your site's server logs: if you have the need for more detailed look at where visitors are coming from, where they are going, and what they are doing when they are at your site, programs are available that will analyze and create reports from your server logs.

PROVIDING FRESH CONTENT

One of the best ways to attract return visitors is to include content that changes on a minute-to-minute, hourly, daily, weekly, or monthly basis. When creating an online newsletter, the content of your site should revolve with each issue, with earlier articles presented as part of back issues or archives. Updating a multi-page Web site including several articles and other informational pages can require a lot of work, especially if you are doing all of the writing yourself. Another alternative for offering fresh content is to designate certain parts of your site as being changeable on a regular basis, while the rest of your site remains unchanged for a much longer period.

Many sources on the Web provide content that you can include on your site. The following are some ways you can include fresh content in your site that changes on a regular basis:

- Write a featured article on a regular basis.
- Include special announcements, what's new, or upcoming events sections.
- Write a new editorial on a regular basis.
- Include news feeds and weather reports from services online that will target your locale or interest.

Including News Feeds and Weather Reports

By using free services available on the Web, you can incorporate news feeds and weather reports into your site. This can be a great way to include constantly refreshed content in your site, because you just need to include the code in your page and do not need to create the content yourself.

ADDING NEWS FEEDS Many third-party news feeds are available on the Web. The news feeds used in the following example are only a sampling.

Through doing research on the Web, Shirley has discovered that NASA provides daily updated news feeds, as well as a calendar of upcoming events, that she can display in her Web pages. She has also discovered another source, SpaceDaily.com, which provides a news feed. After she incorporates the news feeds and calendar into her site, visitors will only need to click on a headline or item to read the latest news stories about space exploration and astronomy.

Shirley has created two tables to hold the feeds from NASA and SpaceDaily.com and only needs to plug in the JavaScript scripts they provide to activate the feeds.

The example file you are working with already has the tables set up that you will be using. All you need to do is insert the required scripts.

Add the NASA and SpaceDaily.com feeds to the page:

1. Create a script in the HEAD element of your page that imports an external script from the NASA site:

```
</script>
<script language="JavaScript" type="text/JavaScript"
src="http://liftoff.msfc.nasa.gov/content.js"></script>
</head>
```

To view the contents of an external JavaScript script, just type its URL into your browser's Address or Location box and press the Enter key.

2. Add the script that creates the first news feed (see Figure 10.6):

```
<p>Read the latest Space news from NASA and SpaceDaily.com, as
well as my calendar of coming space-related events:</p>

<p><table cellpadding="5" width="100%" border="1" class="news">
<tr><th colspan="2">Latest News from NASA</th></tr>
<tr><td width="50%" valign="top"> 
```

```
<script language="JavaScript" type="text/JavaScript">
<!--
nasaShowHeadline("Science", 1, 5);
//-->
</script>
</td>
```

FIGURE 10.6 • *Headlines from a current NASA news feed of science stories appear in the first table.*

3. Add the script that creates the second news feed (see Figure 10.7):

```
<tr><td width="50%" valign="top">
<script language="JavaScript" type="text/JavaScript">
<!--
nasaShowHeadline("Science", 1, 5);
//-->
</script>
</td>
<td width="50%" valign="top"> 
<script language="JavaScript">
<!--
nasaShowHeadline("Liftoff", 1, 5);
//-->
</script>
</td>
</tr>
```

FIGURE 10.7 • *A second news feed of stories from NASA appears in the first table.*

4. Add the script that creates a calendar of coming events (see Figure 10.8):

```
<td width="50%" valign="top">
<script language="JavaScript">
<!--
nasaShowHeadline("Liftoff", 1, 5);
//-->
</script>
</td>
</tr>
<tr>
<td valign="top" colspan="2"> 
<script language="JavaScript">
<!--
nasaShowCal();
//-->
</script>
</td>
</tr>
</table>
</p>
```

FIGURE 10.8 • *A calendar of coming events from NASA appears in the first table.*

NASA event calendar

NOTE The actual news feed headlines and calendar items you will see in your browser will differ from what is shown in Figures 10.6 through 10.8, because you are viewing the feeds on a different day, which is, of course, the whole point of providing fresh content that changes on a daily basis.

5. The SpaceDaily feed does not provide a heading for its feed. To have it look more like the NASA feeds, create a heading for the feed and insert a script to display the month and day (this script uses the date script you created in the document's HEAD element earlier):

```
<p>
<table cellpadding="5" width="100%" border="1" class="news">
<tr><th>Latest News from SpaceDaily.com</th></tr>
<tr>
<td valign="top"> 
```

```
<a href="http://www.spacedaily.com/"><b>SpaceDaily Headlines</b> -
<script language="JavaScript">
<!--
document.write ("<b>"+ themonth +" "+ date +"</b>"
);
//-->
</script></a>
</td></tr>
</table>
</p>
```

6. Add the script that creates the SpaceDaily.com news feed (see Figure 10.9):

```
<p>
<table cellpadding="5" width="100%" border="1" class="news">
<tr><th>Latest News from SpaceDaily.com</th></tr>
<tr>
<td valign="top">
<a href="http://www.spacedaily.com/"><b>SpaceDaily Headlines</b> -
<script language="JavaScript">
<!--
document.write ("<b>"+ themonth +" "+ date +"</b>"
);
//-->
</script></a>
<br>
<script language="JavaScript" src="http://www.spacedaily.com/
portals/spacedaily-headlines-briefs.js">
</script>
</td></tr>
</table>
</p>
```

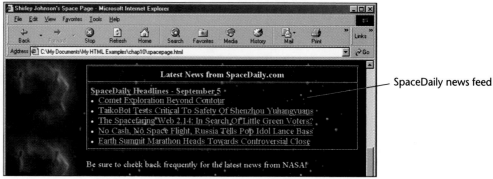

SpaceDaily news feed

FIGURE 10.9 • *A date script is used to display the month and day of the SpaceDaily.com news feed.*

When you depend on content from a third party, be aware that if their server is down or the feed is interrupted for some other reason, visitors to your site will not be able to see the feeds. Third parties that provide content you can insert in your pages might also simply stop providing the content, so you should always closely monitor pages that contain third-party content to make sure the content continues to be available.

Also, including third-party content in a page can impact how quickly the page loads, because each external script or program that needs to be accessed represents an additional download. Remember, a slow load-time for a page is a decidedly *unsticky* feature, so when adding third-party scripts and programs to increase stickiness, you need to be careful they do not overly slow down the load-time for your page.

ADDING WEATHER REPORTS Many sources also are available for weather reports and weather maps that you can display as part of your pages. Depending on the focus and topic of your site and the interests of your audience, a weather report or weather map can be an effective sticky feature that can help motivate visitors to come back for return visits.

action

Add free weather maps to the example page:

1. Visit this chapter's section at the IRC for this book at **www.emcp.com/** and go to the listing of resources.
2. Go to the "Weather Reports and Maps" section, where you will find a listing of free remotely hosted weather reports and maps you can include in your page.
3. Visit as many of the different providers of free weather reports and maps as you like. When you find a weather report or map that you like, sign up for it and then follow the provider's directions to copy and paste the script code they provide into the example page.
4. For instance, to sign up for the free weather maps from Intellicast, go to **www.intellicast.com/About/IntellicastOnYourSite/** and click on the Free Content link in the left sidebar. The links that allow you to add weather maps are arrayed along the top of the page. For instance, click on the Current Conditions link and then click on the Sample Thumbnail Image. You can choose to include a variety of different national and local weather maps. For instance, check the National Current Conditions Map check box and the National Radar check box, and then click the Submit button. Next, just copy the provided code and paste it into the example page at the location where you want it to be displayed.
5. Add additional formatting and text to enhance the display and meaningfulness of your weather report. For instance, if you have pasted in the code for the free weather maps from Intellicast, you can add the following formatting (see Figure 10.10):

```
<p>Be sure to check back frequently for the latest news from
NASA!</p>
<p><table align="center" cellpadding="5">
<tr><th colspan="2"><font size="4" color="#99ffff">View the
Latest Satellite Weather Maps</font></th></tr>
<tr><td width="170" align="center">
<iframe SRC="http://www.intellicast.com/zip/thumbnail?code=1"
NAME="radsat" WIDTH="166" HEIGHT="100" hspace=0 vspace=0
scrolling=no marginheight=0 marginwidth=0 frameborder=0
NORESIZE> <ilayer
SRC="http://www.intellicast.com/zip/thumbnail?code=1"
NAME="radsat" WIDTH="114" HEIGHT="90"> </ilayer> </iframe>
</td>
<td width="170" align="center">
<iframe SRC="http://www.intellicast.com/zip/thumbnail?code=USA"
NAME="natrad" WIDTH="166" HEIGHT="100" hspace=0 vspace=0
scrolling=no marginheight=0 marginwidth=0 frameborder=0
NORESIZE> <ilayer
SRC="http://www.intellicast.com/zip/thumbnail?code=USA"
NAME="natrad" WIDTH="114" HEIGHT="90"> </ilayer> </iframe>
</td></tr>
</table></p>
```

satellite weather maps

FIGURE 10.10 • *Thumbnail images of current satellite weather maps are displayed as part of the page, formatted side-by-side, and centered using a table.*

Many other sources of free content can be included in a Web site, including articles, jokes, comic strips, word definitions, daily horoscopes, and more. For additional resources that provide free content for your pages, see this chapter's section at the IRC for this book at **www.emcp.com/**.

When using third-party Java applets, you must use a Java-enabled browser to see the applets. Many users are not using Java-enabled browsers. Versions of Internet Explorer 6 or greater do not include support for Java—you must go to Sun's site to install support for Java in those browsers from **java.sun.com/**. Other browsers might only provide support for Java as an option.

You can test a page that includes a Java applet by opening it in a browser with support for Java turned off. For instance, in Internet Explorer 6, select Tools, Internet Options, and click the Advanced tab. Find the section that includes check boxes for Java support (this will vary based on which version of the Java Virtual Machine you are running) and uncheck them. In Mozilla 1, select Edit, Preferences, click the Advanced category, and uncheck the Enable Java check box. If you find that including a Java applet in a page causes an undesirable result in a browser in which Java is not enabled, you might need to eliminate the applet. You might also be able to include it in such a way that the space the applet occupies is closed up if Java is not available, such as inserting the applet inline, rather than in a table cell, so visitors using browsers in which Java is not enabled will not notice the absence of the applet.

Including a What's New Section or Page

Including a "What's New" section or page in your site is one way to indicate that your site contains new and fresh content. The disadvantage is that you have to create the new and fresh content on a fairly frequent basis. However, even if you do not update your site's content on a frequent basis, a "What's New" section or page will give the impression to new visitors to your site that you do.

MAKING IT EASY FOR VISITORS TO FIND WHAT THEY WANT

The easier you can make it for visitors to find the information or resource they are looking for at your site, the more likely it is that they will spend extra time there or return for future visits.

Adding a Search Form

A search form that allows visitors to search the pages in your site can make it easier for them to find and access information on your site. You can have a lot of valuable information in your site, but if much of it is buried deep within your site or difficult to find, visitors will be less inclined to linger or return. The easier you make it for visitors to find the information they are looking for, the more likely they are to spend more time at your site or return to your site and use it as a resource in the future.

When adding search capability to your site, you are actually adding your own search engine. Maintaining a search engine means indexing your site and saving the results in a database. The database is then queried when a search is made. You can set up your own search engine in a number of different ways. You can use one of the many free remotely hosted search engines. You also can install a ready-made search engine CGI application or write your own.

NOTE To add a functioning search form to your site, you will need to publish it to the Web, along with the other pages that compose the rest of the site (in this case, two additional pages, mercurycols.html and spacegallery.html, would also need to be published to the Web). Your site needs to be on the Web before it can be indexed by a search engine provider's spider. If you do not presently have Web space where you can publish the example pages, just skip adding a search form to the example page for the time being. Finding a Web host to host your pages was covered in Chapter 6, *Working with Multi-Page Web Sites*. For a list of Web hosting resources that can help you find a free or inexpensive Web hosting service, see the list of resources for Chapter 6 at the IRC for this book at **www.emcp.com/**.

action

Add a free site search form to the example page:
1. Visit this chapter's section at the IRC for this book at **www.emcp.com/** and go to the listing of resources.
2. Go to the "Search Forms and Site Maps" section, where you will find a listing of free remote search forms you can include in your page.
3. Visit as many of the different providers of free search forms as you like. When you find a search form that you like, sign up for it and then follow the provider's directions to copy and paste the script code they provide into the example page. For instance, FreeFind.com will e-mail set-up information to your e-mail address, after which you can log into their control panel, tell their robot to index your site (it will need to be online), select the type of search form you want to include, and then copy the provided HTML codes and paste them into your page. To insert the search form shown in Figure 10.11, just scroll down on the page and copy the codes for the fourth search form provided by FreeFind.com, and then paste them into the page you are working on (above the H1 element, for instance).

4. Add additional formatting and text to enhance the display and meaningfulness of your search form. For instance, if you have pasted in the search form code from FreeFind.com, you can add the following formatting to the search form (see Figure 10.11):

```
<table align="center">
<tr><td>
<center>
<FORM ACTION="http://search.freefind.com/find.html"
METHOD="GET" target="_self">
<font size=1 face="arial,helvetica" >
<A HREF="http://search.freefind.com/find.html?id=xxxxxxxx">
Search this site</a>
powered by <A HREF="http://www.freefind.com">FreeFind</A><br>
<INPUT TYPE="HIDDEN" NAME="id" SIZE="-1" VALUE="xxxxxxxx">
<INPUT TYPE="HIDDEN" NAME="pid" SIZE="-1" VALUE="r">
<INPUT TYPE="HIDDEN" NAME="mode" SIZE="-1" VALUE="ALL">
<INPUT type="HIDDEN" name="n" value="0">
</td></tr>
<tr valign="baseline"><td>
<INPUT TYPE="TEXT" NAME="query" SIZE="20">
 <INPUT TYPE="SUBMIT" VALUE=" Find! "> <input
type="SUBMIT"
name="sitemap" value="Site Map">
</center>
</font></FORM></td></tr></table>
<h1 align="center" style="margin-top: -10px">Shirley Johnson's
Space Page</h1>
```

site search form

FIGURE 10.11 • *A search form can make it easier for visitors to find information they are looking for on your site.*

Creating a Site Index or Site Map

Another way to make it easier for visitors to your site to find information or content that is relative to their interests is to create a site index or site map. A *site index* is a listing of the contents of your site (the page titles) in alphabetical order, and a *site map* is hierarchical representation, often in the form of a tree structure, of the contents of your site. A site map is similar to a detailed table of contents.

Many HTML editing tools can generate site indexes and site maps, such as Microsoft FrontPage or Macromedia Dreamweaver, for instance. You also can manually create your own site index or site map and then link to it from your front page. The search form provided by FreeFind.com shown in Figure 10.11 also includes the option to generate a site map.

CREATING A WEB COMMUNITY

An excellent way to retain visitors and encourage them to return frequently is to create a Web community through your site. This can be done in a number of ways, including:

- Adding a guestbook to your site that allows visitors to share their comments with other visitors.
- Using a message board that allows visitors to your site to discuss with each other issues related to the topic of your site.
- Set up a chat room or rooms that allow visitors to your site to chat with each other on a real-time basis.
- Set up instant messaging that allows visitors to your site to send you instant messages.
- Create a mailing list through which subscribers can post messages and respond to the messages of others on any topic or issue.
- Conduct Web polls on questions and issues related to the topic of your site.

Adding a Guestbook

Adding a guestbook is an easy way to allow visitors to your site to post comments and read the comments of other visitors. Some Web authors use a guestbook to allow visitors to provide feedback, rather than using a mailto e-mail address, in order to limit their exposure to spammers. The easiest way to add a guestbook to your site is to use one of the free remotely hosted guestbook services. You also can install your own guestbook CGI script, if you want a guestbook that does not display somebody else's banner ads.

Add a free guestbook to the example page:

1. Visit this chapter's section at the IRC for this book at **www.emcp.com/** and go to the listing of resources.
2. Go to the "Guestbooks" section, where you will find a listing of free guestbooks you can include in your page.
3. Visit as many of the different providers of free guestbooks as you like. When you find a guestbook that you like, sign up for it and then follow the provider's directions to copy and paste the script code they provide into the example page.
4. Add additional formatting and text to enhance the display and meaningfulness of your guestbook. For instance, if you have pasted in the guestbook code from Dreambook.com, you might add the following formatting (see Figure 10.12):

```
<p><table align="center" border="1" cellpadding="10"
bgcolor="navy"><tr><td>
<center>
<table>
<tr>
<td align=right>
<font face=helvetica>
<a href="http://books.dreambook.com/username/bookname.html">Read
</a> my Dreambook guestbook!<br>
```

```
<a href="http://books.dreambook.com/username/bookname.sign.html">
Sign</a> my Dreambook!
</font>
</td>
<td>
<a target=_top href="http://www.dreambook.com"><img
src="http://buttons.dreambook.com/dbnow.gif" width=88 height=31
border=0 alt="Dreambook"></a>
</td>
</tr>
</table>
</center>
</td></tr></table></p>
<hr>
<address align="center">
Shirley Johnson<br>
```

FIGURE 10.12 • *A guestbook provides two links, one for reading the visitor comments and the other for signing the guestbook (adding your own comment).*

NOTE

For links to resources and tools for creating guestbooks, see this chapter's section at the IRC for this book at **www.emcp.com/**.

Adding a Message Board

A message board (also called a discussion forum) is a great way to help turn your site into the hub of a Web community. A message board also provides the added benefit of letting your visitors create fresh content for your site.

One of the downsides of including a message board on your site, however, is that it might require more time than you want to spend to monitor and maintain it. Because anyone can post a message, you might need to delete messages that contain offensive content or attack, or "flame," other posters. A message board that contains offensive content or is dominated by flame wars between posters might drive away more visitors than it will attract. Requiring that posters register and log in using a username and password can help control unwanted content, but that capability is not as likely to be included in free message board applications and can require additional time and effort to install, configure, and maintain.

It is also a good idea to wait until you have already created significant traffic for your site before you add a message board. A message board with few messages or messages that are outdated gives entirely the wrong impression, tending more toward creating an unsticky, rather than a sticky, site. In other words, before adding a message board to your site, you need to weigh the benefits that might be derived (creating a Web community and encouraging return visits) against any of the negative factors that can be associated with using a message board (extra time required to monitor and maintain, unwanted content, disruptive participants, low participation, and so on). If the pluses only partially outweigh the minuses, you might want to hold off including a message board in your site. Generally, you want to create a sticky site first that is already attracting a fair amount of return traffic; in that case, adding a message board can make your site even stickier. A message board by itself, however, might not make your site sticky; it might, in fact, make your site less sticky.

Add a free message board to the example page:

1. Visit this chapter's section at the IRC for this book at **www.emcp.com/** and go to the listing of resources.

2. Go to the "Message Boards (Discussion Forums)" section, where you will find a listing of free message boards you can include in your page.

3. Visit as many of the different providers of free message boards as you like. When you find a message board that you like, sign up for it and then follow the provider's directions to copy and paste the script code they provide into the example page, adding any additional formatting you think will enhance the presentation. For instance, if you signed up for the free message board from CreationCenter.com, you might insert the link they provide to your page's sidebar menu and format it as follows (see Figure 10.13):

```
<h4 class="menu">Menu:</h4>
<p class="menu"><b>
<a href="#sect1">Space News</a></b></p>
<p class="menu"><b>
<a href="#sect2">My Space Pages</a></b></p>
<p class="menu"><b>
<a href="#sect3">Space Links</a></b></p>
<p class="menu"><b>
<a href="http://creationcenter.com/boards/spaceforum">Message
Board</a></b></p>
```

message board link —

FIGURE 10.13 • *Hosting a message board can be a great way to encourage visitors to your page to come back frequently.*

4. When you click on the link to the message board you have added to the example page, the message board page is displayed. Figure 10.14 shows a message board page that has already had a couple of messages added to it.

message threads

form for posting a new message

FIGURE 10.14 • *A visitor to the message board can read any of the messages, post a response to a message, or start a new message thread.*

A lot of options are available online for adding free message boards to your Web site. For links to resources and tools for creating message boards, see this chapter's section at the IRC for this book at **www.emcp.com/**.

Adding a Chat Room

Adding chat room capability to your site is another way to encourage interaction between visitors to your site. Anyone who is in the "room" can immediately see and respond to any remarks posted by anybody else in the room. Chat room capability works well in conjunction with a message board; you can announce through the message board when you will be available for chatting and how to join the chat room, for instance.

The same drawbacks that were previously mentioned relative to including a message board in your site also apply to setting up chat rooms. Unless you have some way to restrict access or ban participants, it might be difficult to control distasteful or offensive messages and interchanges from occurring. As with adding a message board, it is probably wise to wait until you have sufficient visitors to your site before adding chat capability, since empty chat rooms merely show your site's lack of popularity and contributes more to the creation of an unsticky, rather than a sticky, site.

A lot of options are available online for adding free chat rooms to your Web site. For links to resources and tools for creating chat rooms, see this chapter's section at the IRC for this book at **www.emcp.com/**.

Adding Instant Messaging

Providing instant messaging capability to visitors to your site allows them to send you messages and get back immediate responses, carrying on a kind of electronic conversation that is more immediate (or "instant") than can be achieved by using e-mail alone.

A downside of providing instant messaging capability is that you have to be online and available for messages, on the one hand, and willing to be interrupted in whatever else you may be doing to respond to messages from visitors. One possible way to deal with this is to post a schedule on your site for when you will be available to respond to instant messages. To find out more about instant messaging services, go to Yahoo! at **www.yahoo.com/** and do a search on "instant messaging."

Creating a Mailing List

A mailing list is similar to a message board, except that the messages are e-mailed to the subscribers on the list. Some mailing lists are just one-way e-mailings, in which someone signs up to subscribe to a newsletter, for example. Other forms of mailing lists, sometimes referred to as *listservs* (or *listbots*), allow subscribers to respond to any of the mail list messages, with their responses then relayed to all the other subscribers.

A listbot mailing list, especially, can be time-consuming to monitor and maintain. You might need to review responses, for instance, before resending them to the other participants on the list. If you end up running a large mail list, that can require a lot of time. Running a listserv mailing list can be an effective way to solidify a Web community around your site as a hub, but you should not underestimate the amount of time and effort that is required to make it work. A listserv mailing list also works best when the visitors to your site are highly interested in and focused on a particular topic or issue.

A listserv mailing list lets you keep visitors informed of the latest changes and features of your site; it also can help keep your message in front of visitors long after they first visited your site. If running a large mailing list, you can sell banner advertising to be displayed along with the messages, which can help compensate for some of the extra time involved in running a listserv mailing list.

NOTE

For links to resources and tools for creating mailing lists, see this chapter's section at the IRC for this book at **www.emcp.com**/.

Using Web Polls

Another way to help create a Web community and encourage return visitors is to conduct Web polls on issues and questions related to the topic of your site. Several third parties provide Web polls that you can easily add to your pages. You also can install Web poll CGI applications on your site.

Add a free Web poll to the example page:
1. Visit this chapter's section at the IRC for this book at **www.emcp.com/** and go to the listing of resources.
2. Go to the "Web Polls" section, where you will find a listing of free Web polls you can include in your page.
3. Visit as many of the different providers of free Web polls as you like. When you find a Web poll that you like, sign up for it, fill out any options required to create a the Web poll (create your own poll question and options or use those shown in

Figure 10.15), and then follow the provider's directions to copy and paste the script code they provide into the example page, adding any additional formatting you think will enhance the presentation.

4. For instance, if you signed up for a Sparklit Web poll (at www.sparklit.com/), you might add it to your page and format it as follows:

```
<div class="poll">
<!-- Begin Sparklit HTML Code -->
<FORM ACTION="http://vote.sparklit.com/poll.spark?pollID=idcode"
METHOD="POST">
 <INPUT TYPE=hidden NAME=ID VALUE="idcode">
 <TABLE BORDER="1"  WIDTH=123  BGCOLOR="#FFFFCC"
CELLPADDING="3" CELLSPACING="0">
<TR><TD BGCOLOR="#006633"><FONT FACE="ARIAL,HELVETICA"
COLOR="#FFCC00"  SIZE="-1" >
<CENTER><B>Instant Poll</B></CENTER></FONT></TD></TR>
<TR><TD>
<FONT FACE="ARIAL,HELVETICA" COLOR="#000000"  SIZE="-1">How long
before humans walk on Mars?</FONT><BR><BR>
<FONT FACE="ARIAL,HELVETICA"  SIZE="-1"  COLOR="#000000"><INPUT
TYPE="radio" NAME="ballot"  VALUE="0">10 years<BR>
<INPUT TYPE="radio" NAME="ballot"  VALUE="1">25 years<BR>
<INPUT TYPE="radio" NAME="ballot"  VALUE="2">50 years<BR>
<INPUT TYPE="radio" NAME="ballot"  VALUE="3">100 years<BR>
<INPUT TYPE="radio" NAME="ballot"  VALUE="4">100+ years<BR>
<INPUT TYPE="radio" NAME="ballot"  VALUE="5">Never<BR>
</FONT><BR><CENTER><INPUT TYPE="submit" VALUE="Submit Vote"
NAME="submit"><BR><FONT FACE="verdana, arial, geneva"><SMALL><A
HREF="http://vote.sparklit.com/poll.spark/676095" >Current
Results</A></SMALL></FONT><BR><A
href="http://www.sparklit.com/pc/?ID=676095"><IMG
SRC="http://www.sparklit.com/images/sparklitpowered.gif"
WIDTH=113 HEIGHT=24 BORDER=0></a></CENTER></TD></TR></TABLE>
</FORM>
<!-- End Sparklit HTML Code -->
</div>
```

5. Add a style to the page's style sheet to format the "webpoll" division (see Figure 10.15):

```
div.poll { margin-left: 10px; }
div.poll a { color: navy; }
</style>
```

Web poll

FIGURE 10.15 • *A Web poll is added to the page's left sidebar where it is readily visible and available.*

NOTE For links to resources and tools for creating Web polls, see this chapter's section at the IRC for this book at **www.emcp.com/**.

Adding an Event Calendar

Another feature you can add to your site that will help foster the creation of a Web community is an event calendar. You can add a calendar for which you control the contents, or you can add one that lets visitors add their own announcements. Various free calendar applications are available on the Web that you can add to your site. You also can install JavaScript and CGI calendar applications.

NOTE For links to resources and tools for creating event calendars, see this chapter's section at the IRC for this book at **www.emcp.com/**.

ADDING VIRAL MARKETING FEATURES

The visitors you are already getting to your site can be a great resource for generating future traffic. You can leverage the current traffic to your site to create increased traffic in the future in many ways, including by using link referrers and bookmark scripts. These kinds of features are often referred to as *viral marketing*, which encourage visitors or customers to spread the word about your site, products, or services.

Using Link Referrers

A link referrer, sometimes called a "tell-a-friend" tool, is an option on your site that lets visitors refer your site to friends and associates. If visitors like your site they can tell their friends, who can tell their friends, and so on. Word of mouth is a great way to get the word out about your site.

NOTE You might also run into instances on the Web where this kind of application is referred to as a "link referer," with the word "referer" being a misspelling of "referrer." The main reason for this is that when Tim Berners-Lee wrote the original version of one of the most fundamental specifications for the Web, the HTTP specification, he misspelled the word in referring to one of the most fundamental functions of HTTP (the creation of a request-header field, called the "Referer field," that "allows the client to specify, for the server's benefit, the address (URI) of the resource from which the Request-URI was obtained"). From this, the use of "referer" in place of "referrer" has become extremely common on the Web, so common, in fact, that "referer" might eventually become an accepted alternative spelling, especially when used in the context of the Web. For the time being, however, it is still a misspelling.

action

Add a link referrer to the example page:

1. Visit this chapter's section at the IRC for this book at **www.emcp.com/** and go to the listing of resources.
2. Go to the "Link referrer" section, where you will find a listing of free link referrers you can include in your page.
3. Visit as many of the different providers of free link referrers as you like. When you find one that you like, sign up for it, fill out any options required to create the link referrer, and then follow the provider's directions to copy and paste the script code they provide into the example page. Add any additional formatting you think will enhance the presentation.

   For instance, if you signed up for the Free CGI Recommend link referrer (at www.free-cgi.com) and included it in your page, you might further format it as follows (see Figure 10.16):

```
<p align="center">Do you like this page? <a href="http://www.free-
cgi.com/freecgi/recomend/recomend.asp?User=username">Refer it to
a friend!</a></p>
<hr>
<address align="center">
Shirley Johnson<br>
```

link referrer

FIGURE 10.16 • *A link referrer, or "tell-a-friend" tool, lets visitors recommend your page to friends and associates.*

NOTE — Note that you need to include, in place of *username* in the previous example, the actual username you received when you signed up for the Free CGI Recommend link referrer. If not, you can see how the link referrer link will be formatted on the page, but you will not be able to actually test it by clicking on the link.

A link referrer is one of the simplest, but also one of the most effective, examples of viral marketing. Viral marketing is simply word of mouth, in that one person telling another person about your site can lead to that second person telling a third person about your site, passing the word on about your site like a virus. If a person is particularly enthusiastic about your site, they might tell all their friends about your site, and those friends might tell all their friends about your site, and so on.

Using a Bookmark Script

A bookmark script can be a handy way to encourage visitors to make return visits, by making it easy for them to add your site to their list of Favorites. A bookmark script is not directly a viral marketing feature, but can become one in conjunction with a link referrer, in that someone who saves your site to their Favorites is much more likely to make a return visit and, thus, be more likely to tell others about your site.

Creating a bookmark script in JavaScript is actually very simple. It only works in Internet Explorer, but that likely includes the majority of visitors to your site.

Add a bookmark script to the example page that encourages users of Internet Explorer to add the page to their Favorites:

1. Add the following script to your page's HEAD element:

```
<script language="JavaScript" type="text/JavaScript">
<!--
var address = "http://www.myspacepage.com/";
var title = "Shirley Johnson's Space Page";

function addLink(){
if(document.all)
window.external.AddFavorite(address,title)
}
// -->
</script>
</head>
```

2. Add the following inside your page's body (see Figure 10.17):

```
<table align="center" border="1" cellpadding="10" bgcolor="navy">
<tr><td align="center">
<p><a href="JavaScript:addLink()">Add My Site to Your
Favorites</a><br>(Internet Explorer Only)</p>
</td></tr>
</table>
<h2><a name="sect2"></a>Visit My Pages on Space Exploration</h2>
<p>I've only created a couple of pages about space exploration
so far, but I plan to add more pages in the future. Just click
on the link to go to any of these pages:</p>
```

bookmark script

FIGURE 10.17 • *A link encouraging visitors to add your site to their Favorites is a good way to get more return visitors.*

Using Other Viral Marketing Features

You can incorporate many other viral marketing features into your Web pages or sites, such as e-postcards, opt-in e-mail newsletters, the providing of free content others can include in their Web sites (with a link back to yours), inclusion of a blurb to promote your page or site, along with a link to it, your e-mail signature, and other means and methods for encouraging others to spread the word about your site, products, or services.

Actually, many of the add-ons covered in this chapter are, themselves, examples of viral marketing. You receive the benefit of being able to include free content or services in your site (helping to make it stickier) in return for helping to spread the word about the providers of the content and services. Most of these providers have additional products or services, including more advanced or varied features, which they offer for a price or fee. For instance, if you have created a software program but do not have a lot of money to spend on advertising, one way to help your program get noticed on the Web is to offer a stripped down version (or "basic" version) free. The free version helps spread the word about the non-stripped down version (or "pro" version) that you are offering for a price or fee.

This form of viral marketing is also sometimes referred to as *pull marketing*, as opposed to *push marketing*. Pull marketing offers an incentive for responding to a marketing effort, usually something of value for free (or significantly below its market value). Push marketing tries to push the benefits of the product or service, even unfavorably comparing a competing product or service, to elicit a purchase or subscription.

NOTE

To find more information about viral marketing, see this chapter's section at the IRC for this book at **www.emcp.com**/.

CHAPTER SUMMARY

You should now be familiar with the use of some of the tools and features that can help make your pages stickier, so that visitors to your pages will want to spend more time at your site and be more likely to make return visits. You also should have some idea of what viral marketing is and how it might be used to help spread the word about your site (or a product or service you are offering). You should have gained some practical experience in incorporating sticky features into an example Web page, including:

- Providing visitor feedback and creating immediacy with counters and date stamps.
- Featuring continually refreshed content by adding news feeds, weather reports and maps, and other third-party content.
- Creating a Web community by using guestbooks, message boards, Web polls, and other features that encourage interaction and communication between visitors.
- Leveraging your site's traffic by using link referrers and bookmark scripts.

Code Review

stickiness	Features that encourage visitors to remain at a site and make return visits.
hit or access counter	A script or application that displays the number of hits (or page accesses) to a page, usually at the bottom of a page.
third-party content	Content provided by a third party, including news feeds and weather reports.
search form	An application that allows visitors to search the contents of a site.
site index	An alphabetized listing of the contents of a site.
site map	A hierarchical representation, often in the form of a tree structure, of the contents of a site.
guestbook	An application that allows visitors to post comments about the site and read comments posted by other visitors.
message board	Also called a discussion forum. An application that allows visitors to read messages, post messages, and reply to messages posted by other visitors.
chat room	An application that allows visitors to communicate to others within a group (or room). Anyone in a room can direct messages to, or see and respond to messages from, anybody else who is in the room.
instant messaging	A technology that enables two or more individuals on the Web to exchange messages on an immediate (or "instant") basis.
mailing list	An application that allows the distribution of messages to a group of subscribers, with responses to messages from anyone in the group also sent to everyone included in the list.
Web poll	An application that polls the opinions of visitors on any question, with the current results (votes) of the poll immediately displayed.
link referrer	An application that lets visitors refer or recommend your site to friends, relatives, and associates. Also called a "tell-a-friend" application.

bookmark script	A script that reminds and makes it easy for visitors to add your site to their Favorites (for Internet Explorer only).

ONLINE QUIZ

Go to this text's IRC at **www.emcp.com/** and take the online self-check quiz for this chapter.

REVIEW EXERCISES

This section provides some hands-on practice exercises to reinforce the information and material included within this chapter.

1. Open **spacepage_ex.html** in your text editor and save it as **spacepage_practice.html** in the chap10 folder in your working folder or disk. Open **spacepage_practice.html** in your browser, as well.

2. Use the practice page to gain additional practice incorporating features that create immediacy, feedback, and stickiness, including a date and time stamp, a counter, news feeds, weather reports, a site search form, a guestbook, a message board, a Web poll, a link referrer, and a bookmark script.

3. If you have access to a Web hosting account that provides you with your own cgi-bin folder, use the practice page to gain experience using CGI scripts to add sticky and community-creation features, including a counter, a site search form, a guestbook, a message board, a Web poll, and a link referrer, for instance. Look for other CGI scripts you can install that will enhance the stickiness of your page. The advantage of using CGI scripts is that you control your own code sources, which should generally result in a Web site that is quicker to load than a Web site using multiple third-party sources. For guidance on setting permissions for CGI scripts you install in your own cgi-bin folder on UNIX or Linux servers, see Chapter 7, *Working with Forms*. To test features added using CGI scripts, first publish your practice page to your Web site's folder on the Web. If using a Windows-based or Macintosh-based server, check with your Web host's support documentation for more detailed instructions on what you have to do to install CGI scripts.

4. Visit this chapter's section at the IRC for this book at **www.emcp.com/** and research additional features not mentioned or shown in this chapter that can create immediacy and feedback, add stickiness to your site, or promote the viral marketing of your site over the Web. Practice adding at least three of these features to your practice page. If you have access to your own cgi-bin folder, you can practice using CGI scripts to add one or more features not mentioned or shown in this book.

WEB-BASED LEARNING ACTIVITIES

In this book's text, Find It icons inserted in the margin highlight the Web addresses of additional resources you might find helpful or informative. To further extend your learning using the Web, you can:

- Visit this book's IRC at **www.emcp.com/** to find additional Web addresses of resources related to the material covered in this chapter that you can further investigate and explore.

- Look for additional resources and information that add to your understanding and knowledge of the material covered in this chapter. Use Yahoo!, Google, AltaVista, or other directories and search engines to expand your research. When you find a relevant page or site with information or resources you might want to access later, add it to your Favorites (in Internet Explorer) or your Bookmarks (in Netscape or Mozilla).

- For instance, you can further research the concepts of stickiness or viral marketing. Compile the results of your research into a report that can be shared with your fellow students or team up with other students to create a class presentation or demonstration.

PROJECTS

These projects can be done in class, in a computer lab, or at home. Use the skills you have developed in this and the previous chapters to create any of the following projects.

Project 1. Enhance the stickiness of a Web site by incorporating third-party services and features.

Start out by using Yahoo!, Google, AltaVista, and other directories and search engines to further research the topic you would like to use. Look to see whether there are niches you can fill within a general topic area that are not already being served by other Web sites, or within which you think you can do a better job than sites that already exist. Look at what other sites covering the same or similar topics are doing to add features that create immediacy, feedback, and stickiness, as well as what features they are using to help engender the viral marketing of their sites or services over the Web.

1. After you have settled on a topic for your site, conceptualize, plan, and design your site. A key part of this process should be the creation of textual or graphical content you want to include. Remember, the most important factor in creating a sticky Web site is interesting and compelling content.

2. After creating your Web site design and content, incorporate additional features into your site that create immediacy, provide visitor feedback, create stickiness, and further the viral marketing of your site over the Web. To do this, use local scripts and third-party (remotely hosted) scripts and services.

3. After creating your Web site, ask at least three classmates to critique your efforts. Incorporate any helpful suggestions they provide.

4. You also can include a Web poll in your site that will allow your classmates to rate your efforts. Conceptualize and design a poll that will provide you with useful feedback. Publish your Web site or page to the Web and then provide your classmates with its Web address so they can rate your efforts.

Project 2. Enhance the stickiness of a Web site by incorporating CGI scripts.

If you have access to a Web hosting account that provides you with a cgi-bin folder, follow the same guidelines provided for Project 1, but use CGI scripts that you install on your own server whenever possible to add immediacy, feedback, and stickiness to your site, as well as engender the viral marketing of your site over the Web.

1. After creating your Web site, ask at least three classmates to critique your efforts. Incorporate any helpful suggestions they provide.

2. You also can include a Web poll in your site that will allow your classmates to rate your efforts. For this project, add a Web poll using a CGI script that you install on your own server. Conceptualize and design a poll that will provide you with useful feedback. Publish your Web site or page to the Web and then provide your classmates with its Web address so they can rate your efforts.

Project 3. Create a Web site focused on fostering a Web community.

Design a Web site from scratch or update a Web site you have already designed so that it is focused on the creation and nurturing of a Web community. Web communities are best created based on topics and issues that elicit a passionate and caring response from many individuals. Look for ways you can effectively implement third-party and original content, guestbooks, message boards, chat rooms, and other means for fostering a Web community. For instance, here are some examples of different kinds of Web communities you might try to use in a project:

- Create a site in support of your favorite sports team. This type of site is a natural for incorporating message boards and chat rooms, for instance. There is also an abundance of sports-related third-party content available that you can include in your site.
- Create a site that is focused on a hobby that you are passionately involved with. People often take their hobbies more seriously than their careers or, at least are more emotionally involved in them. For instance, if your favorite hobby is gardening, you will find no lack of individuals on the Web with a similar level of passionate interest and involvement. The same holds true for just about any other hobby whether it be chess, coin or stamp collecting, macramé, model trains, baseball cards, or any number of other popular hobbies.
- Create a site that is focused on fostering a Web community that is passionately interested in a particular issue, pro or con, such as saving the whales, stopping world hunger, global warming, post modernism, deconstruction, political correctness, small government, abortion, or gun control, to name just a few of the "hot button" issues that are liable to elicit a strong response from others on the Web.
- Create a site that is focused on fostering a Web community based on any other topic or area that elicits a lot of response and passion from a lot of people, such as favorite celebrities, political or religious leaders, popular fads, cult or classic movies, music genres, recording groups, artists, sports figures, historical or local trivia, or any number of other popular topics.

TEAM PROJECT
Designing for the Web

In this section you participate in a team project, cooperating with others in planning, preparing, creating, and publishing a Web site that effectively incorporates features and components covered in the chapters in Part Two. Remember, that it is not just the performance of the team that matters, but also your performance as a member of the team. Learning how to cooperate, communicate, and coordinate is just as important as learning how to code a page or design a graphic.

For this team project, you can include any element or feature covered in Part One and Part Two. You should focus, however, on creating a team project that shows main elements and features covered in Part Two. Your team project should implement at least two out of the three following focuses:

- A layout created using CSS positioning, rather than tables, as shown in Chapter 8, *Designing with Style Sheets*.
- A graphical front end or wraparound interface, using an image map or sliced images (or both), as shown in Chapter 9, *Designing with Graphics*.
- The effective incorporation of sticky elements and features to retain visitors, encourage return visits, and implement viral marketing, as shown in Chapter 10, *Adding Bells and Whistles*.

1. BRAINSTORM TOPICS, AUDIENCES, AND OBJECTIVES

With your teammates, brainstorm the kinds of topics, audiences, and objectives you might want to target. Come up with at least six topics for possible projects (with each teammate suggesting at least two topics). For each project topic, define the audience you want to address and the goal you want to achieve by addressing that audience with the topic. Try to come to a consensus on the topic, target audience, and objective.

If you have difficulties coming up with ideas or cannot agree on a topic, audience, and objective, use Yahoo! at **www.yahoo.com/**, Google at **www.google.com/**, or any other search engine to search for sites that can suggest ideas to you.

See the team project section at the end of Part One for further details about how to brainstorm the topics, audiences, and objectives of your project.

2. SUBMIT YOUR PROJECT PROPOSAL FOR APPROVAL

Try to incorporate everything that is most relevant about your project in a single concise mission statement. Following your mission statement, include further information about your project. Include information about the topic of the project, the audience you will be addressing, the goals you hope to achieve, and the methods and techniques you plan to implement to achieve those goals. Keep it to less than one page, double-spaced. Be sure to share responsibility for formulating and creating this proposal.

Submit this proposal to your instructor for approval.

3. CREATE AN OUTLINE

Break down your approved project into parts. Create an outline of your site's planned content that is at least two levels deep, with the first level signifying the major branching subpages within your project's site and the second level signifying major section headings within those pages. After creating your outline, you should have a good idea of what the content of your site will be and how it will be organized.

4. ESTABLISH LAYOUT AND NAVIGATION SCHEMES

Discuss which layout and navigation schemes are appropriate and best suited for your project. See the team project section at the end of Part One for further details about determining which layout and navigation schemes might be appropriate for your project.

5. CREATE A STORYBOARD

A storyboard is a kind of cartoon of your site, showing how your site's pages are ordered and related to each other. A Web site can be organized in many ways. Creating a pictorial representation of your site helps clarify the major relationships that exist between the different parts of your site. See the team project section at the end of Part One for further details about how to create a storyboard for your project.

6. DRAW A MAP

To visualize the dynamic relationships that can be achieved using hypertext links to create navigation schemes, you can draw a map of your site that shows how its pages are linked together. See the team project section at the end of Part One for further details about how to draw a map for your project.

7. ESTABLISH A COLOR SCHEME

Experiment with different text, link, and background colors to establish an appropriate and effective color scheme for your project. Pay attention to legibility and accessibility when choosing color combinations. Optionally, incorporate a background image into your color scheme. Come to a team consensus on the color scheme you want to implement.

8. DEFINE RESPONSIBILITIES AND SET A TIMELINE

Responsibilities for creating the site should be shared coequally among team members. When you start to actually create your project, however, you will need to agree on who will be responsible for which tasks, the order in which those tasks need to be completed, and a timeline detailing the milestones (along with their respective target dates) that need to be achieved to complete the project. Be prepared to renegotiate these agreements, if necessary, as work on the project commences, to take into account unexpected exigencies that might arise. In planning and executing the project, you also need to take into account any overall due date that your instructor has set for the project.

See the team project section at the end of Part One for further details about ways in which you can allocate responsibilities for your project.

No matter how responsibilities are assigned, it is important that each team member gain experience in all aspects of creating the project. Taking a leadership role for a particular area does not mean excluding others from participating in that area.

9. BUILD THE SITE

Begin building the site, considering the timeline and assignment dates provided by your instructor. See the team project section at the end of Part One for further details about different activities that might be involved in building your project's Web site.

10. TEST AND TROUBLESHOOT

All team members should participate in testing and troubleshooting the project's site. Test the project's site in several browsers. For instance, you can test your project's site in the most recent Internet Explorer, Netscape, Mozilla, and Opera browsers. You also can test your project's site for backward compatibility in a version of Netscape Navigator 4.

When you run into problems, you might have to selectively comment out code to isolate the problem code. If you are not able to get a code to work across browsers, you should consider not using the code.

Validate your site's pages using the W3C HTML Validation Service at **validator.w3.org/**. If using Cascading Styles Sheets in your project, also validate your site's style sheets using the W3C CSS Validation Service at **jigsaw.w3.org/css-validator/**.

11. PUBLISH TO THE WEB

Using Web space provided by your school or by another provider of free Web space, publish your project's site so it can be viewed over the Web. Get suggestions, comments, and other feedback from fellow classmates on how you can improve your site. Make revisions to your site that incorporate positive changes suggested by your fellow classmates.

Submit your site to search engines so you can get feedback and comments from visitors to your site who are not fellow classmates.

12. CRITIQUE YOUR WORK

Write a self-critique of your participation in the team project. List some of the important lessons you learned while doing the project. Spell out where you think you performed well and where you think you performed less well, detailing some of the reasons that determined your performance. Point out areas in which you feel you need to improve and what you need to work on in order to improve.

Include a critique of your team's performance. Evaluate your team's ability to communicate, work cooperatively, complete assigned responsibilities in a timely and satisfactory manner, and any other factors you believe made either a positive or negative contribution to completing the project in a satisfactory fashion.

As part of your critique, indicate whether the site fulfilled the approved mission statement and support your evaluation with examples. Report your recommendations for improving or further enhancing the site developed by your team.

PART THREE
Web Design Technologies

HTML/CSS/DHTML

Working with JavaScript

PERFORMANCE OBJECTIVES

In this chapter, you will learn how to use JavaScript to enhance the effectiveness of your Web page or site, including how to:
- Specify when a Web page was last modified.
- Create and control pop-up windows.
- Create jump menus.
- Confirm form submissions and validate form input.
- Perform calculations.
- Generate HTML code and content.
- Link to external JavaScript files.

You have already worked with some examples of using JavaScript in this book, including preloading images, creating rollover buttons, setting date and time stamps, and creating a bookmark script. These examples were meant to illustrate adding certain key functions to HTML files that can be achieved using JavaScript, without delving too deeply into what JavaScript is or how it works.

In this chapter, you will learn about JavaScript in more depth. After an introduction to the basics of JavaScript, you will learn additional ways you can use JavaScript to add functionality and interaction to your Web pages.

USING THE EXAMPLE FILES

If you have created a working folder for storing files you create, you will find the example files for this chapter in the **chap11** folder within your working folder. Save any HTML files you create in this chapter in that folder.

If you have created a working disk, copy the chap11 folder to your working disk from the **HTML_Examples** folder that you or your instructor downloaded from this book's Internet Resource Center (IRC), or from a CD-R disc or floppy disk provided by your instructor. Save any HTML file you create in this chapter in the chap11 folder that you have copied to your working disk.

INTRODUCTION TO JAVASCRIPT

JavaScript is a *client-side scripting language* that was originally developed by Netscape for its Navigator 2 browser. The original name of JavaScript was LiveScript, but the name change was made in conjunction with Netscape's support for Sun Microsystems' Java programming language. This has caused some to believe that JavaScript is a subset of Java, although other than in name, there is little similarity or relation between JavaScript and Java. The only relation between the two is that they both borrow their basic syntax from the C programming language.

JavaScript is a *client-side* technology because servers download JavaScript code (either embedded in HTML files or as standalone files) to a browser (or other user agent) to be interpreted and executed. For a browser to execute JavaScript scripts, it must have a JavaScript interpreter built into it.

JavaScript is a *scripting language* because it is primarily intended for creating relatively short scripts that can easily be downloaded and executed in conjunction with HTML Web pages; it also does not produce compiled programs, such as is the case with Java or C++, for instance, that need to be executed.

Beginning with JavaScript 1.0 in Navigator 2, Netscape has developed additional versions, including JavaScript 1.1 for Navigator 3, and JavaScript 1.2 for Navigator 4. Microsoft has developed its own version of JavaScript, JScript, which is virtually identical to Netscape's. More recently, an attempt has been made to standardize JavaScript in the form of ECMAScript, which is currently supported by the Netscape 6, Mozilla 1, and Opera 6 browsers. Netscape also developed a server-side version of JavaScript, originally named LiveWire, which has since been renamed simply as Server-Side JavaScript.

JavaScript is an *object-oriented* and *event*-driven scripting language. That means that when you work with JavaScript, you are primarily involved in defining and manipulating objects, which can respond to and interact with mouse actions, link activation, form submissions, page loading or unloading, and other user actions or system events. Although JavaScript contains some built-in objects, most objects that you control and manipulate are objects that are part of an HTML Web page, such as the document, windows, frames, and elements (forms, hypertext links, images, and so on).

Writing a Simple JavaScript Script

The SCRIPT element is used to embed or insert JavaScript scripts in Web pages. The SCRIPT element can be used both in the HEAD and BODY elements—scripts that do not output directly to the page or contain functions are generally inserted in the HEAD section, so they will be loaded and parsed before the page body is loaded and displayed. The following is an example of a simple JavaScript script that displays an alert message (see Figure 11.1):

```
<body>
<script language="JavaScript" type="text/javascript">
<!-- start hiding script
document.write("<h2 align='center'>Hi There!</h2>")
// end hiding script -->
</script>
```

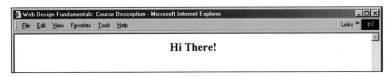

FIGURE 11.1 • *In this simple JavaScript script, the words, "Hi There!", are displayed and centered at the top of the page.*

Here are some things you should note in the previous example:

- The SCRIPT element is nested inside the BODY element. In this case, the script writes directly to the page, and thus needs to be included in the body of the page.
- Both LANGUAGE and TYPE attributes are included in the SCRIPT element. The first is deprecated in HTML 4, but is required by some earlier browsers; the second is required by the HTML 4 specification, but is not recognized by many earlier browsers. The TYPE attribute specifies the content type (or MIME type) of the script language; the TYPE attribute value is case insensitive.
- The `<!--` and `-->` comment codes bracket the content of the SCRIPT element, but as with the STYLE element, they only hide the content from browsers that do not support JavaScript. The `//` code at the start of the last script line signals to the JavaScript interpreter that any text on that same line is treated as a single-line comment, rather than as part of the JavaScript code. (Additionally, `/*` and `*/`, as with CSS, can be used to mark multi-line comments in JavaScript scripts.)
- The code line, `document.write("<h2 align='center'>Hi There!</h2>")`, instructs that the text string (including HTML codes) be written to the document (`document.write`) at the point at which the script is located.
- Notice that the ALIGN attribute value within the JavaScript text string is single-quoted. That is because the text string within which the attribute value is located is already double-quoted.
- Unlike HTML, JavaScript is case-sensitive. In the code line, `document.write` is correct, but `Document.Write` is not.
- A JavaScript interpreter ignores spaces, tabs, and non-breaking spaces (or), which can be used freely to format JavaScript scripts to render them more readable.

NOTE To include quotes within a text string, you need to escape them. To do that, just precede the quote character you want to escape with a backward slash (\) character. For instance, to display quotes around the text message in the previous example, you would do the following:

```
document.write("<h2 align='center'>\"Hi There!\"</h2>")
```

Understanding Variables

Unlike many other programming languages, JavaScript is *untyped*. That means that you do not have to declare the data type of a variable when it is declared. This is also sometimes referred to as being *dynamically typed*. For instance, the following are all variable declarations, but for different data types:

```
<script language="JavaScript" type="text/javascript">
<!-- start hiding script
var course = "Web Design";        // string value
var credits = 5;                  // integer value
```

```
var tuition = 199.99;              // floating point value
var descript = document;           // object
var signup = true;                 // boolean value (true or false)
var school                         // null value

descript.write("<h3>Course Description: "+course+"</h3>");
descript.write("<p>Credits: "+credits+" </p>");
descript.write("<p>Tuition: "+tuition+" </p>");
descript.write("<hr>");
// end hiding script -->
</script>
```

A variable name can start with an underscore or a letter, but not with a number.

EXPRESSIONS AND OPERATORS An *expression* assigns a value to a variable. For instance, the following expression assigns a value of 5 to a count variable:

```
var count = 5;
```

You also can omit the var keyword, although including it makes the variables you have assigned easier to track. Null values should always be assigned using the var keyword; if it is absent, such a variable will result in a runtime error when it is evaluated.

An *operator* performs an operation on a variable or value, such as adding, subtracting, multiplying, dividing, and so on, or compares one value with another. Table 11.1 shows the most commonly used JavaScript operators.

TABLE 11.1 • *Basic JavaScript Operators*

Operator	Action	Example
=	Assigns a variable value	`var time = 60;`

+	Addition (or string concatenation)	`var cost = 50;`
		`var ship = 5;`
		`var total = cost + ship;`
		`document.write("Total: "+total);`
		`document.write("E-Mail: "+name+"@": "+domain);`

-	Subtraction	`var rev = 1000;`
		`var exp = 650;`
		`var profit = rev - exp;`

*	Multiplication	`var price = 1000;`
		`var tax = 0.08;`
		`var cost = price + (price*tax);`

/	Division	`var miles = 125;`
		`var hours = 3;`
		`var mph = miles/hours;`

%	Modulo (remainder after division of one value by another)	`var a = 10;`
		`var b = 45;`
		`var c = a%b;`

++	Increment (increase a value by 1)	`var day = 1;` `var day2 = day++;`
--	Decrement (decrease a value by 1)	`var count = 100;` `var down = count--;`
-[value/var]	Negative (changes value from positive to negative)	`var start = -100;` `var flip = -start;`

continues

TABLE 11.1 • *Basic JavaScript Operators—Continued*

Operator	Action	Example

==	Returns true if equal	`if (a == b)`
		`    document.write("same");`
		`else`
		`    document.write("different");`

!=	Returns true if not equal	`if (a != b)`
		`    document.write("different");`
		`else`
		`    document.write("same");`

>	Greater than	`if (a > b)`
		`    document.write("more");`
		`else`
		`    document.write("not more");`

<	Less than	`if (a < b)`
		`    document.write("less");`
		`else`
		`    document.write("not less");`

>-	Greater than or equal to	`if (a >- b)`
		`    document.write("same or more");`
		`else`
		`    document.write("less");`

<-	Less than or equal to	`if (a <- b)`
		`    document.write("same or less");`
		`else`
		`    document.write("more");`

&&	Both true (Boolean AND)	`if (x==0 && y==1)`
||	Either true (Boolean OR)	`if (x==0 || y==1)`
!	Not true (Boolean NOT)	`if (x==0 || !(y==1))`

RESERVED KEYWORDS JavaScript uses certain keywords that it reserves for its own use and which cannot be used in naming variables or functions. Additional keywords are reserved for future use. Tables 11.2 and 11.3 show keywords that are currently reserved in JavaScript and keywords that are reserved for use in future versions of JavaScript.

TABLE 11.2 • *JavaScript Reserved Keywords*

break	false	new	var
continue	for	null	while
delete	function	return	with
else	if	this	
eval	in	true	

TABLE 11.3 • *Keywords Reserved for Future Use*

abstract	do	instanceof	switch
boolean	double	int	synchronized
byte	extends	interface	threadsafe
byvalue	final	long	throw
case	finally	native	transient
catch	float	package	try
class	goto	short	void
const	implements	static	
default	import	super	

USER-DEFINED VARIABLES You can include user-defined variables in your Web pages in a number of ways, including assigning variables using a prompt window, a form input field, or a designated user action. Variables also can be assigned based on polling various aspects of the user's system, such as the operating system and browser that are being used. For instance, to prompt the user for his or her name, you can use the following script (see Figure 11.2):

```
<script language="JavaScript" type="text/javascript">
<!-- start hiding script
var visitor = window.prompt("Please enter your name: ", "");
// end hiding script -->
</script>
```

FIGURE 11.2 • *The user is prompted to enter his or her name.*

The previous script example first prompts the user for a name and then assigns whatever the user has entered at the prompt as the value of the user variable. In this example, the second pair of double-quotes lets you specify a default content for the prompt box.

Using Conditional Statements

A *conditional statement's* execution is dependent upon one or more conditions. You can create a variety of conditional statements using JavaScript.

USING IF/ELSE STATEMENTS You can use IF/ELSE statements to create conditional statements that are executed (or not executed) based on a condition or set of conditions. For instance, the following example uses a combination of IF, ELSE IF, and ELSE statements to display a different alert message depending on the time of the day (see Figure 11.3):

```
<script language="JavaScript" type="text/javascript">
<!-- start hiding script
var visitor = window.prompt("Please enter your name: ", "");
thismoment = new Date();
hour = thismoment.getHours();
if (hour >= 18) {
    alert("Good evening, "+ visitor +"!");
}
else if (hour >= 12) {
    alert("Good afternoon, "+ visitor +"!");
}
else {
    alert("Good morning, "+ visitor +"!");
}
// end hiding script -->
</script>
```

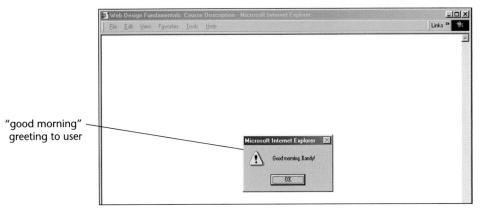

"good morning" greeting to user

FIGURE 11.3 • *Depending on the time of day, the user is wished good morning, good afternoon, or good evening.*

USING WHILE LOOPS A while statement can be used to perform a conditional loop. The instruction is performed until a certain condition is no longer true. For instance, the following script assigns a value of 1 to the count variable and then increments that value by 1 for each loop, until the value reaches 5 (see Figure 11.4):

```
<script language="JavaScript" type="text/javascript">
<!-- start hiding script
var count = 1;
    while (count <= 5 ) {
        document.write("The count is now "+count+".<br>");
        count++;
}
// end hiding script -->
</script>
```

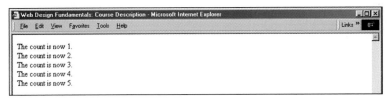

FIGURE 11.4 • *A series of five numbered lines is written to the document.*

As shown in Figure 11.4, the result of the previous script is a series of numbered lines, running from 1 to 5. After the fifth line is reached, the WHILE loop is terminated.

USING FOR LOOPS A FOR loop is similar to a WHILE loop, except that you get to set a start value, an end value, and a count value. The following is an example of a FOR loop (see Figure 11.5):

```
<script language="JavaScript" type="text/javascript">
<!-- start hiding script
document.write("<p>")
for (a=1;a<=10;a=a+1) {
    document.write("Number " + a + ".<br>")
}
document.write("</p>")
// end hiding script -->
</script>
```

Number 1.
Number 2.
Number 3.
Number 4.
Number 5.
Number 6.
Number 7.
Number 8.
Number 9.
Number 10.

FIGURE 11.5 • *The FOR loop continues, incrementing the value of the a variable by 1, as long as its value is less than or equal to 10.*

In this script, the **a=1** part sets the starting point (the value of 1 is assigned to the *a* variable), the **a<=10** part sets the stopping point (the loop continues as long as the value of *a* is less than or equal to 10), and the **a=a+1** sets how much *a* is incremented in each loop (for each new loop, *a* is equal to *a* plus 1).

Working with Functions

A *function* assigns a series of commands to be performed to a name. Later, the function's commands can be executed simply by calling its name. A function consists of the following parts:

```
function function_name(argument1, argument2,...n) {
    statement_1;
    statement_2;
    .
    .
    .
    statement_n;
}
```

For example, the following function is nested in the HEAD element; it defines a variable (*ident*) and then specifies that variable as the content of an alert message:

```
<script language="JavaScript" type="text/javascript">
<!-- start hiding script
function HiThere() {
    ident = window.prompt("Please enter your name: ", "");
    alert("Welcome to my page, "+ident+"!");
}
// end hiding script -->
</script>
```

You can then cause this function to run automatically when the document is loaded, like this:

```
<body onLoad="HiThere()">
```

This example uses an onLoad event handler that calls the HiThere() function when the document is loaded. An event handler allows scripts to respond to user actions or system events (see the upcoming section called "Using Event Handlers"). After the user enters his name at the prompt, an alert message appears welcoming him to the Web page (see Figure 11.6).

user's name in alert message

FIGURE 11.6 • *The user is welcomed to the page, using the name provided by the user.*

To call the function when a link is clicked, you might do the following:

```
<a href="#" onClick="HiThere()">This is the link text</a>
```

or you can do the following:

```
<a href="javascript: HiThere()">This is the link text</a>
```

You also can create a function and then pass values to it. The value can be evaluated by the function and a response produced based on the value. Later in this chapter, you will create a jump menu that does just that; depending on the value that is passed to the function, the jump menu either jumps to a destination or does nothing.

Working with Objects

Every element within an HTML document is an object, starting with the browser window (the window object), proceeding to the document (the document object), and then to every other object that is included in an HTML document. Objects also have properties (or attributes). For instance, an object might have a name, an ID, a size, a URL, a color, and so on.

For instance, you can refer to the VALUE property (or attribute) that belongs to an object; a BUTTON element named "mybutton", that is nested inside another object; and a FORM element named "myform", in the following manner:

```
window.document.myform.mybutton.value
```

The window object can be assumed, and thus can be omitted. The reference also can be stated in this manner:

```
document.myform.mybutton.value
```

JavaScript also includes a number of built-in objects that are not part of the document. These include the window, navigator, frames, location, history, document, Math, and Date objects. Table 11.4 shows the built-in JavaScript objects that are not part of the document.

TABLE 11.4 • *Built-In JavaScript Objects*

Object	Description	Examples
window	The browser window	window.alert("Hi!")
navigator	Browser information	navigator.userAgent navigator.appVersion navigator.platform
frames	Frames in a window	window.frames[1] window.frames[2]
location	Document address	window.location
history	History list	window.history window.history.previous history.back()
document	The current document	window.document document.lastModified document.bgColor
Math	Math functions and constants	Math.PI Math.SQRT2 Math.log() Math.sin()
Date	Date and time	today = new Date()

Working with Arrays

An array allows you to assign a series of values to a variable. For instance, you might assign the names of the 12 months to a *monthname* variable or the names of the days of the week to a *dayname* variable.

```
<script language="JavaScript" type="text/javascript">
<!-- start hiding script
thisdate = new Date();
day = thisdate.getDay();
month = thisdate.getMonth();
year = thisdate.getYear();
date = thisdate.getDate();

var dayname = new Array
("Sunday","Monday","Tuesday","Wednesday","Thursday","Friday",
"Saturday");
var theday = dayname[day];
var monthname = new Array
("January","February","March","April","May","June","July",
"August","September","October","November","December");
var themonth = monthname[month];
var theyear;
    if (year >= 100 && year <= 1999) theyear = 1900 + year;
        else theyear = year;
// end hiding script -->
</script>
</head>
```

You can then write values to the document that correspond to specific values within the array. For instance, the following writes the day and date to the document (see Figure 11.7):

```
<body>
<script language="javascript">
<!-- start hiding script
document.write ("<h2>Today is "+ theday +", "+ themonth +" "+
date +", "+ theyear +".</h2>");
// end hiding script -->
</script>
```

```
┌──────────────────────────────────────────────────────────────────────┐
│ Web Design Fundamentals: Course Description - Microsoft Internet Explorer   _ □ × │
├──────────────────────────────────────────────────────────────────────┤
│ File  Edit  View  Favorites  Tools  Help                    Links »  ▓ │
├──────────────────────────────────────────────────────────────────────┤
│ Today is Monday, September 23, 2002.                                   │
└──────────────────────────────────────────────────────────────────────┘
```

FIGURE 11.7 • *The day and date are written to the document.*

Using Event Handlers

Event handlers allow JavaScript scripts to respond to user actions or system events, such as clicking on a link or passing the mouse cursor over or off an image. Event handlers can be expressed both as HTML attributes and as JavaScript code. For instance, the following is an example of using an event handler as an HTML attribute:

```
<img src="myimage.jpg" name="myimage"
onMouseOver="alert('That/'s me!');"
```

Alternatively, this could also be expressed in JavaScript like this:

```
document.myimage.onmouseover = function() {
    alert('That/'s me!');
}
```

Table 11.5 shows the different event handlers, along with their descriptions.

TABLE 11.5 • *JavaScript Event Handlers*

Event Handler	Description
onAbort	When the loading of an image is aborted by the user.
onBlur	When an element loses focus, such as when a user tabs from one form input element to another. The flip-side of onFocus.
onFocus	When an element is given focus, such as when a user tabs to a form element or when a window is brought to the foreground.
onChange	When a list menu option or input control is selected or deselected, or when the content of a textarea box is changed.
onSelect	When a user selects text in a text input field.
onClick	When the user clicks once on an element.
onDblClick	When the user double-clicks on an element.
onError	When an error occurs while an image is loading.
onKeyDown	When a key is pressed and held down over an element.
onKeyPress	When a key is pressed and released over an element.
onKeyUp	When a key is released by a user.
onLoad	When a document is loaded into a browser window.
onUnload	When a document is unloaded.
onMouseDown	When a mouse button is pressed down over an element.
onMouseUp	When a mouse button is released over an element.

continues on next page

TABLE 11.5 • *JavaScript Event Handlers—Continued*

Event Handler	Description
onMouseOut	When the mouse pointer passes off of an element.
onMouseOver	When the mouse pointer passes over an element.
OnMouseMove	When the mouse pointer is moved while positioned over an element.
onReset	When a form is reset.
onResize	When the window is resized.
onSubmit	When a form is submitted.

NOTE

To find out more about using variables, conditional statements, objects, functions, arrays, and event handlers, see this chapter's section at the IRC for this book at **www.emcp.com/**.

CASE EXAMPLE: CREATING A SCHOOL COURSE SITE

As a student, you have probably often visited pages and sites for classes or courses you have taken. If you choose teaching as a profession, for instance, you might need to create a page or site to provide information, support, and feedback for the courses you will be teaching.

Ruth Clearwater is a Web and graphic design instructor at Flat-Iron College. She is creating a Web site for a course she will be teaching, Web Design Fundamentals, and is specifically looking at ways in which she can use JavaScript in her pages.

action

To start working with this example:
1. Open **webdesign_ex.html** in your text editor from the chap11 folder in your working folder or disk.
2. Save webdesign_ex.html as **webdesign.html** in the chap11 folder.
3. Open **webdesign.html** in your Web browser from the chap11 folder.

AUTOMATICALLY SPECIFYING WHEN A PAGE WAS LAST UPDATED

Specifying when a page was last updated can be helpful to visitors to your site. They can easily see if there have been any changes since their last visit, for instance. If you make frequent changes to a page, however, it can be a hassle and you can easily forget to manually update the "last updated" line.

A better idea is to use a JavaScript script to automatically insert the date when a page was last updated.

action

Insert the date when the document was last updated by using a JavaScript script (see Figure 11.8):

```
<address>
Course: Web Design Fundamentals<br>
Instructor: Ruth Clearwater<br>
```

```
E-Mail: <a href="mailto:rclearwater@flat-
iron.edu">rclearwater@flat-iron.edu.com</a><br>
Web Address: <a href="http://www.flat-iron.edu/web-design/
fundamentals/">http://www.flat-iron.edu/web-design/fundamentals/
</a><br>
<script language="JavaScript" type="text/javascript">
<!-- start hiding script
if (Date.parse(document.lastModified) > 0) {
    document.write("Page Last Modified: "+document.lastModified)
}
// end hiding script -->
</script>
</address>
```

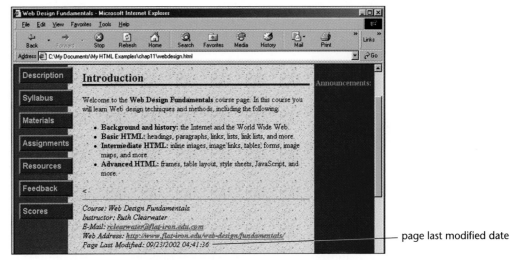

page last modified date

FIGURE 11.8 • *The date and time when the page was last modified appears at the bottom of the screen.*

You could simply insert the **document.write("Page Last Modified: "+docu-ment.lastModified)**, except that some systems will mistakenly report a date of 1970 (which is equal to year 0 in UNIX time). As such, by using the IF statement, the last modified line is only inserted if the parse value for the lastModified date is greater than 0.

CREATING POP-UP WINDOWS

Although you can open a page in a new browser window using just HTML (by using the **target="_blank"** attribute in the link's A element), you cannot control the size and position of the window, nor can you specify whether or not menu bars, status bars, scroll bars, or other window elements will be displayed. You can control all of these features, however, when using JavaScript to open a new window. In the following sections, you will be creating two different kinds of pop-up windows, first a pop-up window that displays an HTML file and then a pop-up window that seamlessly displays an image.

Creating a Pop-Up Window Using an HTML File

You can display an HTML file within a pop-up window. The main concern is that the content of the HTML file fit within the dimensions of the pop-up window you create.

Create a pop-up window that displays an HTML file:

1. Create a script in the document's HEAD section that defines a function (PopWin) that will cause the pop-up window to open when it is called:

```
</style>
<script language="JavaScript" type="text/javascript">
<!-- start hiding script
function PopWin(url) {
    newwindow=window.open(url,'name','height=150,width=150');
    if (window.focus) {
        newwindow.focus()
    }
}
// end hiding script -->
</script>
</head>
```

2. Edit the following text in the document's BODY element, setting up the text, "Background and history:", as a link that calls the PopWin(url) function:

```
<p>Welcome to the <b>Web Design Fundamentals</b> course page. In
this course you will learn Web design techniques and methods,
including the following:</p>
<ul>
<li><b><a href="javascript:PopWin('popup1.html')">Background and
history:</a></b> the Internet and the World Wide Web.
```

3. Save your HTML file and then refresh it in your browser. Click on the "Background and history:" link to cause the pop-up window to appear (see Figure 11.9).

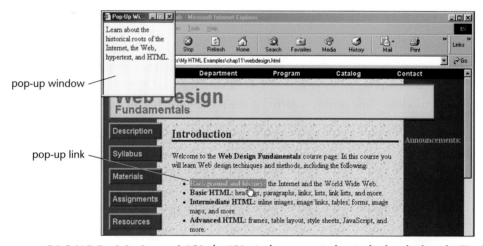

pop-up window

pop-up link

FIGURE 11.9 • *A 150- by 150-pixel pop-up window is displayed when the "Background and history:" link is clicked.*

CONTROLLING THE POP-UP WINDOW'S APPEARANCE AND POSITION By default, the pop-up window's toolbar, menu bar, status bar, directory bar, location bar, and scroll bars are turned off, at least in most current browsers. It is worthwhile, however, to specifically turn them off, if only so you can easily turn them on again, if you wish. You also can specify whether you want the pop-up window to be resizable; because some users may want to increase the size of their text, it is a good idea to allow resizing of the pop-up window.

You can control the position of the pop-up window by specifying an offset from the top and left sides of the screen.

Add parameters to your script that control the appearance of different window elements and position the pop-up window on the screen, offset from the top and left sides of the screen:

1. Edit the PopWin(url) function script in the document's HEAD element:

```
<script language="JavaScript" type="text/javascript">
<!-- start hiding script
function PopWin(url) {
    newwindow=window.open(url,'name','height=150,width=150'
    + ',toolbar=no,status=no,menubar=no,directories=no'
    + ',location=no,resizable=yes,scrollbars=auto'
    + ',top=225,left=325');
    if (window.focus) {
        newwindow.focus()
    }
}
// end hiding script -->
</script>
```

2. Resave **webdesign.html** in your text editor and then refresh the display of the page in your browser (Ctrl+R).
3. Click the "Background and history:" link to display the pop-up window (see Figure 11.10).

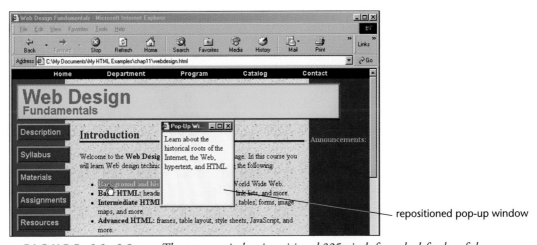

repositioned pop-up window

FIGURE 11.10 • *The pop-up window is positioned 325 pixels from the left edge of the screen and 225 pixels from the top edge of the screen.*

4. Resize the window by grabbing one of the sides (or the corner) of the window with the mouse and pulling it.
5. Close the pop-up window.

CLOSING THE POP-UP WINDOW AFTER A SET TIME You can save the user the bother of closing the pop-up window by causing it to automatically close after a specified period of time.

Set the pop-up window to close automatically after 5,000 milliseconds:

1. Open **popup1.html** in your text editor from the chap11 folder and edit the page's BODY start tag as follows:

```
<body class="popup" onLoad="setTimeout(window.close, 5000)">
```

2. Resave popup1.html as **popup1a.html** in the chap11 folder.
3. Return to or reopen **webdesign.html** in your text editor. Edit it so that the new file (popup1a.html) will be displayed in the pop-up window:

```
<li><b><a href="javascript:PopWin('popup1a.html')">Background
and history:</a></b> the Internet and the World Wide Web.
```

4. If it is not already open in your browser, reopen **webdesign.html** in your browser from the chap11 folder. If webdesign.html is already open in your browser, refresh the display of your page.
5. Click on the "Background and history:" link to open the pop-up window. The pop-up window should automatically close after 5,000 milliseconds.

INCLUDING A CLOSE WINDOW LINK Another option is to include a link in the pop-up window that enables the user to close the pop-up window when she has finished reading its content.

1. If it is not already open, open **popup1a.html** in your text editor from the chap11 folder and edit the content of the page as follows:

```
</head>
<!--
<body class="popup" onLoad="setTimeout(window.close, 5000)">
-->
<body class="popup">
<p>Learn about the historical roots of the Internet, the Web,
hypertext, and HTML.</p>
<p align="center"><a href="javascript:window.close();">Close the
Window.</a></p>
```

2. Resave popup1a.html as **popup1b.html** in the chap11 folder.
3. Return to or reopen **webdesign.html** in your text editor. Edit it so that the new file (popup1b.html) will be displayed in the pop-up window:

```
<li><b><a href="javascript:PopWin('popup1b.html')">Background
and history:</a></b> the Internet and the World Wide Web.
```

4. If it is not already open in your browser, reopen **webdesign.html** in your browser from the chap11 folder. If webdesign.html is already open in your browser, refresh the display of your page.
5. Click on the "Background and history:" link to open the pop-up window. Notice the link added to the pop-up window's page that lets the user close the window (see Figure 11.11).

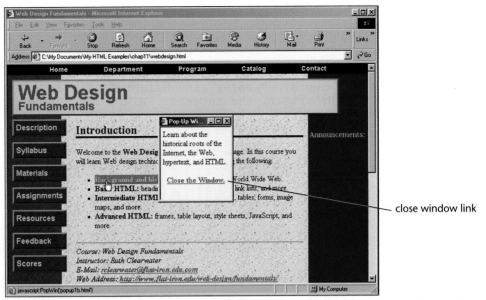

FIGURE 11.11 • *A link is added to the pop-up window's page so the user can close the window.*

close window link

6. In the pop-up window, click on the "Close the Window." link to close the window.

Popping Up an Image Window

A common use for a pop-up window is to display an image. A browser window, however, inserts margin space around an image if you link directly to the image. The same is true if you insert the image inside of an HTML file and then link to that file instead, but because you are linking to an HTML file and not an image, you can edit it to get rid of the margins.

Create a "seamless" pop-up image:

1. Add the following JavaScript function to your document's HEAD element:

```
<script language="JavaScript" type="text/javascript">
<!-- start hiding script
function PopImg(url) {
    newwindow=window.open(url,'name','height=268,width=364'
    +',top=166,left=218');
    if (window.focus) {
        newwindow.focus()
    }
}
// end hiding script -->
</script>
</head>
```

2. Add the following link to your document that will open the pop-up window:

```
<li><b><a href="javascript:PopWin('popup1b.html')">Background
and history:</a></b> the Internet and the World Wide Web.<br>See
<a href="javascript:PopImg('popimg.html')"></a>.
```

3. Resave your document.

4. Open **popimg_ex.html** in your text editor from the chap11 folder. Edit the file as shown here:

```
<body class="popup" marginheight="0" marginwidth="0"
topmargin="0" leftmargin="0" style="margin: 0; padding: 0">
<img src="popimg.gif" height="268 width="364" alt="Diagram:
Hypertext, the Internet, HTML, and the Web">
</body>
```

5. Resave popimg_ex.html as **popimg.html** in the chap11 folder.
6. In your browser, refresh the display of your page. Click on the "image" link to cause the pop-up image to be displayed (see Figure 11.12).

pop-up image window

FIGURE 11.12 • *A seamless pop-up image is displayed.*

Reusing the Pop-Up Function

The two pop-up functions you have created so far (PopWin and PopWin2) differ only in the specified window name (popup1 and popup2), window dimensions (height and width), and screen positions (left and top). The empty quotes at the start of the window.open statement leave open the identity of the HTML file's URL—this has the effect of defaulting to the URL specified in the pop-up link. As long as you do not need to change any of the common characteristics (window name, window dimensions, or screen positions), you can easily reuse the same function to open pop-up windows containing different HTML files. Example HTML files (popup2.html, popup3.html, and popup4.html) that you will be using in this exercise are included with the other example files in the chap11 folder.

Set up a second pop-up window, re-using the PopWin(url) function:

1. Create a new link that pops up the popup2.html example file:

```
<li><b><a href="javascript:PopWin('popup2.html')">Basic
HTML:</a></b> headings, paragraphs, links, lists, link lists,
and more.
```

2. Save the file, refresh it in your browser, and then click on the "Basic HTML:" link to open the pop-up window (see Figure 11.13).

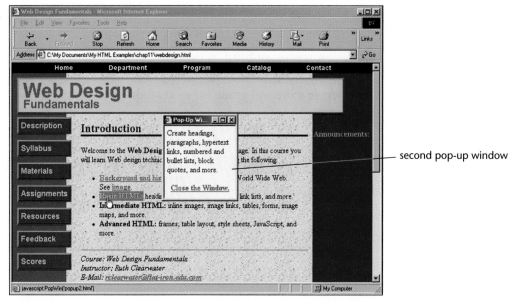

second pop-up window

FIGURE 11.13 • *The popup2.html file is opened in a pop-up window.*

The link you created in this example only differs from the previous link you created in that a different file name is specified for the link URL (popup2.html instead of popup1.html). Everything else is the same. You only need to create a different function, PopWin2(url), for instance, if you want to display a pop-up window with different display properties (size, positioning, toolbars, and so on), or if you want to assign a different name to the pop-up window. You might want to create a different function if the content of your pop-up windows requires differently sized windows. You might want to assign a different name if you do not want the second pop-up window to replace the first pop-up window.

Gain additional practice creating pop-up windows:
1. Create pop-up links for the two additional list headings ("Intermediate HTML" and "Advanced HTML") that link to popup3.html and popup4.html, respectively.
2. Edit popup3.html and popup4.html and add a link that allows the user to close the window.

CALCULATING TEST SCORES

Performing calculations is one of the most useful things you can do with JavaScript. You can do addition, subtraction, multiplication, division, and other simple or complex calculations.

Ruth Clearwater has decided she wants to post her students' test scores on the Web so they can easily check their scores and see how they stack up with their fellow students. She has assigned each student a confidential code name and will identify each student only by that code name, not by the student's real name, when she posts the test scores.

Create a table that calculates test scores and grades:

1. Open **scores_ex.html** in your text editor from the chap11 folder.
2. Add the script that creates the table rows, displays the scores, and calculates the average score and grade for each student:

```
<p><table border="1" width="400" align="center">
<tr style="color: black; background: #ccffcc"><th
colspan="7">First Quarter Test Scores</th></tr>
<tr style="color: black; background: #ffcc99"><th
width="75">Student</th><th width="50">Test1</th><th
width="50">Test2</th><th width="50">Test3</th><th
width="50">Test4</th><th width="75">Avg</th><th
width="50">Grade</th></tr>

<script language="JavaScript" type="text/javascript">
<!-- start hiding script
function TableRow(student, test1, test2, test3, test4) {
    if ((test1+test2+test3+test4) < 240) {rowbg = "<tr
style='color: white; background: black'>";}
    else if ((test1+test2+test3+test4) < 280) {rowbg = "<tr
style='color: yellow; background: #666666'>";}
    else if ((test1+test2+test3+test4) < 320) {rowbg = "<tr
style='color: #006600; background: #99ffff'>";}
    else if ((test1+test2+test3+test4) < 360) {rowbg = "<tr
style='color: #000099; background: #ccff66'>";}
    else if ((test1+test2+test3+test4) < 401) {rowbg = "<tr
style='color: red; background: #ffcc00'>";}
    else {rowbg = "<TR>";}
    if ((test1+test2+test3+test4)/4 < 60) {grade = "F";}
    else if ((test1+test2+test3+test4)/4 < 63) {grade = "D-";}
    else if ((test1+test2+test3+test4)/4 < 68) {grade = "D";}
    else if ((test1+test2+test3+test4)/4 < 70) {grade = "D+";}
    else if ((test1+test2+test3+test4)/4 < 73) {grade = "C-";}
    else if ((test1+test2+test3+test4)/4 < 78) {grade = "C";}
    else if ((test1+test2+test3+test4)/4 < 80) {grade = "C+";}
    else if ((test1+test2+test3+test4)/4 < 83) {grade = "B-";}
    else if ((test1+test2+test3+test4)/4 < 88) {grade = "B";}
    else if ((test1+test2+test3+test4)/4 < 90) {grade = "B+";}
    else if ((test1+test2+test3+test4)/4 < 93) {grade = "A-";}
    else if ((test1+test2+test3+test4)/4 < 98) {grade = "A";}
    else if ((test1+test2+test3+test4)/4 < 101) {grade = "A+";}

    document.write(rowbg, "<td> ", student, " </td><td
align='right'>", test1,
    "</td><td align='right'>", test2, "</td><td align='right'>",
test3,
    "</td><td align='right'>", test4, "</td><td align='right'>",
    (test1+test2+test3+test4)/4, "</td><td align='center'>",
grade, "</td></td>\n") }
TableRow("red2154", 95, 90, 85, 92);
TableRow("blue3215", 75, 70, 80, 65);
TableRow("aqua2701", 99, 92, 98, 95);
TableRow("lime6589", 90, 85, 75, 88);
TableRow("orange1044", 55, 60, 65, 75);
TableRow("purple1595", 82, 80, 81, 86);
TableRow("yellow3110", 45, 50, 55, 40);
TableRow("brown4905", 65, 75, 78, 80);
```

```
TableRow("olive1285", 100, 98, 97, 99);
// end hiding script -->
</script>
</table></p>
```

3. Save your file as **scores.html** in the chap11 folder.
4. Return to or reopen **webdesign.html** in your Web browser. If returning to it, refresh the display of the page in your browser.
5. Click on the Scores button in the left sidebar to display the Scores page. Scroll down to see the table of test scores (see Figure 11.14).

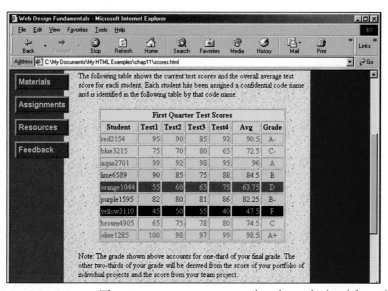

FIGURE 11.14 • *The test scores, average score, and grade are displayed for each student.*

6. Add an additional student, along with some hypothetical scores. For instance, you might key in the following (see Figure 11.15):

```
TableRow("brown4905", 65, 75, 78, 80);
TableRow("olive1285", 100, 98, 97, 99);
TableRow("white7357", 75, 80, 82, 76);
// end hiding script -->
```

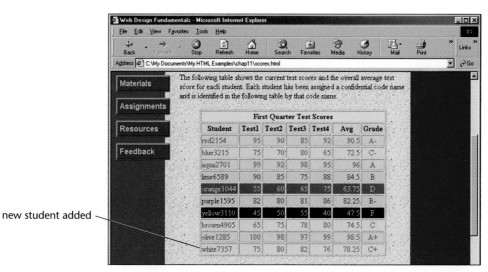

new student added —

FIGURE 11.15 • *A student, "white7357," is added to the table of student scores.*

VALIDATING FORM INPUT

You can create a form using HTML, but you cannot check to make sure that a user has entered valid information. Using a JavaScript script, however, you can check user input to make sure it is valid. The following example checks to make sure that the Name field is not left blank and that an e-mail address (or at least a text string that includes the "@" and "." characters) has been entered.

Create a self-validating form:

1. Open **descript_ex.html** in your text editor from the chap11 folder and resave it as **descript.html**.

2. Add the following JavaScript script to the page's HEAD element:

```
<script language="JavaScript" type="text/javascript">
<!-- start hiding script
function validForm(){
if (document.myform.name.value==document.myform.name.defaultValue)
{
    alert('You have not entered your name.');
    document.myform.name.select();
    document.myform.name.focus();
    return false;
}
if (document.myform.email.value.indexOf('@',0)==-1 ||
document.myform.email.value.indexOf('.',0)==-1) {
    alert('Please enter a valid e-mail address.');
    document.myform.email.select();
    document.myform.email.focus();
    return false;
}
    else {
        {
        return true;
        }
}}
// end hiding script -->
</script>
</head>
```

3. Edit the form so that it calls the validForm() function:

```
<form name="myform" action="/cgi-bin/formSend.pl" method="post"
onSubmit="return validForm()">
<p>Name: <input name="name" type="text" size="35"></p>
<p>E-Mail: <input name="email" type="text" size="35""></p>
<p>Comments:</p>
<p><textarea name="comment" rows="5" cols="40"></textarea></p>
<p><input type="hidden" name="recipient"
value="rclearwater@flat-iron.edu"></p>
<p><input type="submit" value="Submit"> <input type="reset"
value="Reset"></p>
</form>
```

4. Save the file in the chap11 folder. In your browser, open **descript.html** from the chap11 folder.

5. Do not key anything into the Name box (leave it blank).

6. In the E-Mail box, key in any combination of letters or numbers that does not contain a "@" character or a "." character. For instance, key **no e-mail** in the E-Mail box. Click the Submit button. An alert box is displayed telling you that you have not entered your name (see Figure 11.16). Click OK.

F I G U R E   1 1 . 1 6 • *Because the Name field is blank, an alert message is displayed telling the user to enter his or her name.*

If after clicking the Submit button, a new page is displayed in Internet Explorer saying "The page cannot be displayed," it is likely you have made a mistake when keying in the code for the validForm() function (under Step 2 in this Action section). (In Mozilla 1, nothing will happen after clicking the Submit button.) Carefully examine the code you keyed to locate the error. Look particularly for any regular parentheses ("(" or ")") that may have been keyed instead of squiggly brackets ("{" or "}"). Also, look for any missing quotation marks.

7. Key your name in the Name field. For instance, you might key **Portia Quain** in the Name field. Click the Submit button again. Now, you will see an alert message asking you to enter a valid e-mail address (see Figure 11.17).

F I G U R E   1 1 . 1 7 • *Because the E-mail field does not contain both an "@" character and a "." character, an alert message is displayed asking the user to enter a valid e-mail address.*

8. Key an e-mail address in the E-Mail field. For instance, key **portia@quain.com** in the E-Mail field. Click the Submit button again. This time you will not get any more alerts, which means that the form has been validated and submitted.

The example form is a CGI form, so you cannot actually submit it. In Internet Explorer 6, a page is displayed, displaying the text, "The page cannot be displayed," which just means that it cannot find the FormMail.pl CGI script. In the Mozilla 1 browser, you will not see any response at all after clicking the Submit button, although if the form was published on the Web, the CGI script would send a confirmation page that the form had been submitted.

CREATING A JUMP MENU

A *jump menu* is a just a pull-down menu, created using the FORM, SELECT, and OPTION elements, that lets a user select an option and then go to the specified Web page that is associated with that option. There are two basic types of jump menus: a menu that automatically goes to a URL when a destination is selected, or a menu that requires the user to click a "Go" button after selecting a destination.

Creating an Automatic Jump Menu

This kind of jump menu requires a user to execute a minimum of mouse clicks to select and go to a destination. The user only needs to click on the drop-down menu to unfold it and then click on the desired destination.

Create a jump menu at the top of the front page's right column that automatically jumps to a destination when it is selected:

1. Re-open **webdesign.html** in your text editor from the chap11 folder, if it is not already open. Add a JavaScript script to that document's HEAD element that defines a function that will execute the jump:

```
<script language="JavaScript" type="text/javascript">
<!-- start hiding script
function goDestination(a){
    if (document.mymenu.menuopts.value != "null") {
        document.location.href = a
    }
}
// end hiding script -->
</script>
</head>
```

2. Add a form to the right table column that uses an onChange event handler to pass a value, based on the destination selected by the user, to the function defined in Step 1:

```
<td width="130" bgcolor="maroon">
<div class="right">
<div class="rightpad">
<form name="mymenu" style="margin-top: 0">
<select name="menuopts" onChange="goDestination
    (document.mymenu.menuopts.options
    [document.mymenu.menuopts.options.selectedIndex].value)">
<option>Jump to page--&gt;</option>
<option value="webdesign.html">Introduction</option>
```

```
<option value="descript.html">Description</option>
<option value="syllabus.html">Syllabus</option>
<option value="materials.html">Materials</option>
<option value="assignments.html">Assignments</option>
<option value="resources.html">Resources</option>
<option value="feedback.html">Feedback</option>
<option value="scores.html">Scores</option>
</select>
</form>
<h2class="right">Announcements:</h2>
</div>
</div>
</td>
```

3. Save your file, switch over to your browser, and refresh the display of your page. A pull-down list menu should now be displayed at the top of the right column (see Figure 11.18).

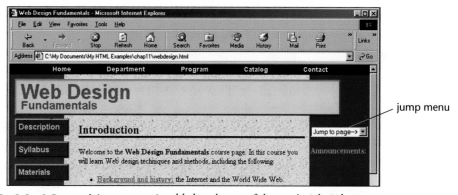

FIGURE 11.18 • *A jump menu is added to the top of the page's right column.*

4. Click on the pull-down list (or on the list's down arrow) to unfold the menu options. Pass the mouse over the unfolded menu to highlight any of the options (see Figure 11.19).

FIGURE 11.19 • *A series of destination options is displayed when the user clicks on the jump menu's box.*

5. Click on the Description option. Your browser should automatically load the page that is specified as that option's value (see Figure 11.20).

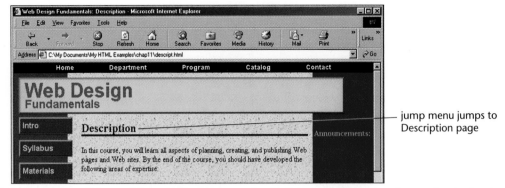

jump menu jumps to
Description page

FIGURE 11.20 • *When the Description option is clicked on, the associated page, descript.html,
is automatically opened in the browser window.*

6. Click the browser's Back button to return to the front page (webdesign.html).

You should note the following about this script:

- This script works by passing a value from the onChange event handler in the form's SELECT element to the script in the document's HEAD element. The value that is passed is assigned to the "a" function argument. As long as the value of "a" is not equal to "null", the passed value is executed as the value of the `document.location.href` statement. That is, if the Description option is clicked, "descript.html" is assigned as the value of `document.location.href`.

- The FORM and SELECT elements are named "mymenu" and "menuopts", respectively. You can name these elements anything you wish, but script in the document's head and the value of the onChange event handler in the SELECT element must match the names that you use.

- An inline style is inserted that turns off the top margin for the FORM element. The top margin is turned off because Internet Explorer 6 adds a top margin above the FORM element, whereas other browsers, such as Mozilla 1, do not. To insure consistent formatting, the best solution is to simply turn off the top margin of this element for all browsers. The document's style sheet (webdesign.css) sets a top padding value for the div.rightpad selector that moves any content down 125 pixels (so it is displayed below the overlapping banner heading).

- A dummy option (an OPTION element without a VALUE attribute) is set as the default selected option. If this option is selected, a "null" value is passed to the script function in the document's HEAD element. This option is used to identify the purpose of the jump menu, which is to jump to a page within the site. Notice that an arrow is created by inserting two hyphens followed by the entity code (`&lt;`) for a right-arrow bracket. You can key in whatever you want as the content of this option, as long as it concisely and accurately conveys the purpose and function of the list menu.

Using a jump menu that automatically jumps to a destination when it is selected poses a potential accessibility concern. Using keyboard input, rather than mouse actions, does not work for this kind of jump menu—a user can access the form and select an option using only keyboard input, but pressing the Enter key after selecting an option does not do anything. For this reason, especially in an educational situation, you should consider not using this kind of jump menu. The following section, "Creating a Jump Menu with a Go Button," covers a different way to create a jump menu, which is accessible using only keyboard input.

Creating a Jump Menu with a Go Button

With this type of jump menu, a user must first unfold the list menu and select an option, and then click on a "Go" button to cause the browser to open the selected destination page. Although this does require an extra step from the user, it has some advantages that help compensate for the additional step:

- You do not need to include a dummy option because the "Go" button label conveys the function and purpose of the jump menu (that it is a jump menu) to the user.
- Users can access the menu and activate any of its options using only keyboard input, which means that this kind of jump menu does not pose the same kind of accessibility concern that the automatic jump menu does.

Create a jump menu that uses a "Go" button to jump to a selected destination:

1. Comment out the function script you added previously to the HEAD element:

```
<!--
<script language="JavaScript" type="text/javascript" >
<!-- start hiding script
function goDestination(a){
    if (document.mymenu.menuopts.value != "null") {
        document.location.href = a
    }
}
// end hiding script -->
</script>
-->
</head>
</script>
```

2. Edit the previous jump menu that you created, as follows:

```
<form name="mymenu" style="margin-top: 0">
<select name="menuopts" style="margin-bottom: 5px"
onChange="goDestination
    (document.mymenu.menuopts.options
    [document.mymenu.menuopts.options.selectedIndex].value)">
<option>Jump to page &gt;</option>
<option value="webdesign.html">Introduction</option>
<option value="descript.html">Description</option>
<option value="syllabus.html">Syllabus</option>
<option value="materials.html">Materials</option>
<option value="assignments.html">Assignments</option>
<option value="resources.html">Resources</option>
<option value="feedback.html">Feedback</option>
<option value="scores.html">Scores</option>
</select>
<input type="button" onClick="location=document.mymenu.menuopts.
options[document.mymenu.menuopts.selectedIndex].value;" value="
Go ">
</form>
```

3. Save your file, switch to your browser, and refresh the display of the page. You will see the new jump menu, this time using a Go button (see Figure 11.21).

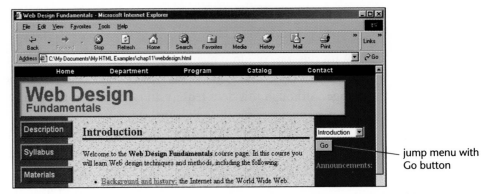

FIGURE 11.21 • *A jump menu, using a Go button, is displayed in the right sidebar.*

4. Click the list menu to unfold its options and click on the Scores option to select it. Click the "Go" button to go to the Scores destination page, scores.html (see Figure 11.22).

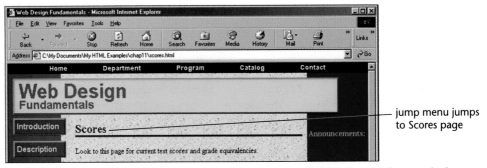

jump menu jumps to Scores page

FIGURE 11.22 • *After the user selects the Scores option and clicks the "Go" button, the browser opens the option's destination file, scores.html.*

GENERATING HTML CODE USING JAVASCRIPT

You can use JavaScript to generate any codes or text that can be included in a Web page. You might want to do this for at least a couple reasons. By generating a whole jump menu, including the HTML form elements:

- You can hide the jump menu from browsers that do not recognize JavaScript or in which it has been turned off.
- You can save the resulting JavaScript script as an external script and easily insert it in as many other pages as you want.

Generating the Jump Menu Using JavaScript

You use the document.write method to write codes and other text to the document (the HTML file).

Set up the jump menu codes and text so that they are written to the document using JavaScript:

1. Use the document.write method to write the form's HTML codes and text to the document:

```
<div class="rightpad">
<script language="JavaScript" type="text/javascript">
<!-- start hiding script
document.write('<form name="mymenu" style="margin-top: 0">');
document.write('<select name="menuopts" style="margin-bottom:
5px">');
document.write('<option
value="webdesign.html">Introduction</option>');
document.write('<option
value="descript.html">Description</option>');
document.write('<option value="syllabus.html">Syllabus</option>');
document.write('<option
value="materials.html">Materials</option>');
document.write('<option
value="assignments.html">Assignments</option>');
document.write('<option
value="resources.html">Resources</option>');
document.write('<option value="feedback.html">Feedback</option>');
document.write('<option value="scores.html">Scores</option>');
document.write('</select>');
document.write('<input type="button" onClick=');
document.write('"location=document.mymenu.menuopts.options');
document.write('[document.mymenu.menuopts.selectedIndex].value\;"');
document.write('value=" Go ">');
</select>
document.write('</form>');
// end hiding script -->
</script>
```

2. Save your file, switch to your browser, and refresh the display of your page.
3. Test the jump menu. Click on it to unfold it, select one of the options, and then click the "Go" button. Your browser should open the destination page for the option you have selected. Click the Back button to return to the front page.

Using an External JavaScript Script

Now that you are generating the jump menu's HTML codes and text by using JavaScript, you can save the JavaScript to a file and link to it, instead of inserting it directly inside the document. You can then insert it in the document simply by linking to it.

Save the jump menu's JavaScript script as an external JavaScript file and then link to it from within the current page:

1. In the jump menu's script code, highlight and copy everything that is below the **<!-- start hiding script** line and above the **// end hiding script -->** line.

2. Open a new blank window in your text editor and paste in the JavaScript code you copied in Step 1, as shown here:

```
document.write('<form name="mymenu" style="margin-top: 0">');
document.write('<select name="menuopts" style="margin-bottom:
5px">');
document.write('<option
value="webdesign.html">Introduction</option>');
```

```
document.write('<option
value="descript.html">Description</option>');
document.write('<option value="syllabus.html">Syllabus</option>');
document.write('<option value="materials.html">Materials</option>');
document.write('<option
value="assignments.html">Assignments</option>');
document.write('<option value="resources.html">Resources</option>');
document.write('<option value="feedback.html">Feedback</option>');
document.write('<option value="scores.html">Scores</option>');
document.write('</select>');
document.write('<input type="button" onClick=');
document.write('"location=document.mymenu.menuopts.options');
document.write('[document.mymenu.menuopts.selectedIndex].value\;"');
document.write('value=" Go ">');
document.write('</form>');
```

3. Save the document as **jumpmnu.js** in the chap11 folder.

4. Return to or reopen **webdesign.html** in your text editor. Delete the contents of
   the jump menu's script:

```
<script language="JavaScript" type="text/javascript">
<!-- start hiding script
document.write('<form name="mymenu" style="margin-top: 0">');
document.write('<select name="menuopts" style="margin-bottom:
5px">');
document.write('<option
value="webdesign.html">Introduction</option>');
document.write('<option value="descript.html"
selected>Description</option>');
document.write('<option value="syllabus.html">Syllabus</option>');
document.write('<option value="materials.html">Materials</option>');
document.write('<option
value="assignments.html">Assignments</option>');
document.write('<option
value="resources.html">Resources</option>');
document.write('<option value="feedback.html">Feedback</option>');
document.write('<option value="scores.html">Scores</option>');
document.write('</select>');
document.write('<input type="button" onClick=');
document.write('"location=document.mymenu.menuopts.options');
document.write('[document.mymenu.menuopts.selectedIndex].value\;"');
document.write('value=" Go ">');
document.write('</form>');
// end hiding script -->
</script>
<h2 class="right">Announcements:</h2>
```

5. Edit the SCRIPT element's start tag so it is linked to the external JavaScript script
   you saved in Step 3:

```
<script language="JavaScript" type="text/javascript"
src="jumpmnu.js">
</script>
<h2 class="right">Announcements:</h2>
```

6. Resave your file. Switch to your browser and refresh the display of your page. Test
   your jump menu by selecting any of its options and then clicking the Go button.
   Click the Back button to return to the front page.

Including the Jump Menu on Other Pages

Now that you have saved your jump menu's JavaScript script as an external JavaScript file, you can easily add it to the other pages in the site.

Add the jump menu to the course description page:

1. With webdesign.html open in your text editor, highlight and copy the SCRIPT element that links to the jumpmnu.js script file.

2. Open **descript.html** in your text editor and paste the SCRIPT element you copied in Step 1 at the top of the right column:

```
<script language="JavaScript" type="text/javascript"
src="jumpmnu.js">
</script>
<h2 class="right">Announcements:</h2>
```

3. Resave **descript.html**.

4. Switch to your browser, which should still be displaying webdesign.html (if not, reopen it). Use the jump menu to go to the Description page, where you will see that the jump menu is also displayed on that page (see Figure 11.23).

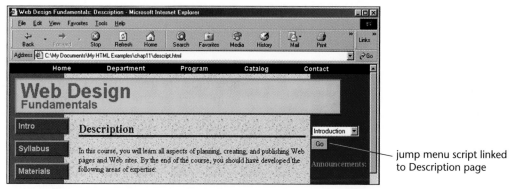

jump menu script linked to Description page

F I G U R E   1 1 . 2 3   •   *The jump menu, by being linked to in an external JavaScript file, is now also displayed on the Description page.*

5. Test the jump menu on the Description page. For instance, select the Introduction option and then click the "Go" button to go back to the Introduction page.

CHAPTER SUMMARY

You should now be familiar with JavaScript, how it works, and how it can be used to provide user feedback, organize and present data, increase interactivity, create dynamic effects, and improve navigation. You should be familiar with the different key aspects and features of JavaScript, including using variables, IF/ELSE statements, WHILE loops, FOR loops, functions, objects, arrays, event handlers, and more. You also gained practical experience using JavaScript to display a date-last-modified date stamp to a page, create and control pop-up windows (for Web pages and images), automatically close a window after a specified period of time, create a link to close a window, and create jump menus that either automatically jump to an option's destination or do so after a "Go" button is clicked. Previously in this book, you also worked with adding date and time stamps to Web pages (including creating date and time stamps as computers like to output them and, using arrays, as humans like to read them), as well as JavaScript rollover buttons.

The purpose of this chapter is not to teach you everything you need to know to start creating your own JavaScript scripts, but simply to introduce you to JavaScript and show you some practical examples of how JavaScript can be used in Web pages. Becoming proficient in using JavaScript requires further study and experimentation on your part. To find links to further JavaScript resources, tutorials, guides, and script repositories, be sure to visit this chapter's section at the IRC for this book at **www.emcp.com/**.

Code Review

client-side script	A script that is downloaded to a Web browser or other user agent, before being parsed and executed. A server-side script, such as one created using Perl, for instance, is parsed and executed on the server, with the results of the script then downloaded to the browser.
SCRIPT element	Inserts an embedded or linked script into an HTML document.
event handler	An attribute in an element that responds to user or system events, such as clicking, double-clicking, moving the mouse over, moving the mouse off, loading, unloading, and so on. Can trigger a function, for instance.
LANGUAGE attribute	In the SCRIPT element, identifies the script language that is being used. For instance, `language="JavaScript"` identifies the language being used as JavaScript. Other client-side script languages, such as VBScript, for instance, also can be referenced. Deprecated in HTML 4, but required by some earlier browsers.
TYPE attribute	In the SCRIPT element, identifies the MIME type of the script language being used. Required in HTML 4, but not recognized by many earlier browsers. The LANGUAGE and the TYPE attributes can be used together in the SCRIPT element.
document.write()	A JavaScript method for writing text to a document.
//	Marks a point on a line after which all text is considered a comment. Can be inserted at the start of a line to specify the whole line as a comment, or it can be inserted within a line to indicated that remaining text on the line is a comment and not to be parsed or executed.

\	Signals that the following character should not be parsed, but should be displayed as it is. For instance, \" signals that the double quote should be displayed and not parsed. To insert a "\" character to be displayed as is, you would insert \\ into the code.
\n	An escape code for inserting a new line (or line break).
variable	A name that may have variable values assigned to it; for instance, `a = 1`, `a = b + 1`, and `a = a * 1`.
operator	A symbol that represents the performance of an operation on a variable or value. Commonly used operators include + (add), - (subtract), * (multiply), and / (divide).
window.prompt()	A JavaScript method for creating a window that prompts the user for input.
IF statement	Executes a statement or statement block only if a specified condition is true.
IF/ELSE statement	The basic mechanism for creating decision branches. If a specific condition is true (the IF statement), one statement block is executed; otherwise, another statement block is executed (the ELSE statement).
ELSE IF statement	A shorthand means for nesting an IF statement within an ELSE statement. Allows the linking of a series of IF statements.
alert()	JavaScript method for displaying an alert message in a window. Short for `window.alert()`.
WHILE statement	Executes a statement or statement block as long as a specified condition remains true. Also referred to as a WHILE loop.
FOR statement	Similar to a WHILE statement, in that it allows the execution of a loop. In a FOR loop, however, the initializing value, the testing value (true/false), and the counter (increment) value are explicitly stated at the start.
function	Performs a function or series of functions based on one or several arguments. Is generally defined in the HEAD element and then can be called from other scripts or event handlers within the BODY element.
object	Elements (identified by name or ID), element properties, or various objects that are built into JavaScript (the window, frames, navigator, document, location, history, Math, and Date objects). Objects form a hierarchical tree (`window.myform.mybutton.value`, for instance).
array	Allows the assignment of a series (or array) of values to a variable. By combining variables and arrays, complex statements can be created that are similar to records and fields in a database, or rows and columns in a spreadsheet, for instance.
window.open()	A method in JavaScript that opens a new window.
setTimeout()	Sets a delay (in milliseconds) before a specified statement or statements are executed. Short for `window.setTimeout()`.

ONLINE QUIZ

Go to this text's IRC at **www.emcp.com/** and take the online self-check quiz for this chapter.

REVIEW EXERCISES

This section provides some hands-on practice exercises to reinforce the information and material included within this chapter.

1. Open **webdesign_ex.html** in your text editor and save it as **webdesign_practice.html** in the chap11 folder in your working folder or disk. Open **webdesign_practice** in your browser, as well.

2. Review the instructions provided in the "Displaying the Date and Time" section of Chapter 10, *Adding Bells and Whistles*, for inserting date stamps, both the way computers like to output them and the way humans like to read them, in Web pages. Experiment with adding both kinds of date and time stamps.

3. Experiment further with creating pop-up windows, but create your own content instead. Create a short HTML file and then create a link that displays it in a pop-up window. Experiment with setting different window dimensions, and turning on and off the display of various window elements, including the toolbar, status bar, menu bar, location box, directory listing, and scroll bars. Also, experiment with positioning the pop-up window relative to the left and top sides of the browser window.

4. Create a second pop-up window (you can re-use the same HTML file) that automatically closes after a specified period of time (stated in milliseconds).

5. Create a third pop-up window (you can re-use the same HTML file) that contains a link that a user can click on to close the window.

6. Create your own image or find an image that you want to use, and then use the directions provided in this chapter as a guide to create a pop-up window that seamlessly displays the image (without visible margins around the image).

7. Open **scores_ex.html** in your text editor and save it as **scores_practice.html** in the chap11 folder in your working folder or disk. Open **scores_practice** in your browser, as well. Follow the instructions provided in this chapter for creating a table that calculates test scores, displays an average score, and displays the equivalent grade. However, modify the example by changing the student code names and the score numbers. Experiment with changing colors and background colors.

8. For a more challenging exercise, start with the table of grade scores you created in exercise 7, but see if you can figure out how to add a fifth set of test scores to the table. You will need to adjust how the average scores, grade colors, and letter grades are figured, since you will be dealing with five test scores instead of four. You will also need to add an additional column of table cells, both to the initial table code that is provided and to the JavaScript-generated table code. Do not forget to adjust the COLSPAN value in the first row's table cell.

9. Experiment further with creating jump menus. Previously in this chapter, you added a jump menu to the Description page (descript.html) that was automatically generated by an external JavaScript file. Do the same for the other example pages (syllabus.html, materials.html, assignments.html, resources.html, and feedback.html).

10. Visit this chapter's section at the IRC for this book at **www.emcp.com/** and research additional features you can add to Web pages using JavaScript. Visit sites that feature repositories of free JavaScript scripts and find at least two additional scripts you would like to use and then add them to webdesign_practice.html.

WEB-BASED LEARNING ACTIVITIES

In this book's text, Find It icons inserted in the margin highlight the Web addresses of additional resources you might find helpful or informative. To further extend your learning using the Web, you can:

- Visit this book's IRC at **www.emcp.com/** to find additional Web addresses of resources related to the material covered in this chapter that you can further investigate and explore.
- If you are new to working with JavaScript or programming, visit this chapter's section at the IRC for this book to find links to several JavaScript tutorials that are aimed at beginners. Do one or more of the tutorials listed. Create a report that you can share with your fellow students about what you like or do not like about the tutorials you do; highlight what you learned and what you feel you still need to learn.
- If you already have programming experience, look for more advanced JavaScript tutorials that match the abilities and experience you already have. Create a report that you can share with your fellow students about what you like or do not like about the tutorials you do; highlight what you learned and what you feel you still need to learn.
- Look for additional resources and information that add to your understanding and knowledge of the material covered in this chapter. Use Yahoo!, Google, AltaVista, or other directories and search engines to expand your research. When you find a relevant page or site with information or resources you might want to access later, add it to your Favorites (in Internet Explorer) or your Bookmarks (in Netscape or Mozilla).

PROJECTS

These projects can be done in class, in a computer lab, or at home. Use the skills you have developed in this and the previous chapters to create any of the following projects.

Project 1. Incorporate JavaScript into a Web page or site you have already created.

Use JavaScript to enhance a Web page or site you have already created. Use any of the JavaScript examples illustrated in this chapter, such as displaying the date and time a page was last updated, adding links to pop-up windows, formatting a table that does calculations, or adding a jump menu. You also can find an example of using JavaScript rollover buttons in Chapter 9, *Designing with Graphics*, and examples of displaying the current date and time using JavaScript in Chapter 10, *Adding Bells and Whistles*.

Visit this chapter's section at the IRC for this book at **www.emcp.com/** to find links to many more JavaScript examples you can incorporate into your Web page or site.

Incorporate any other Web design features covered in this book that you have mastered or want to gain more experience using.

After creating your Web site, ask at least three classmates to critique your efforts. Incorporate any helpful suggestions they provide.

Project 2. Design a Web page or site from scratch that uses JavaScript scripts.

Design a new Web page or site from scratch that makes use of JavaScript to enhance immediacy, interaction, and navigation. Look for original ways that you can incorporate JavaScript scripts, without simply copying examples covered in this book; add your own originality and style. Visit this chapter's section at the IRC for this book at **www.emcp.com/** and look for links to where you can find additional JavaScript examples you can modify and expand.

Implement any other features or techniques covered in the prior chapters of this book that you feel will enhance your Web page or site.

After creating your Web site, ask at least three classmates to critique your efforts. Incorporate any helpful suggestions they provide.

Working with Dynamic HTML

PERFORMANCE OBJECTIVES

In this chapter, you will learn how to use Dynamic HTML (DHTML) to enhance the effectiveness of your Web page or site, including how to:

- Create a dynamic slide show.
- Create dynamic styles that change in response to mouse actions.
- Create multi-object dynamic effects that are triggered from a single mouse action.
- Dynamically position objects in the browser window.
- Cause objects to appear and disappear within the browser window in response to mouse actions.
- Dynamically move objects within the browser window.
- Create dynamic drop-down menus.

You also will learn how to combine JavaScript, Cascading Style Sheets (CSS), and the Document Object Model (DOM) to create dynamic Web pages using Dynamic HTML.

USING THE EXAMPLE FILES

If you have created a working folder for storing files you create, you will find the example files for this chapter located in the **chap12** folder within your working folder. Because this chapter uses two fairly complex examples, the files for this chapter are further organized in two additional folders, the **slideshow** and **dynamenu** folders, which are located inside the chap12 folder. Save any HTML files you create in this chapter in one or the other of those folders, depending upon which example you are working on.

If you have created a working disk, copy the chap12 folder to your working disk from the **HTML_Examples** folder that you or your instructor downloaded from this book's Internet Resource Center (IRC), or from a CD-R disc or floppy disk provided by your instructor. Save any HTML file you create in this chapter in the chap12 folder that you have copied to your working disk. Alternatively, you can copy the slideshow and dynamenu folders to two separate disks.

INTRODUCTION TO DYNAMIC HTML

The first thing you need to know is that there are no official standards for Dynamic HTML (DHTML). That is because there are no official DHTML specifications. Rather, DHTML is a combination of different standards that can be implemented in concert with each other to create dynamic effects in Web pages. The four principal parts that comprise DHTML are a markup language (HTML, XHTML, and XML), a style sheet language (CSS and XSL), a scripting language (JavaScript and VBScript), and a Document Object Model (DOM). Standards are established for HTML, XHTML, XML, CSS, XSL, and JavaScript (through ECMAScript), and an initial standard DOM (DOM1) has been established by the W3C.

Recent browsers that support DHTML are largely in agreement in their support for the HTML/XHTML, CSS, and JavaScript standards, but differ in the DOM versions they support. Microsoft originally coined the term *Dynamic HTML* when it released Version 4 of its Internet Explorer browser to describe the ability to create dynamic effects in that browser using CSS, JavaScript (or VBScript), and its DOM version. Netscape soon followed suit, releasing its own version called *dynamic HTML*, lowercasing the word "dynamic" to distinguish its version from Microsoft's. Netscape's version relied upon using a proprietary HTML element, the LAYER element, to manipulate document objects. Since then, the W3C has released the first official standard DOM version, which has gained support from most current browsers (including Netscape 6, Opera 6, Mozilla 1, and Internet Explorer 6). These different versions of the DOM are generally referred to as the Microsoft DOM, the Netscape DOM, and the W3C DOM. Table 12.1 shows the support by browsers for these different versions of the DOM.

TABLE 12.1 • *Versions of the Document Object Model (DOM)*

DOM Version	Browser Support
Microsoft DOM	Internet Explorer 4, 5, 5.5, and 6
Netscape DOM	Netscape 4
W3C DOM	Netscape 6 Opera 5 and 6 Mozilla 1 Internet Explorer 5, 5.5, and 6

 NOTE

To view all of the examples presented in this chapter, you should use a browser that supports the W3C DOM. All of the screen captures in this chapter were created using Internet Explorer 6 for Windows.

Understanding What Dynamic HTML Does

Dynamic HTML gives you access to all objects (or nodes) within a document, allowing you to:
- Dynamically change an element's CSS properties.
- Change the z-index (or stacking order) of elements.
- Hide and show elements.
- Position and move elements within a document.
- Let users move elements.
- Re-clip an element's visible area.

Understanding the Three DOM Methods

The different DOM versions, however, implement different methods for accessing document objects. The Microsoft DOM accesses document objects using the document.all method:

```
document.all[object].property
```

The Netscape DOM accesses document objects using the document.layers method:

```
document.layers[object].style.property
```

The W3C DOM accesses document objects using the document.getElementById method:

```
document.getElementById[object].style.property
```

You will be working more with these different DOM methods later in this chapter.

Creating a Cross-Browser DHTML Script

If you want to create DHTML scripts that run in all DHTML-supporting browsers, regardless of the specific DOM they support, you must create scripts that can substitute the correct DOM statements depending on which DOM a browser supports.

The following is an example of an HTML file that uses a series of JavaScript functions to dynamically change the background color of an object within the browser window. Branching routines are included that test for which DOM is supported and then output the correct DOM statements:

```
<!DOCTYPE HTML PUBLIC "-//W3C//DTD HTML 4.01 Transitional//EN"
 "http://www.w3.org/TR/html4/loose.dtd">
<html>
<head>
<title>Change the Object's Background Color</title>
<script language="JavaScript" type="text/javascript">
<!-- start hiding script
function newColor1() {
    if (document.getElementById)
        document.getElementById('object1').style.backgroundColor =
'red';
    else if (document.all)
        document.all.object1.style.backgroundColor = 'red';
    else if (document.layers)
        document.object1.bgColor = 'red';
}
function newColor2() {
    if (document.getElementById)
        document.getElementById('object1').style.backgroundColor =
'blue';
    else if (document.all)
        document.all.object1.style.backgroundColor = 'blue';
    else if (document.layers)
        document.object1.bgColor = 'blue';
}
function newColor3() {
    if (document.getElementById)
        document.getElementById('object1').style.backgroundColor =
'green';
    else if (document.all)
        document.all.object1.style.backgroundColor = 'green';
    else if (document.layers)
        document.object1.bgColor = 'green';
}
```

```
// end hiding script -->
</script>
<style type="text/CSS">
#object1 { position: absolute; left: 250px; top: 100px; width:
300px; height: 200px; z-index: 1; background-color: green;
layer-background-color: green; border: 1px none #000000; }
</style>
</head>
<body>
<p><a href="JavaScript:;" onMouseOver="newColor1()"
onMouseOut="newColor3()">Change Object's Background Color to
Red.</a></p>
<p><a href="JavaScript:;" onMouseOver="newColor2()"
onMouseOut="newColor3()">Change Object's Background Color to
Blue.</a></p>
<div id="object1">
</div>
</body>
</html>
```

NOTE

Notice that the **"JavaScript:;"** is used for the value of the HREF element. Some authors use a # sign here (**href="#"**), but that inserts a # character at the end of the page's address in the browser's Address (or Location) box if the prompt link is clicked on, whereas **href="JavaScript:;"** has no impact on the browser display if the prompt link is clicked on.

The three functions work by first testing to see which DOM is supported by the browser being used. If the W3C DOM is supported, then the appropriate statement is issued. For instance:

```
if (document.getElementById)
    document.getElementById('object1').style.backgroundColor =
'red';
```

If the Internet Explorer DOM is supported, then the appropriate statement is issued. For instance:

```
if (document.all)
    document.all.object1.style.backgroundColor = 'red';
```

If the Netscape DOM is supported, then the appropriate statement is issued. For instance:

```
if (document.layers)
    document.object1.bgColor = 'red';
```

In the document body, onMouseOver event handlers are added to the prompt links, calling the newColor1() and newColor2() functions when the mouse cursor is passed over the links, changing the background color of the "object1" object to a red and a blue color, respectively. Additionally, onMouseOut event handlers are added to the prompt links, calling the newColor3() function when the mouse cursor is passed off of the link, changing the object's background color back to a green color.

This example is available as crossbrowser.html, along with the other example files, in the chap12 folder. If you have both a version of Netscape 4 and Internet Explorer installed, you can test how the script works in both browsers even though they are using different DOMs. The figures for this example have been created using Netscape 4.

You can download and install an earlier version of the Netscape 4 browser at **wp.netscape.com/download/archive.html** to test how your pages will display in that browser. It will not interfere with any later version you may have installed.

If you are using Windows, you can only have one version of Internet Explorer installed at any one time. You will not be able to test your pages on Internet Explorer 3, for instance, if you already have Internet Explorer 6 installed, unless you are running more than one copy of Windows (on separate computers or in separate partitions on the same computer).

The same restriction does not apply to the Macintosh versions of Internet Explorer, where you can have versions of both Internet Explorer 4 and 5, for instance, installed at the same time. On the Macintosh, however, you will need to have an earlier version of Internet Explorer already installed; unlike Netscape, Microsoft does not make earlier versions of its browser available for download.

Test the cross-browser script example:

1. Open **crossbrowser.html** in your browser from the chap12 folder (see Figure 12.1).

initial object background is green

FIGURE 12.1 • *When the page is first loaded, the object's background color is green.*

2. Pass the mouse over the first link ("Change Object's Background Color to Red."). The object's background color is changed to red (see Figure 12.2).

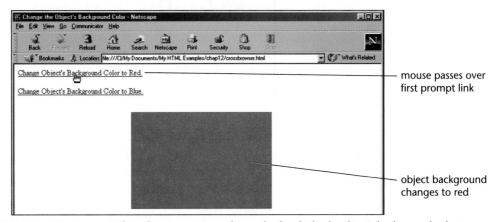

mouse passes over first prompt link

object background changes to red

FIGURE 12.2 • *When the mouse is passed over the first link, the object's background color is changed to red.*

3. Pass the mouse over the second link ("Change Object's Background Color to Blue."). The object's background color is changed to blue (see Figure 12.3).

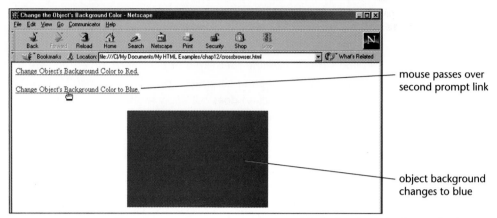

mouse passes over
second prompt link

object background
changes to blue

FIGURE 12.3 • *When the mouse is passed over the second link, the object's background color is changed to blue.*

4. Notice that when the mouse is passed off either of the prompt links, the object's background color is changed back to its original green color (refer to Figure 12.1).
5. Test the example in other browsers you may have installed that include support for DHTML. If you first tested the example using Internet Explorer 6, for instance, you can try testing it in a version of the Netscape 4 browser if you have it installed on your machine.

The previous example is a simple cross-browser DHTML script. If you need to create more sophisticated cross-browser DHTML scripts, several cross-browser APIs (Application Programming Interfaces) are available online, which are scripts that automate specifying browser-specific codes and that can make creating cross-browser scripts more efficient. For links to resources for cross-browser DHTML scripts and APIs, see this chapter's section at the IRC for this book at **www.emcp.com/**.

CASE EXAMPLE: CREATING A DYNAMIC SLIDE SHOW

You can use HTML's TARGET attribute in a link to cause the link's object to be displayed in a specific named frame. You cannot independently control the content of more than one frame in that manner. By using JavaScript and the DOM, however, you can use a mouse event, for instance, to control the contents of multiple frame windows.

Shirley Johnson is experimenting with using Dynamic HTML to add more interactivity and action to her site. She has decided to create a slide show of NASA images that will allow visitors to simply pass the mouse cursor over thumbnail images in a sidebar frame to display the corresponding full-sized images in a second frame (the "main" frame), while at the same time displaying a corresponding caption describing the image in another frame (the "caption" frame).

As stated previously, the example files for this chapter are organized in two separate folders. The example files for this example can be found in the spaceshow folder that is included inside the chap12 folder.

To start working with this example:

1. Open **spaceshow_ex.html** in your text editor from the spaceshow folder in your working folder or disk.
2. Save spaceshow_ex.html as **spaceshow.html** in the slideshow folder.
3. Open **spaceshow.html** in your Web browser from the chap12 folder.

The example page, spaceshow.html, only contains an empty FRAMESET element, so you will not see anything in your browser when you open the page in your browser.

CREATING THE FRAME LAYOUT FOR THE SLIDE SHOW

A frame layout is ideal for creating a slide show, because the objects or links that direct the show can remain visible at all times within their own frame window, while the pages containing the images that compose the show can be shown in their own separate window. A third frame window also can be employed to display the caption text that describes each image in the show.

Create a frame layout for the slide show:

1. Define the characteristics for the top-level frameset, specifying an initial two-column layout, with the first column set to a width of 160 pixels and the second column set to expand or contract along with the browser window:

```
<!DOCTYPE HTML PUBLIC "-//W3C//DTD HTML 4.01 Frameset//EN"
  "http://www.w3.org/TR/html4/frameset.dtd">
<html>
<head>
<meta http-equiv="Content-Type" content="text/html; charset=ISO-
8859-1">
<title>Shirley Johnson's Space Slide Show</title>
</head>
<frameset cols="160,*">
<noframes>
<h3>A frames-compatible browser is required to view this page.
Please visit the <a href="noframes.html">non-frames version</a>
of this site.</h3>
</noframes>
</frameset>
</html>
```

2. Inside the top-level frameset, create the first two columns for the layout, including a FRAME element to contain the sidebar page (sidebar.html) for the first column, as well as a FRAMESET element into which you will later be inserting the "main" and "caption" frames:

```
<frameset cols="160,*">
  <frame src="sidebar.html" name="sidebar" marginheight="0"
marginwidth="10px">
```

```
<frameset>
</frameset>
<noframes>
<h3>A frames-compatible browser is required to view this page.
Please visit the <a href="noframes.html">non-frames version</a>
of this site.</h3>
</noframes>
</frameset>
```

3. Set the nested frameset to contain two rows and then add two FRAME elements to form the rows, composing the "main" and "caption" frames for the layout:

```
<frameset cols="160,*">
  <frame src="sidebar.html" name="sidebar" marginheight="0"
marginwidth="10px">
  <frameset rows="*,30">
    <frame src="main.html" name="main" scrolling="no">
    <frame src="caption.html" name="caption" scrolling="no"
marginheight: "0">
  </frameset>
```

NOTE

The three pages that are linked to in the frameset page (sidebar.html, main.html, and caption.html) have already been created for you and are included with the example files for this example.

4. Save your file, switch over to your browser, and refresh the display of the page (see Figure 12.4).

FIGURE 12.4 • The three-frame layout features "sidebar," "main," and "caption" frame windows.

PRE-LOADING THE SLIDE SHOW IMAGES

Example pages that display the full-size slide show images have already been created for you and are included with the example files for this example. Currently, the thumbnail images displayed in the "sidebar" frame are set up as image links that can be clicked on to display the corresponding full-size images in the "main" frame. In this example, however, you also will be setting up the thumbnail images so that simply passing the mouse over an image causes the corresponding full-size image to be displayed in the "main" frame. To avoid a noticeable delay between when the mouse first passes over a thumbnail image and when the corresponding full-size image is displayed, you must pre-load the images that will be displayed in the "main" frame window.

Add a JavaScript script to the initial page, caption.html, which is displayed in the "caption" frame:

1. In your text editor, open **caption.html** from the chap12\spaceshow folder and edit it as follows to add a script to preload the images and assign them to variables:

```
</style>
<script language="JavaScript" type="text/javascript">
<!-- start hiding script
img1=new Image();
    img1.src="spacecapsules.jpg";
img2=new Image();
    img2.src="flagonmoon2.jpg";
img3=new Image();
    img3.src="apollo_soyuz.jpg";
img4=new Image();
    img4.src="shuttle_launch.jpg";
// end hiding script -->
</script>
</head>
```

2. Resave your file.

If you are pre-loading more than just of a handful of images, JavaScript scripts are available on the Web that will display a progress bar or other indicator that images are being pre-loaded. For links to resources that provide more sophisticated pre-loading scripts to use in your pages, see this chapter's section at the IRC for this book at **www.emcp.com/**.

CREATING THE SLIDE SHOW EFFECTS

Currently, the thumbnail images are set up as image links which, when clicked, load the specified image in the "main" frame. A more dynamic effect is to have the mouse passing over a thumbnail image cause the corresponding full-size image to be displayed in the "main" frame. For added feedback, you also can have the same mouse-over action trigger the display of an appropriate caption in the "caption" frame.

Changing the Caption Text

Currently, the caption text reads "Click the mouse on the thumbnails in the sidebar.", which would be fine if you only want the user to click on a thumbnail image to display a full-sized image in the "main" window. Enabling the user to simply pass the mouse over a thumbnail image to display its full-sized image, however, is not only a more dynamic effect, but requires less effort from the user.

Some earlier browsers, however, do not support mouse-over effects. For those browsers, it would be helpful to have the first caption text remain, prompting users of those browsers to click on the thumbnail images to see their full-sized images, while another caption, reading, "Pass the mouse cursor over the thumbnails in the sidebar.", would be visible to users of browsers that do support mouse-over effects. To do that, you can use the display style property to hide the first caption from browsers that support mouse-over effects, while browsers that do not support them will display the first caption. This works because the same browsers that do not support mouse-over effects also do not support the display style property.

Edit caption.html so that the current caption is hidden from browsers that support the display style property, while displaying a different caption for browsers that support the display style property:

1. In your text editor, open **caption.html** from the chap12\spaceshow folder.
2. Create a style using a class selector that will hide elements belonging to the specified class:

```
.hideme { display: none; }
</style>
```

3. Add a CLASS attribute to the caption's paragraph element that includes it in the "hideme" class:

```
<p align="center" class="hideme">Click the mouse on the
thumbnails in the sidebar.</p>
</body>
```

4. Save your file, switch to your browser, and refresh the display of your page. As shown in Figure 12.5, the caption is now hidden from browsers that support the display style property.

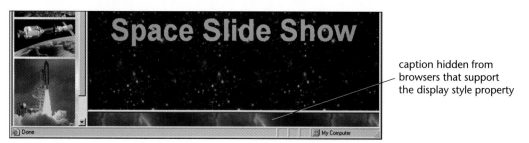

caption hidden from browsers that support the display style property

FIGURE 12.5 • *The initial caption text is now hidden from browsers that support the display style property.*

5. Add another caption to caption.html that tells users of browsers that support the display property to pass the mouse cursor over the thumbnail images.

```
<p align="center" class="hideme">Click the mouse on the
thumbnails in the sidebar.</p>
<p align="center">Pass the mouse cursor over the thumbnails in
the sidebar.</p>
```

6. Save your file, switch to your browser, and refresh the display of the page (see Figure 12.6).

new caption displayed for
browsers that support the
display style property

FIGURE 12.6 • *In browsers that support the display style property, a different caption is displayed, while the initial caption is hidden from view.*

The first caption (telling the user to click on the thumbnail images) is hidden from users of browsers that support the display style property, with a second caption (telling the user to pass the mouse over the thumbnail images) moved up and displayed in its place. For users of browsers that do not support the display property, the second caption falls below the bottom margin of the "caption" frame and is thus hidden from the view of those users.

Creating the Mouse-Over Effect

You can use the onMouseOver event handler to cause one or more effects to occur when the mouse cursor is passed over an image or other object.

Set up the first thumbnail image, spacecapsules_th.jpg, so that passing the mouse over the image causes new pages to be displayed in the "main" and "caption" frames:

1. In your text editor, open **sidebar.html** from the chap12\spaceshow folder and edit it as shown here:

```
<p><a href="main1.html" target="main"
onMouseOver="parent.frames[1].location.href='main1.html';
parent.frames[2].location.href='caption1.html'; return true;">
<img src="spacecapsules_th.jpg" border="0" width="130" height="108"
alt="Space Capsules"></a></p>
```

2. Save the file, switch to your browser, and refresh the display of the page.
3. Pass the mouse cursor over the top thumbnail image in the sidebar. A new page, main1.html, displaying the full-sized image, spacecapsules.jpg, should be displayed in the "main" frame (see Figure 12.7).

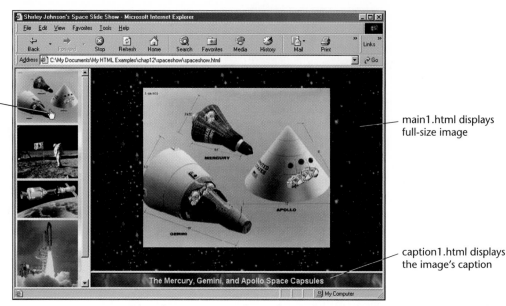

mouse passes over
first thumbnail image

main1.html displays
full-size image

caption1.html displays
the image's caption

The Mercury, Gemini, and Apollo Space Capsules

FIGURE 12.7 • *When the mouse is passed over the top thumbnail image, new pages, main1.html and caption1.html, are displayed in the "main" and "caption" frames.*

In the previous example, the document hierarchy is referenced to create the actions:

- The **parent** code references the current document's parent object (the frameset page, spaceshow.html).
- The **frames[1]** and **frames[2]** codes reference frame objects (FRAME elements) that are located in the frameset page (the parent object). Frame objects are numbered from 0, so the first frame object is **frames[0]** (the "sidebar" frame), the second is **frames[1]** (the "main" frame), and the third is **frames[2]** (the "caption" frame).
- The **location.href='main1.html'** code specifies the URL of the file to be displayed in the specified frame.
- The onMouseOver event handler is applied to the A element, not to the IMG element, so that the effect will also work in the Netscape 4 browsers, which only recognize event handlers that are applied to the A element, but not to the IMG or other elements.
- A **border="0"** attribute value is set for the thumbnail images' IMG elements, so that they will not be outlined with a "link" border. Alternatively, you could apply a style (**style="text-decoration: none"**, for instance) to the IMG elements.

Creating the Mouse-Out Effect

You can use the onMouseOut event handler to cause main.html and caption.html to redisplay in the "main" and "caption" frames when the mouse cursor is passed off of a thumbnail image.

Add an onMouseOut event handler that redisplays the original content of the "main" and "caption" frames when the mouse cursor is passed off of the top thumbnail image:

1. Edit the example, adding an onMouseOut event handler:

```
<p><a href="main1.html" target="main"
onMouseOver="parent.frames[1].location.href='main1.html';
parent.frames[2].location.href='caption1.html'; return true;"
```

```
onMouseOut="parent.frames[1].location.href='main.html';
parent.frames[2].location.href='caption.html'; return true;">
<img src="spacecapsules_th.jpg" border="0" width="130" height="108"
alt="Space Capsules"></a></p>
```

2. Save the file, switch over to your browser, and refresh the display of the page. The frameset should now be returned to its initial state, with main.html and caption.html displayed in the "main" and "caption" frames (as shown previously in Figure 12.6).

For current browsers, such as Internet Explorer 6 or Mozilla 1, for instance, you can add the onMouseOver and onMouseOut event handlers to either the A element or the IMG element. The mouse-over and mouse-out effects, however, only work in the Netscape 4 browsers if they are added to the A element, instead of to the IMG element.

Creating the Remaining Mouse Effects

You create the mouse-over and mouse-out effects for the other thumbnail images in exactly the same way as you did for the first thumbnail image, except that the resulting pages that are displayed in the "main" and "caption" frames are different.

practice To gain additional practice, using the first thumbnail image effect as a guide, create mouse-over and mouse-out effects for the other three thumbnail images:

1. Use an onMouseOver event handler to cause main2.html and caption2.html to be displayed in the "main" and "caption" frames when the mouse is passed over the second thumbnail image. In your browser, pass the mouse over the second thumbnail image to test the mouse-over effect (see Figure 12.8).

mouse passes over second thumbnail image

main2.html displays full-size image

caption2.html displays the image's caption

FIGURE 12.8 • *When the mouse is passed over the second thumbnail image, new pages, main2.html and caption2.html, should now be displayed in the "main" and "caption" frames.*

2. Use an onMouseOver event handler to cause main3.html and caption3.html to be displayed in the "main" and "caption" frames when the mouse is passed over the third thumbnail image.

3. Use an onMouseOver event handler to cause main4.html and caption4.html to be displayed in the "main" and "caption" frames when the mouse is passed over the fourth thumbnail image.
4. Use an onMouseOut event handler to cause main.html and caption.html to be redisplayed in the "main" and "caption" frames when the mouse is passed off any of the last three remaining thumbnail images.
5. Test each thumbnail image by passing the mouse over and then off of it.

USING DYNAMIC STYLES

Microsoft originally coined the term *dynamic styles* to denote a set of methods for dynamically altering the style properties of document elements in response to user actions or system events. Dynamic styles are supported in most recent browsers, with the exception of the Netscape 4 browsers.

The two methods for applying dynamic styles to an element are to use class selectors to define the dynamic style characteristics or to apply the dynamic styles directly to the elements.

Setting Dynamic Styles Using Class Selectors

In the following example, you will use class selectors to define and apply dynamic style characteristics to an element.

Create two dynamic styles that change the display characteristics of the H2 element when the mouse is passed over and then off of the element:

1. In your text editor, open **main.html** from the chap12\spaceshow folder.
2. Create two class-selectors, .over1 and .over2, that specify the display characteristics for the mouse-over and mouse-off effects:

```
.over1 { color: fuchsia; background: navy url(back_nebula.jpg);
font-family: Impact, Arial, Helvetica, sans-serif; font-weight:
bold; font-size: 85px; text-align: center; margin-top: 56px;
width: 90%; margin-left: auto; margin-right: auto; border: 1px
white solid; }
.off1 { color: aqua; background: transparent; font-family: "Comic
Sans MS", Arial, Helvetica, sans-serif; font-weight: bold; font-
size: 62px; text-align: center; margin-top: 56px; width: 90%;
margin-left: auto; margin-right: auto; border-bottom: 3px lime
ridge; }
</style>
```

3. Add onMouseOver and onMouseOut event handlers to the H2 element that will switch in the "over1" class name when the mouse passes over the element and the "out1" class name when the mouse passes off of the element:

```
<h2 onMouseOver="this.className = 'over1'"
onMouseOut="this.className = 'off1'">Shirley Johnson's</h2>
<h1>Space Slide Show</h1>
```

4. Save the file, switch over to your browser, and refresh the display of the page.

5. Pass the mouse over the H2 element's text ("Shirley Johnson's"). The display characteristics of the element should be switched to those defined for the "over1" class (see Figure 12.9).

mouse passes over
H2 element

FIGURE 12.9 • *The H2 element's display characteristics are switched to those defined for the "over1" class when the mouse is passed over it.*

6. Pass the mouse off the H2 element. The display characteristics of the element should be switched to those defined for the "out1" class (see Figure 12.10).

mouse passes off of
H2 element

FIGURE 12.10 • *The H2 element's display characteristics are switched to those defined for the "out1" class when the mouse is passed off of it.*

In the **this.className** code used in the previous example, **this** is a keyword that references the current object (the H2 element, in this case), while **className = 'over1'** references the CLASS attribute of the current object and swaps in "over1" as the value (same as setting a **class="over1"** attribute value for the H2 element).

Applying Dynamic Style Characteristics Directly to an Element

You also can apply dynamic style characteristics directly to an element, without first creating a class selector.

Apply dynamic styles directly to the H1 element ("Space Slide Show"):

1. Add onMouseOver and onMouseOut event handlers to the H1 element that directly switch in different display characteristics when the mouse is passed over or off of the element:

```
<h1 onMouseOver="this.style.color = 'blue'; this.style.background
= 'yellow';" onMouseOut="this.style.color = 'lime';
this.style.background = 'transparent';">Space Slide Show</h1>
```

2. Save the file, switch to your browser, and refresh the display of your page.
3. Pass the mouse over the H1 element's text ("Space Slide Show"). The foreground and background colors for the element should be switched to blue and yellow (see Figure 12.11).

mouse passes over
H1 element

FIGURE 12.11 • *The H1 element's foreground and background colors are changed when the mouse passes over the element.*

In this case, the **this.style.color = 'blue'** code, for instance, sets the color style property of the current element to a "blue" value.

Because they are not allowed in statements, you cannot use hyphens when directly applying style characteristics to elements. For instance, the following will not work:

```
this.style.margin-bottom = '10px'
```

Instead, you need to use an uppercase letter to indicate where the hyphen is located in a style property name. For instance, the following will work (at least in browsers that support dynamic styles):

```
this.style.marginBottom = '10px'
```

The following are some examples of how to refer to other hyphenated style property names:

```
background-image = backgroundImage
background-attachment = backgroundAttachment
font-family = fontFamily
font-style = fontStyle
font-weight = fontWeight
```

```
line-height = lineHeight
list-style-image = listStyleImage
padding-top = paddingTop
text-align = textAlign
z-index = zIndex
```

The second method (direct application of dynamic styles) is primarily useful for switching in a few display characteristics for a single instance of an element, because full statements (**this.style.color = 'blue'**, for instance) have to be expressed for each style characteristic you want to change and they have to be repeated for each instance of an element in which you want them to have effect.

To apply a larger assortment of display characteristics to be activated in response to mouse actions, use the first method, which uses class selectors to define the display characteristics to be switched in.

practice

To gain additional practice setting dynamic styles, do the following:

1. Delete the direct dynamic styles you set in the H1 element, as shown here:

```
<h1 onMouseOver="this.style.color = 'blue';
this.style.background = 'yellow';" onMouseOut="this.style.color
= 'lime'; this.style.background = 'transparent';">Space Slide
Show</h1>
```

2. Using the .over1 class sector as a guide, create a second class selector, .over2, in the style sheet that defines these display characteristics:

> color: purple
> background: aqua url(back_clouds.jpg)
> font-family: Impact, Arial, Helvetica, sans-serif
> font-size: 65px
> text-align: center
> margin-top: 56px
> width: 90%
> margin-left: auto
> margin-right: auto

3. Using the H2 element as a guide, add an onMouseOver event handler to the H1 element that switches it to the .over2 class when the mouse is passed over the element.

4. Save the file, switch to your browser, and refresh the display of your page. Pass the mouse over the H1 element ("Space Slide Show"). The display characteristics should be switched to those you defined for the .over2 class selector (see Figure 12.12).

mouse passes over
H1 element

FIGURE 12.12 • *When the mouse passes over the H1 element, the display characteristics are switched to those defined for the .over2 class selector.*

5. Using the .out1 class sector as a guide, create a second class selector, .out2, in the style sheet that defines these display characteristics:

> color: #ffcc66
> background: transparent
> font-family: Arial, Helvetica, sans-serif
> font-size: 62px
> text-align: center
> margin-top: 62px
> width: 95%
> margin-left: auto
> margin-right: auto
> padding-bottom: 5px
> border: 3px ridge aqua

6. Using the H2 element as a guide, add an onMouseOut event handler to the H1 element that switches it to the .out2 class when the mouse is passed over the element.

7. Save the file, switch to your browser, and refresh the display of your page. First pass the mouse over the H1 element ("Space Slide Show"), and then pass the mouse off of the element. When the mouse is passed off of the H1 element, the display characteristics should be switched to those you defined for the .out2 class selector (see Figure 12.13).

mouse passes off of the H1 element

FIGURE 12.13 • *When the mouse passes off of the H1 element, the display characteristics are switched to those defined for the .out2 class selector.*

8. Copy and paste the .over1, .out1, .over2, and .out2 styles and then comment out one of the copies (using /* and */). In the copy that is not commented out, experiment further with setting different or new display characteristics.

TRIGGERING DYNAMIC EFFECTS

You can create some nice effects using dynamic styles, but you cannot apply an effect to an element other than the element in which the mouse action takes place. You cannot, for instance, pass the mouse over one element to cause a change in another element. To do that, you need to access the DOM more directly.

NOTE The following examples focus on using the W3C DOM, which is the standard DOM that all current browsers should support. These examples, however, will not work in Internet Explorer 4 or Netscape 4, which support separate proprietary versions of the DOM (the IE and Netscape DOMs).

When incorporating DHTML scripts into your pages and sites, you must decide whether you need to support one DOM method (the W3C DOM) or all three DOM methods. If you choose not to support all three DOM methods, the percentage of users of the affected browsers is relatively small and will only continue to diminish in the future. One of the Web Standard Project's methods can easily be used to alert or redirect users of browsers that do not support the W3C DOM.

You might have a client, however, that requires you to support all browsers, from the "version 4" browsers up. In that case, you must implement scripts that can shuffle DOM methods, depending on a browser's DOM support. A basic example of that method was shown earlier in the "Creating a Cross-Browser DHTML Script" section of this chapter. In this chapter's section at the IRC for this book at **www.emcp.com/** you can also find links to additional DHTML resources focused on using the different DOM methods.

Creating a Multi-Object Mouse-Over Effect

You can create DHTML scripts that define display characteristics for multiple objects that can be triggered by a single mouse-over action.

Create a mouse-over effect that changes display characteristics of the document body, the "myname" object, and the "mytitle" object:

1. Open **spaceshow.html** in your text editor and edit it as follows:

```
<frameset cols="160,*">
   <frame src="sidebar2.html" name="sidebar" marginheight="0"
marginwidth="10px">
   <frameset rows="*,30">
      <frame src="mainshow.html" name="main" scrolling="no">
      <frame src="caption.html" name="caption" scrolling="no"
marginheight: "0">
   </frameset>
```

2. Resave the file as **spaceshow2.html** in the chap12\spaceshow folder. Switch to your browser and open **spaceshow2.html**.
3. Open **mainshow_ex.html** in your text editor and resave it as **mainshow.html** in the chap12\spaceshow folder. Edit **mainshow.html**, as shown here:

```
<title>Space Slide Show</title>
<script language="JavaScript" type="text/javascript">
<!-- start hiding script
isW3 = (document.getElementById) ? true : false;
if (!isW3) {
parent.frames[1].location.href='nodom.html';
}
// end hiding script -->
</script>
```

NOTE The previous script example checks to determine whether the browser being used supports the W3C's DOM. If not, a substitute page, nodom.html, is displayed in the "main" window. If the W3C's DOM is supported, the current page, mainshow.html, is displayed.

4. Create a function, Change1(), which specifies object properties to be called in response to a mouse action:

```
<!-- start hiding script
isW3 = (document.getElementById) ? true : false;
if (!isW3) {
parent.frames[1].location.href='nodom.html';
}

function Change1() {
    w0 = document.getElementById('mypage').style;
        w0.background = 'url(back_nebula.jpg) #333300';
    w1 = document.getElementById('myname').style;
        w1.color = 'fuchsia';
        w1.background = 'url(starcluster.jpg) black';
        w1.marginTop = '25px';
```

```
        w2 = document.getElementById('mytitle').style;
            w2.color = 'maroon';
            w2.background = 'url(back_clouds.jpg) #ccffff';
    }
    // end hiding script -->
    </script>
```

NOTE

Notice that the first part of the object statements
(`document.getElementById('`*objectname*`').style`) is assigned to a variable (w0, w1, or w2), so it can be repeated by inserting the variable. Otherwise, you would have to rekey the entire phrase for every style property value you want to assign to the function.

NOTE

Notice that both a background image and a background color are specified for the background property. Whenever specifying a background image for an element, you should also specify a background color that is similar in color and tonality to the most common colors in the background image. That is because some surfers have the display of images turned off in their browsers—those surfers will see the background color you specify instead of the background image.

5. In the body of the document, add an onMouseOver event handler that calls the Change1() function:

```
<body id="mypage">
<div id="myname" onMouseOver="Change1()">
Shirley Johnson's
</div>
<div id="mytitle">
Space Slide Show
</div>
```

6. Save the file, switch to your browser, and refresh the display of the page. Pass the mouse cursor over the first DIV element ("Shirley Johnson's"). In response, display properties for both DIV elements are changed to those defined in the Change1() function (see Figure 12.14).

FIGURE 12.14 • *When the mouse is passed over the top element, the display properties for three different elements are changed.*

Adding Padding and Borders

As has been mentioned previously in this book, Internet Explorer 5.5 for Windows has a bug that causes it to miscalculate the width or height of an element if borders or padding are included in the element—it calculates the element's width or height as including, rather than excluding, any borders or padding that are defined for the element. When using the W3C DOM to set style properties for elements, you also need to be aware of this bug. One solution to this problem is to include any borders or padding you want to define for an element within a nested DIV element. In this example, for instance, DIV elements are used, rather than the H1 and H2 elements that were used in the previous example—this is necessary because you are not allowed to nest a block element inside an H1 or H2 element.

Set widths for the "myname" and "mytitle" objects and use nested divisions to set padding and borders for those objects:

1. Nest two new divisions ("padname" and "padtitle") for which padding and borders can be defined:

```
<body id="mypage">
<div id="myname" onMouseOver="Change1()">
<div id="padname">
Shirley Johnson's
</div>
</div>
<div id="mytitle">
<div id="padtitle">
Space Slide Show
</div>
</div>
```

2. Add statements to the Change1() function that define padding and borders for the "padname" and "padtitle" divisions, as well as additional display characteristics for the "myname" and "mytitle" divisions:

```
function Change1() {
    w0 = document.getElementById('mypage').style;
        w0.background = 'url(back_nebula.jpg) #333300';
    w1 = document.getElementById('myname').style;
        w1.color = 'fuchsia';
        w1.background = 'url(starcluster.jpg) black';
        w1.marginTop = '25px';
        w1.width = '75%';
    w1a = document.getElementById('padname').style;
        w1a.padding = '10px';
        w1a.border = 'red 4px groove';
    w2 = document.getElementById('mytitle').style;
        w2.color = 'maroon';
        w2.background = 'url(back_clouds.jpg) #ccffff';
        w2.fontSize = '44px';
        w2.width = '80%';
    w2a = document.getElementById('padtitle').style;
        w2a.padding = '5px';
        w2a.border = 'lime 4px ridge';
}
```

3. Save the file, switch to your browser, and refresh the display of the page. Pass the mouse over the top division ("Shirley Johnson's"). The two document divisions should now display the borders, padding, and other display characteristics that you set in Step 2 (see Figure 12.15).

padding and borders are added to "myname" and "mytitle" objects

FIGURE 12.15 • *Padding and borders are displayed as part of the mouse-over effect.*

Creating a Multi-Object Mouse-Out Effect

You create a mouse-out effect that triggers changes in multiple objects in exactly the same way you created the previous mouse-over effect.

Create a mouse-out effect that triggers display changes in the "mypage," "myname," and "mytitle" objects:

1. Create a second function, Change2(), that changes the background images displayed in "mypage," "myname," and "mytitle" objects when the function is called:

```
function Change2() {
    w0 = document.getElementById('mypage').style;
        w0.background = 'url(starcluster.jpg) black';
    w1 = document.getElementById('myname').style;
        w1.background = 'url(back_nebula.jpg) #333300';
    w2 = document.getElementById('mytitle').style;
        w2.background = 'url(back_aqua.jpg) aqua';
}
// end hiding script -->
</script>
```

2. Add an onMouseOut event handler to the "mytitle" division that calls the Change2() function:

```
<body id="mypage">
<div id="myname" onMouseOver="Change1()" onMouseOut="Change2()">
```

3. Save the file, switch to your browser, and refresh the display of your page. Pass the mouse over the "myname" object ("Shirley Johnson's") and then pass it back off again. When the mouse is passed off of the object, the background images of the "mypage," "myname," and "mytitle" objects are changed (see Figure 12.16).

mouse moves off "myname" object

FIGURE 12.16 • *When the mouse is passed off of the "myname" object ("Shirley Johnson's"), the background images are changed for all three objects ("mypage," "myname," and "mytitle").*

Positioning and Revealing Objects

You also can create mouse effects that position or reposition objects and cause invisible objects to become visible within the browser window.

Position two invisible objects in the browser window, create a function that makes them visible, and then add an onMouseOver event handler that calls the function:

1. Add two objects to the page:

```
<div id="mytitle">
<div id="padtitle">
Space Slide Show
</div>
</div>
<div id="object1">
</div>
<div id="object2">
</div>
```

2. Define two ID-selector styles for the new objects (with both objects set as hidden):

```
#object1 { position: absolute; top: 350px; left: 50px;
visibility: hidden; background: #ffffcc; border: 3px blue groove;
z-index: 1; height: 20px; width: 556px;
/* Start Box Model Hacks  - Required for Internet Explorer 5.5 */
voice-family: "\"}\""; voice-family: inherit; height: 14px;
width: 550px; }
html>body #object1 { height: 14px; width: 550px }
/* End Box Model Hack */
#object2 { position: absolute; top: 50px; left: 125px;
visibility: hidden; background: aqua url(back_clouds.jpg);
padding: 10px; border: 6px lime ridge; z-index: 2; height: 250px;
width: 162px;
/* Start Box Model Hack  - Required for Internet Explorer 5.5 */
voice-family: "\"}\""; voice-family: inherit; height: 238px;
width: 150px; }
```

```
html>body #object2 { height: 238px; width: 150px; }
/* End Box Model Hack */
</style>
```

3. Create a new function, Change3(), which reveals the hidden objects and sets the position and stacking order of the "myname" and "mytitle" objects:

```
function Change3() {
    w1 = document.getElementById('myname').style;
        w1.position = 'absolute';
        w1.top = '50px';
        w1.left = '50px';
        w1.textAlign = 'left';
        w1.zIndex = '3';
    w2 = document.getElementById('mytitle').style;
        w2.position = 'absolute';
        w2.top = '200px';
        w2.right = '50px';
        w2.zIndex = '4';
        w2.width = '300px';
    w4 = document.getElementById('object1').style;
        w4.visibility = "visible";
    w5 = document.getElementById('object2').style;
        w5.visibility = "visible";
}
// end hiding script -->
</script>
```

4. Add an onMouseOver event handler to the "mytitle" object that calls the Change3() function:

```
<div id="mytitle" onMouseOver="Change3()">
<div id="padtitle">
Space Slide Show
</div>
</div>
```

5. Save the file, switch to your browser, and refresh the display of the page. Pass the mouse over and off of the "myname" object. Next, pass the mouse over the "mytitle" object ("Space Slide Show"). The two original objects should be repositioned in the browser window and two new, previously hidden, objects should now be stacked behind the original objects (see Figure 12.17).

"object1" object

"object2" object

mouse moves over "mytitle" object

FIGURE 12.17 • *When the mouse is passed over the "mytitle" object ("Space Slide Show"), two previously hidden objects are displayed behind the "mytitle" and "myname" objects.*

Animating Objects

Not only can you create DHTML effects that cause objects to appear and disappear in the browser window, but you also can create animation effects that cause objects to move within the browser window.

Create a DHTML effect that causes the "object1" and "object2" objects to move diagonally across and off the page:

1. Add the following script to the document's HEAD element:

```
// end hiding script -->
</script>
<script language="JavaScript" type="text/javascript">
<!-- start hiding script
var xp1 = 50;
var yp1 = 350;
var xp2 = 125;
var yp2 = 50;
var a = -2;
var b = 2;

function moveobj() {
if(xp1 <= -600) {
    xp1 = 0;
    }
if(yp1 > 600) {
    yp1 = 0;
    }
if(xp2 > 600) {
    xp1 = 0;
    }
if(yp2 <= -600) {
    yp1 = 0;
    }
```

```
xp1 = xp1 + 2 * a;
yp1 = yp1 + 2 * a;
xp2 = xp2 + 2 * b;
yp2 = yp2 + 2 * b;

document.getElementById("object1").style.left = xp1 + "px";
document.getElementById("object1").style.top = yp1 + "px";
document.getElementById("object2").style.left = xp2 + "px";
document.getElementById("object2").style.top = yp2 + "px";

if ( xp1 <= -400 ) {
    document.getElementById('object1').style.display = 'none';
    document.getElementById('object2').style.display = 'none';
    }
else {
    window.setTimeout("moveobj();",100);
    }
}

// end hiding script -->
</script>
<style type="text/css">
```

2. Save your file, switch to your browser, and refresh the display of your page. Pass the mouse over the "myname" object ("Shirley Johnson's") and pass the mouse over the "mytitle" object ("Space Slide Show").
3. Pass the mouse off of the "mytitle" object. You should see the two background objects ("object1" and "object2") moving diagonally in opposite directions on the screen (see Figure 12.18) until they exit the browser window.

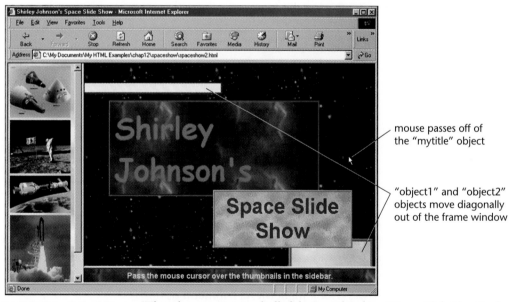

mouse passes off of the "mytitle" object

"object1" and "object2" objects move diagonally out of the frame window

FIGURE 12.18 • *When the mouse is passed off of the "mytitle" object ("Space Slide Show"), the two background objects move diagonally across the screen in opposite directions.*

This is a fairly complex example, so some explanatory comments are in order:
• The first part of the script sets a number of variables, which are used as initial values later in the script.

- The xp1 and yp1 variables set the starting *x* and *y* coordinates of the "object1" object, while the xp2 and yp2 variables set the starting *x* and *y* coordinates of the "object2" object. These coordinate positions are the same that are set for the left and top style properties for those objects.

- The *a* and *b* variables set the direction of the movement. A negative value of 2 is set for the *a* variable, for instance, which can be used to negatively increment either the *x* or the *y* coordinate for an object. By increasing the value (positive or negative), you can increase the amount that the coordinate positions are incremented in each loop.

- The moveobj() function is called to start the animation. It uses IF statements to set ranges for the coordinate values, within which the animation continues, but beyond which it ceases.

- Following the IF statements, a series of expressions set how the coordinate values are incremented. For instance, `xp1 = xp1 + 2 * a` increments the value assigned to the xp1 variable on each loop of the moveobj() function, adding 2 to it, and then multiplying the result by the value of the *a* variable. In this case, the *x* coordinate of the "object1" object is increased by 2 and then multiplied by −2, which when applied in the following part of the script, causes the object to be moved to the left along its *x* axis.

- The next part of the script lists a series of statements that use the incremented coordinate value to reposition the object in each loop of the function. Note that the variable for the coordinate value is followed by a plus sign and a "px" text string (`style.left = xp1 + "px"`). That is because the xp1 variable value is an integer (which can be incremented), while the resulting value of the concatenation is a text string (`350px`, for instance, which cannot be incremented).

- The final part of the function is an IF/ELSE conditional statement that determines whether the loop will continue or end. In this case, it checks to determine whether the value of the object's *x* coordinate is less than or equal to −400. If it is, the display property value for both objects is set to **none**. If the value of the object's *x* coordinate, however, is not less than or equal to −400, the loop continues.

- The ELSE branch that continues the loop uses JavaScript's window.setTimeout method to set a delay, in nanoseconds, before the loop is continued (by recalling the moveobj() function). To speed up the progress of the objects' movement, just decrease the numerical value (from 100 to 10 nanoseconds, for instance).

CASE EXAMPLE: CREATING A DYNAMIC DROP-DOWN MENU

In the previous example, you worked with hiding and then turning on the visibility of objects in the browser window. In this example, you will create a dynamic menu that displays submenu options when the mouse passes over the menu's main options. You will also create a second level of submenu options that is displayed when the mouse passes over a higher-level submenu option.

Ruth Clearwater has included a ribbon menu at the top of the page she has created for the Web Design Fundamentals *course she is teaching. The menu links to administration and department pages that have been set up by her school. She has decided to experiment with using DHTML to turn the ribbon menu into a dynamic drop-down menu, with additional submenu options dropping down when the mouse is passed over the main ribbon menu options.*

As stated previously, the example files for this chapter are organized in two separate folders. The files for this example can be found in the dynamenu folder that is included inside the chap12 folder.

To start working with this example:

1. Open **dynamenu_ex.html** in your text editor from the dynamenu folder in your working folder or disk.
2. Save dynamenu_ex.html as **dynamenu.html** in the dynamenu folder.
3. Open **dynamenu.html** in your Web browser from the chap12 folder.

This example is similar to the example you created in Chapter 11, *Working with JavaScript*, except that the ribbon menu is not centered, but left-aligned, and the pop-up window links and jump menu example have been removed.

Adding a Drop-Down Menu to the Page

Adding a drop-down menu to the page involves several steps, including creating a JavaScript function that toggles the visibility of the drop-down menus object on and off, adding onMouseOver and onMouseOut event handlers that call the function, and adding the actual drop-down menus to the page.

Create a function, event handlers, and drop-down menu elements:

1. Create a JavaScript function in the HEAD element that toggles the visibility of objects on and off:

```
<script language="JavaScript"> type="javascript">
<!-- start hiding script
isW3 = (document.getElementById) ? true : false;
if (!isW3) {
    document.location.href='webdesign_alt.html';
}
function showHide(id, toggle) {
    eval("document.getElementById(id).style.visibility = \"" +
toggle + "\"");
}
// end hiding script -->
</script>
</head>
```

Notice that the showHide() function defines two parameters (id and toggle) that allow values to be passed to it. JavaScript's built-in eval function is then used to evaluate the following string, substituting the variable values (id and toggle) where indicated. Note the two backward slash characters, which are used to escape the following double-quote marks.

2. Create the objects for the drop-down menus ("menu1," "menu2," and so on):

```
<a href="dummy.html"><span>Contact</span></a>
</p>

<div class="dropmnu">
```

```
<div id="menu1" class="mnuform"
onMouseOver="showHide('menu1','visible')"
onMouseOut="showHide('menu1','hidden')">
<a href="dummy.html">Administration</a>
<a href="dummy.html">Directory</a>
<a href="dummy.html">Contact</a>
</div>

<div id="menu2" class="mnuform"
onMouseOver="showHide('menu2','visible')"
onMouseOut="showHide('menu2','hidden')">
<a href="dummy.html">Communication</a>
<a href="dummy.html">Computer Science</a>
</div>

<div id="menu3" class="mnuform"
onMouseOver="showHide('menu3','visible')"
onMouseOut="showHide('menu3','hidden')">
<a href="dummy.html">Web Design</a>
<a href="dummy.html">Tech Writing</a>
</div>

<div id="menu4" class="mnuform"
onMouseOver="showHide('menu4','visible')"
onMouseOut="showHide('menu4','hidden')">
<a href="dummy.html">Day Classes</a>
<a href="dummy.html">Night Classes</a>
</div>

<div id="menu5" class="mnuform"
onMouseOver="showHide('menu5','visible')"
onMouseOut="showHide('menu5','hidden')">
<a href="dummy.html">Faculty</a>
<a href="dummy.html">Students</a>
</div>
</div>

</div>
</div>
</div>
```

NOTE

Notice that each menu object ("menu1," "menu2," and so on) has onMouseOver and onMouseOut event handlers set that pass values to the showHide() function created in Step 1. For instance, the "menu1" object's onMouseOver event handler passes values of 'menu1' and 'visible' to the showHide() function's id and toggle parameters, toggling on the visibility of the "menu1" object when the mouse is passed over it. The result of this, essentially, is that "menu1" is assigned as the value of the id variable, while "visible" is assigned as the value of the toggle variable.

Likewise, the "menu1" object also includes an onMouseOut event handler that works very similarly to the onMouseOver event handler, with the only difference being that a value of "hide" is passed to the function's toggle parameter, toggling off the visibility of the "menu1" object when the mouse is moved off of it.

3. Add onMouseOver and onMouseOut event handlers to the main menu options that call the showHide() function you created in Step 1, to turn the display of the appropriate drop-down menu on and off when the mouse is passed over and off of the corresponding main menu option:

```
<p>
<a href="dummy.html"
   onMouseOver="showHide('menu1','visible')"
   onMouseOut="showHide('menu1','hidden')"
><span>Home</span></a>

<a href="dummy.html"
   onMouseOver="showHide('menu2','visible')"
   onMouseOut="showHide('menu2','hidden')"
><span>Department</span></a>

<a href="dummy.html"
   onMouseOver="showHide('menu3','visible')"
   onMouseOut="showHide('menu3','hidden')"
><span>Program</span></a>

<a href="dummy.html"
   onMouseOver="showHide('menu4','visible')"
   onMouseOut="showHide('menu4','hidden')"
><span>Catalog</span></a>

<a href="dummy.html"
   onMouseOver="showHide('menu5','visible')"
   onMouseOut="showHide('menu5','hidden')"
><span>Contact</span></a>
</p>
```

NOTE

Notice that the onMouseOver and onMouseOut event handlers call the showHide() function, while passing on values that are to be assigned to the id and the toggle variables, respectively. For the first menu option ("Home"), for instance, the onMouseOver event handler passes **'menu1'** and **'visible'** as the values of the id and toggle variables, calling for the "menu1" object to be rendered visible. Conversely, the onMouseOut event handler works in reverse, calling for the "menu1" object to be hidden.

4. Create styles to format the drop-down menus:

```
<link rel="stylesheet" type="text/css" href="webdesign.css">
<style type="text/css">
.mnuform { color: #ffce63; background: red; font-family: Arial,
Helvetica, sans-serif; font-size: 14px; font-weight: bold;
padding: 0; margin: 0; border: black 1px solid; z-index: 9; }
#menu1 { position: absolute; left: 50px; top: 17px; visibility:
hidden; text-align: left; padding: 0; margin: 0; }
#menu2 { position: absolute; left: 166px; top: 17px; visibility:
hidden; text-align: left; padding: 0; margin: 0; }
#menu3 { position: absolute; left: 357px; top: 17px; visibility:
hidden; text-align: left; padding: 0; margin: 0; }
#menu4 { position: absolute; left: 495px; top: 17px; visibility:
hidden; text-align: left; padding: 0; margin: 0; }
#menu5 { position: absolute; left: 625px; top: 17px; visibility:
hidden; text-align: left; padding: 0; margin: 0; }
```

```
div.dropmnu a, div.dropmnu a:link, div.dropmnu a:visited,
div.dropmnu a:active { display: block; margin: 0; padding: 2px
5px; color: #ffce63; background: red; font-weight: bold; text-
decoration: none; font-family: Arial, sans-serif; }
div.dropmnu a, div.dropmnu a:link, div.dropmnu a:visited,
div.dropmnu a:active { width: 140px; voice-family: "\"}\"";
voice-family: inherit; width: 130px; }
html>body div.dropmnu a { width: 130px }
div.dropmnu a:hover { color: black; background: white; margin-
bottom: 0; margin-top: 0; }
</style>
```

5. Save the file, switch to your browser, and refresh the display of the page. Pass the mouse over the Home link on the ribbon menu. A menu should drop down below the Home link, displaying three menu options (see Figure 12.19).

"menu1" object —

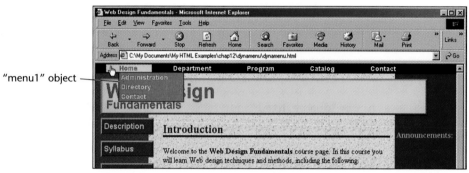

FIGURE 12.19 • *When the mouse is passed over the Home link, a drop-down menu with three additional options is displayed.*

6. Move the mouse cursor down through the menu options. As the mouse cursor moves over each menu option, its foreground and background colors should roll over to black on white (see Figure 12.20).

menu option
rollover effect —

FIGURE 12.20 • *When the mouse is passed over the menu options, their foreground and background colors change to black on white.*

7. Click on any of the three menu options. A dummy page (dummy.html) should appear. Click the Back button to return to the example page.
8. Pass the mouse cursor over the other ribbon menu links. Notice that passing the mouse off one of the ribbon menu links hides its drop-down menu again. Move your cursor down to test the display of the drop-down menu options (see Figure 12.21).

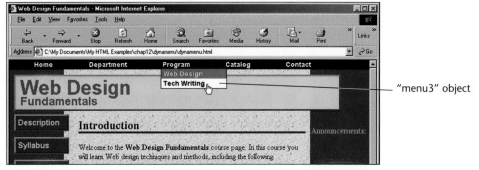

FIGURE 12.21 • *After the Program option's drop-down menu is displayed, the "Tech Writing" option is highlighted by passing the mouse cursor over it.*

Adding a Cascading Submenu

You also can have any of the drop-down menu options trigger the display of a cascading submenu.

Add a cascading submenu that is triggered when the mouse passes over the "Administration" option on the first drop-down menu:

1. Add event handlers to the "Directory" option of the first drop-down menu, as well as a right-arrow to show the option displays a further submenu:

```
<div class="dropmnu">
<div id="menu1" class="mnuform"
onMouseOver="showHide('menu1','visible')"
onMouseOut="showHide('menu1','hidden')">
<a href="dummy.html">Administration</a>
<a href="dummy.html"
onMouseOver="showHide('menu1_a','visible')"
onMouseOut="showHide('menu1_a','hidden')"
>Directory
           
  &gt;</a>
<a href="dummy.html">Contact</a>
</div>
```

2. Create the new submenu:

```
<a href="dummy.html">Contact</a>
</div>

<div id="menu1_a" class="mnuform"
onMouseOver="showHide('menu1','visible')"
onMouseOut="showHide('menu1_a','hidden')"
onMouseOut="showHide('menu1','hidden')"
>
<a href="dummy.html"
onMouseOver="showHide('menu1_a','visible')"
onMouseOut="showHide('menu1','hidden')"
>Departments</a>
<a href="dummy.html"
onMouseOver="showHide('menu1_a','visible')"
onMouseOut="showHide('menu1','hidden')"
```

```
>Campus Map</a>
<a href="dummy.html"
onMouseOver="showHide('menu1_a','visible')"
onMouseOut="showHide('menu1','hidden')"
>Index</a>
</div>
```

3. Create the styles that format and hide the new menu:

```
#menu1 { position: absolute; left: 50px; top: 17px; visibility:
hidden; text-align: left; padding: 0; margin: 0; }
#menu1_a { position: absolute; left: 191px; top: 37px;
visibility: hidden; text-align: left; padding: 0; margin: 0; }
#menu2 { position: absolute; left: 166px; top: 17px; visibility:
hidden; text-align: left; padding: 0; margin: 0; }
```

4. Save the file, switch to your browser, and refresh the display of your page. Move the mouse cursor down to the "Directory" option. A further submenu, displaying three additional options, should be displayed to the right of the option (see Figure 12.22).

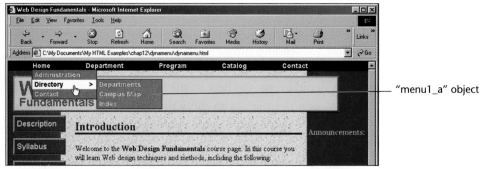

—— "menu1_a" object

FIGURE 12.22 • *When the mouse is passed over the "Directory" option, a submenu containing three additional options is displayed.*

5. Pass the mouse over any of the options in the submenu (see Figure 12.23).

—— submenu option rollover effect

FIGURE 12.23 • *When the mouse is passed over any of the submenu options, their foreground and background colors roll over to black on white.*

CHAPTER SUMMARY

You should now be familiar with DHTML and some of the more common ways it can be effectively used in Web pages. You should be aware that DHTML is not a standard, but is a combination of other standard Web technologies, including Cascading Style Sheets (CSS), JavaScript (or ECMAScript), and the Document Object Model (DOM).

You should now be familiar with a number of different methods for creating dynamic effects in response to user actions and system events. These include targeting content to be displayed in multiple frames, dynamically changing style properties, making objects appear and disappear, and moving objects in response to mouse-over and mouse-off actions, for instance.

 The purpose of this chapter is not to teach you everything you need to know to start creating your own DHTML scripts, but to introduce you to some practical examples of how DHTML can be used in Web pages. To become proficient with DHTML requires further study and experimentation on your part. To find links to further DHTML resources, tutorials, guides, and script repositories, be sure to visit this chapter's section at the IRC for this book at **www.emcp.com/**.

Code Review

document.getElementById ('*objectname*')	The W3C DOM method for addressing a document object, with *objectname* corresponding to an object's ID attribute value. Supported by all current browsers, such as Internet Explorer 5 and 6, Netscape 6, and Mozilla 1.
document.all.*objectname*	The Internet Explorer DOM method for addressing a document object, with *objectname* corresponding to an object's ID attribute value. Supported by the Internet Explorer 4, 5, and 6 browsers.
document.layers.*objectname*	The Netscape DOM method for addressing a document object, with *objectname* corresponding to an object's ID attribute value. Supported by the Netscape 4 browsers (but not the Netscape 6 browsers).
parent.frames[*integer*]. location.href='*address*'	Specifies that a file at the specified address should be displayed in a specified frame within the current document's parent frameset file, where *address* is a file name or a URL and *integer* indicates the position of the frame within the sequence of frames in a frameset (starting with `frames[0]`).
onMouseOver	An element attribute, or event handler, that specifies an action to be performed when the mouse cursor is passed over the element (or object).
onMouseOut	An element attribute, or event handler, that specifies an action to be performed when the mouse cursor is passed off of (or out of the area of) an element (or object).
this.className	The first part, `this`, is a JavaScript keyword that refers to the current object, while `className` refers to that object's CLASS attribute value.

this.style.*property*	Refers to a style property belonging to the current object (such as the color property of the H2 element, for instance).
eval("*string*")	A built-in JavaScript function that evaluates a text string containing JavaScript code.
ID attribute	In DHTML, the ID attribute is used to identify an object within a document, so that dynamic behaviors and display characteristics can be assigned to it.
visibility	A style property that toggles the visibility of an object off and on (with the "visible" and "hidden" values). A `visibility: hidden` property value differs from a `display: none` property value in that the first still occupies space within the document, while the second does not.
document.write()	A JavaScript method for writing text to a document.

ONLINE QUIZ

Go to this text's IRC at **www.emcp.com/** and take the online self-check quiz for this chapter.

REVIEW EXERCISES

This section provides some hands-on practice exercises to reinforce the information and material included within this chapter.

1. Add two more slide show images to the dynamic slide show example. Two additional thumbnail and full-size image pairs (eagle_nebula_th.jpg and eagle_nebula.jpg, and saturn_rings_th.jpg and saturn_rings.jpg) are included with the example files in the chap12\spaceshow folder. To add the two new slide show images:

   1. Open **spaceshow.html** in your text editor and edit it as shown here:

      ```
      <frameset cols="160,*">
          <frame src="sidebar_practice.html" name="sidebar"
      marginheight="0" marginwidth="10px">
      ```

   2. Save spaceshow.html as **spaceshow_practice.html** in the chap12\spaceshow folder.

   3. Open **sidebar.html** in your text editor and edit it to add the two new full-sized images to the images that are pre-loaded when the page is loaded. Resave the file as **sidebar_practice.html** in the chap12\spaceshow folder.

   4. Still editing sidebar_practice.html, set up the thumbnail images for the two new slide show images, including the appropriate onMouseOver and onMouseOut event handlers to control the display of the full-size images' pages in the "main" frame. Save the file.

   5. Open **spaceshow_practice.html** in your browser and test your new slide show images. If you added the thumbnail images to the bottom of sidebar_practice.html, scroll the frame to show the two new thumbnail images, and then pass the mouse over and off of the images to test them. For instance, when passing the mouse over the eagle_nebula_th.jpg thumbnail image, a Web page displaying the eagle_nebula.jpg full-size image should be displayed in the

"main" frame. When passing the mouse off of the eagle_nebula_th.jpg thumbnail image, the initial front page, main.html, should be redisplayed in the "main" frame.

2. Experiment further with using dynamic styles to create dynamic effects by following these steps:

    1. Open **main_ex.html** in your text editor from the chap12/spaceshow folder and save it as **main_practice.html**.

    2. Create class-selector styles that define display characteristics to be displayed when the mouse is passed over and off of an element in the page. Do not simply repeat the same style properties that were defined in main.html, but create new and different effects.

    3. Add onMouseOver and onMouseOut event handlers to the H2 element that use the `this.className` method shown earlier in this chapter to call the class-selector styles you created in Step 2. Save the file.

    4. Open **main_practice.html** in your browser and test the dynamic styles you have created. Pass the mouse over and off of the H2 element to test the effects you created in Steps 2 and 3.

    5. Repeat Steps 2 and 3, but creating dynamic styles that are displayed when the mouse is passed over and off of the H1 element. Save your file and test the two new dynamic styles you have just created in your browser.

3. Experiment further with creating multi-object dynamic effects that can be triggered using onMouseOver and onMouseOut event handlers:

    1. Open **mainshow_ex.html** in your text editor and resave it as **mainshow_practice.html**.

    2. Using the mainshow.html file you created in the chapter example as a guide, create a JavaScript function in the page's HEAD element that can be called to trigger multi-object effects in response to a mouse action (an onMouseOver event handler, for instance). Do not just repeat the same effects you previously created in mainshow.html, but define different effects. Look for additional background images you can use in the chap12\spaceshow folder, or find and use other background images of your own choice.

    3. Add an onMouseOver event handler to the "myname" object that calls the function you created in Step 2. Save your file and then open it in your browser. Pass the mouse over the "myname" object ("Shirley Johnson's") to test the effect you have created.

    4. Create an additional JavaScript function that can be called to trigger more multi-object effects in response to a mouse action (an onMouseOut event handler, for instance). Do not just repeat the same effects you previously created in mainshow.html, but define different effects.

    5. Add an onMouseOut event handler to the "myname" object that calls the function you created in Step 4. Save your file and then open it in your browser. Pass the mouse over and then off of the "myname" object ("Shirley Johnson's") to test both effects you have created.

4. Experiment further with creating functions that position and reveal objects in the browser window:

    1. Add a new object to the page, define an id-selector that defines its initial display characteristics, set a style property to hide the object, and set z-index properties to set the stacking order of the objects in the page.

2. Create a function that absolutely positions all objects on the page, sets their z-index properties if they are not already set, and turns on the visibility of the new object.

3. Add an onMouseOver event handler to the "mytitle" object that calls the function you created in Step B when the mouse is passed over the "mytitle" object.

4. Create a function that turns off the visibility of the new object. Add an onMouseOff event handler to the "mytitle" object that calls the function to turn off display of the new object when the mouse is passed off of the "mytitle" object.

5. Experiment further with creating a dynamic drop-down menu:

   1. Open **dynamenu_ex.html** from the chap12\dynamenu folder and resave it as **dynamenu_practice.html**.

   2. Using the example in the book as a guide, create a JavaScript script that includes a function that can be used to toggle the visibility of the menu elements on and off.

   3. Create the drop-down menu elements, including onMouseOver and onMouseOut event handlers that turn their visibility on and off when the mouse is passed over and off of them. Try to think of submenu options to be used in the drop-down menus that are different from those used in the chapter's example.

   4. Add onMouseOver and onMouseOut event handlers to the main menu options that turn the visibility of the corresponding drop-down menus on and off when the mouse is passed over and off of the main menu options.

   5. Add at least one cascading submenu that is displayed when the mouse is passed over one of the drop-down menus' submenu options. Do not create it for the same submenu option that was used in the chapter's example, but create it for a different submenu option, positioning it in a different position in the browser window. For the cascading submenu, create different options than were used in the chapter's example.

WEB-BASED LEARNING ACTIVITIES

In this book's text, Find It icons inserted in the margin highlight the Web addresses of additional resources you might find helpful or informative. To further extend your learning using the Web, you can:

- Visit this book's IRC at **www.emcp.com/** to find additional Web addresses of resources related to the material covered in this chapter that you can further investigate and explore.

- Look for additional resources and information that add to your understanding and knowledge of the material covered in this chapter. Use Yahoo!, Google, AltaVista, or other directories and search engines to expand your research. When you find a relevant page or site with information or resources you might want to access later, add it to your Favorites (in Internet Explorer) or your Bookmarks (in Netscape or Mozilla).

PROJECTS

These projects can be done in class, in a computer lab, or at home. Use the skills you have developed in this and the previous chapters to create any of the following projects.

Project 1. Create your own dynamic slide show using images you have created or selected.

Using images you have either created or selected, create your own dynamic slide show. Create the frameset file, sidebar file, front page, and caption file. Create and size the thumbnail images and size the full-size images in your image editor. Create HTML files to display the full-size images and then set onMouseOver event handlers for the thumbnail images that display the corresponding full-size images' HTML files in the main frame window and the corresponding caption file in the caption frame window. Set onMouseOut event handlers that redisplay the front page file in the main frame window when the mouse is passed off of the thumbnail images.

Project 2. Incorporate dynamic styles into a Web page or site you have already created.

Use dynamic styles to enhance a Web page or site you have already created, setting different display characteristics that are displayed when the mouse is passed over and off of document objects. Ask at least three classmates to critique your efforts. Incorporate any helpful suggestions they provide.

Project 3. Design a Web page or site from scratch using dynamic HTML effects.

Design a new Web page or site from scratch that makes use of Dynamic HTML effects to enhance its functionality and responsiveness. Implement any other features or techniques covered in the prior chapters of this book that you feel will enhance your Web page or site. Ask at least three classmates to critique your efforts. Incorporate any helpful suggestions they provide.

Project 4. Design a dynamic drop-down menu for a site you have already created or create from scratch.

Design a dynamic drop-down menu and incorporate it into a site you have already created or create from scratch. Ask at least three classmates to critique your efforts. Incorporate any helpful suggestions they provide.

Working with XHTML and XML

PERFORMANCE OBJECTIVES

In this chapter, you will learn how to use the XHTML (Extensible Hypertext Markup Language) and XML (Extensible Markup Language) to deliver content over the Web, including the following:

- Understand what XHTML is and why it exists.
- Understand the differences between XHTML 1.0 and HTML 4.01.
- Use XHTML DocType declarations and other document declarations.
- Declare character encodings and sets in XHTML documents.
- Create XHTML documents that are compatible with HTML 4.01.
- Understand what XML is and how to use it.
- Create XML documents that are styled using Cascading Style Sheets (CSS).

In this chapter, you also will learn how to work with XHTML and XML documents. These topics are much larger than a single chapter can comprehensively cover, so the discussion and examples provided in this chapter are focused on providing a basic introduction to these technologies and some practical examples of how they can be used. Links are provided to online resources where you can find more comprehensive coverage of these topics.

USING THE EXAMPLE FILES

If you have created a working folder for storing files you create, you will find the example files for this chapter located in the **chap13** folder within your working folder. Save any HTML files you create for this chapter in this folder.

If you have created a working disk, copy the chap13 folder to your working disk from the **HTML_Examples** folder that you or your instructor downloaded from this book's Internet Resource Center (IRC), or from a CD-R disc or floppy disk provided by your instructor. Save any HTML file you create in this chapter in the chap13 folder that you have copied to your working disk.

INTRODUCTION TO XHTML

The XHTML (Extensible Hypertext Markup Language) 1.0 specification was recommended on January 26, 2000, so it is not a new technology, at least in terms of Internet time. XHTML is a reformulation of HTML 4.0 and 4.01 to conform to XML (Extensible Markup Language).

The W3C defines XHTML as "a family of current and future document types and modules that reproduce, subset, and extend HTML 4" and that XHTML document types are "XML based, and ultimately are designed to work in conjunction with XML-based user agents" (see **www.w3.org/TR/xhtml1/#xhtml**). XHTML 1.0, therefore, defines only one of many possible XHTML document formats. The primary purpose of XHTML 1.0 is to subset HTML 4.01 within the overall context of conformance with XML. What this means is simply that XHTML 1.0 is HTML 4.01, but brought into conformance with XML.

Understanding XHTML Modules

Currently, three XHTML versions or modules have been defined: XHTML 1.0, XHTML 1.1, and XHTML Basic. It is important to note that a module is not simply a sequential version of HTML that supplants a previous version. Rather it is a parallel specification that may be intended to implement more specialized purposes than was initially the case with XHTML 1.0 (which was defined before the focus on modularity was instituted).

XHTML 1.1 is a reformulation of the strict definition of XHTML 1.0 as an XHTML module (and, as such, does not allow the use of deprecated or frameset elements and attributes). The purpose of XHTML 1.1 is to facilitate the integration and interoperability of XHTML with other future XHTML modules and other markup languages. For instance, a separate document type might be defined that combines XHTML 1.1 with MathML 2.0. In other words, while the focus of XHTML 1.0 is primarily on backward compatibility with HTML 4.01, while still remaining conformant with XML, the focus of XHTML 1.1 is on extensibility, modularization, and forward compatibility with future XHTML modules and new XML-based markup languages.

XHTML Basic defines the minimal features required to implement the XHTML document type and is targeted at Web clients that do not support the full gamut of features defined in XHTML 1.0, such as cell phones, personal digital assistants (PDAs), pagers, TV set-top boxes (WebTV, for instance), and other platforms or devices. XHTML Basic can interact with other XHTML modules as they are developed. The primary reason for defining a separate XHTML module for this is that these platforms are accessed through user interfaces that do not use the traditional mouse/keyboard paradigm that is more typical of computer-based browsing. Instead, users may need to rely on using a keypad or a remote to navigate pages, activate links, select options, and so on. It is anticipated, for instance, that a set of event-handlers will be developed for XHTML Basic that will be more generic than those already defined for HTML 4.01, which assume a mouse/keyboard interface. The same event handler, in other words, might have a different meaning, depending on whether a cell phone keypad or a television set-top remote is being used.

Understanding the Roots of XHTML/HTML/XML: SGML

XML is formulated to conform to SGML (Standard Generalized Markup Language), so XHTML documents, especially when declared to be compatible with the "strict" XHTML DTD, should be more or less compatible with SGML as well. SGML is a much more generic markup language that is targeted at marking up computer-generated documents in general, primarily for printing or reproduction. Note that the intention behind the original versions of HTML was for HTML to be an SGML-conforming markup language, but due to proprietary vendor extensions (as implemented in the Mosaic, Netscape Navigator, and Microsoft Internet Explorer browsers), HTML evolved into something other than an SGML-conforming markup language. Still, all of the essential characteristics of HTML, such as elements, tags, attributes, character references (entity codes), comments, and document type definitions (DTDs), are derived directly from SGML. To learn more, see the "On SGML and HTML" section from the HTML 4.01 specification at **www.w3.org/TR/html4/intro/sgmltut.html**.

Understanding the Differences between XHTML and HTML

The latest HTML specifications (HTML 3.2, 4.0, and 4.01) were aimed more at trying to capture current practice than at roping HTML back into the SGML camp. As such, three separate DTDs (Document Type Definitions) are defined for these later versions of HTML: strict, transitional, and frameset, with the more obviously non-SGML-like elements and attributes segregated within the latter two definitions. The same is repeated for the XHTML 1.0 specification, which also has strict, transitional, and frameset DTDs for which document authors can declare conformance.

The differences between XHTML 1.0 and HTML 4.01 are mostly syntactical. Apart from these syntactical differences, as well as differences in how XHTML and HTML documents are declared, the XHTML 1.0 specification relies upon the same element and attribute definitions defined by HTML 4.01. If you already know how to code HTML 4.01 documents, you should have no trouble learning how to code XHTML 1.0 documents, because most of XHTML 1.0 is simply HTML 4.01.

Apart from differences between how XHTML and HTML documents are declared (which is treated separately in a following section), the primary differences between the two markup languages are as follows:

- Element and attribute names are not case-sensitive in HTML, but they are in XHTML. All element and attribute names in XHTML documents must be stated in all lowercase letters (`<h1>...</h1>`, but not `<H1>...</H1>`, for instance).
- In HTML documents, the quoting of attribute values is often optional, but in XHTML documents it is mandatory.
- The use of implied end tags, which is permitted for several elements in HTML, is not permitted in an XHTML document. In an XHTML document, every `<li>` start tag must be followed by an `</li>` end tag.
- Empty elements, such as the BR, HR, and IMG elements, for instance, must end with `/>` or be stated as a start tag/end tag pair (`<br></br>`, for instance). The first approach is recommended, because some earlier HTML-only user agents might not properly parse empty tags when they are stated as start tag/end tag pairs. HTML-only user agents might also trip over an ending / character within an empty element's tag, but will ignore it if it is preceded by a space (`<br />` rather than `<br/>`, for instance).
- HTML 4 allows Web authors to entirely omit both the start and end tags for the HTML, HEAD, and BODY elements as being implied, but inclusion of both the start and end tags for these elements is required within XHTML documents.
- In HTML 4, the TBODY element is implied if it is not present, but in XHTML, the TBODY element must be present for styles properties to be applied to it.
- HTML 4 allows the use of minimized attributes, such as the HR element's NOSHADE attribute (`<hr noshade>`, for instance), but in XHTML, all attributes must have values (`<hr noshade="noshade" />`, for instance).

- In XHTML, the ID attribute supercedes the NAME attribute, with `<a id="part1"></a>` used to specify a target anchor in XHTML, instead of `<a name="part1"></a>` as used in HTML. Non-XML user agents, however, might not recognize the use of ID attributes in place of NAME attributes, so the NAME attribute is also included in XHTML for transitional purposes. Both can be used for maximum compatibility (`<a id="part1" name="part1"></a>`, for instance).

- In XHTML, the XML:LANG attribute supercedes the LANG attribute. For transitional purposes, both are included in XHTML 1.0 and can be used in combination for maximum compatibility (`<html xml:lang="en" lang="en">`, for instance).

- In HTML 4, standalone ampersands (&) and left angle brackets (<) are allowed in element attributes and elsewhere within the document. In an XHTML document, any standalone ampersands and left angle brackets need to be inserted using their entity codes (`&amp;` and `&lt;`). This is also an issue for embedded scripts, which can contain & and < characters as operators; a way around this is to link to an external script, instead of using an embedded script.

- Commonly, HTML 4 documents hide the content of style sheets and scripts from earlier browsers that do not recognize the STYLE and SCRIPT elements by bracketing it inside HTML comment codes. A browser's HTML parser will ignore the comment codes in this situation, but its XML parser likely will not. This is not a problem with current browsers, which all parse XHTML files using their HTML parser, but could be a problem in future browsers that might choose to parse XHTML files using their XML parser instead. For that reason, in XHTML documents, you should either not use HTML comment codes to hide the content of STYLE and SCRIPT elements or you should link to external style sheets and scripts, instead.

Understanding the Reasons for Using XHTML

Web authors might want to consider migrating their Web documents from HTML 4.01 to XHTML 1.0 for a number of reasons:

- Because the core of XHTML 1.0 is simply HTML 4.01, with the primary differences between the two being in the area of syntactical markup, a Web document written in XHTML should perform in current browsers as well or better than if it were written in HTML 4.01.

- As the family of XHTML document formats evolves, XHTML documents will be better able to interoperate with other XHTML modules as they are developed, introducing new functionality that will be less likely to be available through HTML 4.01.

- As alternative ways of accessing the Internet and the Web are developed, XHTML is better poised to add additional modules that extend its capability to facilitate alternative modes of access than is the case with HTML 4.01, which is not modularized and thus not as easily extended.

In reality, almost all current browsers treat XHTML 1.0 and HTML 4.01 documents alike, using their HTML parser to render both, rather than any XML parser that might also be included in the browser. A new MIME-type, application/xhtml+xml, has been designated by the W3C for serving up XHTML documents as XML, so they will be parsed by a browser's XML parser, instead of its HTML parser, but using it might render the document unreadable or deliver it as a straight text dump in browsers that do not support the new MIME-type or do not provide a separate XML parser.

So the primary differences between XHTML 1.0 and HTML 4.01 come down to the syntactical differences, with the syntactical requirements imposed by XHTML 1.0 being more restrictive than those imposed by HTML 4.01. Because the same HTML parser is used to render either in all current browsers, for the time being this is primarily a concern when validating an XHTML document, which might generate additional errors that validating an HTML document will not.

There is no need, however, to convert legacy documents from HTML to XHTML, because future browsers will undoubtedly continue to support the display of HTML document indefinitely into the future to account for the millions of HTML documents on the Web that browsers will need to continue to display. Individual Web authors should also not feel constrained to move from HTML 4.01 to XHTML 1.0, because the differences between the two are relatively minor. Current browsers, treat HTML 4.01 and XHTML 1.0 documents identically (that is, simply as HTML documents). The vast majority of individual Web authors have continued to code their pages using HTML, rather than XHTML, so the vast majority of Web pages on the Web will likely continue to be HTML documents, rather than XHTML documents, for many, many years to come (and it is possible that the majority of Web pages on the Web may always be HTML, rather than XHTML, documents).

Corporate users, however, might want to decide to standardize on XHTML, rather than HTML, to be positioned to take advantage of the increased functionality that XML will likely provide in the future. Those looking forward to a possible career in the Web design or Web development fields should be knowledgeable and proficient in both HTML 4.01 and XHTML 1.0, because either might be required in a specific employment scenario.

CASE EXAMPLE: UPDATING A PERSONAL WEB PAGE TO XHTML

Because the differences between HTML 4.01 and XHTML 1.0 are not that significant, updating a Web page from one to the other is fairly easy.

> *Johnny Watson feels he has developed a proficiency in creating Web pages that conform to the HTML 4.01 standard. From doing further research, he knows that the differences between HTML 4.01 and XHTML 1.0 are not that great and he has decided to experiment with updating his personal Web page to XHTML 1.0.*

To start working with this example:
1. Open **watson-x_ex.html** in your text editor from the chap13 slideshow folder in your working folder or disk.
2. Save watson-x_ex.html as **watson-x.html** in the chap13 folder.
3. Open **watson-x.html** in your Web browser from the chap13 folder.

Inserting the XML Declaration

The XHTML 1.0 specification requires that an XML declaration be included at the head of an XHTML document only if the character encoding used in the document is other than UTF-8 or UTF-16 (8-bit or 16-bit Unicode). UTF-8 and UTF-16 are inclusive of both the US-ASCII and ISO-8859-1 (or Latin-1) character sets, which form the first 128 and 256 character positions, respectively, in UTF-8 and UTF-16. Therefore, if you have not included any special character references to character positions above `&#255;` (the y-umlaut character), so that all characters included within the document are included and allowed within the ISO-8859-1 character set, there is no absolute requirement that an XML declaration be inserted at the head of an XHTML document.

NOTE

UTF stands for Unicode Transformation Format. UTF-8, UTF-16, and UTF-32 represent characters as 8-bit, 16-bit, and 32-bit code sequences. UTF-8 can represent up to 64,000 characters. UTF-16 can use surrogate pairs of 16-bit codes to achieve the same result as UTF-32, which is the representation of over one million possible characters. To find out more about Unicode, see the Unicode home page at **www.unicode.org/**.

However, the W3C also recommends strongly that an XML declaration declaring the document's character encoding system be included, even if no non-ISO-8859-1 characters are included in the document. The reason for the strong recommendation is that in XHTML documents that are served up as HTML documents (as a text/html media type), rather than as XML documents, no default character encoding system can be automatically assumed. In the absence of a specific declaration, the default character set employed by a browser can vary from browser to browser. For that reason, the W3C recommends that you explicitly declare the encoding method for any XHTML documents that you create and not assume that the encoding value will default to UTF-8 or UTF-16 if such a declaration is absent.

action

Insert an XML declaration at the head of the document:

```
<?xml version="1.0" encoding="UTF-8"?>
<html>
<head>
<title>Johnny Watson's Home Page: Sports and Gardening</title>
```

The XML declaration declares that the current document conforms to XML 1.0 and that the character encoding system used in the document is UTF-8 (8-bit Unicode).

Other character encodings might be declared. For instance, the following encoding declaration could be used to declare that the language used in the document is Japanese:

```
<?xml version="1.0" encoding="EUC-JP"?>
```

To find out more about character encodings that can be declared in XHTML documents, see **www.w3.org/International/O-charset.html**. For a listing of the character sets that are most typically used in Web pages, see **www.w3.org/International/O-charset-lang.html**.

Declaring the XHTML DocType

In XHTML documents, you are required to include a DocType declaration prior to the root element that declares your document to be in conformance with one of the DTDs (document type definitions) for XHTML. As is the case with HTML 4.01, three different levels of conformance to XHTML 1.0 can be declared: strict, transitional, and frameset.

To declare your document to be in conformance with the strict definition of XHTML 1.0, you would insert the following DocType Declaration:

```
<!DOCTYPE html
    PUBLIC "-//W3C//DTD XHTML 1.0 Strict//EN"
    "http://www.w3.org/TR/xhtml1/DTD/xhtml1-strict.dtd">
```

To declare your document to be in conformance with the transitional definition of XHTML 1.0, you would insert the following DocType Declaration:

```
<!DOCTYPE html
    PUBLIC "-//W3C//DTD XHTML 1.0 Transitional//EN"
    "http://www.w3.org/TR/xhtml1/DTD/xhtml1-transitional.dtd">
```

To declare your document to be in conformance with the frameset definition of XHTML 1.0, you would insert the following DocType Declaration:

```
<!DOCTYPE html
    PUBLIC "-//W3C//DTD XHTML 1.0 Frameset//EN"
    "http://www.w3.org/TR/xhtml1/DTD/xhtml1-frameset.dtd">
```

You need to key the DocType declarations exactly as they are shown here, including all upper-case and lowercase characters. If you do not, the DocType declaration will not be valid.

As is also the case with HTML 4.01, you should declare your document to be in conformance with the strict definition of XHTML 1.0 only if it contains no deprecated elements or attributes and no frameset elements or attributes. If your document contains deprecated elements or attributes (such as FONT elements or ALIGN attributes, for instance), but no frameset elements or attributes, you should declare it to be in conformance with the transitional definition of XHTML 1.0. If your document contains frameset elements or attributes (including the A element's TARGET attribute, which is considered a frameset attribute), you should declare it to be in conformance with the frameset definition of XHTML 1.0.

The deprecated elements and attributes, as well as the frameset elements and attributes, are identical for both XHTML and HTML 4.01.

For a full listing of all deprecated elements, see the W3C's index of HTML 4.01 elements at **www.w3.org/TR/html4/index/elements.html**. For a full listing of all deprecated attributes (and the contexts in which they are deprecated), see the W3C's index of HTML 4.01 attributes at **www.w3.org/TR/html4/index/attributes.html**. Frameset elements and attributes, for both XHTML 1.0 and HTML 4.01, include the FRAMESET, FRAME, and NOFRAMES elements, and the A element's TARGET attribute.

Declare the document to be in conformance with the transitional definition of XHTML 1.0:

```
<?xml version="1.0" encoding="UTF-8"?>
<!DOCTYPE html
    PUBLIC "-//W3C//DTD XHTML 1.0 Transitional//EN"
    "http://www.w3.org/TR/xhtml1/DTD/xhtml1-transitional.dtd">
<html>
<head>
```

Declaring the XML Namespace for XHTML Documents

XHTML documents are also XML documents. In XML documents, the root element (the HTML element, in this case) must include a declaration of the XML namespace to which the document-type belongs. The namespace for XHTML is defined as `http://www.w3.org/1999/xhtml`.

In the document's root element (the HTML element), declare the document-type as belonging to the XHTML namespace:

```
<?xml version="1.0" encoding="UTF-8"?>
<!DOCTYPE html
    PUBLIC "-//W3C//DTD XHTML 1.0 Transitional//EN"
    "http://www.w3.org/TR/xhtml1/DTD/xhtml1-transitional.dtd">
<html xmlns="http://www.w3.org/1999/xhtml">
<head>
```

In XML, a *namespace* defines the naming convention of elements and attributes that belong together. If a document is declared as belonging to the XHTML namespace, for instance, then only names belonging to that namespace can be used, unless you change the declared namespace. You can mix namespaces within a single document, declaring different sections as belonging to different namespaces, but you cannot mix names belonging to different namespaces without switching the namespace. For instance, an XML document can contain XHTML code, but that code must be inserted in separate sections that are declared as belonging to the XHTML namespace.

NOTE For more information on the use of namespaces in XML documents, see **www.w3.org/TR/REC-xml-names/**.

Declaring the Document's Language

Web pages can be presented with content using a variety of different languages. When creating XHTML documents, you can use the XML:LANG and LANG attributes in the document's root element to declare the language being used in the document.

Declare the language being used in the document to be English:

```
<html xmlns="http://www.w3.org/1999/xhtml" xml:lang="en" lang="en">
```

In XHTML, the XML:LANG attribute is intended as replacing HTML 4.01's LANG attribute. For transitional purposes, the LANG attribute is also included in XHTML 1.0, but might not be included in future versions of XHTML. For the sake of backward compatibility with earlier browsers that do not recognize XHTML (and treat the document as simply an HTML document), both of these attributes can be used at the same time. The value of either of these attributes is a two-letter or three-letter country/language code. For instance, to declare the document's language as being Japanese, you would do the following:

```
<html xmlns="http://www.w3.org/1999/xhtml" xml:lang="jp" lang="jp">
```

NOTE

For the official listing of two-letter and three-letter country/language codes (ISO 639-2), see the Codes for the Representation of Names of Languages at the Library of Congress site at **lcweb.loc.gov/standards/iso639-2/langcodes.html**. For a listing of just the two-letter country/language codes (ISO 3166), see **www.iso.org/iso/en/prods-services/iso3166ma/02iso-3166-code-lists/list-en1.html**.

Specifying the Character Set

Browsers that support XML and XHTML will recognize the encoding value in the XML declaration, but older browsers that treat XHTML documents simply as HTML documents will ignore the XML declaration. For those older browsers, you can declare the document's character set using a META element, just as you can when creating HTML 4.01 documents.

Insert a META element that declares the character set of the document to be UTF-8:

```
<html xmlns="http://www.w3.org/1999/xhtml" xml:lang="en" lang="en">
<head>
<meta http-equiv="Content-Type" content="text/html; charset=utf-8" />
<title>Johnny Watson's Home Page: Sports and Gardening</title>
```

Following are some of the issues you may need to consider when specifying character sets for XHTML documents:

- The META element character set declaration should be inserted at the start of the HEAD element, before any other elements. Although that is not necessarily critical, especially when declaring a UTF-8 or ISO 8859-1 character set, it could be if you are declaring a non-Western character set, for instance, especially if the server delivering your page is assuming that a Western character set is being used.
- Notice that, because the META element is an empty element, a "/" character has been inserted at the end of the element's tag, preceded by a space.
- In the XHTML 1.0 specification, the W3C states that the best approach is to declare the correct character encoding for a document in the HTTP header that is downloaded by the server, but that in the absence of such a declaration both an XML declaration and a META HTTP-EQUIV statement should be included that declare the correct character set to be used to display the document.

NOTE

In most cases, as long as your server and your HTML document assume the same default language (such as English or another language that makes use of the Latin-1/ISO 8859-1 character set), the character encoding declaration in the HTTP header and the language used in the HTML document should agree.

However, if your server and your HTML document assume different default languages (such as when encoding Web pages written in English that are hosted on a server in Russia, for instance, you might want to include a different character encoding declaration in the HTTP header. For links to resources on the Web that provide further detail about how to create and edit HTTP headers that are associated with XHTML documents, as well as other information about specifying character encodings, see this chapter's section at the IRC for this book at **www.emcp.com/**.

Updating XML to XHTML

To create a proper XHTML document, you need to update its syntax and exclude any other prohibited features that are legal in HTML 4.01 documents but are not legal in XHTML 1.0 documents.

---

action

Update the document's syntax so it conforms to the XHTML requirements:

1. Add a closing "/" character, preceded by a space, to the empty META elements in the document's head:

```
<meta name="description" content="A Web page focused on my
personal involvements and interests, including a biography, my
resume, sports and gardening resources, and links to Web pages
created by my friends." />
<meta name="keywords" content="sports, gardening, espn, bbc,
football, baseball, indoor gardening, house plants, container
gardening, plant diseases" />
```

2. Add a closing "/" character, preceded by a space, to the empty HR and BR elements that are present in the "oops" IFRAME element:

```
<iframe class="oops">
<center><font size="5" color="maroon">This site will look much
better in a browser that supports
<a href="http://www.webstandards.org/upgrade/"
title="Download a browser that complies with Web standards.">
Web standards</a>,<br />but it is accessible to any browser
or Internet device.</font>
</center>
<hr />
</iframe>
```

3. In the IMG element's ALT attribute, replace the "&" character with the **&**, the entity name for the ampersand character and add a closing "/" character:

```
<p><img src="banner.gif" alt="Banner Image: Sports &amp;
Gardening" height="75" width="300" /></p>
```

NOTE

An HTML 4.01 document that contains standalone ampersands will still validate if you validate it using the W3C HTML Validator, but an XHTML 1.0 document will not. For that reason, all instances of ampersands in XHTML documents that do not signal the start of an entity reference should be changed to the entity name for the ampersand character (**&**) or your document will not be a valid XHTML document.

The same prohibition applies to standalone "<" characters, which should always be inserted as **<**.

4. Delete the **align="justify"** attributes from the document's P elements (because **justify** is an allowed value for the P element's ALIGN attribute in HTML 4.01, but not in XHTML 1.0) and set inline styles to achieve the same effect:

```
<p align="justify" style="text-align: justify;">Welcome to my home
page! My name is Johnny Watson and I'm a big nut about two things:
<a href="http://www.espn.com/"><span class="link">sports</span></a>
and <a href="http://www.bbc.co.uk/gardening/"><span
class="link">gardening!</span></a> You may think that is an odd
combination, but they really have more things in common than you
```

might suppose. First they are both largely outside activities: I enjoy participating in, rather than just watching, sports, for one thing. When the weather is bad, there can be an indoor component to both activities. I enjoy following some of my favorite teams on TV, while watering my indoor plants at the same time!</p>

```
<h2 align="center">Biography, Interests, and Friends</h2>
<p align="justify" style="text-align: justify;">In the following
list, I've included links to biographical and career info,
resources focused on topics that I'm especially interested in,
and pages that have been created by friends of mine:</p>
```

NOTE ── You can also set a `text-align: justify` property value for the P element within the document's style sheet, which would justify the content of all P elements within the document.

5. Add end tags to the page's LI (List Item) elements:

```
<ul>
<li><a href="mybio.html">My biography</a></li>
<li><a href="myresume.html">My resume</a></li>
<li><a href="http://www.usatoday.com/sports/scores.htm">Get the
latest sports scores</a></li>
<li><a href="http://www.about-house-plants.com/">Get indoor
gardening tips and advice</a></li>
<li><a href="http://www.blank.com/jshmoe/">My friend Joe's
site</a></li>
<li><a href="http://www.wherever.com/jdoe/homepage.html">My
friend Jane's site</a></li>
</ul>
```

6. Add a closing "/" character to the empty HR and BR elements that precede and are contained in the ADDRESS element:

```
<hr />
<center>
<address>
Johnny Watson<br />
E-mail: <a
href="mailto:jwatson@whatnot.com">jwatson@whatnot.com</a>
</address>
</center>
```

7. Add an example of an expanded minimized attribute to the HR element:

```
<hr size="5" noshade="noshade" />
<center>
<address>
```

8. Save your file, switch over to your browser, and refresh the display of your page (see Figure 13.1).

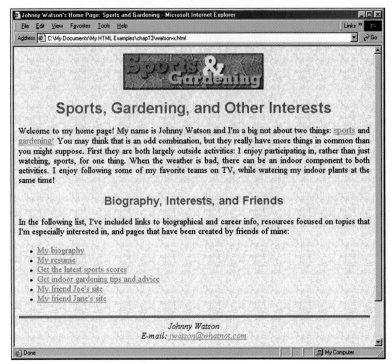

FIGURE 13.1 • *This page should display the same even though it is now coded as an XHTML 1.0 document rather than as an HTML 4.01 document.*

Other minimized attributes that are legal in HTML 4 but must be expanded in XHTML 1 include the CHECKED, COMPACT, DECLARE, DISABLED, ISMAP, MULTIPLE, NORESIZE, NOSHADE, NOWRAP, READONLY, and SELECTED attributes. Most browsers have no trouble handling these minimized attributes in their expanded form, but some earlier browsers might not recognize minimized attributes in their expanded form. These types of attributes are sometimes referred to as *boolean attributes*, most likely because they toggle a particular attribute value state (such as a check box being checked) on or off based upon their presence or absence.

Creating Nested Lists in XHTML

Because you need to include closing tags for all LI elements when creating lists in XHTML documents, creating nested lists is a little more complicated and easier to get wrong in XHTML documents than in HTML documents.

Johnny Watson has decided to add more links to his list of links. He also wants to organize them in nested lists, so the links will be listed according to their type.

Create a properly nested two-level bulleted list:
  1. Revise the current single-level list so it is a two-level nested list, with the top-level list items indicating the different link list categories:

```
<ul>
<li>Personal links:
    <ul>
    <li><a href="mybio.html">My biography</a></li>
    <li><a href="myresume.html">My resume</a></li>
    </ul>
</li>
```

```
<li>Sports links:
    <ul>
    <li><a href="http://www.usatoday.com/sports/scores.htm">Get
the latest sports scores</a></li>
    <li><a href="http://www.cnnsi.com/">Read the latest sports
news at CNN/Sports Illustrated</a></li>
    </ul>
</li>
<li>Gardening links:
    <ul>
    <li><a href="http://www.about-house-plants.com/">Get indoor
gardening tips and advice</a></li>
    <li><a href="http://www.gardenweb.com/">Participate in
GardenWeb, the Internet's garden community</a></li>
    </ul>
</li>
<li>Friends' links:
    <ul>
    <li><a href="http://www.blank.com/jshmoe/">My friend Joe's
site</a></li>
    <li><a href="http://www.wherever.com/jdoe/homepage.html">My
friend Jane's site</a></li>
    </ul>
</li>
</ul>
```

2. Revise the page's style sheet to make allowance for the second level of nested LI elements:

```
<style type="text/css">
body { color: navy; background: #ffffcc url(back_light.jpg); }
p, blockquote, li, address { font-size: 1.1em; }
li { font-family: Arial, Geneva, Helvetica, sans-serif; color:
maroon; background: transparent; margin-bottom: 10px; }
li li { font-family: 'Times New Roman', Times, serif; font-size:
1em; margin-bottom: 0; }
span.link { font-size: 1.1em; }
```

3. Save the file, switch to your browser, and refresh the display of the page (see Figure 13.2).

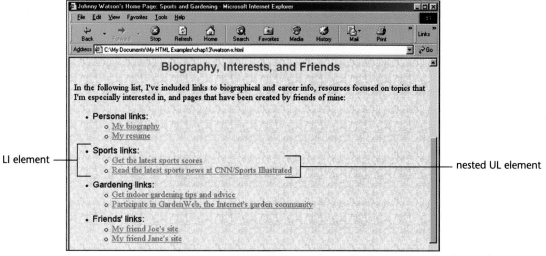

FIGURE 13.2 • *Nested lists in XHTML documents need to be nested inside of a bracketing LI element.*

The main thing to keep in mind is that in an XHTML document, in which you must include the `</li>` end tag for list items, you need to insert any nested lists (UL or OL elements) inside of a bracketing LI element, and not simply inside of a bracketing UL or OL element.

The revision of the document's style sheet was necessary primarily to counteract the font size of 1.1 ems that is set for the LI element, which would otherwise concatenate itself for each nested level, causing list items in the nested lists to be displayed in a larger font (1.1 times larger) than those in the non-nested lists. This was counteracted by setting the font size for list items that are nested within other nested list items to 1 em.

When creating style sheets for XHTML documents, you need to be cognizant of the case-sensitivity of XHTML element names, which should always be keyed in lowercase. In HTML documents, you can key HTML element names in lowercase in the document body, while referring to them in a style sheet in uppercase, because regular HTML is not case-sensitive. In XHTML documents, however, any references to element or attribute names must be keyed in lowercase characters, matching how they must be keyed within the document body.

Validating Your XHTML Document

The W3C Validator can validate both HTML and XHTML documents. Whenever updating an HTML document to XHTML, you should always revalidate it, even if it previously passed as a valid HTML 4.01 document, for instance. That is because the requirements for a valid XHTML 1.0 document are more restrictive than those for a valid HTML 4.01 document.

Validate watson-x.html using the W3C's HTML Validator:

1. In your browser, go to the W3C site at **www.w3.org/** and click the HTML Validator link in the left sidebar.
2. Scroll down on the page and click the "upload files" link.
3. Click the Browse button to the right of the File text box.
4. Navigate to the location of watson-x.html (in the My Documents\My HTML Examples\Chap13 folder, for instance) and then double-click on watson-x.html (or single-click on it and then click Open; see Figure 13.3).

FIGURE 13.3 • *The file, watson-x.html, is specified to be uploaded to the HTML Validator for validation.*

5. Because you have included a DocType declaration in your XHTML document that declares it to be compatible with the transitional definition of XHTML 1.0, leave the Document type option as it is ["(specified inline)"]. Leave all of the check boxes unchecked.

6. Click the Validate this document button. If you have successfully updated the document from HTML 4.01 to XHTML 1.0, you will be told that your document validates as XHTML 1.0 Transitional (see Figure 13.4).

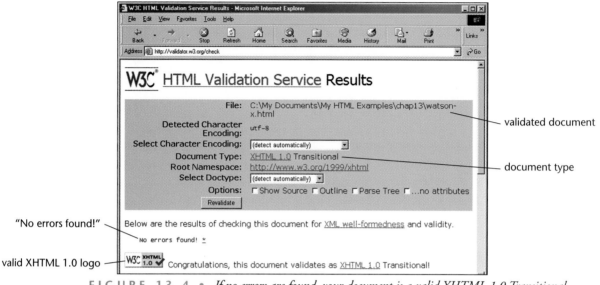

FIGURE 13.4 • *If no errors are found, your document is a valid XHTML 1.0 Transitional document.*

Declaring Your Document's XHTML Validity

Now that your document has been validated as a valid XHTML document, you can insert the code provided by the W3C to display the XHTML 1.0 logo on your page.

Declare that your document conforms to XHTML 1.0:

1. Add the W3C's XHTML 1.0 logo below the ADDRESS element in watson-x.html:

```
</address>
<p>
  <a href="http://validator.w3.org/check/referer"><img
      src="http://www.w3.org/Icons/valid-xhtml10"
      alt="Valid XHTML 1.0!" height="31" width="88" /></a>
</p>
</center>
```

2. Save your file. Switch to your browser; connect to the Internet, if you are not already connected. Refresh the display of your page. The W3C's XHTML logo should now be displayed at the bottom of the page (see Figure 13.5).

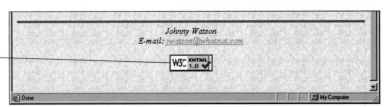

logo declaring the page to be a valid XHTML 1.0 document

Johnny Watson
E-mail: jwatson@whatnot.com

FIGURE 13.5 • *The W3C XHTML 1.0 logo is displayed at the bottom of the page, declaring that the document is a valid XHTML 1.0 document.*

NOTE For additional links to XHTML resources, see this chapter's section at the IRC for this book at **www.emcp.com/**.

INTRODUCTION TO XML

XHTML is considered a bridge between HTML on the one hand and XML (Extensible Markup Language) on the other. You also can use XML by itself to create documents for display on the Web. XML differs from XHTML in that XML does not contain pre-defined elements for which default display characteristics might be assumed. In XML, you can create any element that you want—the only restriction is that all elements must be properly nested. This means that a P element in one XML document might refer to a text paragraph, as it does in HTML, for instance, while in another XML document it might refer to the document page, a technological process, or to pastries. In other words, in an XML document, the author determines how elements are named and what those element names mean.

While this gives you a lot of freedom when creating XML documents, it also means that you need to specify *all* of the display or formatting characteristics that you want an XML element to have. When creating an HTML or XHTML document, on the other hand, you only need to specify display characteristics that are not already presumed by whichever element is being displayed.

In an XML document, the appearance of elements is entirely handled using an attached style sheet. There are a number of style sheet languages that can be used with XML, including DSSSL, XSL/XSLT, and CSS:

- DSSSL (Document Style Semantics and Specification Language) is a style sheet language that can be used with SGML documents and, by extension, with XML documents as well, since XML documents should also be valid SGML documents. DSSL style sheets can be attached to XML documents, but not to XHTML or HTML documents.
- XSL/XSLT (Extensible Stylesheet Language and Extensible Stylesheet Language Transformations) enables the specification of style characteristics for XML or XHTML documents, as well as the transformation of XML documents into other output formats. XSL (Extensible Stylesheet Language) encompasses XSLT (XSL Transformations), XPath (XML Path Language), and XSL-FO (XSL-Formatting Objects). XSLT is a language for transforming the output of XML documents, such as into XHTML with CSS styling, for instance. XPath is a language for addressing objects within the XML document tree. XSL-FO is a collection of formatting objects, along with their associated properties, that can be associated with XML documents.
- CSS (Cascading Style Sheets) works in XML and XHTML documents in exactly the same way as it does in HTML documents. CSS style sheets, however, must be attached as external style sheets to XML documents rather than being embedded.

Of the three XML style sheet options, CSS style sheets are by far the easiest to learn and maintain. There are also many inexpensive and free software tools available that can generate CSS-formatted XHTML and XML documents, while software tools for creating XSL/XSLT-formatted documents are less numerous and more expensive. XSL/XSLT allows you to do things you cannot do with CSS, such as dynamically generating element content, but it is much more complex and technically demanding than CSS. By and large, it is expected that XSL/XSLT will only be used by Web authors who require the additional functionality it provides, while everyone else will use CSS instead to style XML documents. It is not expected that DSSSL will be extensively used with XML documents, although those who are already versed in its application to SGML documents may choose to use it in XML documents as well.

The following case example provides an example of attaching a CSS style sheet to an XML document.

NOTE

To learn more about the different factors that go into which style sheet technology to use, CSS or XSL/XSLT, see CSS and XSL at **www.w3.org/Style/CSS-vs-XSL**. Also, see this chapter's section at the IRC for this book at **www.emcp.com/** for links to additional resources covering the use of XSL/XSLT and CSS with XHTML and XML documents.

CASE EXAMPLE: CREATING A BIBLIOGRAPHY DOCUMENT USING XML AND CSS

The easiest way to add style to XML documents is to use CSS. This choice is made all the more likely since most Web authors who are moving from creating HTML (and XHTML) documents to creating XML documents will already be either knowledgeable about or proficient in the use of CSS. If there is no need for the additional functionality provided by XSL/XSLT, there is really little point in using it instead of CSS to style XML documents.

Crystal Porter is researching a paper on the culture and religion of ancient Egypt. She is also experimenting with using XHTML and XML to format documents on the Web. She has decided to experiment with creating a bibliography of books on ancient Egypt as an XML document, utilizing a CSS style sheet to control the document's appearance when displayed in an XML-supporting browser.

To start working with this example:
1. Open **biblio.txt** in your text editor from the chap13 folder in your working folder or disk.
2. Save biblio.txt as **biblio.xml** in the chap13 folder.

Creating the XML Declaration

Starting out, the biblio.xml document simply includes lines of text, containing the text that will compose the separate bibliography information. It is not yet an XML document, however, because it contains only text.

Add an XML declaration to the top of the document:

```
<?xml version="1.0" encoding="UTF-8" standalone="yes"?>

The British Museum Book of Ancient Egypt
Stephen Quirke, Jeffrey Spencer
Thames & Hudson
1996
```

The **standalone="yes"** attribute declares that the document is a standalone document and that only internal declarations need to be processed.

Creating the Root Element

For an XML document to be well-formed, all elements must be nested, with only a single root element.

Bracket the content of the document within a root element:

1. Insert the root element's start tag at the top of the document:

```
<?xml version="1.0" encoding="UTF-8" standalone="yes"?>
<biblio>
The British Museum Book of Ancient Egypt
Stephen Quirke, Jeffrey Spencer
Thames & Hudson
1996
```

2. Insert the root element's end tag at the bottom of the document:

```
The Priests of Ancient Egypt
Serge Sauneron
Cornell University Press
2000
</biblio>
```

You can name the root element whatever you want. If you wanted to create a root element using the **<whatever>** and **</whatever>** start and end tags, that would be perfectly legal.

All other elements that you designate must be nested inside of the root element (the BIBLIO element, in this case).

Creating the Item Elements

Next, you can create XML elements that designate the individual items that compose the bibliography.

Nest the bibliography items within their own elements:

1. Nest the first bibliography item within an ITEM element:

```
<?xml version="1.0" encoding="UTF-8" standalone="yes"?>
<biblio>
```

```
<item>
The British Museum Book of Ancient Egypt
Stephen Quirke, Jeffrey Spencer
Thames & Hudson
1996
</item>
```

2. Repeat for the remaining bibliography items, nesting each of them inside an ITEM element.

Creating the Item Fields

The bibliography items are composed of different types of information that can be categorized, similar to defining the fields in a database record. Using XML, you can define element names that describe their content.

Create element names that categorize the different types of information included in the bibliography items:

1. Add descriptive elements to the first bibliography item:

```
<item>
<title>The British Museum Book of Ancient Egypt</title>
<author>Stephen Quirke, Jeffrey Spencer</author>
<publisher>Thames & Hudson</publisher>
<date>1996</date>
</item>
```

2. Repeat for the remaining bibliography items.

Creating a Document Title

At this point, the document is just a listing of bibliographical information, with nothing to indicate the import of that information.

Add a new element at the top of the document that contains a document heading:

```
<?xml version="1.0" encoding="UTF-8" standalone="yes"?>
<biblio>
<heading>Bibliography for Ancient Egypt</heading>
<item>
<title>The British Museum Book of Ancient Egypt</title>
<author>Stephen Quirke, Jeffrey Spencer</author>
<publisher>Thames & Hudson</publisher>
<date>1996</date>
</item>
```

Replacing Ampersands with Their Character Entities

You cannot include raw ampersands (&) in an XML file. All ampersands need to be replaced by their character entity code.

Replace any ampersands included in the text with the ampersand character entity code:

1. Replace the ampersand in the first bibliography item with its character entity code:

```
<item>
<title>The British Museum Book of Ancient Egypt</title>
<author>Stephen Quirke, Jeffrey Spencer</author>
<publisher>Thames &amp; Hudson</publisher>
<date>1996</date>
</item>
```

2. Find any other ampersands (&) in the remaining bibliography items and replace them with character entity codes.

LINKING TO A CSS STYLE SHEET   By themselves, XML elements have absolutely no formatting. They merely define the structural hierarchy and the semantic meanings of the document's data, but do not specify how the content of those elements is to be formatted or presented. In other words, all XML elements start out the same, without any formatting at all. If you open an XML file that is not linked to a style sheet in Internet Explorer 6 for Windows or Internet Explorer 5 for the Macintosh, for instance, the raw XML file is displayed, including all declarations and elements (see Figure 13.6). Other browsers, such as the Mozilla 1 browser, for instance, display the file's unformatted text, without displaying any of the XML code (see Figure 13.7).

FIGURE 13.6 • *When a style sheet is not attached, Internet Explorer 6 for Windows displays the raw XML code.*

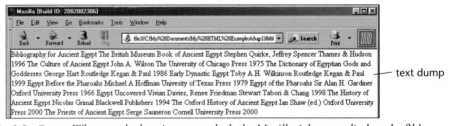

FIGURE 13.7 • *When a style sheet is not attached, the Mozilla 1 browser displays the file's unformatted text.*

Link the XML document to a CSS style sheet:

```
<?xml version="1.0" encoding="UTF-8" standalone="yes"?>
<?xml-stylesheet type="text/css" href="bibl.css"?>
<biblio>
<heading>Bibliography for Ancient Egypt</heading>
```

Creating the Style Sheet

You create an external CSS style sheet for an XML document just as you would for an HTML 4 or XHTML 1 document. The only difference is that for an XML document, you create styles for XML element names, instead of for HTML 4 and XHTML 1 element names.

Create the external CSS style sheet that is attached to your XML document:

1. In your text editor, open a new blank document. Create the following style sheet:

```
biblio {
    display: block;
    position: absolute;
    left: 0px; top: 0px;
    width: 103%;
    color: navy; background: white url(back_paper.jpg);
    padding: 16px;
    }
heading {
    display: block;
    font-size: 28px;
    font-family: 'Comic Sans MS', Arial, Helvetica, sans-serif;
    text-align: center;
    border-bottom: lime ridge 5px;
    margin-bottom: 16px; padding-bottom: 5px;
    }
item {
    display: block;
    border-bottom: 1px solid black;
    margin-bottom: 8px; padding-bottom: 10px;
    }
title {
    display: block;
    color: red; background: transparent;
    font-style: italic; font-weight: bold;
    font-family: Arial, Helvetica, sans-serif;
    }
author {
    display: block;
    color: purple; background: transparent;
    }
publisher {
    display: block;
    }
date {
    display: block;
    }
```

2. Save the file and switch to your browser. Open **biblio.xml** in your browser as **biblio.xml** in the chap13 folder (see Figure 13.8). (In Internet Explorer, select All Files from the Files of type list box to see files with a .xml extension in the Open dialog box.)

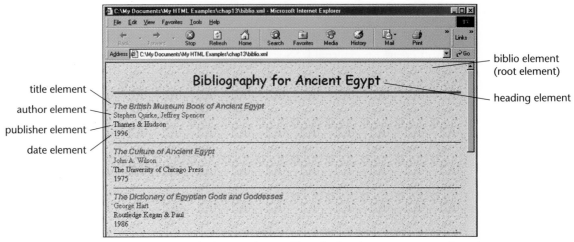

title element
author element
publisher element
date element

biblio element (root element)
heading element

Bibliography for Ancient Egypt

The British Museum Book of Ancient Egypt
Stephen Quirke, Jeffrey Spencer
Thames & Hudson
1996

The Culture of Ancient Egypt
John A. Wilson
The University of Chicago Press
1975

The Dictionary of Egyptian Gods and Goddesses
George Hart
Routledge Kegan & Paul
1986

FIGURE 13.8 • *The formatted XML file is displayed in an XML-compliant browser.*

A few comments about this style sheet are in order:

- The BIBLIO element is absolutely positioned in the document window. The reason for doing this is that Internet Explorer 6 for Windows, for instance, inserts a default margin around the page, while the Mozilla 1 browser does not. Setting the element's margin to zero does not eliminate the default margins set by Internet Explorer 6. The effect of this is to display a white border space around the tiled background image that is also set for the BIBLIO element. Absolutely positioning the element at the top-left corner of the document window eliminates the problem.

- A **width: 103%** property is set for the BIBLIO element. Setting this to **100%** results in a white margin space appearing along the right edge of the document window in Internet Explorer 6, but increasing the width property to a value of **103%** eliminates the white margin space.

- The **padding: 16px** property set for the BIBLIO element creates the visual margin space that is seen around the bibliography content (with the background image displayed behind it).

- All of the style sheet elements have a **display: block** property set. Without this being set, the elements would default to being inline elements (**display: inline**).

- Pixel-measurement units, rather than em-measurement units, are used throughout the style sheet because browsers are highly inconsistent in how they handle em-measurement units in XML documents.

This is, of course, a simple example of an XML document formatted using a CSS style sheet. It is a perfectly valid XML document, however, and should at least give you a taste of what it is to work with an actual XML document. A great deal more can be learned about using XML, but pursuing that here would go far beyond the primary focuses of this chapter.

NOTE

To display XML documents, a browser must have an XML parser built into it. The most current browsers, such as Internet Explorer 6, Netscape 6, Mozilla 1, and Opera 6, among others, can all display XML documents, although they may not all equally support the latest XML technologies, such as XLink (for including hypertext links directly in XML documents). Mozilla 1, for instance, supports XLink, but Internet Explorer 6 for Windows does not. Earlier browsers, however, such as Internet Explorer 4 or Netscape Navigator 4, for instance, lack XML parsers and cannot display XML documents.

See this chapter's section at the IRC for this book at **www.emcp.com/** for links to resources on the Web where you learn more about working with XML documents

CHAPTER SUMMARY

You should have an understanding of what XHTML is, why it has been developed, and what some of the advantages are of using XHTML to create Web pages. You have had hands-on experience updating an HTML file so that it conforms to the XHTML 1.0 specification, as well as validating an XHTML file using the W3C's HTML Validator. You should be familiar with the more strict syntax requirements that are required to create a valid XHTML 1.0 document, as well as other factors that differentiate a valid XHTML document from a valid HTML document.

This chapter provided examples of creating XHTML and XML files that use CSS style sheets to specify presentation and formatting. Additional discussion was also provided of using other style sheet languages with XML documents, such as DSSSL (Document Style Semantics and Specification Language) and XSL/XSLT (Extensible Style Sheet Language and XSL Transformations.

Code Review

ID attribute	In XHTML documents, replaces the NAME attribute as a fragment identifier target. The NAME attribute is included in XHTML 1.0 for transitional purposes and can be used at the same time as the ID attribute, for browsers that recognize the NAME attribute, but not the ID attribute.
XML:LANG attribute	In XHTML documents, replaces the LANG attribute for identifying the language content of a document or element. The LANG attribute is included in XHTML 1.0 for transitional purposes and can be used at the same time as the XML:LANG attribute.
`<?xml version="1.0" encoding="UTF-8"?>`	The XML declaration that should be inserted at the top of all XML (and XHTML) documents. The encoding attribute value specifies the character encoding system.
`xmlns="http://www.w3.org/1999/xhtml"`	The XMLNS attribute, when inserted in the HTML element, declares that elements and attributes contained within it belong to the XHTML namespace.
noshade="noshade"	Expansion of a minimized attribute (the NOSHADE attribute), which is required for XHTML documents.
` `	In XHTML, empty elements must be closed with a "/" character. The space is inserted to allow for earlier HTML browsers, which otherwise ignore the "/" character.
`standalone="yes"`	In the XML declaration, declares that the document is a standalone document and that only internal declarations need to be processed. The default value is **no**.
`style="text-align: justify"`	Required in XHTML documents to justify paragraph text, because `align="justify"` is not allowed in XHTML documents.

`<?xml-stylesheet type=` `"text/css" href="bibl.css"?>`	An XML style sheet declaration, with the TYPE attribute specifying the style sheet language (CSS, in this case) and the HREF attribute specifying the location (optional) and name of the style sheet file.

ONLINE QUIZ

Go to this text's IRC at **www.emcp.com/** and take the online self-check quiz for this chapter.

REVIEW EXERCISES

This section provides some hands-on practice exercises to reinforce the information and material included within this chapter. For this chapter, you will be working with an example XHTML document, watson-practice_ex.html, that is included with the other example files in the chap13 folder. It contains errors that will cause it not to validate as a valid XHTML 1.0 document. You will upload the document to the W3C HTML Validator to discover the validation errors, correct the errors, and then successfully validate the document as valid XHTML 1.0.

1. Open **watson-practice_ex.html** in your text editor and resave it as **watson-practice.html** in the chap13 folder.
2. Run your browser and go to the W3C site at **www.w3.org/**. Click the HTML Validator link in the sidebar, and then scroll down the page and click the "upload files" link.
3. Click the Browse button to the right of the File text box. Navigate to and open the chap13 folder where you saved watson-practice.html. Double-click on **watson-practice.html** (or single-click on it and click the Open button).
4. Click the Validate this document button. A "Results" page reports conditions in the document that cause it to be an invalid XHTML 1.0 document (see Figure 13.9).

FIGURE 13.9 • *The W3C HTML Validator reports that there are errors in watson-practice.html that cause it not to validate as an XHTML 1.0 document.*

5. Read and interpret the first error (for line 7, column 67). In your text editor, correct the problem that is causing the error and resave the document.

6. In your browser, click the Back button to return to the HTML Validator's upload page. If necessary, click the Browse button to reselect watson-practice.html as the document to be uploaded. Click the Validate this document button. If you have corrected the error condition, the first two error reports (for line 7, column 67, and for line 7, column 0) will have disappeared. If the error is not corrected, return to your text editor to correct the error and then revalidate the document.

7. Repeat this process for each of the errors that the HTML Validator reports. To help you locate where the error is occurring, the HTML Validator provides a numbered line listing for the document at the bottom of the error report.

8. When you manage to eliminate all of the errors, receiving a report that there are no more errors in the document and that it validates as a valid XHTML 1.0 document, in your browser, select File and Save As to save a copy of the page to the chap13 folder. (In Internet Explorer 6, click Yes at the Save Web Page dialog box and then add .html extension to the file name.) If you are connected to a printer, you also can print out a copy of the page to show that you have corrected all errors in the page.

WEB-BASED LEARNING ACTIVITIES

In this book's text, Find It icons inserted in the margin highlight the Web addresses of additional resources you might find helpful or informative. To further extend your learning using the Web, you can:

- Go back and visit any of the Web addresses highlighted in this chapter that you have not yet visited. Look for additional resources and information that add to your understanding and knowledge of the material covered in this chapter. When you find a relevant page or site with information or resources you might want to access later, add it to your Favorites (in Internet Explorer) or your Bookmarks (in Netscape or Mozilla).

- Visit this book's IRC at **www.emcp.com/** to find additional Web addresses of resources related to the material covered in this chapter that you can further investigate and explore.

- Look for additional resources and information that add to your understanding and knowledge of the material covered in this chapter. Use Yahoo!, Google, AltaVista, or other directories and search engines to expand your research. When you find a relevant page or site with information or resources you might want to access later, add it to your Favorites (in Internet Explorer) or your Bookmarks (in Netscape or Mozilla).

- For instance, you might do additional research on the relationship between SGML and HTML (and XHTML), or you might research issues involved with using different character sets in HTML and XHTML documents. You also can research the continuing development of XHTML, CSS, the DOM, XML, XSL/XSLT, and other related cutting-edge Web technologies and what that might mean for the future of the Internet and the Web. Compile the results of your research into a report. You also can team up with other students to create a presentation on a topic you and your teammates have researched.

PROJECTS

These projects can be done in class, in a computer lab, or at home. Use the skills you have developed in this and the previous chapters to create any of the following projects.

Project 1. Update a Web page or site that you have already created to XHTML 1.0.

Update a Web page or site that you have already created so that it is coded using valid XHTML 1.0 code. Use the pointers provided in this chapter as guides to updating elements and attributes to the proper syntax that is expected in an XHTML document. When finished updating a page, upload it to the W3C's HTML Validator to test its validity. When you succeed in validating your page, print out or save the results page declaring that your page is a valid XHTML 1.0 document, so you can show that you have successfully completed the project. After validating your page as a valid XHTML 1.0 document, include the W3C's XHTML logo at the bottom of your page (or anywhere else on your page where you want to display it). If updating a Web site, repeat for each page in the site.

Project 2. Create a Web page or site from scratch using XHTML 1.0.

Create a Web page or site from scratch that is coded using valid XHTML 1.0 code. When finished creating your page, upload it to the W3C's HTML Validator to test its validity. When you succeed in validating a page, print out or save the results page declaring that your page is a valid XHTML 1.0 document and insert the code to display the W3C's XHTML logo at the bottom of the page (or anywhere else on your page where you want to display it).

Incorporate any other features you have learned in previous chapters that you feel will enhance your project.

Project 3. Create a Web page using XML.

Create a Web page that is coded using XML code. To take the best advantage of the strengths of XML in presenting structured data, create a Web page that presents data that is organized in repeatable subsets (such as the items in the bibliography example that was demonstrated in the chapter body). For instance, you might choose to format a listing of meal recipes (ingredients, preparation directions, and so on), favorite movies (release date, studio, director, actors, and so on), or a catalog of classes required to finish your certificate or degree. When creating your XML page, be sure to include an XML declaration that declares the version of XML your page is using. Define a root element within which all other elements are nested. Create element names that describe their content. Test your XML page in a browser that contains an XML parser, such as Internet Explorer 6 for Windows or Mozilla 1, for instance.

TEAM PROJECT
Web Design Technologies

In this section, you participate in a team project, cooperating with others in planning, preparing, creating, and publishing a Web site that effectively incorporates features and components covered in this part's chapters. Remember, it is not just the performance of the team that matters, but also your performance as a member of the team. Learning how to cooperate, communicate, and coordinate is just as important as learning how to code a page or design a graphic.

Your work on this project should demonstrate all of the skills you have learned in this text. For this team project, you can include any element, feature, or technology covered in any part of this book, including Part One, Part Two, and Part Three. One of your main focuses should be on creating a team project that shows main features covered in Part Three, but other features covered in other areas of the book also should be included in your project.

Your team project should implement and show some or all of the following features that were covered in Part Three:

- JavaScript scripts that help enhance feedback, interactivity, immediateness, usability, and navigation. Find and adapt scripts or create your own scripts from scratch. Show how external scripts can be applied to several pages within a site.
- Dynamic HTML effects that involve causing objects to change, appear, disappear, jump from one location to another, or move along a trajectory in response to user actions or system events.
- Optionally, create your project using only valid XHTML 1.0 code, including all required and recommended declarations, properly nested elements, closed empty elements, quoted attribute values, lowercase element and attribute names, and other required and strongly recommended XHTML 1.0 features. Validate your code. Creating XHTML 1.0 Web pages that also include JavaScript scripts and Dynamic HTML (DHTML) effects might pose additional challenges.

In addition, your team project should also show many of the following features that were covered in the other parts of this book:

- Basic proficiency in HTML, including using heading-level elements, paragraph elements, hypertext links, bulleted and numbered lists, link lists, horizontally aligned elements, inline images, and address elements. Other features that should be demonstrated include the use of inline highlighting (bold, italic, and monospaced text), block quotes, and superscripts (and/or subscripts).
- The proper use of DocType statements to identify the version (HTML 4.01 or XHTML 1.0) and level conformance (strict, transitional, or frameset) of your project's Web pages. The use of META elements to declare the character set used in a page, provide a page description, and enumerate a list of relevant keywords that can be used by search engines and directories to index your page.

- Menu links that jump to sections within a page (or within another page) and return links (or loop back links) that return users to their starting position. You also can demonstrate the use of footnote or endnote links.

- The proper insertion of non-keyboard characters, including the copyright symbol, the registered symbol, or other characters from the ISO 8859-1 character set. You also can demonstrate the display of verbatim HTML code in Web pages by substituting the proper entity code names for the <, >, &, and " characters. For an added challenge, include Unicode characters (such as characters from the Greek, Hebrew, or other non-Latin languages).

- The effective use of the FONT element and its SIZE, COLOR, and FACE attributes, as well as the use of the BODY element's TEXT, LINK, VLINK, ALINK, BGCOLOR, and BACKGROUND attributes to set text colors, link colors, background colors, and background images. Optionally, use Cascading Style Sheets (CSS) to set foreground colors, link colors, background colors, and background images.

- The effective use of graphics, horizontally aligning images on the page; flowing text and other elements around images; using graphic rules, buttons, banners, and logos; and creating your own optimized GIF and JPEG Web graphics. Optionally, use or create your own GIF animations to add movement, dynamism, and visual interest to your pages. For a bigger challenge, demonstrate the effective embedding of audio, video, or animation in a page.

- The effective use of the PRE or TABLE elements in the presentation of tabular data in rows and columns. Demonstrate table features, such as setting the table width, aligning horizontally on the page, spanning rows and columns, setting the width and appearance of table columns, controlling the appearance of table rows and cells, and other table features. Optionally, show how to use styles to control the appearance of tables. Use a table to create a two-column or three-column page layout.

- Use of frames to create a multi-windowed Web site. Create a two-row, two-column, or combination row-column framed layout. Optionally, demonstrate using styles to control the appearance of your framed site. Use relative URLs to link to pages and images in multiple folders.

- Use of valid HTML or XHTML code, as well as valid CSS code. After validating a page's HTML (or XHTML) and CSS code using the W3C's HTML Validator and CSS Validator, display the W3C's logo images to declare the validity of your page's code.

- Use of FTP to publish your project's site to a server on the Web, using Web space provided by your school or by a free Web space provider. Thoroughly test your site after publishing, to make sure that links are still working and images are still displaying.

- Incorporation of a form in your project, showing the effective use of text boxes, radio buttons, check boxes, list menus, text area boxes, submit and reset buttons, and other form features. Create your form as either a mailto or CGI form.

- Creation of a Web site where presentation is entirely controlled by CSS style sheets, with HTML elements controlling only the structural organization of the pages. Try to avoid using deprecated elements, such as FONT elements or ALIGN attributes, for instance, relying instead upon styles to achieve the same or better results. Demonstrate the use of simple selectors, group selectors, contextual selectors, class selectors, ID selectors, DIV and SPAN elements, absolute or relative positioning, and the z-index property to set the stacking order of objects. Use link and dynamic pseudo-classes to create CSS rollover links and buttons.

- Creation of a graphical front-end using an image map or a table layout using sliced images. If creating an image map, be sure to ensure the usability of the page even if the display of graphics is turned off. If creating a wraparound graphical interface, for instance, using sliced images, be sure to test your page in several browsers (including recent versions of the Internet Explorer, Netscape, Mozilla, and Opera browsers). Alternatively, use a JavaScript to preload images and create a rollover button effect.
- Use of "sticky" and other features to create immediacy and feedback, provide new and changing content, and enhance navigation, using counters, date and time stamps, news and weather feeds, and search forms, for instance. Demonstrate the creation of Web communities using guestbooks, message boards, chat rooms, Web polls, and other add-ons that encourage visitors to your site to become engaged and interact with each other. Exhibit the use of viral marketing techniques, such as using link referrers, bookmark scripts, and other ways of encouraging return visits and word of mouth recommendations.

1. BRAINSTORM TOPICS, AUDIENCES, AND OBJECTIVES

With your teammates, brainstorm the kinds of topics, audiences, and objectives you might want to target. Come up with at least six topics for possible projects (with each teammate suggesting at least two topics). For each project topic, define the audience you want to address, and the goal you want to achieve by addressing that audience with the topic. Try to come to a consensus on the topic, target audience, and objective.

If you have difficulties coming up with ideas or cannot agree on a topic, audience, and objective, use Yahoo! at **www.yahoo.com/**, Google at **www.google.com/**, or any other search engine to search for sites that can suggest ideas to you.

See the team project section at the end of Part One for further details about how to brainstorm the topics, audiences, and objectives of your project.

2. SUBMIT YOUR PROJECT PROPOSAL FOR APPROVAL

Try to incorporate everything that is most relevant about your project in a single concise mission statement. Following your mission statement, include further information about your project. Include information about the topic of the project, the audience you will be addressing, the goals you hope to achieve, and the methods and techniques you plan to implement to achieve those goals. Keep it to less than one double-spaced page. Be sure to share responsibility for formulating and creating this proposal with the members of your team.

Submit this proposal to your instructor for approval.

3. CREATE AN OUTLINE

Break down your approved project into parts. Create an outline of your site's planned content that is at least two levels deep, with the first level signifying the major branching subpages within your project's site, and the second level signifying major section headings within those pages. After creating your outline, you should have a good idea of what the content of your site will be and how it will be organized.

4. ESTABLISH LAYOUT AND NAVIGATION SCHEMES

Discuss which layout and navigation schemes are appropriate and best suited for your project. See the team project section at the end of Part One for further details about determining which layout and navigation schemes might be appropriate for your project.

5. CREATE A STORYBOARD

A storyboard is a kind of cartoon of your site, showing how your site's pages are ordered and related to each other. A Web site can be organized in many ways. Creating a pictorial representation of your site helps clarify the major relationships that exist between the different parts of your site. See the team project section at the end of Part One for further details about how to create a storyboard for your project.

6. DRAW A MAP

To visualize the dynamic relationships that can be achieved using hypertext links to create navigation schemes, you can draw a map of your site that shows how its pages are linked together. See the team project section at the end of Part One for further details about how to create a map for your project.

7. ESTABLISH A COLOR SCHEME

Experiment with different text, link, and background colors to establish an appropriate and effective color scheme for your project. Pay attention to legibility and accessibility when choosing color combinations. Optionally, incorporate a background image into your color scheme. Come to a team consensus on the color scheme you want to implement.

8. DEFINE RESPONSIBILITIES AND SET A TIMELINE

Responsibilities for creating the site should be shared coequally among team members. When you start to actually create your project, however, you will need to agree on who will be responsible for which tasks, the order in which those tasks need to be completed, and a timeline detailing the milestones (along with their respective target dates) that need to be achieved to complete the project and the due dates for those tasks. Be prepared to renegotiate these agreements, if necessary, as work on the project commences, to take into account unexpected demands that might arise. In planning and executing the project, you also need to take into account any overall due date that your instructor has set for the project.

See the team project section at the end of Part One for further details about ways in which you can allocate responsibilities for your project.

No matter how responsibilities are assigned, it is important that each team member gain experience in all aspects of creating the project. Taking a leadership role for a particular area does not mean excluding others from participating in that area.

9. BUILD THE SITE

Begin building the site, considering the timeline and assignment dates provided by your instructor. See the team project section at the end of Part One for further details about different activities that might be involved in building your project's Web site.

10. TEST AND TROUBLESHOOT

All team members should participate in testing and troubleshooting the project's site. Test the project's site in several browsers. For instance, you can test your project's site in the most recent Internet Explorer, Netscape, Mozilla, and Opera browsers. You also can test your project's site for backward compatibility in a version of Netscape Navigator 4.

When you run into problems, you might have to selectively comment out code to isolate the problem code. If you are not able to get a code to work across browsers, you should consider not using the code.

Validate your site's pages using the W3C HTML Validation Service at **validator.w3.org/**. If you are using CSS in your project, also validate your site's style sheets using the W3C CSS Validation Service at **jigsaw.w3.org/css-validator/**.

11. PUBLISH TO THE WEB

Using Web space provided by your school or by another provider of free Web space, publish your project's site so it can be viewed over the Web. Get suggestions, comments, and other feedback from fellow classmates on how you can improve your site. Make revisions to your site that incorporate positive changes suggested by your fellow classmates.

Submit your site to search engines so you can get feedback and comments from visitors to your site who are not fellow classmates.

12. CRITIQUE YOUR WORK

Write a self-critique of your participation in the team project. List some of the important lessons you learned while doing the project. Spell out where you think you performed well and where you think you performed less well, detailing some of the reasons that determined your performance. Point out areas in which you feel you need to improve and what you need to work on in order to improve.

Include a critique of your team's performance. Evaluate your team's ability to communicate, work cooperatively, complete assigned responsibilities in a timely and satisfactory manner, and any other factors that made either a positive or negative contribution to completing the project.

As part of your critique, indicate whether the site fulfilled the approved mission statement and support your evaluation with examples. Report your recommendations for improving or further enhancing the site developed by your team.

APPENDIX A

HTML Quick Reference

This HTML quick reference consists of two parts. The first part includes a listing in alphabetical order of all of the standard elements of HTML 4.01 and their most commonly used attributes. The second part covers generic and other attributes that are applied to many elements.

Elements and attributes that were first standardized in HTML 3.2 and HTML 4.0 are marked with "3.2" and "4.0." All recent browsers should support HTML 3.2 elements and attributes. Use of HTML 4.0 elements and attributes requires more care, however, because some HTML 4.0 elements and attributes are widely supported, but others are currently only supported by a few browsers or not at all.

HTML ELEMENTS

A (Anchor)	**Type:** Inline/Container	**Content:** Inline

Attributes	name="*destination anchor name*"	See note
	href="*URL and/or fragment identifier*"	See note
	target="*frame name*"	Optional

Note: Either NAME or HREF is required.

Example	`<a href="http://www.somesite.com/somedir/somepage.html">Go to my page.</a>`

ABBR (Abbreviation) (4.0)	**Type:** Inline/Container	**Content:** Inline

Specifies the expanded form of an abbreviation. If the letters of a shortened expression are individually pronounced, such as ABC, FBI, BBC, NCAA, NAACP, WWW, CSS, and so on, it is an abbreviation.

Attributes	title="*expanded term*"

Example	`<p>J. Edgar Hoover was the first Director of the <abbr title="Federal Bureau of Investigation">FBI</abbr>.`

ACRONYM (4.0)

Type: Inline/Container   **Content:** Inline

Specifies the expanded form of an acronym. If the shortened expression is pronounced as a word, such as NATO, CERN, radar, laser, SOHO, SCUBA, and so on, it is an acronym.

Attributes	`title="expanded term"`
Example	`<p>The World Wide Web was invented by Tim Berners-Lee at <acronym title="Conseil European pour la Recherche Nucleaire/European Organization for Nuclear Research">CERN</acronym>.</p>`

ADDRESS

Type: Inline/Container   **Content:** Inline

Identifies the author/owner of a Web page, along with a means to contact or provide feedback, such as a link to a contact page.

Note: The ALIGN attribute is not a legal attribute for the ADDRESS element, although many browsers recognize it. Block elements are not allowed within the ADDRESS element (although browsers do not care).

Example	`<address>` `Roger Dodger ` `E-mail: <a href="mailto:rogdodg@blutto.com">rogdodg@blutto.com</a>` `</address>`

APPLET (3.2) (Deprecated)

Type: Inline/Container   **Content:** Inline

Inserts a Java applet inline within an HTML document.

Attributes		
	`code="applet class file"`	See Note
	`object="applet class resource"` (4.0)	See Note
	`alt="alternative text description"`	Recommended
	`codebase="URL"`	Optional
	`archive="comma-delimited list of URLs"` (4.0)	Optional
	`width="n|n%"`	Optional
	`height="n|n%"`	Optional
	`name="applet name"`	Optional
	`align="top|middle|bottom|left|right|center"`	Optional
	`hspace="n"`	Optional
	`vspace="n"`	Optional

Note: Either CODE or OBJECT is required. If both are present, they must reference the same applet class file name.

PARAM (3.2) (Deprecated in APPLET)

Type: Inline/Empty   **Content:** N/A

When nested inside an APPLET element, passes parameters to a Java applet. Also can be nested inside an OBJECT element. *See also* OBJECT.

Attributes		
	`name="parameter name"`	Required
	`value="parameter value"`	Required

Note: The NAME attribute value must start with a letter (A–Z or a–z), with the remainder of the value composed of letters, numbers, hyphens, or periods.

AREA (3.2)

See MAP.

B (Bold)
Type: Inline/Container   **Content:** Inline

Specifies that nested text should be bolded. *See also* EM (Emphasis), STRONG (Strong Emphasis), and I (Italic).

Example
```
<p>It is <b>important</b> that assignments be turned in on time.</p>
```

BASE

See HEAD.

BASEFONT (3.2) (Deprecated)
Type: Inline/Empty   **Content:** N/A

Sets font characteristics for following text. BASEFONT is not implemented in many recent browsers and should be avoided. *See also* FONT.

Attributes		
`size="1|2|3|4|5|6|7"`		Optional
`color="color name|RGB color code"` (4.0)		Optional
`face="font name|font name list"` (4.0)		Optional

BDO (4.0)
Type: Inline/Container   **Content:** Inline

Changes the direction in which nested text is displayed.

Attributes		
`dir="LTR|RTL"`		Required
`lang="language code"`		Optional

BIG (3.2)
Type: Inline/Container   **Content:** Inline

Increases the size of nested text by one font size. The sizes correspond to the seven font sizes that can be set with the FONT and BASEFONT elements. *See also* SMALL.

Example
```
<p>In case of a fire alarm, walk, don't run, to the nearest
<big>Exit</big> sign.</p>
```

BLOCKQUOTE
Type: Block/Container   **Content:** Block/SCRIPT

Displays a long quotation as an indented block.

Attributes		
`cite="URL"`		Optional

Example
```
<p>When starting a chess game, one should keep in mind the following
basic principles, enumerated by the great American Grandmaster,
Frank J. Marshall, in his book, <em>Chess Step by Step</em>:
<blockquote>
```

```
<p>In selecting a Sphere of Action, always move the pieces where
they will command the greatest number of squares, have the greatest
freedom of action, where they cannot be readily attacked or driven
away, and where they will restrict or delay the opponent's
development.</p>
</blockquote>
```

BODY
Type: Container   **Content:** Block

In a non-frameset page, one of two elements (along with HEAD) that is nested directly inside the HTML element. Both the start tag and end tag are optional in HTML 4.01.

Attributes	text="*color name*|*RGB color code*" (Deprecated)	Optional
	link="*color name*|*RGB color code*" (Deprecated)	Optional
	vlink="*color name*|*RGB color code*" (Deprecated)	Optional
	alink="*color name*|*RGB color code*" (Deprecated)	Optional
	bgcolor="*color name*|*RGB color code*" (Deprecated)	Optional
	background="*image URL*" (Deprecated)	Optional

Example
```
<body text="navy" link="red" vlink="#666600" alink="#666600"
bgcolor="#ffffcc" background="images/back_light.jpg">
```

BR (Break)
Type: Inline/Empty   **Content:** N/A

Causes a line break to be displayed.

Attributes	clear="left|right|all" (Deprecated)	Optional

Note: The CLEAR attribute causes text flowing around a floating image to move down until the left, right, or both margins are clear (not obstructed by the floating image).

Example
```
<h2>From "Auguries of Innocence" by William Blake:</h2>
<blockquote>
<p>To see a World in a Grain of Sand<br>
And a Heaven in a Wild Flower,<br>
Hold Infinity in the palm of your hand<br>
And Eternity in an hour.</p>
</blockquote>
```

BUTTON (4.0)

See FORM.

CAPTION (3.2)

See TABLE.

CENTER (3.2) (Deprecated)
Type: Block/Container   **Content:** Block/Inline

Centers nested text or elements horizontally on the page. In HTML 3.2 and HTML 4, the CENTER element is equivalent to a DIV element with an `align="center"` attribute set.

Example
```
<center>
<h2>Announcement:</h2>
<p>You can sign up for volunteer positions starting on Friday at
8:00 a.m.</p>
</center>
```

CITE   **Type:** Inline/Container   **Content:** Inline

Indicates that nested text is a citation of a source. Text nested in the CITE element is generally displayed in italics. EM or I can be used to achieve the same effect.

Example
```
<p>"There is no safe trusting to dictionaries and definitions," as
Charles Lamb stressed, in "Popular Fallacies," <cite>Essays of
Elia</cite>.
```

CODE (Computer Code)   **Type:** Inline/Container   **Content:** Inline

Indicates that nested text is a fragment of computer (or program) code. Text nested in the CODE element is generally displayed in a monospaced font. The TT (Teletype Text) element can alternatively be used to format computer code.

Example
```
<p>Start by declaring a variable that sets a starting value for the
count: <code>var count = 1;</code>.</p>
```

COL (Column) (4.0)

See Table.

COLGROUP (Column Group) (4.0)

See Table.

DD (Definition Data)

See DL (Definition List).

DEL (Delete) (4.0)   **Type:** Inline/Container   **Content:** Inline

Marks nested text as a deletion. In browsers that support this element, nested text is generally displayed as strikeout text (with a line drawn through it). STRIKE and S also can be used to display strikeout text, with STRIKE being the most widely supported. *See also* INS (Insert).

Example   `<h1><del>My </del>Frequently Asked Questions Page</h1>`

DFN (Definition) (3.2)   **Type:** Inline/Container   **Content:** Inline

Marks nested text as the defining instance of a term. Nested text is generally displayed in italics, but some earlier browsers might bold it.

Example
```
<p>JavaScript is an <dfn>object-oriented</dfn> scripting language,
which means that when you work with JavaScript, you are primarily
involved in defining and manipulating objects.</p>
```

DIR (Directory List) (Deprecated)   **Type:** Block/Container   **Content:** Block

The DIR element was originally intended for displaying multi-column directory lists, but this was never implemented in browsers. The UL element produces exactly the same result in all browsers and should be used instead. *See also* UL (Unordered List).

DIV (Division) (3.2)   **Type:** Block/Container   **Content:** Inline/Block

Marks a division within a document (a document division).

Attributes   align="**left**|right|center|justify" (Deprecated)   Optional

Note: The ALIGN attribute is the only HTML formatting that can be applied to a DIV element. All other formatting must be applied using an inline style (using the STYLE attribute), an embedded style sheet (the STYLE element), or an externally linked style sheet (using the LINK element).

Example
```
<div align="center">
<h1>Causes of the American Revolution</h1>
<h2>by William Jefferson</h2>
</div>
```

DL (Definition List)   **Type:** Block/Container   **Content:** Block

Designates that nested text is a definition list (or glossary). Nested DT (Definition Term) and DD (Definition Data) elements designate the terms and definitions.

Attributes   compact (Deprecated)   Optional

Note: The COMPACT attribute is a hint to a browser that a definition list can be displayed in a more compact way. Browsers that support this, such as Internet Explorer 6, for instance, display the DT and DD elements on the same line, as long as the DT text does not include more than four characters. Most browsers, however, ignore the COMPACT element, so it is best avoided.

DT (Definition Term)   **Type:** Block/Container   **Content:** Inline

Designates nested text as a term in a definition list. The end tag is optional.

DD (Definition Data)   **Type:** Block/Container   **Content:** Inline/Block

Designates nested text as a definition in a definition list. The DD element is generally indented in from the left margin. The end tag is optional.

Example
```
<dl>
<dt>crippleware
<dd>A form of shareware software program in which one or more key
functions have been crippled.
<dt>demoware
<dd>A form of shareware software program that is distributed for
demonstration purposes only, usually with an evaluation period,
```

```
                      after which the software stops functioning.
                      </dl>
```

EM (Emphasis)   **Type:** Inline/Container   **Content:** Inline

Marks nested text as emphasized, which is displayed in italics in all browsers. Alternatively, the I (Italics) element can be used to achieve the same result. *See also* STRONG (Strong Emphasis), I (Italic), and B (Bold).

Example
```
<p>When moving, it is very <em>important</em> to submit a Change of
Address form at the post office.</p>
```

FIELDSET (4.0)

See FORM.

FONT (3.2) (Deprecated)   **Type:** Inline/Container   **Content:** Inline

Designates font characteristics, including size, color, and face, that are to be applied to nested text.

Attributes
```
size="n[1|2|3|4|5|6|7] or +n|-n"                        See Note
color="color name|RGB color code"                       Optional
face="font name|font name list"                         Optional
```

Note: The default font size is equivalent to `size="3"`, unless it has been reset by a preceding BASE-FONT element or a bracketing FONT element. A + or - sign preceding the size number designates a font size that is relative to the default font size.

Example
```
<h1><font size="7" color="blue" face="Arial">Upcoming
Schedule</font></h1>
```

FORM   **Type:** Block/Container   **Content:** Block

Designates that nested elements are part of a form.

Attributes
```
action="URL"                                            Required
method="get|post"                                       Optional
enctype="content type"                                  Optional
```

Note: ACTION attribute should specify an HTTP URL; behavior of user agents resulting from use of non-HTTP URLs (such as a mailto URL) is undefined. For user-input forms, use the **post** value with the METHOD attribute.

INPUT   **Type:** Inline/Empty   **Content:** N/A

Defines various input controls that can be included in forms, including text boxes, radio buttons, check boxes, and more.

Attributes
```
type="text|password|checkbox|radio|submit
     |reset|file|hidden|image|button"                   See Note
name="control name"                                      See Note
value="initial value"                                    See Note
```

`size="n"`	See Note
`maxlength="n"`	See Note
`checked`	See Note
`src="URL"`	See Note

Note: The TYPE attribute is optional when creating text boxes, but required when creating other input controls. When submitted, values input by the user are associated with the NAME attribute value. The VALUE attribute is required for check boxes and radio buttons, but optional otherwise. The SIZE and MAXLENGTH attribute number specifies the width in character spaces for text box and password input controls, but in pixels for other input controls. The CHECKED attribute is recognized only for radio button and check box controls. The SRC attribute, specifying the location of an image, is required only when creating an image input control.

Example

```
<form action="http://www.mysite.com/cgi-bin/sendform.pl"
method="post">
<p><input type="hidden" name="recipient" value="bonzo@bedtime.com">
First Name/Initial: <input type="text" name="FirstName"
size="30"><br>
Last Name: <input type="text" name="LastName" size="30"><br>
Gender: <input type="radio" name="Sex" value="Male"> <input
type="radio" name="Sex" value="Female">
Allergies: <input type="checkbox" name="Allergies" value="Food">
<input type="checkbox" name="Allergies" value="Pets"> <input
type="checkbox" name="Allergies" value="Trees/Plants"> <input
type="checkbox" name="Allergies" value="Molds/Fungi"> <input
type="checkbox" name="Allergies" value="Chemicals"><p>
<p><input type="submit" value="Submit"> <input type="reset"
value="Reset"></p>
</form>
```

SELECT

Type: Inline/Container   **Content:** OPTGROUP/OPTION

Creates a list menu, in combination with the OPTION element and, optionally, the OPTGROUP element.

Attributes

`name="control name"`	Optional
`size="n"`	Optional
`multiple`	Optional
`disabled`	Optional

Note: The SIZE attribute value specifies the number of visible rows (options) that will be displayed; the default value is **1**. MULTIPLE allows the selection of multiple options.

OPTION (Required in SELECT)

Type: Inline/Container   **Content:** Inline

Specifies an option in a list menu (required in the SELECT option). The end tag is optional.

Attributes

`selected`	Optional
`value="initial value"`	Optional
`label="option label"` (4.0)	Optional

Note: The VALUE attribute specifies the initial value for an option; otherwise, the option value defaults to the OPTION element's content. The LABEL attribute is supposed to specify a label for an option, but this attribute is not widely supported; otherwise, the option label defaults to the OPTION element's content.

Example	```<select name="menu">```
	```<option selected>Eenie</option>```
	```<option>Meenie</option>```
	```<option>Minie</option>```
	```<option>Moe</option>```
	```</select>```

TEXTAREA

Type: Inline/Container   **Content:** Text

Creates a multi-line text input box.

Attributes	```name="control name"```	Optional
	```rows="n"```	Required
	```cols="n"```	Required
	```disabled```	Optional
	```readonly```	Optional

Note: Browsers should display text nested within the element, if there is any, as its initial value.

Example	```<textarea name="comment" rows="20" cols="80">```
	```Type your comment here.```
	```</textarea>```

OPTGROUP (4.0) (Optional in SELECT)

Type: Inline/Container   **Content:** Inline

Specifies a group of options to be displayed in a list menu.

Attributes	```label="option group label"```	Required
	```disabled```	Optional

Example	```<select name="Foods" size="13" multiple>```
	```<optgroup label="Breakfast">```
	``` <option value="cereal">Cold Cereal w/Milk</option>```
	``` <option value="bacon">Bacon and Eggs</option>```
	``` <option value="fruit">Fresh Fruit</option>```
	```</optgroup>```
	```<optgroup label="Lunch">```
	``` <option value="bologna">Bologna w/Cheese Sandwich</option>```
	``` <option value="soup">Soup w/Salad</option>```
	``` <option value="peanut">Peanut Butter Sandwich</option>```
	```</optgroup>```
	```<optgroup label="Dinner">```
	``` <option value="steak">Steak w/Potatoes</option>```
	``` <option value="fish">Broiled Fish w/Rice</option>```
	``` <option value="chicken">Fried Chicken w/Fries</option>```
	``` <option value="vegetable">Vegetable Tempura</option>```
	```</optgroup>```
	```</select>```

BUTTON (4.0)

Type: Inline/Container   **Content:** Inline

This alternative to using the INPUT element to create Submit and Reset buttons has richer rendering possibilities. Also can be used to create push buttons that trigger scripts.

Attributes	```type="submit|reset|button"```	Optional
	```name="control-name"```	Optional

```
                       value="initial value"                                        Optional
                       tabindex="n"                                                  Optional
                       accesskey="character"                                         Optional
                       disabled                                                      Optional
```

Note: The button label is provided by the text nested inside the BUTTON element; if an image is nested inside the BUTTON element, it is displayed as the button.

Example
```
<p><button type="submit" name="submit" value="submit">
  <font size="5" color="red">Submit</font></button>  
<button name="reset" type="reset">
  <font size="5" color="purple">Reset</font></button></p>
```

LABEL (4.0)   **Type:** Inline/Container   **Content:** Inline

Associates a label with a form control.

Attributes   for="control ID"   Optional

Note: Although visual browsers do nothing with the LABEL element, its use can help non-visual browsers and screen readers identify the purpose and function of a form control. This can be especially useful when using a table to lay out form controls in which the text identifying the control's purpose and function is located in a separate table cell. The FOR value references the ID value of the associated form control.

Example
```
<tr>
<th><label for="fname">First Name/Initial:</label></th>
<td><input name="first" id="fname"></td>
</tr>
```

FIELDSET (4.0)   **Type:** Block/Container   **Content:** Inline/Block

In conjunction with the LEGEND element, specifies a set of thematically related form controls and labels.

LEGEND (4.0)   **Type:** Container   **Content:** Inline

In conjunction with the FIELDSET element, provides a legend for a set of thematically related form controls.

Example
```
<fieldset>
<legend>Academic Interests</legend>
<input type="checkbox" name="Interest" value="arts"> Arts
<input type="checkbox" name="Interest" value="science"> Science
<input type="checkbox" name="Interest" value="business"> Business
</fieldset>
```

FRAME (4.0)

See FRAMESET.

FRAMESET (4.0)
Type: Container   **Content:** FRAMESET, FRAME, NOFRAMES

Defines a set of framed windows to be displayed in a browser window. A page containing one or more FRAMESET elements is usually referred to as a frameset page and requires a DocType declaration declaring it to be compliant with the frameset definition of HTML 4.01 or XHTML 1.0.

Attributes	`rows="n,n,..."`	See Note
	`cols="n,n,..."`	See Note

Note: A FRAMESET element must contain either a ROWS or a COLS attribute, or it can contain both. The ROWS or COLS attribute value is a comma-separated list of two or more values specifying the vertical dimension of rows or the horizontal dimension of columns. The individual values can be of three types: pixel, percentage, or relative. A pixel value states a dimension in pixels; a percentage value states a dimension as a percentage of width or height of the browser window; a relative value expresses a dimension that is a ratio of the available vertical or horizontal space. For instance, `rows="25,1*,5%"` specifies a height of 25 pixels for the top row, a height of 5% of the browser window for the bottom row, and a height equivalent to 1 times the available space in the browser window for the middle row. The values 1* and * are equivalent. Likewise, `cols="50,5*,1*"` would set a width of 50 pixels for the first column, and then allot 5/6 and 1/6 of the remaining available browser space to the second and third columns.

FRAME (4.0)
Type: Empty   **Content:** N/A

Defines a single framed window within a frameset.

Attributes	`src="URL"`	See Note
	`name="frame name"`	See Note
	`frameborder="1|0"`	Optional
	`marginheight="n"`	Optional
	`marginwidth="n"`	Optional
	`scrolling="auto|yes|no"`	Optional
	`noresize`	Optional
	`longdesc="URL"`	Optional

Note: SRC is required to display content within a frame; an empty frame is displayed if an SRC URL is not specified. NAME is required if you want to target a frame's name in a hypertext link using the TARGET attribute. NORESIZE stops the user from manually resizing frame dimensions using the mouse cursor. LONGDESC specifies the URL of a document that provides a long description of the contents of the frame, which can improve accessibility for individuals with visual impairments.

Example

```
<!DOCTYPE HTML PUBLIC "-//W3C//DTD HTML 4.01 Frameset//EN"
 "http://www.w3.org/TR/html4/frameset.dtd">
<html>
<head>
<meta http-equiv="Content-Type" content="text/html; charset=ISO-
8859-1">
<title>NuShark Scuba Gear</title>
</head>
<frameset rows="85,*">
  <frame src="top.html" scrolling="no" marginheight="0">
  <frameset cols="150,*">
    <frame src="side.html">
    <frame src="front.html" name="main">
```

```
        </frameset>
      </frameset>
    </html>
```

NOFRAMES (4.0) **Type:** Container **Content:** BODY (optional), BLOCK

Provides content to be displayed in browsers that do not support frames (such as Internet Explorer 2.0, the default browser for Windows NT 4.0, for instance). The NOFRAMES element can be inserted inside the top-level FRAMESET element. The BODY element and any other elements normally nested inside the BODY element can be nested inside the NOFRAMES element. A hypertext link should be included in the NOFRAMES element that allows visitors using non-frames-capable browsers to access the rest of the site.

Example
```
<frameset rows="85,*">
  <frame src="top.html" scrolling="no" marginheight="0">
  <frameset cols="150,*">
    <frame src="side.html">
    <frame src="front.html" name="main">
  </frameset>
  <noframes>
  <p>A frames-capable browser is required to view this page. Please
go directly to my site's <a href="front.html">front page</a>.</p>
  </noframes>
</frameset>
```

H1, H2, H3, H4, H5, H6 (Heading Elements) **Type:** Block/Container **Content:** Inline

Allows the hierarchical organization of a document using six different heading levels. In practical terms, however, only the first four are likely to be used, because the H5 and H6 elements are displayed by default in most browsers in a font that is smaller than the default text size. The H1 element is generally only inserted once, as the document's top-level heading (or title).

Attributes   `align="left|center|right|justify"`   Optional

Example
```
<h1 align="center">My Life as an Emergency Room Attendant</h1>
<h2 align="center">by Ralph Green</h2>
```

HEAD (Header) **Type:** Container **Content:** HEAD elements

Along with the BODY element, one of two top-level elements that are nested directly inside the HTML element. The HEAD element is intended to contain elements that identify, describe, or direct the display of the page, whereas the BODY element contains all elements that are actually displayed within the page. Both the start tag and end tag are optional in HTML 4.01.

TITLE (Required) **Type:** Container **Content:** Inline

Specifies the title for a page, which is displayed on a browser's title bar.

Example
```
<html>
<head><title>Peter Locke's Political Science Site</title>
</head>
```

BASE
Type: Empty   **Content:** N/A

Specifies the absolute URL for the document that acts as a base for resolving relative URLs.

| *Attributes* | `href="URL"` | Required |

Example	

```
<head><title>John Peters' Political Science Site</title>
<base href="http://www.somewhere.com/peters/polysci/index.html">
</head>
<body>
<p align="center">Visit John Peter's <a href="../index.html">Home
Page</a></p>
<hr>
```

Note: Because of the BASE URL, the relative URL in the BODY element correlates to an absolute URL of http://www.somewhere.com/peters/index.html.

ISINDEX (Deprecated)
Type: Empty   **Content:** N/A

Creates a one-line text-input control. The W3C recommends that Web authors use the INPUT element to create text-input controls.

| *Attributes* | `prompt="prompt string"` | Optional |

LINK
Type: Empty   **Content:** N/A

Defines a link in the HEAD element. A primary use for the LINK element is to link to external style sheets.

Attributes	`type="content-type"`	Optional
	`rel="link-type"`	Optional
	`rev="link-type"`	Optional
	`href="URL"`	Optional
	`media="media-descriptor"` (4.0)	Optional

Note: REL and REV can be used in combination with HREF to specify forward and reverse links. TYPE can be used in combination with HREF to specify a link to an external style sheet (`type="text/css"`). When linking to an external style sheet, MEDIA can be used to target a linked style sheet for a particular media. Because Netscape Navigator 4 ignores any LINK element with a MEDIA attribute other than **screen** set, the LINK element's MEDIA attribute can be used to block Netscape 4 users from accessing an external style sheet. Current allowable values for MEDIA include screen (the default), all, print, projection, handheld, tv, tty, aural, braille, and embossed.

Example	

```
<head><title>Peter Locke's Political Science Site</title>
<link href="mystyles.css" rel="stylesheet" type="text/css"
media="all">
```

META
Type: Empty   **Content:** N/A

Specifies meta-information about the document.

Attributes	`name="meta-data identifier"`	See Note
	`http-equiv="refresh"`	See Note
	`content="meta-data data"`	Required

Note: Either NAME or HTTP-EQUIV is required.

Example

```
<head><title>John Peters' Political Science Site</title>
<meta name="description" content="Opinions and discussion of
political science, including the theory of representative government,
political constitutions, popular sovereignty, and other topics.">
<meta name="keywords" content="political science, polysci, politics,
constitution, civil rights, free speech, bill of rights, inalienable
rights, liberty">
</head>
```

or

```
<meta http-equiv="refresh"
content="3;url="http://www.somewhere.com/peters/polysci/index.html">
```

STYLE (3.2)   **Type:** Container   **Content:** Style Codes

Embeds a style sheet in the document's HEAD element. Multiple STYLE elements can be embedded.

Attributes   `type="content-type"` (4.0)   Required
               `media="media-descriptor"` (4.0)   Optional

Note: Only CSS style sheets can be used with HTML documents, so `type="text/css"` is always set for the STYLE element in HTML documents. In XHTML, however, other style sheet languages can be used, such as XSL, for instance. The MEDIA attribute allows the creation of style sheets that target specific media; current allowable values include **screen** (the default), **all**, **print**, **projection**, **handheld**, **tv**, **tty**, **aural**, **braille**, and **embossed**. This allows the embedding of a style sheet that will only be used when printing the document. Because only recent browsers support the MEDIA attribute, STYLE elements with a MEDIA attribute value other than **all** should precede any other STYLE elements in the HEAD element. Similar to the SCRIPT element, comment codes (`<!--` and `-->`) can be used to shield the content of the STYLE element from browsers that do not support it; style-aware browsers will ignore the comment codes.

Example

```
<head><title>Peter Locke's Political Science Site</title>
<style type="text/css">
<!--
h1, h2, h3 { color: blue; background: transparent; }
p { font-family: Arial, Helvetica, sans-serif; }
-->
</style>
```

HR (Horizontal Rule)   **Type:** Block/Empty   **Content:** N/A

Draws a horizontal rule across the page.

Attributes   `size="n"` (Deprecated)   Optional
               `width="n|n%"` (Deprecated)   Optional
               `align="left|center|right"` (Deprecated)   Optional
               `noshade`   Optional

Note: SIZE specifies the height of the rule in pixels. ALIGN horizontally aligns the rule within the browser window, if WIDTH is set to a value of less than **100%** or a pixel-width is set that is less than the width of the browser window. NOSHADE turns off the 3-D shading for rules that is otherwise generally displayed by browsers.

| **Example** | `<hr size="5" width="75%" align="center" noshade>` |

HTML
Type: Container   **Content:** HEAD elements, BODY, FRAMESET

The top-level element in an HTML document. HTML 4.01 requires that a DocType declaration specifying the document's HTML conformance be inserted above the HTML element.

| **Example** | ```
<!DOCTYPE HTML PUBLIC "-//W3C//DTD HTML 4.01 Transitional//EN"
 "http://www.w3.org/TR/html4/loose.dtd">
<html>
All other elements in the document are nested here.
</html>
``` |

I (Italic)
Type: Inline/Container   **Content:** Inline

Causes nested text to be displayed in italics.

| **Example** | `<p>One of my favorite books is <i>The Brothers Karamazov</i> by Fyodor Dostoevsky.</p>` |

IFRAME (Inline Frame) (4.0)
Type: Inline/Container   **Content:** Inline

Creates an inline windowed frame within a Web page.

Attributes	`src="URL"`	Required
	`width="n"`	Optional
	`height="n"`	Optional
	`align="`**bottom**`|middle|top|left|right"`	Optional
	`name="frame name"`	Optional
	`marginheight="n"`	Optional
	`marginwidth="n"`	Optional
	`scrolling="`**auto**`|yes|no"`	Optional
	`frameborder="1|0"`	Optional
	`longdesc="URL"`	Optional

Note: Netscape 4 does not support inline frames. Content can be included in the IFRAME element to alert users of browsers that do not recognize the IFRAME element. NAME allows the targeting of an inline frame by a link using the TARGET attribute. The **left** and **right** values for the ALIGN attribute float the inline frame at the left or right margins, with following text flowing around the other side of the inline frame.

| **Example** | ```
<p><iframe src="insert.html" align="top" width="200" height="100">
[Note: This page uses inline frames, which is a feature not
supported by your browser. To find out how to upgrade to a browser
that supports current Web standards, see the <a
href="http://www.webstandards.org/upgrade/">Web Standard Project's
Browser Upgrade Campaign</a>.]
</iframe></p>
``` |

IMG (Image)
Type: Inline/Empty   **Content:** N/A

Inserts an image inline within a Web page.

`src="`*URL*`"`		Required
`alt="`*alternate text*`"`		Required
`height="`*n*`|`*n%*`"`		Recommended
`width="`*n*`|`*n%*`"`		Recommended
`align="`**bottom**`|middle|top|left|right"`		
(3.2) Deprecated		Optional
`hspace="`*n*`"` (3.2) Deprecated		Optional
`vspace="`*n*`"` (3.2) Deprecated		Optional
`name="`*image name*`"`		Optional
`usemap="#`*mapname*`|`*URL*`"`		Optional
`border="1|0"`		Optional

Note: ALIGN with **left** or **right** set floats the image on the left or right margin with following text or elements flowing around the other side of the image. VSPACE and HSPACE are used with floating images to add vertical horizontal spacing outside the image. NAME allows the image to be targeted by a script. USEMAP links the image with the name of a client-side image map and is only used in conjunction with a fragment identifier that points to the NAME attribute of a MAP element or the URL of an external HTML file containing the associated MAP element. BORDER can turn the image border off (**border="0"**) when the image is an image link (nested inside the A element).

Example
```
<p align="center"><img src="mybanner.jpg" alt="Banner image"
height="125" width="175"></p>
```

INPUT

See FORM.

INS (Insert) (4.0)
Type: Inline/Container   **Content:** Inline

Marks nested text as an insertion. In browsers that support this element, nested text is generally displayed as underlined. INS can be used in combination with DEL (Delete) to display insertions and deletions in an HTML document. *See also* DEL (Delete).

Attributes   `cite="`*URL*`"`   Optional

Note: CITE can link to an HTML file providing details about why the document was revised, who revised it, when it was revised, and so on. No browser currently supports CITE.

Example
```
<h1><del>My </del><ins>Most </ins>Frequently Asked Questions
Page</h1>
```

ISINDEX

See HEAD.

KBD (Keyboard)
Type: Inline/Container   **Content:** Inline

Can be used to indicate keyboard input. Text nested in the KBD element is generally displayed in a monospaced font. To distinguish KBD from the other monospaced text elements, it can be nested inside of (or bracket) a B (Bold) element.

| *Example* | `<p>At the prompt, key <b><kbd>newuser</kbd></b> and press the Enter key.</p>` |

LABEL (4.0)

See FORM.

LEGEND (4.0)

See FORM.

LI (List Item)

See OL (Ordered List) *or* UL (Unordered List).

LINK

See HEAD.

MAP (Client-Side Image Map) (3.2)   **Type:** Inline/Container   **Content:** Block/AREA

In conjunction with the AREA element, defines a client-side image map.

| *Attributes* | `name="`*`mapname`*`"` | Required |

Note: In NAME, *mapname* must match (including uppercase and lowercase letters) the pointer included in the USEMAP attribute (`usemap="#`*`mapname`*`"`) of the IMG element being used for the image map.

AREA (3.2)   **Type:** Inline/Empty   **Content:** N/A

Defines an area within a client-side image map that functions as a hotspot link.

Attributes	`shape="`**`rect`**`	circle	poly	default"`	Optional
	`coords="`*`coordinates`*`"`	Optional
	`href="`*`URL`*`"`	Optional
	`nohref`	Optional
	`alt="`*`alternative text`*`"`	Required

| *Example* | `<p align="center"><img src="mymap.jpg" height="135" width="450" alt="Image Map: Navigation Menu" usemap="#mymap" border="0"></p>`
`<map name="mymap">`
`<area shape="rect" alt="Previous" coords="15,15,145,120" href="page1.htm">`
`<area shape="rect" alt="Contents" coords="160,15,290,120" href="toc.htm">`
`<area shape="rect" alt="Next" coords="305,15,435,120" href="page3.htm">`
`<area shape="default" nohref>`
`</map>` |

MENU (Deprecated)

Type: Block/Container   **Content:** Block

Originally intended for specifying a single-column menu, in contrast to the DIR element, originally intended for specifying a multi-column menu. Browsers treat MENU and DIR elements exactly like UL (Unordered List) elements and the W3C recommends that Web authors use UL instead.

META (Meta Data)

See HEAD.

NOFRAMES (4.0)

See FRAMESET.

NOSCRIPT (4.0)

See SCRIPT.

OBJECT (4.0)

Type: Inline/Container   **Content:** Block/Inline

Generic mechanism for inserting inline objects into a Web page. Optionally used in conjunction with the PARAM (Parameter) element.

Attributes		
	`classid="URL"`	Optional
	`codebase="URL"`	Optional
	`codetype="content-type"`	Optional
	`data="URL"`	Optional
	`type="content-type"`	Optional
	`standby="standby message"`	Optional
	`id="objectname"`	Optional

PARAM (Parameter) (4.0)

Type: Empty   **Content:** N/A

Sets initial parameters for an object displayed by the OBJECT element.

Attributes		
	`name="parameter name"`	Required
	`value="parameter value"`	Optional
	`valuetype="`**`data`**`|ref|object"`	Optional
	`type="content-type"`	Optional

Note: NAME's value and case-sensitivity depends on the specific object implementation. VALUE is the value of the run-time parameter specified by NAME; the actual value is determined by the object implementation. VALUETYPE specifies the type of value being passed by the VALUE attribute; if **data**, the value is passed as a string; if **ref**, the value is passed as a URL; and if **object**, the value is passed as the ID value of the object.

Example
```
<object data="intro.wav" type="audio/wav" width="200" height="45"
vspace="5">
<param name="src" value="intro.wav">
<param name="autostart" value="true">
<param name="controller" value="true">
```

```
<param name="loop" value="false">
Audio introduction to site.
</object>
```

OL (Ordered List)
Type: Block/Container   **Content:** Block

Creates an ordered (or numbered) list.

Attributes   `type="1|a|A|i|I"`   Optional
                      `start="n"`   Optional
                      `compact (Deprecated)`   Optional

Note: TYPE specifies the numbering system, whether Arabic (**1**), lowercase alphabetic (**a**), uppercase alphabetic (**A**), lowercase Roman (**i**), or uppercase Roman (**I**). START can specify a starting number other than **1**.

LI (with OL)
Type: Block/Container   **Content:** Inline/Block

Specifies a list item, within an OL element in this case. The end tag for LI is optional. See also *UL (Unordered List)*.

Attributes   `type="1|a|A|i|I"`   Optional
                      `value="n"`   Optional

Note: VALUE specifies a value for the current list item. For instance, if **A** is the value of the TYPE attribute, `value="4"` corresponds to a value of D.

Example
```
<ol type="A">
<li>Breakfast
<li>Lunch
<li>Dinner
</ol>
```

OPTGROUP (Option Group) (4.0)

See FORM.

OPTION

See FORM.

P (Paragraph)
Type: Block/Container   **Content:** Inline

Indicates that nested text is a paragraph. The end tag is officially optional, but should be included to avoid problems that can arise otherwise.

Attributes   `align="left|center|right|justify" (3.2) (Deprecated)`   Optional

Example   `<p>Welcome to my home page!</p>`

PARAM (Parameter) (3.2/4.0)

See APPLET *and* OBJECT.

PRE (Preformatted Text)　　　　　　　**Type:** Block/Container　　**Content:** Inline

Specifies that nested text be treated as preformatted text, with all included spaces and hard returns displayed by the browser. Inline elements that cannot be nested in a PRE element include IMG, OBJECT, BIG, SMALL, SUB, and SUP. Text in a PRE element is generally rendered in a monospaced font.

Attributes　　width="*n*" (Deprecated)　　　　　　　　　　　　　Optional

Example
```
<pre>
                QTR 1      QTR 2      QTR 3      QTR 4      Score
Madison State      7         14          0          3         24
Concord Tech       0          7         14          7         28
</pre>
```

Q (Quote) (4.0)　　　　　　　　　　　**Type:** Inline/Container　　**Content:** Inline

Marks nested text as an inline quotation. Browsers that support the Q element should automatically render quotation marks delimiting the quotation. Because few browsers support the Q element (Mozilla 1 does, but Internet Explorer 6, does not) and quotations marked by the Q element do not degrade gracefully in browsers that do not support the Q element (because no quotation marks at all are displayed), the Q element probably should be avoided.

Attributes　　cite="*URL*"　　　　　　　　　　　　　　　　　Optional
　　　　　　　　lang="*language-code*"　　　　　　　　　　　　Optional
　　　　　　　　dir="LTR|RTL"　　　　　　　　　　　　　　　Optional

Note: CITE references the URL of the source of the quote. LANG specifies the language of the quotation (**lang="fr"**, if the language of the quotation is French, for instance).

S (Strike) (4.0) (Deprecated)　　　　　**Type:** Inline/Container　　**Content:** Inline

Marks nested text as strikeout text, displayed with a line drawn through it. Previously proposed as part of the HTML 3.0 proposal, S (Strike) was included in HTML 4.0, but deprecated at the same time. STRIKE is more universally supported by earlier browsers and should probably be used instead.

SAMP (Sample Code)　　　　　　　　　**Type:** Inline/Container　　**Content:** Inline

Marks nested text as sample code. All browsers display SAMP text in a monospaced font. The TT (Teletype Text) element can be used instead to achieve the same result.

SCRIPT (3.2)　　　　　　　　　　　　**Type:** Container　　　**Content:** Script Code

Allows inclusion or linking of client-side scripts. The SCRIPT element can be inserted in either the HEAD or the BODY element.

Attribute

　　　　　　　type="*content type*"　　　　　　　　　　　　Required
　　　　　　　language="*script language*" (Deprecated)　　　　Optional
　　　　　　　src="*URL*"　　　　　　　　　　　　　　　　Optional

Note: TYPE identifies the MIME type of the scripting language (**text/javascript**, for instance). LANGUAGE is deprecated because it references non-standard script language identifiers. Some older browsers, however, recognize LANGUAGE, but not TYPE, in the SCRIPT element, so good practice dictates including both. Comment codes, `<!--` and `//-->`, can be used to shield browsers that are not script aware from displaying the content of the SCRIPT element. Script-aware browsers ignore the comment codes.

Example

```
<script type="text/javascript" src="mainscript.js"></script>
```

or

```
<script type="text/javascript" language="JavaScript">
<!-- start hiding script
function HiThere() {
    ident = window.prompt("Enter your name: ", "");
    alert ("Welcome to my page, "+ident+"!");
}
// end hiding script -->
</script>
```

NOSCRIPT (4.0)   **Type:** Container   **Content:** Block

Specifies content to be displayed in a browser that does not support the specified script language or is not script-aware. A script-aware browser ignores the content of the NOSCRIPT element, while a script-unaware browser displays the content of the NOSCRIPT element.

Example

```
<body>
<noscript>
<p>This page includes JavaScript scripts. Please go to the <a
href="no-js.html">non-JavaScript version</a> of this page.</p>
</noscript>
```

SELECT

See FORM.

SMALL (3.2)   **Type:** Inline/Container   **Content:** Inline

Marks text for display in a smaller font. Text is displayed in a font size that is one size smaller than the default font size, based on the seven font sizes specified by the FONT and BASEFONT elements' SIZE attribute. Nesting SMALL elements, although legal, is not recommended, because it can result in an illegible font size in some Macintosh browsers, for instance.

Example

```
<h1><big>M</big><small>y</small> <big>H</big><small>ome</small>
<big>P</big><small>age</small></h1>
```

SPAN (4.0)   **Type:** Inline/Container   **Content:** Inline

Marks a span of text, to which formatting using styles can be applied. By itself, the SPAN element has no formatting.

Example

```
<p>Registration for <span style="font-family: Arial; color: maroon;
background: transparent">Winter Quarter</span> classes will begin
on January 5.</p>
```

STRIKE (Strikeout) (3.2) (Deprecated)
Type: Inline/Container   **Content:** Inline

Marks nested text as strikeout text, displayed with a line drawn through it. STRIKE is more universally supported than either the S (Strike) or the DEL (Delete) element and should probably be used instead.

Example   `<p>Text to be deleted is marked as <strike>strikeout</strike>.</p>`

STRONG (Strong Emphasis)
Type: Inline/Container   **Content:** Inline

Marks nested text as strongly emphasized. Browsers display STRONG text identically to B (Bold) text. Either can be used.

Example   `<p><strong>Note:</strong> When creating Web sites, the unexpected is to be expected.</p>`

STYLE (3.2)

See HEAD.

SUB (Subscript) (3.2)
Type: Inline/Container   **Content:** Inline

Marks nested text as subscripted. To allow for earlier browsers that do not support SUB, subscripted text can be enclosed inside parentheses. *See also* SUP (Superscript).

SUP (Superscript) (3.2)
Type: Inline/Container   **Content:** Inline

Marks nested text as superscripted. To allow for earlier browsers that do not support SUP, superscripted text can be enclosed inside parentheses. *See also* SUB (Subscript).

Example   `<p>Eat Crumpies<sup>(tm)</sup>, the greatest thing since H<sub>(2)</sub>O!</p>`

TABLE (3.2)
Type: Block/Container   **Content:** Table Elements

Specifies that nested code is a table (arranged in columns and rows).

Attributes
```
width="n|n%"                                          Optional
border="n"                                            Optional
cellpadding="n"                                       Optional
cellspacing="n"                                       Optional
align="left|center|right"                             Optional
bgcolor="color name|RGB color code"                   Optional
frame="void|above|below|hsides|
        lhs|rhs|vsides|box|border" (4.0)              Optional
rules="none|groups|rows|cols|all" (4.0)               Optional
```

Note: The ALIGN values of **left** and **right** have the effect of floating the table to the left or right margin and flowing following text or elements around the other side of the table. Current browsers also support the BACKGROUND attribute for specifying a background image for a table, but it is not a standard attribute, primarily due to differences in how it is implemented in browsers.

CAPTION (Table Caption)   **Type:** Block/Container   **Content:** Inline

Marks nested text as a table caption.

Attributes	`align="`**`top`**`|bottom|left|right"` (Deprecated)	Optional

Note: A **top** value centers the caption above the table. A **bottom** value for ALIGN causes the caption to be displayed below the table. Values of **left** and **right** left-aligns or right-aligns the caption (in the caption space) above the table.

TR (Table Row) (3.2)   **Type:** Container   **Content:** TH/TD

Delineates a row of cells in a table. The end tag is officially optional in HTML 4.01, but leaving it off might cause problems in earlier browsers.

Attributes	`align="left|center|right|justify"`	Optional
	`valign="top|middle|bottom|baseline"`	Optional

TH (Table Heading) and TD (Table Data) (3.2)   **Type:** Container   **Content:** Block/Inline

Designates a table heading (TH) or table data (TD) cell. TH content is centered and bolded, whereas TD content is left-aligned and displayed in a regular font. The end tag for TH and TD is officially optional in HTML 4.01, but leaving it off might cause problems in earlier browsers.

Attributes	`align="left|center|right|justify"`	Optional
	`valign="top|middle|bottom|baseline"`	Optional
	`colspan="`*`n`*`"`	Optional
	`rowspan="`*`n`*`"`	Optional
	`width="`*`n`*`|`*`n`*`%"` (Deprecated)	Optional
	`height="`*`n`*`|`*`n`*`%"` (Deprecated)	Optional
	`nowrap` (Deprecated)	Optional

THEAD (Table Head), TBODY (Table Body), and TFOOT (Table Foot) (4.0)   **Type:** Container   **Content:** TR

Designates the head, body, and foot sections (or row groups) in a table. These elements have no formatting, by themselves, but can have styles applied to them to control their presentation. If not present, the whole table defaults to displaying styles set for TBODY (in HTML 4, but not XHTML 1). The end tags for THEAD, TBODY, and TFOOT are optional.

Attributes	`align="left|center|right|justify"`	Optional
	`valign="top|middle|bottom|baseline"`	Optional

Example

```
<style type="text/css">
<!--
thead tr.border th { border-bottom: 1px solid black; }
tbody tr.border th, tbody tr.border td { border-bottom: 3px double
black; }
tfoot th, tfoot td { color: red; background: transparent; }
-->
</style>
</head>
<body>
<table align="center" width="450" cellspacing="0">
<thead>
<tr><th></th><th colspan="3">Semi-Annual Sales Report</th></tr>
```

```
<tr class="border" align="right"><th>Salesperson</th><th>1st
Qtr</th><th>2nd Qtr</th><th>Totals</th></tr>
</thead>
<tbody>
<tr align="right"><th>Brady</th><td>$   525,000</td>
<td>$   365,000</td><td>$   890,000
</td></tr>
<tr align="right"><th>Crawford</th><td>400,000</td><td>500,000</td>
<td>900,000</td></tr>
<tr class="border" align="right"><th>Peters</th><td>250,000</td>
<td>400,000</td><td>650,000</td></tr>
</tbody>
<tfoot>
<tr align="right"><th>Totals</th><td>$1,175,000</td><td>$1,265,000
</td><td>$2,440,000</td></tr>
</tfoot>
</table>
```

COLGROUP (Column Group) (4.0)

Type: Container   **Content:** COL

Designates a group of columns (specified by the COL element). The end tag is optional.

COL (Column) (4.0)

Type: Empty   **Content:** N/A

Example
```
<table width="75%" align="center" border="1">
<colgroup id="colg1">
  <col id="col1">
</colgroup>
<colgroup id="colg2">
  <col id="col2">
  <col id="col3>
  <col id="col4">
</colgroup>
<colgroup id="colg3">
  <col id="col5">
  <col id="col6>
  <col id="col7">
</colgroup>
```

TEXTAREA

See FORM.

TFOOT (Table Foot) (4.0)

See TABLE.

TH (Table Heading) and TD (Table Data)

See TABLE.

THEAD (Table Head) (4.0)

See TABLE.

TITLE

See HEAD.

TR (Table Row)

See TABLE.

TT (Teletype Text/Typewriter Text)   **Type:** Inline/Container   **Content:** Inline

Marks nested text to be displayed in a monospaced font.

Example   `<p>The message, <tt>Wait while downloading</tt>, is displayed.</p>`

U (Underline) (3.2)   **Type:** Inline/Container   **Content:** Inline

Marks nested text to be displayed as underlined.

Example   `<p>The commissary will be <u>closed</u> on Friday.</p>`

UL (Unordered List)   **Type:** Block/Container   **Content:** Block

Creates an unordered (or bulleted) list.

Attributes	`type="`**`disc`**`	circle	square"`	Optional
	`start="`*`n`*`"`	Optional
	`compact (Deprecated)`	Optional

Note: TYPE specifies the numbering system, whether Arabic (1), lowercase alphabetic (a), uppercase alphabetic (A), lowercase Roman (i), or uppercase Roman (I). START can specify a starting number other than 1.

LI (with OL)   **Type:** Block/Container   **Content:** Inline/Block

Specifies a list item, within an OL element in this case. The end tag for LI is optional. See also *UL (Unordered List)*.

| ***Attributes*** | `type="`**`1`**`|a|A|i|I"` | Optional |
| | `value="`*`n`*`"` | Optional |

Note: VALUE specifies a value for the current list item. For instance, if **A** is the value of the TYPE attribute, **`value="4"`** corresponds to a value of D.

Example
```
<ol type="A">
<li>Breakfast
<li>Lunch
<li>Dinner
</ol>
```

VAR (Variable)

Type: Inline/Container   **Content:** Inline

Marks nested text as a variable. The VAR element is generally displayed in italics. Alternatively, the I (Italic) and EM (Emphasis) elements can be used to achieve the same effect.

Example

```
<p>The <var>count</var> variable is incremented by one each time
the loop is executed.</p>
```

GENERIC AND OTHER ATTRIBUTES

Core Attributes

```
id="unique ID"
class="class name"
style="style properties"
```

Language Attributes (i18n)

```
lang="language code"
dir="ltr|rtl"
```

Event Handler Attributes

```
onBlur="script" (See Note 1)
onChange="script" (INPUT, SELECT, and TEXTAREA)
onClick="script" (See Note 2)
onDblClick="script" (See Note 2)
onFocus="script" (See Note 1)
onLoad="script" (BODY, FRAMESET)
onKeyDown="script" (See Note 2)
onKeyPress="script" (See Note 2)
onKeyUp="script" (See Note 2)
onMouseDown="script" (See Note 2)
onMouseUp="script" (See Note 2)
onMouseOver="script" (See Note 2)
onMouseMove="script" (See Note 2)
onMouseOut="script" (See Note 2)
onReset="script" (FORM)
onSelect="script" (INPUT, TEXTAREA)
onSubmit="script" (FORM)
onUnload="script" (BODY, FRAMESET)
```

Note 1: A, AREA, BUTTON, INPUT, LABEL, SELECT, and TEXTAREA.

Note 2: All elements, except for APPLET, BASE, BASEFONT, BDO, BR, FONT, FRAME, FRAMESET, HEAD, HTML, IFRAME, ISINDEX, META, PARAM, SCRIPT, STYLE, or TITLE.

accesskey="*character*" (A, AREA, BUTTON, INPUT, LABEL, LEGEND, and TEXTAREA)

align="**top**|bottom|left|right" (CAPTION) (Deprecated)

align="top|middle|bottom|left|right" (APPLET, FRAME, IMG, INPUT, and OBJECT)
       (Deprecated)

align="**left**|center|right|justify" (DIV, H1, H2, H3, H4, H5, H6, and P)
       (Deprecated)

align="left|center|right|justify|char" (COL, COLGROUP, TBODY, TH, THEAD, and
       TR) (Not Deprecated)

bgcolor="*color name*|*RGB color code*" (BODY, TABLE, TR, TD, and TH) (Deprecated)

border="*n*" (IMG, OBJECT, and TABLE)

charset="*character set*" (A, LINK, and SCRIPT)

class="*class name*" (All, except for BASE, BASEFONT, HEAD, HTML, META, PARAM,
       SCRIPT, STYLE, and TITLE)

dir="ltr|rtl" (All, except for APPLET, BASE, BASEFONT, BDO, BR, FRAME,
       FRAMESET, IFRAME, PARAM, and SCRIPT)

id="*unique ID*" (All, except for BASE, HEAD, HTML, META, SCRIPT, STYLE, and
       TITLE)

lang="*language code*" (All, except for APPLET, BASE, BASEFONT, BDO, BR, FRAME,
       FRAMESET, IFRAME, PARAM, and SCRIPT)

style="*style properties*" (All, except for BASE, BASEFONT, HEAD, HTML, META,
       PARAM, SCRIPT, STYLE, and TITLE)

tabindex="*n*" (A, AREA, BUTTON, INPUT, OBJECT, SELECT, and TEXTAREA)

target="*frame name*" (A, AREA, BASE, FORM, and LINK)

title="*title*" (All, except for BASE, BASEFONT, HEAD, HTML, META, PARAM,
       SCRIPT, and TITLE)

valign="top|middle|bottom|baseline" (COL, COLGROUP, TBODY, TD, TFOOT, TH,
       THEAD, and TR)

APPENDIX

B

Special Characters Chart

Because HTML documents are ASCII text documents, the number of characters that should be inserted directly from the keyboard is limited to the 128 ASCII characters. The ISO 8859-1 character set defines an additional 128 characters.

ASCII (KEYBOARD) CHARACTERS

The ASCII character set has 128 (0 through 127) positions. Positions 0 through 31 in the ASCII character set are control characters (Backspace, Tab, Cancel, and so on) that do not result in a displayable character. Positions 32 to 126 are characters that can be entered directly from the standard ASCII keyboard. Position 127 is a control character (Delete).

The displayable ASCII characters run from position 32 to 126. These constitute the only characters that should be directly entered from the keyboard into an HTML document.

tip

Keyboards for some Macintosh computers marketed in the United Kingdom substitute the British pound currency symbol (£) for the number sign (#). On those computers, press Option+3 (or Alt+3) to insert the number sign (#).

NOTE

For links to resources showing where you can learn more about the ASCII character set, as well as charts showing all of the characters that are included in the ASCII character set, see the Appendixes' section at the IRC for this book at **www.emcp.com/**.

RESERVED CHARACTERS

A number of characters are used to indicate HTML codes and, depending on the circumstance, might need to be inserted into an HTML document using their entity number or entity name.

Character	Entity Number	Entity Name	Description
"	"	"	quotation mark
&	&	&	ampersand
<	<	<	less-than sign
>	>	>	greater-than sign

When displaying a < or > character in a Web page, always insert the character using either its entity number or entity name. Generally, standalone " and & characters do not need a substitute, unless they are part of an HTML code that you want to display, as is, in a Web page.

EXTENDED CHARACTERS (UNUSED)

Positions 128 through 159 reference extended characters that are in addition to the ASCII character set. Which characters in these positions are actually available depends upon the computer system and default character set being used. In the ISO 8859-1 character set, which is the standard character set for displaying Western European languages on the Web, the positions 128 through 159 are referenced as "unused" (or not to be used in Web pages). A number of browsers on the UNIX platform ignore entity numbers for all characters within this range. The following table shows the extended Latin-1 (ISO-8859-1) character set that is used in Microsoft Windows.

Character	Entity Number	Entity Name	Description
	&#128;		unused
	&#129;		unused
‚	&#130;		single quote (low)
ƒ	&#131;	&fnof;	function of, florin
„	&#132;		double quote (low)
…	&#133;	&hellip;	horizontal ellipsis
†	&#134;	&dagger;	dagger sign
‡	&#135;	&Dagger;	double dagger sign
ˆ	&#136;		small circumflex accent
‰	&#137;	&permil;	per thousand (mille) sign
š	&#138;	&Scaron;	S-caron[*]
‹	&#139;	&lsaquo;	left single quillemet
Œ	&#140;	&OElig;	capital OE ligature
	&#141;		unused
	&#142;		unused
	&#143;		unused
	&#144;		unused
'	&#145;	&lsquo;	left single quote
'	&#146;	&rsquo;	right single quote
"	&#147;	&ldquo;	left double quote
"	&#148;	&rdquo;	right double quote
•	&#149;	&bull;	round filled bullet
–	&#150;	&ndash;	en dash
—	&#151;	&mdash;	em dash
˜	&#152;	&tilde;	small tilde
™	&#153;	&trade;	trademark
š	&#154;	&scaron;	s-caron[*]
›	&#155;	&rsaquo;	right single guillemet
œ	&#156;	&oelig;	small oe ligature

[*] S-caron and s-caron characters are not available in the Macintosh's default character set.

Character	Entity Number	Entity Name	Description
	&#157;		unused
	&#158;		unused
Ÿ	&#159;	&Yuml;	Y-umlaut

SPECIAL CHARACTERS (ISO 8859-1)

The positions 160 through 255 include characters from the ISO 8859-1 (or Latin-1) character set that can be displayed in Web pages. Most of these characters are supported by most browsers.

Versions of Netscape Navigator prior to version 4 only support using the entity names for the non-breakable space, copyright, registered trademark, and the accented characters (A-gravé, c-cedilla, and so on).

Character	Entity Number	Entity Name	Description
[ ]			non-breakable space (brackets added)
¡	&#161;	&iexcl;	inverted exclamation
¢	&#162;	&cent;	cent sign
£	&#163;	&pound;	British pound sign
¤	&#164;	&curren;	currency sign
¥	&#165;	&yen;	Japanese yen sign
¦	&#166;	&brvbar;	broken vertical bar*
§	&#167;	&sect;	section sign
¨	&#168;	&uml;	umlaut
©	&#169;	&copy;	copyright symbol
ª	&#170;	&ordf;	feminine ordinal
«	&#171;	&laquo;	left double guillemet
¬	&#172;	&not;	logical not sign
-	&#173;	&shy;	soft hyphen
®	&#174;	&reg;	registered trademark
¯	&#175;	&macr;	macron accent
°	&#176;	&deg;	degree
±	&#177;	&plusmn;	plus/minus sign
²	&#178;	&sup2;	superscript 2*
³	&#179;	&sup3;	superscript 3*
´	&#180;	&acute;	acute accent
µ	&#181;	&micro;	micro sign
¶	&#182;	&para;	paragraph sign
·	&#183;	&middot;	middle dot
¸	&#184;	&cedil;	cedilla accent
¹	&#185;	&sup1;	superscript 1*
º	&#186;	&ordm;	masculine ordinal

* This character is missing from the native Macintosh character set. Internet Explorer 5 for the Macintosh substitutes the Latin-1 (ISO-8859-1) character set, so this character is displayed in that browser, but might not be displayed in other Macintosh browsers.

Character	Entity Number	Entity Name	Description
»	&#187;	&raquo;	right double guillemet
¼	&#188;	&frac14;	quarter fraction*
½	&#189;	&frac12;	half fraction*
¾	&#190;	&frac34;	three-quarter fraction*
¿	&#191;	&iquest;	inverted question mark
À	&#192;	&Agrave;	A-gravé
Á	&#193;	&Aacute;	A-acute
Â	&#194;	&Acirc;	A-circumflex
Ã	&#195;	&Atilde;	A-tilde
Ä	&#196;	&Auml;	A-umlaut
Å	&#197;	&Aring;	A-ring
Æ	&#198;	&AElig;	AE ligature
Ç	&#199;	&Ccedil;	C-cedilla
È	&#200;	&Egrave;	E-gravé
É	&#201;	&Eacute;	E-acute
Ê	&#202;	&Ecirc;	E-circumflex
Ë	&#203;	&Euml;	E-umlaut
Ì	&#204;	&Igrave;	I-gravé
Í	&#205;	&Iacute;	I-acute
Î	&#206;	&Icirc;	I-circumflex
Ï	&#207;	&Iuml;	I-umlaut
Ð	&#208;	&ETH;	capital Eth*
Ñ	&#209;	&Ntilde;	N-tilde
Ò	&#210;	&Ograve;	0-gravé
Ó	&#211;	&Oacute;	O-acute
Ô	&#212;	&Ocirc;	O-circumflex
Õ	&#213;	&Otilde;	O-tilde
Ö	&#214	&Ouml;	O-umlaut
×	&#215;	&times;	multiplication sign*
Ø	&#216;	&Oslash;	O-slash
Ù	&#217;	&Ugrave;	U-gravé
Ú	&#218;	&Uacute;	U-acute
Û	&#219;	&Ucirc;	U-circumflex
Ü	&#220;	&Uuml;	U-umlaut
Ý	&#221;	&Yacute;	Y-acute*
Þ	&#222;	&THORN;	capital Thorn*
ß	&#223;	&szlig;	sharp s, sz ligature
à	&#224;	&agrave;	a-gravé
á	&#225;	&aacute;	a-acute
â	&#226;	&acirc;	a-circumflex
ã	&#227;	&atilde;	a-tilde
ä	&#228;	&auml;	a-umlaut
å	&#229;	&aring;	a-ring
æ	&#230;	&aelig;	ae ligature

*This character is missing from the native Macintosh character set. Internet Explorer 5 for the Macintosh substitutes the Latin-1 (ISO-8859-1) character set, so this character is displayed in that browser, but might not be displayed in other Macintosh browsers.

Character	Entity Number	Entity Name	Description
ç	&#231;	&ccedil;	c-cedilla
è	&#232;	&egrave;	e-gravé
é	&#233;	&eacute;	e-acute
ê	&#234;	&ecirc;	e-circumflex
ë	&#235;	&euml;	e-umlaut
ì	&#236;	&igrave;	i-gravé
í	&#237;	&iacute;	i-acute
î	&#238;	&icirc;	i-circumflex
ï	&#239;	&iuml;	i-umlaut
ð	&#240;	&eth;	small eth[*]
ñ	&#241;	&ntilde;	n-tilde
ò	&#242;	&ograve;	o-gravé
ó	&#243;	&oacute;	o-acute
ô	&#244;	&ocirc;	o-circumflex
õ	&#245;	&otilde;	o-tilde
ö	&#246;	&ouml;	o-umlaut
÷	&#247;	&divide;	division sign
ø	&#248;	&oslash;	o-slash
ù	&#249;	&ugrave;	u-gravé
ú	&#250;	&uacute;	u-acute
û	&#251;	&ucirc;	u-circumflex
ü	&#252;	&uuml;	u-umlaut
ý	&#253;	&yacute;	y-acute[*]
þ	&#254;	&thorn;	small thorn[*]
ÿ	&#255;	&yuml;	y-umlaut

[*] This character is missing from the native Macintosh character set. Internet Explorer 5 for the Macintosh substitutes the Latin-1 (ISO-8859-1) character set, so this character is displayed in that browser, but might not be displayed in other Macintosh browsers.

TROUBLE *spot*

Do not directly insert non-keyboard characters into an HTML file by using the Windows Character Map utility, for instance, because what displays as one character on one platform might display as another character on another platform.

HTML 4 UNICODE CHARACTERS

ISO 8859-1 provides a total of 95 characters that can be inserted into HTML documents in addition to the ASCII "keyboard" characters that also can be used. This means, however, that many characters that desktop publishers, for instance, are accustomed to including in documents are not available in the ISO 8859-1 character set.

To overcome the limited number of characters that are available in ISO 8859-1, HTML 4 supports including characters in HTML documents from the Unicode character set. Unicode 3.0 supports the inclusion of over 49,000 characters from a wide range of languages, including from the Americas, Europe, the Middle East, Africa, India, Asia, and the Pacific.

The Unicode characters shown in the following sections should be available on most recent Windows and Macintosh systems and display in most recent browsers. Other Unicode characters, however, might require additional Unicode-supporting fonts that include the characters be installed on the system.

To display most of the following Unicode characters in Netscape 4, declare the document's character set to be UTF-8:

```
<html>
<meta http-equiv="Content-Type" content="text/html; charset=UTF-8">
```

Be aware that non-keyboard characters that have been directly inserted into an HTML file, instead of being inserted using the characters' entity codes, might display entirely different characters or not display any characters at all. This is one more reason not to directly insert non-keyboard characters into an HTML file.

Latin Extended-A and Extended-B

Character	Entity Number	Entity Name	Description
Œ	&#338;	&OElig;	capital ligature OE
œ	&#339;	&oelig;	small ligature oe
Š	&#352;	&Scaron;	S-caron
š	&#353;	&scaron;	s-caron
Ÿ	&#376;	&Yuml;	Y-diaeresis
ƒ	&#402;	&fnof;	function, florin

Greek Capital Characters

Character	Entity Number	Entity Name	Description
A	&#913;	&Alpha;	capital Alpha
B	&#914;	&Beta;	capital Beta
Γ	&#915;	&Gamma;	capital Gamma
Δ	&#916;	&Delta;	capital Delta
E	&#917;	&Epsilon;	capital Epsilon
Z	&#918;	&Zeta;	capital Zeta
H	&#919;	&Eta;	capital Eta
Θ	&#920;	&Theta;	capital Theta
I	&#921;	&Iota;	capital Iota
K	&#922;	&Kappa;	capital Kappa
Λ	&#923;	&Lambda;	capital Lambda
M	&#924;	&Mu;	capital Mu
N	&#925;	&Nu;	capital Nu
Ξ	&#926;	&Xi;	capital Xi
O	&#927;	&Omicron;	capital Omicron
Π	&#928;	&Pi;	capital Pi
P	&#929;	&Rho;	capital Rho
	&#930;		unused

Character	Entity Number	Entity Name	Description
Σ	&#931;	&Sigma;	capital Sigma
Τ	&#932;	&Tau;	capital Tau
Υ	&#933;	&Upsilon;	capital Upsilon
Φ	&#934;	&Phi;	capital Phi
Χ	&#935;	&Chi;	capital Chi
Ψ	&#936;	&Psi;	capital Psi
Ω	&#937;	&Omega;	capital Omega

Greek Small Characters

Character	Entity Number	Entity Name	Description
α	&#945;	&alpha;	small alpha
β	&#946;	&beta;	small beta
γ	&#947;	&gamma;	small gamma
δ	&#948;	&delta;	small delta
ε	&#949;	&epsilon;	small epsilon
ζ	&#950;	&zeta;	small zeta
η	&#951;	&eta;	small eta
θ	&#952;	&theta;	small theta
ι	&#953;	&iota;	small iota
κ	&#954;	&kappa;	small kappa
λ	&#955;	&lambda;	small lambda
μ	&#956;	&mu;	small mu
ν	&#956;	&nu;	small nu
ξ	&#958;	&xi;	small xi
ο	&#959;	&omicron;	small omicron
π	&#960;	&pi;	small pi
ρ	&#961;	&rho;	small rho
ς	&#962;	&sigmaf;	small sigma final
σ	&#963;	&sigma;	small sigma
τ	&#964;	&tau;	small tau
υ	&#965;	&upsilon;	small upsilon
φ	&#966;	&phi;	small phi
χ	&#967;	&chi;	small chi
ψ	&#968;	&psi;	small psi
ω	&#969;	&omega;	small omega

Miscellaneous Characters and Symbols

Character	Entity Number	Entity Name	Description
–	&#8207;	&ndash;	en dash
—	&#8212;	&mdash;	em dash
'	&#8216;	&lsquo;	left single quotation mark
'	&#8217;	&rsquo;	right single quotation mark
‚	&#8218;	&sbquo;	single low-9 quotation mark
"	&#8220;	&ldquo;	left double quotation mark
"	&#8221;	&rdquo;	right double quotation mark
„	&#8222;	&bdquo;	double low-9 quotation mark
†	&#8224;	&dagger;	dagger
‡	&#8225;	&Dagger;	double dagger
•	&#8226;	&bull;	bullet
…	&#8230;	&hellip;	horizontal ellipsis
‰	&#8240;	&permil;	per mille sign
′	&#8242;	&prime;	prime, minutes, feet
″	&#8243;	&Prime;	double prime, seconds, inches
‹	&#8249;	&lsaquo;	single left angle quotation mark
›	&#8250;	&rsaquo;	single right angle quotation mark
⁄	&#8260;	&frasl;	fraction slash
€	&#8364;	&euro;	euro sign
™	&#8482;	&trade;	trademark
←	&#8592;	&larr;	left arrow
↑	&#8593;	&uarr;	up arrow
→	&#8594;	&rarr;	right arrow
↓	&#8595;	&darr;	down arrow
↔	&#8596;	&harr;	left-right arrow
⇒	&#8658;	&rArr;	right double arrow
⇔	&#8660;	&hArr;	left-right double arrow
∀	&#8704;	&forall;	for all
∂	&#8706;	&part;	part differential
∃	&#8707;	&exist;	there exists
∇	&#8711;	&nabla;	nabla/backward difference
∈	&#8712;	&isin;	element of (is in)
∋	&#8715;	&ni;	contains as member
∏	&#8719;	&prod;	product sign
∑	&#8721;	&sum;	n-ary summation
−	&#8722;	&minus;	minus sign
√	&#8730;	&radic;	square root/radical sign
∝	&#8733;	&prop;	proportional to
∞	&#8734;	&infin;	infinity
∠	&#8736;	&ang;	angle
∧	&#8743;	&and;	logical and
∨	&#8744;	&or;	logical or
∩	&#8745;	&cap;	intersection, cap
∪	&#8746;	&cup;	union, cup
∫	&#8747;	&int;	integral

Character	Entity Number	Entity Name	Description
∴	&#8756;	&there4;	therefore
~	&#8764;	&sim;	similar to, tilde operator
≈	&#8776;	&asymp;	asymptomatic, almost equal
≠	&#8800;	&ne;	not equal
≡	&#8801;	&equiv;	equivalent
≤	&#8804;	&le;	less than or equal
≥	&#8805;	&ge;	greater than or equal
⊂	&#8834;	&sub;	subset of
⊃	&#8835;	&sup;	superset of
⊆	&#8838;	&sube;	subset of or equal to
⊇	&#9939;	&supe;	superset of or equal to
⊕	&#8853;	&oplus;	direct sum
⊥	&#8869;	&perp;	perpendicular
◊	&#9674;	&loz;	lozenge
♠	&#9824;	&spades;	spades suit
♣	&#9827;	&clubs;	clubs suit
♥	&#9829;	&hearts;	hearts suit
♦	&#9830;	&diams;	diamonds suit

NOTE

For additional resources and information on using character sets on the Web, see the Appendixes' section at the IRC for this book at **www.emcp.com**/.

APPENDIX C

Web-Safe Colors Chart

The Web-safe color palette contains 216 colors that display without being dithered on computer systems with display adapters that are limited to 256 colors. This color palette was originally called the "Netscape palette," because Netscape originated it. The 216 colors specified should all be present on the 256-color system palettes of most computers, whether running Windows, Macintosh OS, or UNIX. The Web-safe color palette also can help make it easier to select a color, because you only have to choose between 216 colors, whereas the full True Color palette includes 16.3 million possible colors.

FFFFFF	FFFFCC	FFFF99	FFFF66	FFFF33	FFFF00
FFCCFF	FFCCCC	FFCC99	FFCC66	FFCC33	FFCC00
FF99FF	FF99CC	FF9999	FF9966	FF9933	FF9900
FF66FF	FF66CC	FF6699	FF6666	FF6633	FF6600
FF33FF	FF33CC	FF3399	FF3366	FF3333	FF3300
FF00FF	FF00CC	FF0099	FF0066	FF0033	FF0000

CCFFFF	CCFFCC	CCFF99	CCFF66	CCFF33	CCFF00
CCCCFF	CCCCCC	CCCC99	CCCC66	CCCC33	CCCC00
CC99FF	CC99CC	CC9999	CC9966	CC9933	CC9900
CC66FF	CC66CC	CC6699	CC6666	CC6633	CC6600
CC33FF	CC33CC	CC3399	CC3366	CC3333	CC3300
CC00FF	CC00CC	CC0099	CC0066	CC0033	CC0000

99FFFF	99FFCC	99FF99	99FF66	99FF33	99FF00
99CCFF	99CCCC	99CC99	99CC66	99CC33	99CC00
9999FF	9999CC	999999	999966	999933	999900
9966FF	9966CC	996699	996666	996633	996600
9933FF	9933CC	993399	993366	993333	993300
9900FF	9900CC	990099	990066	990033	990000

66FFFF	66FFCC	66FF99	66FF66	66FF33	66FF00
66CCFF	66CCCC	66CC99	66CC66	66CC33	66CC00
6699FF	6699CC	669999	669966	669933	669900
6666FF	6666CC	666699	666666	666633	666600
6633FF	6633CC	663399	663366	663333	663300
6600FF	6600CC	660099	660066	660033	660000

33FFFF	33FFCC	33FF99	33FF66	33FF33	33FF00
33CCFF	33CCCC	33CC99	33CC66	33CC33	33CC00
3399FF	3399CC	339999	339966	339933	339900
3366FF	3366CC	336699	336666	336633	336600
3333FF	3333CC	333399	333366	333333	333300
3300FF	3300CC	330099	330066	330033	330000

00FFFF	00FFCC	00FF99	00FF66	00FF33	00FF00
00CCFF	00CCCC	00CC99	00CC66	00CC33	00CC00
0099FF	0099CC	009999	009966	009933	009900
0066FF	0066CC	006699	006666	006633	006600
0033FF	0033CC	003399	003366	003333	003300
0000FF	0000CC	000099	000066	000033	000000

NOTE For additional resources and information on using color on the Web, see the Appendixes section at the IRC for this book at www.emcp.com/.

APPENDIX

D
CSS Quick Reference

This two-part appendix provides an alphabetical listing of all properties in CSS1 (Cascading Style Sheets, level 1), and then lists some of the most commonly used properties that were introduced as part of CSS2 (Cascading Style Sheets, level 2). CSS1 is supported by all current browsers; parts of CSS2 are widely supported, but other parts are not. The parts of CSS2 that are featured in this appendix are supported by current browsers (except where otherwise noted).

NOTE — Initial values for properties (when they have them) are indicated by bold type. Anything other than a literal value is indicated by italics (such as *length*, for instance, to indicate measurement values such as **10px** or **3em**).

CSS1 PROPERTIES

background	**Inherited:** no	**Application:** all elements

A shorthand property for setting the background-color, background-image, background-repeat, background-attachment, and background-position properties.

Property Values   *background-color\background-image\background-repeat\background-attachment\background-position*

Example
```
body { color: blue; background: black url(back_dark.jpg) fixed; }
h1, h2, h3 { color: yellow; background: transparent; }
p { color: #ffffcc; background: transparent; }
```

background-attachment	**Inherited:** no	**Application:** all elements

Specifies whether a background image is fixed relative to the canvas or scrolls with the Web page.

Property Values   fixed|**scroll**

Example
```
body { color: maroon; background: white; background-attachment: fixed; }
```

The background-attachment property is not included in *CSS1 core*, which defines the core functionality required for a browser to be CSS1-compliant. Of CSS-aware browsers, however, only Netscape 4 does not recognize the background-attachment property.

background-color
Inherited: no　　**Application:** all elements

Specifies a background color for an element.

Property Values　　*color*|**transparent**

color = a color name, a hexadecimal RGB color code, a decimal RGB color code, or a percentage RGB color code (see the color property listing for examples of using these).

Example　`div.box { color: navy; background-color: #ccffcc; }`

Some earlier CSS-aware browsers do not support using the background-color property; to allow for these earlier browsers, you should use the background property, and not the background-color property, to set background colors.

background-image
Inherited: no　　**Application:** all elements

Specifies a background image for an element.

Property Values　　url(*URL*)|**none**

Example　`body { color: black; background-color: white; background-image: url(back_light.jpg); }`

When parsing a relative URL for a background image in an external style sheet file (.css), Netscape 4 wrongly locates the background image relative to the location of the HTML file, instead of relative to the location of the external style sheet file. Redirect or shield Netscape 4 users, or specify the relative URL in an embedded style sheet.

background-repeat
Inherited: no　　**Application:** all elements

Specifies whether and how a background image should be repeated in a Web page's background.

Property Values　　repeat-x|repeat-y|**repeat**|no-repeat

Example　`body { color: black; background-color: white; background-image: url(back_twocol.jpg); background-repeat: repeat-y; }`

The repeat-x repeat-y properties repeat the background image horizontally and vertically, respectively. The repeat property (the initial value) repeats (or tiles) the background image along both horizontally and vertically. The no-repeat property causes the background image to not be repeated and is usually used in conjunction with the background-position property (to position a watermark image, for instance).

background-position
Inherited: no　　**Application:** block and replaced elements

Positions a background image in a Web page's background. Used in conjunction with a **no-repeat** value for the background-repeat property.

Property Values　　*length length*|*n% n%*|*length*|*n%*|*length n%*|*n% length*|*keyword keyword*| *length*|*n%*|*keyword*|0% 0%

length = pixels (px), em units (em), ex units (ex), centimeters (cm), inches (in), millimeters (mm), points (pt), picas (pc) (negative values allowed).
keyword (horizontal) = left, center, right.
keyword (vertical) = top, center, bottom.

n% = a percentage value.

Negative percentages (-n%) are allowed.

A replaced element's intrinsic dimensions are relied upon to display the element. Examples of replaced elements include the IMG, INPUT, TEXT AREA, SELECT, and OBJECT elements.

Example
```
body { color: black; background-color: white; background-image:
url(watermark.gif); background-repeat: no-repeat; background-
position: 50% 150px; }
```

or

```
div { color: black; background-color: white; background-image:
url(logo.gif); background-repeat: no-repeat; background-position:
top center; }
```

The background image is positioned relative to the padding edge of the containing block. When two length values or two percentage values (or combinations of the two) are specified, the first value specifies the horizontal position and the second value specifies the vertical position. If only one length or percentage value is specified, a horizontal position is assumed, with a vertical position of **50%** (or **center**) assumed. Keyword values cannot be combined with length or percentage values.

border
Inherited: no   **Application:** all elements

A shorthand property for setting the border-width, border-style, and border-color properties.

Property Values   *border-width|border-style|border-color*

Example   `div.frame { border: 4px solid red; }`

border-color
Inherited: no   **Application:** all elements

Specifies the border color to be drawn around the four sides of an element.

Property Values   *color*|transparent|***color property value***

color = a color name, a hexadecimal RGB color code, a decimal RGB color code, or a percentage RGB color code (see the color property listing for examples of using these).

If a border style has been specified, but no border color, the color property value is applied as the initial value.

One to four values can be specified. One value applies to all four sides; two values apply to the top/bottom and right/left borders; three values apply to the top, right/left, and bottom borders; and four values apply to the top, right, left, and bottom borders.

Example
```
div.alert { border-color: green #0066ff rgb(48,200,5)
rgb(10%,25%,50%); }
```

border-style
Inherited: no   **Application:** all elements

Specifies the style of border to be drawn around an element.

Property Values   dotted|dashed|solid|double| groove|ridge|inset|outset|**none**

One to four values can be specified. One value applies to all four sides; two values apply to the top/bottom and right/left borders; three values apply to the top, right/left, and bottom borders; and four values apply to the top, right, left, and bottom borders.

Example   `div.announce { border-color: green; border-style: groove; }`

Other than when setting a **solid** border-style property value, there is little consistency in how different browsers handle the other border-style property values. *CSS1 core*, which defines the core functionality required for a browser to be CSS1-compliant, allows CSS1-compliant browsers to display dotted, dashed, double, groove, ridge, inset, and outset borders as solid borders.

Because the initial border-style value is **none**, a border-style property (or a border property with a border-style value set) must be set for a border to be displayed. The border-style property can be used by itself to set an element border; the border color defaults to the color property value; the border width defaults to a **medium** value (3 or 4 pixels, depending on the browser).

border-top, border-right, border-bottom, border-left
Inherited: no   **Application:** all elements

Shorthand properties for setting the border width, style, and color for the top, right, bottom, or left sides of an element. The border-top property is shorthand for the border-top-width, border-top-style, and border-top-color properties, for instance.

Property Values   *border width, border style, border color*

border width = border-top-width, border-right-width, border-bottom-width, or border-left-width property values.
border style = border-top-style, border-right-style, border-bottom-style, or border-left-style property values.
border color = border-top-color, border-right-color, border-bottom-color, or border-left-color property values.

One to four values can be specified. One value applies to all four sides; two values apply to the top/bottom and right/left borders; three values apply to the top, right/left, and bottom borders; and four values apply to the top, right, left, and bottom borders.

Example   `div.topbottom { border-top: groove green 5px; border-bottom: ridge olive 3px; }`

border-top-color, border-right-color, border-bottom-color, border-left-color
Inherited: no   **Application:** all elements

These properties specify the color of the top, right, bottom, and left borders of an element.

Property Values   *color*|transparent|*color property value*

color = a color name, a hexadecimal RGB color code, a decimal RGB color code, or a percentage RGB color code (see the color property listing for examples of using these).

One to four values can be specified. One value applies to all four sides; two values apply to the top/bottom and right/left borders; three values apply to the top, right/left, and bottom borders; and four values apply to the top, right, left, and bottom borders.

See below for example.

border-top-style, border-right-style, border-bottom-style, border-left-style   **Inherited:** no   **Application:** all elements

These properties specify the width of the top, right, bottom, and left borders of an element.

Property Values   *length*|thin|**medium**|thick

length = pixels (px), em units (em), ex units (ex), centimeters (cm), inches (in), millimeters (mm), points (pt), or picas (pc).

One to four values can be specified. One value applies to all four sides; two values apply to the top/bottom and right/left borders; three values apply to the top, right/left, and bottom borders; and four values apply to the top, right, left, and bottom borders.

See below for example.

border-top-width, border-right-width, border-bottom-width, border-left-width   **Inherited:** no   **Application:** all elements

These properties specify the width of the top, right, bottom, and left borders of an element.

Property Values   *length*|thin|**medium**|thick

length = pixels (px), em units (em), ex units (ex), centimeters (cm), inches (in), millimeters (mm), points (pt), or picas (pc).

One to four values can be specified. One value applies to all four sides; two values apply to the top/bottom and right/left borders; three values apply to the top, right/left, and bottom borders; and four values apply to the top, right, left, and bottom borders.

Example   `h2 { border-top-color: blue; border-top-width: 3px; border-top-style: solid; }`

border-width   **Inherited:** no   **Application:** all elements

A shorthand property for setting values for the border-top-width, border-right-width, border-bottom-width, and border-left-width properties. Specifies the width of the borders around an element.

Property Values   *length*|thin|**medium**|thick

length = pixels (px), em units (em), ex units (ex), centimeters (cm), inches (in), millimeters (mm), points (pt), or picas (pc).

One to four values can be specified. One value applies to all four sides; two values apply to the top/bottom and right/left borders; three values apply to the top, right/left, and bottom borders; and four values apply to the top, right, left, and bottom borders.

Example   `h2 { border-color: blue; border-top-style: solid; border-width: 6px 3px; }`

clear
Inherited: no   **Application:** block elements

Used in conjunction with the float property, this property causes an element to clear a floating element, moving down on the page until the left, right, or both margins are clear (not blocked by the floating element).

Property Values   left|right|both|**none**

See *float* for an example of using the clear property.

color
Inherited: yes   **Application:** all elements

Specifies the foreground color for an element.

Property Values   *color*

color = a color name, a hexadecimal RGB color code, a decimal RGB color code, or a percentage RGB color code (see the color property listing for examples of using these).

Example
```
h2 { color: navy; background: #ccffcc; }
span { color: rgb(128,255,0); background: transparent; }
```

display
Inherited: no   **Application:** all elements

Specifies how or whether an element will be displayed, allowing an inline element to be displayed (and treated) as a block element (and vice versa), for instance. The display of an element also can be turned off.

Property Values   **block**|inline|list-item|none

Example
```
a.button { display: block; padding: 5px; border: ridge blue 3px;
color: red; background: yellow; }
.noshow { display: none; }
```

The **display: none** property declaration is distinguished from the **visibility: hidden** property declaration—in the first instance, the element is not present and does not affect the page's layout, whereas in the second instance, the element is still present, although invisible, and thus affects the page's layout. The display property also is not inherited, whereas the visibility property is.

The display property is not included in *CSS1 core*, which defines the core functionality required for a browser to be CSS1-compliant. Internet Explorer 3 does not support the display property. Internet Explorer 4 only supports the **none** value. Internet Explorer 5, Internet Explorer 5.5, and Opera 3 do not support the **list-item** value. Netscape Navigator 4 does not support the **inline** value.

float
Inherited: no   **Application:** all elements

Floats an element to the left or right margin, with following text or other elements flowing around the other side of the element.

Property Values   left|right|**none**

Example
```
div.left { float: left; width: 200px; margin-right: 5px; }
h1, h2, h3 { clear: left; }
```

The float property works similarly to the deprecated **align="left"** and **align="right"** HTML attributes, except that it can be applied to any element (except for positioned or generated elements), rather than just to the IMG, TABLE, OBJECT, and APPLET elements, as is the case with using the ALIGN attribute.

The clear property can be used in conjunction with the float property to cause following elements to clear a floating element. It also can be inserted in an inline style to cause a specific element to not flow around a floating object (`style="clear: both"`).

font

Inherited: yes   **Application:** all elements

A shorthand property for setting the font-family, font-size, font-style, font-variant, font-weight, and line-height properties.

Property Values   *font-family*, *font-size*, *font-style*, *font-variant*, *font-weight*, and *line-height*

Example
```
h2 { font: Arial, Geneva, Helvetica, sans-serif bold italic small-
caps 110%/125%; }
```

In the **110%/125%** code, the **110%** sets the font size, while the **125%** sets the line height.

font-family

Inherited: yes   **Application:** all elements

Specifies a font-family name or comma-separated list of font-family names. Either specific or generic font-family names can be specified.

Property Values   *font-family\generic font-family*

A specific font-family name should match the actual name of a font in use, such as Times New Roman, Trebuchet MS, Comic Sans MS, Palatino, New Century Schoolbook, and so on. Font-family names with spaces in them must be quoted.

Five generic font-family names can be used: **serif**, **sans-serif**, **monospace**, **cursive**, and **fantasy**. The actual font displayed is determined by the default font assigned by browsers to these generic font-families. Serif fonts include Times New Roman, Times, and Palatino, for instance. Sans serif fonts include Arial, Geneva, and Helvetica, for example. Monospaced fonts include Courier New and Courier, for instance. There is consistent browser support only for the serif, sans-serif, and monospace generic font-families; specifying the cursive or fantasy generic font-family names produces widely differing results in different browsers.

Example   `h2 { font-family: 'Courier New', Courier, monospace; }`

A specific font-family has to be available on a local system to be displayed. In the code example, if the Courier New font (a TrueType font) is available, it is displayed. If Courier New is not available, but Courier (an Adobe Postscript font) is available, then the Courier font is displayed. If neither Courier New nor Courier is available, then a browser's default monospaced font is displayed.

Although not required, it is good practice to list font-family names exactly, including any uppercase letters, because font names on some platforms are case-sensitive. It is also good practice to list PostScript fonts after TrueType fonts, because some Windows browsers will display the embedded bitmap font if a PostScript font is listed first and Adobe Type Manager is not installed (more recent Windows browsers simply ignore PostScript fonts).

font-size

Inherited: yes   **Application:** all elements

Specifies the font size in which an element is to be displayed.

Property Values   *length\n%\relative-size\
absolute-size* (**medium**)

length = pixels (px), em units (em), ex units (ex), centimeters (cm), inches (in), millimeters (mm), points (pt), picas (pc).

relative-size = larger, smaller.

absolute-size = xxsmall, x-small, small, **medium**, large, x-large, xx-large.

Important: Font sizes set in em units, ex units, and percentages are relative to the parent element's font size. Thus a font size of 1.5 ems set for an element would be one and a half times the font size set for that element's parent element.

When setting font sizes, em units and percentages are equivalent (with 1.5 em and 150% both representing a font size that is one and a half times the font size of the parent element). Ex-unit font sizes should be relative to the x-height of the parent element's font, but many current browsers simply treat an ex unit as one-half of an em unit.

Example
```
h2 { font-size: 6.5em; }
p { font-size: 110%; }
address { font-size: smaller; }
```

Points (pt), picas (pc), centimeters (cm), inches (in), and millimeters (mm) should never be used to set font sizes for display on the Web because display dimensions, screen resolutions, and dot-pitches are variable and indeterminate; they should only be used where the dimensions of the output media are known, such as when creating a "print" media style sheet for printing to an 8.5 × 11.5-inch piece of paper.

Absolute-size keywords (xxsmall, x-small, small, medium, large, x-large, and xx-large) for setting font sizes are interpreted differently in different browsers, with some browsers (Internet Explorer 5.5 for Windows and Opera 5/6, for instance) incorrectly displaying a small font in the same size as the default text font size (`size="3"`), while others correctly display a medium font in the same size as the default text font size. For this reason, absolute-size keywords should probably be avoided when setting font sizes.

font-style   **Inherited:** yes   **Application:** all elements

Specifies whether an element is displayed in an italic, oblique, or normal font style.

Property Values   italic|oblique|**normal**

An italic font is a separate typeface that has been individually crafted, while an oblique font is a normal font that has been slanted. Current browsers, however, do not seem to distinguish between the two, displaying an italic font, if available, regardless of whether an italic or oblique font style is specified.

Example   `span.stress { font-style: italic; }`

font-variant   **Inherited:** yes   **Application:** all elements

Specifies whether an element is displayed in small caps.

Property Values   small-caps|**normal**

Example   `h3 { font-variant: small-caps; }`

The font-variant property is not included in *CSS1 core*, which defines the core functionality required for a browser to be CSS1-compliant. Correspondingly, Internet Explorer 5.5 for Windows, for instance, does not support this property. An element set in small caps is displayed in Internet Explorer 5.5 in capital letters that are all of the same size. Internet Explorer 6 for Windows, however, does support the font-variant property.

font-weight

Inherited: yes   **Application:** all elements

Specifies the weight of an element's font.

Property Values   bold|bolder|lighter|**normal**|
                             100|200|300|400|500|600|700|800|900

A 400 font-weight should be equal to a normal font-weight and a 700 font-weight should be equal to a bold font-weight. Most current browsers do not distinguish the other font-weights, displaying them in either a normal or a bold font-weight. Stick to specifying bold or normal font-weights, in other words, and do not bother with the rest.

Example   `blockquote { font-weight: bold; }`

height

Inherited: no   **Application:** block and replaced elements

Specifies the height of an element's font.

Property Values   *length*|**auto**

CSS2 also allows for a *percentage* (*n%*) value for the height property, which is supposed to be relative to the height of the element's containing block, but browsers are inconsistent in how they handle this. Internet Explorer 5.5 for Windows, for instance, applies percentage heights to all block elements. Internet Explorer 6 for Windows ignores percentage heights set for block elements, unless a `height: 100%` property declaration is also made for the BODY element. Mozilla 1 and Netscape 6 only recognize percentage heights for absolutely positioned elements (`position: absolute`) and truncates the width of the element to its content unless a width of 100% is also set. In Mozilla 1 and Netscape 6, as well, text can overflow an element height, which is correct according to the CSS2 specification, but in Internet Explorer 6, the setting of a height for an element is a minimum setting that is overridden if the element content extends farther down the page.

Example   `div.box { color: navy; background: aqua; height: 10ems; }`

When setting heights or widths using CSS, be aware that Internet Explorer 5.5 for Windows misapplies the CSS box model, including any border or padding amounts within the calculated width or height of an element (the calculated width of an element should exclude any border or padding amounts). One way to deal with that is to set any borders or padding for an element in a separate, bracketing, DIV element. Another way is to use the Box Model Hack. For an example of using the Box Model Hack, see the *width* property listing.

CSS1 core, which defines the core functionality required for a browser to be CSS1-compliant, allows browsers to ignore the height property if the element is not a replaced element, as is the case with Internet Explorer 3 or Windows and the Macintosh.

letter-spacing

Inherited: yes   **Application:** all elements

Specifies additional spacing to be added between letters within an element.

Property Values   *length*|**normal**

A negative value (`letter-spacing: -2px`, for instance) can be set to reduce spacing between letters, but browsers can set implementation-specific limits (such as when also justifying text, for instance).

Example   `h2 { letter-spacing: 2px; }`

The letter-spacing property is not included in *CSS1 core*, which defines the core functionality required for a browser to be CSS1-compliant.

line-height   **Inherited:** yes   **Application:** all elements

Specifies the height of an element's line.

Property Values   *length|n|n%|***normal**

n = an integer value that sets the line-height as a multiplication of the element's font size (with a value of 2, for instance, corresponding to double-spacing).

A percentage value (*n%*) differs from an integer value in that the computed value is inherited by a child element, while for an integer value, the specified value is inherited.

Example   `p { letter-height: 1.5; }`

list-style   **Inherited:** yes   **Application:** List item elements

A shorthand property for setting values for the list-style-type, list-style-position, and list-style-image properties.

Property Values   *list-style-type, list-style-position, list-style-image*

Example   `ul { list-style: circle url(bullet.gif) inside; }`
            `ol { list-style: A; }`

list-style-image   **Inherited:** yes   **Application:** list item elements

Specifies the URL of an image to be displayed in place of an unordered list's bullet character.

Property Values   url(*URL*)|**none**

Example   `ul { list-style-image: url(bullet.gif); }`

list-style-position   **Inherited:** yes   **Application:** list item elements

Specifies whether the list bullet or number is displayed inside or outside of a list item's element box.

Property Values   inside|**outside**

Example   `ol { list-style-position: inside; }`
            `ol ul { list-style-position: outside; }`

list-style-type   **Inherited:** yes   **Application:** list item elements

Specifies the type of unordered or ordered list to be displayed.

Property Values   **disc**|circle|square (for UL elements)
                    decimal|lower-roman|upper-roman|
                    lower-alpha|upper-alpha|none (for OL elements)

Example
```
ol { list-style-type: square; }
ol ol { list-style-type: disc; }
ol ol ol { list-style-type: circle; }
ul { list-style-type: upper-roman; }
ul ul { list-style-type: upper-alpha; }
ul ul ul { list-style-type: decimal; }
```

margin   **Inherited:** no   **Application:** all elements

A shorthand property for setting the margin-top, margin-right, margin-bottom, and margin-left properties for an element.

Property Values   *length*|*n*%|auto|**0**

One to four values can be specified. One value applies to all four sides; two values apply to the top/bottom and right/left sides; three values apply to the top, right/left, and bottom sides; and four values apply to the top, right, left, and bottom sides.

For inline text elements, such as EM, STRONG, I, B, and so on, margin values are only applied to the left and right sides of the element. For the IMG element, however, which is also an inline element, margins are applied to all four sides.

Example
```
body { margin: 2em; }
div.inset { margin: 10px 20px; }
```
Margin spacing is displayed outside of any borders or padding space that are set for an element.

margin-top, margin-right,
margin-bottom, margin-left   **Inherited:** no   **Application:** all elements

These properties specify the amount of margin spacing to be display outside of the four sides of an element.

Property Values   *length*|*n*%|auto|**0**

Adjacent horizontal margins of nested elements are added together, while vertical margins between abutting elements collapse to the highest value of the two.

In CSS, an element with a width less than 100% of the browser window can be centered by setting the left and right margins to **auto**. Because of a bug, however, this does not work in Internet Explorer 5.5 for Windows. The workaround is to nest the element inside of a DIV element with a **text-align: center** property set, while setting **text-align: left** on the nested element. See the *text-align* listing for more information on using the text-align property.

Example
```
div.center { text-align: center; }
div.centered { width: 75%; margin-left: auto; margin-right: auto;
text-align: left; font-size: 110%; }
</style>
</head>
<body>
<div class="center">
<div class="centered">
<h2>Announcement:</h2>
<p>This semester's field trip is scheduled for next Friday. To be
excused, you must have a signed statement from a parent or
physician stating the reason you should be excused. Be sure to wear
```

```
proper walking shoes and bring protection against the rain, since
rain is not unheard of at this time of the year.</p>
</div>
</div>
```

Negative values can be set to reduce the margin spacing that would otherwise be displayed for an element. A problem can result, however, when trying to do this to reduce the default indenting of ordered or unordered lists because Internet Explorer and other browsers that follow its example indent a list by adding margin space to the left of the list, while Netscape and Mozilla indent a list by adding padding space to the left of the list. The workaround is to nest the list inside a DIV element and then set a negative left-margin on that element to reduce the default indenting of a list.

padding	**Inherited:** no	**Application:** all elements

A shorthand property for setting the padding-top, padding-right, padding-bottom, and padding-left properties for an element.

Property Values   *length*|*n*%|auto|**0**

One to four values can be specified. One value applies to all four sides; two values apply to the top/bottom and right/left sides; three values apply to the top, right/left, and bottom sides; and four values apply to the top, right, left, and bottom sides.

Example   `div.inset { margin: 10px 20px; border: 4px red groove; padding: 5px 10px 8px; }`

Padding is displayed outside of the element's content box, but inside of any border.

padding-top, padding-right,		
padding-bottom, padding-left	**Inherited:** no	**Application:** all elements

These properties specify the amount of padding to be displayed around the four sides of an element.

Property Values   *length*|*n*%|auto|**0**

Example   `div.center { text-align: center; }`
`div.centered { width: 75%; padding-left: 10px; padding-right: 10px;`
`border: 4px ridge maroon; margin-left: auto; margin-right: auto;`
`text-align: left; font-size: 110%; }`

text-align	**Inherited:** yes	**Application:** block elements

Specifies how the content is horizontally aligned within an element.

Property Values   left|right|center|justify

Example   `p { text-align: justify; }`

The **justify** value is not included in *CSS1 core*, which defines the core functionality required for a browser to be CSS1-compliant. Internet Explorer 3 for Windows and Internet Explorer 3 and 4 for the Macintosh ignore the **justify** value, enforcing the default text-alignment instead (left or right, depending on the default writing direction of the language in use).

text-decoration

Inherited: no   **Application:** all elements

Specifies how text is decorated (or highlighted) within an element.

Property Values   underline|overline|line-through|blink|**none**

A common use of the text-decoration property is to turn off display of the default underlining that most browsers display under hypertext links.

Browsers are not required to support the **blink** value. Generally, blinking text on the Web is considered to be irritating and rude and is best avoided.

Example
```
h2 { text-decoration: overline; }
a { text-decoration: none; }
```

text-indent

Inherited: yes   **Application:** block elements

Sets the amount of space the first line of an element is to be indented. Can be used to format tabbed paragraphs, for instance.

Property Values   *length*|*n%*|**0**

Example
```
p { text-indent: 10px; margin-top: 0; margin-bottom: 0; }
```

text-transform

Inherited: yes   **Application:** all elements

Transforms the case or capitalization of an element.

Property Values   capitalize|uppercase|lowercase|**none**

Example
```
h1 { text-transform: lowercase; }
```

The text-transform property is not included in *CSS1 core*, which defines the core functionality required for a browser to be CSS1-compliant. Of CSS-aware browsers, only Internet Explorer 3 does not support the text-transform property.

vertical-align

Inherited: no   **Application:** inline and table-cell elements

Vertically aligns an element relative to its parent element.

Property Values   **baseline**|sub|super|top|text-top|middle|bottom|text-bottom|*n%*

The **baseline** value aligns the element with the parent element's baseline. The **sub** and **super** values subscript or superscript the element relative to the parent element. The **top**, **middle**, and **bottom** align the element with the top, middle, or bottom of the parent element. The **text-top** and **text-bottom** values align the top or bottom of the element with the top or bottom of the parent element's text. A percentage value allows the incremental lowering or raising of the element relative to its parent element's box, with the percentage value being relative to the element's line-height. CSS2 also allows a length value (pixels or ems, for instance) to be specified.

Example
```
h3 { font-size: 2em; }
h3 em { font-size: 2.5em; vertical-align: middle; }
```

white-space   **Inherited:** yes   **Application:** block elements

Specifies how *whitespace* within an element is to be treated. In CSS, whitespace is defined as being formed by spaces (Unicode 32), tabs (Unicode 9), line feeds (Unicode 10), carriage returns (Unicode 13), and form feeds (Unicode 12), but not by other characters forming spaces, such as em spaces (Unicode 8195), for instance.

Property Values   nowrap|pre|**normal**

The **nowrap** value causes the line to not wrap at white space characters, causing the line to extend past the right margin until a BR element is encountered. The **pre** value causes the element's content to be treated as though it were in a PRE element, with all spaces and hard returns preserved. The **normal** value causes whitespace characters to be treated as they normally are, with lines wrapping at the farthest white space character within a browser window and multiple white space characters, for instance, being collapsed to a single space.

In CSS, white space is defined as being formed by spaces (Unicode 32), tabs (Unicode 9), line feeds (Unicode 10), carriage returns (Unicode 13), and form feeds (Unicode 12), but not by other characters forming spaces, such as em spaces (Unicode 8195), for instance.

Example   `code { display: block; white-space: pre; }`

The white-space property is not included in *CSS1 core*, which defines the core functionality required for a browser to be CSS1-compliant. It is not supported by Internet Explorer 3 through 5 for Windows, Internet Explorer 3 for the Macintosh, or Opera 3. Internet Explorer 5.5 for Windows supports the **nowrap** value, but not the **pre** value, whereas Netscape 4 supports the **pre** value, but not the **nowrap** value.

width   **Inherited:** no   **Application:** block and replaced elements

Specifies the width of the content area within an element.

Property Values   *length*|*n*%|**auto**

The width of an element is exclusive of any additional padding, borders, or margins that are defined for the element. When the width is undefined (or when **auto** is explicitly defined), the width is equal to the available space, minus any padding, borders, or margins. When a specific (or percentage) width is defined, the right margin is adjusted to fill the available space (assuming that the parent element is left-aligned), unless both the margin-left and margin-right properties are set to **auto**, in which case both the left and right margins are adjusted to fill the available space (in effect, centering the element).

A percentage width is relative to the width of the containing block (the parent element).

Example   `div.insert { width="75%"; margin-left: auto; margin-right: auto; }`

As mentioned previously in the *height* listing, Internet Explorer 5.5 for Windows incorrectly calculates the width of an element as including any padding or borders that have been set. The result of this is that borders and padding are set for an element along with a specific width; the displayed element will be less wide in Internet Explorer 5.5 than in other browsers that do this correctly. This can be important, for instance, when creating a button that must be wide enough to contain its content (its text label). There are two workarounds for this, the first being simply to nest the affected element inside a DIV element with `text-align: center` set (while setting `text-align: left` for the nested element, if the maintenance of left-alignment is desired). The second workaround is commonly referred to as the *box model hack*. The box model hack works by taking advantage of a parsing error in Internet Explorer 5.5 that causes it to ignore style properties that follow **voice-family: "\"}\"";** **voice-family: inherit;** in a style rule, as shown in the following example:

```
div.top { width: 600px; height: 200px; border: maroon ridge 5px;
padding: 10px;
/* Start box model hack
voice-family: "\"}\""; voice-family: inherit; width: 570px; height:
170px;
html>body div.top { width: 570px; height: 170px; }
/* End of box model hack
```

Internet Explorer 5.5 ignores anything in the style rule that follows **voice-family: "\"}\"";** **voice-family: inherit;** and thus retains the initial width and height settings of 600 and 200 pixels, while browsers without the parsing error reset the height and width to the values following the voice-family property instances (to 570 and 170 pixels). The following line, beginning with **html>body div.top** takes care of one remaining exception, the Opera 5/6 browser, which has the same parsing error as Internet Explorer 5.5, although it correctly interprets the CSS box model, by making use of a CSS2 selector that Opera 5/6 recognizes, but Internet Explorer 5.5 does not.

word-spacing	**Inherited:** yes	**Application:** all elements

Increases or decreases the amount of space displayed between words within an element.
Specifies the width of the content area within an element.

Property Values   *length*|**normal**

The *length* value can be negative (**word-spacing: -2px**), although results can differ between browsers.

Example   h2 { letter-spacing: 2px; }

The word-spacing property is not included in *CSS1 core*, which defines the core functionality required for a browser to be CSS1-compliant. Accordingly, Internet Explorer 5.5 for Windows, for instance, does not support the word-spacing property, although Internet Explorer 6 for Windows does.

SELECTION OF CSS2 PROPERTIES

border-collapse	**Inherited:** yes	**Application:** table elements

Specifies the formatting model for displaying adjacent borders in tables.

Property Values   **collapse**|separate|inherit

A **collapse** value collapses adjacent table borders to a single border, while a **separate** value retains separation between adjacent borders.

Example
```
table { border-collapse: collapse; border-spacing: 0; border: 1px
solid black; margin-left: auto; margin-right: auto; }
th, td { padding: 4px; border: 1px solid black; }
```

Netscape 6 does not recognize the border-collapse property, but does recognize **border-spacing: 0** to achieve the same result. See *border-spacing* for more information on this property.

border-spacing	**Inherited:** yes	**Application:** table elements

Specifies the amount of spacing to be displayed between adjacent table borders when **border-collapse: separate** is set.

Property Values   *length1* [*length2*]|inherit|**0**

One or two *length* values can be specified; if two, then the first specifies the horizontal spacing and the second specifies the vertical spacing to be displayed between table borders.

Example
```
table { border-collapse: separate; border-spacing: 3px; border: 1px
solid black; margin-left: auto; margin-right: auto; }
th, td { padding: 4px; border: 1px solid black; }
```

Internet Explorer 6 for Windows and Internet Explorer 5 for the Macintosh do not support the border-spacing property. To control spacing between adjacent table borders in those browsers, you must use the CELLSPACING attribute in the TABLE element.

clip	**Inherited:** no	**Application:** block and replaced elements

Specifies an area within an element to be displayed (with the "clipped" areas rendered invisible).

Property Values   rect(*top right bottom left*)|**auto**|inherit

The rect values (*top*, *right*, *bottom*, and *left*) specify offsets (in pixels, ems, or percentages, for instance) from the respective sides of the element. Negative values can be used. An **auto** offset value also can be used to specify that an offset should be unchanged from what it would normally be.

Example   `div.banner img { clip: rect(5px 20px 15px 30px); }`

font-size-adjust	**Inherited:** yes	**Application:** all elements

Adjusts the size of fonts based on their x-heights. A Verdana font, for instance, has a much larger x-height (as a ratio of the font-size) than Arial or Geneva.

Property Values   *x-height ratio*|**none**|inherit

The *x-height ratio* specifies the ratio of the x-height to the font size of the preferred font. If a font other than the preferred front in a font list is displayed, its x-height will be adjusted to match that of the preferred font.

Example   `p { font-family: Verdana, Geneva, Arial, sans-serif; font-size-adjust: .55; }`

Of current browsers, the Mozilla 1 browser supports the font-size-adjust property, but other browsers do not. In the above example, an x-height ratio of .55 matches the default x-height ratio for a Verdana font in Mozilla. One way to find out the x-height ratio for a font is to compare two versions of the same element displayed using the same font, but with an x-height ratio set for one, but not for the other; if the correct x-height ratio is set, you will not notice any difference in the two elements' fonts. The x-height ratios as they are displayed in the Mozilla browser for some of the other more commonly used TrueType fonts include Comic Sans MS/.53, Arial/.52, Times New Roman/.44, Tahoma/.54, and Trebuchet MS/.52 (note: these ratios are slightly less than those suggested in the CSS2 specification).

overflow   **Inherited:** no   **Application:** block and replaced elements

Specifies how content that overflows the dimensions of an element is to be treated.

Property Values   **visible**|hidden|scroll|auto|inherit

A **visible** value indicates the element's content can overflow and be rendered outside of the element's boundaries. A **hidden** value hides content that overflows the element's boundaries. A **scroll** value causes scroll bars to be displayed, even if an element's content does not overflow its boundaries, while an **auto** value displays scroll bars only if the element's contents overflows its boundaries.

Example   `div.wnd { height: 25em; overflow: auto; }`

position   **Inherited:** no   **Application:** all elements (but not

generated content)

Used in conjunction with the top, right, bottom, and left properties to position an element within the browser window.

Property Values   **static**|relative|absolute|fixed|inherit

A **relative** value positions the element relative to its current position. An **absolute** value positions the element relative to the top, right, bottom, and left edges of the containing block's padding area. A **fixed** value works the same way as an **absolute** value, except the element remains fixed on the screen when the page is scrolled. See *top, right, bottom, and left* for an example.

Netscape 6, Mozilla 1, and Opera 5/6 support the **fixed** value, but Internet Explorer 6, and earlier versions, does not.

top, right, bottom, and left   **Inherited:** no   **Application:** positioned elements

Used in conjunction with the position property to position an element within the browser window.

Property Values   *length*|*n*%|**auto**|inherit

When absolutely positioning an element, the top, right, and left properties indicate the distance of the element's position from the top, right, and left edges of the containing block's padding area, while the bottom property positions it relative to the bottom of the browser window. When relatively positioning an element, the top, right, left, and bottom properties indicate the distance of the object from its current position. Negative values can be used.

Example   `div.pos1 { position: absolute; top: 24px; left: 100px; }`

visibility   **Inherited:** no   **Application:** all elements

Specifies whether an element's generated box is rendered.

Property Values   visible|hidden|collapse|**inherit**

The **visible** value renders the element's box visible, while the **hidden** value hides it. A `visibility: hidden` property value differs from a `display: none` property value, in that the first merely renders the element from being visible, which continues to occupy space within the document flow; while the second stops the element's box from being generated at all, without affecting the layout or positioning of surrounding elements. A **collapse** value applies only to table rows or columns; relative to other elements, a **collapse** value is equivalent to a **hidden** value.

Example   `div.hide { visibility: hidden; }`

z-index   **Inherited:** no   **Application:** all elements

Specifies the stacking order of positioned elements.

Property Values   *n*|**auto**|inherit

Normally, a following positioned element is stacked on top of a preceding positioned element. A positioned element with a higher z-index value is stacked on top of one with a lower z-index value.

Example
```
height: 125px; width: 98.7%; background: aqua; }
div.left { z-index: 2; position: absolute; top: 135px; left: 10px;
height: 85em; width: 150px; background: lime; }
div.main { z-index: 1; position: absolute; top: 135px; left: 160px;
height: 85em; width: auto; background: yellow; }
```

NOTE For additional resources and information on using CSS, see the Appendixes' section at the IRC for this book at **www.emcp.com/**.

E

Miscellaneous Technologies and Features

This appendix includes brief rundowns, including some examples, of various technologies and features not covered previously, but which students might find of interest or value in further pursuing the development of their Web design and authoring knowledge and skills. Features and technologies covered in this appendix include:

- Server-side includes (SSI)
- Cookies
- Password protection
- Server-side scripting and programming
- ASP, ASP.NET, and PHP
- Online databases
- Secure forms and servers
- Wireless Web protocols

USING SERVER-SIDE INCLUDES

Many Web servers allow you to include files within other files by means of *server-side includes* (SSI). Your Web host, however, must configure your account to allow the use of server-side includes. Server-side includes enable you to easily include updateable content within any page.

Server-side includes date back to when virtually all Web servers were UNIX machines. Although server-side includes (or a close variant) are supported on some Windows-based and Macintosh-based servers, the commands and syntax that they require can differ significantly from what is required on a UNIX server. Although different UNIX-based servers can support slightly different implementations of server-side includes, the commands and syntax they use are generally the same. The code examples and information provided in this section applies only to UNIX-based servers.

There are some drawbacks to using server-side includes, however. A server must parse the file that contains the server-side include, rather than simply delivering it to the Web browser. Each include that is present within a file generates a separate server process. Because of the extra load that enabling server-side includes places on the server, some Web hosts, especially the inexpensive or free ones, do not allow server-side includes.

Because files that include server-side includes must first be parsed by the server, before they are delivered to a browser (or other client-side agent), a special file extension, .shtml, is generally used to identify files that include server-side includes. Otherwise, a server would have no way of knowing which files contain server-side includes and which do not. By using a special extension, a server only needs to parse files with a .shtml extension before delivering them, while files with a .html extension can be delivered unparsed.

Server-side includes are inserted in HTML documents using HTML comment codes. The general format used is as follows:

```
<!--#command attribute=value attribute=value ...-->
```

Specifying the Date and Time

You can use a server-side include to specify the current date. For instance, the following server-side include causes a supporting server to display the current date:

```
<p><!--#echo var="DATE_LOCAL" --></p>
```

The previous example simply echoes the default date format, which might not be in the format that you prefer. You can use the CONFIG command to change the time format. For example:

```
<p><!--#config timefmt="%A, %B %d, %Y - %R %p" -->
Today is <!--#echo var="DATE_LOCAL" --></p>
```

Besides displaying the date in a different format, the previous example also displays the time. It is important to note, however, that the time reported through a server-side include corresponds to the time on the server and not to the time on a user's local computer, and so might not correspond to a user's own local time.

Displaying the Last Time a Document Was Modified

Another handy thing you can do using a server-side include is display the date when a document was last modified. The server-side include enables you to include that information in your document without manually updating it each time you make a change to the document. The following is an example of using a server-side include to display the last time the document was updated:

```
<!--#config timefmt="%A, %B %d, %Y" -->
This document was last modified on <!--#echo var="LAST_MODIFIED"
-->.
```

Including a File

Probably the most common use for server-side includes is to include a file inside a document. This can allow you, for instance, to create a document that contains a page's address block and then automatically include that file inside other pages within a site. This can be useful if sections or parts are duplicated across many pages (such as an address block, for instance). By using a server-side include, you only need to edit the file being included to update your entire site, in other words. The following is an example of using a server-side include to include a file within an HTML document:

```
<!--#include file="inclfile.html"-->
```

The previous example uses a relative URL to specify that the file to be included is located in the same folder as the document in which it is to be included. You cannot, however, use "../" to step back up the folder tree when using the file attribute. To specify the folder where a file to be included is located, use the virtual attribute, as shown here:

```
<!--#include virtual="/includes/inclfile.html"-->
```

In this case, if the file to be included is located at the address, **http://www.yourdomain.com/includes/inclfile.html**, just eliminate the first part of the URL. If you do not have your own domain name, but have a folder within someone else's domain, you might use the following code (where *username* corresponds to your user name):

```
<!--#include virtual="/username/includes/inclfile.html"-->
```

USING COOKIES

A cookie is a file that is saved on a user's computer when a Web page is visited. Later, when a user visits the same page, the cookie can be read and updated. Cookies can keep track of when you last visited or how many times you have visited a page, as well as many other kinds of information. A shopping cart application, for instance, might save a cookie to your computer to remember what you have placed in your shopping cart. A cookie also can be used to remember a password or user name, for instance.

Cookies can be set either using a server-side program (a CGI script written in Perl, for instance) or a client-side script or program (a JavaScript script or a Java applet, for instance).

There is a great deal of misinformation and myth in regards to what cookies can and cannot do. Cookies are not programs, but simple text files, so they cannot be executed to perform actions or look for information on a user's computer. One serious concern, however, is that a cookie can be used to track and monitor users' browsing history over many sites, rather than simply track their history and preferences relative to a single page or site. This is generally done through a third party that provides an advertising banner on another site; when the advertising banner is displayed, the third party sets a cookie tracking the banner being shown, if the person clicks on the banner, the page from which the banner originated is displayed, and so on. The information gathered is generally used to then tailor ads to the specific interests or preferences of that individual. Some are concerned that this type of gleaning of personal information could possibly be exploited in the future for less benign purposes. It is important to stress, however, that unless users volunteer their names or e-mail addresses, for instance, there is no way that cookies can discover that kind of information.

A number of proposals are in the works to change the protocol that enables the use of cookies to make it more difficult for third parties to track users' Web browsing habits. The most recent browsers also provide users with more capability to control how cookies are set and read on their computers. For instance, to change how cookies are handled in Internet Explorer 6 for Windows:

1. Access the Control Panel (click the Start button and select Settings and Control Panel) and double-click the Internet Options icon. Click the Privacy tab.
2. To control how cookies are set and accessed on your computer, either use the slider to set a higher or lower level of privacy or click on the Advanced button. You also can choose to override the cookie parameters you have set for individual sites by clicking the Edit button.

3. If you click on the Advanced button, you can select the check box to override automatic cookie handling. For instance, you might choose to accept cookies from first parties (set directly by sites that you visit and only readable by those sites), but choose to block cookies from third parties (set by third-party advertisers on a first-party site, for instance).

ADDING PASSWORD PROTECTION

There are many reasons why you might want or be called upon to password protect a Web page, a folder, or an entire site. For instance, you might be running a service that requires users to log in to use your service, so you can charge a subscription fee. You may also be running an administrative site that you do not want to be available to the general public. If running a subscription service, you may also want to implement automated sign-ups and authentication, so subscribers can sign up and receive a username and password, which they can then use to log into your site.

Setting up password protection that is relatively secure needs to be done on the server, but if you do not require strong security, JavaScript scripts for password protecting files can be used. Most JavaScript password-protection scripts work by requiring you to know the name of the file you are trying to access, which serves as the password. If you cannot provide the correct password, you get a "file not found" response.

If setting up password protection on the server, on a UNIX server, you will need—at a minimum—to create or edit a .htaccess file for the folder or page you want to protect that points to another file, .htpasswd, which lists one or more usernames and passwords that can be used to access the folder or page. When users try to access the protected page, they will be prompted to enter a username and password.

To get more sophisticated, you will need to use an application that allows for automated sign-ups and updating of the password file. This can involve using a form and a CGI script (a Perl script, for instance) to process the data submitted with the form, which could then be automatically written to the password file to update it. If charging a fee or price for signing up, you may also need to have access to a secure server for gathering sensitive data, such as a credit card number. Larger sites with a large number of subscribers might need to access a MySQL database, for instance, for storing and updating user name and password data.

SERVER-SIDE SCRIPTING AND PROGRAMMING

JavaScript is a client-side scripting language, as is VBScript. Java is a client-side programming language, as is ActiveX (Java programs are called "applets," whereas ActiveX programs are called "controls"). Scripting languages create scripts, which are text-based lists of codes that can be embedded in Web pages or linked to externally. Java and ActiveX programs, on the other hand, are compiled, which means they are downloaded to your browser as binary data, instead of as text code.

CGI (Common Gateway Interface) is not a programming language but a gateway protocol that allows a browser to access scripts and programs residing on a server. Such scripts and programs are server-side applications, in that they run on the server, rather than first being downloaded and run in the browser. One of the most common server-side scripting languages is Perl, which owes its popularity partly due to its availability on most UNIX computers (and most servers on the Web still run some variant of UNIX).

Other server-side scripting and programming languages can be used, however, including C, C++, Visual Basic, TCL, UNIX Shell, ASP, PHP, ActiveX, Server-Side JavaScript, Enterprise Java (Java Servlets), and more (see the next two sections for descriptions of ASP and PHP).

ASP and ASP.NET

ASP (*Active Server Pages*) uses server-side scripting to dynamically generate Web pages. Most commonly, ASP is used with VBScript (*Visual Basic Script*), but also can be used with JScript (Microsoft's version of JavaScript) or other scripting languages. ASP Web pages have an extension of .asp, instead of .html or .htm. ASP requires server support to be used—ASP is supported by Windows-based Web servers, such as Microsoft Internet Information Server (IIS). To test ASP Web pages on your local Windows machine, you need to install a Personal Web Server (PWS), which is available for Windows 2000/XP Pro (Add/Remove Programs in the Control Panel), Windows 98 (under "add-ons" on the Windows 98 CD), and Windows 95/Windows NT 4 (download the NT4 Option Pack at www.microsoft.com/ntserver/nts/downloads/recommended/NT4OptPk/default.asp).

ASP pages can include HTML codes, client-side scripts (such as JavaScript scripts, for instance), and server-side scripts. When a user accesses an ASP page, the ASP server is called by the Web server, which then scans the page from top to bottom, parsing any server-side scripts. After executing the server-side scripts, it outputs the resulting HTML file and downloads it to the client (the browser).

ASP.NET is an expansion of the basic idea behind ASP into a server-side programming framework or platform which is designed to facilitate the building, deploying, and running of distributed Web applications that can run in any browser and on any platform. ASP.NET takes advantage of the .NET Common Language Runtime that is built into all newer versions of Windows and which provides access to lower-level services, such as user authentication, file management, network mapping, and so on. ASP.NET pages, unlike regular ASP pages, are compiled, which speeds up performance considerably. ASP.NET pages have an extension of .aspx.

PHP

PHP stands for *PHP: Hypertext Preprocessor* (it is a recursive acronym, which is an acronym which refers to itself). PHP is a scripting language that runs on a server (a server-side scripting language). PHP is used to dynamically generate HTML pages on-the-fly. PHP code is embedded directly in HTML pages. Web servers that support PHP scan HTML files, parsing any PHP codes they contain before downloading them to clients. A `<?php ... ?>` code alerts the server that a PHP command is enclosed. Some common uses of PHP include working with cookies and online databases (such as MySQL, SyBase, ODBC, Oracle, and more). PHP is an open-source scripting language that can be used on most platforms and server software.

ONLINE DATABASES

There are two basic approaches to publishing databases to the Web. The first is to export or convert database records to HTML documents before publishing them to the Web.

The second is to actually publish a database to the Web that users can then query (using SQL, PHP, ASP, and so on).

The simplest way to publish information from databases to the Web is to format a report form that includes the necessary HTML codes. You then just need to generate a database report, which is then published to the Web. This is especially useful for formatting catalogs, for instance, as HTML documents. Additionally, various utilities can convert database data (such as in comma-delimited CSV files, for instance) to HTML documents. Many database software programs, such as FileMaker Pro or Microsoft Access, can export data in HTML format.

You can approximate the look-and-feel of an online database by generating HTML-formatted documents for various queries and then linking to them.

Actually publishing a database to the Web that can be queried by users can be either relatively simple or complex. Relatively simple options for publishing data to the Web include simple text-based and table-based datasets that can be queried using scripts, while more complex options include creating databases using MySQL with ASP and PHP. Some database programs, such as FileMaker Pro, for instance, also facilitate publishing flat-file or relational databases to the Web that can be queried by users.

SECURE FORMS AND SERVERS

If you want to add a form or a shopping cart application to your site that needs to collect and transmit credit card or other sensitive information, you should have access to a secure server running SSL (Secure Sockets Layer). Web pages located through a secure server usually start with "https://," instead of "http://," as is the case with pages on a regular Web server. When you link to a page on an SSL server, any data transmitted between you and the server (or from the server to you) is encrypted and is next to impossible to intercept or decipher.

You will also need access to a digital certificate, either your own or one provided by the provider of your secure server space. A digital certificate authenticates the identity of a Web site to browsers. Generally, using a digital certificate provided by your secure server provider is less expensive, but does not uniquely identify you when users view your digital certificate information (it identifies the provider of the secure server instead). In other words, if you want to instill the maximum degree of confidence in your customers when using a secure form or shopping cart application on your site, you should purchase your own digital certificate. For a smaller site that will not be handling a large number of orders, however, this is not necessary. Accounts that provide secure server access cost somewhat more per month (from $35 to $50 a month, if using your provider's digital certificate) than a regular virtual hosting account.

Different levels of encryption can be provided via SSL: 128-bit, 56-bit, and 40-bit encryption. 128-bit encryption is, by far, the more secure and, in fact, was considered so secure that the U.S. government until recently forbid the export of software programs that included 128-bit encryption capability. Most recent Web browsers support 128-bit encryption.

WIRELESS/WAP/WML

Not everyone connects to and surfs the Web using a computer. More and more people are connecting to the Web using other devices, such as mobile phones, PDAs, set-top boxes (such as WebTV, for instance), and other devices that do not feature the screen or resolution size necessary to present a Web page as it might normally be displayed on a computer screen. These devices also often do not use keyboard/mouse interfaces, which requires the specification of different means, such as using a keypad or a remote, for accessing menus, links, scrolling, and so on.

Initially, the WAP (Wireless Application Protocol) and WML (Wireless Markup Language) standards were developed to enable the publishing of content on the Web that is tailored to presentation on wireless and other small-format devices. More recently, support is migrating to the use of XHTML (XHTML Basic) and CSS (CSS Mobile Profile) to enable presenting text, images, forms, basic tables, and other objects on wireless/mobile devices.

NOTE For links to many resources that further discuss the topics covered in this appendix, see the Appendixes' section at the IRC for this book at **www.emcp.com**/.

Index